The Free Speech Mo

IN MEMORY OF MARIO SAVIO (1942–1996)

Diogenes said: "The most beautiful thing in the world is the freedom of speech." And those words are in me, they're sort of burned into my soul, because for me free speech was not a tactic, not something to win for political [advantage]. . . . To me, freedom of speech is something that represents the very dignity of what a human being is. . . . That's what marks us off from the stones and the stars. You can speak freely. It is almost impossible for me to describe. It is the thing that marks us as just below the angels. I don't want to push this beyond where it should be pushed but I feel it.

MARIO SAVIO, 1994

The Free Speech Movement

Reflections on Berkeley in the 1960s

EDITED BY

Robert Cohen and Reginald E. Zelnik

UNIVERSITY OF CALIFORNIA PRESS

Berkeley   Los Angeles   London

2-13-2004
WW
₱ 19.95

University of California Press
Berkeley and Los Angeles, California

University of California Press, Ltd.
London, England

Library of Congress Cataloging-in-Publication Data

The free speech movement : reflections on Berkeley in the 1960s /
edited by Robert Cohen and Reginald E. Zelnik.
      p.   cm.
   Includes bibliographical references and index.
   ISBN 0-520-22221-0 (cloth : alk. paper)—ISBN 0-520-23354-9
(pbk. : alk. paper)
      1. University of California, Berkeley—Students—History.
2. College students—California—Berkeley—Political activity—
History.   3. Student movements—California—Berkeley—
History.   4. Savio, Mario.   I. Cohen, Robert, 1955 May. 21- II.
Zelnik, Reginald E.

LD760.F74   2002
378.1'981'0979467—dc21   2002016554

Manufactured in the United States of America
10   09   08   07   06   05   04   03   02
10   9   8   7   6   5   4   3   2   1

The paper used in this publication meets the minimum requirements of ANSI/NISO Z39.48-1992 (R 1997) *(Permanence of Paper)*.∞

CONTENTS

Illustrations follow page 226

ACKNOWLEDGMENTS

As stated in the introductory chapter, this book could not have been written without Mario Savio, to whose memory it has been dedicated. Our thanks to Lynne Hollander Savio, both for providing us with the tape of Mario's speech at the University of California at Santa Cruz and for granting us permission to publish it in this volume. Thanks as well to Kim Friedlander for her deft transcription of the tape. We join with the publishers in gratefully acknowledging the generous contribution to this book provided by Stephen M. Silberstein.

Our book grew out of a special panel on Mario Savio and the Free Speech Movement held at the annual convention of the Organization of American Historians in April 1997, following Mario's untimely death in November 1996. We were able to organize the panel on very short notice thanks to the enthusiastic assistance rendered by Mary Ryan, cochair of the convention's Program Committee, and by Linda Kerber, who chaired both the panel and the convention itself.

We are grateful to former University of California president Clark Kerr, who, though well aware that many of the other authors would be critical of his role in the 1964 campus crisis, agreed to contribute to our book and thereby become a part of this dialogue. We would also like to thank two key members of his staff, research associate Marian Gade and editorial assistant Maureen Kawaoka, for their kind and eager cooperation.

We are indebted to the staff of the Bancroft Library and especially Elizabeth C. Stephens, project archivist for its Free Speech Movement collections, for their assistance and cooperation. By releasing Mario's disciplinary file, William M. Roberts, then the University archivist, made it possible to write a more complete history of Mario's Berkeley years. We are also very grateful to Jesse Lemisch for his close and thoughtful reading of our manuscript.

A grant from New York University's School of Education enabled us to obtain copies of the FBI files on the FSM and Mario and defrayed some of the cost of our bicoastal research and editing. We thank Charles Sprague for helping to expedite this crucial funding. Athan Theoharis, the nation's leading historian of the FBI, shared some additional FBI documents on the FSM with us, and we wish to thank him for his generosity. We are also grateful for research support from the University of California at Berkeley and the encouragement and assistance provided by NYU faculty colleagues Joel Westheimer and Diana Turk.

We are in debt to several of the contributors to this volume, including David Hollinger and Larry Levine, for giving us badly needed advice on how to deal with some difficult, sensitive issues at critical moments.

Much encouragement and many good suggestions were given us by staff at the University of California Press, most notably Naomi Schneider, Annie Decker, Sheila Levine, Jim Clark, and Marilyn Schwartz. Michael Bass and his skilled professional staff, headed by Steven B. Baker, did a splendid job copyediting the manuscript.

Our wives, Rebecca Hyman and Elaine Zelnik, constantly provided us with their wise counsel and amazing patience. Robby Cohen also wants to thank his son Daniel for joining him on his Berkeley research trips. The years it has taken to bring this book to fruition have roughly coincided with the first years of the Zelniks' grandson, Jaxon Zelnik Stuhr, who has been a source of inspiration. Finally, each of us would like to thank the other for working so well together and for collaborating on this project with such energy, enthusiasm, professionalism, and such a consistently friendly disposition.

PERMISSIONS AND CREDITS

The editors and publishers are grateful to the publishers and authors who have given permission to reproduce the following materials. There are minor editorial changes in some of the reproduced essays.

Margot Adler, "My Life in the FSM: Memories of a Freshman," excerpted from Margot Adler, *Heretic's Heart: A Journey through Spirit and Revolution* (Beacon Press, 1997), chapter 4. Reprinted here by permission of the author.

Wendy Lesser, "Elegy for Mario Savio," first published in *New York Times Book Review*, December 15, 1996; reprinted in Wendy Lesser, *The Amateur: An Independent Life of Letters* (Pantheon Books, 1999). Reprinted here by permission of the author.

Greil Marcus, "On Mario Savio," first published in *Rolling Stone*, December 26, 1996–January 9, 1997, copyright 1996 by Straight Arrow Publishers. Reprinted here by permission of the author.

Reginald E. Zelnik, "Mario Savio: Avatar of Free Speech," first published in *New York Times Magazine*, 29 December 1996. Reprinted here by permission of the author and the New York Times.

The editors and publishers are grateful to the Bancroft Library for permission to quote from its manuscript collections and to the Bancroft Library's Regional Oral History Office for permission to quote from the oral histories listed in the selected bibliography.

Photos 5a and b, 6a, 8, 9, 11–15, 17–19, and 23 were taken by Steven Marcus and are reproduced here with the permission of the Bancroft Library. Photos 1–4, 6b, 7, 10, 16, 20–22, and 24 were taken by Ronald L. Enfield and are reproduced with the permission of Medford Software Works, Inc., acting as his agent. Photo 28 was taken by Anita Medal and is reproduced here with her permission. Other photos are from the personal collections of the editors.

PREFACE

Beginning in 1969, the Berkeley campus of the University of California chose to revamp the traditional graduation exercises. The reason for the change attested to the continuing impact of student activism unleashed by the Free Speech Movement (FSM) of 1964. The director of public ceremonies, a faculty member, summed up the problem in a memo to the chancellor: "Before this year, the campus accepted our choice of 'representative' student speakers. From now on, we are in trouble." The message could not have been clearer, and its implications went far beyond the choice of graduation speakers. In the 1960s, first on the Berkeley campus and then nationally and internationally, students tested the limits of permissible dissent, challenged the conventional wisdom in unprecedented ways, and insisted on participating as active agents in the shaping of history. That is the achievement of the FSM, and each new class at Berkeley inherits that legacy.

But if free expression and social activism are now revered Berkeley traditions, they have led a precarious life. For much of the twentieth century Berkeley, like most campuses, tended to be a white, middle-class enclave, a haven of privilege and conformity. When I was an underclassman there, the mechanisms of repression and surveillance were very much in place, along with overly protective and vigilant administrators. In our political science and history classes we studied the Constitution, but outside of the classroom we were advised to be cautious and prudent in practicing the freedoms the Bill of Rights guaranteed. Controversial speakers were excluded from campus, University rules forbade using the college grounds for partisan political activity, and the Board of Regents insisted on monitoring the loyalty of each faculty member through an oath. Under these conditions, student activism was not simply inhibited; it was intimidated. One searched with difficulty for a rebel or a reformer, let alone a Marxist, and it became increasingly difficult to find anyone who felt very strongly about anything. Curious pollsters circulated a petition on campus containing the Bill of Rights—nothing more; most students, equating petitions with political commitment and the endangerment of their careers, refused to sign. Throughout this period, the University performed its traditional role— producing, by and large, the adaptable, conventional, uninteresting kinds of people demanded in a highly organized corporate society. "These men don't question the system," *Fortune Magazine* said gleefully of my class, the Class of '51. "Their aim is to make it work better—to get in there and lubricate the machinery. They're not rebels; they'll be social technicians for a better society."

When Robert Gordon Sproul, as president of the University, addressed my graduating class, we were told to avoid "misguided" conservatives and "insane" radicals, and we knew who they were and that it was better to be misguided than insane. We were admonished to be loyal to our government and prepared to serve our country. (My draft notice would soon be on its way.) Ever since the 1930s, in the hope of making Berkeley a certifiably Communist-free campus, the Sproul administration had employed an elaborate intelligence network that included Bay Area law enforcement officials, the FBI, and Army Intelligence, all of whom cooperated in gathering intelligence data on suspect (radical) students and monitoring radical political activism.[1] Administrators at Berkeley and elsewhere could always defend their actions by warning that, if campus officials did not act, legislatures would impose even harsher restrictions. Even the best universities succumbed. The president of Yale, for example, could portray his institution as a bastion of academic freedom, once he had purged it of subversives. "There will be no witch-hunts at Yale," he boasted, "because there will be no witches."

Until the mid-1960s, the entrenched hierarchy that governed universities like UC seemed ageless and enduring, immune to ideological contamination. Like most college presidents, Sproul viewed students paternalistically. He deemed political activism, particularly when it assumed a radical face, incompatible with the acknowledged goals and professionalism of an institution of higher learning. He tried to make certain that the young men and women entrusted to his care were protected from threatening ideologies and manipulation by radical agitators. (Students in the 1950s were not said to be *influenced* by radical ideas; they were said to be *infected* by them.) That meant for Sproul "freedom within the framework of public good" and "liberty with order." There were limits to freedom. "No society," Sproul proclaimed, "will tolerate for long those among its own servants who give aid and comfort to enemies seeking its destruction." In the atmosphere of the Cold War, that left little room for ambiguity. Yet several decades later, on

December 3, 1997, what had been called Sproul Steps (the approach to Sproul Hall, the administration building) were renamed Savio Steps to celebrate—in name and in implementation—a very different conception of freedom and dissent in a university community.

In keeping with that spirit, the book you are about to read, *The Free Speech Movement: Reflections on Berkeley in the 1960s*, offers a range of perspectives, as the Movement meant and came to mean very different things to many different people. What this volume makes clear is that the rights enjoyed by UC students in the late twentieth century did not come easily. The University—regents and administrators alike—did not yield power quickly or graciously. (It has been said of administrators that they act wisely once they have exhausted all other alternatives.) The victories required extraordinary commitment, they had to be fought for, they had to be won by unrelenting agitation, and much of the credit belongs to a generation of students often denigrated for their excesses—the generation whose presence and historical legacy is the centerpiece of this book.

No doubt the sixties will always evoke, as it does in this volume, mixed memories for students, alumni, faculty, and administrators. The majority of students, like most Americans, did not protest or demonstrate. That is not surprising. After all, social activism and dissent are rare qualities in human life; passivity and accommodation are far more characteristic. Throughout our history, however, men and women have braved unpopularity and both state and private violence to make a commitment to social justice. Inspired and moved by the example of the Civil Rights Movement, between 1960 and 1972 at places like Berkeley significant numbers of young people came to believe that direct, personal commitment to social justice was a moral imperative and that social inequities are neither inevitable nor accidental but reflect the assumptions, beliefs, and decisions of certain people who command enormous power. These were important perceptions. What began at Berkeley as a movement of protest to obtain a traditional liberal freedom, freedom of speech and advocacy, soon brought into question the official version of reality.

Whatever the mixed legacy of the FSM generation, whatever the attempts to revise perceptions of the sixties to accord with the politics of more conservative periods, few generations in our history have been more irreverent, candid, or creative. Few so engaged themselves in the struggle for social justice. Few cared more deeply about their country. Eschewing the conventional flag-waving, mindless, orchestrated patriotism, they opted for the highest kind of patriotism and loyalty. They defined loyalty to one's country as disloyalty to its pretenses, a willingness to unmask its leaders, and a calling to subject its institutions, government, and wars to critical examination, not only the decisions made by rulers but often their indecision. In making these commitments, they gave America a much needed

LIST OF ABBREVIATIONS

AAUP   American Association of University Professors
ACLU   American Civil Liberties Union
AFT   American Federation of Teachers
ASUC   Associated Students of the University of California
BED   Board of Educational Development
B of A Bank of America
CAF   Committee on Academic Freedom
CCNY   City College of New York
CCPA   Committee on Campus Political Activity
CIA   Central Intelligence Agency
CIO   Congress of Industrial Organizations
CORE   Congress of Racial Equality
CPE   Center for Participant Education
DC   *Daily Californian,* also referred to as the *Daily Cal*
DEC   Division of Experimental Courses
EEC   Emergency Executive Committee
EEOC   Equal Employment Opportunity Commission
FPC   Faculty Peace Committee
FUC   Free University of California
GCC   Graduate Coordinating Committee
HUAC   House Committee on Un-American Activities
        (accurately, HCUA)
ILWU   International Longshoremen's and Warehousemen's
        Union
IIR   Institute of Industrial Relations
ILE   Intensive Learning Experience
IWW   International Workers of the World

KKK   Ku Klux Klan
MLK   Martin Luther King, Jr.
NAACP   National Association for the Advancement of Colored People
ROTC   Reserve Officer Training Corps
SCOE   Special Committee on Education
SDS   Students for a Democratic Society
SLATE   Short name for a radical student group active at UCB before
          and during the FSM
SNCC   Student Non-Violent Coordinating Committee
SCPF   Study Committee on Political Freedom (later renamed CCPA)
SRE   Students for Racial Equality
SSU   Sonoma State University
UC   University of California
UCB   University of California at Berkeley
UNC   University of North Carolina at Chapel Hill
VDC   Vietnam Day Committee

The Many Meanings of the FSM

In Lieu of an Introduction

Robert Cohen

Were it not for Mario Savio, the book you now hold in your hands would never have been written. As a young man, Savio played a key role in leading the Free Speech Movement (FSM) to victory in its struggle to end the restrictions the University of California had placed on campus political activity. He was the Berkeley student rebellion's most eloquent orator, the one who first spoke from atop the police car that his fellow protesters surrounded and immobilized on October 1, 1964, to prevent the arrest of Jack Weinberg, a civil rights activist whose only crime had been to defy the administration's prohibition against political advocacy on University property. Savio's rousing words and the mass protest around the police car on Sproul Plaza (the central campus thoroughfare) helped to launch the Free Speech Movement. And Savio's "operation of the machine" speech, just before the December Sproul Hall sit-in, not only set the tone for the non-violent occupation of the administration building—which culminated in the largest mass arrest of students in American history—but also became the most famous oration in the early history of the New Left. Savio's daring attempt to speak at an administration-run meeting in Berkeley's Greek Theatre days after the sit-in electrified thousands of students, who were shocked to see campus police drag him from the podium. As both a speaker and a symbol, then, Savio helped to make the Berkeley student rebellion a memorable event, one that inspired campus activists across the country and the globe in the 1960s and that still has the power to attract the attention of scholars and writers such as those represented in this book. Savio refused, however, to present himself as the Berkeley rebellion's indispensable leader. Like so many other FSMers, he preferred to see the movement as too democratic to need leaders, stressing instead that its strength came from the moral principles that gave it mass appeal. When, soon after memory from movement veterans and their opponents to historians. Mario's death was a reminder that the task of probing the meaning of the FSM cannot forever be left to the sixties generation; if we are to advance our understanding, historians must probe the memories and documents of those events and begin to draw their own conclusions about that revolt's historical significance.

Readers of this volume will no doubt be struck by the polemical edge to many of the memoirs and the contrast between these passionate participant accounts and the more staid essays by the historians. Although time has changed much about the authors and the world, both FSM vets and the former University president have been remarkably true to their collective pasts—carrying with them many of the ideals, heroes, demons, joys, and regrets that they held in 1964. Regardless of their political stance, to various degrees they communicate the historical sensibility, the folklore, and the logic of their respective sides of the Berkeley barricades with emotion and immediacy. And, as one would expect of partisans, both sides have difficulty expressing any significant degree of empathy or understanding for their old foes. It is our hope that historians will ultimately provide some of the balance that may be lacking in the memoirs.

Most of the scattered writings that historians have published about the FSM appear in their accounts of the New Left and the 1960s. Usually they offer a few pages or at most a chapter on the FSM, placing it in the context of the larger national campus insurgency of the 1960s, which centered on opposition to the Vietnam War. Berkeley is depicted, much as it was in the Scranton Commission report, as a prototype for this national student rebellion. It was the site of the first massive display of civil disobedience on campus. In this sense, Berkeley served as a bridge between the Civil Rights Movement, which pioneered the use of nonviolent civil disobedience, and the campus world, where it empowered student dissenters and enabled them as never before to question the authority and challenge the power of campus administrators.

New Left historiography has also, in a variety of ways, credited Berkeley's student rebels with helping to pioneer a new style of radical political thought. Wini Breines, for example, in her important book *Community and Organization in the New Left* (1989), sees the FSM's ideas and forms of revolt as "expressions of a radical utopian upsurge." Breines cites approvingly an argument that former SDS leader Todd Gitlin made about the FSM in 1970: This "mass movement is not simply 'about' free speech, nor even simply 'about' the right to organize for political action, but finally it is 'about' the necessity of revolt from the gargantuan, depersonalized, mass-production multiversity.... A social movement is never simply 'about' its object, but is always 'about' the deeper identities of the participants ... who ... stoke it and shape it." Again stressing the need to look beyond the free speech issue, Breines cites a New Left slogan, "The Issue is not the issue." In the FSM, Berkeley students were, in her view, engaged in a form of "prefig-urative" politics in which they "prefigured in lived action and behavior" the society they desired, a society radically different from capitalist America. According to Breines, the students' alienation from the university and its bureaucracy led them to a radical critique of the multiversity, "facilitated their formulation of a condemnation of their society," and provoked them to search for a new form of community. "A basic . . . purpose of the move-ment," she writes, "was to create communities of equality, direct democracy and solidarity." These were "in bold contrast to the [mainstream American] values of competition, individualism, and efficiency."[8] To Breines, the FSM had anticapitalist implications, as "students expressed opposition to a face-less and inhumane bureaucracy organized for industry and profit" and resisted having their freedom "constrained in the interests of profit, prop-erty, and efficiency." In this reading of Berkeley's revolt, the students understood it as an event in which "thousands of individuals . . . say 'no' to the structures and politics of the dominant society, . . . refuse to take part and in so doing create a crisis of legitimacy that stops the machine." The FSM enabled the left to "kick the labor metaphysic," meaning that instead of relying upon the "proletariat" to be the agent of radical change, this role could be played by middle-class students, "a new working class," who would revolt not out of material deprivation but out of a "radical consciousness" that presumably emerged from alienation and an existential crisis over the lack of freedom and meaningful work. Similar interpretations of the FSM have been advanced in other cogent historical accounts, such as those by Stanley Aronowitz and James J. Farrell.[9]

These New Left histories are right to explore the radical implications of the FSM. Part of what makes the FSM story so memorable is its place in American radical history as one of the few times when a left-led movement was so profoundly effective. As Savio declared on the FSM's twentieth anniversary, the Free Speech Movement "has remained for me a brilliant moment when, as a friend put it, we were 'both moral and successful.'" The image of that police car being immobilized by a student crowd on Sproul Plaza has special resonance in the context of a left that was so often on the losing end politically. Here was a moment when a mass movement held off the emissaries of state violence and accomplished this nonviolently, using as its only weapon the solidarity of people willing to "put their bodies on the line" to stop the arrest of a civil rights activist. "It was," in Savio's words, "really important" that the police car "was taken," because it was then that the

> community of the Free Speech Movement was founded. Even if you only sat there [around the car] your role was crucial. . . . It's hard to describe the feel-ing of the beauty of it. "If I don't do this it will fail." That's the feeling. The

reflects—united student radicals with liberals, centrists, and even some conservatives. Looking back, some vocal FSM veterans tend to see the story the way Breines does. They worry, understandably enough, that the canonization of Savio as a civil liberties saint will obscure his radical egalitarianism, and they fear that the FSM's radical implications will be forgotten. By contrast, some former faculty allies of the FSM, especially but not exclusively those who became passionate critics of the late-sixties Berkeley left, look back at the FSM as a more moderate movement, committed to nonviolence and rational discourse in a way that the post-FSM left was not.[16] This is just one example of the competing interpretations, the layers of analysis and opinion, that still abound. While each of them points to a partial truth, the editors of the present volume have tried to eschew the single-minded pursuit of any unidimensional interpretation of the FSM and to present a wider range of sometimes conflicting stories that together constitute the history of the FSM, stretching from Mario Savio's account to Clark Kerr's.

Part of what is at issue here is, of course, the ownership of the past. Whose historical memory of the FSM gets privileged over all the others? Since the FSM was indeed (among other things) a milestone in the evolution of the New Left, there has been a natural tendency to privilege the voices of those leaders who helped build the radical movement and then became the more prominent interpreters of the Berkeley revolt. Indeed, we must confess to having done some of that privileging ourselves, since many of the FSM veterans who appear in this volume were movement leaders. Such people often speak of the FSM as a life-changing experience. John Searle, an avid faculty supporter of the FSM who later became a critic of the campus left, has written of the "religious character" of the experiences of those activists (a view echoed, if from a very different perspective, in Michael Rossman's essay in this book). "Even after the FSM," Searle writes,

> many of its veterans wanted to continue the style of the movement after the issues had been resolved.... They did not see the FSM as a limited political organization seeking free speech, as was stated in its platform; they saw in it the possibility of a whole new attitude to life.... What they... wanted for themselves was a whole new set of values and a new way of life. Their rhetorical style was not one of saying "Here is our platform and here is how we intend to achieve our objectives," but rather in effect of saying "Here is our style and it is itself the objective, for it offers you meaning, fulfillment, and community, a chance in short to find yourself and meaning in your life, a chance to avoid the bankrupt materialism of the world around you."[17]

Whether used to praise or to bury the FSM, this mode of thinking about it overflows with excitement and historical drama, for it implies the advent of a whole new worldview and can be linked easily to post-FSM developments. But, though perhaps less dramatic or exciting and though surely less of a fit with the standard post-FSM historiography, the story of vast numbers of involved students for whom the FSM was *not* a quasi-religious experience, not a moment replete with life-transforming consequence, the story of those who were drawn to the Berkeley revolt "merely" because it spoke the language of rights, must also be told. Those who viewed the FSM as a struggle for free speech and due process, a struggle to protect the Civil Rights Movement, focusing on limited if vital demands, and for whom the winning of those demands meant that a return to one's studies and career pursuits was now both possible and desirable were a very significant component. The FSM, as Martin Roysher's essay and my own essay on the rank and file will argue, succeeded as a mass movement not only because it had a dynamic radical minority in its leadership but also because it could draw so reliably at certain key moments upon such non-radical students, the campus majority.

We often hear from those at the center of the movement but rarely from those on the periphery. In his essay historian David Hollinger, who at the time was a history graduate student and viewed the FSM from the periphery, reminds us that the movement had an impact and a history that affected even students far removed from the FSM's activist core. It had a "prodigious circumference," recalls Hollinger, who challenges historians to recognize that the Berkeley revolt's historical significance may rest as much with its political and intellectual effect on those on its margins as with those in its leadership. In exploring this hitherto hidden history, Hollinger shows us that it can lead in surprising directions. For example, reading the long and fascinating memoir of David Goines, a prominent FSMer, can leave one with the impression that the FSM was a kind of antiacademic rebellion, one that left activists thoroughly disillusioned—as he was—with academia. Hollinger, on the other hand, as an intellectually intense graduate student viewing and supporting the movement from its circumference, came away from the FSM proud of the way that faculty had rallied to the FSM to preserve free speech, and strengthened in his professional goal: an academic career devoted to the life of the mind, educational reform, and faculty self-government.

Such new perspectives suggest how important it is to open the door to a wide variety of historical interpretations. Far from claiming to offer a "definitive" volume on the Berkeley student revolt, what we seek to do is spark the broadest possible discussion and debate about the movement's causes, character, and consequences. In this spirit, we are pleased to report that the contributors to this volume disagree on many aspects of the story. The views range from movement veterans who think the FSM changed the world to skeptics who argue that the FSM failed even to achieve significant change on the Berkeley campus. None of them "owns" this part of the American past. The movement's history belongs to all whose lives it touched, even those who opposed it, as well as to those who study it. Drawing upon conflicting memories and documentary sources, and influenced by a variety of political assumptions, these writers point us toward an understanding that the FSM's history intersects not only with that of the New Left but also with the history of liberalism, Cold War America, civil liberty, higher education, California politics, the New Right, and the rise of neo-conservatism.

If for the moment we start reading the FSM story within a local rather than a national narrative frame, in the context of the University's own history one can see the FSM as much as a culmination as a beginning. In the local context, the FSM may reasonably be seen as representing the final act of Cold War Berkeley's 1950s, which is why when many Berkeley faculty, alumni, and administrators speak of the FSM they often begin by reading it backwards into UC's past rather than forward into the New Left's future. That past centers around the political tensions and repression of a campus scarred by an anti-Communist loyalty oath that in 1949 and the early 1950s drove away prominent faculty members and inhibited student activism. The demand that all faculty sign a loyalty oath had been imposed by an administration (headed by President Robert Sproul) that was so fearful of losing control of the campus to the legislature that it sought to preempt a right-wing attack from Sacramento by essentially initiating a political purge of its own. The remainder of the 1950s found Berkeley liberals and radicals trying to recover from this disaster and restore political freedom on campus. The best-known facet of this struggle is that of the students who in the late 1950s established and built SLATE, a student political party devoted to fostering left-liberal activism and debate.* SLATE was continually running afoul of a Berkeley administration wary of public controversy. SLATE activists and other students made their most dramatic stand against the domestic Cold War and McCarthyism in 1960, when they attracted national headlines protesting the hearings of the House Committee on Un-American Activities (HUAC) in San Francisco, protests that culminated in the authorities using high-powered fire hoses to wash the protesters down the City Hall steps.[18]

Although Berkeley faculty had done nothing as dramatic as the students who demonstrated at City Hall, they too had an active minority that in the late 1950s and early 1960s resisted what the historian Carl Schorske termed "administrative harassment of political expression." As Reginald

---

*SLATE's name derived from its fielding of a slate of candidates in Berkeley student government elections in the late 1950s on a common plank opposing racial discrimination in campus organizations (at a time when most of UC's Greek-letter social organizations had discriminatory clauses in their constitutions).

Zelnik shows in his essay on the role of the faculty, Schorske and other liberal faculty opposed the campus administration's suspension of SLATE and challenged existing restraints the administration had placed on the use of the University's name, such as the barring of faculty from identifying themselves as UC professors when endorsing a political cause. Schorske and his colleagues were also involved in challenging the University's policy of banning Communist speakers, a policy they later saw as part of a continuous set of restrictions on political expression that culminated in the 1964 crisis. Attesting to this history of faculty solidarity with the struggle of students for free speech, Schorske links an admittedly small cohort of like-minded professors to faculty involvement in the conflicts of 1964: "[We] were in a certain sense the forerunners trying to get the policies changed in order to overcome the liabilities that clung on from the past, including the oath, but reaching farther back."[19]

Since faculty members were usually older and tended to have been at Berkeley longer than most students, it is not surprising that professors such as Schorske would see the FSM as the culmination of a long-term battle. Nor was this long view of the struggle for free speech at Berkeley confined to faculty. One of the central documents of the FSM was the "Rossman Report," a detailed exploration of earlier attempts to squelch political expression on the campus. Written collaboratively by a large group of FSMers—a process illuminated in Michael Rossman's essay in this volume—the report documents student and faculty battles for free political expression dating all the way back to the loyalty oath.[20]

Though it may seem odd that students would have so long a collective memory of campus political conflict, it must be noted that a significant group of FSM activists, including Rossman, were graduate students. Some, having been at Berkeley for several years, carried with them knowledge that, as Rossman then put it, "the conflict of these past two weeks began in the '50s," a view the report persuasively developed in more than one hundred well-documented pages.[21]

Nor was Rossman the first graduate student to focus attention on this pattern of political conflict. Two years prior to the FSM, David Horowitz, a Berkeley teaching assistant (TA) in English, had published the book *Student.* Written in the wake of the anti-HUAC protests and the HUAC-produced film *Operation Abolition,* which red-baited Berkeley campus activists, *Student* sympathetically recounted the story of the students' struggle for freedom of inquiry. As the book's cover blurb explained, "Millions of dollars have been spent to accuse them falsely of being under Communist domination. But the future of this country will be decided by the courageous students who don't accept the mistakes of their elders, and who seek new solutions to the political problems which, if left unsolved, can in this decade mean the destruction of all life."[22]

Taken together, the Horowitz book and the Rossman Report demonstrate that the best-informed activists had grounds for claiming that the FSM's victory was the culmination of a long struggle, a long-delayed moment when Berkeley's activists finally won a major battle—maybe even the war—for their First Amendment rights, exorcised the ghost of Joseph McCarthy, and helped Berkeley to rid itself of scars left by the Cold War and the loyalty oath. This sense of history framed the way that Bettina Aptheker, a key member of the FSM Steering Committee, remembers the FSM's outcome. She is speaking here of that triumphant day when the Academic Senate passed the December 8 resolutions endorsing the FSM's position.

> There were thousands of us gathered outside, listening to that debate—...
> one of the really courageous moments in the history of the faculty which has
> not always been courageous. And as it [the vote] was announced, the roar of
> approval rumbled across the plaza, and moments later, the faculty emerged.
> We students parted ranks, forming an aisle through which the faculty seemed
> to formally march, in a new kind of academic procession. Many of us were
> crying and so were many of them. *There were many among them, and among us,*
> *who finally came to believe that the repression of the 1950s was truly at an end.*
> [emphasis added][23]

The 1950s also played a role in shaping the FSM's political style. First and most obviously, the movement rebelled against the prejudices of Cold War America by refusing to ban Communists from its leadership. There was an ethical commitment to judging people on the basis of their current political behavior rather than their party affiliations. But if the FSM rejected any purging of the Old Left, it also rejected the political style of that earlier left, which had been so discredited in the 1950s. Savio in particular recalled his determination to avoid both the sloganizing that had isolated the Old Left and the tendency of these earlier radicals toward a vanguard mind-set and closed-door decision making by an elite group. In other words, to avoid the undemocratic political style that had rendered the Old Left vulnerable to 1950s-style red-baiting, the FSM had to be sure it operated in so open a manner that it could not even appear to be manipulated by a secretive elite. Thus Savio insisted that the movement "had to be *scrupulously* democratic." This meant not merely being democratic "in the sense of elections"—though, as Savio put it, "we did that"—but also finding ways to continuously "get *direct feedback* from people," including those unaffiliated students who entered the FSM with no representative organizations. In short, the revolt against both McCarthyism and the undemocratic features of the Old Left worked together with the model of democratic decision making that key FSM leaders had learned from a new generation of civil rights workers in SNCC to yield an unusually open and inclusive approach to leadership. For FSMers such as Robert Hurwitt, it was this style of politics that made the FSM so attractive: "The continuing experiment in developing a workable form of representational democracy for the burgeoning, mostly unorganized masses of demonstrators was one of the most exciting day-to-day aspects of the FSM and one of its major contributions to the development of the movements that followed."[24]

A very different reading of the FSM comes from Clark Kerr, who in the 1950s had been elevated from Berkeley chancellor to president of the statewide university system. Like both Schorske and Rossman, Kerr, who as a faculty member had opposed the loyalty oath, starts with the proposition that Berkeley had inherited a legacy of political repression from the Cold War era. The difference, however, is that Kerr sees himself not as a source of that repression but as a liberal reformer who had inherited illiberal campus regulations from President Sproul, regulations that Kerr deliberately and consistently worked to change. In his essay for this volume Kerr proudly (and accurately) points to his leadership in convincing the Regents to lift the campus ban on Communist speakers, and he invokes this important accomplishment as a symbol of the progress he was making in expanding free speech at the University. In Kerr's narrative it is not the FSM that looms as the heroic force that finally ended the repressive 1950s at Berkeley but Kerr himself, who, before there ever was a mass movement claiming to stand for free speech, battled the Regents and the legislature in defense of that principle. But Kerr sees his liberal heroism as ending tragically after he is undermined by the FSM (with the support of many faculty), which scoffs at his reforms, demands total change overnight, employs illicit methods to achieve this, and in the process alienates the public from the University and its liberal values. In the Kerr narrative, it is the FSM and its heirs that set in motion the political backlash that allowed Ronald Reagan to capture the California governorship by promising to "clean up the mess in Berkeley." According to Kerr, the FSM's significance rests less with its role in the emergence of the New Left than with its displacing of his careful, effective liberalism by a reckless mass movement that inadvertently facilitated the ascendancy of the New Right. It should be noted, however, that Kerr's depiction of the FSM is not entirely negative; in addition to praising what he calls its more moderate faction, he does give credit to the FSM for having placed some important issues on the University's agenda.[25]

Kerr's interpretation raises important questions about the process of change in educational institutions. Is it best, as he suggests, to go slow, focusing on incremental change? Is it reasonable to assume that, absent the FSM, Kerr would still have moved to eliminate all or some of the remaining restrictions on political advocacy? Although the question is counterfactual and no one can be sure, there are grounds for skepticism. Kerr had come of age as an administrator under President Sproul.[26] While serving as the Berkeley chancellor, he observed and generally admired how Sproul had welcomed by many because of his tenacious escalation of the Vietnam War, shattered the socially democratic dreams of Great Society reformers. The crisis of liberalism also carried Richard Nixon to the White House and ensured that the great era of social justice and support of civil rights presided over by Chief Justice Earl Warren's Supreme Court would end prematurely.[54]

The FSM's role in the weakening of liberal politics in California is a complex and challenging subject. Kerr tends to see it as an unambiguous story with himself cast as the liberal educator who expanded free speech on campus and promoted the liberal dream of widely accessible public higher education. At the height of his success in expanding the University into a multicampus institution, Kerr finds himself blindsided by a student left that refuses to work with him and by a rightward-drifting public that elects Ronald Reagan, who in turn delivers on his campaign promises by firing Kerr. In Kerr's telling, the FSM and some of its faculty sympathizers were largely to blame for this debacle, their impetuous and militant actions driving a progressive reformer from power and awakening the sleeping dogs of reaction. Kerr does candidly acknowledge that he erred in his failure to immediately overrule the chancellor's ban on advocacy on the Bancroft strip, a ban that sparked the Berkeley revolt. But that ban had implications that Kerr does not explore. If one sees in Berkeley 1964 the beginning of the end of Kerr's era of liberal reform, one must also acknowledge that some of the seeds of that debacle were sown by Kerr's continued entanglement in aspects of President Sproul's illiberal approach that—however effective in fending off a backlash from the legislature—inhibited robust forms of free expression on campus in a way that offended and threatened those engaged in the crusade for civil rights.

Some of Kerr's accusatory rhetoric during the early stages of the free speech crisis surely contributed to the rift between establishment liberalism and student radicals. In early October Kerr was quoted in the *San Francisco Examiner* as having declared that "forty-nine percent of the [FSM's] hard core group are followers of the Castro-Mao line." Kerr has consistently denied ever uttering these words (a denial that strikes us as credible), but even his *corrected* version of that quote during the crisis opened the door to more aspersions on the loyalty of the protesters: "[S]ome elements active in the demonstrations have been impressed with the tactics of Fidel Castro and Mao Tse-tung"; "[the] hard core group of demonstrators contained . . . persons identified as being sympathetic with the Communist Party and Communist causes." These intimations of Communist influence, coming as they did in the Cold War atmosphere of 1964, were yet another obstacle to open dialogue with students and may even have been grist for the mill of those who fomented the very anti-Berkeley backlash that facilitated the rise of Reagan. After all, if the campus was really infiltrated with dangerous subversives, why shouldn't voters demand that extreme measures be used to contain Communism at California's premier public university? Be that as it may, there can be little doubt that FSMers were left with a sense of betrayal, convinced that they had been red-baited by their own University president. Savio, though granting the inaccuracy of the 49-percent quote, went so far as to tell an FSM rally that Kerr's other words linking the FSM to Communists reminded him of his days in Mississippi, where the racist press sought to demonize civil rights volunteers by tarring them with the same brush.[55]

At first glance it may seem puzzling that Kerr, the master negotiator whose specialty was labor mediation, would risk alienating student activists by introducing this theme. It appears that somehow his political and diplomatic skills failed him, rendering him unable to prevent a bitter split with the students that might have been avoided. But the problem that may have been insurmountable was that Kerr was attempting to play two virtually incompatible roles—that of the FSM's political adversary and that of the flexible arbitrator. As its adversary he was prepared to disparage the movement, and in so doing he may well have built support with the public, but in the process he undermined his role of mediator in the eyes of students, who strongly resented his rhetoric (many do even to this day, as some of the memoirs in this volume illustrate). Indeed, a common rhetorical excess in some of these memoirs, one that we urged their authors to reconsider, concerned the alleged 49-percent quote, the "memory" of which had left some of them so angry that even approaching late middle age they were still quite eager to hurl invectives at their old nemesis.

This bitterness over Kerr's intimations of Communist influence is rooted in a sixties-vintage radical distrust of establishment liberalism. In this view Kerr appears as a corporate manager seeking to stifle dissent by means of red-baiting rather than as a benign progressive who respected the right of dissent. Many militants saw ample grounds for believing that, as Savio once put it, "there was a kind of a strain of authoritarianism within liberalism."[56] But such a conclusion, however effective as a rebuke to Kerr for his role in the FSM—and however understandable coming from activists denounced by a liberal university president and jailed by a liberal governor—can hardly do justice to the complexity of Kerr's earlier political history, which includes his pre-FSM battles against the loyalty oath, abolition of compulsory ROTC, and lifting of the Communist speaker's ban. It will obviously require more than the epithet *authoritarian* to explain Kerr's handling of the FSM crisis, and to reconcile it with the UC president's earlier history as a reformer—a daunting task that awaits Kerr's biographers.

But Kerr was hardly alone in attacking the FSM. Much of the press was, if anything, way ahead of him, behaving quite outrageously throughout the crisis, attacking the student rebels relentlessly and with little regard for the facts. In those days it would have been true to form for the *San Francisco Examiner* to have doctored a Kerr quote in order to make the FSM look as bad as possible. This was the same newspaper, after all, that ran Ed Montgomery's three-part series slandering the FSM as a "Marxist dominated" enterprise whose Communist leadership was dedicated to "draw[ing] young blood for the vampire which is international communism." FBI documents later released under the Freedom of Information Act showed that Montgomery colluded with the FBI in red-baiting the student movement—though he claimed that on this particular series he acted alone.[57]

Front-page editorials in other newspapers, such as the *Oakland Tribune,* denounced the FSM as lawless rioters and failed to give the public a real chance to examine the students' grievances. In the words of Carl Schorske, press treatment of the FSM was "very bad." "In a crisis in which freedom and order were both involved," he continued, "those whose basic concern was with order . . . were always favored [by the press] over those primarily concerned with freedom. It was much like the civil rights movement, where the protest marches were 'illegal,' but fundamental to the realization of new freedoms. . . . [T]he press focused on the worst student behavior, not the issues." Ranking among the most egregious examples of press misconduct was the *Tribune*'s doctored photo of an FSM rally, made to appear as if a demonstrator was carrying a Marxist text. Such methods of demonization managed to take their toll, as seen in a February 1965 Field poll showing that 74 percent of Californians disapproved of the Berkeley student movement. With such polling numbers, it is little wonder that, even before the rise of Reagan, California politicians began to build and ride a backlash against Berkeley's "subversive" activists. Among the first out of the starting block were assembly speaker Jesse Unruh and Berkeley assemblymember Donald Mulford, who called for a state legislative probe into Berkeley's campus "agitators."[58]

Given the post-FSM trajectory of national politics during the Vietnam era, one might conclude that the rift between radicals and establishment liberals was inevitable, with the Berkeley conflict serving simply as its logical precursor. Here again, however, one must be cautious about reading the future back into the past, for there are ways in which the FSM can still be seen as a moment that represented hope of at least a limited kind of cooperation between liberals and radicals. It was, after all, a mostly liberal faculty—with a mixture of motives, to be sure—that on December 8 rejected the use of excessive force on campus and finally ended the immediate crisis by endorsing the central FSM positions. It should go without saying that this faculty action was not a denial but an *affirmation* of liberal principles. There was no inherent reason why a movement that carried the banner of the Bill of Rights, uniting liberal and radical students both with each other and with like-minded faculty, had to culminate in a bitter schism. Indeed, it is possible to see the faculty resolutions as the most powerful assertion of faculty liberalism and the greatest moment of student-faculty cooperation in the history of the University. The FSM also enjoyed support from the campus's liberal clergy—as campus minister Keith Chamberlain's essay attests—and from prominent off-campus liberals in the labor, Civil Rights, and civil liberties movements.[59]

Still there is no denying that, just as a fundamentalist minority of campus activists rejected positive relations with liberal faculty almost as a matter of principle, an articulate segment of liberals, both in and outside the University, was deeply hostile to the FSM and to its principled militancy. Since FSMers saw themselves as championing a cause with great liberal appeal, in the words of two Berkeley protesters, it "came as a shock to the FSM that the analysis of the Berkeley events in liberal magazines was overwhelmingly hostile." Lead articles in what were then considered moderately liberal magazines—the *New Leader*, the *Reporter*, and *Commentary*—denounced the FSM as a threat to law and order, and many students were "stunned" to find that the articles were written by four prominent UC faculty members (Lewis Feuer, Seymour Martin Lipset, Paul Seabury, and Nathan Glazer). There was in all these critics a fear of disorder and a revulsion at the FSM's use of civil disobedience, sentiments that led them to denounce the movement harshly; Lipset compared the FSM to the KKK (since both promoted disorder!). These faculty opponents of the FSM and critics of the faculty actions of December 8 were harbingers of something new on the American ideological scene, neoconservatism, a movement of disillusioned liberals. Here again the story of the FSM reaches beyond the history of the New Left: in ways we do not yet fully understand, it seemed to impel at least a vocal minority within the liberal intelligentsia onto a conservative trajectory.[60]

No assessment of the FSM would be complete without taking into account its effect on the local Berkeley political scene. As W. J. Rorabaugh's essay informs us, veterans of the FSM and new participants in the ongoing Berkeley student movement soon became active in local electoral politics, running antiwar candidates, founding leftish political parties, initiating rent control and a host of reforms which pushed the city leftward well beyond its more conventionally liberal profile of the early 1960s. This kind of shift, as the historian David Farber suggests, was not unique to Berkeley but was part of a larger national trend that began to take hold in those politically embattled years. Farber speaks of "the relevance of university towns to the process of social change." Most flagship state universities, he points out, have structural characteristics that are certain to make them local agents of broader social change: the presence of large numbers of autonomous youth, the continuous generating of new knowledge, the universities' influence via their nationally and internationally recruited faculties. If, as Farber concludes, university towns have by their very nature been "spaces in which people experiment politically and culturally," his conclusion certainly applies to Berkeley and the Bay Area, where the FSM itself functioned as a palpable source of such experimentation and change.[61]

The FSM was also important in its links to other social protest movements. Inspired and energized by movements that preceded it, the FSM in turn inspired and energized many future movements. As Jo Freeman's and Waldo Martin's essays suggest, the FSM was immeasurably strengthened because its leadership included veterans of both the Bay Area and southern civil rights movements, movements that brought to the Berkeley campus a level of political daring and tactical boldness that University administrators had never seen before, and that made the leaders of the FSM such formidable political organizers. They also carried from the Civil Rights Movement a political style that was highly democratic and participatory, attracting masses of often politically inexperienced students, some of whom would soon be using the new political space created by the FSM to rally their classmates to the emerging antiwar movement. In the mid-sixties FSM veterans played a key role in organizing a massive antiwar teach-in, anti-ROTC and antidraft agitation, and Robert Scheer's peace candidacy for Congress, making Berkeley a center of resistance to the escalating war in Vietnam. Moreover, the FSM's demand for a student voice in university governance, for free speech, and for a less regulated campus environment soon spread to other colleges and universities as well as some high schools, and the decade ended with the U.S. Supreme Court ruling in *Tinker v. Des Moines* (1969) that even middle- and high-school students had free speech rights guaranteed by the First Amendment.[62] Further, in a different, less direct way the FSM can be linked to the rebirth of American feminism. The FSM included several women in its leadership circles, but, as Margot Adler, Bettina Aptheker, and Suzanne Goldberg each note in their respective essays, not usually on the basis of true equality. It was largely a white, male-dominated movement. The feminist sensibility that female movement veterans began to develop later in the decade grew in part out of their reaction to the subordination they had experienced even as they worked for progressive change in the FSM, SNCC, SDS, and the antiwar movement.[63]

The connections between the FSM and the forces of political and educational change on other campuses remain to be explored in adequate depth. One suspects that those connections occurred on at least two levels. With regard to administrators at other universities, the FSM seems to have spawned a certain degree of change by raising their level of apprehension. Much as inner-city rebellions spurred governmental action in the area of race relations, the FSM heightened university officials' concern about the ominous prospect of mass protests at their own institutions, and the "We don't want another Berkeley here" syndrome seems to have sensitized them to the need for educational reform. To students, however, the FSM suggested that mass protest might become the royal road to political effectiveness. On the left this empowering insight was read positively, as a facilitator of an idealism that could better both the campus and society. Thus proponents of student activism were happy to hear that in the semester after the FSM, Ohio State students formed a Free Speech Front and sat in at the administration building to demand an end to that university's ban on Marxist speakers. Similar FSM-style protests soon erupted at UCLA, UC Riverside, and elsewhere.[64]

For critics of the student movement, however, this mimetic impulse was a danger sign, placing new power in the hands of thrill-seeking youths who were all too capable of abusing it. As one such critic, John Searle, complained:

> Once a full-scale revolt takes place at one university, the urge to imitate it elsewhere becomes irresistible. . . . That a group of students and a mere handful of faculty could overthrow the system of authority of one of the richest and most powerful universities in the land stimulated students elsewhere to enact a similar drama. Even detailed features of Berkeley were imitated. . . . A glamorous, rewarding, and exciting role for students to play had been created, and as long as it continues to be rewarded—by prestige, absence of penalties, media, especially TV glamorization, and inner meaningfulness and significance—it will continue to flourish. At present there is no more rewarding role for students than that of rebel. The rebel student leader is one of the most glamorized and romanticized figures in America—he is constantly in demand for TV interviews; movies are made about his heroism, his face is on the cover of countless magazines. . . . The life of the student acquires much of the excitement that it is capable of possessing through the imitation and re-creation of certain romantic models—the football hero, the student president, Joe College, etc. In the past decade, we have created a new and much imitated ceremonial psychodrama of the student revolt.[65]

Although not without its grain of truth, this argument is open to criticism in that it suggests a narrow, almost monocausal explanation (reducing national student protest to a mere fad) for a complex national phenomenon, the advent of a national wave of campus insurgencies. At the same time, to the extent that Searle is correct about the movement attaching a kind of allure and even glamour to the role of student activist, this characteristic of many social movements is neither surprising nor a reason to discount their value. Mario's contribution to this volume, for example, concedes that he went to his first civil rights demonstration because "there was this girl I wanted to impress." Although not particularly proud of this incident, Savio seems to grasp the utility to the movement of people's acting in accord with such human motivations. Instead of impressing your friends by driving a fancy car or winning a football game, you did so by showing that you were sufficiently serious-minded to protest racism. "I think it was actually a healthy thing," Savio recalled. "We were creating an alternative society, and so in an alternative society, you impress people you want to go out with by doing things that are alternative, right?" But of course Mario's desire to impress a young woman was soon supplanted by deeper social concerns as he came face to face with the challenge of racism. One suspects that such was also the case with other activists who, however their involvement may have been launched, would require something more enduring than shivers of excitement or thrills of social recognition to sustain an activist role over the course of an entire college career.

Another problem with Searle's argument is the uncertainty of its empirical foundation. We simply do not yet know enough about how the Berkeley revolt was perceived by the student generation of the mid- and late 1960s (including students in other countries) or even by its activist minority. The ways in which the FSM did or did not inspire them, the degree to which Berkeley student rebels, who often were not romanticized but *demonized* in the press and who faced real penalties, suffused the role of student protester with glamour and lent it a romantic aura—these are important questions that still await their historian.

It may be useful to think of the FSM as one of the first in a long series of waves that began to wash away some established political and cultural traditions. This process of change in the 1960s, which the FSM helped to expedite, went beyond political discourse and impacted such aspects of daily life as dress, deference, and—as Lawrence Levine's essay suggests—the prevalent speech codes. Schorske recalled how the civil liberties issue soon opened the door to cultural innovations:

> The simple civil liberties thing was the beginning and the heart of the first push, but then it became an empowerment question for students.... The minority rights movements fueled the ethnic studies movements. The political revolution, as so often happens, begins to develop cultural ramifications and begins to erode structures of authority.... The modes of deference suddenly change. What kind of clothes do you wear when you speak to the chancellor?... Getting your tie off was the first step; throwing your jacket away was the second.... Men and women began to dress alike, with jeans; unisex came. These things...became quickly generalized so that even people who were not in the movement adopted the new loose style (sometimes even a kind of studied sloppiness). It wasn't possible for me any longer...to tell who was a child of a farmer in the Valley from who was a child of the San Francisco elite or who was from a [predominantly] Jewish high school in Los Angeles... because everybody began to dress alike.[66]

It is possible, then, to see the FSM as a little Lexington or Concord in what historian Arthur Marwick has depicted as a broader cultural revolution that broke down rigid social rules and hierarchies. After all, it was Berkeley that first circulated the phrase "don't trust anyone over thirty," a challenge to the hierarchies of age that would be repeated many times over in a decade known for its iconoclastic youth culture and the "generation gap" it helped to promote.[67]

In this cultural realm, however, as in the political arena, one must be cautious about excessive conflating of the histories of the late and early 1960s. Of course there was youthful antiauthoritarianism in the FSM and some students whose political rebellion was linked to a countercultural version of personal liberation that included shabby clothes, facial hair, sex, drugs, and rock and roll. However, for every FSMer who, like David Goines, saw the student revolt as an avenue for R-rated acts of personal-sexual rebellion, there were others whose memoirs would be rated PG. Margot Adler recalls in her essay that for her the FSM had none of the sexual significance that Goines dwells upon. She left the FSM as she had entered it, she tells us, as a virgin and saw it as being "about ideas," not sexual revolution. Similarly, Schorske, though speaking about the FSM as the first step en route to major cultural change, also recalls that even in 1965 the move toward informality in dress was far from complete. In answer to his own question about what clothes one wore to meet with the chancellor, he recalls with some surprise that when he met the FSM leadership for a dinner with the new chancellor, "they were all dressed up in a conventional way."[68] Schorske might have been less surprised, however, had he looked back at the famous FSM photo of the student protesters marching through Sather Gate on their way to the November Regents' meeting; there we see the male FSM leaders carrying aloft a "Free Speech" banner while wearing coats and ties. Kate Coleman's essay reminds us that the FSM erupted early enough in the (precounterculture) sixties that many rebellious students like her still cared about appearing respectable, and consequently dressed in a tidy and fastidious way so as to refute their negative stereotype as "dirty beatniks." Thus, even if one concedes that Berkeley was an early chapter in the history of Woodstock nation, one still must come to grips with the fact that it is a long way from coats and ties at Sather Gate to tie-dye and nudity on Yasgar's farm.

One purpose of this volume is to alert the reader to the persistence of free speech as a live issue on the Berkeley campus well after 1964. Despite the victory of December 8, there was considerable uncertainty over just what rights had been won and who controlled the "facts on the ground" with regard to political regulation. This uncertainty evolved from the Regents' response to the faculty resolutions, or perhaps more accurately, to the absence of a clear response. Neither at their meeting ten days later nor on any subsequent occasion did the Regents fully or formally endorse the December 8 settlement, and in the immediate aftermath of the FSM it was not entirely clear if the administration would adhere to its libertarian spirit. At best it may be said that at that meeting, by underscoring their acknowledgment of the applicability on campus of the First and Fourteenth Amendments and by failing to rebuke the faculty's advice to reduce restrictions on political advocacy to the parameters of "time, place, and manner," the Regents were signaling their *de facto* acquiescence. Nevertheless, the meaning of their language was sufficiently ambiguous to lend itself to both liberal and conservative interpretations, while the "time, place, and manner" concept, though borrowed from the words of the U.S. Supreme Court, could itself be subject to varied interpretations in different situations. It should therefore come as no surprise that free speech controversies at Berkeley endured into 1965 and beyond and included far more than the obscenity debate (the "Filthy Speech Movement") of the spring semester.[69]

In 1965, for example, attempts by a Regental committee (headed by Thomas Meyer) to codify a set of specific rules for speech on campus evoked considerable controversy. Both students and faculty demanded that the committee's recommendations be rejected, for once again they included restrictions on outside speakers, restrained student government from taking positions on off-campus issues, and left open the possibility of disciplining students for the content of their speech. Clashes over campus rules grew very contentious in April when—as students protested the chancellor's interim rules for campus political activity—police confiscated an FSM table and a defiant Savio publicly shredded a speaker's permit, symbolizing his defiance. In tearing up this permit, required for nonstudents to speak on campus, Mario told the crowd: "When we are able to give our consent, then we will abide by specific regulations. . . . We will continue with our own rules until then."[70]

Perhaps no issue attested more to the reluctance of UC administrators to completely drop the restrictions inherited from the 1950s than the conflicts over student government during the spring 1965 semester. Despite the FSM revolt, University administrators still hoped to continue the part of the old "Kerr Directives" of 1959 that, in the name of political neutrality, barred student governments from taking positions on off-campus issues. In February 1965 antiwar activists sought to challenge the Kerr Directives by getting the ASUC (student) senate to adopt a resolution calling for an end to U.S. intervention in Vietnam. When the chancellor's representative urged the senate not to so defy the regulation, his pressure helped to sway more-traditional students, leaving the senate hopelessly divided nine to nine.[71] The same issue came up again in March, this time in connection with the Civil Rights Movement in the South. The brutal attack on civil rights marchers in Selma had evoked a wave of sympathy for the marchers and their cause. This time the ASUC senate was prepared to defy the administration; it voted to endorse federal enforcement of voting rights and protection for civil rights workers in Selma. Here was a case where fresh memory of the FSM seemed to make a difference, for this time the administration did not seek to reverse this senate action (unlike the chancellor at Riverside, whose order disallowing a similar resolution prompted the resignation of the student body president).[72]

As late as spring semester 1966 Berkeley activists were struggling with the campus administration over how much control it could exercise over the "time, place, and manner" of political speech. This time the administration ignited another battle when it sought to ban amplified rallies from Sproul Plaza. This battle, which Mario dubbed "the little free speech movement" (analyzed in my essay on that event) briefly returned him to the Berkeley political stage and ended in another victory for free speech advocates. Even as this struggle to preserve Sproul Plaza heated up, other controversies flared over political space and political rules. The administration was still trying to do some political policing when in October 1966 it barred an SDS-sponsored conference on black power.[73] In short, though the FSM and the December 8 resolutions brought a major free speech victory, it was one whose parameters remained contested for a few more years. If Berkeley had attained an uneasy truce, as yet there was no peace.

Nevertheless, the momentum was on the side of free expression as the administration repeatedly backed down in the face of student (and, though to a smaller extent, faculty) opposition, dropping its ban on the black power conference, its threat to ban the amplified rallies, and its refusal to allow the ASUC to take political positions. Hence by 1967 it had finally become evident that in practice, at least, the libertarian principles championed by the FSM and affirmed by the faculty were determining the behavior of the campus administration. The FSM had demanded that activists be free to advocate even potentially unlawful acts of protest so as to open the campus to the Civil Rights Movement, whose community organizing sometimes involved civil disobedience. In 1967 that mode of protest and similarly robust forms of political advocacy were able to proceed unabated on campus; as Leon Wofsy's essay shows, Berkeley faculty and students managed to convene, with no administration restrictions or reprisals, a symbolically potent antiwar graduation ceremony on campus in which civil disobedience—the aiding and abetting of draft resistance—was openly advocated.

Although the FSM was a mass movement, its interior life will never be understood simply by analyzing it en masse. Because in the last analysis a mass movement is composed of individuals, the historian who seeks deeper insights into the motivations of FSMers will have to look at individual stories. In other words, the tools of autobiography and biography, including psychobiography, must be integrated into the historiography. The many memoirs included in this volume represent attempts to illuminate the FSM experience via these personal stories. Not surprisingly, the figure most discussed in those memoirs is Mario. His celebrity status as leader in a movement that liked to think of itself as leaderless, his eloquence, militancy, and evident brilliance, his retreat from the limelight and no doubt very troubled personal life, his reemergence as a political activist decades after the 1960s—all these elements conspire to make him an enigmatic figure of great historical interest. Some of the essays by those who were closest to him, most notably Suzanne Goldberg's, raise important questions about the relationship between political activism and individual psychology. The editors of this volume are wary of the dangers of reductionism—and of superficial studies that have used psychology as a weapon to denounce 1960s radical activists as unstable, disturbed individuals who vented their personal and generational rage into irrational and harmful protests. But if handled sensitively and respectfully, psychological exploration can illuminate some of the important, and not always fully conscious, motivations that fostered student activism, especially when integrated into the social and political context in which these individuals developed. Adding to the insights of these memoirs, not all of which are in accord with the views of the editors, are essays by historians Waldo Martin and Doug Rossinow that explore Mario's distinctive mode of democratic leadership and its links to religious impulses and to the Civil Rights and existentialist movements. The memoirs by Lynne Hollander, David Hollinger, and Jeff Lustig, among other contributions to this volume, attest to Mario's faith in reason, his love of ideas and language, and his rare ability as an orator to engage undergraduates, graduate students, and faculty alike in serious political thought. Jonah Raskin, a colleague of Mario's at Sonoma State, explores the final chapter in Savio's political life, his return to activism in the 1990s in defense of student rights, immigrant rights, and affirmative action. This volume also brings into print for the first time an autobiographical speech that Mario Savio gave just a year before his untimely death. In it Mario speaks of the way the Holocaust, the bomb, and the Civil Rights Movement shaped the political consciousness of his generation of activists, and how his Catholic background and training in philosophy established an intellectual and moral foundation for his own activism.

In the realm of biography perhaps the most unexplored area of the FSM's story concerns ethnicity. The old order at Berkeley was predominantly Anglo-Protestant. The administrators who codified and then enforced restrictions on political advocacy at Berkeley were men of solid American pedigree, who sought to keep the peace with their cousins in the California political establishment. But as Berkeley emerged as America's premier public university, it drew faculty and students from across the nation (and the globe). These newcomers, among whom Jews and others of (mostly) white ethnic origins figured prominently, were in some cases too "cosmopolitan" in their thinking to identify closely with California's tra-ditional power elite in the legislature. Their eyes were more on Selma, the Tonkin Gulf, or Greenwich Village than on Sacramento. One could say, then, that a more politically *reserved* campus, whose tone was set by old-stock officials like Sproul, Kerr, and Strong, was being transformed into a politically *expressive* environment—more open to national and interna-tional political discourse and to new forces of change. Among politically active students and especially among the FSM leaders, one now began to encounter such "exotic" names as Anastasia, Aptheker, Goldberg (not one but three), Iiyama, Savio, and Weinberg. In this sense one might think of President Kerr as a victim of his own success. He wanted to build a great university; but in doing so he helped to attract students and faculty too diverse and cosmopolitan to accept the political compromises of the past, people who thought that a university could not be great unless it could be more engaged in the quest for social justice. Though it would be foolish and misleading to explain the FSM merely by invoking changes in demog-raphy, it cannot be denied that at Berkeley, as at Wisconsin and many other campuses, the new student activism was often led by Jewish students, some of whose families had experienced leftist politics of a kind with which rela-tively few California-born Anglo-Protestants were familiar.[74]

"Free speech . . . represents the very dignity of what a human being is. . . . That's what marks us off from the stones and the stars. You can speak freely. . . . It is the thing that marks us as just below the angels." These words uttered by Mario Savio in 1994 say much about his ongoing commitment to the cause he championed as a twenty-one-year-old student in 1964.[75] But if with regard to free speech in 1964 Mario and the FSM were First Amend-ment purists, by the end of the 1960s and in succeeding decades, including our own, the relationship between the left and freedom of speech would grow more problematic. At moments of great excitement and high passion, and especially when a brutal and unpopular war was raging or when cen-turies-old traditions of racial oppression and exclusion were being chal-lenged, there were (and are) radical activists who cringe at the idea that their political foes or rivals should be free to promote their views. A left that had rallied so boldly to defend its *own* free speech rights sometimes hesi-tated or refused to extend those rights to others. More recently, the issue of hate codes, the regulation of bigoted speech on campus, has posed a fur-ther quandary for radicals who have been forced to choose between their fidelity to free speech on one hand and, on the other, their rejection of racism, sexism, and, more recently, homophobia. As the essay by Jonah Raskin and my final essay suggest, Mario himself in the 1980s and 1990s sometimes found it difficult to think like a free speech absolutist when faced with public expression that involved racial insensitivity or the defense of imperialism. In the wake of all these post-FSM controversies over free speech—and one is raging even as I write—one must ask whether the free speech principles defended at Berkeley in 1964 are still germane in the present context, an issue explored in the essay by constitutional scholar Robert Post. It is our firm conviction that they are.

Although the best-known chapters of the FSM's history cover events that occurred on campus, the movement's final chapter unfolded in the courts. As FSM lawyer Malcolm Burnstein's essay discloses, the FSM sought to use the 1965 trial of its arrested members to defend its political principles. There were certainly some important similarities between the FSM's struggles in the courts and on the campus. In both venues the movement championed free speech, challenged the administration's credibility, sought to maintain group solidarity in the face of punitive threats, and resisted efforts to demonize its members. But there were also important differences. FSM leaders who had been so quick to challenge authority in the campus world initially found it harder to do so when that authority came from their attorneys. Those attorneys worked pro bono, were well intentioned, and of course had much greater legal expertise than their clients. As Burnstein's essay recounts, the lawyers successfully resisted the FSM leadership's desire for jury trials and much of its other tactical advice about how to use the legal proceedings to further a political agenda, advice that Burnstein now believes the lawyers would have been wise to heed. There was a tension between the lawyers' function as guardian of individual rights and the movement's need for solidarity.[76] The legal case also taught the FSM that its dismal relations with University officials may have made the off-campus venues for adjudicating disputes look better from a distance than they were in fact up close—that court authorities were initially no more inclined than their campus counterparts, and perhaps even less so, to lend a sympathetic ear to the FSM and student rights.

In much of the recent historiography of the New Left there has been a tendency to depict movement history as a tale of decline and degeneration. The student movement, so the argument goes, went from being open, democratic, nonviolent, and pragmatic in the early 1960s to being authoritarian, violent, dogmatic, and delusional in its revolutionary expectations in the late 1960s and beyond. The movement shifted, as the subtitle to Todd Gitlin's widely read narrative of the sixties put it, from its constructive "years of hope" to its final and destructive "days of rage."[77] If we were to adhere to this declension model and its division between "good" and "bad" eras, the FSM would clearly fall into the first category. This is what David Burner had in mind in *Making Peace with the Sixties* (1996) when he contrasted Mario with Mark Rudd, leader of the Columbia University student revolt of 1968: "Mario's rhetoric had drawn on Herodotus; Rudd favored obscenity." (Rudd had challenged Columbia's president with the words "Up against the wall, motherfucker. This is a stick up.") Burner praised

Mario's famous Sproul Hall speech as "poetry that combines the exaltation of the civil rights movement with the splendor of the existential vision . . . with no suggestion of violence, thinking of concrete change . . . discourse as yet unthickened by dogmatic pseudorevolutionary verbiage."[78]

The FSM certainly did have a political style that commands respect from people who care about democracy, reasoned discourse, and a principled approach to political change. The nonviolent yet militant spirit of the Civil Rights Movement was glaringly present in the FSM. It can be seen in small but revealing ways, as when the speakers who sought to use the captured police car's roof as a platform thoughtfully took off their shoes before climbing atop the car and later raised funds to repair its dented roof. Searle has noted that notwithstanding Mario's famous speech about stopping the University machine, the ensuing occupation of Sproul Hall was a relatively mild affair: "[S]tudents sat peaceably in the hallways, taking care not to interfere with traffic or to block the doorways. . . . However annoying, such scenes are unlikely to seriously impair much less halt, the operation of a vast university." Searle mocked the administration for overreacting and for believing that "Mario Savio was going to huff and puff and blow the house down." He pointed out that it was "not the sit-in but the arrests and the aftermath" that led to the strike that brought "the university to a grinding halt."[79] The ability of the FSM's leadership to exercise restraint was also visible when, in the hopes of *avoiding* violence—that is, a potentially violent confrontation with the police—it negotiated an end to the October police-car capture, even agreeing as part of that settlement to a moratorium on further peaceful acts of civil disobedience.

Further, the FSM's open and democratic style of political leadership involved activists in endless meetings that often featured genuine discussion and debate rather than dogmatic pronouncements. Mario himself displayed a level of political candor that was highly unusual in mass movements or for that matter in any form of politics. On the eve of the aborted sit-in of November 23, for example, when the FSM seemed deeply divided and on the verge of defeat and was holding an open debate about what strategy to follow, Mario spoke in a manner that few who attended will ever forget. Although he personally favored a sit-in (on moral grounds), he aired his doubts and misgivings about his own position. He presented the best arguments against his own position to enlighten students about what the significant contingencies were and then spoke to the pro-sit-in position. Other pro- and anti-sit-in speeches followed, so that both sides could be well represented before the group made its final decision. This is not to deny that there were moments—on November 9, for example, as the FSM moved to resume civil disobedience—when moderates felt that they were treated scornfully by the FSM leadership.[80] Nevertheless, the FSM's fundamentally open and trusting form of political leadership did contrast sharply with some of the manipulative vanguard tendencies that developed later in the Berkeley antiwar movement. As Martin Roysher points out in his essay, Vietnam Day Committee leader Jerry Rubin embodied this new tendency when, for example, he conveyed his lack of interest in consulting movement rank-and-filers about the potential violence they might encounter on a planned march, since if the marchers were injured it would supposedly radicalize them.

If the difference, then, is real, there is still a danger in drawing too neat and sharp a contrast between the FSM and its successors. Anyone who has listened to Mario's most militant speeches and heard his outbursts of anger, however justified, knows better than to depict the FSM as an always gentle rebellion. If Burner is right about Mario being far more cultured and intelligent than so crude a political leader as Mark Rudd, he is wrong to imply that Rudd alone resorted to obscenities; Mario did so as well, publicly and on several occasions. Nor were the FSMers, hard as they tried, always successful in restraining themselves physically. These were, after all, young men and women in a stressful situation facing arrest and contending with the opposition of campus police. So when, for example, police stepped on demonstrators in the October Sproul Hall sit-in, a scuffle ensued during which Mario bit a campus policeman on the leg (an act for which he later apologized!).[81] Although thankfully this kind of physical contact never recurred during the FSM, its occurrence can serve to remind us that the spirit of Gandhiism may not always prevail.

In presenting an image of an ever gentle, polite, and civil FSM, Burner also overlooks the views of the FSM's detractors. Kerr, Glazer, and other critics of the student revolt charged that the FSM was guilty of physical coercion. Even if no blood was spilled, in their view, leaders of the FSM involved students in such acts as storming buildings, acts that were unlawful and unnecessary and set a dangerous precedent. They also charged that the conflict could have been resolved through negotiation and that when people occupy buildings instead of going through established channels the norms of a democratic society are trampled.[82] The FSM of course rejected this view, insisting that no real channels of communication had been opened to them by an administration that failed to negotiate in good faith. The rebels argued that in a hierarchical university run by an aloof, unresponsive bureaucracy, civil disobedience was the only way powerless students could make themselves heard.

Since such discussions of coercion are so often weighted with ideology, they tend to be unnuanced, framed as an all-or-nothing proposition. Either the students *did* use physical coercion and are therefore portrayed negatively, or they did not and are therefore valorized. Lost in such discussions is the notion of coercion as a continuum with points along the way that can range from mild to extreme. At the lower end of the continuum is the kind of coercion that comes only from highly charged, emotional rhetoric, and at the other end is genuine violence. In the case of the FSM not all sit-ins and sleep-ins were at the same location on that continuum. Even though the December sit-in was the one that led to mass arrests, it was arguably the least coercive and most orderly of these events, with students sitting peacefully, talking, studying, singing, and sometimes dancing in the halls, and with most of the building's occupation occurring after the end of the official work day. This contrasted with the sit-in of October 1, which, because it blocked a dean's office, came to be known as a "pack-in" and at one point precipitated a shoving match with police.[83] Critics made much of the fact that Mario bit a police officer during this scuffle, but failed to note that this brief physical clash was about the only one in which students could be charged with any violence at all. So one is left with choosing whether the movement should be judged on the basis of its months of nonviolence or its few moments of physical conflict and coercion. Almost inevitably, this choice is linked to the political sympathies of the person sitting in judgment, which is why Kerr can color the movement coercive while Mario lauds it as a "non-violent army."[84] Indeed, seen from the vantage point of the FSM, the threat of violence and then violence itself was injected into the dispute not by the FSM but by the administration and the governor, who responded to the movement's nonviolent civil disobedience by calling police onto campus and thereby setting a dangerous precedent.[85] And in fact, this massive display of police power, which yielded the largest mass arrest in California history, did set a precedent. In any case, no matter which side one may prefer to blame, there is no question that the FSM conflict raised the physical stakes in campus politics, a trend that was to spread faster than tear gas in mid- and late-1960s America.

These considerations make the contrasts between 1964 and the later 1960s seem a bit less stark and leave the "good sixties/bad sixties" framework looking somewhat simplistic. Moreover, there is something inherently unfair about using figures like Rudd or Rubin to represent the full array of students who mobilized to protest the Vietnam War and other injustices. As Terry Anderson has shown in his informative chronicle, *The Movement and the Sixties* (1995), at the very time in the late 1960s when revolutionary posturing was paralyzing New Left organizations, most notably SDS, the antiwar movement grew at an unprecedented rate, and millions of students demonstrated in the same mostly nonviolent way that the FSM had done back in 1964.[86] It may be that as historians follow up on Anderson's pioneering work, they will find that for most student activists who came along later in the decade, the nonviolent approach that the FSM popularized in the early sixties never went out of style, a conclusion reinforced by the finding of the President's Commission on Campus Unrest.[87] We will know that for certain, however, only if and when historians wake up to the task of completing grassroots studies of student revolts on the many campuses whose sixties protest have never been examined. We hope that our volume will encourage a new generation of historians to undertake such studies, so that we can shed the old clichés and assumptions in favor of fresh thinking, yielding a history of the sixties that is free of both condescension and romanticism.

Given the topic of this book, however, strictly academic or historiographical goals seem somehow insufficient. The editors believe that the significance of the issues raised in these essays, and by the FSM itself, transcend both the sixties and the task of historically reconstructing that turbulent era. The volume invites us to reconsider our assumptions about words and institutions that are familiar but too often unexamined: free speech, the First Amendment, political neutrality, democracy, academic freedom, academic governance, student rights, interracial solidarity, the university, movement sexism, educational reform, radicalism, liberalism, community, backlash, leadership. We hope that in the spirit of the FSM, when a police car was converted into a podium for examining the world surrounding students, this collection will provoke a dialogue between the present and the past and will generate much free speech about the ways in which the issues raised by a long-ago campus rebellion can make us more reflective and critical of ourselves and the world we live in today.

ADDENDUM

Lost in all the controversy regarding Kerr's alleged 49-percent quote were the actual facts regarding the Communist role in the FSM. Although Communists and people close to the Communist Party, including FSM Steering Committee member Bettina Aptheker, participated in the FSM, their numbers were very small. Not even FBI Director Hoover, always eager to unearth signs of Communist influence, could find many "reds" in the FSM. Indeed, an obviously disappointed Hoover reported that the FBI investigation had identified only thirty-nine students and five faculty "with subversive backgrounds" in FSM's often huge demonstrations. But Hoover, unwilling to admit the uselessness of his investigation, argued that the FSM, "while not Communist originated or controlled, had been exploited by a few Communists for their own ends."[88]

On the 49-percent quote itself Kerr, convincingly insisting in our recent interview that he would never have made such a "stupid" statement, blamed the misquote on sloppy reporting. In print, Kerr has acknowledged two occasions when he did raise the Communist issue. Since the issue has caused so much controversy, it is worth noting his exact words. On October 2, 1964, at a San Francisco press conference: "I am sorry to say that some elements active in the demonstrations have been impressed with the tactics of Fidel Castro and Mao Tse-tung. There are very few of these, but there are some." Then, at an October 6 press conference in Los Angeles: "Experienced on-the-spot observers estimated that the hard core group of demonstrators—those who continued as part of the demonstrations through the night of October 1—contained at times as much as 40 percent off-campus elements. And within that off campus group, there were persons identified as being sympathetic with the Communist Party and Communist causes."[89] In our interview Kerr still was reluctant to confront the negative implications of his remarks. While expressing anger at having been misquoted, he focused on the words that had been inaccurately attributed to him rather than on what the FSM reasonably saw as the red-baiting overtones of what he had actually said. When we pointed out that even without the 49-percent misquote the words he actually *did* use, given the Cold War atmosphere of 1964, would tar the FSM as un-American, Kerr conceded that it had "probably been a mistake" to have so focused attention on the Communist issue.[90]

Nevertheless, the erroneous story of a 49-percent statement has involved some FSMers and others in inaccurate allegations. For example, Hal Draper in his ardently pro-FSM *Berkeley: The New Student Revolt* offers a chapter on red-baiting in which he claims that "there is no record that he [Kerr] ever sent a denial to the papers" in which the quote appeared.[91] In fact, Kerr *did* send such a clarifying statement; it was published in the *Examiner* on November 27, 1964. Savio himself had a mixed record in responding to the quote. At a Sproul Plaza rally on October 6, 1964, he spoke to the crowd about two conflicting reports of Kerr's remarks—the 49-percent quote from the October 3 *Examiner* and a report of Kerr's remarks, also October 3, in the *San Francisco Chronicle* that, in Savio's words, "treated us a good deal better," since it lacked the wildly inflated 49-percent figure. After comparing this situation to the Mississippi press's red-baiting of the Civil Rights Movement, Savio then told the crowd that he had called Kerr's office to find out whether the *Examiner* story or the "less provocative" *Chronicle* story was more reliable. Savio reported Kerr's response that the "less provocative" *Chronicle* story was more reliable. Savio graciously accepted Kerr's denial and, alluding to the press's anti-FSM bias, acknowledged that "we have no reason at all to suppose" that Kerr was lying, that "there were plenty of people who could very easily have influenced that article—the more provocative one—and would have been very happy to do so." Yet shortly after the end of the FSM crisis, Savio, responding to an interviewer's question about red-baiting, said that "to a very large extent" Kerr began it when he spoke about "the 'hard core of the FSM being 49 percent Castroite-Maoists'"; here Mario was ignoring the denial he had personally obtained from Kerr's office.[92]

If the historiography of the FSM is to deepen our understanding of the relationship between the left and the Berkeley rebellion, it must begin to transcend both this old 49-percent controversy and its underlying premises. Once we dispense with the Cold War obsession (dating at least as far back as Joe McCarthy) about counting Communists, we can begin to see the Berkeley campus left in all of its complexity. That left, after all, included not only SDS and the civil rights organizations that we associate with the new student radicalism but also Berkeley's wide spectrum of Old Left groups, ranging from the Communist-led Du Bois Club to its counterparts in the anti-Stalinist left, including the Independent Socialist Club (IS) and the Young People's Socialist League. Although none of these Old Left affiliates were mass organizations, they did have politically experienced and articulate organizers who had participated in civil rights protests and had connections with community organizers, politicians, and left intellectuals (such as Hal Draper, who provided ideological inspiration to the IS). Given these connections, it makes sense for historians to explore Jack Weinberg's contention that the Old Left organizational presence in Berkeley was essential to the FSM, especially in its networking beyond the campus. In other words, rejecting Cold War caricatures of Communist control of the FSM should not lead us to the other extreme: ignoring the role of Old Left organizations, a role that historians have barely mentioned and that few memoirs in this volume touched upon.[93]

NOTES

1. Savio, "Commentary on Memorandum Prepared by Dean of Men Arleigh Williams," n.d., Free Speech Movement records, CU-309, University Archives, Bancroft Library, University of California at Berkeley (hereafter cited as FSM Records). Many documents in this archive are available at <lib.berkeley.edu/BANC/FSM>. For a typical Savio statement indicating his reluctance to be seen as *the* FSM leader, see Raskin, "The Berkeley Affair: Mr. Kerr vs. Mario Savio and Co.," in *Revolution at Berkeley: The Crisis in American Education,* ed. Michael V. Miller and Susan Gilmore (New York: Dell, 1965), 79. See also *Daily Californian* (hereafter *DC*), 27 Apr. 1965.

2. On Savio's leadership skills and his discomfort with the celebrity status those skills conferred upon him, see the tributes to him paid by fellow movement activists and friends following his death in 1996: "Remembering Mario Savio," essays by Mark Shechner et al., *Tikkun* 12 (Jan. 1997): 27–30, 75–76; Zelnik, "The Avatar of Free Speech," *New York Times Magazine,* 27 Dec. 1996 (also in this volume); "Remembering Savio," *Nation,* 2 Dec. 1996, 7. See also Arthur Gatti, "Mario Savio's Religious Influences and Origins," *Radical History Review,* no. 71 (1998): 122–32, and the eulogies at www.fsm-a.org.index.html.

3. The 1996 OAH session on Savio and the FSM was chaired by Linda Kerber and organized by Robert Cohen, Mary Ryan, and Reginald Zelnik. Papers were given by several contributors to this volume (Freeman, Hollinger, Lustig, Martin, Cohen, Zelnik). The only book-length study of the FSM to appear in the last thirty years was written not by a historian but by graphic artist and FSM veteran David Lance Goines, *The Free Speech Movement* (Berkeley: Ten Speed Press, 1993). In

contrast to the 1960s, in which there were—according to Philip Altbach and David Kelly—more than 150 books, articles, and dissertations on the FSM, the post-1960s era generated little new research by historians, with the exception of the chapter in W. J. Rorabaugh, *Berkeley at War* (New York: Oxford University Press, 1989), and Bret Eynon's "Community in Motion: The Free Speech Movement, Civil Rights, and the Roots of the New Left," *Oral History Review* 17 (spring 1989): 39–69. Eynon's article draws upon a superb interview he did with Savio for the Columbia Oral History Project in 1985, now available at <lib.berkeley.edu/BANC/FSM>.

4. *Report of the President's Commission on Campus Unrest* (Washington, D.C.: U.S. Government Printing Office, 1970), 22–23. Despite the Commission's claim that the FSM invented a new style of campus politics, there were a number of precedents for student use of civil disobedience in the early 1960s, though most of these were directed toward off-campus civil rights targets (and, in the case of the 1960 anti-HUAC protests in San Francisco, civil liberties targets). The most extensive use of civil disobedience on campus prior to the FSM occurred at the University of Chicago in 1962, where CORE activists sat in outside the president's office for two weeks protesting racial discrimination in university-owned housing. However, compared to the FSM, the Chicago protest was a mild affair involving a small number of students and lacking the FSM's large-scale civil disobedience, mass arrests, and strike activity. Hence, though its tactics were not unprecedented, in terms of its scale and its disruptiveness the FSM was, as the Commission suggested, something new in American student politics. On the Chicago protest, see *New York Times*, 26, 28 Jan., 4, 6, 7 Feb. 1962.

5. *DC*, 1 Oct. 1984; Robert Cohen, ed., "The Free Speech Movement and Beyond," 1994; Mario Savio to friends, 29 Aug. 1984, in my possession. Another outcome of this twentieth anniversary commemoration was that the California State Legislature, after extensive lobbying by Berkeley's graduate student government, declared October 1 "Free Speech Day" in California, adopting a free speech bill to honor the FSM, coauthored by state assemblymember Tom Bates. See *DC*, 1 Oct. 1985.

6. *DC*, 28 May, 1, 2 June 1982. The FBI was not the only government agency spying on the FSM. The Mississippi Sovereignty Commission, an intelligence agency created by that state's legislature in 1956 to help protect segregation, had a paid agent taking photos and gathering other information on the FSM. See Jo Freeman, "The Berkeley Free Speech Movement and the Mississippi Sovereignty Commission" (2001), available at <www.JoFreeman.com>.

7. "Berkeley in the Sixties" (Emeryville, Calif.: Kitchell Films, 1984, brochure); Leon Litwack, "On the Dedication of the Mario Savio Steps," UC Berkeley, 3 Dec. 1997, typescript in author's possession. Parts of the 1994 commemoration were recorded along with interviews of activists in the documentary film *Free @30*. The FSM website launched by Rossman may be accessed at www.fsm-a.org.index.html.

8. Wini Breines, *Community and Organization in the New Left* (New Brunswick, N.J.: Rutgers University Press, 1989), xiv, 18, 20, 23, 26–27, 30–31.

9. Ibid., 23–24, 30–31; Stanley Aronowitz, *The Death and Rebirth of American Radicalism* (New York: Routledge, 1996), 65–68; James J. Farrell, *The Spirit of the Sixties: Making Postwar Radicalism* (New York: Routledge, 1997) 156–64.

10. Savio interview with Robert Cohen and David Pickell, Berkeley, 29 Sept. 1984, transcript in FSM Records.

11. Savio to friends, 24 Aug. 1984, copy of letter in my possession. Note, however, that, though Savio understood the historical significance of the FSM, he consistently stressed that Mississippi Freedom Summer and the Civil Rights Movement were even more important in facilitating the rise of campus activism. He recalled that in summer 1964 there was still no mass movement of white students until the surge of volunteers who joined in the Mississippi Freedom Summer. He credited Freedom Summer (and organizer Bob Moses) with prodding white students to seek a deeper meaning in their own lives—what Doug Rossinow would later term a "search for authenticity"—through a commitment to political action. Savio explained that "the thing that I think turned the '60s as we know them loose was that interface between the poorest stratum of society that was on its own struggling for liberation and...white students, [from the] privileged stratum...who had all sorts of comforts but...the notion of a wasteland really...applied—a very hollow kind of existence" (Savio interview with Cohen and Pickell).

12. There is ample evidence that many FSMers did not share the confrontational style and political radicalism of the more militant leaders. Note, for example, that the FSM's more militant leaders won a key vote to resume civil disobedience in early November *by a single vote* (Goines, 303–25); and later that month, when the FSM's more radical leaders held a sit-in after the regents made some compromises that placated many moderates, the sit-in had to be aborted. There were organizations, such as Particle Berkeley, a math and science club, that, though part of the FSM from the start, opposed the use of civil disobedience on campus until the December sit-in (Barbara Goldberg, "Recollections of December 2nd," Malcolm Burnstein papers, BANC MSS 99/294(c) [hereafter cited as Burnstein Papers], carton 2, Bancroft Library). An example of the nonradical mind-set can be seen in the comments an FSM activist jotted down on the back of an information card he had completed in volunteering to donate labor to the movement. He wrote, "Some comments by Savio in particular have been snide and ill-advised. When talking of the administration we should all remember that equal status in the affairs of the university is what we want—not hegemony. If we demand respect and dignity, we must logically extend this to those with whom we differ" (Information Card, Barry Glick, carton 1, FSM Records). Also see Joseph La Pointe Probation Report by D. Fenn, 23 July 1965, carton 2, Burnstein Papers. Little has been written on the post-FSM politics of FSM activists, and most of this literature starts from the misleading assumption that all or almost all FSMers were radicals in 1964. See, Alberta J. Nassi, "Survivors of the Sixties: Comparative Psychosocial and Political Development of Former Berkeley Student Activist," *American Psychologist* 36 (July 1981): 753–61; idem and Stephen I. Abramowitz, "Transition or Transformation? Personal and Political Development of Former Berkeley Free Speech Movement Activists," *Journal of Youth and Adolescence* 8 (1979): 21–35; Michael Maidenberg and Philip Meyer, "The Berkeley Rebels Five Years Later," *Public Opinion Quarterly* 24 (1970): 477–78; Wade Green, "Where Are the Savios of Yesteryear?" *New York Times Magazine,* 12 July 1970, 6–9, 35–37.

13. Breines, 18.

14. As I see it, Breines makes too much of remarks Savio made during a 1965 interview, where he said that "Free Speech was in some ways a pretext.... Around that issue the people could gain the community they formerly lacked." Though not

insignificant, this remark needs to be set in historical context. It was made *after* the FSM revolt had ended, when Savio and other militants pondered the movement's radical implications as they thought about how to sustain a left political momentum on campus. Savio never made such an argument *during* the FSM, when his speeches, memos, and leaflets as well as those by virtually all FSMers highlighted the centrality of the free speech issue. The 1965 interview was also very brief, with no follow-up on the "pretext" quote and no attempt to press Savio to elaborate on the relative weight of the free speech issue. Two more extensive interviews with Savio, which elicited a far fuller analysis of the FSM's genesis and meaning, indicate that he saw the free speech and civil rights issues as absolutely central and never repeated the "pretext" argument. See Savio interview with Bret Eynon, 5 March 1985, Columbia University Oral History Project; Savio interview with Cohen and Pickell, 29 Sept. 1984, FSM Records. Savio, upon learning that the FBI had been spying on him, mocked the very idea that the FSM had been a revolutionary event and insisted on the primacy of the movement's free speech cause: "We weren't engaged in overthrowing the government. We were engaged in trying to set up our little tables with the cups for money and handing out literature and making speeches about civil rights. We were doing a perfectly legitimate thing in Thomas Jefferson–constitutional type terms" (*DC,* 1 June 1982).

15. See defendants' statements in box 3, Burnstein Papers. On these concerns about free speech and due process, see Cohen, "This Was *Their* Fight," this volume, where my inability to cite these statements by name is explained in the footnote on pages 230–31.

16. See John Searle's remarks in the film directed by Mark Kitchell, *Berkeley in the '60s* (New York: First Run Features, 1990); and Lynne Hollander's remarks at the memorial session, UC Berkeley, 6 Dec. 1996, Bancroft Collection.

17. John Searle, *The Campus War: A Sympathetic Look at the University in Agony* (New York: World Publishing, 1971), 58–59.

18. Ernest Kantorowitz, *The Fundamental Issue: Documents and Marginal Notes on the University of California Loyalty Oath* (San Francisco: Parker Printing, 1950; reprint, 1999); Clark Kerr, *The Gold and the Blue: A Personal Memoir of the University of California, 1949–1967,* vol. 2: *Political Turmoil* (Berkeley and Los Angeles: University of California Press, 2003); Kerr interview with Amelia Fry, 29 Sept. 1969, in "Earl Warren: Views and Episodes, Oral History transcript/tape-recorded interviews conducted 1969–1975 by K. Baum and Amelia Fry" (University of California at Berkeley, 1976), 2–13; Michael Rossman, *The Wedding Within the War* (Garden City, N.Y.: Doubleday, 1971), 30–123.

19. Carl E. Schorske, "Intellectual Life, Civil Libertarian Issues, and the Student Movement at the University of California, Berkeley, 1960–1969," oral history conducted in 1996 and 1997 by Ann Lage, Regional Oral History Office, The Bancroft Library, University of California at Berkeley, 2000 (hereafter, Schorske Oral History), 28.

20. "Administrative Pressures and Student Political Activity at the University of California: A Preliminary Report" [1964], FSM Records. As Rossman indicates in his essay in this volume, the naming of this report for him had sexist overtones, since it was coedited by Lynne Hollander and should have been known as the "Hollander-Rossman Report." To Rossman and other organizers of this report the his-

tory of political repression at UC Berkeley was so familiar that they began the research for it already knowing all the major instances of repression that they wanted to study. Indeed, they began their study knowing what its conclusion would be—a conclusion they discussed in an information sheet as they started to organize groups of student researchers. See "Information Sheet for Research on Repression at Berkeley," 1964, Free Speech Movement files of the FBI.

21. Rossman, *Wedding,* 94–95, 107. It was with this long view in mind that Rossman, in describing the police car incident, wrote that "we realize simply that we have to hold that car. That car is the only thing we have gotten in six years" (ibid., 110). Students did not have to read the Rossman Report to learn of the history of repression at UC but heard about it on Sproul Plaza from SLATE veterans. See Art Goldberg's remarks at a 6 Oct. 1964 rally, in the transcript of that rally, FSM Records. Also, see FSM press release, 23 Nov. 1964, The Center for Higher Education papers regarding the Free Speech Movement, CU 310.2 (hereafter Center for Higher Education Papers), box 1, Bancroft Library. Savio too referred back to the 1950s during the December occupation of Sproul Hall, when he warned that "some of our best faculty were forced to leave in the 1950 [*sic*] loyalty oath controversy. Some of our best students may be expelled now" (Max Heirich, *The Spiral of Conflict: Berkeley 1964* [New York: Columbia University Press, 1971], 272).

22. David Horowitz, *Student* (New York: Ballantine Books, 1962). This book played a significant role in Savio's decision to attend Berkeley; its political narrative convinced him that it "was an exciting place to be" (Savio interview with Eynon, 5 March 1985, p. 10).

23. Bettina Aptheker essay in Cohen, "Free Speech Movement and Beyond," 66.

24. Savio interview with Cohen and Pickell; Savio interview with Eynon; Robert Hurwitt, "How Red Was My Berkeley," *Berkeley Express,* 15 Sept. 1989, 15. Note, however, that while small in number Communists in the FSM did—as Steve Weissman's essay in this volume suggests—play a significant role in the movement; but that role was the opposite of the one imagined by red-baiters in that the Communists were often a voice of tactical moderation.

25. Kerr's views are expressed in the interview cited in note 18, in his essay in this volume, and in his forthcoming book *Political Turmoil.*

26. Although the Rossman Report and most students linked the restrictions of 1964 to the Cold War years of the 1950s, these restrictions actually date back to the early days of the Sproul administration. Sproul's codification of limitations on student expression and outside speakers began in 1934 as an outgrowth of the red scare that beset the Bay Area in the aftermath of the San Francisco general strike and the West Coast waterfront strike. See Max Heirich and Sam Kaplan, "Yesterday's Discord," in *The Berkeley Student Revolt: Facts and Interpretations,* ed. Seymour Martin Lipset and Sheldon S. Wolin (Garden City, N.Y.: Doubleday, 1965), 10–16; C. Michael Otten, *University Authority and the Student: The Berkeley Experience* (Berkeley: University of California Press, 1970), 106–135; Robert Cohen, *When the Old Left Was Young: Student Radicals and America's First Mass Student Movement, 1929–1941* (New York: Oxford University Press, 1993), 100–108, 118–29.

27. As Vice Chancellor Alex C. Sherriffs explained, one of Kerr's "preoccupations" was how to win "maximum free speech and still not get the university involved in politics which could bring the university to its knees, distort it, or give

the legislature the right to tell us how to behave. The public wouldn't understand [if we had political advocacy on campus]. They would come in to control you. If someone came in to control you, you're much less of a university because you're that much less free to pursue the truth"; Alex C. Sherriffs, "The University of California and the Free Speech Movement: Perspectives from a Faculty Member and an Administrator," oral history conducted in 1978 by James H. Rowland, Regional Oral History Office, Bancroft Library, University of California at Berkeley, 1980 (hereafter Sherriffs Oral History), 42–43. On Kerr's support for the "no political advocacy" policy on campus, see especially his essay in this volume.

28. Savio interview with Cohen and Pickell.

29. Kerr interview with Cohen and Zelnik, 12 July 1999, tape in editors' possession.

30. Philip Selznick, "Reply to Glazer," in Lipset and Wolin, 304.

31. In his study of the 1960s, David Burner makes a useful observation regarding the contrast between the era's insurgent movements—especially the Civil Rights and Free Speech Movements—and Cold War liberals, who favored compromise, "self-control and emotional constraint": "The liberal relish[ed] . . . the virtues of sobriety and restraint. . . . Underlying the particular quarrels between liberals and radicals was a basic difference in temperament and perception. Liberals favored the legal formalities that movement rebels scorned. . . . The liberalism of the Berkeley administration, disposed to compromise, crashed head-on into the moral objectives of the student movement, as the liberalism of the Kennedy and Johnson administration collided with the moral purity of the civil rights activists" (Burner, *Making Peace with the '60s* [Princeton, N.J.: Princeton University Press, 1996], 5, 7, 140).

Kerr's sometime strategy of compromising certain student political rights in order to liberalize other policies is nowhere more evident than in his codification of campus political rules, beginning in 1959, via a series of policy pronouncements which came to be known as the "Kerr Directives." He wanted to liberalize the rules for bringing outside speakers to UC but had to get conservative Regents to buy into this policy. So, while liberalizing the speaker rules, he offered the Regents rules that barred student governments from taking positions on off-campus issues. For a brilliant discussion of Kerr's political maneuvering with these directives, see Glenn T. Seaborg (Berkeley's chancellor when Kerr issued the directives) with Ray Colvig, *Chancellor at Berkeley* (Berkeley: Institute of Governmental Studies Press, 1994), 423–33.

32. Samuel Kaplan, "Revolt of an Elite: Sources of the FSM Victory," *Graduate Student Journal*, no. 4 (spring 1965): 77.

33. For examples of students who, like Mayer, linked their outrage over UC's new political restrictions to disappointment that UC was not behaving like the freer universities they had previously attended, see defendants' statements to Judge Crittenden, boxes 3, 4, Burnstein Papers.

34. See defendants' statements in boxes 3, 4, Burnstein Papers.

35. Lipset and Seabury, "The Lesson of Berkeley," in Lipset and Wolin, 349.

36. "Byrne Report to the Forbes Committee of the Board of Regents," 7 May 1965, Appendix B, *Appellants' Opening Brief: People of the State of California, Plaintiff and Respondent vs. Mario Savio and 571 Others, Defendants and Appellants*, 329–92; *Education at Berkeley: Report of the Select Committee of Education* (Berkeley: University of

California Press, 1968); Caleb Foote, Henry Mayer, and Associates, *The Culture of the University: Governance and Education* [report of the Study Committee on University Governance] (San Francisco: Jossey-Bass, 1968).

37. Goodman, "Berkeley in February," in Miller and Gilmore, 292.

38. Schorske Oral History, 51, 53, 102. See also Elinor Langer, "The Berkeley Scene, 1966 (II): Educational Reform," *Science* 152 (May 1966), 1220–23; *DC*, 17 Feb. 1965.

39. Rossman, lecture, Berkeley, 5 Sept. 1984, tape in my possession; Michael Rossman, "The Movement and Educational Reform," *American Scholar* 36 (Autumn 1967): 594–600; Mario Savio, "The Uncertain Future of the Multiversity: A Partisan Scrutiny of Berkeley's Muscatine Report," *Harper's*, Oct. 1966, 88–94. For an account by a TA exhilarated by the class he taught at "the free University of California" during the Sproul Hall occupation and equally excited by the cause of educational reform, see Michael Klein probation report, 19 July 1965, carton 2, Burnstein Papers. On another FSM defendant who came away from the sit-in impressed that the free speech crisis had "aroused a new intellectual curiosity. The marriage of politics and education meant a new vitality for the university," see Andrea Snow probation report, 22 July 1965, loc. cit.

40. Nathan Glazer, "Reply to Selznick," in Lipset and Wolin, 315.

41. Kerr, address at commencement exercises, Berkeley campus, 12 July 1965, series 8, carton 4, FSM Records.

42. Kerr, *The Uses of the University* (Cambridge: Harvard University Press, 1963). Also see Kerr, "The Unique Role of the State University," 1 Oct. 1964, Center for Higher Education Papers.

43. On October 2, 1964, Kerr told the American Council on Education (ACE), "We do not permit meetings on campus for planning social and political action against the surrounding community." Coming at a time when students were organizing against racial discrimination in the "surrounding community," these remarks gave the impression that Kerr opposed such organizing. Note also that Kerr's formulation, "against the surrounding community," assumes a unitary "community." But in fact, organizing to protest employment discrimination involved students in demonstrations *against* employers yet *in support of* the local black community. Since Kerr opposed the use of the campus as a vehicle for organizing civil rights protests, one might mistakenly conclude—as some FSMers did—that he opposed the Civil Rights Movement. But as a liberal, Kerr, prior to the FSM, had at times acted as a friend of that movement. Thus in Kerr's October 2 ACE speech at the Sheraton Palace Hotel, site of the largest pre-FSM civil rights protest involving Berkeley students, he indicated that he had stood up to the enemies of civil rights: because "some Berkeley students participated . . . in illegal activities [a civil rights sit-in] in this hotel, . . . a few leading legislators" had demanded that the students be expelled. "We refused to do so on the grounds that they had acted as citizens, not as students. However, if they had recruited on campus or had made their plan on campus, we could not have drawn such a distinction." Clearly Kerr's problem was not with the Civil Rights Movement itself, but with the use of the campus as its base. For the text of Kerr's speech, see Center for Higher Education Papers.

44. Raskin, "Berkeley Affair," 83–84. See also Savio, "The Multiversity vs. the Free University," FSM Conference, 9 Jan. 1965, FSM Records.

45. Goines, 187–88.

46. Statement to Judge Crittenden, [July 1965], box 3, Burnstein Papers.

47. Sol Stern, "A Deeper Disenchantment," in Miller and Gilmore, 237.

48. Robert Starobin, "Graduate Students in the FSM," *Graduate Student Journal*, no. 4 (spring 1965): 17–26; Robert Cohen, "The Making of a New Left Labor Union: Berkeley's Union of University Employed Graduate Students (AFT Local 1570), 1964–1965," in Cohen, "Free Speech Movement and Beyond," 217–21.

49. See Kerr's essay in this volume; he makes the same point in more detail in *Political Turmoil.*

50. Sherriffs Oral History, 15–62; Katherine Towle, "Dean of Students, "Administration and Leadership," interview in 1967 by Harriet Nathan, series director, University History Series, Bancroft Collection, University of California at Berkeley, 1970, pp. 143, 195, 198, 200, 208, 217, 218.

51. *FSM Newsletter,* 12, 20 Oct. 1964; "President Kerr," FSM song, words by Genevieve Hailey, and Kerr caricature from FSM Christmas Card, in Goines, 723, 728; see also the treatment of Kerr in an untitled short skit by Barbara Garson, script in carton 2, FSM Records.

52. J. Edgar Hoover to Tolson, Belmont, De Loach, Sullivan, 28 Jan. 1965, copy in my possession.

53. Savio used this term in the preface to his "operation of the machine" speech in December 1964 (Goines, 361). The Weinberg quote is from Calvin Trillin, "Letter from Berkeley," in Miller and Gilmore, 275.

54. On the theme of liberal breakdown, see Allen J. Matusow, *The Unraveling of America: A History of Liberalism in the* 1960s (New York: Harper and Row, 1984), xiv, 395–439.

55. The 49-percent quote appeared in the *San Francisco Examiner,* 3 Oct. 1964; Kerr's attempts to correct this statement can be found in ibid., 27 Nov. 1964, and *DC,* 1 Dec. 1964. On Savio's remarks concerning Kerr's reported statements about the FSM's links to Communism and for further discussion of the controversy over those alleged links, see Addendum to this Introduction.

56. Savio interview with Cohen and Pickell.

57. The series, by Ed Montgomery, ran in the *Examiner* on 25–27 Nov. 1964. On Montgomery's relationship with the FBI, see *DC,* 1 June 1982.

58. *Oakland Tribune,* 2 Oct. 1964 (the editorial attacking the FSM); Schorske Oral History, 91–92, 94. The Field poll on the FSM is in Lipset and Wolin, 199; for an illuminating discussion of the doctored photo that appeared in the *Tribune* on 2 Oct. 1964, see Goines, 174–75; also see Colin Miller, "The Press and the Student Revolt," in Miller and Gilmore, 313–48; on Unruh and Mulford, see *San Francisco Chronicle,* 4 Dec. 1964; *Berkeley Daily Gazette,* 5 Dec. 1964.

59. Press release, California State Council of Building Service Employees, 3 Dec. 1964; Executive Committee, Central Labor Council of Alameda County AFL-CIO to Governor Brown, 3 Dec. 1964; James Farmer's statement reprinted in *DC,* 15 Feb. 1965; John Lewis, SNCC press release, 3 Dec. 1964, carton 3, FSM Records.

60. James F. Petras and Michael Shute, "Berkeley '65," in Miller and Gilmore, 208–9; Joseph Dorman, *Arguing the World: The New York Intellectuals in Their Own Words* (New York: Free Press, 2000), 144–56.

61. David Farber, "New Wave Sixties Historiography," *Reviews in American History* 27 (June 1999): 300.

62. John W. Johnson, *The Struggle for Student Rights:* Tinker v. Des Moines *and the* 1960s (Lawrence: University Press of Kansas, 1997).

63. Ruth Rosen, *The World Split Open: How the Modern Women's Movement Changed America* (New York: Viking, 2000), 94–140.

64. In his memoir of the FSM, Berkeley historian Henry May noted that because of the FSM "the word 'Berkeley' . . . like Pearl Harbor or Sarajevo even entered the language in the middle sixties as a common noun, as in 'For God's sake, don't do that; we don't want another Berkeley on our hands here'" (Henry May, *Ideas, Faiths, and Feelings: Essays on American Intellectual and Religious History,* 1952–1982 [New York: Oxford University Press, 1983], 90). On the FSM's immediate impact on other campuses, see *DC,* 2, 7, 21, 28, 30 April 1965; [UCLA] *Daily Bruin,* 1, 2, 4 Dec. 1964. See also the report of FSM leaders' speaking tour of other campus, *Los Angeles Times,* 14 Dec. 1964. SDS leader Tom Hayden responded to the FSM by arguing that "the way to support students at Berkeley is not to send telegrams . . . but to go down to the administration building and take it over. . . . I mean that literally" (*Daily Bruin,* 10 Dec. 1964). On the SDS's response to the FSM, see also James Miller, *"Democracy Is in the Streets": From Port Huron to the Siege of Chicago* (New York: Simon and Schuster, 1987), 223. On a movement similar to the FSM at the University of Texas, see Doug Rossinow, *The Politics of Authenticity: Liberals, Christians, and the New Left in America* (New York: Columbia University Press, 1998), 215–16. An early sign that students beyond America's shores were watching the FSM came to Kerr's attention in April 1965 when student protesters in Scotland demonstrated against him during his visit there. Thanks to these protesters, "the famous initials 'FSM' were everywhere" during his visit to Strythclide University, where he had come to receive an honorary degree; the student government, citing Kerr's "illiberal views on the rights of students," voted against granting the degree and then boycotted the ceremony; *DC,* 30 April 1965.

65. Searle, *Campus War,* 181.

66. Schorske Oral History, 104–5.

67. Arthur Marwick, *The Sixties: Cultural Revolution in Britain, France, Italy, and the United States, c.* 1958–1974 (New York: Oxford University Press, 1998), 17–20. The folk music and dance that were part of the FSM's final sit-in led the *San Francisco Examiner* (3 Dec. 1964) to refer to the occupation as the "Sproul Hall Hootenany."

68. Schorske Oral History, 104. Note that the most hostile segments of the press played up and wildly exaggerated the FSM's cultural radicalism as a device for discrediting the movement, so that, in addition to red-baiting, the Berkeley revolt was subjected to what one might call beatnik-baiting. Hearst columnist Lucius Beebe, for example, in one of his diatribes, "A Dim View of Berkeley's Red Square," referred to FSMers as "uncouth, verminous, screaming beatniks" (*San Francisco Chronicle,* 12 Oct. 1964), an image FSMers repeatedly denounced. Rossman's essay in this volume evokes both the countercultural element and its limitations. He indicates that half the FSM Steering Committee had smoked marijuana yet also shows that the leadership was too worried about the FSM's public image to defend Lenny Glazer, a controversial Berkeley-area figure who was being harshly prosecuted for marijuana use.

69. Verne A. Stadtman, *The University of California, 1868–1968* (New York: McGraw-Hill, 1970), 469–72.

70. *DC*, 8, 23 April 1965; on student editorial and faculty attacks on the Meyer committee recommendations, see *DC*, 3–6 and 17 May 1965.

71. Ibid., 17 Feb. 1965.

72. Ibid., 16–18, 23 Mar. 1965.

73. Martin Klein to Roger Heyns, 11 Oct. 1966; Henry Mayer to Heyns, 5 Oct. 1966, Records of the Office of the Chancellor, University of California, 1952–1971, CU-149 (hereafter Chancellor's Records), University Archives, Bancroft Library.

74. According to Stanley Rothman and S. Robert Lichter, a majority of the Steering Committee was Jewish. Their further claim to know that "half the membership" was Jewish seems dubious; the FSM was not a membership organization but a mass movement in constant flux. See Rothman and Lichter, *Roots of Radicalism: Jews, Christians, and the New Left* (New York: Oxford University Press, 1982), 81. A survey of participants in the December sit-in found that 32 percent of the participants in the sit-in were Jewish, a significant figure but well below the "half" imagined by Rothman and Lichter. See Rorabaugh, 33–34. The prominence of Jews in the FSM and the post-FSM Berkeley campus left did not escape the notice of antiradicals, whose attacks on campus radicalism were sometimes tinged with anti-Semitism. For example, a Berkeley placement officer, upset by the radical protests led by "Typhoid Mario," complained that the University was in danger of being "Latin Americanized by beatniks, peacenicks, Selznicks or Skolnicks" (Brinton H. Stone to Earl F. Cheit, 2 Dec. 1966, Chancellor's Records). Although it is interesting to note the prominence of Jews in the FSM and among its faculty supporters, the overall picture was more complex. Jews, for example, figured prominently among the FSM's faculty critics, including some prominent scholars who attacked the revolt in national magazines and books.

75. *In Memory ... Mario Savio: December* 8, 1942–*November* 6, 1996 (memorial service program in author's possession).

76. Marvin Garson, untitled article on the FSM defendants, n.d., 1–14, FSM Records. Garson's essay offers a scathing radical critique of the legal strategy employed by FSM attorneys, arguing that they were too much a part of a legal system oriented toward compromise and deal making and so waived jury trials and in other ways undermined the efforts of FSM militants to make theirs a political trial true to the sprit of the Berkeley rebellion.

77. Rick Perlstein, "Who Owns the Sixties? The Opening of a Scholarly Generation Gap," *Lingua Franca* 6 (May/June 1996): 30–37; Todd Gitlin, *The Sixties: Years of Hope, Days of Rage* (New York, Bantam Books, 1987).

78. Burner, 141, 147. Burner is correct about Savio quoting Herodotus. During the FSM Savio referred to another ancient Greek historian as well, citing Thucydides in a revealing rebuttal to something Kerr had said earlier that fall. Kerr, criticizing the FSM for insisting that political advocacy should be a part of college life, had argued that such activity was foreign to a university's mission: "Collecting money and picketing ... are not necessary for the intellectual development of students. If they were so, why teach history? We can't live in ancient Greece." Savio during the FSM trial recalled that, taking issue with Kerr, he gave a speech in which he argued "that in my opinion ... president [Kerr] had no understanding of the need

for student political activity, nor any understanding of the need for the study of history, and I mentioned specifically *The Peloponnesian Wars* of which Thucydides makes it clear in his writing of it that the future generations [who] wouldn't be able to take part in the war may learn something from it in terms of action of war" (FSM trial transcript, Mario Savio testimony, 13 May 1965, p. 47, FSM Digital Archive and Oral history Project, <www.lib.berkeley.edu/BANC/FSM>; *DC*, 3 Feb. 1965).

79. John Searle, "The Faculty Resolution," in Miller and Gilmore, 98. Searle was correct about the minimally disruptive character of the December sit-in. In the accounts of the arrests they wrote for their defense team, participants noted that they "cleared an aisle" for administrators, secretaries, and others to permit them to enter and leave their offices at will. Indeed, it was this very nondisruptive quality to the sit-in that led some of the protesters to believe that their demonstration in Sproul was lawful and to think they ought not to have been arrested. See arrested-student questionnaires, BURN, carton 1.

80. On this criticism of the FSM leadership by moderates in the movement, see Jo Freeman's remarks in note 27 of Cohen, "This Was Their Fight," in this volume.

81. Goines, 177–83; Heirich, *Spiral of Conflict*, 163–64.

82. Nathan Glazer, *Remembering the Answers* (New York: Basic Books, 1970), 100–130.

83. Searle, "Faculty Resolution," 98; Goines, 177–83. Probably the greatest test of the FSM's commitment to nonviolence in the December sit-in came during the police invasion of Sproul Hall when various levels of physical force were used to remove protesters from the building. Although such physical pressure could have easily sparked violent resistance by protesters who were being manhandled, almost everyone remained nonviolent. Describing the struggle to remain calm amidst such a provocative and chaotic scene, one of the protesters reported that "I was standing up, shouting to people not to touch them [the police], to keep quiet, to remain non-violent and orderly. A few people were throwing paper at the police and shouting at them and occasionally a fist would reach out to strike one. But everyone around such a person pulled him back or somehow stopped him. It was an incredible thing. I think if someone had tried to make any attack on the police, he would first have had to fight his way through a wall of students. . . . [P]erhaps 90% of those present were non-violent and would police the others" (arrested-student questionnaires, carton 1, Burnstein Papers).

84. See Kerr's essay in this volume; Savio quote is from the *Save the Steps Rally: Friday Nov. 4, 1966: A Complete Transcription* (Bancroft Library, University of California at Berkeley, photocopy).

85. If there was a violent element in Sproul Hall it was police. Student accounts of the arrests strongly suggest that the police used excessive force: "kicking" and "hitting" protesters, throwing them down stairs, stepping on them, applying choke holds. See arrested-student questionnaires, carton 1, Burnstein Papers.

86. Terry Anderson, *The Movement and the Sixties* (New York: Oxford University Press, 1995), i–xii.

87. *President's Commission on Campus Unrest*, 8, 43–45; for example, the commission cited a Harris poll from the end of the 1960s that found that 68 percent of college students rejected violence as an effective means of change (p. 49). Moreover, according to White House figures, from 1968 to 1970, the period in which SDS-

centered historiography focuses upon the Weather Underground brand of revolutionary violence, violent campus incidents actually declined from 452 in 1968, to 245 in 1969, to 195 in 1970. See Rhodri Jefferey-Johns, *Peace Now! American Society and the Ending of the Vietnam War* (New Haven: Yale University Press, 1999), 87.

88. *DC,* 18 May 1965.

89. Kerr, letter to *DC,* 1 Dec. 1964.

90. Interview in Berkeley, 12 July 1999, tape in editors' possession.

91. Hal Draper, *Berkeley: The New Student Revolt* (New York: Grove Press, 1965), 59.

92. See transcript of the Oct. 6 rally, Kerr office files on the FSM, CU 495, box 1, Center for Higher Education Papers; Mario Savio, "Comments on Berkeley," *Free Student News,* 1965.

93. Jack Weinberg made the case for the importance of the Old Left's organizational talents in his talk on 13 April 2001 at the Bancroft Library's symposium "Taking Part: FSM and the Legacy of Social Protest" (video recording and audio cassette, Bancroft Library, University of California at Berkeley) and in a subsequent conversation with Reggie Zelnik.

PART ONE

Roots

Thirty Years Later

Reflections on the FSM

Mario Savio

On November 15, 1995, at the invitation of historian Barbara Epstein, Mario Savio gave a talk on the FSM to the History of Consciousness Department colloquium at UC Santa Cruz. Mario did not have a prepared text for this talk, but—as was his usual practice—worked from notes and spoke in an extemporaneous fashion. Capturing on paper Savio's uniquely dialogic style of speaking is like trying to cover the concert of a jazz musician or singer by transcribing the notes they hit. What follows is not a full verbatim account of the speech but a somewhat abridged version that faithfully relays its central ideas and, we hope, a good deal of its texture.

I'd like to share with you some ideas about how my consciousness, my piece of collective consciousness and that of my friends, developed. We had our beginnings in the 1940s and 1950s. [I was born in] 1942. I was a war baby. But spiritually speaking, [our consciousness formed largely] in reaction to the 1950s. It was in reaction to the 1950s that we did the kinds of things that we did.

[The television sit-com] *Roseanne* recently had a program where [Roseanne Barr] did Roseanne of the 1950s. It's really quite remarkable because Roseanne's caricatured version of the 1950s is in some ways the pretend world that we were reacting to. Now it had some darker things in it too, and they didn't make their way into the *Roseanne* episode, but I thought [overall her rendering of the 1950s] was really wonderful. Here on the tube, this major [source] of information is disseminating stereotypes of the left. It's interesting because most of the media that disseminate stereotypes disseminate stereotypes of the right. And now, it would be nice if we could get beyond the stereotypes, but at least we should have some of ours up there, not always theirs. So I loved it. It was really marvelously done.

The fact that Roseanne could do that and that it would be very popular, canned laughter and all, means that it is no longer possible to be, to unself-consciously accept being, "normal." You see the fifties were "normal." The fifties are bizarre, but they were the last normal decade, [when] everything was still just in place the way it ought to be. The man thought he was in charge, the woman let him think that while making certain decisions in the house (she took care of the kids, made sure they were all washed and went to school, everything went just right), and the only black man they knew was the one who came around collecting money for charity. And that was what happened in the episode. It was tremendous.

That was the last normal decade. Those were the last normal people. [Today] there are hardly any normal people left. And I think that's really significant. Bill Clinton is not normal because after all he is married to Hillary and Hillary is not normal, right? That is, she's not part of that normal world, thank goodness. And Newt Gingrich is not normal. He's less normal but certainly not normal. It's now the case that even people in positions of power are clearly [not normal]. Here's a president playing the saxophone. There's something really abnormal about it. All of us who grew up in normal times know that that's so. That's really quite significant. It's no longer possible to be unself-consciously normal. We are in a very strange period of transition. In periods that are not periods of transition, everybody's normal, right? Now, hardly anybody is.

How did such a strange state of affairs begin? You could imagine back, say, in the time of the Reformation: you want your own church? Abnormal, right? You see, that kind of a revolutionary situation is where the abnormal, the crazy people, people who want their own church, get to have one. And I can just imagine, coming out of the church that I came out of, how it must have made the cardinals really go ballistic that any of [these reformers, who] previously would [have been dismissed as] kooks, would be in charge of a kingdom or a principality. You know, this crazy person nails these theses to the door of the church, and soon there were people saying, "That's great! Go for it Luther!"

But we are in that kind of strange situation now. That is one of the reasons that the right is so "strong" now. They're not strong because they are actually strong. They're strong because the world is not any longer the normal world that they're trying to preserve. That's why we call them "reactionaries." They're trying to go [back] into the nineteenth century. But we're much closer to the twenty-first. They seem stronger than they are because they recognize [that they are losing ground]. Why, for example, are they so gung ho for family values? Because most of the families aren't like those families of the fifties. Even the ones that are as close as possible are not really like that. I think it's important to keep that in the back of one's mind when we feel really oppressed by how strong they are, just think how weak they actually are. And one clear example of that to bear in mind is the following: Colin Powell is going to run as a Republican. . . . I was gearing up to decide whether I would vote for the first time for a Republican . . . because the country could use a black male president. I mean it's fantastic. Fortunately I didn't have to make that decision. But look, all of these right-wing Republicans up on a stage, a whole phalanx of them, denouncing this Republican. Denouncing him. That's not a sign of strength. That is a sign of terrible weakness. Why would they have to do such a thing? They were afraid. Why? They are trying to pull us back from what they imagine is sort of a pit, [a loss of their own institutions]. Trying to pull us back, and here they think, "We've got it, we've got the Republican Party," and they realize they can lose it just like that. They're very scared. So the situation may not be quite what it seems to be. How did it get this way?

Well, I'll tell you how it got this way for me. I grew up as a Catholic. I was an altar boy. I was going to be a priest. Now obviously the eldest son in an Italian Catholic family, a person who would become a priest if anyone was going to be—and I was going to be that person. My two aunts are nuns. I came into it from liberation theology. I read things that probably most people in this room have not read. I read [Jacques] Maritain, I read [Emmanuel] Mounier, I read things put out by *Catholic Worker* people; I was very much immersed in that sort of thing. And that was how I came at it. By virtue of my Catholicism and the particular character it was taking, for me a major decision was whether to be a priest. Therefore I was not a careerist. I couldn't be a careerist. I had something more important to do. I was trying to save my soul. And I made pacts with myself repeatedly. "If you can just believe these things, then you will have to apply to become a Jesuit." That was the image I had—a romantic image. But the point is, I certainly could not become a careerist.

Now it turns out that from various other paths, many people I met at Berkeley were in the same situation. Not all Catholics—mostly not. But they, for one reason or another, were in some kind of peripheral relationship to the society, not really able to put career first but rather to put ideas first. There were a remarkable number of people there at that time of that kind. And not just at Berkeley. Some of them were from Jewish families, some from Protestant families even, which is really remarkable to me because I don't think of there being that many Protestants in America because where I grew up [Queens, New York] there were only Catholics and Jews. But in any case, I understand there are a lot of Protestants in America and we, in fact, encountered some. And in any case, whichever background they came from, they were not set on being careerists. The ideas actually mattered. For me it was because of the reasons I've described, but for others with different backgrounds it would have been for other reasons. That was a significant part of that time. And maybe one of the reasons it was possible was because they were prosperous times. It's harder to eschew an excessive concern with career when you want to make sure you have one, right? We knew, no problem, you can get student digs for thirty-five dollars. Astonishing. So one didn't worry about the material world. One could afford to be above the material world, and a lot of people at that time really were, and I think fortunately.

We also were the first generation to grow up under the threat of the bomb. That actually was special. We were the first generation to do that. They exploded them on the [TV] tube. See, they hadn't yet put them [under] the ground. Periodically there would be an explosion of the hydrogen bomb or the latest device there, chow, boom! Right on the news. And I remember even as a little child they had us ["take cover"] under desks. There were periodically drills in the schools as I was growing up in the fifties and you would go under desks. Now, I ultimately took degrees in physics, so even then I asked myself questions like "Will it actually do the job?" And I made up these stories. Maybe it's the flash, so maybe the desk could keep me from going blind. You try to think, "What could this wooden desk [do to protect me in a nuclear attack]?" So I would actually try to think, what would it do? and I never raised the issue with the teacher. I mean, one could, right? One could say, "You know, I don't want to make a big thing about this, but will it really work? Could you maybe explain it to me?" But I did think about it, you see. Lots of people did. One of the reasons they put [fallout shelters] underground was because people were super scared. People were more scared of the bombs than of the Commies. [Even people] like me, coming from a background where, [for] Catholics of a certain kind, J. Edgar Hoover was a person to take seriously as an intellectual almost, from a sort of a Catholic point of view. So, in other words, the Commies, I knew, were bad. I later met some and discovered they were very warm human beings, but it took me a while. But the bomb, you knew that was bad, right? So that was part of the background.

And then, part of the background for me and, I think, for others was the Holocaust. I'm not Jewish but I saw those pictures. And those pictures were astonishing. Heaps of bodies. Mounds of bodies. Nothing affected my consciousness more than those pictures. And those pictures had on me the following impact, which other people maybe came to in a different way. They meant to me that *everything* needed to be questioned. Reality itself. Because this was like opening up your father's drawer and finding pictures of child pornography, with adults molesting children. It's like a dark, grotesque secret that people had that at some time in the recent past people were being incinerated and piled up in piles. I saw those pictures. I couldn't believe them. And I thought as a [high school] kid looking at those pictures: "If this really happened, then everything must have changed." Germany must absolutely have been a transformed government—from sinners to saints. They must actually have rooted out the possibility of such a thing happening—totally rooted it out—[and] have totally transformed society where even the least possibility that anyone could do anything bad again is prevented just from the fear of what once happened. Otherwise this couldn't be real. It must be a fake. I mean how could it possibly [be]? But I knew it was real. And this affected me more than any other single thing. I started to get the idea that people weren't really coming completely clean about things. In other words, that there was almost a conspiracy not to tell the truth to oneself, even on a mass scale. Because I knew that if the kind of transformation that would have to have happened in Germany, reflective of taking these pictures seriously, [actually happened,] we'd know about it. You'd hear about it on the news: "German chancellor just nominated for sainthood," or something like that. Some sort of absolutely astonishing things would be happening in Germany if there were any human response to these heaps. So it's clear that that hadn't happened, and that's [the] point. And that was the thing that started me questioning everything about reality. It was really those pictures. And I'll bet you that those pictures had such an effect on thousands and thousands of people, whether they were Jewish or not. This is not the good that comes out of the bad—à la Saint Augustine—that justifies the Holocaust. But this is the good that comes out of the bad because we've got to get on into our next millennium or something. Those pictures had an impact on people's lives. I know they had an impact on mine, something not as strong but akin to a "never again" feeling which Jews certainly have had. But non-Jews had that kind of feeling, too.

In the midst of all this, the Civil Rights Movement exploded. To me that was very important at that moment because I had had this confrontation with the ideas of the Holocaust. I was not a careerist. I was someone who took good and evil exceptionally seriously. I had two aunts who were nuns. I could have been a priest. And, suddenly, there's the Civil Rights Movement. And since I'm breaking away from the Church, I see the Civil Rights Movement in religious terms. [In the] Civil Rights Movement there were all those ministers; it was just absolutely rife with ministers, bristling with ministers. And so, to me, this was an example of God working in the world. Allying myself in whatever way I could with that movement was an alternative to the Church because I couldn't actually believe those [biblical] stories. Not that things couldn't have happened that way, but there seemed to be lots of reasons to think maybe they hadn't happened that way. I couldn't bring myself to believe the religion I was born into on a factual basis. But the spirit of "do good" and "resist evil" was an important part of my religious upbringing. I saw [that] present in the Civil Rights Movement—and I wanted to ally myself with that. I believe that thousands of people from different religious points of view who no longer believed in their religions literally still kept with them that germ of truth, part of which is do good and resist evil. And for them the Civil Rights Movement was the thing they were waiting for—a real counterbalance to the evil that they had seen or imagined, to the bombs exploding and [telling people], "This is just normal; we have to protect ourselves from the Communists and so we create a weapon that could destroy the world." And everyone knows it. And they said it. Here finally was, in counterpoint to palpable evil, something that was palpably good and that was an example of resisting evil and doing good.

I was drawn to it in that way, and I think lots of other people were, for these kinds of very positive, ethical reasons. What makes it possible to be drawn to something for ethical reasons? You've got to be in a position of relative prosperity. If you're not in a position of relative prosperity, then economic concerns do assert themselves and become more overtly determinative of your behavior. But the sixties was a period of comparative prosperity and so lots of kids, especially from middle-class families or, in my case, upper working-class families, could orient a large segment of their lives along a moral axis because they could afford to do so.

I then went to Berkeley. I was a philosophy student, and this was the case of "philosophy student goes South." I'd been studying physics. I then realized that I had to take a little sojourn into philosophy because I had to finally make the decision—am I a Catholic or not? So I decided to do it in this very systematic way. I became a philosophy student. That was interesting, and I am now toying with the idea of finally getting a Ph.D. in philosophy because I might as well actually complete this and make some kind of late career move which I wasn't able to do at all [in the 1960s]. And let me say something about the spirit of philosophy at Berkeley in those days. There were two main branches to philosophy at Berkeley in [the sixties]. There was the analytic tradition out of British empiricism and as developed by the philosophies of ordinary language—especially J. L. Austin, whom I was very taken by, actually moved by. And then versus that was a very strong countertrend which was based at least in the early [sixties] on existentialism, only later [in that decade] on Marxism. And so, at the very beginning, in the early sixties, the two trends in philosophy at Berkeley were analytic philosophy and existentialism. Existentialism had the coffeehouses and analytic philosophy had the lecture halls. But they were both present, and people who were interested in those things could get both and did. I remember that the term just before the FSM broke, Jean Wahl from the Sorbonne was [in Berkeley] giving a lecture on philosophy of existence, a series of lectures. I took those lectures, and then I wrote a paper based on a comparison of Gabriel Marcel to G. E. Moore. It was mostly about Moore, and the person who read the paper said, "This isn't about existentialism." It's an interesting little sidelight. I was more drawn to the analytical side because I was always more in favor of giving precise answers to small questions [than] excessively imprecise ones to big questions—although I was aware that the questions were small. Other people not only liked the precise answers but also thought those were the only questions. That's another story. I was never suckered into that.

So, it was in this environment. And what was the environment then? It was back to basics intellectually, trying to get precise about the kinds of questions that the existentialists were asking. Among the students a serious contender for sainthood at that time was Albert Camus. [He was] Everyman's saint. Much later in life I went to Provence and put some flowers at his grave. The combination of analyzing everything to the root and the [notion that the] really important things are the decisions you make and the life you choose—that was the spirit of existential philosophy, combined with the Civil Rights Movement going on outside the campus.

People on the Berkeley campus got very involved in the Civil Rights Movement. And there was a local branch of it. The Bay Area civil rights movement was tremendously attractive to students and a minority of [them] took part. There were demonstrations all over the Bay Area, often the same faces, and they're faces now that I see elsewhere at demonstrations, same people, a little grayer. And, here's what's interesting: they were successful demonstrations, militant demonstrations that brought results. And that was very energizing to people, the fact that you could compel a store to hire people [of color] they weren't previously hiring. And there were consequences if they didn't do that. That's, by the way, how affirmative action got started. Affirmative action got started in the streets in the sixties. We called it in those days a response to "de facto" discrimination. De facto discrimination means, you didn't have to prove the [employer] actually hated people of a certain kind; just that he didn't have any of them working for him was enough. And now, they're trying to do away with that idea. It's a very important idea, we felt. We put the burden effectively on the business. You either hire these people or you show us why you shouldn't hire them, and they couldn't [justify their discriminatory practices]. In which case they get closed down. When people say that affirmative action is counter to democracy, they better recognize that filling in boxes with your particular kind of ethnicity and so forth, if that isn't liberal democracy, I don't know [what is]. It really is quite a liberal democratic alternative to fill in boxes with your ethnicity, right? It's very orderly. The alternative is back to the streets. That's where it came from, in those days.

I was at one of those demonstrations [against discriminatory employment practices in San Francisco]. I got [recruited] to the demonstration by being handed a leaflet on the Berkeley campus, at this strip of land [at Bancroft and Telegraph]. They gave me this leaflet. I said, "Oh. Demonstration, okay." These demonstrations had the moral cachet of the campus. Absolutely. They had won out over football games, no question about it.

And so, I believed in all this, and, in addition, there was this girl I wanted to impress, so I didn't become a football star, I went to this demonstration. It's true. I can say it now right because what's the big deal? But I think it was actually a healthy thing. We were creating an alternative society, and in the alternative society, you impress people you want to go out with by doing things that are alternative, right? And so, that's how that happened. Well, so I took this leaflet. I read it. I knew I had to go there. I went to the demonstration, got arrested for the first time, and I remember we were all holding hands, locking arms and stuff like that. There was this lady [a guest at the hotel]; she was looking down, "You go back to Russia!"

"I don't come from Russia."

"Well, just go back to where you belong, go back to Russia. You're a Communist."

"My parents are from Italy." This actually happened.

I was, as a result of getting that leaflet, arrested. I'm in the holding pen when someone named John King, whom I've never met, says, "Oh, are you going to Mississippi?" Well, that summer was going to be Mississippi Freedom Summer. This, if the good guys win, is the seminal event of the twentieth century. When you get past the Second World War, this is it. This is what determines the rest of the history of the country in this century. This particular event, the Mississippi Freedom Summer. That created the cadre [of student activists] for the whole country. Fantastic event. That doesn't mean that you had to be there. You just had to know somebody who was there. It was electric. So if I'm nominating people for sainthood, Bob Moses wins hands down. I was, on this trip, then [a philosophy student suspecting that] nothing is [real], [wondering] what is real. They tell you [one thing while] they pile bodies. I was really on a "doubt all things" trip, in part fed by analytic philosophy. I tended in the worst moments to believe it's all sense data that's just a patch of purple, and so I was [on] a super-Human trip combined with this tremendous ethical drive. It's a terrible combination actually to be faced with, and so I wanted to come into contact with some reality. I had to go to Mississippi. That was obviously the proof. Okay, you had to go to Mississippi.

So I went and I had my touch with reality. And my touch with reality was one particular moment that summer. All that effort to get one particular moment. I brought somebody to register to vote. You weren't supposed to say a word. This guy comes. The guy was about sixty, seventy years old. There's the sheriff's wife behind the counter. 'Doffs his hat and he just stands there. Silent. She goes about her business. Finally, finally, she comes over: "What do you want, boy?" Head down. "Wanna reddish." "*Boy*, what do you want?" "Wanna reddish." "Reddish, what's that boy?" Here—he's obviously older than she is. He's worked all his life—such silence, such dignity, such composure. And meanwhile I cannot say anything. We're not allowed to say a word—going to watch that's all. And this went on for a long time. "What do you want, boy?" "Wanna reddish, ma'am." They all said "reddish." The word *register* became a two-syllable word in Mississippi and that's what they said: "Wanna reddish. Wanna reddish." Finally she throws the thing at him, and now he has to interpret a section of the Mississippi constitution in order to qualify as a registered voter. And that was my moment of reality. And you don't need that many. I only needed that one.

I endangered people by bringing them down to register. I was into chutzpah, okay? I made up a line. How did I get this guy to register? I would go round to the houses. We'd go in teams of two, and I talked oftentimes. Knock, knock—person comes to the door: "What do you want, sir?" It's always "sir." So, "May I speak to the head of the family?" And there always was one, it was always either the father or the grandfather. "What do you want?" [I'd] explain we're here to organize people to go down to the courthouse to vote. "I don't wanna vote." They were afraid, obviously. Didn't want to lose his job or worse. And I got to say the following line. I couldn't believe it; I'd say, "Did your father vote?"

"No sir."

"Did your grandfather vote?"

"*No* sir."

"Do you want your children to vote?"

That's all. I don't know where I got the nerve to say such a thing. And always then, when I came to the third question, they were ready to register and that was it. Change was in the air and they wanted to be on that freedom train. And I do not know how I got . . . I mean it was almost an effrontery to ask those questions. But I asked them. Nobody told me to.

Obviously I endangered people. When I went back to Berkeley, back to California, nice, sunny California—home of none of that, right? [And] lots of other people were in the same boat. I was then the incoming president of University Friends of SNCC, and when we came back to California, the [campus] administration sent out letters to all these various organizations saying "that strip of land," the very place where I'd gotten the first leaflet, "we have now discovered that this is University property," and so we're not allowed to have advocacy of anything on University property and therefore there will no longer be these card tables to distribute literature. No more distribution of leaflets, no more collecting of money, no more doing all of the things that had gotten me to go to the demonstration where I was first arrested and ultimately to Mississippi to endanger these people. And to me it was a very clear question, "Am I a Judas?" I'm going to betray the people whom I endangered now that I'm back home? Forget all about that. Was that reality? Or is it just a fantasy? A little childish game? I did my little childish game in Mississippi, and now I'm back to the serious stuff of becoming whatever I was going to become (I had no idea what that was anyway)? And all the other students seemed to feel the same way: the ones who could do something about it, all the people who received the letter, *all* the people [opposed the ban], including the Republicans for God's sake, and not for civil rights reasons, for strictly libertarian reasons.

The letter said, "Please come and we'll explain; if you want to have this explained to you, what this policy change means, we'll be glad to explain." And this [letter] was [from] Dean Katherine Towle, a lovely person, really, and so we went. We didn't go one by one. We went together, en masse. We did that from the beginning, and we never did it any other way. It was always together. So here we are together [with] the dean. "How do we change this?" That's all we wanted to know. [She says,] "This is University policy. You can't change that." And I remember asking questions like this at that very meeting. I said, "Okay, I'd at least like to know something." (My training was in philosophy.) "Does the law require the University to forbid these tables here? Show that to us. Or does the law simply grant the University the *right* to forbid these tables here? Is this discretionary?" I made it quite clear what I was asking. She said, "Oh, it's discretionary. But that's our policy."

I say, "Oh, so in other words, this is a matter of discretion and you've adopted this as a matter of policy. What's the justification for it? [We are] willing to listen. You need a reason. If you exercise discretion, you need a reason and we insist on getting a reason."

"We're not required to give a reason, the law doesn't require it."

"Oh yes, but we require it. This is discretionary and therefore you made a decision to do this. You're not obliged to make that decision. You have to have a reason. I mean, you surely didn't make it in an arbitrary fashion. You must have had a reason. What was the reason?"

Well, there wasn't any reason that could really stand muster there. They'd been pressured by the *Oakland Tribune,* by these sort of right-wingers who were peripheral then and are now making a bid for national power. That was their reason. But that reason they couldn't put forward. I guess if she knew what was coming, she would never have agreed to the first premise that this was discretionary. But, of course, it was and everyone knew it. So here's how the FSM [arose] in the simplest [terms]: We insisted on a reason. They said the only reason is that this is University property. But, as I and others pointed out in the very first meeting, "That's not a reason. That's a fact."

Now that was, that was really decisive. They got spiked right there: "That's not a reason. That's a fact." How'd they get spiked? See this was the "end of ideology" era. And we just had turned the tables on them. They were attacking people who were taking moral action on the basis of "well, you're just emoting, just making value judgments." As if this were not a normal human thing to do. That the only real solid things were facts. So when

you tell me that the reason you're doing this is because it's University property, then I'm at perfect liberty to say, "Choup! That's a fact. That's not
a reason." And of course that's exactly right, it was just a fact. What made
it just a fact? The fact that they had discretion. That is, we had learned
our end-of-ideology lessons very well. And in learning the lessons, we had
honed a very, very sharp knife. And that knife was now turned at them. I
hope this point is really clear because it is extremely important. Why is this
business about end of ideology important here and relevant to this? What
was this end of ideology about? It was about destroying socialism. Because
what were the alternatives? The alternative was a perfectly "natural" commercial society in which everything happened according to the laws of
nature's god, or whatever. There it is. You couldn't tamper with that. The
alternative was tampering with the market, maybe even elements of a command economy. All of that was against nature, and based upon an ideology.
We here, in the land of nature's god, we have no ideology. It's just according to the facts. This is the natural way to do things, right? Buying and selling is natural. The market price, that's the natural price. It's only you
wicked people over here who tamper with the laws of nature's god, and you
have ideologies behind you. Okay. Very well. But then if you say that you
have a policy, and you have discretion to develop that policy in this particular way, then, and you have no reason for that, and you offer as your reason
that it's University property, I have learned very well what answer you need.
"That's not a reason. That's just a fact. And facts can't be argued into reasons. No way." And we told them those things. It's quite remarkable to realize now. Now we're past those debates; they're in the past. But it was super
powerful at that time. We talked their language but not to their purpose.

   I'd like to say how I was drawn into the FSM personally. You may say,
"Haven't you said enough about that?" No. Everyone needs his own personal hook. We had a meeting early in the movement, and we had to
choose a name. We were "name tripping." Anybody who's chosen names
knows you can go crazy choosing names. There were various revolutionary
organizations then with letters, and so someone finally said "Free University." No. "Free Speech Movement" and "FSM"—okay, and that sounded
almost like some Latin American revolutionary [organization]. I think Jack
Weinberg proposed that name, and I asked him years later, "Why did you
like it?" "Oh, it sounded like some Latin American revolutionary organization." But that's not why it appealed to me. I personally had a tremendous
stammer all through high school. I couldn't speak. And that name, as soon
as he said it, I said "Aw!" It's a pun. For me it was really a tremendous pun,
which meant a lot to me [as it signified the free movement of my own
speech]. And I must say that free speech meant a lot to me and means a lot
to me. There's this wonderful saying of Diogenes the Cynic. "Cynic" meant
something different in those days—it was where he came from. Anyway,

Diogenes, who supposedly had the lantern during the daytime to see if there were any honest people around, said, "the most beautiful thing in the world is the freedom of speech," and I really feel that. And we weren't going to let go of it. I wasn't going to let go of it.

We almost lost. This is important to understand. To people today [the FSM seems] successful. [But] we were almost unsuccessful. We worked our little hearts out—our little tushes—for a whole term. We worked like crazy to mobilize the students and to educate the faculty. Above all we had to educate the faculty. Students come and go. Faculty had position there, they had jobs, they had tenure in many cases. And if we could educate them, we could win. There was no hope of educating the Regents, okay? And that's why there's a problem today. The faculties are in favor of affirmative action but the Regents aren't. So this is a serious problem. [We] wanted to educate the faculty. And we worked so hard at it. The FSM had almost run its course. It was toward the end. Things were still very touch and go. There was this meeting at the Greek Theatre. Clark Kerr had decided on the solution. He had his plan. His plan had nothing in it about free speech. No correspondence at all between his plan for solving the "campus chaos," which was all he was concerned about, [and the FSM's free speech position]. Nothing at all in his plan that was responsive to any of the things that we had said. So the Greek Theatre. Very, very, very nice. The symbolism was beautiful. They had this stage, they had these *baronial* chairs and sitting on them were the department heads. The chairs on the chairs and there they were like the barons. And so he made a speech. The speech was over. They turned off the microphone. I walked to the center of the stage to tell people, to announce simply that we're going to have a meeting down in [Sproul] Plaza. That was my intention. To discuss these issues. We were afraid of losing it at that very moment. And we could have. And fortunately, they had ready their cops, and they came and they pulled me down. Astonishing!

We lucked out time after time, and that was our final luck out. We had argued it all beautifully; we presented all of the facts, the arguments, the reasons and theories. We talked to everybody, and yet at the very last moment we could have lost the whole thing. But they saved us in that way just as earlier they had saved [us]; luck had saved us. During the original gathering, they [had] put a police car on the campus to arrest one of our people. You've really got to be bereft of all sense to do that! We could not anticipate that they would do such a thing, that they would arrest a former student on the campus with a police car, that they [would] drive right in the middle of the Plaza, kaplunk! That'd be bereft of all sense. They do this. Okay, great, that's a plus. Just falls into our laps. Here it is. Then what happens? The next day is "Parents Visiting the Campus Day." We were around that car for thirty-two hours, for God's sake. We could have been around that car for another seventy, and that would have really been very upsetting to the trustees and the people who contribute money, the rich alumni; the whole little ball of wax would have just melted, just like that. What were they going to do? They had police ringing the campus. They threatened to come in bludgeoning people. Well, there would have been blood on the pavement, and they wouldn't have gotten the blood off the pavement so easily. That was luck, sheer luck. We knew how to take advantage of luck, but it was luck. And then likewise at the very end. They come [to the Greek Theatre]; I go up to make an announcement, whew! [The] police [drag me] down. I'm in a different place. I'm talking to one of the cops in Italian at this point, true. So I'm really just now in a different world. That's what won it for us.

A couple of days later [December 8] there's the meeting of the Berkeley Academic Senate, and we have worked with these guys, trying to tell them about free speech. These are smart guys. To be on the Berkeley faculty you can't be that dumb. [Yet] it took us a very long time to explain to them the niceties of civil liberties issues where they could understand [them]. But we didn't know even then whether they would understand. And we had done our all. If we'd lost it at that point, it would have been gone. And they voted by about eight to one. In those days it wasn't a representative body [of delegates]; it was a one person–one vote senate and they had a real debate. We had opened up a space for the faculty to have a debate. And that's really a side of the FSM which isn't understood. We had to work like crazy, disrupting the University, taking over buildings, having sit-ins, marches, all this sort of thing to just open up a little space where people would have a real debate. That was America. This is a free country here, and [yet] you had to go crazy so we can have an actual, real debate that could really decide something. Astonishing! And they voted the right way. And we were outside. And [the faculty] came walking through, and I remember we were clapping and tears were just streaming down our faces because, if we had not won at that point, if they didn't get it at that point, I wouldn't be here right now.

It was that close right to the very end, and that gets me talking about where we are now. History works that way. Right—a very, very fine cut. It's not one million workers gathering together and three bosses in a room, you see—it ain't like that. It's usually a very, very fine cut. We had to work like maniacs. I was exhausted and so were the other people. I'm talking personally because I can remember my own experience, but all the people I worked with, Bettina [Aptheker], whom you know, I'm sure, Jack [Weinberg], whom I mentioned, and so many others, we were meeting around the clock. If we had lost it then, and we could have, it would have been all over. There would not have been free speech. The anti–free speech forces would have prevailed. The silence of the silent fifties would have prevailed.

It might have, it would have, broken out some other way but not so cleanly and finely—and not so early on, as things go. That was 1964. It would have been a messier event, as many of the other campus movements were. The clear confrontation of the issues, the clear victory, was the product of a tremendous effort, and it almost missed. Have we had other experiences like that? There was a dictatorship in Germany, but there was also a dictatorship in Russia. I wouldn't want to have lived in either place. One was clearly worse than the other. At some point Stalin wasn't so sure which side he wanted to be on. There was bickering whether there should be a pact between the Russians and the Nazis and then maybe the West would sort of wipe itself out and then—very [close], too close. That's how history really is. There was a good side, there was a bad side, but they weren't like that [*Savio shows a big distance with his hands*]; they were like this [*brings his hands close together*]. It was a very, very fine cut. The Nazis were defeated. When you think of it in those terms, then you say, "Oh, gulp! Real history is usually a very, very fine cut, and if the right side wins, if you are on the ground, actually involved in the struggle, you are not sure that you are going to win."

We are involved in that situation today. Those people who lost in the South are now making a bid for national power; it's much the same people. I mean, where does Newt Gingrich come from? Where does Jesse Helms come from? Where does Phil Gramm come from? They don't come from Maine, okay? They lost in the South. We beat them in the sixties, actually. They're making a bid for national power. They are in an end-game situation. *They*, not us. If they don't win it now, they don't win it. Why? I'll tell you. The issues that we fought for and developed over the sixties and seventies, mostly the sixties, actually are the issues of today. The national agenda [today] is the agenda that we created. What is that agenda? The simple version is, it's antihierarchy. But what does it mean? Antihierarchy in race, antihierarchy in gender, antihierarchy in class, antihierarchy in the environment. It's not one species *über alles*. Antihierarchy in the empire [means] not one nation *über alles*. Those five [points] that Cornel West is happy to name: race, gender, class, environment, empire. That is the agenda that we began the creation of, and that is today's agenda.

Where do you learn to obey and that some people are worse than others? You learn it in the family; you don't learn it out of a book. You learn in the family that it's not what you do but what you are. If you have the wrong kind of genitalia, then you are in one class. And if you have the right kind, you are in another class. Later on, you can easily transfer that learning to other things, but it is a very important lesson learned in the home and very early. Because it's not going to take if you don't learn it early: that it's okay for whole classes of people to be above another on the basis of what they are, not what they do. If you have a woman physicist and a male national football hero, it's right to say that he's better—at football. That's correct. But it's not right to say that he's better because he is a better kind of person. He shouldn't have a higher status. If status breaks down in the home, they've lost it—absolutely lost it. It's very, very serious; this is an end-game situation, as I see it. Well, we began to break the whole idea of status down about everything. It was true about race. People who have dark skin in America were not regarded as normal. The norm was a white male. That's not true anymore. Everybody here knows that's not true. Roseanne knows it's not true, and all her viewers know it's not true. So this is very serious for them, and therefore, they are panicky. They're making a bid for power at the last moment. When Colin Powell said, "I want to be president. Maybe, I'm going to think about it," this whole phalanx of guys make these speeches denouncing him [and] his character. Why? Because he's not a Ward Connerly, he's not a me-too in the trustees. He has his own mind. Okay, his mind is not my mind or your mind. It's his own mind, though, and he's not allowed to do that. They were hysterical. They were afraid. It's because it's the last moment.

If you believe you've got to win by blueprinting a new kind of society and having everyone do that, you're not going to win. History doesn't work that way. We won in '64 very, very closely. The Russians defeated the Nazis at Stalingrad, but you wouldn't have wanted to live in either society. That's really true. What is a similar thing here? Last week I read in the [San Francisco] *Chronicle* a study of hierarchy in wealth and income in industrialized countries. There've been a million such studies. They compare wealth and income hierarchies in the industrial democracies of Europe, Japan, Canada, the U.S. The studies always come out the same. They compare various different scales, let's say income, of the poorest person in the top tenth and the richest person in the bottom tenth. That's the gap, that's the so-called income gap and wealth gap. The gap is always greatest in the U.S. In Finland it's right now lowest, [where] there's a 2.8-fold difference between that poorest rich guy and richest poor guy. In the U.S. it's around 15-fold. Tremendous, tremendous. What does that mean? Say, that's terrible, [and it can leave you] pessimistic. How could you bring [more equality to America]? [But it is possible to be] optimistic. We only need to shift resources very modestly. If the U.S. had a 5-fold income or wealth gap, that would start us down the right road. It's like this tremendous boat, an ocean liner. You only have your little tugboat. But if you only have to move it a few degrees to port—you see, just a bang! One bang will start [the boat] going the right way, and they're not going to be able to steer it back because this is the end of the line for them. This is their last generation, guys. We just have to give it one good, solid slam in the right direction and then watch and see where it goes. [But] that's going to be tremendously hard to do. Lots of people died so that Stalin could defeat the Nazis, so that the Russians could prevail at Stalingrad. Lots of people died. They died in Stalingrad. They died in the ovens. Lots of people died. It's an agony to make a very, very slight change, and we don't know how this is going to come out. But, what is hopeful is, we don't have to do a miracle. We only have to give the boat a very solid push in one direction and it will do the rest of the job.

From Freedom Now! to Free Speech

The FSM's Roots in the Bay Area Civil Rights Movement

Jo Freeman

In late March or early April 1964 Mario Savio filled out his application to participate in the Mississippi Summer Project. Asked to list his arrests, he wrote: "The Sheraton-Palace Hotel in San Francisco (a demonstration organized by the Ad Hoc Committee to End Discrimination). At about 4 A.M. on the morning of March 7, 1964, the police began making arrests after the demonstrators, lying down with arms linked, began blocking the exits of the hotel. We were charged with disturbing the peace . . . and are presently out on bail awaiting trial. Our attorneys will probably enter a plea of not guilty." The demonstration at the Sheraton Palace was one of a series of actions that rocked the Bay Area from October 1963 through summer 1964. UC Berkeley and San Francisco State students were abundant among the roughly five hundred arrested in these demonstrations, which generated headlines and debate. These protests broke the ground for the FSM by sensitizing students to civil rights and providing a model for action. They taught students that sitting in was a logical response to injustice. They created a community of involved students, much larger than the band of political activists only the year before. And they set the standards for commitment.

The Bay Area demonstrations were one consequence of the Birmingham protests led by Martin Luther King, Jr., and the Southern Christian Leadership Conference (SCLC) in spring 1963. The Birmingham struggle inspired civil rights agitation in the North. During that year almost a thousand civil rights demonstrations occurred in at least 115 cities; more than twenty thousand people were arrested; ten were killed; there were thirty-five bombings. We Berkeley students learned of all this from the newspapers, TV, and visits from participants. James Baldwin lectured to nine thousand students during the May Birmingham confrontations. James Farmer, national director of the Congress of Racial Equality (CORE) since 1961, addressed a thousand students on the day classes began in fall 1963 and another five thousand in San Francisco a few days later. Berkeley CORE revived that year and Campus CORE was founded in October 1963.

Campus and Berkeley CORE worked together to pressure local merchants to hire more African Americans. Documentation of discrimination had been established several years earlier. In 1960 the U.S. Civil Rights Commission found that "only 1.5 percent of a total of 269 employees in a representative sample of 35 Berkeley grocery stores were black. Similarly, in 20 banks, the only black employee observed was a maintenance man. Only two blacks held sales positions in a representative sample of 24 department, variety, and specialty stores." CORE went after the merchants on Telegraph and Shattuck Avenues, the two main commercial strips in Berkeley. Agreements were reached, then canceled, then reached again. Race and civil rights issues were on the front page of the *Daily Californian* three days out of five during the fall 1963 semester.

The first big demonstration was at Mel's Drive-In, organized by a new group called the Ad Hoc Committee to End Discrimination. It was in fact organized by members of the Du Bois Club, a youth group loosely associated with the Communist Party. Du Bois Club members worked with African American youth in San Francisco and from them learned that they could eat at Mel's but not work there. The first picket lines appeared in October. Though Mel's had eateries on both sides of the Bay, its co-owner was Harold Dobbs, a San Francisco supervisor who was running for mayor. The climax came the weekend before the election. On Saturday the Ad Hoc Committee picketed Dobbs' home. That night, and again on Sunday, the demonstrators at Mel's held the first mass sit-ins of the Bay Area civil rights movement. They occupied all the seats and refused to order. Over one hundred were arrested. When Dobbs lost the election many said the picketing was politically motivated, though the organizers denied this. Dobbs signed an employment agreement with the Ad Hoc Committee the next week to hire "Negroes" in "up front" positions.

After Mel's, CORE took the lead by organizing a "shop-in" at Lucky's supermarkets. Lucky's was an old adversary, having been picketed successfully by CORE in 1948. CORE had negotiated another agreement in the summer of 1963, but no additional jobs for African Americans appeared. In February 1964 CORE set up picket lines at several markets. A week later it started the shop-in. Although new to Berkeley students, it was a classic form of nonviolent disruption; all the actions were legal but interfered with Lucky's ability to conduct business. Demonstrators went shopping, piling their carts with goods, and changed their minds at the checkout counter. The cashiers were left with ringing cash registers and a counter full of unwanted goods. The managers had no way of separating the real shoppers from the ringers. And the real shoppers didn't want to stand in lines forever, waiting for cash registers to be cleared and goods to be returned to the shelves. After a few days of this the mayor of San Francisco, John Shelly, negotiated an agreement in which the parent company promised to hire at least sixty "Negroes," ending the shop-in.

The week the Lucky's agreement was announced, a picket line appeared outside the Sheraton Palace Hotel in San Francisco. The NAACP had been contemplating legal action against the hotel industry for some time because so many local blacks had complained to it of discrimination. But after the successful Mel's action, demonstrations seemed a quicker route to jobs. The most logical targets for action were the three most elegant hotels in the city—the Sheraton Palace, the Mark Hopkins, and the Fairmont. If one of them agreed to hire more African Americans the other hotels would follow. The Sheraton's location made it the easiest one to bring masses of demonstrators. At this time, the many civil rights groups worked closely together; their leaders knew each other well, and blacks and whites in the movement did walk "hand in hand." The Ad Hoc Committee wrote a letter to the Sheraton management asking for a racial breakdown of its employees. This led to two months of discussion between the committee and the hotel. During this time a few African Americans were hired, but the Hotel Owners Association stepped in and effectively dared the civil rights organizations to do something. It obtained a court injunction limiting the number of pickets to a mere handful and slapped the Ad Hoc Committee and its leaders with a $50,000 lawsuit.

The lawsuit prompted the Ad Hoc Committee to raise the stakes. It asked supporters to picket the Palace on February 29. The Ad Hoc Committee said that Sheraton Palace employed only 19 blacks, all in menial jobs, on a staff totaling 550. About five hundred protesters came. After a couple hours of picketing and chanting, several went inside. First they stood around without signs. Then other demonstrators brought their signs inside. Gradually getting bolder, more of the picket line went in, the demonstrators now quietly forming a circle in, outside, and around the hotel. To this was soon added singing, chanting, and clapping hands. Toward the end of the afternoon the whole picket line moved inside the hotel.

Two hours later the court issued an injunction prohibiting picketing inside the hotel and limiting the number of pickets outside to nine. The monitors read the injunction to the demonstrators and asked them to leave and disperse, which they did. The next day they again picketed outside the hotel, in excess of the number allowed; 81 were arrested. Another demonstration was held late that night outside the Hall of Justice, from which several people marched over to the Sheraton Palace to resume picketing. They were promptly arrested. This brought the total to 123. Negotiations resumed in a heightened atmosphere of tension. On March 5 the Sheraton Palace Hotel hired its first black waitress, but refused to sign an agreement ensuring that this was not just tokenism.

The Ad Hoc Committee leafleted the campuses, inviting students to join the picket line on March 6. Thousands came from all over the Bay Area—but mostly from Cal and San Francisco State—to show their commitment to civil rights. The usual procedure at Cal was to go to Stiles Hall, the YMCA building on Bancroft a couple of blocks from Telegraph. Those with cars loaded them with people. A joint press conference in support of the demonstration was held by Dr. Thomas N. Burbridge, who headed the San Francisco NAACP, CORE head William Bradley, and the three leaders of the Ad Hoc Committee—Mike Myerson, Tracy Sims, and Roy Ballard. Myerson had graduated from Cal in 1961, where he had been SLATE chairman. Sims had graduated from Berkeley High School in 1963, and dropped out of San Francisco State to become a full-time civil rights activist. Ballard was in CORE. Myerson was the only white in this leadership group, and he stayed behind the scenes. Sims was the primary spokesperson.

The demonstration started quietly enough, around dinner time. As the night wore on we became louder, singing freedom songs and chanting. Our numbers surged and then thinned to about fifteen hundred as picketers grew cold, tired, and bored. Around 10:00 P.M. we moved inside. The hotel secured another injunction but did not enforce it, and we proceeded to "sleep in" in the lobby. We sat down, occupying the entire lobby except for a pathway left for hotel guests and police. The leadership went upstairs to negotiate with the Hotel Owners Association. Negotiations dragged on while we were entertained by comedian Dick Gregory and led in song by songwriter Malvina Reynolds. Thrice the leaders announced that agreement had been reached to hire more African Americans in thirty-three hotels. Thrice that turned out to be wrong; each time lawyers for the hotel owners said they could not sign because of some procedural problem. First they wanted the unions to agree, then other African American leaders; finally they insisted that all thirty-three hotel owners had to be consulted.

Between 3:00 and 4:00 A.M. we were instructed on how to be arrested. We were told that those willing to be arrested should cluster at the three main doors, while the rest should stay out of the way. Those under age eighteen were asked not to be arrested, though no one checked IDs. In order to lengthen the process, we were told to link arms and legs until we were separated and to go limp so we would have to be carried out. This also made good camera copy for the TV stations and newspapers.

It was all very orderly. A large group of demonstrators sat down and linked themselves together while the police waded in and tore us apart. Line after line of protestors walked to the front, sat down, and linked up.

We could see the zeal on the faces of the cops as they pulled us apart. They could see the stubborn resistance on ours. Those who had chosen not to get arrested began to sing. After six arrests, Willie Brown made a speech in which he asked the demonstrators to leave the doorway and simply hold a sleep-in. The demonstrators did not move until the members of the Ad Hoc Committee voted on this proposal, and they cheered when it was voted down. After about forty arrests, Tracy Sims announced that bail had been set at $600. She said that those who could not afford to remain in jail until Monday should hold a sleep-in but asked as many as could to let themselves be arrested. The threat of high bail later turned out to be a rumor circulated by the police to scare us into leaving.

During the night, 167 of us were arrested and charged with disturbing the peace, while another few hundred continued to picket. International Longshoremen's and Warehousemen's Union (ILWU) leaders phoned Mayor Shelly, who had enjoyed major union support for his recent election, and urged him to resolve the conflict. Several children of ILWU leaders were in the Sheraton demonstrations, and many blacks were among the union's members. The mayor called all parties into his office and kept them there until they signed an agreement. It required affirmation of a nondiscrimination policy by thirty-three hotels, regular "statistical analysis" of job categories, a goal of 15 to 20 percent minority employees, inspections to determine compliance, and amnesty. It was signed by Myerson, Sims, and Ballard and a lawyer for the Hotel Owners Association, and was "endorsed, ratified and approved" by four African American leaders in San Francisco. We cheered and sang after the agreement was read to us. Dick Gregory asked us to clean up the debris in the lobby. We did so and left.

The arrestees included 127 men, 34 women, and 6 juveniles (4 boys, 2 girls). Eight arrestees were black. Half the demonstrators were women, and 60 to 80 percent were white. The arrestees seemed slightly younger than the demonstrators as a whole. Two-thirds of the men and three-fourths of the women were between the ages of eighteen and twenty-three; 93 men and 22 women said they were students. Of the rest, a handful of the men said they were laborers, clerks, or unemployed. Most of the remaining women were clerks or secretaries. There were very few professional workers (teachers, attorneys). The *Berkeley Daily Gazette* identified 78 local residents.

We were denounced by almost everyone in authority. Governor Pat Brown said we endangered people's lives by blocking entrances at the Palace, set back the civil rights cause, and made it more difficult to defeat Proposition 14, which would be on the ballot that fall (designed to void the Fair Housing Act). On March 12 prominent churchmen warned, "The hope that these tactics have produced a victory for the Negro is a dangerous illusion." Our elders came up with a litany of reasons to discredit us, the most frequent of which was that the demonstrators were mostly white, even though the leaders and spokespeople were black. The clergymen said, "To the credit of our Negro fellow citizens, let it be noted that their part in these unfortunate events has been minimal." *San Francisco Chronicle* columnist Charles Denton asked how "responsible Negro leaders really expect to be taken seriously when they allow themselves to be represented in their struggle by an 18 year old girl in the full flush of adolescent arrogance, some students who figure getting their heads cracked is easier than cracking a book and a few retired beatniks who think anything at all beats working?" And the Du Bois Club's connection with the Ad Hoc Committee exposed us to red-baiting. All the daily newspapers denounced our outrageous tactics, including the student newspapers at Cal and San Francisco State. Our only press support came from two *Chronicle* columnists—Herb Caen and Arthur Hoppe. Hoppe normally wrote in a humorous vein, but he was quite serious when he compared us favorably with the "firebrands" of the Boston Tea Party. "[O]ne man's heroes are another man's bums," he wrote. "It just depends on which side you're on."

Demonstrations continued throughout the spring. The next targets were the car dealerships on Auto Row. On March 14, 107 people were arrested in front of the Cadillac agency, including 20 Cal students and/or Berkeley residents. The mayor negotiated a moratorium on civil disobedience, but picketing continued. The dealers published their own "Declaration of Policy" emphasizing that they were already equal opportunity employers. The NAACP asked the auto dealers to agree to a goal of "16 to 30 percent employment of minority group persons in future job turnover openings." When they did not do so, demonstrations were called for April 11. This time 226 were arrested. Mario Savio was not among them. I was. The Auto Row sit-ins had more adults and fewer students than those at the Palace, and many more African Americans. Though the papers described the pickets as "predominantly white," we thought whites were only half. More blacks were arrested, though I do not have an exact count. Sixty percent of the arrestees gave their occupation as student, though those listed as "teacher" were probably TAs. As before, laborers, clerks, secretaries, printers, and unemployed were the only other occupations listed by more than one or two people. Only 65 percent were between the ages of eighteen and twenty-three.

Once more we were condemned. Once more the demonstrations had their intended effect. The pickets continued. On April 13 the national NAACP announced it would hold demonstrations against auto dealers in fifty cities, beginning on May 4 with a protest at General Motors headquarters in Detroit. The Lincoln-Mercury dealer, who had received the worst of the April 11 sit-in, settled on April 17. That same day William Bradley promised there would be two thousand demonstrators on Saturday and possibly some "creative destruction." With thousands of people massed on

Auto Row ready to go in again, a sit-in was avoided at the last minute when both sides made pledges to the mayor's Interim Committee on Human Relations, created because neither side would negotiate with the other. The NAACP got the promises it wanted, and the auto dealers got peace.

Other employers were also under investigation and on the agendas of different civil rights organizations. CORE was looking into the Bank of America, which had twenty-nine thousand employees in California. CORE had found that minorities were only 2.4 percent of its employees and blacks only 1.9 percent, with none in executive positions. Of course B of A disagreed, but the bank's general counsel said "we are always ready at any time to sit down and discuss the problems with responsible representatives of any minority group." CORE began picketing B of A around the end of May. In June CORE began a version of the shop-in. Although insisting that its hiring of minorities was ongoing and laudable, B of A signed an agreement with the California Fair Employment Practices Commission under which it would provide regular reports of its recruitment activities and success rates. CORE was not mentioned, and the Bank's general counsel said he didn't care if CORE approved. In late summer William Bradley announced the B of A action was suspended; nearly 240 African Americans had been hired in white collar jobs between May and July.

This was the end of the big civil rights demonstrations, in part because employers were more willing to sign agreements and in part because the civil rights organizations had exhausted their human resources. In April the city of San Francisco put us on trial in groups of ten to fifteen. The trials went on for four months, taking up a lot of our time. The outcomes varied widely. Mario's trial group was acquitted, as was mine, but both of us spent weeks in court. Many others were convicted, receiving both fines and jail time. Tracy Sims served sixty days. Dr. Burbridge was sentenced to nine months. The Ad Hoc Committee continued to demonstrate but shifted to Oakland, where it picketed the *Oakland Tribune* and the restaurants around Jack London Square, until it fell apart from exhaustion and internal acrimony in the fall of 1964. Even as it did so, student activists shifted their focus to building the FSM and its protests against new University rules on political activity.

Mario Savio exemplified the straight line many students walked from the Civil Rights Movement to the FSM. In the fall of 1963 he was a newcomer to Berkeley and to the Civil Rights Movement but not to social justice. Mario was raised in Queens, New York, by a devoutly Catholic Italian family. Deeply religious, he served as an altar boy and might well have become a priest. However, after a year at a Jesuit College in Manhattan he lost his faith in the Church, transferring it to a more abstract sense of social justice. "Resist evil" was the message he had received from his family. If you see an injustice, it is your obligation to remove it. He spent the next year at

Queens College and in summer 1963 went to Mexico to work on an aid project arranged by the Newman Club. In Mexico he saw abject poverty and experienced the barriers raised by government officials to the project's efforts to build a public facility where people could wash their clothes.

In fall 1963 Mario became a student at Berkeley and moved into a nearby boardinghouse. He began attending meetings of Friends of SNCC, a group founded by former SLATE chairman Mike Miller. Mario's interest in civil rights and antipathy to racial discrimination may have come from his mother. During World War II, he would later learn, she had worked in a dime store where she found out that an African American friend and fellow worker was getting three cents less an hour than she was. Her boss told her he paid the woman less because "Negroes" got less, but agreed to pay equal rates after Dora Savio threatened to demonstrate. With these values firmly entrenched, when Mario saw pickets around Mel's while walking down the street one day, he felt a solidarity with the Civil Rights Movement and joined the line. But he was not ready to be an activist and only picketed a couple of times. He tutored black junior-high and high-school students in Berkeley. The tutorial project was using a room provided by a Berkeley women's group. Some of the tutors were also involved in CORE. After CORE began picketing the Berkeley merchants, the women's group asked them to leave. In the spring Mario joined SLATE but was not particularly active in it.

Mario found himself at the Sheraton Palace on March 6 by the same route as most of the Berkeley students—he was handed a leaflet at Bancroft and Telegraph. In 1964 student political groups were not allowed on campus except for limited purposes. On campus they could not hold regular meetings, advocate political action, collect money, or solicit members. They could put up posters advertising their off-campus meetings at eight specific locations. And they could invite speakers to address the University community, provided space was reserved and a faculty member agreed to preside at least three days in advance. The privilege of inviting speakers was a recent one; only a year before, the University had finally abolished its "Communist speaker ban," which had permitted the administration to veto any possible speaker it deemed too controversial, even if not a Communist.

At Bancroft and Telegraph several pillars marked the entrance to the University. Between these and the public street there was a twenty-six-foot strip of sidewalk that, though technically University property, was treated as if it belonged to the city. The student groups that were not allowed on campus put up their tables, passed out leaflets, and solicited money from this strip. In September 1964 the campus administration decided to reclaim the space as part of the University, subject to its rules and hence to its prohibitions on political groups. The decision to take away this "political space" sparked the FSM.

Why the administration chose this moment to reclaim that strip is unsettled to this day, but we all thought it was an attempt to curb the Civil Rights Movement. This was the spot from which we solicited students to participate in demonstrations, to picket, to disrupt business, and at times to break the law. Without this spot we could still function, but not as easily. Whether we could ask students to engage in illegal action from what was technically University property became the sticking point in the negotiations with the administration. We did not know the Bay Area civil rights movement was over; we thought we would need this space to solicit students for future off-campus demonstrations.

By the time the administration handed down its edict, Mario had changed from a cautious, inquisitive do-gooder who thought the Lucky Market shop-ins lacked "self-restraint and dignity" and the CORE campaign against Berkeley merchants was "a little bit too outlandish" to a self-confident activist who thought that several thousand students sitting around a police car was "very beautiful and very wholesome." He had gone from a shy stutterer who did not impress the person who interviewed him for Mississippi Summer to an inspired leader who galvanized others into action by speaking what was in their hearts. What transformed him was the time he spent in Mississippi helping local black residents register to vote during Freedom Summer. He learned about the Mississippi Summer Project, and decided to go, while sitting in jail after being arrested at the Sheraton Palace.

When Mario went to the Palace he did not intend to spend the night there, let alone several hours in jail. In fact, he had been at a "Welcome to Spring" party with his girlfriend when someone brought up the demonstration scheduled for that evening and several students there, including Mario, decided to go. They went to Stiles Hall and jumped into one of the many cars taking students across the Bay. After Tracy Sims asked the demonstrators to submit to arrest, Mario walked around for a while, trying to decide what to do. He watched others sit down and be arrested, with some anxiety and curiosity. And then he sat down himself. In his mind this was something of an initiation rite. In the act of letting himself be arrested he had crossed an invisible line, which somehow made him a different person, one with a sense of obligation to act on his beliefs beyond what he had felt before. When he got out of jail a few hours later, Mario was a committed political activist. Upon returning from Mississippi in late August he was more than committed; he was a political missionary.

On September 16 Mario attended a Campus CORE meeting that focused on Dean Katherine Towle's controversial letter announcing that, after September 21, University rules would be "strictly enforced" on the Bancroft strip. "University facilities may not, of course, be used to support or advocate off-campus political or social action." Mario thought this ruling "totally absurd." He was one of several representatives of student organizations who met with Dean Towle the following day to negotiate the matter. But Towle could not negotiate. She lacked the power. She had not made the decision; she could not change it. We could not talk with whomever had made it; indeed we were not even told who had made it or why. Mario immediately connected the ruling with his own experiences of the past few months. Without that twenty-six feet of political space he might not have known about the Palace demonstration, might not have been arrested, might not have gone to Mississippi. "It seemed fantastic that the University would presume to cut this off," he said later, "one of the main outlets in the free part of the country . . . for information, [or] recruiting."

The world of the University in September 1964 was not the same as it had been a year previous. The Civil Rights Movement had expanded our consciousness and our commitment. Probably in 1963, and certainly in 1962, we would have accepted with resignation what the University bureaucrats decreed, knowing that we lacked the power to do otherwise. But by September 1964 the Bay Area civil rights movement had transformed a critical mass of students into a community of concern. Thus, when campus police arrested Jack Weinberg for sitting at a CORE table illegally put in front of Sproul Hall, Berkeley students spontaneously surrounded the police car in which he was placed. A little over two weeks after the discouraging meeting with Dean Towle, ten of us were sitting in the conference room of President Kerr, negotiating the fate of several thousand students holding the police car hostage. Two-thirds of the student negotiators had been arrested in the civil rights demonstrations of the previous spring.

NOTE ON SOURCES

I was an undergraduate at Berkeley in 1961–1965 and a participant in most of the events I recount. (Some of these events I described in a term paper written in the spring of 1964, from which I have borrowed freely.) I knew Mario only slightly in 1963–1964. The information about him comes from research done in 1997, including interviews with friends and family and reading transcripts of interviews he did with the Columbia Oral History Research Center on March 5, 1985, and with Max Heirich on June 9, 1965. All quotes from Mario except the Mississippi Summer application are from the Heirich interview.

Holding One Another

Mario Savio and the Freedom Struggle in Mississippi and Berkeley

Waldo Martin

In the early afternoon of July 22, 1964, on the streets of Jackson, Mississippi, Berkeley student Mario Savio and Robert David Osman, another white volunteer in the Mississippi Summer Project, were walking toward the project's downtown headquarters. The summer project was the brainchild of Robert Moses, head of the Student Nonviolent Coordinating Committee's (SNCC's) Mississippi program. The Mississippi Summer Project's aim was to bring several hundred white volunteers into the freedom struggle on a short-term basis as a way to catalyze the movement. The idea was to use the expected added publicity to force the federal government to do more for the locals engaged in the struggle. Moses saw the participation of white college youth in the Mississippi struggle as a means to enhance outside support, especially among the white American majority.[1]

While on their way to project headquarters, Savio and Osman befriended a black male teenager and eagerly agreed to walk with him to the office. Proudly wearing the official "One Man—One Vote" button of the Summer Project, Mario had just returned from a round of voter registration work in Holmes County and needed to get back to the office to find out what his next assignment would be. Besides voter registration work, Savio participated in SNCC's Freedom Schools. These alternative educational institutions featured instruction in African American history and culture as well as the academic basics. Empowerment through education was the thrust of the Freedom Schools, which also included leadership training and recreation.[2]

Shortly prior to 4:00 P.M., before Savio, Osman, and their African American acquaintance could reach their destination, two Klansmen pulled up in an older-model white Chevy. The Klansmen apparently saw Savio and Osman as "Yankees," "nigger lovers," outside agitators bent on stirring up racial trouble. Seemingly ignoring the unidentified black male teenager who escaped unharmed, the southern "good ole boys," armed with billy clubs, each seized upon a white victim and took out after Mario and Robert. Mario escaped with a few glancing blows to his left shoulder before his assailant left him to join in the attack on Robert.

While Mario ran to an intersection, Robert fled to a field where both assailants cornered him. In his official statement to police officials, Robert recalled that in the heat of battle he, apparently like Mario, had neglected to warn his assailants that voting rights activities were "protected by Federal laws." One suspects that the two attackers could not have cared less. Indeed, for them the federal government was an integral part of the problem. Like so many white southern opponents of the Black Freedom Struggle, they surely viewed the federal government as supportive of that struggle in Mississippi and elsewhere, in spite of a good deal of evidence to the contrary.

Still reeling from the attack, Mario nonetheless felt no need for immediate medical attention. Robert was not so lucky. He remembered, "I covered my head with my arms to protect that area from attack. I was unable to observe the attack, . . . but I suffered hard, vicious blows from the club upon my right arm, right wrist, right knee, my ribs to the right side and the right side of my back." His wounds required immediate medical attention.[3]

Robert's official statement spoke pointedly to the philosophy animating his response to the violence of his attackers. Once it became clear that escape was impossible, he prepared himself for the attack. "I am committed to nonviolence and fell to the ground trying to protect myself as best I could. I made no attempt to do him [an attacker] any kind of physical harm."[4]

Fortunately for Robert and Mario, both escaped alive. But many black and white victims of anti–civil rights violence were not so lucky. Summer Project volunteer Andrew Goodman, black CORE activist James Chaney, and white CORE activist Michael Schwerner had been missing since June 21. Their murdered bodies were not discovered until August 4 in an earth-fill dam near Philadelphia, Mississippi. These young martyrs inspired those like Savio to continue the Mississippi freedom struggle. Indeed, within a month of the attack on Robert and Mario, at least one of the assailants, based on the testimony of Mario and Robert, was tried, convicted, and sentenced to thirty days in jail and a $100 bond for misdemeanor assault. Again, unfortunately, innumerable perpetrators of anti–civil rights crimes went, unlike this episode, undetected and unpunished.

Mario's participation in the Mississippi Summer Project affected him deeply. So much of the moral passion, principled commitment, and piercing insight he soon came to be known for as an FSM leader became evident in the wake of that fateful summer experience. That moment was critical to

Savio's transformation from what his colleague Jo Freeman has described as "a cautious, inquisitive do-gooder" to a "self-confident" activist. Indeed a scholarly consensus acknowledges the importance of the Mississippi Summer Project for the subsequent activist lives of many more of the participants.[5]

What is lacking in these scholarly discussions is an adequate understanding of the larger context of the Black Freedom Struggle of this period at the local as well as the national level. That context encompasses two realities. The first is the intrinsic interconnectedness of various progressive movements for social change, including movements for civil rights, civil liberties, human rights (both international and national), and economic rights. Typically, the fundamental issue tying these struggles together was a deep-seated commitment to the expansive and empowering notion of American democracy.

Put another way, the work of realizing American freedom, equality, and justice—in often different ways—animated these related movements. Nowhere is the interrelationship among progressive social movements better glimpsed than in the triangulation across the southern and Bay Area civil rights movements and the FSM. The powerful impact on the FSM of the Black Freedom Struggle in both its national and local phases demonstrated the inherent linkages of civil liberties and civil rights, political liberty and political speech, student rights and human rights. Mario Savio's activism personified and illuminated these linkages.

The second, closely related reality I would point to is the vital importance of the Black Freedom Struggle in representing the nature and direction of social change. In 1964 Michael Rossman noted that because of its utter seriousness and its searing impact on national consciousness, "the Civil Rights struggle interlocks with and binds together the whole spectrum of new student activity." The increasingly successful black struggle to destroy Jim Crow emboldened white youth to envision that they too could join movements to change the surrounding world.[6]

Undeniably, the engine pushing the progressive social movement agenda forward in the 1950s was the Black Freedom Struggle, highlighted by the Montgomery Bus Boycott (1955–1956) and the black college student sit-in movement emanating out of Greensboro, North Carolina, after February 1, 1960. African Americans themselves were tackling head-on America's seemingly intractable racial dilemma and, in the process, demanded that white Americans like Savio do likewise.

The crucial point is that whites like Savio listened to African Americans, learned from them, followed African American leadership, and in the process were forever transformed. That African Americans benefited from the sacrifices of those like Savio who gave so unstintingly to the Black Freedom Struggle, especially that summer, goes without saying. Both races gained immeasurably from the experience, and it ultimately redounded to the benefit of the nation as well as American race relations. Mississippi Summer allowed whites like Savio to confront "up close and personal" the antiblack racism of themselves and others. As a result, they were able to grapple with and get beyond white racism in ways most white Americans can hardly begin to fathom. This extraordinary empathy made Savio an even more impressive leader.

It was clear to partisans of the black liberation insurgency that race was the key division keeping the American nation from realizing its better self. White and black partisans of the Black Freedom Struggle came to see that the struggle was as much if not more about the meanings and prerogatives of whiteness as it was about black self-determination. The Black Freedom Struggle was not just a recent and short-term racial liberation movement; it represented the continuation of an ongoing African freedom struggle dating back to the arrival of the first Africans on these shores.

Thus, even though the American revolutionary movement of the late eighteenth century slighted the contemporaneous black freedom struggle, in time the inseparability of the two would help empower the black struggle. Building upon that understanding, Savio, like so many of his comrades, came to see the revolutionary nature of black freedom claims. His intense involvement in the black liberation insurgency that momentous summer only intensified this evolving awareness of the profound reach and power of the Black Freedom Struggle. He now understood that the insurgency was not just about black freedom, or white freedom, but American freedom.

·   ·   ·

Mario Savio's development as an activist illustrated the importance of engagement in local civil rights struggle as a springboard to broader realms of activism. While his participation in the Mississippi Summer Project clarified, sharpened, and deepened his commitment to the Black Freedom Struggle, that experience built directly upon his previous work in the Bay Area civil rights movement. When Mario arrived in Berkeley in fall 1963, he already possessed a finely honed moral sensibility. Raised a devout Catholic and keenly aware of the Christian imperative to fight against evil and injustice, his early religiosity pushed him in the direction of social activism. His mother's egalitarianism seems to have fostered his burgeoning social conscience and ethical awareness.

Mario was a serious student of philosophy, and his analytical and logical skills enhanced his moral reasoning and social understanding. Committed to making a positive difference in the real world, the summer before he matriculated at Berkeley he worked on an antipoverty project in Mexico. Once he arrived at Berkeley, he encountered a Bay Area civil rights movement energized by local protests in part inspired by the explosive and well-publicized Birmingham campaign. Bay Area visits by James Baldwin and CORE leader James Farmer further spurred local civil rights activism.

The Bay Area civil rights movement nurtured Savio's evolving civil rights commitment. The local movement energized a small yet growing number of Berkeley students because, like its southern counterpart, it proved morally righteous and politically viable. "Students have turned to the civil rights movement," campus CORE activist Jack Weinberg observed at the time, "because they have found it to be a front on which they can attack basic social problems, a front on which they have some real impact."[7]

In Berkeley, as elsewhere in the West and North, local civil rights work attracted a broad swath of white student support, especially when the movement was threatened. Like Savio, many white students now supported the Black Freedom Struggle not only because it was the moral thing to do but because it dignified their own lives and offered hope for a better future. Rossman observed that, for white student advocates, "The Civil Rights Movement represents a symbolic promissory note upon their own futures, upon the chances that their own lives . . . will be less futile than they feel those of the previous generation to have been." White students, he predicted, would support the Civil Rights Movement "not only because it is meaningful per se, but also because it is a promise of meaning in their own lives and work."[8] That search for meaning played nicely into Savio's civil rights activism.

Furthermore, by fighting antiblack prejudice and discrimination from Berkeley to Birmingham, white college youth began the very difficult process of repudiating white supremacy. In turn, they joined the ranks of the neoabolitionist movement, harkening back to the interracial nineteenth-century abolitionist movement to emancipate the black slave. This earlier phase of the Black Freedom Struggle had also been notable for its strong black phalanx, for its equally strong yet very small number of white allies, and for its interracialism. Whereas the nineteenth-century struggle eventually achieved success through the Civil War, the twentieth century struggle triumphed over Jim Crow principally because of the southern black-led grassroots insurgency that spread throughout the nation.[9]

In the South, black activists battled legal (de jure) as well as customary (de facto) forms of discrimination. Outside the states of the former Confederacy, especially in the Far West and the North, in places like Berkeley, the struggle was typically against structural and customary manifestations of racism. In 1960, Berkeley was a thriving yet racially segregated university town. While the world-class University of California gave the city a liberal patina, fundamentally the city was a Manichean world divided into black and white sections. The University and North Berkeley, including the exclusive Berkeley Hills area, were white enclaves.[10]

Berkeley's black residents made up about a fifth of the city's population and lived almost exclusively in southwest Berkeley. Many were relatively recent migrants from the South, especially Louisiana, Texas, and Mississippi. For most black Berkeleyans, the University was an alien world. As historian W. J. Rorabaugh observes, in 1960 they "lived in a corner of the city remote from the University. One seldom saw a black on campus, black shoppers were not welcome in downtown Berkeley, and both school segregation and discrimination in employment and housing were common. In 1963 Berkeley voters rejected an open housing ordinance, 22,750 to 20,456, and in October 1964 the school board was nearly recalled over desegregation."[11]

Not surprisingly, a critical component of the Bay Area civil rights movement took root in Berkeley and flowered in the accommodating soil of progressive students and faculty. It was this rapidly evolving "community of concern," as Freeman labels it, that nurtured Savio's civil rights activism. Before 1963 and Savio's arrival on the scene, the local civil rights movement took its cue from the southern movement and tackled the most visible and onerous forms of local Jim Crow.

During the late fifties and early sixties, a small number of Berkeley students engaged in a variety of protests featuring such traditional tactics as passing resolutions, forming investigating committees, and toward the end of this period, picketing. After the February 1960 outbreak of the black college student sit-in movement, there were a series of sympathy boycotts of local Woolworth and Kress stores. These kinds of actions persisted throughout the Bay Area for roughly a year. In spring 1960 Students for Racial Equality (SRE) emerged to collect money and food for the southern movement. Administration opposition soon crippled the work of SRE, and after a very promising beginning and thirteen months of hard work and modest success, the group dissolved. The tension between the administration and the students over on-campus political activity was heating up. It would soon boil over. And when it boiled over, the issue of the right of students to speak out on campus on behalf of the black civil rights struggle proved decisive.[12]

SLATE was the first prominent Berkeley student group in the 1950s to work on behalf of civil rights. Its founding dated back to 1957, the year of the explosive integration of Little Rock's Central High School by nine courageous black students, an event that created a national calamity as well as an international media moment. That same year Berkeley's student activists tackled the issue of racial discrimination in the fraternity system. The name "SLATE" denoted a new coalition of progressive students that was fielding a *slate* of candidates for student government who were committed to abolishing discrimination in all campus organizations. SLATE promoted civil rights politicization and education among Berkeley students and the surrounding community, leading, in Rossman's words, "the first real [off-campus] student activity in Civil Rights: support of a 1959 Fair Housing Ordinance." Foreshadowing the FSM conflict, the UC administration, rattled by SLATE's aggressive political style, especially its militant actions in support of black civil rights, clashed often with the group, and by February 1961 had thrown it off campus.[13]

The CORE-led 1961 southern Freedom Rides to test compliance with new federal laws mandating integrated interstate bus travel garnered Berkeley student support, and a few student volunteers. The following year SLATE's summer conference led to the creation of Bay Area Friends of SNCC. Former SLATE chair Mike Miller spearheaded the formation of this SNCC support network. There were soon eleven Bay Area chapters. Meetings of a Berkeley's Friends of SNCC chapter provided one of Savio's initial points of entry into the local civil rights struggle in fall 1963.[14]

SLATE was critical in opening up the Berkeley student body and the campus to student activism, including the Black Freedom Struggle. Previously the Greek system and its conservative politics had dominated the student government and the campus's undergraduate culture. Although its membership was relatively small, SLATE pushed student politics beyond the narrow strictures of post-McCarthyite anxiety and Cold War conformity. It was controversial, according to Rorabaugh, because it included both leftists and moderates. In addition, he explained, it was "the first post–McCarthy era organization to reject anticommunism," and it "established a working model for later Berkeley umbrella groups."[15]

Nowhere did SLATE's influence germinate more effectively than in the escalating Berkeley student involvement in the Bay Area civil rights movement. Of course, many Berkeley students came to support that movement without any connection to SLATE. But for those who did, SLATE offered a multi-issue progressive agenda. It also offered a forward-looking political education, demonstrating in effect the interrelationships among contemporary social movements. Understanding those interrelationships, activists were better able to constitute a multi-issue agenda, though often making the black freedom insurgency a priority. In addition to its civil rights campaigns, SLATE was active in grassroots anti–capital punishment agitation centered on the unsuccessful effort to prevent the execution of Caryl Chessman in 1960. The group was also prominent in the mobilization that year against the House Un-American Activities Committee investigations in San Francisco.[16]

This was the activist student world that Savio entered in fall 1963. The southern wing of the Black Freedom Struggle was hurtling along, fueling the struggle outside the South. The Birmingham campaign, which in spring 1963 generated TV news coverage that exposed Americans and the world to the brutality of southern racism, riveted the attention of Berkeley civil rights activists.[17] On August 28 over 250,000 Americans thronged the Lincoln

Memorial for the March on Washington for Jobs and Freedom. It was a momentous occasion, with prayer, music, and grand speech making. Martin Luther King, Jr., electrified that powerful historic moment with his now classic "I Have A Dream" speech, emerging as an iconic world historical figure as he revivified the enduring hope for freedom, equality, and justice.

The year 1963 witnessed the resurgence of extremely dangerous southern forces of massive resistance to black freedom. These militant racists still operated with relative impunity in some areas of the South. On June 11 the highly respected and influential Mississippi civil rights leader Medgar Evers was murdered in his driveway by Klan member Byron De La Beckwith. A few weeks after the March on Washington, as the nation still floated along on the emotional high of that awesome moment, four little black girls were murdered by a bomb blast while attending Sunday School at Birmingham's Sixteenth Street Baptist Church. A shocked world recoiled in horror at another dastardly deed perpetrated by the racist counterrevolution. The terrifying reality of this violent racist counterinsurgency made the escalating black insurgency all the more urgent and dangerous.

.   .   .

The further cementing of the southern, northern, and western wings of the Black Freedom Struggle led by those in the central theater of action, the South, also occurred in 1963. In Berkeley, in particular, the local civil rights struggle had by now come to be fully identified with the struggle in the South. That summer and fall over five hundred Berkeley students labored to defeat the statewide pro–housing discrimination measure, Proposition 14. While the measure passed, in Berkeley it lost by a margin of almost two to one. In 1963 Berkeley students also founded Campus CORE.[18]

It was within this context that Berkeley students joined civil rights activists throughout the Bay Area in protests organized by the Ad Hoc Committee to End Discrimination. The Ad Hoc Committee, inspired by the example of southern black activists, was an interracial movement that aimed at ending local job discrimination. The committee promoted active black leadership and participation, and its sensitivity to this imperative ensured the eventual success of the revitalized interracial Bay Area civil rights movement.[19] Following the tactics of the southern movement, especially pickets, boycotts, and sit-ins, the committee pressured offending employers to come up with plans to integrate their workforces. The overriding objective of the committee's plan of action was straightforward yet potentially transformative. The goal was to seek equal job opportunities and placements for blacks at all realistic levels, not just further expansion within lower-level categories, most notably service staffs—where institutionalized racism had left blacks clustered in the least desirable and worst-paid jobs.

There was an impressive series of well-orchestrated protests between October 1963 and the summer of 1964 against job discrimination at Bay Area businesses, including several in Berkeley. Overall, the Ad Hoc Committee's strategy proved highly effective. Businesses like the Lucky supermarkets were increasingly willing to enter into employment agreements with the committee rather than endure protests and public censure. It was clear, however, that the initial protests and intense pressures were necessary to achieve the desired results. In time, more and more businesses voluntarily signed such agreements. The high point of the committee's activity was the protracted and intense struggle with the downtown San Francisco hotels, especially the Sheraton Palace. The settlement with the Hotel Owners Association came out of a particularly heated confrontation, after a marathon sit-in at the Sheraton Palace on the night of March 6, 1964. Subsequent protests spread to other institutions including auto dealerships and the Bank of America. The key action, however, was the protest at the Sheraton Palace.[20]

Here Savio enters the story. He was one of 167 arrested during the sit-in at the Sheraton Palace. It was while in jail after his arrest that he first heard of the Mississippi Summer Project and decided to participate. Jo Freeman, also a Berkeley student, was similarly transformed by her participation in the Bay Area movement. "These demonstrations," she notes, "were highly publicized and much talked about." She recalls that the demonstrations led by the Ad Hoc Committee galvanized Berkeley student activism, showing students that through civil disobedience they could win battles against injustice, a lesson that paved the way for the FSM. For Savio himself the decision to become a part of the Mississippi Summer Project reflected a determination to do something positive about what he saw as America's most critical problem, the state of black-white relations. His decision marked his commitment to serious political action. As Freeman suggests, when Savio left the jail after being arrested at the Sheraton Palace, he did so as a "committed political activist"; and in the fall he returned from Mississippi as "a political missionary."[21]

In addition to involvement with a local branch of Friends of SNCC, Savio's education and politicization around the race question in Berkeley also grew out of his tutorial work with youngsters at Berkeley schools. Ironically, one interviewer, charged with selecting participants for the Mississippi Summer Project, a civil rights activist who knew Savio, rated him average at best and gave him a marginal and guarded recommendation while criticizing Savio's work on what she called the "abortive tutorial project." The interviewer found him to be "not a very creative guy altho [*sic*] he accepts responsibility and carries it through if you explain to him exactly what needs to be done; not exceedingly perceptive on the movement, what's involved, etc."[22] Clearly, however, this unflattering portrait of Savio contrasts sharply with his extraordinary FSM leadership, as well as with the portrait drawn of him by those who came to know him in the course of his work in Mississippi. Dorothy Smith, for example, a thirteen-year-old student at a McComb Freedom School when she met Savio and another northern volunteer, recalled being "highly impressed" with them, partially because "I had not had any dealings with whites prior to that, . . . so this was an entirely different experience for me." Another young black Mississippi student told of an exciting intellectual moment—an extended philosophical discussion with Savio the philosophy major. A black leader on the Summer Project recalled his surprise at the Savio of FSM fame: "Is this the Mario we knew? Speaking out like that? He was so quiet and self-effacing here." And a fellow volunteer remembered that his personal interactions with Savio had "opened up his eyes and mind in a way he was . . . in awe of."[23]

Savio's experiences in Mississippi gave him a wealth of insight into the nature, meanings, and consequences of American-style apartheid. Working within the SNCC tradition of developing local black initiative and leadership, Savio carefully observed how those on the other side of the racial divide negotiated their daily lives, from the mundane to the highly political. Unlike the vast majority of whites, he came to understand black history and culture in personal and revealing ways. The endurance, grace under pressure, dignity, and bravery of the black Mississippians whom he worked with taught him volumes about black people, working-class struggle, and working-class agency. Education and politicization in the Summer Project were dynamic and interactive; they cut both ways. Indeed, white volunteers learned as much as, if not more than, the Mississippi blacks whose freedom struggle they so unabashedly supported.[24]

White volunteers in Mississippi had to confront the ubiquity of white supremacist ideologies and practices. Likewise, they had to confront their own complicity in structures of white privilege as well as their *own* racial beliefs and practices. It was often a searing experience, and it certainly was for Mario. He came away a profoundly changed person, more in sync than ever before with the egalitarian and antiracist imperatives of the Black Freedom Struggle. Like the best of the volunteers, he increasingly understood the necessity of following the people themselves, in this case the black leadership at all levels in the black freedom insurgency. Similarly, he came to see that the most viable practices of grassroots social movements came from the bottom up, out of the day-to-day exigencies of organizing, or what Charles Payne in the title of his book calls "the organizing tradition." This tradition had to be respected, tapped into, and cultivated. Decisions about how best to meet the demands of black grassroots struggle had to be made by local blacks. They could not be imposed from without by others, especially not white others.[25]

Awareness that it was the local people, at all levels of the community, who ultimately had to accept the lion's share of the responsibility for reshaping their own lives was crucial to the fomenting of serious change. A guiding principle of SNCC and especially of the Mississippi Summer Project, therefore, was the development and support of local black grassroots agency. As Clayborne Carson has argued, "SNCC had been at the center of an experience based on the belief that people of every social status could play significant roles in determining their destiny, and people associated with it had learned lessons that were of lasting value for anyone who shared the belief."[26] Savio obviously learned all this, and his egalitarian leadership style had "SNCC" written all over it.

Savio also learned a great deal from his brush with southern white violence and racist intimidation in the harrowing episode recounted at the outset of this essay. That brutal assault graphically illustrated the terror and violence at the heart of Jim Crow and captured the vicious extremity of southern white opposition to the Black Freedom Struggle. It illustrated the bitter hatred of racist whites toward those they considered race traitors and outside agitators. While Savio seldom spoke of this moment, one has to assume that he never forgot it.

The Freedom Summer moment that Savio did speak of as having profoundly influenced him was classic in its stark representation of African American bravery in rural Mississippi in the teeth of state-sponsored white supremacy. Mario had been talking with an elderly black man for some time, trying to convince him to register to vote. After several tactics had failed, Mario stumbled upon another—he asked the slightly stooped gentleman a series of questions. Had his father ever voted? Had his father's father voted? To both of these queries the gentleman responded, "No." Next, Mario asked him if he wanted his children to vote. At this moment it all came together for that old black warrior, as the travails of his family's and his people's past merged with the promise of an African American future. He decided to go with Mario to the registrar's office, where he stoically endured the racist taunts of the female official who referred to him as "boy" ("What do you want, boy?"). Mario remembered that to receive a copy of the necessary voter registration form, "she made him eat shit for it. She humiliated him." Still, the black man persevered, and his courage, his willingness, after hearing Mario's words, both to risk his life and endure humiliation to register to vote, Mario would recall, "changed my life."[27]

The uncommon moral courage and physical bravery of black Mississippians made evident in this episode helps explain why Mario's Mississippi experiences were so deeply inspiring. His own personal interactions with the racist enemy only intensified his awareness of the uncommon strength and commitment required to go forward in the struggle. Like so many white and black comrades, he too had faced the possibility of death, and this common experience forged a close bond among them. Fortunately, Mario survived his ordeal even more committed to "the struggle that must be," as sociologist Harry Edwards titled his autobiography. As Jack Weinberg, a close friend and collaborator of Mario's in the FSM and, like him, a Civil Rights Movement veteran, has observed, "Mario had been inspired . . . by the courage and commitment of young African Americans, in the deep South and elsewhere, who were struggling for basic human, civil, and economic rights with little or no broad public recognition, often in the face of extreme violence and brutality. Mario's personal identification with the Black struggle was an important reality that the mass media could never satisfactorily capture. Nor did Mario seek to display that side of himself."[28] Instead, he evinced an exemplary lifelong commitment to black freedom, to equality and justice.

Over time the necessity of fearlessness in the African American liberation struggle was becoming painfully clear. A key to this rising fearlessness was the recognition of the power that both the individual and the group could gain through concerted social action. The force of collective protest empowered the disempowered. Speaking of his black Mississippi comrades as a vital inspiration to the FSM, Savio would later note that they "overcame their fears *by holding one another.* Against the snapping and snarling dogs, against the torrents of water, they held one another. That was a lesson that what we need we can find in one another, the strength we need. I was shamed and inspired to do what I could do."[29] In a similar vein, FSM veteran Mark Shechner recalled that Mississippi Freedom Summer taught Savio and his volunteer comrades "to live with fear, and fear became the rock on which they founded their moral stamina, their tactical savvy, their commitment, their analysis. They had seen firsthand how entrenched power perpetuates injustice and came home prepared to wage war against it."[30]

Indeed, after Mississippi the opposition of the Berkeley campus administration, state officials, and much of the media to the free speech rights of students proved far less intimidating. As one student activist explained, "A student who has been chased by the KKK in Mississippi is not easily scared by academic bureaucrats." The shy Savio came out and literally found a public voice on behalf of a vital cause. One observer viewed Savio's Mississippi work as crucial to his confident leadership during the FSM: "No way, he ever would have . . . stepped forward if it hadn't been for Mississippi. Part of it was confidence. He was really a pretty shy guy." The turning point was the Summer Project. "Freedom Summer tended to boost you," this observer said; "you felt like you had been there and you know what you were talking about. . . . [T]hat seemed to happen to him." The "moral outrage" at what he experienced in Mississippi drove Savio to a "total commitment to the movement . . . and no stupid bureaucratic rules were going to get in the way."[31]

SNCC'S guiding organizational philosophy and practice as well as Savio's interpersonal interactions with blacks and whites in Mississippi deeply influenced his own evolving activism. From SNCC he imbibed three defining attributes. First, he carefully observed the organization's emphasis on group-centered leadership rather than leader-centered groups. This collective sensibility extended to early SNCC's emphasis on group-centered rather than leader-centered movements. His emphasis on democratic leadership and what historian Ruth Rosen has characterized as his "reluctant leadership" style reflect the influence of SNCC. Second, he was very impressed by SNCC's devotion to grassroots democracy and consensual decision making. This cultivation of grassroots initiative and leadership was a model of the kind of participatory democracy that came to mark organizational structure as well as decision making within the FSM. Third, there was the stress SNCC placed on taking seriously the distinction between the long-term, often arduous work of organizing as against the short-term, tactical work of mobilization for a specific action.[32] Again, this was a crucial distinction that significantly influenced how Savio helped to plan and implement the FSM's strategies and tactics.

The emphasis here on the impact of the Freedom Summer Project on Savio's evolving activism should not obscure the considerable contributions that he and other volunteers made in southwest Mississippi, particularly in the Pike County town of McComb, under extremely oppressive conditions. This was an especially racist and repressive part of the state where only a few years earlier the local black movement had suffered a crushing setback. In 1961 the murder of black activist Herbert Lee in broad daylight by a white state congressman rocked the movement. This event had signaled the intensification of a local racist counterinsurgency, which helps account for the fact that for the next two years or so campaigns to desegregate public facilities and register blacks to vote were stillborn. White supremacism was especially vicious in this area, even by Mississippi standards. It was the kind of area that gave special urgency to singer Nina Simone's striking lamentation—"Mississippi Goddam!"[33]

The Freedom Summer project revitalized the local movement in McComb. The volunteers, including Savio, Marshall Ganz, and Gene Guerrero, played crucial roles in this revitalization. John Dittmer has called the rebirth of the movement in McComb "a major achievement of the [SNCC] summer project," carried out "in the face of the most violent and sustained campaign of intimidation and terror in the state." In Dittmer's words, the SNCC workers who returned to Pike County that summer "were assisted by a talented group of white volunteers, several of whom became full-time organizers after leaving Mississippi. McComb demonstrated the possibility that 'black and white together' could be more than a movement slogan." Soon thereafter Savio returned to Berkeley and his involvement in the

FSM, Ganz worked for a time with the United Farm Workers in California, while Guerrero helped organize the Southern Student Organizing Committee (a white-led student group modeled after SNCC).[34]

After Freedom Summer the interracial tensions simmering within the Civil Rights Movement escalated. The problem of white involvement, and particularly white leadership, in a movement for black freedom became more pronounced. Growing numbers of blacks, and some whites, became increasingly concerned about how white involvement obscured and at times undermined black leadership and agency. White and black activists debated how best in this context to maintain and extend black autonomy over their own freedom struggle. This concern flared into a burning issue. During Freedom Summer, Savio observed within SNCC not just the expected political in-fighting but also a burgeoning fracture of the white-black coalition, in part along race lines. In retrospect, he observed that "this was really the swan song of the white-black coalition within the Civil Rights Movement." By 1966 SNCC would expel whites and adopt a black nationalist philosophy. Within a few years, the interracial "beloved community" of the Civil Rights years had given way to the increasingly separatist thrust of the Black Power insurgency.[35]

.   .   .

Mario Savio brought similar lessons from his early Catholic moral training and his civil rights activism into the FSM, lessons that strengthened his recognition of white Americans' responsibility for participating in the antiracist struggle. From his religious upbringing and from his experience in Mississippi, he came to see the urgency of working within one's own community to ameliorate the oppression of the least fortunate. He also came to see that it was necessary to battle concurrently against the oppression in one's own life. The battle was both personal and political, internal and external. The key was the constancy and ubiquity of struggle, indeed of lifelong struggle, on behalf of others as well as oneself. It is critical for those truly committed to progressive social change to embrace the reality, as legendary SNCC leader Robert Moses recently argued, that "our lot is struggle."[36]

In his important book *Freedom Summer,* Doug McAdam has persuasively argued that "for most of the leaders of the Berkeley revolt, the movement was seen as an extension of the civil rights struggle and the Summer Project in particular. The tactical, ideological, and personnel imprint of Freedom Summer was everywhere evident in the events of Berkeley." Similarly, Jo Freeman has cogently argued that Savio exemplified "the straight line many students walked" from the Civil Rights Movement to the FSM. Twelve of Berkeley's twenty-one volunteers in the Summer Project were later active in the FSM. The impress of the movement culture of the Black Freedom Struggle was omnipresent. Civil Rights–inspired and especially SNCC-inspired rallies, sit-ins, songs—most notably "We Shall Overcome"— and participatory democracy–inflected leadership, organizational structure, and practice marked the FSM. It is not surprising, therefore, that, when the FSM mobilized a march to coincide with a University Regents meeting, the male attire was recognizable. "Borrowing an idea from the civil rights movement in the South," Rorabaugh has written, "Savio insisted that male marchers wear coat and tie."[37]

The intense, committed, cerebral yet grounded and highly ethical leadership of Savio also had a clear Civil Rights Movement parallel in Robert Moses. As a mathematics major with a fondness for philosophy, Moses, like Savio the philosophy major, had a penchant for logical concision, theoretical clarity, and tactical/strategic thinking. Moses, too, was a reluctant yet charismatic and highly effective leader. Moses not only helped lead the Mississippi campaign that affected Savio so deeply but was also a principal architect of the immensely important yet failed effort of the insurgent and integrated Mississippi Freedom Party to unseat the all-white Mississippi delegation at the 1964 Democratic Convention. In Moses, Savio saw a visionary student leader he both admired and emulated.[38]

If the civil rights struggle was both text and subtext in the FSM, it was not just the Freedom Summer experience that framed the FSM's emergence. McAdam's singular attention to the Summer Project in relationship to the development of the FSM implies as much, but his broader argument belies that rather restricted focus. Granted the huge influence of the national Civil Rights Movement, the local civil rights movement was surely of comparable significance to the history of the FSM. It was the combined and interactive impact of the local civil rights movement and the Freedom Summer Project that prepared the ground for the FSM's appearance. As Freeman has put it, redressing the balance, "The civil rights movement had expanded our consciousness and our commitment. Probably in 1963 and certainly in 1962, we would have accepted with resignation what the University bureaucrats decreed, knowing that we lacked the power to do otherwise. But by September 1964 the Bay Area civil rights movement had transformed a critical mass of students into a community of concern." In a related vein, Michael Rossman has made the point that, "The recent successes of the Civil Rights movement left a deep impression as to the immediate relevance of Constitutional rights."[39]

That "community of concern" understood quite well what was at stake in the University's efforts to prevent students and others from advocating, organizing, and mobilizing on campus on behalf of the Civil Rights Movement. Such University efforts to suppress student speech and action constituted egregious violations of constitutionally protected rights. In September

1964 the institution of rules to regulate students' political advocacy and push it off campus ignited a firestorm of controversy.

But it was a controversy that had been brewing for quite some time. In 1961, for example, Malcolm X had been prevented from speaking on campus by University officials on the grounds that he was a religious proselytizer. Yet earlier that year the same officials had approved an on-campus speaking engagement by James Pike, Episcopal Bishop of San Francisco. The intention was clear: the on-campus agitation of controversial black civil rights leaders was to be avoided at all costs.

By fall 1964 even Berkeley's chancellor, Edward Strong, could grasp that the latest crackdown on activism on campus was likely to provoke a strong student backlash. He anticipated protests in large part because "hardcore demonstrators—the students who spent the summer in Mississippi civil rights work— . . . are going to try to open up the campus." As he saw the problem, these student activists "returned to Berkeley thinking the University should become more involved in social justice."[40]

He could not have been more accurate. When returning students heard of the new, restrictive rules and of stricter enforcement of old ones, large numbers refused to accept what they correctly viewed as unconstitutional restrictions on their rights of free speech and assembly. And throughout the three-month struggle of the FSM, the free speech activists led by Savio had no trouble interpreting the administration's actual motive—to decouple the Berkeley campus from the civil rights actions taking place in the surrounding community. Most of those singled out for punishment during the protests had a strong commitment to civil rights, including all eight of those who were initially suspended. At the time, Rossman wrote that "the 'reinterpretations' of the Administration's regulations this semester (and in the past five years!) hit most strongly at the organizational heart of the Civil Rights movement on campus. Both the vehemence and breadth of the protest stemmed partly from this fact." Similarly, Freeman recalled that "we all thought it was an attempt to curb the Civil Rights Movement." She then went on to explain that the Bancroft-Telegraph sidewalk strip, which the administration withdrew from use as a "free-speech area" that September, was "the spot from which we solicited students to participate in [civil rights] demonstrations, to picket, to disrupt business, and at times to break the law. Without this spot, we could still function, but not as easily."[41]

Savio obviously agreed. In fact, he saw the FSM as a continuation of his Mississippi work specifically and his civil rights activism in general. As he explained at the time:

> Last summer I went to Mississippi to join the struggle there for civil rights. This fall I am engaged in another phase of the same struggle, this time in Berkeley. The two battlefields may seem quite different to some observers, but this is not the case. The same rights are at stake in both places—the right

to participate as citizens in democratic society and the right to due process of law. Further, it is a struggle against the same enemy. In Mississippi an autocratic and powerful minority rules, through organized violence, to suppress the vast, virtually powerless, majority. In California the privileged minority manipulates the University bureaucracy to suppress the student's political expression. That "respectable" bureaucracy masks the financial plutocrats: that impersonal bureaucracy is the efficient enemy in a "Brave New World."[42]

When Savio gave the speech that elevated him to legendary and heroic proportions, the example of the civil rights struggle empowered him. When he spoke of "a time when the operation of the machine becomes so odious, makes you so sick at heart that you can't take part . . . and you've got to make it stop," he spoke profoundly to all engaged in progressive social struggle. Not just the FSM. When he further explained that "you've got to indicate to the people who run it, to the people who own it, that unless you're free, the machine will be prevented from working at all!" he spoke to all engaged in modern freedom struggle everywhere.[43] Yet precisely because of Savio's exemplary civil rights activism, in this classic utterance there was a special resonance for partisans of the struggle against the ideology and mechanisms of white supremacy.

If it is necessary to acknowledge the achievements of the FSM, it is equally necessary to recognize its limitations. In light of its close ties to the Civil Rights Movement, one glaring limitation in the FSM's vision is the participants' relative silence regarding the near absence at the time of black students and faculty at Berkeley. In part this was the limitation of an essentially white movement. Even on the relatively enlightened and sympathetic Berkeley campus, the crying need to greatly expand the black and, more generally, the nonwhite presence on the campus was insufficiently understood. Only a few years later, however, Berkeley's students of color would mount a struggle to promote the recruitment and retention of minority students and faculty. These activists necessarily sought out and frequently gained the support of white students, most notably the most sensitive white civil rights activists. That group often coincided with those most committed to keeping alive the democratic spirit of the free speech struggle. This growing commitment to the recruitment and retention of students and faculty of color, though it had its own historical antecedents and its own genesis, thus signified a logical extension of the expanding struggle to make Berkeley a more open and tolerant community.

.   .   .

In 1994, on the occasion of the thirtieth anniversary of the FSM, Savio and other FSM veterans vividly recalled the centrality of the African American Civil Rights Movement to their movement. Two years later, on the sad occasion of the memorial service for Savio, on December 8, 1996, the inspiring memory of his principled and exemplary civil rights activism was everywhere. In the last years of his life, graphically demonstrating the continuity of his commitments, he had vigorously participated in the movements to defeat California Propositions 187 and 209. The former forbade the provision of state services to illegal immigrants, mostly Latinos. The latter undid the state's commitment to affirmative action in programs under its aegis, including education, contracting, and hiring. Together with like-minded activists, Savio had helped create an alliance across California's community college, state college, and university systems to defeat these propositions. Clearly the rights of peoples of color in California were under siege and remained so when Mario died of cardiac arrest in November 1996.

Ruth Rosen has given us a revealing description of the 1996 gathering on Sproul steps in Mario's memory:

> [A] huge crowd gathered outside on the unofficially renamed Savio Steps of famous Sproul Plaza. Led by freedom singers, hundreds of middle-aged people and their children put their arms around each other, sang civil rights songs, and swayed to the memories of a more hopeful era. And somehow it seemed neither maudlin nor sentimental, but just the right way to say farewell.[44]

Fittingly, the appreciation and the memory of the ties between both struggles—the struggle for civil rights and the struggle for free speech— endure, as do the history and memory of Mario Savio's important role in illuminating those ties and keeping them alive.

NOTES

1. Solid primary accounts of the Summer Project include Len Holt, *The Summer That Didn't End: The Story of the Mississippi Civil Rights Project of 1964* (New York: William Morrow, 1965; reprint, with a preface by Julian Bond, New York: Da Capo Press, 1992); Sally Belfrage, *Freedom Summer* (New York: Viking, 1965). Excellent secondary accounts include Doug McAdam, *Freedom Summer* (New York: Oxford University Press, 1988); Mary Aickin Rothschild, *A Case of Black and White: Northern Volunteers and the Southern Freedom Summers, 1964–1965* (Westport, Conn.: Greenwood Press, 1982); John Dittmer, *Local People: The Struggle for Civil Rights in Mississippi* (Urbana: University of Illinois Press, 1994), 215–302; Charles M. Payne, *I've Got the Light of Freedom: The Organizing Tradition and the Mississippi Freedom Struggle* (Berkeley and Los Angeles: University of California Press, 1995), 300–316; Clayborne Carson, *In Struggle: SNCC and the Black Awakening of the 1960s* (Cambridge: Harvard University Press, 1981), 111–29.

2. Holt, 97–128; Rothschild, 93–126.

3. My narrative of this event has been pieced together from statements Savio and Osman gave to police and FBI officials. See FBI file of Savio, July–August 1964,

file 44-26027 (copy in editors' possession). I thank Robert Cohen for sharing the relevant portions of this file with me.

4. Ibid., Osman's statement to FBI officers, 23 July 1964.

5. Jo Freeman, "From Freedom Now! to Free Speech: The FSM's Roots in the Bay Area Civil Rights Movement," in the present volume; see also McAdam, passim; Rothschild, passim; David DeLeon, *Leaders from the 1960s; A Biographical Sourcebook of American Activism* (Westport, Conn.: Greenwood Press, 1994).

6. Michael Rossman, *The Wedding Within the War* (Garden City, N.Y.: Doubleday, 1965), 84, 82.

7. Ibid., 84; Jack Weinberg, "The Free Speech Movement and Civil Rights," *Campus CORE-lator,* Jan. 1965, reprinted in Hal Draper, *Berkeley: The New Student Revolt* (New York: Grove Press, 1965), 187.

8. Rossman, 85.

9. Howard Zinn, *SNCC: The New Abolitionists* (Boston: Beacon Press, 1965); Paul Goodman, *Of One Blood: Abolitionism and the Origins of Racial Equality* (Berkeley and Los Angeles: University of California Press, 1998).

10. Gretchen Lemke-Santangelo, *Abiding Courage: African American Migrant Women and the East Bay Community* (Chapel Hill: University of North Carolina Press, 1996); W. J. Rorabaugh, *Berkeley at War* (New York: Oxford University Press, 1989).

11. Rorabaugh, 18.

12. Rossman, 86.

13. Ibid., 85–87.

14. Ibid., 87; Freeman 80.

15. Rorabaugh, 15.

16. Ibid., 15–16; Rossman, 85–87.

17. Glenn Eskew, *But for Birmingham: The Local and National Movements in the Civil Rights Struggle* (Chapel Hill: University of North Carolina Press, 1997).

18. Rossman, 87–88; Rorabaugh, 58–60.

19. Freeman, 74–75.

20. Ibid., 75–78; Rossman, 88; Rorabaugh, 72–73.

21. Freeman, 81.

22. Interview, quoted in McAdam, 165.

23. Dorothy Smith quoted in Rothschild, 172; the other remembrances quoted in Virginia Steele, "Remembering Mario" (unpublished essay in the author's possession, Dec. 1996), 5, 7, 6.

24. See McAdam and Rothschild for further details.

25. For Payne's title see note 1.

26. Carson, 302.

27. Savio interview with Bret Eynon, 5 March 1985, Columbia University Oral History Research Project, FSM Archive, Bancroft Collection, University of California at Berkeley (also available at www.lib.berkeley.edu/BANC/FSM).

28. Harry Edwards, *The Struggle That Must Be: An Autobiography* (New York: Macmillan, 1980); Jack Weinberg, in "Remembering Mario Savio," *Tikkun* 12 (Jan.–Feb. 1997): 29.

29. Savio quoted in insert by the *Journal's* editors in "Remembering Mario Savio," *The Journal of Blacks in Higher Education* 15 (Spring 1997): 52 (emphasis added).

30. Mark Shechner quoted in "Remembering Mario Savio," *Tikkun,* 12 (Jan.–Feb. 1997): 28.

31. The student activist is quoted in Rorabaugh, 20; subsequent quotes are from an interview with an anonymous volunteer quoted in McAdam, 166.

32. The influence of unheralded and pioneering activist Ella Baker in bringing these ideas into SNCC is developed in Joanne Grant, *Ella Baker: Freedom Bound* (New York: Wiley, 1998); Payne, 67–68, 92, 271, 277, 331–32; 83–89, 93–94, 369–70, 379–80; and Carson, 19–20, 24–6, 30. For the impact of SNCC on the FSM more generally see McAdam, 161–71.

33. Dittmer, 103–15; Payne, 111–31; Nina Simone, "Mississippi Goddam," on *Nina Simone in Concert* (Philips, 1964).

34. Dittmer, 270–71; 486, note 63.

35. Interview with Savio, 5 March 1985, Columbia University Oral History Research Project.

36. Shechner, 27–28; Freeman, 8–9; McAdam, 171; Robert Moses, "The Algebra Project" (presentation for the NEH Civil Rights Seminar, Harvard University, July 1999).

37. Freeman, 79; McAdam, 162–71; Rorabaugh, 29.

38. Eric R. Burner, *And Gently He Shall Lead Them: Robert Parris Moses and Civil Rights in Mississippi* (New York: New York University Press, 1994), chaps. 7 and 8.

39. McAdam, 162–71; Freeman, 82; Rossman, 91; see also Rorabaugh, 16–17, 25.

40. Chancellor Edward Strong, *DC,* 20–21 Oct. 1964, quoted in Robert Cohen, "The Issue Is the Issue: Mario Savio and Free Speech" (paper delivered at the annual meeting of the Organization of American Historians, April 1997), 9–10.

41. Rossman, 89, 90–91; Freeman, 81.

42. Mario Savio, "An End to History," *Humanity,* Dec. 1964, reprinted in Draper, 179.

43. Mario Savio, quoted in David Lance Goines, *The Free Speech Movement: Coming of Age in the 1960s* (Berkeley: Ten Speed Press, 1993), 361.

44. Ruth Rosen, "A Passion for Justice: A Gentle Warrior's Fight for Free Speech," *Chronicle of Higher Education,* 10 Jan. 1997, B7.

PART TWO

Experience

Fall 1964

War Is Declared!

Jackie Goldberg

Whomp! Whomp! Whomp! The rhythmic sound of the printer's paper cutter provides the background beat for our work. It's a warm, early September morning. We're feverishly racing the clock to get out the SLATE *Supplement* before classes begin. There are only ten to twelve of us, but we will still put out ten thousand copies of this bulletin—a guide to help UC Berkeley students choose professors and TAs for their classes. I am becoming skilled as a book stitcher myself, a job that's elegant in its repetitiveness. The comradely feeling of working on a concrete task together always helps deepen our personal relationships as well as our political ones.

The "ox" cuts through huge numbers of booklets with a single blow on the cutter. Whomp! Whomp! Whomp! The ox's strength is unbelievable. Because of it, he grows even more in everyone's esteem, since many people stereotype political leftists as pale, thin, weak, and hopelessly intellectual. But like the ox, we are all doing *manual labor* and—to the surprise of some of us—we find the satisfaction from it to be immense. Here we are, September 1964; a new school year is about to begin. My senior year. Last spring was an active one for most of us. I was arrested for the first time in a civil rights protest at the Sheraton Palace Hotel in San Francisco. From that I found out a great deal about myself and about the criminal injustice system in America. But that's another story.

Today the challenge is getting the *Supplement* on the street before registration. This year we are adding a new feature—a student manifesto, written by Brad Cleveland. Brad had led his own campaign in SLATE last spring. He thought the *Supplement* should contain a "call to action" to the students of Berkeley. As for me, I think his article is a pipe dream at best and somewhat adventurist at worst. I mean, Goldwater is the GOP presidential nominee, the right wing is making big gains, and Cleaveland thinks his manifesto will turn twenty thousand apathetic Cal students into social activists. Ha! But Brad won the vote at the meeting, and so his article is in the front of the very *Supplement* we are now assembling.

I remember that meeting where Cleaveland handed out copies of his student manifesto. The debate was not going well from his point of view among the forty to fifty people in the room. Most people objected to his adventurism; you know when an idea is too far ahead of the consciousness of the people who are the audience. It would only give our enemies a chance to smear us as conspirators. We had no chance of activating even two thousand students, much less twenty thousand.

But some argued against Brad's article from the right as well as from the left. SLATE had all kinds of people in it—Communists, socialists, liberals, social democrats, Democrats, and a wide assortment of undifferentiated anticapitalists. The liberals thought Brad's article too simplistic and much too radical. The left in SLATE thought it too idealistic—not grounded in reality. Building a consensus in SLATE is always a difficult task because of the wide range of views of people in the group. And Brad's manifesto was pushing us to deal with ideological differences. Now mind you, I have no objection to debating ideology. In fact I think it's essential. But the left wing of SLATE has as many objections to printing the manifesto in the SLATE *Supplement* as SLATE's center and its right wing.

Brad does have his support. And as the meeting wears on, more people shift to side with him, because the liberals are being out-front anti-Communist in their arguments. It is a very difficult meeting. At some point I noticed that Brad was beginning to stall and keep the vote from taking place. It's an old apartment dwellers' tactic in SLATE. You know, drag on the debate until the women in the dorms and other living groups have to go home for curfew. Then, since the apartment dwellers tend to be more radical, when the vote is taken, they are at an advantage. And indeed that is what Brad did. I remember leaving the meeting to get home on time thinking, "I bet this Manifesto ends up in the *Supplement*." Though I actually liked what Brad wrote, I thought putting it in print would make SLATE look silly and out of touch with reality. I knew there would never be an uprising involving tens of thousands of students at UC Berkeley. Students were just too afraid for their careers—that they would be blacklisted. Or they were just too apathetic.

I was right. Here I am, stitching away on SLATE *Supplements*, with Brad's manifesto placed boldly in the front. Well, at least I know that most of the students won't bother reading it anyway (not that it wouldn't be challenging if they did). All they bought it for was to know who the good professors are, and which courses are the most interesting, and which relied more heavily on research papers and which relied more on exams to determine one's grade. I guess we will survive this momentary leap into fantasy.

With a sense of great expectations we collate, stitch, cut, count, and sell these popular little booklets. Sales are already brisk, and money for this year's political projects should be somewhat more plentiful than in previous years. Maybe we will have to screen *Casablanca* only four or five times instead of seven or eight.

I am happy and content that my senior year at Cal is going to be one of better progress in organizing fellow students to be politically involved. After stitching books, and then selling them for many hours, I trek up the long hill to have lunch at Delta Phi Epsilon, my sorority. I take a lot of guff for living here, because most people do not understand how important the women at Delta Phi Epsilon are to me. I've been living here already for two years, and this year I am pledge mother. But I really don't care if they "get it." This place is home for me, and it gives me joy and good times as well.

As always, I pick up my mail on the way to the dining room. I go into lunch with the few other sorority sisters who have returned to school early. As I sit down, I notice that in addition to a welcomed letter from my mother in Los Angeles there is a letter from the dean of student's office. I am not surprised to get mail from Dean Katherine Towle. We have had a friendly relationship ever since I helped her engineer a nondiscrimination clause in the bylaws of all sororities here at Cal. During Panhellenic meetings last year, we cooked up a way to get it done. But that too is another story. She has always been honest with me and I with her.

Lunch is simple, vegetable soup, chili and beans, cheese corn bread, and make-it-yourself deli sandwiches. Everything is hot and homemade. The food sure beats anything the dorms have to offer. While waiting for dessert, I decide to see what Dean Towle has in mind to send me. I open the letter, which is very brief. It says that the rules have been reinterpreted and our normal place for setting up card tables at Bancroft and Telegraph is no longer to be used by student organizations to raise money, recruit members, or pass out literature advocating action. OH MY GOD! THE UNIVERSITY HAS DECLARED WAR!

For me and thousands of others this was just the beginning. After lunch, I called my brother Art. He checked and found that SLATE got a letter, too. We divided the list of political groups, Art taking the left and I taking the right, and we arranged to gather everyone at Art's apartment that very afternoon. This first meeting was an historic event, to be sure. Groups that would shout at each other from card tables at Bancroft and Telegraph were suddenly potential allies. Only the University administration could have accomplished that.

In one room, there were people from the Young Democrats and the College Young Republicans, the DuBois Club, Young Socialist Alliance, SLATE, Campus Women For Peace, Campus CORE, University Society of Individualists, Young Peoples Socialist League, Committee for "NO" on

Proposition 14, University Friends of SNCC, University Youth for Goldwater, Students for Independent Political Action, the Independent Socialist Club, SDS, and the Youth Committee Against Proposition 14. In one room! I don't think anything like this had ever happened before.

It was a stormy meeting, to be sure. Everyone was full of mistrust. And we had people there who would have supported arresting, deporting, jailing, and even expelling others in the room. How to work together, that's the rub! The discussions were hot and heavy. What to do? Some felt we should sue the University. Some wanted to just ignore the letter and do what we've always done—set up our tables at Bancroft and Telegraph. Some wanted to set up tables anywhere on campus, now that it was all illegal! There was very little coming together on tactics.

People were smoking cigarettes. Some had brought food. But after several hours of wrangling, we were no closer to agreement than when we walked in the door. Our ideological differences were largely about tactics, for once, because there was absolute agreement that the ban on political activity at the free speech area at Bancroft and Telegraph would put all of us out of business. It is truly amazing that the University administration accomplished a degree of unity and cooperation among us in one letter that would otherwise have been inconceivable to members of every group present.

My own personal hero in these early meetings was Paul Cahill from one of the Republican groups. He was so thoughtful, articulate, and statesmanlike. I was astonished. For me it meant I could no longer look at all Republicans alike. That of course was a "blow." But Paul was committed to working for his candidate, Barry Goldwater, for president. And he believed that it was his perfect right to do so on the campus of the University of California. He was willing and able to articulate a position that kept many center and right-wing folks in this early coalition.

We wrangled for interminable hours. Finally, we settled on where to begin. We would write a collective response to Dean Towle with our position on the matter. We would send a small delegation to meet with her and see if the matter could be resolved. Personally, she did not support the position she took in the letter. I knew that from talking with her by phone. She also believed that, if she refused to send the letter, her superiors would not find it difficult to have some other administrator send it. I personally believe she feared for her job, when she was less than a year or two from retirement.

We decided to call ourselves the United Front. This was pretty funny, given the history of the phrase and its association during much of the twentieth century with left-wing, socialist, and Communist causes. But, unfortunately for the right, they did not know their history, so they accepted the name without objection.

The final decision was to name a spokesperson. This almost undid the entire coalition. At one time or another, almost every person in the room was nominated. Many declined the nomination. Groups threatened to "walk out" if a certain person were to be named. Around and around we went. When it was narrowed to about five or six names, I was "outed" as a sorority member and pledge mom of Delta Phi Epsilon. Well, that did it. The right wingers were convinced that someone from a Greek sorority who lived in the sorority house could not be all bad. I had not mentioned the fact myself because it always seemed to make the left-wing folks, who did not really know me, very suspicious. Each side was involved in stereotyping. The left thought it meant I could not be completely trusted. The right believed it made me trustworthy. Of course neither was true. Where I lived had to do with not getting into the dorms when I first came to Cal and with my making lifelong friends once I joined D Phi E. But of course, through-out the FSM, I was never able to convince anyone of that.

Be that as it may, everyone very reluctantly agreed that I would be the first spokesperson of the United Front. We wrote the letter to the dean and launched what became the Free Speech Movement or, as it was better known, the FSM.

Eventually Mario Savio purged me after our meetings with President Clark Kerr at the time of the police car sit-in. But that too is another story.

If I were looking for further research to do on the FSM, I would say that too little of what is contained here in this wonderful collection of essays truly examines how the FSM was able to keep together so many different people from groups representing such diverse ideologies. I think the leadership of Paul Cahill and literally fifty to a hundred students must be explored and written about. The hundreds of pages in this volume mention only a very few people, and then not in much depth. But what was amazing was how many people stepped forward to spend endless hours forging compromises and strategies that kept people together instead of dividing us. I think it would also be useful for researchers to explore the actual organization of the FSM. We were able to write, publish, and distribute ten to twenty thousand leaflets within hours. We communicated regularly with the press, with other campuses, with elected officials, and with an enormous Berkeley campus. We fed people at mass rallies and at long meetings. We were able to speak to living groups, apartment dwellers, and commuters at a variety of venues. All this with no real money coming in and while under attack from virtually all corners of mainstream society. It was a most remarkable, sustained organizing drive. And many could learn from the nuts and bolts of the "Centrals" including "Central Central" that kept us all pretty well-informed.

Finally, I hope that the entire role of Mario Savio is explored more thoroughly. I can say that I loved the man, like so many others. But I do not believe his judgment was infallible. And I do believe there were moments when he suffered from the "cult of personality," largely due to the overexposure he had to endure. His was a complicated role of leadership, and it has yet to be critically discussed. This would in no way diminish the role of his ability to articulate what most of us felt nor his incredible capacity to help us understand what was happening and what he believed these events meant in the context of the campus, of philosophy, and of the larger society. I do not believe we could have had the success we had without Mario Savio's leadership. But it is essential to understanding what happened to look at all that he and his closest collaborators said and did, if we truly want to understand how leadership was developed and exercised and what the consequences were of taking a position other than that of Mario and those closest to him.

My Life in the FSM

Memories of a Freshman

Margot Adler

It's a sunlit morning in 1964. My mother and I are traveling across the country on our way to Berkeley, and she is slowly coming to terms with the departure of her only child for college. I'm floating in a swimming pool somewhere in the Midwest, saying various syllables over and over, like "Oregon" and "all." I am trying to lose my New York accent; like so many immigrants, I am trying to remake myself.

Living in New York City, I looked upon Berkeley as so many Americans have looked throughout history upon the West—as an escape from everything that defined my past. For me Berkeley was not only an excellent school, and a place with a rich history of student activism; going to Berkeley meant also fleeing New York, my parents, the memories of four depressing high school years during which I had few real friends. Most of all, I was fleeing from myself and from the large one-hundred-and-eighty-pound body that encased me. California, a place I had never seen, seemed a place of open space, infinite possibilities—radicals, surfers, palm trees, the Beach Boys, and not necessarily in that order. I was determined to enter this mythical realm and to claim it as my own.

Although no one (including myself?) would admit it at the time, I was the kind of applicant that gives college administrators pause. Visibly overweight and wearing dark, oversized tent dresses, with my hair short and shapeless, I was not the type to inspire confidence, despite an energetic, even bubbly nature. And I was sure every interviewer could see through my outer facade, into the dark, angst-filled, daydream-laden creature below who was secretly spending two or three hours a day living out various historical and science fiction fantasies.

Going to Berkeley was my own attempt—which seemed feeble at the time—to find a rich and interesting life of my own. And it worked: for the next eight years, everywhere I went I found myself mysteriously at the center of extraordinary events. True, my Berkeley was not the only one. It was a center of bohemianism, yet Ronald Reagan was the governor of the state when I graduated, in 1968, and his signature is on my diploma. Berkeley had the largest number of Nobel laureates and Peace Corps volunteers of any university but also the largest number of federal contracts for nuclear weapons research. The 1968 yearbook portrays the conventional Berkeley I did not know—sports teams and glee clubs, cheerleaders—but not a single mention of anyone I knew. The student protests are relegated to one or two snapshots. The seven professors who inspired me are neither listed nor photographed. I am not there, either. It almost seems as if the Berkeley I knew was purposely rubbed out by the official chroniclers of the time, its radical legacy denied.

Berkeley was like a fantasy of the agora in ancient Athens (forgetting for the moment that there were slaves in Athens and women were second-class citizens expected to stay indoors). Much of Berkeley's social life took place outside, and except for the three-month rainy season, the sky seemed eternally blue. The older structures on the campus, white buildings with Spanish terra-cotta tile roofs, glistened in the sunlight. As dusk approached and the sky darkened into an intense and vibrant blue, the cedars and fir trees were tinged with a golden light and the entire campus seemed bathed in radiance. Sproul Hall, with its four huge Doric columns, looked out on our agora, Sproul Plaza. At noon it often seemed that the entire population of thirty thousand students would pour into the plaza. No stranger to crowds and large city life, I found Berkeley an appropriate size—like a Greek polis.

As an only child I had lived alone most of my life, and unlike many students whose thirst for independence is symbolized by the quest for their own apartment, I had no desire to live on my own. What I desperately wanted was company. Living in a boardinghouse for young women, mostly freshmen, brought the comfort of neighbors and friends—an entry into an instant and easy community I had never had. I privately exulted at this abundance of companionship.

Even those things that irked radical students the most and were the seeds from which rebellion was already sprouting—the machinelike quality of some of the education, the huge lecture classes with eight hundred students, the small sections led by bored and immature teaching assistants, the inadequate counseling, the invisibility of each person among a student body of almost thirty thousand—those things, at least at the beginning, were liberating. "There is something wonderful about being able to lose oneself in a crowd," I wrote to my mother two weeks after school began. "Knowing that no one knows me, . . . there is a beautiful feeling knowing that I *am like a thousand normal people!*"

The part of campus life that quickly became confusing was the dizzying array of choices. "This school is beginning to overwhelm me," I wrote home only a week later.

> I want to try everything! But already I wonder if I am taking too much? I guess I am in a weird mood because a girl who lives in this house just had something akin to a nervous breakdown. I hear that this is a common enough occurrence in college, . . . so it makes you wonder, . . . [W]hen you are assigned over one weekend 400 pages of reading from Plato, Sophocles, Epic of Gilgamesh, Homer and modern political analysis, it's fair to cry out, "My God, give me a little time to do this, so that I can go folk dancing or go to a movie." There are so many choices each night—a party, a meeting, a movie, or realistically, getting some of this damn reading done.

I realize only now, reading *her* letters from 1964, that my mother tried to help me see the larger aspects of life:

> October 4th, 1964
> Dearest Margot:
> I have complete trust in your good sense, . . . so that fun will always be something truly enjoyable and not an extreme attempt to avoid your responsibilities to your work. However, the choice you will have to make is to be a good average student with time to live life to the hilt, or an A student plodding away at the cost of missing the real purpose of college which is to make life more . . . meaningful. The purpose of all those wonderful philosophers you are reading is to give you a sense of values to live by, a way of saying, Yes to life.
> . . . [Y]our biggest problem is that which plagues imaginative people all their lives—CHOICES. You will have to decide of three equally exciting things which one to go to, even if all three are equally intriguing. . . . [N]o one but yourself is pressuring you to be a top student. I only want for your sake that you just get the necessary grades not to be kicked out, that's all. I don't give a damn if you get one A. . . . [I]f college is pressuring people so they crack, we had better say the hell with college and look into what is wrong. The purpose of the humanities is to be able to live a rich, intellectual and emotional life, to be able to embrace life in all its colors, joys and tragedies, but never to be so overburdened that one's senses become deadened and unable to receive the gifts college offers in the first place.

My mother echoed what many students at Berkeley believed in 1964 but what is very hard for today's students to fathom in this era of downsizing and burdensome student debt. The purpose of school was to enlarge oneself, to discover the path to a rewarding and interesting life, to get a liberal education and ponder the meaning of existence; it was only secondarily to get a career. Although living well did not mean having the kinds of material possessions it does today, America was prosperous. Jobs were available, and we assumed that we could get them when the time came. Tuition was low at Berkeley, even for out-of-state students; it was easy to live cheaply, and students paid back loans only when they were able. Later, tuitions would rise, scholarships would be cut, and regulations governing loans would be tightened, all of which would undercut student activism and force many to choose money over meaning.

But we were a generation determined to mine experience for its riches.

Within my first weeks at Berkeley I was involved in a buzz of activities in addition to my studies. I had gone to a fraternity party, had sat behind a table for Students for a Democratic Society, had gone to a meeting of the W. E. B. DuBois Club, had seen films by Eisenstein and Leni Riefenstahl.

In contrast, my "Introduction to Government" course was decidedly at odds with the budding ferment around me. In the early 1960s most political scientists believed that American democracy worked only because most Americans were apathetic. Most Americans, we were told in readings for the course, did not care and did not participate in political activities; they placed their dreams and hopes in the private sector instead. The authors argued that this apathy toward the political prevented extremes and promoted stability. (Why, if Americans truly cared about politics, these experts assured us, our country would be as politically unstable as Italy!) When I asked the professor to suggest readings that took a different view, I was told that there were none. Confused and angry, I began to look for other authorities.

Outside the classroom, politics was the breath of life. Standing around the tables set up in the plaza, students were talking about politics and philosophy, gesturing, shouting each other down. Clusters of students discussed events and ideas for hours. Here politics was seen as a life-and-death struggle, and argument was ecstasy. Caring intensely was not only good; it would surely change the world for the better.

The Free Speech Movement had just begun when I arrived at Berkeley, although it would be another month before there was an organization with that name. Having already taken part in many political activities in New York, I thought the right to political advocacy seemed obvious, and I was soon handing out leaflets, attending rallies, and sitting behind tables filled with political literature—activities that were forbidden under the new campus regulations.

In the beginning, the FSM focused exclusively on campus free speech, but eventually it went much further: it demanded that students be treated like citizens, subject to regulation only by the courts. I embraced that goal since I had become enraged at California's paternalism within days of my arrival. (When my mother and I tried to enter a San Francisco cabaret to see a show, we were told that, since drinks were available and the drinking age was twenty-one, I was too young to attend, even though a parent was accompanying me. I was livid. In those days the drinking age in New York was eighteen, and I was accustomed to being treated as an adult.)

Later, the FSM also mounted a blistering critique of the University as a "knowledge factory" turning out corporate drones for industry. With a student body of nearly thirty thousand, resources at Berkeley were strained; it was easy for students to feel they were being pressed out like so many pieces of sausage. And this idea of the University as a factory that would train bureaucrats, engineers, and politicians to keep the establishment going seemed the antithesis of any real quest for knowledge. (It still does.) Twenty years later, Michael Rossman would bring an audience of Berkeley students to hysterical laughter by framing the FSM critique this way: "We were being prepped to run the society for the students at Harvard and Yale, who were being prepped to *own* it."

But even if the student argument made intellectual sense to me, I felt anything but alienated. I was out on my own. I floated through my first semester, did well in everything, and even defended the large lecture format in letters home. My ever vigilant mother worried about "classes of five hundred and more where you are fortunate if you get a glimpse of your professor." "Remember," she advised me, "it will be the intimate connections and contacts with stimulating people on the faculty through whom the important part of your academic life will have real meaning. I'd hate for you to be swallowed up in a mass of bigness and impersonalness."

I was quick to reassure her. "It's really a myth about how terrible these large lecture classes are," I wrote home. "If you have a really great professor his classes will be stimulating, no matter how many students are in the class." I felt a new sense of freedom and an almost Edenic sense of bliss, and it was a bit hard to see myself as the soulless IBM card depicted in FSM leaflets.

By September 28 the ban on political activity had become so divisive that all classes stopped that day at 11:00 A.M. for an address to all students by Chancellor Edward Strong and President Clark Kerr. As Strong introduced new student officers and gave his views on the controversy—words that seemed turgid and bland—about four hundred students paraded through the aisles carrying signs: "Vote for X (Censored)" and "Ban the Ban." To many of us in the audience, the protesters, unlike the speakers, seemed to radiate life.

On October 1 I wandered over to Sproul Plaza for the noon rally and arrived just after Jack Weinberg's arrest. It was extraordinary to see this police car immobile, surrounded by a growing crowd. As a freshman, I felt too timid to make a speech, although I thought of several as I listened; I felt excited by the sense of community among the protesters. It seemed ridiculous that Weinberg had been arrested for sitting behind a table covered with civil rights literature, something I had been doing myself just days before. It seemed easy and appropriate to sit down on the ground with the other students. The police car, usually such a powerful symbol of authority, seemed tiny and helpless in the face of our growing numbers. As we sat around the car, blocking its movement, preventing this arrest from occurring, I felt a sense of exhilaration. But there were moments of fear and terror as we wondered what action the authorities would take. Most of the protesters had never participated in any political demonstration before. Many cried or laughed, or were uncertain what to do. We had turned the world upside down, stopped the machinery of the state. There was a feeling of instant community and internal power. We had no name for the power that we felt. Years later, spiritual feminists would call it "evoking power-from-within."

Bettina Aptheker, in a book on the student rebellion, writes that while the demonstration was motivated by principle, something more than a principle was needed to "evoke such a display of courage": "There was a shared, if not yet articulated sentiment that the authority of the university itself had to be challenged; that many things about it were wrong: . . . that somehow, somebody, everybody had to straighten it out before we all died for no plausible reason—just as we all seemed to be living for no plausible purpose. There is no other way to explain the presence of that quaking, still joyful, mass of people, clinging to each other."[1]

The moment was what the author (and witch) Starhawk would call magic: "the art of liberation, the act that releases the mysteries, that ruptures the fabric of our beliefs and lets us look into the heart of deep space where dwell the immeasurable, life-generating powers."[2] It was unplanned and spontaneous, and the thousands of students who sat around this symbol of external authority, of the state, could not help but be affected and began to think that their cause was more than a simple fight for free speech, that it encompassed a battle to change the nature of power and authority.

In the end, with almost a thousand police amassed on the campus and protesters negotiating with the administration, an agreement was worked out. Students would end the demonstration: Weinberg would be booked and released, and the University would not press charges. The cases of the suspended students would go before the student conduct committee of the Academic Senate, and a committee of students, faculty, and administration, including leaders of the demonstration, would meet to discuss all aspects of political behavior on the campus and make recommendations to the administration.

Perhaps it was an oversight, perhaps it was a trick, but there *was* no student conduct committee of the Academic Senate; instead, the cases were brought before a committee appointed by the chancellor, which was unacceptable to the protesters and fueled our paranoia. Negotiations and rallies resumed. It was at this point that the FSM adopted its name and really began to organize, creating a Steering Committee, an Executive Committee with representatives from all interested campus political groups, and various centers for press, communication, work, and legal affairs. The FSM published a newsletter, and it put out two different recordings (including a very funny Christmas spoof, "Free Speech Carols") as well as more serious papers attacking the University's paternalistic ideology, arguing that students were citizens and that political expression on campus could only be governed by the Constitution and the courts.

Negotiations with the administration had been lengthy and nonproductive, and students were debating whether to engage in new confrontations. The FSM Steering Committee, led by civil rights organizers, took the more radical position, but although the Steering Committee made many of the day-to-day decisions, most issues had to be brought before the larger Executive Committee. A group of moderates led by a leader of the Young Democrats tried to pack an Executive Committee meeting with a half-dozen inactive organizations so that the moderate position—a vote against renewed civil disobedience—would win out. "I am now on the Executive Committee of the Free Speech Movement," I wrote home. I was representing a college civil liberties organization that didn't seem to do much of anything and that I had never heard of. I had been asked to represent this group by a leader of the Young Democrats. When I had been invited to represent this group it had felt wonderful, but I soon realized that I was being used. When I realized that I was siding with the radicals over the issue of renewed protests but had been placed on the Executive Committee in order to support the moderate position, I left before the vote.

On Monday, November 9, the FSM and eight other off-campus organizations set up tables in front of the main steps of Sproul Hall. Seventy-five people, including me, had their names taken by various administration officials. On November 10 we all received letters and were asked to appear at the dean's office.

"Don't worry, Mom," I wrote in mid-November,

it looks as though everything will be fine. I still don't know what will exactly happen to us, but it looks as if it will be nothing more than a reprimand or social probation, which is no more than a warning. I met with one of the deans and she was a lovely woman. She asked me no questions about my FSM involvement and only wanted to know if there were any individual circumstances that made my case different from the rest—in other words was I unwillingly involved. I said, "no." She asked me how I was doing in school, how I liked "Cal" and even said that if I was aware of the responsibilities I was taking, then "more power to you." Some of the other deans had intimidated students. Anyway, the past week has been terribly exciting. We have constantly set up tables and the administration has done nothing. How many can they cite, after all? There have been rumors about police, but so far nothing.

Eventually the seventy-five cited students were sent letters of formal reprimand. We were warned that future violations would subject us to more serious discipline.

On November 20 there was a large march of several thousand students. Everyone wore dresses or suits and ties. Looking at a picture of that demonstration, like looking at early pictures of the Beatles, reminds me how positively "straight" we looked. The styles that would give the decade its look were still a few years away. We would not have recognized ourselves four years later.

Soon after this, the Regents passed resolutions that students be required to obey state and community laws and that political activities would be permitted in certain campus facilities, as long as they were legal. Four days later the administration announced new rules allowing organizations to get permits and set up tables. Students could solicit donations and advocate political action. Many believed the University had given as much as it could and that the FSM was dead, having won a partial victory. But the movement, led by its civil rights activists, now understood that its primary demand was that only the courts of law could judge the content of speech and impose punishment. Achieving that goal seemed as elusive as ever.

The FSM was at war with a notion that was central to the thinking of many of Berkeley's faculty and even some of its students: that the University was a place outside of space and time, with different rules from those of the society at large. Many University administrators couldn't honestly understand why students would want to give up the loving hand of paternalistic parents for the colder, harder justice of the outside world.[3]

By November the university had agreed to all of the FSM's demands except one: control of the decisions that affected our lives. There was a new notion of politics in the air. Politics wasn't about voting or political parties but, in the words of *The Port Huron Statement*, was all "those social decisions determining the quality and direction of . . . life."[4] Subtle and difficult, this was not an idea that thousands would go to jail for. The movement would have died, if, at the end of November, the administration hadn't made a huge mistake.

On November 27–28, out of the blue, four students—Mario Savio, Art Goldberg, Brian Turner, and Jackie Goldberg—received letters from the administration. They were ordered to attend hearings before an administrative committee for illegal activities back in October, when thousands had surrounded the police car. When these letters became public, almost every student involved in the FSM felt personally betrayed. And when the movement demanded these charges be dropped, arguing that only the courts could regulate the content of speech and insisting that this demand be met by noon on December 2, the stage was set for the extraordinary events that followed.

At a huge demonstration in front of Sproul Hall, thousands of students heard Mario Savio give his famous "operation of the machine" speech. I found his words so powerful that thirty years later I still have most of them committed to memory:

> We have an autocracy which runs this university. It's managed. We asked the following: if President Kerr actually tried to get something more liberal out of the Regents in his telephone conversation, why didn't he make some public statement to that effect? And the answer we received—from a well-meaning liberal—was the following: he said, "Would you ever imagine the manager of a firm making a statement publicly in opposition to his board of directors?" That's the answer! I ask you to consider: if this is a firm, and if the Board of Regents are the board of directors, and if President Kerr in fact is the manager, then I'll tell you something: the faculty are a bunch of employees, and we're the raw material! But we're a bunch of raw materials that don't mean to have any process upon us, don't mean to be made into any product, don't mean to end up being bought by some clients of the University: be they the government, be they industry, be they organized labor, be they anyone! We're human beings! There is a time when the operation of the machine becomes so odious, makes you so sick at heart, that you can't take part; you can't even tacitly take part, and you've got to put your bodies upon the gears and upon the wheels, upon the levers, upon all the apparatus and you've got to make it stop. And you've got to indicate to the people who run it, to the people who own it, that unless you're free, the machine will be prevented from working at all![5]

How strange to think of these words today, when the idea of the university as handmaiden to industry and government is once again unquestioned. But as I stood in the plaza, hearing those words, they came to symbolize for me the life of freedom and joy and mystery I was seeking and I found myself moved to tears.

December 2nd, 1964, 9:00 P.M.
Dear Mom:
This is a really incredible situation. I am sitting on the floor of Sproul Hall. . . .
On each window is a big letter: FSM, so it looks like the building is really ours. Four students were threatened with further disciplinary action and received letters threatening expulsion. We are sitting-in in protest of that, and what started as a demand for free speech and advocacy has changed to include the whole meaning of education. There is anger at being only an IBM card, anger at the bureaucracy, at the money going to technology. The main issue remains that students should have to abide only by the laws of the government and the US Constitution in matters of civil liberties—they should not need to abide by special regulations.

This afternoon, there was an inspired rally where all the FSM leaders spoke, and Joan Baez sang. Everyone called for a tremendous sit-in, and then Joan Baez and Mario Savio led about 2,000 people into Sproul Hall. Charles Powell, the president of the student government, made a feeble statement which was hissed down, telling people to have faith in the administration.

We went into Sproul Hall, and all the employees left. At 7 P.M., the police asked us to leave, but we refused. We were given instructions in non-violent civil disobedience, how to go limp when arrested. Then a truly extraordinary evening began.

We sang songs. There were rooms available for studying. There was a Chanukah service and folk dancing. In another room, they showed the Charlie Chaplin film *The Rink*. Professors and teaching assistants created "Freedom Schools," gave classes in non-violence, political science, mathematics, Spanish, and the history of the civil rights movement in the Bay Area. There's been more singing and speeches. Joan Baez is still here. Food and drink are being passed around. We may be here a long time. If we are still here by tomorrow morning, there may be a strike by students and teaching assistants.

The press is here in droves: newspapers, *Life*, NBC, ABC, KPIX. A reporter saw me reading Thucydides and wrote it down. I swear it is the most stimulating experience I've ever had. It's a pretty mixed group. There are even three Gold-water Republicans here who write for the conservative journal *Man and State*, although the tendency is definitely toward the left.

December 3rd, 6:45 A.M.
Things look quite different at 6:45 A.M. For one thing, I am tired. At 11 P.M., Mario Savio spoke and said it looked as if Clark Kerr was going to stall us out— that is, not bring the police—and that we would have to stay a long time. So at 11:30, after more singing, a bunch of us went to sleep until 2 A.M., when I awoke to hear a complete change in the situation. We were sleeping near the telephone the FSM was using, so we heard all the important news. It seems the Alameda County Sheriff and police will come soon and arrest us. So we were given more instructions in non-violence, and all of us on the first floor went to the second and third and fourth. Then Chancellor Strong came, along with the Chief of Police, and gave us five minutes to leave the building, before being arrested. By 5:00 A.M., they had only arrested thirty people, but by now they have arrested about seventy-five, including all of those on the fourth floor. There are about 1,000 of us altogether. Some people even managed to be hoisted up into the building on ropes, so we have thirty-five new people.

Here's what we have heard: Students for a Democratic Society—remember that's the organization I belonged to—has promised sympathy demonstrations on 100 campuses. Governor Brown plans to come to Berkeley today. Many reporters are still here. Many employees are not going to work, there is a picket line in front of the Student Union and many people will not cross. The Teamsters Union has refused to cross the picket line and therefore the University is without food in the cafeterias. A strike has been moved up to today at noon. Many faculty are with us, including the entire math department, which is the most radical department. They have started arresting people on the third floor.

. . . Dawn has come. Nothing like this has happened, I guess, since the thirties. The people here are really marvelous and hopefully comprise the future. A great number of students seem vitally concerned with education, a true and meaningful education. And of course, this is an educational experience in itself.

12:10 P.M.
I feel sick—inside and out. I feel depressed and ashamed of my society, afraid, sick and weird—a feeling of half not feeling anything and half wanting to cry on someone's shoulder. I am sitting with fifty other girls in an Oakland police station. . . . Now, you must understand that there were two police forces involved. . . . The Berkeley police were quite civil, even kind at times, and, as policemen go, understanding. The Oakland cops were brutal. They ran up and grabbed Jack Weinberg who was speaking over a microphone and dragged him down the stairs. For each arrest, an officer came up, asked us to leave, gave us a number, photographed us and asked if we would walk. We went limp and they (the Berkeley police) dragged us rather nicely to the elevator. The boys got dragged down the stairs. When we got to the basement, we refused to walk, and the Oakland police dragged us horribly. This guy twists my arm back in a hammer lock, and forces me up, so I have to give in and walk. Then came the most Kafkaesque part—you get fingerprinted, photographed against a wall, and searched, they even undid my bra. Then we waited, singing freedom songs, until we were marched with our photos, a group of twelve, into a paddy wagon where, still singing, we were taken to a police station in Oakland where we are sitting, talking, singing, and studying.

But the worst thing we saw was the brutality before our arrest. One boy was clubbed; several were treated brutally. One girl was dragged and thrown crying into the police wagon. The worst moments were when the police went after the PA system. The first time they got Jack Weinberg; the second time, they tried to get Steve Weissman, but he slipped outside and escaped down a rope. At that moment the place went into bedlam, and two or three students threw boxes and books; fortunately they didn't hit anyone and they were told to stop.

I feel weird and scared. Even though I believe in what I did, I still have that weird feeling of being stamped for life, always having a police record next to my name. Of course I am in good company, but still. . . . I will write again when I know more about the future—bail, charges, etc.

2:00 P.M.
I'm still in this room, only 23 of us are left. We have heard that at least 600 were arrested, and there are rumors that the Santa Rita jail can't hold us and we will be put in navy barracks.

9:45 P.M., San Leandro Armory
Finally at about 4:00 P.M. we were put into this bus with barred windows. We were in that 20 by 20 room—a shifting population of 20–55. But our group stayed longest. The facilities were deplorable. There was no toilet paper. We finally got some. There was one toilet, which was open and in full view. We sat on the floor. By 4 P.M., people who hadn't eaten since last night were starved. Then, for the first time, even though I had only been arrested for several hours, I realized what

lack of physical freedom means: the fact that I could not go out that door—that I was completely at their power and mercy, that my world had become 20′ by 20′, and it was packed with others—no room to move. I tried reading Thucydides, but I just couldn't concentrate. I was nervous and had no outlet, not even the usual escape—food. Many of the people around me were smoking, but I had no way to calm myself. And worst of all, I had my period, and it had leaked and there was no way to change, and nothing to do.

So finally we were taken in this barred bus to the armory—it seems the jails were overcrowded—so they created a jail here. We were finally given some tepid tea and a cold cut sandwich at 5 P.M. More people have arrived, but our knowledge of what is going on at the University is limited. Until half an hour ago we had no contact. Now, after we have been booked for the second time, we can use the phone. My fingerprints will go to the FBI. I guess when the thought gets depressing one can always remember that conversation between Thoreau and Emerson when Thoreau was in jail: Emerson: "What are you doing in there?" Thoreau: "What are you doing out there?" So now we are trying to go to sleep on the floor of the Armory with some thin blankets. It's 10:15 P.M., and I only had one and a half hours sleep on the floor last night. I will try to sleep until we go to Santa Rita and get our mug shots.

December 4th, 12:45 A.M., Santa Rita

Nine of us were awakened. We got packed into a car to drive to the Santa Rita jail. I felt sicker than ever, woke up cold, shivering with spasms of cold tiredness. I had only slept an hour and the blanket was thin and the air freezing. We walked out into the cold air and a shivering fit really hit me. I just couldn't stop shaking. We were packed into a police barred car, very tight, which was good because it warmed us and we joked about such things as, "misery is a stone cold floor" and talked about "The Brig" and "Mario, Mario my Savio," until laughter threw off the cold and we were heated by each other's bodies and by the car itself. We arrived at Santa Rita and filed in to be mugged. Funny, I always associated the word "mugging" with the antithesis of police—something that happens in Central Park, for example, but they seem to use it for those pictures, you know, those front and side shots with the numbers below, that make you look like a criminal no matter what. I figured out why. They don't let you smile, and by then we were all so miserable looking anyway. So then we were put in some kind of cell, then taken to another regular room, although it was locked, and now there are rumors that we will get out soon, or that we won't get out soon and will have cold showers. But now it seems we may get out.

December 5th

Eventually we were released and taken in a bus to the gates of Santa Rita; there, a faculty-student carpool was waiting to pick us up. These supporters had raised our bail, and were now driving us home. I finally got home at 2:30 A.M. and managed to get five hours of sleep. I couldn't sleep well, nor do I seem able to study effectively. I keep thinking about the past few days. Last night I was terribly depressed. Everything I had been thinking about the two levels of existence—how at the higher level we are ants in a meaningless universe—seemed true. At the moment, I feel so insignificant. It seems as if the truth will never conquer and that it was of no consequence that there were 800 of us and that the majority of the faculty supported us. The press still shouts, "communist," and there are calls for the FSM to be investigated by a committee like HUAC.

Sometimes I think that I could become an anarchist, if law means the action of the police. Jail affected me. The loss of physical freedom was a shock. The frisking was humiliating; the fingerprinting feels weird. It all has the feel of forever. You feel trapped and powerless. The police have the power to do anything they want to you for 48 hours—after that they must book you. You have practically no rights, and after a while, the police seem to be an evil power, because by this time you no longer associate them with law and order, but with hitting nonviolent students, wrenching, throwing, dragging people down stairs, and you realize that they have the backing of the society and you have nothing but your convictions.

The feelings I experienced inside Sproul Hall and, later, in jail were a complex mix: an ecstasy of community bonding and collective power followed by a sense of total powerlessness. There were moments where all potential and possibility opened, and moments of utter futility when a thousand students seemed nothing more than a thousand grains of sand. A few years later, when I would enter the imposing court buildings in lower Manhattan for political trials—first as a journalist, later as a juror, but never again as a defendant—I was still close enough to the events of the sixties that I retained a clear understanding of the true meaning of the massive structures I was entering: the towering columns of the federal court building; the barred windows rising so high at 100 Center Street, the seat of the criminal courts. And I understood that the rooms within, with their thirty-foot ceilings and the judge sitting many feet above ordinary citizens, had been carefully designed to show the insignificance of the individual human being in the face of government power.

But as a participant in this demonstration and arrest, what I could not see was the view of this event from the outside, a view which did much to increase faculty support for our cause. While we rejected the notion of the university as an ivory tower, our teachers still embraced it. The professors who walked onto campus that morning found their lovely sanctuary ringed with police. It was this shock that caused many a professor to make a final break with the administration and support the FSM's demands. David Goines writes that this was "the first time in American history that the German academic tradition, barring civil authority from the University campus, had been disregarded," and that the faculty felt the administration had treated them with contempt and so, in the end, had allied themselves not so much with the students as against the administration and the government of California.[6]

Back on campus the atmosphere was electric. Most classes were canceled, and there was a very effective student strike. Graduate students picketed many buildings and the almost eight hundred who had been arrested returned to the campus wearing black armbands with a *V* emblazoned on them. You could see their armbands all over the campus. The time felt incredibly special, as if my own action was part of something that had caused a shift in the world.

Two faculty groups, a group of two hundred that supported FSM goals and a council of department chairmen that didn't, met to plan strategy, and President Clark Kerr announced that a University-wide meeting would take place on December 7 at the large Greek Theatre. The FSM met as well and determined to have its own speaker at the gathering.

At the Greek Theatre President Kerr spoke before a huge crowd. His words about order and "lawful procedures" and the continuation of classes seemed curiously detached from the electric reality—reverberating in the amphitheater like dead language from an ancient world. But Kerr did announce an amnesty in the cases against the four students and said that the University would not initiate disciplinary action against those who participated in the sit-in, and would accept the action of the courts. Rules for campus political activity would be liberalized. When Kerr finished his announcement, Mario walked slowly up to the front to speak. To my stunned amazement—and the amazement of thousands of others—two campus policemen grabbed Mario before he could reach the microphone and dragged him off the stage. The effect was sensational. Shocked, we all rose to our feet and roared our disapproval.

Goines believes that this one "lightning-lit instant in the history of the FSM" did more to gain support for the movement than anything else. "We all heard stories of older professors who had escaped Nazi terror," Goines writes, "and who, stunned by what the police had done before their very eyes, expressed shame and rage that they had condoned an administration which resorted to Storm Trooper tactics to prevent one student from speaking to a crowd."[7] Moments later, when the administration realized its mistake and released Savio, the damage was done. Ten thousand people attended the rally in Sproul Plaza later that day.

Meanwhile, a group of liberal faculty members—the Committee of 200—drew up its own proposals, which supported the FSM's demands. The next day, December 8, the Academic Senate met to consider these proposals. Between three and five thousand students listened for three hours as the meeting was broadcast outside over loudspeakers. When the Committee of 200's resolution passed by a vote of 824–115, the students outside roared their approval, and many of us stood holding each other as tears flowed. A week later the Regents voted that political activity would only be regulated by the First and Fourteenth Amendments. Students would be judged as citizens. The FSM had won.

We were jubilant. As I wandered through the fogbound and rainy campus, I found my soul open and ready to receive on all levels. As I inhaled the pungent smell of eucalyptus trees and walked the charming wooden bridges over Strawberry Creek, I kept pinching myself that this place was real. The world seemed deeply good.

Later, the coldness of the law and the brutality of the Oakland police sank in. And as I read the biased reports of our struggle in the newspapers (in which we were portrayed as Communist dupes or outside agitators—accounts which bore no relation to the events we had witnessed), I felt, as if for the first time, that the society around me was a place of distortion, lies, and evil. The FSM gave me a profound understanding of the unseen institutions of this country—the courts, the jails, and the police—institutions which had never before touched my life and which remain hidden for most white middle-class people.

But more importantly, the FSM gave me an experience of a new kind of freedom, not to speak, to act, or to buy, but to claim the power to come together with others in community to transform and to change. And the FSM was emotionally powerful also because it seemed to be a battle to wrest the control of our lives away from the clerks, files, and forms that seemed increasingly to dominate our lives as students—in other words, from the seemingly invulnerable giants of technology and bureaucracy. In my own life, I had gone from a small private school filled with liberty and creativity to a high school where creativity was mixed with bureaucracy and rigidity, to a huge university where the most popular slogan referred to students as IBM computer cards ("Do not fold, spindle, or mutilate!"). The FSM gave me and many others a sense of personal power and control over our lives.

This is true for me even though I was just a grunt, a foot soldier, in this battle. I was a lowly freshman and few people knew my name. I made no speeches from the steps of Sproul Plaza, and I was never quoted in the newspapers. I sat at tables, picketed, went to meetings, listened to speeches, handed out leaflets, marched, sat-in, and went to jail.

I resisted some of the activities of day-by-day political organizing—the staffing of offices, the cooking of food. In part, this was because I knew that I was a person of ideas, not of day-to-day action. I was fascinated by theory and philosophy, but I found many political meetings deadly dull. And I also intuitively knew, without benefit of feminist analysis, that it was the female students (then called "coeds") who were generally making the coffee and running the mimeograph machines. The FSM retained, as did all left movements of the day, its sexist baggage, and few were the women who made names for themselves on their own. Most of the movement's women leaders were some man's sister or lover.

Bettina Aptheker was the one woman who stood entirely on her own, and many years later she would say that she was accepted into the inner circles partly because her father was a famous Communist. I was certainly in awe of Mario Savio's and Jack Weinberg's oratory, but if there was anyone whom I sought as my mentor, a leader whose style I wished to emulate, it was Bettina. Although she was described in the press as an avowed Communist—and was, in fact, the only actual Communist Party member in the FSM leadership—Bettina actually functioned then, as she did throughout the sixties, as a peacemaker between all factions. She was down-to-earth, optimistic, direct, and unpretentious. She could cut through any argument and find the common ground. She radiated goodness, was egalitarian in style despite her party affiliation, and seemed to be without even a drop of adolescent angst. She remained for me a model of righteous politics wedded to good spirits and psychological wholeness. And she became an illustration of an important and recurring lesson in life: outward political affiliation or ideology is never the measure of a human being, and it should never be the basis on which you choose your friends.

Reading Goines's book *The Free Speech Movement: Coming of Age in the 1960s* has made me understand how different my own experience was from his and how different was the experience of women from that of men in the movement. For Goines, political activity was part of his total rebellion against his parents. He hated school and gloried in a kind of young man's liberation; he writes that he quickly saw that radical politics brought him sex and the adoration of young women.

I was a virgin when I arrived on campus in the summer of 1964, and I was still a virgin when the FSM achieved its victory in December. For me, unlike Goines, radical politics had little to do with sex; instead, it was about ideas and, secondarily, about friendships. I weighed 180 pounds, a fact that I now understand was in part a deep feminist protest. My weight was a suit of armor I wore to maintain control of my life, so as to be taken seriously for my ideas and never be seen as a sexual object. And I wasn't. Looking back, I realize that I also protected myself by not putting myself in situations that would be dangerously intimate, like the day-to-day running of a political organization. It was much safer to act from the outside, where I was always in control.

In December 1984, twenty years after our victory, Bettina Aptheker addressed several thousand people at an FSM reunion. It was the first time I had seen her in many, many years. She started by saying that she was often known as the daughter of Herbert Aptheker, the Communist historian and theoretician, but she was also the daughter of Fay Aptheker, and that she would now like to introduce herself by naming herself back through her female line. She noted that most of the histories of the sixties have been written by men and so our history of that era is partial, since the ideas and articulations and reflections of women have been excluded. Because of this, she argued, the histories have emphasized power and control, whereas the women's stories might have emphasized the dailyness of struggle, connection, and the long slow process of meaningful change. She noted that women staffed the offices, while men held the press conferences and did the publicity. This reflected the sexual division of labor in the larger society, "but if we are a radical movement about the business of making change, we need to change how we go about our business of making change."

And then she entered deeper waters: "It was also the case that there were women who, one way or another, found themselves in situations of performing sexual favors for important movement men. That happened. It is also a fact that women activists were more seriously abused, physically and sexually, both by the police, which is to be expected, and also by men within the movement, which is something that is no longer tolerable."

Then Bettina spoke even more personally and her words began to illuminate my own reflections as a woman who went through this experience. She said that as an only child, very cherished by her parents, she was not "gendered female." And when she came to Berkeley, as Aptheker's daughter, "I was ushered into the inner circles of the revolutionary movement in Berkeley despite my sex." She said she was treated as "one of the boys," neutered sexually. The very few times she was looked upon as female she was seen as "an object of sexual prey."

"I also internalized certain aspects of the oppression of women," she continued. "I believed there were men, there were women, and there was me. I didn't want to be like other women, because I saw the women as being subordinated and unable to speak and unable to present their views, so I participated in the oppression of women in the FSM"—and here her voice dropped to a deep whisper—"for which I apologize." Many women in the audience sat with tears streaming down their faces. Bettina ended her speech by saying that, despite the humiliating roles women were forced to play in the movement, "we did march in the morning, and in apprehending the sound of those streets flooded with people we heard the echo of our own liberation. . . . What we learned in the sixties, the great secret as it were, is that people have the inherited wisdom and the collective strength to change the conditions of their lives."[8]

Like Bettina, I was an only child who had not been programmed as readily as others into a female role. For me, as for her, politics was a place I came to through inheritance and tradition, not through anger and rebellion.

At least a hundred former activists attended the twentieth anniversary of the FSM. As we looked around the room at those who had come to this reunion, we realized what we were not: we were not burned-out, drugged-out sixties radicals, the lost generation described so often in studies of this period. We had emerged from the storms of the era for the most part deepened and reasonably unscathed. Most of us had experienced a kind of radiance and now led full and interesting lives, doing more good than harm. Among us there were few regrets.

Many people have attempted to describe the energy that people felt, the intense sense of possibility, the feeling, almost universally shared, that we could change not only our own lives—in itself an amazing idea, for even that seems a fantasy to so many young people today—but the conditions of the world. And because we experienced a victory, most of us have never lost that feeling, despite the inevitable setbacks, tragedies, and changes that may have taken place in our individual lives. Most of us remain incurable optimists and most of us have been able to continue working, in some form, toward efforts of personal and political transformation.

Jack Weinberg, the activist who'd once coined the phrase "Never trust anyone over thirty," explained it this way: We had not only experienced a great battle, we had experienced what it was like to *win* a great battle, and it was the experience of victory that had changed our lives. Unlike the generation that followed, who only experienced the maddening and frustrating battle to end the Vietnam War, our fight, like the civil rights activism that went before and after it, left a trail of positive change.

At the University, we had demanded our rights as citizens, argued for self-directed education, and helped to usher in a whole decade of experimentation. We'd done something to transform the world around us, and we were forever marked by the belief that change was possible. It would affect us for life, making us deep optimists about human possibility and influencing every choice from then on. As W. J. Rorabaugh writes in *Berkeley at War,* "The Free Speech Movement unleashed a restless probing of life."[9]

Six months later I went to Mississippi as a civil rights worker.

NOTES

1. Bettina Aptheker, *The Academic Rebellion in the United States* (Secaucus, N.J.: Citadel Press, 1972), 157–58.

2. Starhawk, *Truth or Dare* (San Francisco: Harper and Row, 1987), 6.

3. David Lance Goines, *The Free Speech Movement: Coming of Age in the 1960s* (Berkeley: Ten Speed Press, 1993), 188.

4. Students for a Democratic Society, *The Port Huron Statement* (2nd printing, Dec. 1964), 7.

5. Savio quoted in Goines, 361.

6. Ibid., 410.

7. Ibid., 429.

8. Aptheker's speech is from her essay in Robert Cohen, ed., "The Free Speech Movement and Beyond: Berkeley Student Protest and Social Change in the 1960s (unpublished manuscript, Berkeley, 1994, available in Bancroft Library), 65.

9. W. J. Rorabaugh, *Berkeley at War* (New York: Oxford University Press, 1989), 47.

Gender Politics and the FSM

A Meditation on Women and Freedom of Speech

Bettina Aptheker

My first speech was from the top of the police car that had been dispatched to Sproul Plaza to take Jack Weinberg to jail. It was Thursday, October 1, 1964. I had just turned twenty. It was the beginning of what was to become the Free Speech Movement, named by Weinberg at marathon meetings that weekend. Jack had been arrested at noon that Thursday for distributing civil rights literature and soliciting donations, activity that had recently been banned from the campus. Hundreds of us, many trained in the nonviolent exigencies of the Civil Rights Movement, spontaneously sat down around the car. We prevented its departure for thirty-two hours, assuring ourselves of Jack's release after protracted negotiations with the campus administration and the University president, Clark Kerr. Mario Savio emerged as our spokesperson.

About 9:00 P.M. that Thursday I joined a stream of speakers who had preceded me. Removing my shoes (we did this so as not to damage the car), I scrambled up the front hood, slithered over the windshield, and finally stood in stocking feet on the roof. Television lights blinded me, so I could not see the crowd, but I could feel the expectant energy of the two thousand students and onlookers now surrounding the car. The only thing I remember saying was a quote from Frederick Douglass: "Power concedes nothing without a demand." The crowd roared its approval. Two fellow students, Mario and Art Goldberg, helped me down from the car, clapping me on the back and saying things like "That was great," their own voices hoarse with exhaustion.

Throughout the months of struggle that followed, Mario always maintained that freedom of speech meant, above all else, the protection of speech with consequences. For example, when the administration first conceded our rights of advocacy, it nevertheless reserved its right to discipline students who advocated that others participate in potentially unlawful political action off campus. In principle this was unacceptable because the advocacy in such cases was still protected by the First Amendment. In practice it was unacceptable because at the height of the Civil Rights Movement it was precisely the advocacy of nonviolent civil disobedience that assured the promise of success.

When I participated in the FSM in 1964 I had no knowledge of women's history, no consciousness of gendered oppression, and no words with which to articulate my own experience of sexual abuse. The field later known as women's studies did not yet exist, and phrases such as "feminist scholarship" had not yet been invented. There were many women prominently associated with the FSM, including, for example, Jackie Goldberg, who has since become a major political figure in Los Angeles and, more recently, in Sacramento. Nevertheless, it was men who dominated our meetings and discussions. Women did most of the clerical work and fundraising and provided food. None of this was particularly recognized as work, and I never questioned this division of labor or even saw it as an issue!

FSM meetings went on for hours. At the end of them, in the wee hours of the morning, Mario and I usually wrote the leaflet to be distributed on campus later that morning. Our words would reflect the consensus reached in our meetings so that students would understand the FSM position. I also spoke at virtually every FSM rally. It never occurred to me that I was often the only woman speaking at these rallies. I had no idea of the extent to which my participation was significant to other women simply because I was female. Years later I learned that there were women who left abusive marriages because they saw me on television, women who decided to speak up in their classes or to say what they really thought to a male companion or lover, because they heard me speak at a rally on Sproul Hall steps. Some women decided to leave their jobs in search of more meaningful work; others returned to school; others joined a union or the peace movement, deciding that they too could act. I learned these stories over the years. But I don't think that any of these changes were related to my personal powers of persuasion. They were a consequence of the perceived absence of women in public life and of the force of the FSM itself as it succeeded in overturning Regental (white/male) authority.

I had no consciousness of myself as a woman because I had been gendered male. That is, I had grown up modeling myself after my father and doing "boy" things. With feminist understandings, I have come to realize that gender (as distinct from a biological sexual designation) is a social construct. We "do gender" every day, reproducing and elaborating "female" and "male" cultural norms. Gender is performative. For example, we "do gender" in the way we style our hair, in the makeup we wear, and in the way we dress. We perform gender in the use of body language. It is enacted in our conversations, in our choice of words, even in our willingness (or *un*willingness) to speak.[1] But at the time, none of us in the FSM had any understanding of these gendered dynamics.

When I say that I was "gendered male" I mean that, having modeled myself after my father, his colleagues, and the male heroes I read about or imagined, like resistance fighters in Europe during World War II, I rejected the expectations of female behavior. I did not consider my mother an appropriate role model, much to her despair. She wanted to dress me in the latest fashions, and I fiercely resisted. She wanted me to take ballet and modern dance, and I wanted to play baseball. My best friends until I was thirteen were the boys on the block with whom I played ball. I wrote school reports with confidence, published my first story when I was fourteen, and spoke with authority in classes and public venues, because it never occurred to me that I couldn't or shouldn't. I arrived in Berkeley two years before the FSM. I was ushered immediately into the revolutionary circles as "Aptheker's daughter."[2] These circles had very, very few women, and if there were women, they were older than I was and in graduate school. I acted as "one of the boys." Sometimes I was treated that way, but at other times I was perceived as an object of sexual prey, which I found confusing and very distressing.

Sex for me was a great enigma. I had no boundaries, no sense of a defined or inviolate self, no (or very limited) personal communication skills, and absolutely no idea about how to relate to men as anything other than "pals." I also knew that I was most attracted to women, but I didn't know what to do about it. The results, of course, were disastrous. My personal demons were close to home; they were the result of impermissible childhood and adolescent sexual abuse. I had no sense even of how traumatized I was, although I enacted a suicide fantasy at the age of twenty-three and very nearly succeeded in killing myself. I advanced a public persona of apparent confidence and bravery but lived in a private world of despair and paranoia. It was many years before I could bring myself into wholeness. While I had little or no fear of administrative or professorial authority—in my childhood world of Communist demarcations the "class enemy" was not to be respected but overthrown—it had not yet occurred to me that the "class enemy" was primarily male or that this situation had anything to do with authority and power.

The FSM was a moment of great personal liberation for me. It gave me a taste of power—not in the sense of power over but in the sense of self-empowerment. I had had so little of this in my life that the feelings were overwhelming, something to be savored. The FSM also created a community such as I had never known. Those of us on the FSM Steering Committee, especially, had tremendous love for each other. This is a very special feeling that comes out of a shared political commitment, a comradeship and devotion—something that is utterly necessary for us as human beings. Most of us rarely if ever experience it. It was an enormous gift to me. And it was through the FSM that I developed a lifelong friendship with Mario. Although the media implied (or claimed outright) that Mario and I were lovers and the right-wing press cast me as the "evil woman" (insert "Communist" and "Jew") who had used her sexual wiles to lead fair-haired Mario astray, in fact this had nothing in common with our actual friendship. Mario was the first serious male relationship I had that was not fraught with sexual tension and the awful pressure for sexual favor. He was also one of the very few people I knew who did not relate to me as "Aptheker's daughter." He loved me for myself and as a human being. As a friend, Mario was available, sympathetic, honest, engaged, and funny. Although later in our lives we were separated for years at a time, we always reconnected with the same intensity we had known in our twenties.

Another very striking fact about the FSM, visible to us in retrospect, is that it was virtually all white. Look at the photographs! One Asian American woman, Patti Iiyama, was on the Executive Committee (a broader group than the Steering Committee). One African American woman, Carolyn Craven, who was then a member of SDS, arrived on the campus and became active there only in the spring following FSM. And I recall only one African American man, Howard Jeter, not a student but a community activist, was arrested in the Sproul Hall sit-in in December, though there may have been one or two others. The involved faculty were all white and almost entirely male. This reflected the racial and gender segregation characteristic of American higher education prior to the affirmative action programs of the 1970s and 1980s. Although the FSM grew out of and was deeply affected by the Civil Rights Movement and although leading civil rights leaders visited the campus to offer their support, the FSM reflected the segregation of the times.

The first stirrings of an organized Women's Liberation Movement began three year after the FSM. Women, both white and black, questioned their treatment within the Civil Rights, student, and New Left movements and the status of and violence against women more generally in society. Men in the New Left and within the liberation movements, almost without exception, ridiculed the women with virtually the same contempt and fury as their liberal and conservative counterparts. This in itself became a significant experience in our understandings of the extent to which patriarchal conventions and male supremacy cut across boundaries of race, ethnicity, and class.[3]

.   .   .

If we consider freedom of speech as a practice rather than as an abstract set of legal rights or an inscribed condition or achievement,[4] it becomes apparent that women have been allowed very little of it. This may seem paradoxical, given how often women are scorned as gossip mongers and nags and their speech is described as excessive, shrill, and hysterical. These descriptions are themselves symptomatic of the pervasive trivialization of women's speech. Women's freedom of speech has been circumscribed historically, politically, and personally. In this respect, attitudes found within the FSM had a long enough pedigree.

In the first half of the nineteenth century, for example, it was unusual and controversial for women even to speak in public. Opposition was especially strong from the church fathers. Maria W. Stewart, a free black woman and schoolteacher whose appearances were sponsored by the Afric-American Female Intelligence Society of Boston in 1832–1833, was the first American-born woman to speak publicly in the United States. The propriety of her right to speak was intensely debated, with even much progressive opinion unfavorable to the idea. For example, an editorial in the abolitionist periodical *The Liberator* opined, "The voice of woman should not be heard in public debates, but there are other ways in which her influence would be beneficial."[5] Nevertheless, Stewart delivered four lectures advocating both the abolition of slavery and equality for women before she succumbed to criticisms she received from so many men, both black and white.

Stewart was followed by other women daring to speak in public, many of them deeply dedicated to the antislavery cause. Among those most articulate in the defense of women's freedom of speech was the southern-born white abolitionist Angelina Grimké. In a letter to abolitionists Theodore Weld and John Greenleaf Whittier, she wrote on August 20, 1837, "If we surrender the right to *speak* to the public this year, we must surrender the right to petition next year & the right to write the year after &c. What *then* can *woman* do for the slave, when she herself is under the feet of man & shamed into *silence?*"[6] Women's arguments eventually held sway in the antislavery movement, and many of the women became distinguished lecturers. Yet as women, their right to speak was continually contested. Sojourner Truth, for example, who was a brilliant orator, was repeatedly confronting male antagonists who attempted to silence her.[7]

In other instances, women were subjected to persecution for publishing controversial opinions or challenging authority. For example, in July 1829 the Washington journalist Anne Newport Royall, America's first roving correspondent, was arrested under a federal warrant as a "common scold." This accusation, an archaic remnant of an old Presbyterian law, was a charge brought against a woman whose speech contravened church doctrine. A fearless muckraker, Royall traveled widely through the states and wrote a series of "Black Books" that offered incisive political commentary on the state of the union. Having uncovered serious corruption among high-ranking government employees, she exposed one of their schemes as a violation of the constitutional separation of church and state. She also discovered and publicized that one of the main culprits was a womanizer who had impregnated an African American woman. Caught in a maelstrom of intrigue and political vendetta, Royall was arrested, tried before a jury (of all white men, of course), and convicted. Appealing her conviction, Royall then argued that being a "common scold" was a nonexistent crime, and that her sentence, prolonged dunking underwater, was reminiscent of the seventeenth-century witch-hunt trials and constituted cruel and unusual punishment. Embarrassed, the judge denied the appeal, withdrew the charge of "common scold," and then convicted Royall of being a public nuisance! He sentenced her to pay a ten dollar fine and court costs. She paid neither and claimed no recollection of how this matter was settled. Thus freed, Royall continued her muckraking, but the charge of a "common scold" remained in legal ambiguity.[8]

Ida B. Wells was an African American teacher and journalist living in Tennessee, where she was co-owner of a paper called the *Memphis Free Speech*. In March 1892, when three of her closest friends, the owners of a highly successful grocery store, were shot to death by a white lynch mob, Wells took up a crusade in her newspaper to condemn the killers. When the white-owned press responded by alleging that the victims had been planning to rape a white woman, she replied in an editorial, "Nobody in this section of the country believes the old threadbare lie that Negro men rape white women. If Southern white men are not careful, they will over-reach themselves and public sentiment will have a reaction; a conclusion will then be reached which will be very damaging to the moral reputation of their women."[9] Addressing the highly flammable issues of sex and race, Wells's editorial infuriated the Memphis establishment. A white mob was prepared to lynch her, but learning that she was out of the state, it instead destroyed the offices of the *Free Speech* and issued a warning: Wells had best not return to Memphis if she valued her life. Wells did not return, but she did initiate a remarkable forty-five-year international crusade against lynching.[10]

These stories represent only a brief and incomplete account of the suppression of women's constitutional freedoms, but they are emblematic of women's historical subordination. Women have been particularly persecuted for both the content of their views and the gendered (and racialized) impropriety of their speech. The question of women's citizenship was legally ambiguous for much of the nineteenth century, and their civil and political rights remain a matter of contention to this day. We have yet, for example, to pass a clearly stated constitutional amendment affirming women's equality. And numerous examples could be cited from as recently as the 1960s wherein collisions of gender and race prevented even the illusion of constitutional protection and made the practice of freedom perilous indeed.

.   .   .

Women's freedom of speech has been particularly circumscribed when women were seeking to redress grievances against themselves. Nowhere can this be seen more clearly than in contemporary movements against sexual harassment, sexual and domestic violence, and incest and other forms of child sexual abuse, and for women's reproductive rights. Likewise, women have been punished, often severely, for advocating and affirming a nonheterosexual standard. In considering freedom of speech as a practice, and in particular a practice with consequences, the suppression or subversion of women's speech comes most clearly into focus.

In a subtle but important way, Anita Hill's testimony before the Senate Judiciary Committee in October 1991 is a case in point. Given the extent of her public exposure, to reflect on Hill's mistreatment as a free speech issue may at first seem paradoxical. Yet this is precisely the point. The paradox lies in Hill's apparently unlimited license to speak while the media, the president, and the Senate simultaneously distorted, demeaned, and subverted her speech by challenging her veracity, coherence, wisdom, and mental balance. Charges such as these are almost always directed against women who overstep the boundaries of patriarchal convention.

Republican President George Herbert Bush, making an appointment to the Supreme Court to replace the legendary African American jurist Thurgood Marshall, sought a conservative successor. He selected a little known federal judge, Clarence Thomas, who had headed the Equal Employment Opportunity Commission (EEOC) under the Reagan administration. Thomas had opposed affirmative action, though he himself had benefited greatly from it. Indeed, he had been able to attend Yale University law school because of its aggressive affirmative action policies. Despite the obvious race-ing of the proposed appointment, Bush insisted that his nomination was "raceless," a curious invocation in a nation obsessed with race.

During the course of the FBI's investigations into the nominee's qualifications, charges of sexual misconduct came to light. Anita Hill, an African American attorney who had served with Thomas on the EEOC, came forward reluctantly, and only with assurances that her privacy would be protected, to question the propriety of Thomas's nomination. She charged that he had repeatedly pressured her for sex, violating their professional relationship. But rather than discreetly withdraw the nomination,

President Bush and his Senate allies pursued it with a vengeance. When the all-white and all-male Senate Judiciary Committee reopened its hearings, Hill was forced to testify before a television audience of some twenty-two million. Despite grueling cross-examination, Hill, speaking with a quiet dignity, recounted Thomas's repeated unwanted advances, his assertions of sexual prowess, and his descriptions of pornographic materials. Other witnesses, white and black, corroborated her testimony. Yet a great deal of the public response to these hearings was not to criticize Thomas but to cast aspersions on Hill's character, motivation, and sexual (mis)conduct. Nevertheless, although the Judiciary Committee voted for Thomas, thanks to Hill's courageous testimony his confirmation was almost defeated, passing the Senate by the extraordinarily close vote of 52–48.[11]

Anita Hill had put the question of sexual harassment on the national agenda. Outraged by her treatment, women now broke their silence about their own sexual harassment. Thousands came forward, testifying before legislative committees and government commissions, speaking out in public forums, and writing about their experiences. Although sexual harassment had long been a general condition of female employment and education, its existence was still contested by men, who loudly protested their innocence while women remained largely silent, a silence that "could only be heard in the moment in which it was breaking."[12] This was speech with consequences, and its suppression, containment, and discrediting were eagerly pursued. While men's speech was granted authority simply because they were men, women's speech was suspect at the very moment of its utterance. Speech by women of color was consigned to the very outskirts of the "speakable."

Hill had been subjected to a kind of treatment that had long been familiar to women and girls who revealed themselves within their families, and in the courts as survivors of rape, incest, and domestic violence. Years of struggle by the Women's Liberation Movement, beginning in the 1970s, had finally brought these issues into political discourse. The perception of Hill "speaking truth to power," as she put it,[13] crystallized a historical moment twenty years in the making. What had been previously considered unspeakable because it was "private" or "shameful" and because women were "unreliable witnesses" had now been publicly and irrevocably spoken. With the failure to return women to their socially mandated silence after Hill's testimony, women's speech was subjected to lawsuits, loud disclaimers, and renewed psychiatric evaluation. Retrieved memories of incest and other forms of childhood abuse, for example, have resulted in fathers' suing their daughters and a new category of pathology known as "false memory syndrome" (to replace or complement the Freudians' timeworn "hysteria"). Therapists, especially feminist ones, have been sued or professionally castigated for "instilling" or "suggesting" such memories.

Yet if these lawsuits and allegations of pathology have had a chilling effect on women's free speech, they have also had an opposite if unintended consequence. In her essay *Excitable Speech: A Politics of the Performative*, Judith Butler urges us to consider that "censorship is implicated in its own repudiated material in ways that produce paradoxical consequences." She argues that in the effort to censor, the explicit "regulation that states what it does not want stated thwarts its own desire. . . . [T]he effort to constrain the term culminates in its very proliferation." Butler is discussing the 1994 statute that put into law the "don't ask, don't tell" policy on homosexuals in the military. She concludes that "The regulation of the term 'homosexual' is . . . no simple act of censorship or silencing. The regulation redoubles the term it seeks to constrain."[14] In an analogous way the effort to censor women's speech on matters of sexual violence and incest has unintentionally proliferated discussion of the issue in a way that was unthinkable twenty or even ten years ago. So many women have written their stories, so many have testified in public forums and in protest marches to "Take Back the Night," that it has not been historically possible to contain that which was once "unspeakable." As the new millennium begins, women seem finally to have propelled the "unspeakable" issue of sexual violence against women and children into public discourse. The effort to censor having failed, the issue now proliferates. And now that the truth about sexual violence has finally been spoken, it can be effectively challenged and collectively resisted. This is the meaning of freedom of speech as a practice.

.   .   .

When I reflect upon the meaning of the Free Speech Movement for women, a line in a poem by Adrienne Rich flashes like the neon it paradoxically rejects: "The longer I live the more I mistrust / theatricality, the false glamour cast / by performance, the more I know its poverty beside / the truths we are salvaging from / the splitting open of our lives."[15] A painting by Frida Kahlo reveals a watermelon split open, the red-pink fruit succulent, black seeds protruding, a metaphor for the ways in which she split open her life so we could see the interiority of her suffering. In 1978, when Susan Griffin, a veteran of the Berkeley student movement, wrote *Woman and Nature*, she began it with the dedication "These words are written for those / of us whose language is not heard / whose words have been stolen or erased."[16]

When I reflect upon the meaning of the Free Speech Movement for women, I feel the heat of the cauldron out of which our voices rose in the years that followed. If that movement is to be called up, let it be in the spirit of sustaining the voices of those who have been silenced, whose words have been denied. May we listen carefully to women's speech, hear its merit, critically assess its claim, be respectful. May we acknowledge the violence done to women, and the injury done to all, by any form of supremacy. The phrase "women's equality" sounds quaint in these postmodern times. Yet it also remains politically elusive. If we were to truly honor the meaning of those words so that the practice of freedom is equally bestowed upon women and men of all races and ethnicities, it would transform our understanding of history and of the human experience.

NOTES

1. There is an extensive feminist literature on the social construction of gender. Among the more interesting works, see: Nancy Henley, *Body Politics: Power, Sex, and Nonverbal Communication* (Englewood, N.J.: Prentice Hall, 1977); Candace West and Don H. Zimmerman, "Doing Gender," *Gender and Society* 1 (June 1987); Judith Butler, *Gender Trouble: Feminism and the Subversion of Identity* (New York: Routledge, 1990); Barrie Thorne, Chris Kramerae, and Nancy Henley, eds., *Language, Gender, and Society* (New York: Newbury House, 1983); Barrie Thorne, *Gender Play: Girls and Boys in School* (New Brunswick: Rutgers University Press, 1993); Daphne Scholinski and Jane Meridith Adams, *The Last Time I Wore a Dress: A Memoir* (New York: Riverhead Books, 1997).

2. My father, Herbert Aptheker, was a prominent member of the U.S. Communist Party and a well-known Marxist historian.

3. See, for example, Rachel Blau DuPlessis and Ann Snitow, eds., *The Feminist Memoir Project: Voices from Women's Liberation* (New York: Three Rivers Press, 1998).

4. See the essay by Wendy Brown, "Freedom's Silence," in Robert C. Frost, ed., *Censorship and Silencing: Practices of Cultural Regulation* (Los Angeles: Getty Research Institute for the History of Art and the Humanities, 1998), 318. Brown is citing an interview with Foucault by Paul Rabinow, "Space, Knowledge and Power," in *The Foucault Reader* (New York: Pantheon, 1984), 245.

5. "Duty of Females," *The Liberator*, May 5, 1832, quoted in Paula Giddings, *When and Where I Enter: The Impact of Black Women on Race and Sex in America* (New York: William Morrow, 1984), 49–50.

6. Gilbert Barnes and Dwight L. Dumond, eds., *The Letters of Theodore Weld, Angelina Grimké Weld and Sarah Grimké, 1822–1844* (New York: Appleton-Century-Croft, 1934), 1:429.

7. Olive Gilbert, ed., *Narrative of Sojourner Truth: A Bondwoman of Olden Times* (1878; reprint, New York: Arno Press and The New York Times, 1968), 138–39. See also the definitive study by Nell Irvin Painter, *Sojourner Truth: A Life, A Symbol* (New York: Norton, 1996).

8. See Alice S. Maxwell and Marion B. Dunlevy, *Virago! The Story of Anne Newport Royall (1769–1854)* (Jefferson, N.C.: McFarland, 1985). In September 1971 a journalist, Marion B. Dunlevy, coauthor of *Virago!*, was arrested as a "common scold," among other charges, and held on $1,000 bail. She was indicted, arraigned, and then brought to trial in Monmouth County Court, Freehold, New Jersey, on April

10, 1972. The charge of "common scold" was severed from the case, and she was eventually acquitted on all charges (ibid., prefatory material).

9. Ida B. Wells, *Southern Horrors: Lynch Law in All Its Phases* (1892; reprint, New York: Arno Press and The New York Times, 1969), 4.

10. For further details, see Bettina Aptheker, *Woman's Legacy: Essays on Race, Sex, and Class in American History* (Amherst: University of Massachusetts Press, 1982), 53–76; Ida B. Wells, *Crusade for Justice*, ed. Alfreda M. Duster (Chicago: University of Chicago Press, 1970); Linda O. McMurray, *To Keep the Waters Troubled: The Life of Ida B. Wells* (New York: Oxford University Press, 1998).

11. For a particularly illuminating anthology, see Toni Morrison, ed., Race-ing Justice, En-gendering Power: Essays on Anita Hill, Clarence Thomas, and the Construction of Social Reality (New York: Pantheon, 1992).

12. These words are from Sheila Rowbotham, *Woman's Consciousness, Man's World* (Middlesex, England: Penguin Books, 1973), 29.

13. Anita Hill, *Speaking Truth to Power* (New York: Doubleday, 1997).

14. Judith Butler, *Excitable Speech: A Politics of the Performative* (New York: Routledge), 130–31.

15. Adrienne Rich, "Transcendental Etude," in *The Dream of a Common Language* (New York: Norton, 1993), 74.

16. Susan Griffin, *Woman and Nature: The Roaring Inside Her* (New York: Harper and Row, 1978).

Recollections of the FSM

Martin Roysher

"The concept of irony doesn't begin to explain what's going on here," Bettina Aptheker (whom we knew as "Tina") told the hundred or so FSM veterans at the March 2000 opening of the Free Speech Movement Café in the University's Moffitt Library. Displaying FSM memorabilia, the Café is part of a $3.5 million gift from Berkeley alumnus Steven Silberstein, who worked in the University Library during the FSM and was one of thousands of FSM sympathizers. His sympathies endured as he went on to invent the software that libraries around the world use to keep track of their books. After Mario Savio's death, Steve decided to make a gift to the library that would commemorate the FSM. He talked with Lynne Hollander, Mario's widow, and concluded that a fitting memorial to the movement and to Mario, the quintessential intellectual, would be an endowment for humanities and social sciences books, along with an FSM archive and a café where students could discuss ideas and revisit the FSM's struggle to shape their university.

The right to conduct political activity on campus is so commonplace today that we forget it was secured at Berkeley only when the University tried to ban it and the FSM won it back in a three-month protest. We who had led that fight in our youth found ourselves gathering early on that March evening as middle-aged, mostly white celebrants of what now seems truly mundane. Tina's brief recounting of the protest stirred memories that seemed oddly out of sync as we enjoyed Chardonnay and Brie in the Café's slick modern surroundings. Malcolm Zaretsky, a stalwart of the graduate student strike, mused that he hardly recognized anybody. "When did our objective change?" he asked with a smile. "Oh," joked Jack Weinberg, "we lost our edge a long time ago." Lynne explained why a café was an appropriate memorial: Mario had so loved the ambiance of cafés that he made a second home of his local one, with its freely flowing conversations, occasional music, and people quietly working. Lynne always knew where to call when he wasn't home and had papers to grade or notes to prepare. The FSM Café, however, meant something else to the current student body president: it was a caffeine recharge station for the intensely competitive, serving late-night concoctions that sounded like they would keep me awake for days. Chancellor Robert Berdahl portrayed the Café as a symbol of reconciliation. He praised Mario for rekindling Berkeley's critical spirit and welcomed back Weinberg, the notorious nonstudent of the police car incident. The old spirit echoed in brief applause when a protester commandeered the microphone and urged the Café operators to serve only unadulterated foods and beverages.

We usually think of the FSM as a student movement, but faculty and staff predominated at the Café opening. The FSM broke down the fears still lingering from loyalty oath controversies and McCarthyism, and faculty discovered the regenerating effect of public debate animated by intellectual richness that perhaps only a university can engender. The line between students and faculty had blurred since the 1960s. Some faculty at the Café's opening had been students or graduate students in the FSM who later went into teaching.

After completing his master's degree in physics at San Francisco State, Mario became a demanding, respected, and popular teacher of science and poetry at California State University's Sonoma campus. Few of today's students attended the dedication. Perhaps they take free speech for granted and do not know that it had to be won in a conflict that made Berkeley the first major campus battleground of the turbulent sixties.

Having been a member of the FSM Steering Committee, I was amused to see our names on an old mimeographed manifesto embedded in a Café tabletop, and wondered what it would all mean to my granddaughters if I ever brought them to the Café. A few veterans have kept the FSM's memory alive by organizing reunions, creating an FSM website, and collecting historical materials (now available in the Bancroft Library's FSM archive, funded from the Silberstein gift). These materials reflect a common view that in protesting a ban on political activity and civil rights work, the FSM prefigured other sixties protests against universities acting in loco parentis, repressive cultural mores, and the Vietnam War. But I remembered a messier picture and began to think about what the FSM actually was and who we, its adherents, really were.

ACCIDENTS HAPPEN; HUBRIS HELPS

In hindsight the FSM seems like a seriocomic accident that played out in a string of administrative blunders abetted by the hubris of President Clark Kerr. The first blunder was the ban on campus political advocacy apparently sparked by William Knowland, publisher of the *Oakland Tribune*, who complained early that fall that the campus had become a base for civil rights protests in Oakland. Defying the ban, representatives of political organizations set up tables in Sproul Plaza to distribute leaflets, solicit contributions, and sign up members. Students quickly gathered, and so many took part that deans gave up citing them. Hundreds more soon presented the dean's office with letters and petitions attesting that they too had violated the ban. The only one at the tables not then enrolled at the University was Weinberg, who had dropped out of UC to become a CORE organizer. Wanting to make an issue of this "nonstudent," administrators out of touch with campus opinion blundered again by ordering a police car onto the Plaza during a crowded noon hour to arrest and remove Weinberg. Instead, the protest mushroomed: Jack went limp and an impromptu sit-in immobilized the car for nearly a day and a half.

Tense negotiations ensued among an ad hoc group of protest leaders, campus and university administrators, and faculty members. Kerr refused to rescind the restrictive rules but agreed to suspend them and negotiate changes with a tripartite committee composed of administrators, students, and faculty. By late the next evening several hundred people had joined the sit-in. "Fratties" (fraternity members) loudly taunted, pushed, and threatened those around the perimeter, while police assembled behind Sproul Hall poised to break up the protest. Mario climbed on the car and outlined the settlement. Wanting above all to prevent violence, he invited no debate and pleaded with us to accept the compromise and leave voluntarily what he called "this terrible scene." I was furious that we were leaving without having won, and felt our nonviolent sit-in had done nothing to make the scene "terrible." I was so angry that the University had called police onto the campus to break up a peaceful demonstration that I found myself shouting curses at the convoy of buses carrying the police away.

The stupidity of this blundering rankles me still. In a sense the sit-in truly was a terrible scene. I am glad the FSM secured the right to conduct political activity on campus, but it should not have had to. The University had capitulated to a local power broker when there was no real need to do so. In striking contrast, in May 1967 a tense but united campus successfully defended a Vietnam Commencement that students had organized to announce their refusal to serve in the war. Governor Reagan publicly vowed to prevent it, but the campus faced him down as thousands gathered peacefully in the Plaza to honor war resisters. In this case the campus governed itself by applying rules resulting from the FSM and conducting a demonstration peacefully, within the regimen of academic life, thus protecting itself from police intervention. But in the FSM the administration called in police and opened the way to National Guard helicopters teargassing the campus a few years later.

These blunders owed much to Kerr's undermining Berkeley administrators and attempting to manipulate public opinion. His special interest in the University's flagship campus led him to tolerate if not maintain an ossified campus administration that in the FSM acted neither independently nor intelligently and patently ignored most of the faculty. The FSM was, for the First Amendment, motherhood and apple pie; but Kerr and the administration tried to marginalize us and by extension our faculty supporters by calling us outsiders, radicals, and, we read in a newspaper report, 49 percent Maoists and Castroites. They packed the negotiating committee with their partisans and groups that had not been involved in the controversy, a stratagem Kerr had described in his labor management writings. Kerr also manipulated the media behind the scenes in ways that impeded emergence of a more balanced view of the FSM. A *Newsweek* reporter fresh from the *Harvard Crimson* editor's chair, Joe Russin, got close enough to the FSM to pass as a Steering Committee member during the sit-in and wrote accurate stories. But he told us that Kerr's office and University Public Information Office officials prevailed on his editors to delete much of his work, even as events proved Russin right and Kerr's responses wrong. The following spring Kerr himself intervened with the president and chairman of the board of CBS to turn a balanced documentary on the FSM into diverting vignettes of groovy hippies. The producer, Arthur Barron, and director, Peter Davis, fought to retain the program's content, but were forced to show us mostly riding horses down local beaches and baking magic brownies.

Kerr later denied having made the 49-percent statement, but he never made a sustained effort to correct the misconception at the time or to acknowledge then that the FSM was an overwhelmingly student movement, no matter how radical it may or may not have been. Nor did he support grassroots faculty efforts to resolve the controversy. In fact, his and his staff's charges feebly evoked McCarthyism, although he may have felt that his liberal reputation would insulate him against that rebuke. A man of noted discretion and media savvy should have known such charges would have consequences. My parents, for instance, lived in a conservative suburb of LA. After a local right-wing rag repeated the charges and printed a photo of me with my home address, they received late-night phone calls impugning their patriotism (which helped turn two loyal Republicans into Democrats).

After the FSM, the faculty sought its own voice and forums. Out-of-touch and discredited campus administrators were replaced or moved, leaving to a new acting chancellor, Martin Meyerson, the job of trying to correct the larger public misunderstanding of Berkeley. But public opinion was so polluted that Meyerson, a cerebral, gentle, and erudite man, could not undo Kerr's words and was ultimately removed for being another Berkeley radical, despite a concerted faculty effort to get a more balanced view of the campus into the state's media coverage.

For all his faults in the FSM affair, Kerr is a learned man who spoke to educational issues. But he propounded a view of the university that ran counter to the spirit of the times on campus in ways that he failed to recognize. In *The Uses of the University* he argued that industrial civilization had transformed the community of professors and students into a "multiversity" servicing scientific and industrial research, agricultural extension, technical and professional training, and the administration of various public and private programs. Many students had come to Berkeley for its distinguished faculty, however, and critics argued that the new missions emphasized by Kerr had damaged, even displaced, undergraduate teaching. Some students resented being channeled into large courses in which professors gave a lecture or two a week while graduate assistants dealt with students, taught discussion sections, and graded exams and papers. Articulate and confident students got to know faculty, but hesitant ones may not even have met their professor. I do not know how many students shared these feelings of alienation, but Mario tapped into them as he called on us to enter Sproul Hall on December 2.

He first explained that he had learned from an informant that Kerr had tried to get a more liberal position out of the Board of Regents but that Kerr would not say so publicly. "Would you ever imagine the manager of a firm making a statement publicly in opposition to his board of directors?" the informant had asked Mario rhetorically. "That's the answer!" Mario announced, and his voice rang out over the Plaza:

> Now, I ask you to consider: if this is a firm, and if the Board of Regents are the board of directors, and if President Kerr in fact is the manager, then I'll tell you something: the faculty are a bunch of employees, and we're the raw material! But we're a bunch of raw material that don't mean to have any process upon us, don't mean to be made into any product, don't mean to end up being bought by some clients of the University, be they the government, be they industry, be they organized labor, be they anyone! We're human beings!

Faculty, too, sensed enough discontent with the University at the time to appoint two commissions to explore its origins and recommend remedies. Charles Muscatine (English) chaired a select committee in 1965 whose report, *Education at Berkeley*, was widely read as a guide for rejuvenating teaching and learning in a mass university. Caleb Foote (law) chaired a Study Commission on University Governance in 1966–1967 whose report, *The Culture of the University*, also drew much attention. (I worked on both efforts, as a researcher for the Muscatine committee and a member of the Foote commission.) Testifying to the depth of the underlying University issues, the FSM also spawned an experimental college that restructured the freshman and sophomore curricula. (Created by philosophy professor Joseph Tussman, the college devoted each semester to a great historical era, exploring its major intellectual, cultural, scientific, and aesthetic aspects. It faltered when Tussman and the faculty could not link it to the established curriculum and students began to fear that they could fall behind in traditional fields of study.)

Facing the challenges of the FSM era, Kerr abjured the role of university president as public leader in the mold of Harvard's James Conant or Berkeley's Benjamin Ide Wheeler. Seeing conflicting demands on the University as inherent, he sought to mediate the FSM conflict without engaging students or faculty in open forums on University issues and was lukewarm in support of others doing so. Instead he seemed to expect formative questions about the University's educational mission and governance to yield to labor negotiating stratagems. In part, his position may have reflected his personality as much as his views; he was a more distant man of less charm and magnetism than Meyerson, and he also feared that the public would grow impatient with universities that retreated behind ivy walls or entangled themselves in loud squabbles as they took more of the public purse to educate growing numbers of baby boomers. The title of his book, *The Uses of the University*, was a plea to recognize the value of universities. But during the FSM, he departed from educating the public to play on its stereotypes to discredit critics. In the end the Regents sacked him too for permitting what the newspapers called the "mess at Berkeley."

In retrospect, one would hope that all university presidents might learn from Kerr's hubris and his accomplishments. But a run of faceless managers since has taken a more deadening measure of his experience, namely, that silence on major public issues assures longer and more peaceful presidencies. Kerr's place in the history of American academia is more complicated than the FSM's partial undoing of his theories may imply. Suffice it for this recollection to say that while some, perhaps much, of the greatness of the University of California today is his legacy, the FSM was not among his finer hours.

DEFENDING RIGHTS

As the FSM gathered steam, the campus administration stumbled more. Besides packing the negotiating committee, it insisted that the committee's recommendations be strictly advisory; it ignored student representations and fidgeted between disciplinary action and inaction, which alienated students and faculty. The canard that the unrest was due to a few outsiders and radicals insulted growing numbers of students, who came to appreciate the issues of constitutional rights, educational policy, and university governance that the FSM had raised. Many participants felt the FSM was simply

defending American liberties. They truly believed they were being fundamentally patriotic, and would return from visits home chafing at the distorted picture of us that had spread beyond Berkeley with media reports of
outsiders they never met and riots that didn't happen. They resented
claims that they fell prey to manipulative FSM leaders when in fact they had
seen us inviting questions and explaining issues while the administration
hid behind obfuscation. Students also rejected media and administration
descriptions of our protests that used words like *riot* and *violence,* because
they saw us apply lessons of nonviolence from the Civil Rights Movement.
We kept our rallies peaceful as the administration's favorite students, the
Fratties, taunted people on the rally fringes and pushed lit cigarettes into
their backs. Many faculty, too, were insulted, finding their advice on ending
the crisis ignored by out-of-touch administrators.

The FSM was both a coalition of political groups spanning the ideological spectrum and an experiment in mass democracy that shaded into a
nascent "politics of feeling." Each group had two representatives on the
Executive Committee, which had some forty members at its high point. It
soon became utterly unwieldy and elected a smaller Steering Committee
of eleven to manage the day-to-day protest. The Steering Committee was
charged with convening the Executive Committee before embarking on
any major change of direction, such as another sit-in or a settlement. This
arrangement was a relief because Executive Committee meetings were
marathons. One, a key debate over a proposed sit-in after the Regents meeting of November 20, dragged on well past midnight. Sit-in advocates felt
that students at large would understand the need for direct action only if
they developed the same feeling of resistance that the Steering Committee
had mustered through a long introspective discussion. Michael Rossman's
entreaty alone, as he sat on the floor in a swirl of intensity and cigarette
smoke, ran on for an hour and a half. A few of us escaped for dinner and
returned to find him still groping his surreal way toward a mood of resistance. A "politics of feeling" was in the air, but the meeting left us so tired
that I wondered how many would show up for the sit-in.

Pragmatism was the FSM's major key, and ideology a minor one. Tina
was the only avowed Marxist on the Steering Committee and didn't care
about advancing her beliefs. She would often stab the air with a pointed finger and exhort, "Dammit, we can win this." Weinberg, too, was a tactician
intent on winning his battles. Even Marxist members did not use the FSM
to propound their views and were savvy enough to know that doing so
would have doomed us. In fact the movement's real leftists thought us
naive and Tina hidebound. We were called "new" radicals because our ideology was not that of the Old Left. But labeling misses the point: we animated thous-ands when we spoke directly to student concerns and did not
propound a larger agenda. Only a few hundred partisans followed when-

ever we were perceived as being radical in ways that we could not show were needed to win the fight. At the Café opening in 2000 I was unexpectedly reminded of how naive some old radicals thought us: Malcolm Zaretsky had just reintroduced himself to Lynne, who remembered him. It turns out that in sorting Mario's papers she had come across Malcolm's recommendation to reject Mario for an internship in community action because, Malcolm had written, he lacked sufficient political acumen. We toasted Malcolm for bringing on the FSM by not removing Mario from the campus.

I was elected to the Steering Committee in early November in what became known as the purge of the moderates, but ideology played little part. I had just that fall transferred as a sophomore to Berkeley from Princeton, where I had joined SDS and helped organize protests against the Vietnam War. A former high-school debater, I was outspoken about political issues and soon found myself one of two SDS representatives on the Executive Committee. My nomination, however, was largely accidental. SDS was then an East Coast group, and Eric Levine (a graduate student in political science) and I may have been its only Berkeley members (though Eric kept reassuring me that our numbers were growing rapidly). Later, when a few Steering Committee members explored a settlement with the administration but failed to tell the committee and were found out, I was among three elected replacements.

Moderates and radicals in the FSM argued about tactics far more than ideology. All urged adherence to three principles: political activity on campus should be permitted; participants should not be punished for activity that a court might later find illegal (like a sit-in); and campus advocacy could be limited only as needed to assure that it did not disrupt the University's academic work. Internally we had a fourth principle: Any settlement must be fully discussed and could be made only by a majority vote of the Executive Committee. There was no further ideological litmus test; even purged moderates remained strong FSM advocates. They defended having sought a compromise way of implementing our principles but did not back down from them. The Young Republican Steering Committee member, Mona Hutchins, shared the FSM's basic rejection of rules and regulations without roots in human needs or defensible social requirements. That surprised some, but Mona's libertarian views were strong; a few years later she forced the San Francisco transit system to arrest her when she insisted on riding a cable car's outside platform and holding the handrail, which only men were then allowed to do. I counted myself among the FSM's radicals. We were willing to be more confrontational because we feared that the administration would consign us to an oblivion of negotiating committees. Many students were angry that administration blunders forced them to support the FSM, and some FSM moderates resented our not holding back to allow the administration more time to come to its senses. But we felt we could not let up without hampering the activities of political action groups and inviting disciplinary reprisals against what the administration might then see as a weakened movement (which is what happened). In the end the administration cemented our unity by trying to discipline moderates and radicals alike because it could not distinguish between them.

Media focused on a "fiery" Mario, and my dear friend was indeed a passionate man given to vivid imagery. But his charismatic calls for action came only after he had carefully developed a case based not on radical ideology but on a thorough understanding of the issues and facts. He had a deep respect for the autonomy of the individual that was rooted in his profoundly humanist instincts and the principles of philosophers he had closely studied (among them I recall Thomas Aquinas and Immanuel Kant). Contrary to the administration's portrayal, he was a contemplative man who took intellectual life as seriously as anyone I ever knew and tried to appreciate day-to-day choices facing students and faculty. His passion had been stoked the previous summer when he went south to work in the Civil Rights Movement, and that experience fired his speeches. But his more frequent words were carefully drawn: "I ask you to consider," he would always say, as he began to painstakingly dissect the failings of the administration's latest position.

Some FSM ideologues thought Mario naive for spending so much time talking to students about free speech in a society whose institutions, in their view, represented powerful economic and political interests that would ignore popular sentiment anyway. But Mario knew as well as anyone that dialogue alone would not bring about social changes: "The trouble with liberals," he remarked, "is that they do not understand there is evil in the world." Learning how that evil played out in human institutions and how to combat it preoccupied him. Like most of us, he didn't think Marxism had the answers. Mario came from a working-class family with limited opportunities and had been schooled by inquiring Jesuit teachers. His radicalism went deeper than Marxism. A concern for the persistence of the underprivileged led him to a core conviction that there is indeed evil in the world and that it can be changed only if each of us understands its implications for himself or herself personally and for other human beings. Only then, he believed, could people forge themselves into a critical community of committed opposition, which the FSM was. Well aware of the distorting yet warming bath of modern media, Mario knew that establishing a common discourse begins with engaging one's opponents and must precede concerted action.

The foreground issues of the FSM were campus based, but they contained a complex mix of legal, political, and academic considerations. The FSM owed more to Mario's genius in explicating complex issues in countless conversations than to his equal gift for charismatic oratory in a crisis. Students and staff began to grasp that their rights were in danger and pressed Berkeley to live up to its image as the Athens of the West. Faculty worried about the viability of campus governance and whether course work really engaged students. Some looked to the FSM as a way for the University to expiate its recent past of loyalty oaths and political firings. It still took great courage for two untenured junior history professors, Reggie Zelnik and Larry Levine, to break official faculty ranks, come to a Steering Committee meeting to hear our views, and begin a dialogue with colleagues that became a larger faculty movement (the Committee of 200). The meeting was at my apartment. I remember the two of them sitting alone on the couch as we arrayed ourselves around the room in an inquisitorial arc that reflected our skepticism that two people hardly older than us could turn around a vaunted faculty, a thought that may have crossed their minds as well. Many half-forgotten conversations—like one I had with Professor Fred Crews when I knocked on his door during an office hour to talk about the FSM—were also needed to convince faculty that FSM leaders did not have horns and that growing numbers of students supported us. Perhaps because I came from an academic family and was thought to speak rationally to faculty concerns, I became a link to some of the more open-minded among them. Ultimately, the FSM spurred many faculty to assume major responsibility for campus governance and educational reform, although some still accused us of intruding on their prerogatives and forcing the FSM position upon them.

Fundamentally, the FSM was a community of thousands of students, faculty, teaching assistants, and staff who came together to affirm fundamental rights. People discovered that in living by their commitment to the FSM's basic principles, they created a new campus community that could effect major changes. A core commitment to democratic processes was intimately bound up with these principles. It was most evident following the November 20 Regents meeting that rejected our petition for an affirmation of FSM principles. Students at large understood that the Regents had upheld the ban, but still felt there was no cause for direct action. The campus administration was not enforcing the ban and seemed to have accepted political activity de facto. The FSM leadership was closely divided over what to do next. Some argued that students would join a sit-in only if the administration moved against the FSM directly. The Executive Committee voted for one anyway. But when only a few hundred students entered Sproul Hall, the Steering Committee ended it by another close vote, 6–5. Mario was so strongly committed to the sit-in that at moments he shook visibly with rage. But he accepted the vote and coaxed fellow dissenters out of the building by patiently arguing that preserving the FSM and respecting the majority will were more important than a show of moral outrage by a few hundred partisans.

The abortive sit-in underlined for me the politics of the FSM, insofar as it had any politics of particular substance. It had begun as a fight by a comparatively few organizations on the left of the spectrum to propound their views, collect funds, and recruit members. Other campus groups, some only marginally political, soon understood that their work was also threatened, and more students realized that the University was asserting a right to limit what they could read and whom they could hear. So there arose many views of the FSM, and because those who have written the history to date have been more political, our legacy has been handed down largely as a political one. People have since seen the FSM as one of the last civil rights movements, a precursor of other rights movements, and a harbinger of cultural changes, alluding first to hippies and rock music, then to the antiwar movement, and later to the women's and gay rights movements. At the time, however, the FSM was fundamentally a constitutional rights crusade, although much of its passion stemmed from its connections to the Civil Rights Movement, which had fought similar battles for basic rights to speak, eat, and rest for the night at places of one's choosing. As our support grew, we had to be careful not to misread what drew students to the FSM. As long as we were fighting for their rights to hear and act on disparate views on campus, as many as five thousand would come to our rallies and another five thousand or more probably supported us. But in the abortive sit-in, we stretched for something more than we could articulate, and only a hundred or so people remained to the end, when the force of Mario's persuasion alone probably drew them out of the building.

At this nadir of the FSM, the administration committed two final blunders that united the campus against it. Instead of letting the FSM die out, the chancellor resumed disciplinary proceedings. Letters went out over Thanksgiving break summoning to disciplinary hearings a few of those who had been cited for sitting at the first "illegal" tables, as if student support for the FSM were so shallow that it would wash away over a long weekend. But the depth of reaction surprised even us. All we had to do was announce the rally for December 2. Students were furious that the administration would think that an apparent consensus for de facto political activity hammered out over two months could be ignored and that they could be intimidated into letting it pick off FSM leaders. Over ten thousand people joined a spirited rally, an estimated fifteen hundred entered Sproul Hall, and about eight hundred stayed to be arrested. The FSM called a campuswide strike. Teaching assistants set up picket lines, and instruction was effectively shut down. Classes that were not canceled or moved off campus were devoted largely to discussing the crisis.

The breakthrough came quickly. Representatives of the Committee of 200 reached an agreement with the FSM, and word spread around campus that an Academic Senate meeting scheduled for December 8 would probably pass resolutions settling the controversy. The FSM suspended the strike in support of the faculty effort. Having infuriated students, Kerr and some senior faculty resorted to yet another stratagem, a second blunder, that cut them off from the larger faculty as well. They tried to steal the initiative from the Senate by calling off classes for a special convocation in the Greek Theatre on the morning of December 6. There they puffed up a body of department chairmen, who arrayed themselves across the stage. Striving for an aura of campus unity behind the new group, the moderator, Robert Scala-pino, chair of political science, refused to give Mario a place on the program or permit him to invite members of the audience to a noon rally that we had called in response to the convocation. As the program ended, Mario strode quietly toward the microphone to make the invitation anyway. Police grabbed him and dragged him away across the stage, much to the consternation of the chairmen, who were trying to make a decorous exit. With the audience shouting in protest and some chairmen complaining furiously that they had been duped, Mario was finally offered the microphone. He took it and simply invited people to depart this second "terrible scene" for our rally.

Even with the campus firmly behind the FSM, students did not engage in civil disobedience lightly. I remember students in countless conversations that fall, in and after class, on the Terrace, over coffee, and in dorms and apartments late into the night, weighing the balance of commitment and career and arguing about whether we were correct in our principles, fair in our tactics, and prudent about our futures. Some did suffer later for their involvement in the FSM, but others did not and many found the FSM label to be a badge of honor. My experience may or may not have been atypical. Years later, in 1976, I was a nominee for a gubernatorial appointment in New York state government and worried about the state police background check. Somewhat to my surprise, the investigator simply asked whether the FSM was a "campus dispute." When I described how it was, he smiled in relief that he would be able to conduct a phone investigation and wouldn't have to cross the country to check me out. His tone suggested that he and his superiors had concluded from similar cases that universities had been chronically unable to manage themselves in those years. A few years later, in the spring of 1981, I had left New York state service and was now a career member of the federal Senior Executive Service (SES), but I thought it prudent to resign and return to New York service. Edwin Meese, President Reagan's incoming attorney general, had been assigned to vet senior federal executives, and I felt that, if he remembered anyone from the FSM, it might be me. I had not been arrested in 1964, because I was designated to leave the sit-in to help run the strike and negotiate bail and other legal arrangements with the very same Edwin Meese, then an assistant district attorney for Alameda County. Our lawyers had driven him nuts requesting individual trials for the eight hundred arrestees, and he never struck me as a forgiving man. My SES appointment was still probationary, and I was well aware that even permanent SES members could be assigned anywhere. Choosing not to risk a posting to Guam or Alaska, I accepted an offer of another New York State executive position.

TIMES CHANGE

After the arrests victory came quickly. At a special meeting on December 8, the faculty passed its resolution affirming the right to engage in political advocacy on campus. The campus celebrated as we broke for Christmas, and, having won, we disbanded the FSM on January 5. Afterwards some FSMers, myself included, propounded the idea of a "new university" and struggled to flesh it out. Faculty talked of a "great university," and the campus began to change for the better. Meyerson's administration was an enlightened one, and sympathetic faculty, including Neil Smelser (sociology) and Robert O'Neill (law) joined it. Several members of the Committee of 200 became informal advisors to the chancellor, among them John Searle (philosophy), who had spoken boldly at our rallies, and Robert Cole (law), a drafter of the December 8 resolutions.

But articulating a vision beyond constitutional rights, democratic principles, and sensible administration was hard. Events quickly foreclosed the effort. Two vignettes capture for me the disarray and distrust. Shortly after Meyerson's appointment, he asked to meet with Mario and the Steering Committee. We went to his office, explained our concerns for the University, listened to his ideas, and were soon off on a two-hour conversation with him (Searle and Smelser were also present). We ranged from the meaning of the classical Greek forum through philosophy and history to what each side would do in the coming weeks. Meyerson was a city planner, and I knew from his writings and projects that he was a many-faceted and humane man with whom we could work. Mario was impressed but characteristically skeptical. As we neared the building exit after the meeting, he wondered aloud whether "even if he [Meyerson] is a good guy, he'd ever be permitted to act that way." At that moment we bumped into Meyerson and Smelser, who had taken a different route to the same exit and were expressing their surprise about how such alleged firebrands could be so reasonable and wondering whether we would remain so. Mario and Meyerson reached out, each about to say something, shook hands, and broke out laughing. As I recall, Meyerson said something about not letting speculation override our experience of each other, and we all went home.

The other vignette is from the 1966 strike, which began with a protest against military recruiting on campus (a government program that some defended as an exercise of free speech). By then Meyerson had been replaced by an academic manager who had neither Kerr's vision nor Meyerson's magnetism. It had become clear, too, that the FSM community was no more. One evening, meetings were called to vote on a strike settlement. Graduate TAs and undergraduates met in different buildings that faced each other across a large lawn. The graduates voted for the settlement and marched out singing the "Internationale," the traditional anthem of the revolutionary left. Moments later, however, the undergraduates, many carrying candles, poured out onto the lawn singing, "We all live in a yellow submarine," the Beatles' recent counterculture hit. A profound change in student culture had already taken place and a unifying vision was hard to see.

This divide had begun to open during the FSM, which attracted some early hippies. For many of them politics was secondary to personal expression, but an FSM couple featured in the CBS documentary discovered that what we now call "lifestyle" could be more threatening to their elders than politics. The young woman's parents were proud of the couple's role in the FSM and had invited mainline Philadelphia society friends into their home to see the broadcast. But the couple, worried that the show would reveal that they were living together, asked me to stop by CBS on a trip East and review the rushes, which I did. Later, when I told them that I was sure the film would reveal the truth to the woman's parents, they pressed me on details and concluded that I was wrong and that the parents would never know. When the program aired, the shock wave hit Berkeley even before the first commercial. The film's creators had chosen to focus on four people who struck them as having what they saw as new lifestyles and attitudes. They may have been right in sensing that the real story in the public mind was about the FSM as a precursor of cultural change, and they depicted the FSM to emphasize that theme, even though the FSM's hippies were certainly no more numerous or consequential than the FSM's political ideologues. If my recollections and letters written by the arrested students are any guide, the large majority of FSM supporters were in fact remarkably middle class in their values and aspirations, which made our success in rallying them to civil disobedience all the more remarkable.

The FSM was fortunate in having relatively clear and simple principles in the limited environment of a university, in contrast to later movements. As far as I could tell, most FSM supporters felt they had won the battle, returned to classes, and resumed whatever political activity they had been involved in, if any. The "new university" also proved an impossible sell. Few students cared about elaborating the notion, not because educational issues turned out to be less important but because faculty seemed to be addressing them. I also sensed that the intensity of the FSM could not be maintained over more than a few months. The Vietnam War loomed as a critical issue, and most students seemed to ration their political time somewhat carefully. Some leaders of the antiwar protest, however, ignored FSM lessons about how to build a mass movement that respected its participants. They assumed instead that anyone enlightened enough to have supported the FSM would of course support their cause and their tactics, and they attacked the nonconverted. Meanwhile, the media built a "filthy speech movement" out of a half dozen or so activists who were preoccupied with uttering provocative profanities and, on a few highly publicized occasions, parading naked on Sproul Plaza. With such help, the media easily tarred the FSM with subsequent fiascoes and soon obscured what we had been about. In fairness, I must acknowledge that the FSM's principles were so widely accepted and the University environment was so isolated and unique that we did not offer much guidance on how to tackle larger, more controversial and intractable issues.

Candor with one's comrades, however, is a simple lesson in which any worthy movement must be grounded. Granted that the challenges facing later movements were more difficult, deception did not make their work easier. An insidious arrogance that perverted the beliefs of some FSM participants ran through the Vietnam Day Committee (VDC). Some had argued that, even if the FSM did not know how to counter a bad policy, we should resist it and disrupt its enforcement in order to make "a moral statement." From this politics of feeling (for feelings are what such politics ultimately appealed to) it was a short step to believing that one need not seek alternatives because they would emerge somehow during the struggle. Finally, by 1966 Jerry Rubin could urge a march on Oakland when the VDC had no plan and knew that the Oakland police would let Hell's Angels through their lines to beat up demonstrators. Rubin rejected any obligation to warn marchers of the impending danger. He argued that we all knew the repressive nature of American society and the episode would merely reveal it, thus radicalizing participants. One cannot exaggerate the contrast between Rubin's duplicity and Mario's forthrightness in carefully extricating thousands of students, police, and bystanders from that first tense, potentially violent standoff around the police car. Denying the obligation to engage, which Mario and the FSM had relished, the VDC degenerated into a series of street disruptions that may or may not be excused by their importance to the antiwar movement, depending on one's view. For publicly rejecting this politics of cynical manipulation, many of us were called finks.

A larger sea change, the loss of a lively and politically engaged student body, ended another important legacy of the FSM. The job market for professors, doctors, and lawyers plummeted at the end of the 1960s. We in the FSM could devote time to out-of-class activity, which taught us as much as classes did. (I remember a student during the big sit-in who began plowing through his history and social science texts in a fruitless search for insights into how he had come to be a midnight trespasser awaiting arrest.) For all our political activity, we could still be assured of going on to professional or graduate school with lower grades than we might otherwise have compiled. But by the end of the 1960s professional openings were in shorter supply and graduate programs harder to get into.

The chilling effect was palpable. In 1973 I returned to Berkeley to pursue my doctoral studies and was a reader for Robert Blauner's sociology course. One day I began a standard drill on good writing by talking to the students about choosing a thesis, breaking down its major points, and marshaling evidence for each. The students' responses surprised me: "You're asking our opinion!" "We don't know; that's why we are here to learn." My suggestion that one learned through discussions with teachers and one's fellow students and by reading critically brought the reply "You're inviting us to disagree with the professor. How do we know he won't mark us down?" Having known Berkeley for years, I felt confident asserting that they misunderstood the rules of the game. Every professor I knew, I tried to reassure them, welcomed a contrary position if it was well argued and supported. Retorts came quickly: "You don't understand. We need to get into graduate school and can't take that risk." "The professor's job is to lay it out, ours is to spoon it back." I was truly unhinged. Were these Berkeley students? Later Blauner noted that I seemed to think the students were strange. "Of course," I said. "I was in Berkeley for five years and never heard students like these." "No," Blauner told me, "You were the strange ones. It's become apparent to us [faculty] that a special kind of student began coming here in the early sixties. They set a tone, but by 1970 they stopped coming. The students you saw today are the ones who were here before and have returned."

The FSM was a complicated experience. A window in time brought an apparently special group of students and faculty together. Students had been raised on the legacy of America as a moral force—championing freedom, helping to defeat Fascism and rebuild Europe, and finally grappling with its own domestic demons of poverty and racial injustice. The faculty emerged from McCarthyism's shadow and reasserted their role in campus governance. Holding the University accountable to the times and its legacy seemed an obvious imperative, and academic reforms at universities throughout the country followed the FSM. But the window closed: Kennedy and King were shot, Vietnam seemed to erase the honor of World War II, and the need for a job overwhelmed students. Motives are always difficult to disentangle, but a few of the most supportive faculty may also have left Berkeley in part because of the taxing pressure of hearing activists insist that they join in each new cause. Historian Carl Schorske's telling me during a concert intermission of his decision to leave for Princeton triggered one of the rare moments when I questioned what we had done.

In retrospect an endowment for books and a café memorializing three months in 1964 when the University came together seem fitting and proper. That relatively few leaders of the FSM's constituent political groups came to the Café opening is not terribly surprising. Many participants, after all, did not share the left's political views, and the FSM's legacy in broader areas faded with the sixties. People came to the Café not so much to reaffirm FSM politics as to remember an intense moment that revitalized the University and launched lifelong commitments and friendships. I realized that I was comfortable with the Café as a legacy. More than reconciliation has taken place. At least in accommodating political activity, the University has changed and now publicly honors the movement that forced it to. These days I also pay my respects at a little bronze plaque in the Plaza where in December 1997 the University memorialized the "Mario Savio Steps," well before any word of Silberstein's gift. Over three decades after the FSM, all of us must struggle with new issues and create new communities of concerned citizens. Some larger political issues of the FSM period have receded, but the underlying problems remain, and new movements must undertake the work of thinking them through and pursuing social change. The Café is there to remind us that this work can be done.

A View from the South

The Idea of a State University

Henry Mayer

I participated in the Free Speech Movement in the certain knowledge that I had exercised my rights as an undergraduate in Chapel Hill more fully than I was permitted to as a graduate student in Berkeley. I also brought to the controversy a vision of the public university as both a haven of freedom and a moral and intellectual beacon for the state that I had absorbed at the University of North Carolina and found distressingly missing from the University of California. Two factors, however, prevented me from expressing these convictions as thoroughly as I wanted. The prevailing stereotypes about the South as a cesspool of prejudice and ignorance made it difficult for people to accept sophisticated, nonconforming reports from the region. Even worse, at that very moment a repressive cloud, for the first time, hung over my alma mater in the form of a ban on Communist speakers imposed by a high-handed faction in the legislature egged on by a rising television editorialist named Jesse Helms. Thirty-five years later I still believe that the North Carolina experience—including the tortuous fight over the "speaker ban"—affords some illuminating comparisons for the FSM and Berkeley.

A personal experience will set the stage. In 1962–1963, my senior year at UNC, I headed the Carolina Forum, an agency of the student government responsible for bringing outside speakers to the campus to discuss political issues. The roster in my tenure had included a broad spectrum of guests such as Norman Thomas, Michael Harrington, William F. Buckley, Ayn Rand, and the UN correspondent for the Soviet news agency Tass, and I had presided at the lectures and conducted the ensuing discussion periods. In early spring 1963 a crisis had sprung up in nearby Durham, where the city council had denied a permit for Malcolm X (in town to dedicate a new mosque for the Nation of Islam) to speak in a city park. I called the newspapers to announce that the Carolina Forum would welcome Malcolm X as a speaker in Chapel Hill, and before nightfall he had accepted for the very next evening.

I don't remember how the connection was made, but the meeting evolved into a debate between Malcolm X and Floyd McKissick, a Durham attorney and head of the local CORE chapter, who was representing the Muslims in the fight with the city and who was one of the first black graduates of the UNC law school. I spent the entire day arranging for a hall and getting out flyers, having only had time to get an announcement into the morning *Daily Tar Heel* that Malcolm X would be speaking somewhere on campus that night. By midafternoon it became clear that the small auditorium I had booked would be inadequate, and I had to rework arrangements to move into the largest hall on campus. When I returned to my dorm room in late afternoon, I had a message that the chancellor wanted to see me as soon as possible.

The staff had gone home by the time I arrived at South Building, and I found the chancellor, a law school professor named William B. Aycock, alone at his desk. He genially asked me a few questions about the arrangements, nodding at the details of my report, and then grew expansive. In his eastern North Carolina drawl, Aycock declared that it would be "an interresting meetin'."

"Ah mean, you're gonna have on stage a Negro segregationist and a Negro integrationist, and in the audience you're gonna have white integrationists and white segregationists and Negro integrationists and maybe even a few Negro segregationists. . . ." He paused and added expansively, "and it takes all kinds."

I laughed, but I knew that the chancellor had not yet gotten to his point. He leaned forward and looked at me narrowly.

"I'll tell you someone else who might be there." He named our local state senator, a reactionary white supremacist. "And if he's there, he'll be drunk," the chancellor went on, "and if he gets up to cause a fuss, don't mess with him. Let Officer Beaumont handle him."

I took his point and went off to chair the meeting. The alcoholic legislator did not make an appearance, and the evening of passionate oratory and searching discussion passed into the record as another routine example of the opportunity for free discussion the Carolina Forum—and the University—had historically provided.

I don't think it could have happened this way at UC Berkeley. Campus regulations forbade the student government from taking positions on "off-campus issues" and left the administration in control of the "off"/"on" switch. To intervene in a free speech dispute in a neighboring city would have breached the rules as either inconsistent with the University's educational mission or an impermissible interjection of the University into politics—perhaps both, or maybe neither, since administrative reasoning could be capricious. (Academic freedom itself might be an interdicted topic; in 1960, when the student government protested the dismissal of a professor at the University of Illinois on the basis of a newspaper article he had written, the Berkeley chancellor, Glenn Seaborg, ruled the action "null and void" and informed the president at Illinois that he had done so.)[1] As a matter of fact, campus officials had barred Malcolm X from speaking on the Berkeley campus in May 1961, because he represented a religious organization.

Even if, for argument's sake, we assume that the rules applied only to the student senate itself and not to a student committee chair, it is highly unlikely that I could have intervened in an off-campus dispute as independently and as quickly as I could have at UNC without provoking an inquiry—and crippling delays—from a dean. The rules, after all, required all student organizations to have faculty advisers, to declare their purposes to be compatible with the University's and free of partisan or religious affiliation, and to abjure the advocacy of positions on off-campus issues. Had Malcolm X been denied permission to speak in Oakland, a Berkeley student group's invitation for him to speak on campus would almost certainly have been construed as a violation of the rule against taking positions on off-campus controversies. Even had my purpose passed muster, the campus rules required a week's notice to reserve a room, the signature of a faculty adviser on the request, and the employment of a tenured faculty member as moderator. To seek a waiver would have involved some form of administrative review and exerted a further chilling effect upon the effort to maintain an open forum. My expeditious campus effort at Chapel Hill to rectify a denial of free speech in the local community would, in all likelihood, have foundered at Berkeley, where campus speech existed largely on sufferance and in a context of prior restraint.

I remember being puzzled when I came to graduate school in September 1963 by the little entryway plaques that proclaimed the campus to be "the property of the Regents of the University of California with permission to pass revocable at will." I assumed the signs to be a product of some dim technical quirk of law and considered them an amusing antique. I did think about them, though, because I had come from a university that prided itself on being "the University of the people" whose boundaries, as the saying went, "were coterminous with those of the state." Not until the FSM began did I realize that the Regents' plaque expressed a philosophy of governance quite different from the democratic populism I had absorbed by osmosis in Chapel Hill.

UNC saw itself as a progressive and moral force in the state, and its one hundred trustees (one for each North Carolina county) understood their role as the protector of the University's freedom. "Whatever the administration," said the University's great New Deal leader, Dr. Frank Porter Graham, "the freedom of the University, gathering momentum across a century, and the democracy of the people, sometimes sleeping but never dead, will rise in majesty to reassert the intellectual integrity and the moral autonomy of the University of North Carolina."[2] The University of California, by contrast, had neither a grand sense of mission in the state nor a public constituency of alumni that defended its autonomy, and it had an oligarchic board of regents who ran the institution in ways that paralleled the corporate boards upon which many of them also sat. The Regency regarded the University not as an open community of intellect but as a domain something like a private shopping mall, a marketplace of ideas amenable to regulations that would exclude potential troublemakers and sustain the established interests of the state.

Carolina had Chancellor Aycock's laconic "It takes all kinds." Berkeley had President Kerr's intrusive declaration that the University is "not engaged in making ideas safe for students [but] in making students safe for ideas."[3] Each officer expressed core values from his campus tradition and a brief comparison will demonstrate the conditions underlying the FSM.

UNC had a 160-year-old history of autonomous student self-government, built upon the foundation of student debating societies and rooted in the responsibility of enforcing the student honor code. (Although imperfect in many respects, the honor system accorded students a measure of respect that mitigated some of the demeaning aspects associated with the doctrine of administrative in loco parentis.) The beloved "Dr. Frank" had explicitly affirmed the University's respect for students in his 1931 inaugural address, saying that academic freedom included "the freedom of students with their growing sense of responsibility and student citizenship to govern themselves, and the right of lawful assembly and free discussions by students of any issues and views whatever."[4]

California, however, regarded its students as "boys and girls" considered too immature for politics. In 1934 President Robert G. Sproul denounced as "insubordinate" UCLA students who had demanded a student-controlled open forum, and in 1936 he promulgated rules that required presidential approval for all off-campus speakers and forbade campus student groups from expressions of partisanship or advocacy of political action. When a professor recently dismissed from the University of Washington for refusing to sign a loyalty oath was scheduled to debate at UCLA in February 1949, the cautious provost felt obliged to confine the meeting to "mature" graduate students. Although undergraduates protested their exclusion from a discussion of matters that ran in all the newspapers, the provost got in trouble with Sproul and the Regents for allowing the man to speak at all. The episode proved one of the precipitating events in the ignominious loyalty oath controversy that further demonstrated the repressive and self-censoring quality of the Sproul administration.[5]

Students at UC, moreover, had no autonomous tradition of government; their organizations were creations of the chancellor and accountable to him. In 1961 a dissenting student party (SLATE), possessed of intellectual acumen and political fortitude, found itself transmogrified by fiat into an "off-campus" organization ineligible to participate further in student government. Two years earlier, to curb a potentially disruptive influence, the administration maneuvered the graduate students out of the ASUC on the basis of an informal poll that retrospectively became a binding referendum. This meant that half the student body at Berkeley at the time of the FSM lacked even the meager political standing accorded undergraduates. In one of the more ludicrous aspects of the post-FSM semester, I had the honor of being elected twice as a graduate student to the ASUC senate, once in a formal election in which the newly energized student government tried to reincorporate graduate students and once in a "freedom ballot" after administrators had concocted ex post facto rules to invalidate the results of the first election.

UNC also had a strong heritage of academic freedom and campus free speech that rested upon Jeffersonian bedrock and had enjoyed regular and powerful renewal under the leadership of two remarkable twentieth-century presidents, Harry Woodburn Chase (1919–1930) and Frank Porter Graham (1931–1949). Chase had recruited the pioneering sociologist Howard Odum, whose hard-hitting studies of regional poverty and the effects of racial discrimination were published by the UNC Press (another Chase innovation), and the president sturdily defended Odum and others from the wrath of the textile industry.[6] When religious fundamentalists tried to pass a law forbidding state-paid employees from teaching about evolution in 1925, Chase led the successful opposition, though he risked the University's budget in the process, saying, "If the university doesn't stand for anything but appropriations, I, for one, don't care to be connected with it." Graham said the "monkey bill" raised issues "older than the state of North Carolina . . . the Inquisition, the Index and the stake are its unclaimed ancestors" and praised Chase for upholding the University standard of "freedom to think, freedom to speak, and freedom to print." Graham inaugurated his own administration in 1931 by rhapsodizing about "the breath of freedom in the air" at Chapel Hill that existed not only for students and faculty but for "the unvoiced millions and the unpopular . . . even hated minorities," and he cautioned that "no abuse of freedom should cause us to strike down freedom of speech or publication, the fresh resources of a free university, a free religion, and a free state." The University motto, "Lux et Libertas," Graham said, meant that the University had a mission "to light up the heavens of the commonwealth with the hopes of light and liberty for all mankind."

At California, the motto, "Fiat Lux," had a more restrictive meaning. When President David P. Barrows defined academic freedom in his inaugural address of 1923 he confined its application to tenured faculty alone and cautioned that "the university is not an open forum [and] its platforms are not free to the uninstructed or to those without repute." Just as the permanent members of the University are "selected with great care and for reasons of confidence in their knowledge," Barrows reasoned, "so those who are invited to speak incidentally or occasionally must be judged with comparable consideration."[7] President Robert G. Sproul said not one word about academic freedom in his lengthy inaugural of 1930 but he quickly made plain his understanding that the campus could enjoy freedom only "within the framework of public good."[8]

The implicit assumption that the president and regents had sole power to define the public good flowed directly from another core assumption. The University had historically construed itself as "nonpartisan" and believed itself constitutionally bound not to exercise intellectual or moral leadership on the issues of the day. That this high-minded presumption of neutrality actually committed the institution to the perpetuation of the status quo and suppression of dissent did not seem to trouble many. However, at the height of the labor struggles of the 1930s, more polarized in California than anywhere else in the nation, the reform-minded editor Chester Rowell grew so appalled at the political intolerance manifested by his fellow Regents that he warned President Sproul (confidentially, of course) that if "we are going to impose the personal opinions of the old and the rich on the education of the young and aspiring, by transforming the University into a propaganda bureau for economic orthodoxy, we shall only be playing into the hands of the most dangerous sect of radicals."[9] When Sproul and the Regents mandated political orthodoxy in 1949–1950 by imposing a loyalty oath, they demonstrated further their understanding that freedom had to be constrained for their conception of the public good and showed that in times of crisis they would be conduits for the most reactionary elements in the state rather than sentinels against them.

By the time I arrived at Berkeley in the early sixties, the loyalty oath controversy had receded in public memory (though it still scarred the faculty in ways students never quite comprehended), and through the magic of federal money, public relations, and a marginally lighter hand on the throttle of campus rule enforcement, UC seemed a bustling, productive institution with an impressive amount of political activity. Indeed, President Kerr had received accolades for liberalizing the rules so that student groups—under the constraints earlier described—could invite outside speakers, including Communists, to the campus. These marginal changes, however much they ventilated the suffocating policy of the Sproul era, nonetheless struck me as stifling any genuine political autonomy for students. In fact, the political pulse beat most strongly at the margins of the campus, literally so at the Bancroft and Telegraph entrance where tables and soapboxes figuratively overshadowed the Regents' little plaque. Far from being honored as part of the University, the activities at the gateway went on in a legal and bureaucratic twilight zone of negotiated rights.

This was a paradox to me. In Chapel Hill the University served as a sanctuary for political dissent, whereas in Berkeley free speech seemed safer on the sidewalk, where it was constitutionally protected, than it did within the University, whose regulations infringed upon free speech ideals and the settled practice I had known down South. For someone who had come to Berkeley to prepare for a teaching career in the liberal arts, the paternalistic university culture I encountered was disheartening.

From my North Carolina perspective I did not sense that California had much soul, and indeed, President Kerr had just delivered an important set of lectures at Harvard proclaiming that the modern "multiversity" could not have, and did not need, a spiritual center. His University was a roiling mass of conflicting interest groups, held together by the much-maligned president who mediated among warring contenders by "being *equally* [emphasis in the original] distasteful to each of his constituencies" and "mov[ing] the whole enterprise another foot ahead in what often seems an unequal race with history."[10] When confronted by the claims of a rising new constituency of activist students intent upon advancing the Civil Rights Movement, the University's repressive history overwhelmed Kerr's theories of management, and he proved unable to accord students and their dissenting ideas equal standing in his managerial calculus. The FSM challenged the political history of the campus, and the University responded by denigrating the issue and disciplining the protesters.

Infuriating to me then, and no less galling today as I review the old documents, was the inability of University officials to hold themselves to the intellectual standards they extolled for the classroom. University spokesmen made assertions about constitutional law that could not be defended, and President Kerr, raised in the tradition of Quaker moral witness, spoke to the American Council on Education about civil disobedience in a manner that smeared its practitioners as "paying merely lip service to democratic ideals while in actuality serving the cause of anarchy."[11] The brass with which Kerr was said to have told the press that "49 percent of the hard-core group [of protesters] are followers of the Castro-Maoist line"[12] forfeited him, I felt, any further claim to intellectual respectability. The blithe manner in which administrators abandoned one set of sophistical distinctions for another would have earned an undergraduate a remedial semester in elementary logic and rhetoric. When Chancellor Strong told the Town and Gown Club, "Arbitrary exercise of authority is always to be challenged, but defamation of authority duly exercised undermines respect for high offices and demoralizes a society," he seemed unaware of his unspoken major premise that the authorities insisted upon controlling the definition of *arbitrariness*. If student government was a training ground, as the deanery proclaimed, its crass manipulation of the graduate student referendum suggested that we were being schooled for sullen participation in a totalitarian society.

I do not say these things facetiously. The culture of an educational community is shaped by the practices of the committee room as well as the classroom, yet I do not believe the responsible officers at Berkeley ever considered the messages inherent in their actions. Whatever their words, they taught submission, and when challenged, as is appropriate in an educational community, they responded with threats and punishment. This is not a lesson plan likely to succeed, yet nothing in the University's process expected its officers to regard their work as a form of teaching.

The FSM was a profound educational experience nonetheless. For thousands of us the long weeks of controversy proved an exhilarating intellectual adventure that examined not only constitutional law and political philosophy but the premises of university education itself. It is in this context that Mario Savio's leadership worked most profoundly, for it was his earnestness, his moral seriousness, his willingness to probe and speculate and examine questions from all sides, that set the standard for the movement. Although the media portrayed him as a demagogic rabble-rouser, he was really the FSM's Socratic teacher, and his oratory succeeded precisely because he voiced the ideas and the aspirations that we all had pondered and probed together. With poetic justice, it was from the steps of Sproul Hall, named for the architect of campus repression, that Mario Savio put into honest and noble practice the values of free speech and political assembly that the University had compromised for decades.

The long process of collaborative self-education in the FSM provided the model for the "teach-in" a few months later as campus communities began to examine the premises of the Vietnam War in forums that broke the boundaries of the classroom and the departments. The "prodigies of work . . . in organization, in research, in writing" evoked by the FSM impressed even its faculty critics, one of whom wrote that "many professors have been given quite a start to discover what stores of energy are locked in our students and untouched by the normal routine."[13] He was echoing a remark of Thomas Paine in *Rights of Man*, equally applicable to universities as to nations:

> It appears to general observation, that revolutions create genius and talents; but those events do no more than bring them forward. There is existing in man, a mass of sense lying in a dormant state, and which, unless something excites it to action, will descend with him, in that condition, to the grave. As it is to the advantage of society that the whole of its faculties should be employed, the construction of government ought to be such as to bring forward, by a quiet and regular operation, all that extent of capacity which never fails to appear in revolutions.[14]

Of course the FSM was not a revolution, but at its heart lay a controversy over citizenship. Would students have to sacrifice their constitutional rights to become subordinate members of a hierarchical academic society, or would the University have to relinquish some control over students in order to honor the fundamental values of the American political culture in which it too existed? The diversionary tactics of the administration made it difficult to pose this question in the state's leading newspapers, which readily bought into the "law and order" interpretation and regarded student activism either as a larky species of political panty raiding or as the harbinger of an alien "Latin Americanizing" tendency. The *San Diego Union* ran a mocking image of "School Daze," with beatniks strumming guitars and singing of "rioting, reading, and 'rithmetic," while the *San Francisco Chronicle*'s artist depicted nasty beret-clad figures named "rebellion," "disrespect," and "anarchy" climbing aboard a bespectacled Trojan horse labeled "phoney 'free speech' issue" poised in front of Sather Gate.[15] Such views epitomized one style of dismissal. The *San Jose Mercury*'s stern conclusion that "the university would be perfectly justified in clamping a lid on all non-school political activities . . . since the campus is, essentially, a place for study" expressed another widespread view that saw scant distinction between grade school and college.[16] Editorialists voiced confidence that few universities extended greater tolerance toward student political activity than UC, although most writers regarded this as a dubious virtue and called for the expulsion of protestors.

In a brief review of the daily newspapers in California's largest cities I found only one—the *San Francisco Chronicle*—that eventually came to an understanding that "universities are teachers, not policemen." On December 9, 1964, the day after the faculty had adopted a free speech policy that foreswore any regulation of content, the *Chronicle* declared that "a great university perforce must provide an arena for the free and open exchange of thought—no matter how repugnant any individual voice may be to anyone among us." The *San Jose Mercury*, by contrast, thought the faculty had "missed the point" that "the proper habitat of the soapbox is the street, not the university campus," while both the *Los Angeles Times* and *San Francisco Examiner* continued to insist that the real issue remained "Who shall run the university?" without any comprehension that the heavy-handedness of the Regency had led to the crisis.[17]

Not until the May 1965 appearance of the Byrne Report, a study of the Berkeley crisis commissioned by the Regents themselves (and whose publication they endeavored to suppress), did the state hear criticism of the rigid and meddlesome character of Regental governance.[18] Here, for the first time during the entire controversy, I heard advanced a conception of the university that resonated with the legacy I had brought from Chapel Hill. "The university is established by a wise society to be its continuing critic," wrote Jerome G. Byrne, a Southern California attorney appointed by the Regents as special counsel, and this function inevitably placed it in a state of creative tension with the larger society. The Regents had failed in their constitutional obligation to provide a system of governance that could cope with the "continuing and inevitable conflict between the values of the academic community and those of the larger society" and could maintain the independence of the life of the mind.

The report attributed the escalation of student dissatisfaction into "unmanageable crisis" to uncertain and divided leadership, hampered both by the Board's excessive involvement in operational decisions and a decades-long legacy of mistrust. To compound the problem, the analysis went on, the University had failed to honor its own principles by excluding students from discourse, prejudging the quality of speech or conduct, and establishing rules that prohibited students from acting on their own responsibility. Byrne made a number of specific proposals involving decentralization and delegation of powers, but the leading recommendation was an eloquent statement of the need for university autonomy. "The crucial power of the Regents is the power to reinvest in others the high faith placed in the Regents by the people," Byrne wrote. "This suggests that the Regents can and must *show the same faith* [emphasis in original] in the individual members of the academic community that the people of California have shown in the Regents, and must accord them the rights due to responsible citizens of a free community."

While the Regents heard, evidently for the first time, that they had misperceived their responsibilities, the trustees of my alma mater endeavored to defend the University of North Carolina from a sneak attack on its autonomy. I had no direct involvement in this, but even at second hand the "speaker ban" story offers a relevant coda. The law prohibiting known Communists or those who had taken the Fifth Amendment before congressional committees investigating subversion from speaking at state-supported campuses was rushed through the North Carolina General Assembly on the last day of its session in June 1963. Propelled by a disgruntled rump of right-wing, John-Birchite legislators who had lost all their other initiatives of the session, the attack surprised normally vigilant University officials. The sponsors made plain that their greatest hostility was directed toward the radicalism of Chapel Hill and the participation of many students in the interracial demonstrations for equality in public accommodations then occurring across the state, including the favorite watering holes of the legislators in Raleigh. (I am proud to say that in the week of my college graduation I marched and picketed in five North Carolina cities, all of which eventually agreed to desegregate.) Yet such was the strength of traditional campus freedom that even the segregationists—and their editorial spokesman Jesse Helms—did not dare to call for disciplining the students, as the right wing would soon seek in California, but rather tried to imprison the University trustees within their fevered theories that subversive outside agitators lay behind the protests.

The University's well-respected president, William C. Friday, backed by the trustees and many of the state's newspapers, whose editors were in many cases Chapel Hill grads, mounted a long campaign for reconsideration and repeal, but the political ground shifted beneath them when an arch-segregationist gubernatorial candidate threw his support to a moderate, Dan K. Moore, in order to defeat the putative liberal successor to the reform-minded Terry Sanford. The best the friends of the University could get—and this only after threats that UNC would lose its accreditation if its independence were breached—was a study commission that brokered a compromise that in 1965 amended the law in a way that let the trustees formulate their own restrictive policy. Though the trustees' new language was vague and gave a good deal of latitude to campus administrators, the statement deviated significantly from the University's traditional openness and provoked the rise of a student protest movement, the Committee on Free Inquiry, which issued speaking invitations to Frank Wilkinson, an opponent of HUAC who had refused to testify before it, and the historian Herbert Aptheker, a member of the Communist Party. When the president and chancellor, despite their personal opposition to the policy, capitulated to the political pressure and denied permission for the appearances, the students brought the visitors to the campus anyway, and after being duly excluded by Officer Beaumont, each speaker proceeded to a lectern on the adjacent town sidewalk while the audience gathered on the campus side of a low stone fence labeled "Governor Dan Moore's wall."

The staged protests led to a legal challenge that in 1968 held the law unconstitutional. "Despite its eventual repeal, the speaker ban was a victory for conservative forces," a recent study concludes, for it seriously compromised the cultural authority of the University as an exemplar of freedom and exposed the weakening power of liberalism in the state.[19] It laid the political basis for the party organization that in 1972 would send Jesse Helms to Washington for the first of his five terms in the U.S. Senate.

Ironies abound. In Berkeley the Regents had laid claim to a strip of sidewalk in order to keep student activism within the disciplinary control of the University. In Chapel Hill students had used the sidewalk to demonstrate the absurdity of drawing a line that could regulate the free flow of ideas. Campus free speech gained ground in the University of California, where it lacked traditional standing, just as it lost ground in North Carolina, where free speech was legendary and central to the University's identity. My alma mater was losing its soul just as my new campus discovered that it needed one.

NOTES

1. Verne A. Stadtman, *The University of California, 1868–1968* (New York: McGraw-Hill, 1970), 436; David Lance Goines, *The Free Speech Movement: Coming of Age in the 1960s* (Berkeley: Ten Speed Press, 1993), chapt. 11. When Chancellor Strong assumed office in 1962, he, too, ruled that the ban on off-campus issues extended to discussions of academic freedom, but he may have relaxed that view later in his tenure. (Eugene Bardach et al., "The Berkeley Free Speech Controversy: A Preliminary Report Prepared by a Fact-Finding Committee of Graduate Students," [1964, unpublished manuscript held in Free Speech Movement records, CU-309, University Archives, Bancroft Library, University of California at Berkeley], p. 18).

2. Frank P. Graham, "The University Today," 11 November 1931, reprinted as Appendix F in John Ehle, *Dr. Frank: Life with Frank Porter Graham* (Chapel Hill: Franklin Street Books, 1994), 276. In recent years, scholars have devoted attention to the accommodations southern liberals like Graham made on racial issues. See, for example, Daniel T. Rodgers, "Regionalists and the Burdens of Progress," in *Region, Race, and Reconstruction: Essays in Honor of C. Vann Woodward,* ed. J. Morgan Kouser and James M. McPherson (New York: Oxford University Press, 1982), 3–26. One might argue that Graham's temporizings on these matters are a parallel to the accommodations made by Clark Kerr and other University officers with the conservatism of the Regents and legislature, but Graham's had the effect of protecting the realm of university freedom, while the Californians' deliberately restricted it. Graham, of course, paid a high political price for his liberalism on racial matters (however circumscribed it appears to historians today) when he lost his U.S. Senate seat to the avowed white supremacist element he had long opposed (see note 6). Kerr ultimately lost his position, too, but to the right-wing forces he had tried, insufficiently as it turned out, to appease.

3. Kerr, Charter Day 1961, quoted in Goines, chapt. 11. The statement was intended as a defense of Kerr's reformed approach to off-campus speakers, specifically an appearance by Frank Wilkinson, against whose anti-HUAC remarks students were, in Kerr's view, satisfactorily inoculated.

4. Graham, "University Today," 275.

5. For UC in the 1930s, see Robert Cohen, *When the Old Left Was Young: Student Radicals and America's First Mass Student Movement, 1929–1941* (New York: Oxford University Press, 1993), 100–105, 118–29; for the 1949 UCLA debate see David P. Gardner, *The California Oath Controversy* (Berkeley and Los Angeles: University of California Press, 1967), 14–21.

6. See William D. Snider, *Light on the Hill: A History of the University of North Carolina at Chapel Hill* (Chapel Hill: University of North Carolina Press, 1992), chapts. 11–13 (quotations from 191–92, 204–5). Graham left the presidency in 1949 when appointed to a vacancy in the U.S. Senate. He was defeated at the next election after a viciously racist campaign orchestrated by the victor's press secretary, Jesse Helms. See Ehle, 174–78; Snider, 234–36; and the classic account, Samuel Lubell, *The Future of American Politics* (New York: Harper, 1952).

7. Barrows's address may be found on the "Days of Cal" website, <http://sunsite.berkeley.edu>.

8. See "Days of Cal" website for Sproul's address, at <http://sunsite.berkeley.edu.> Sproul quoted in Cohen, 105.

9. Quoted in ibid., 128.

10. Clark Kerr, *The Uses of the University* (Cambridge, Mass.: Harvard University Press, 1964), 40.

11. Kerr to the American Council on Education, 2 Oct. 1964, quoted in Terry F. Lunsford, *The "Free Speech" Crisis at Berkeley, 1964–1965: Some Issues for Social and Legal Research* (Berkeley: University of California Center for Research and Development in Higher Education, 1965), 67. The Lunsford volume, an extremely thoughtful survey, deserves to be better known; it is available on the FSM Archives website at <http://www.lib.berkeley.edu/BANC/FSM>.

12. *San Francisco Call-Bulletin*, 3 Oct. 1964.

13. Nathan Glazer, "Reply to Philip Selznick," *Commentary*, March 1965, reprinted in Seymour Martin Lipset and Sheldon S. Wolin, eds., *The Berkeley Student Revolt: Facts and Interpretations* (Garden City, N.Y.: Doubleday, 1965), 315.

14. Thomas Paine, *Rights of Man, Common Sense, and Other Political Writings* (New York: Oxford University Press, 1995), 228–29.

15. *San Diego Union*, 5 Dec. 1964; *San Francisco Chronicle*, 2 Oct. 1964.

16. *San Jose Mercury*, 4 Dec. 1964.

17. Ibid., 10 Dec. 1964; *San Francisco Chronicle*, 9 Dec. 1964; *Los Angeles Times*, 4 Dec. 1964; *San Francisco Examiner*, 2 Dec. 1964. A full study of the FSM coverage in both print and video media would be extremely valuable.

18. The Byrne Report was printed in full (along with stories of the Regents' displeasure and effort to withhold its publication) in the *Los Angeles Times*, 12 May 1965. The newspaper later reprinted the report as a pamphlet, from which edition my quotations are taken (*Byrne Report of the Forbes Committee of the Board of Regents* [Los Angeles: Los Angeles Times, 1965], 4, 9, and 17).

19. William J. Billingsley, *Communists on Campus: Race, Politics, and the Public University in Sixties North Carolina* (Athens: University of Georgia Press, 1999), 240. My account is also based on Snider, 271–79.

Endgame

How the Berkeley Grads Organized to Win

Steve Weissman

When Jack Weinberg, the tactical genius of the FSM, warned us never to trust anyone over thirty, I never imagined that at sixty I would be sitting deep in the French countryside looking back over what we had done at Berkeley so many years before. Was it that important? What, if anything, did we accomplish? And what particular role did our graduate students play?

In my view then and now, the FSM was not a big deal. Only as part of the larger Civil Rights and antiwar movements did our fight for free speech on the Berkeley campus take on any lasting significance.

Many of those most active in the FSM had worked in the South in Freedom Schools and voter registration programs, or across the country in direct action protests with CORE and organizational and support work with Friends of SNCC. Almost all would go on to stop troop trains, march, teach in, dodge the draft, and do whatever else we could to end our country's war in Southeast Asia. These were our experiences, our commitment, our inspiration, and they shaped how we came to understand free speech.

My situation was fairly typical. Before coming to Berkeley, I had been a graduate student at the University of Michigan and a not very active member of SDS. I still remember vividly the night in August 1963 when SNCC chairman John Lewis came to Ann Arbor to speak to us, testing the bombshell he intended to drop the following week at the big civil rights March on Washington. His words left no room to sit on the fence: If President John Kennedy wanted to support meaningful political and economic rights for the poorest black sharecroppers, good. If not, the movement would rise up without him like Sherman marching through Georgia.

I had already considered going to the march, but Lewis's speech ended any doubt. I called home to tell my parents—and ask for money to pay for the trip. My father was horrified. Though quite liberal on civil rights, he feared that I would be branded a radical and lose any chance to get a job as a college professor. "You'll end up a truck driver," he warned. Over the next few years, my father and I would have many opportunities to repeat the same conversation.

Like many of his generation, my father was scared. Our family lived in a midsized southern town where newspaper editorials and commentators regularly tarred Martin Luther King, Jr., as a Communist or Communist dupe. We'd already had a cross burned on our lawn for my daring to introduce an antisegregation resolution in my high-school student senate. And we were Jewish, a tiny minority in a very conservative Christian community. To his credit, Dad sent the money in spite of his reservations, and I trooped off to Washington with a bunch of SDSers. There we were, right in front of the Lincoln Memorial, waiting for John to give his speech and singing that old civil rights favorite "If Kennedy gets in the way, we'll roll right over him."

How wrong we were! On that day at least, Kennedy and his supporters in the March leadership rolled right over us. If John insisted on giving his speech as he had written it, the Reverend Eugene Carson Blake of the National Council of Churches and others threatened to withdraw from the list of speakers. John softened his speech a bit; we continued to sing and no one heard us.

I learned a lot about free speech that day, and about the willingness of so many good-hearted liberals to exercise their own power over who should speak and what they should be allowed to say. My instincts, and I think those of most of my generation, were far more open, libertarian, and anti-authoritarian. Let everyone have his or her say and let the listeners decide for themselves. Among those of us who had seen Bob Moses, Stokely Carmichael, or other SNCC field secretaries stand up in meetings and quietly challenge any unquestioned acceptance of authority, these instincts grew even stronger.

SNCC had come to its attitude the hard way. Organizing the poorest of poor blacks, SNCC organizers worked every day with people who had learned to survive by continually giving in to white authority. SNCC undid their submissiveness by teaching them to ask, "Who made that decision?" SNCC taught the same question to many young white middle-class radicals.

In my own case, I also read too many books by and about Spanish, Italian, Russian, and American anarchists, who still fascinate me in a way no Bolshevik ever did. Does anyone remember Marcello Mastroianni's poignant portrayal of an anarcho-syndicalist in that wonderful Italian film *The Organizer*? For many years, Mastroianni's character was my secret Mickey Mantle.

In the spring of 1964, while teaching and studying in Spain, I sent a letter to the SNCC office in Atlanta applying to work in the movement. I never got a reply. So, faute de mieux, I showed up at Berkeley in September, only to find the University administration bringing a police car onto campus to stop recruiting for civil rights protests in neighboring Oakland and San Francisco. Like thousands of other Berkeley students, I saw a blatant assault on free speech, which I am certain I would have opposed even if the University were trying to ban the American Nazi Party, Ku Klux Klan, or John Birch Society. Apart from my eagerness to defend the First Amendment, my antiauthoritarian bent would have balked big-time at some bureaucrat telling me which groups I could and could not listen to.

But for me and most of the students I came to know—and for the hapless administrators—the issue was far more concrete. What Berkeley bureaucrats were trying to stop was not free speech in the abstract nor the insignificant ranting of some right-wing fringe. They were banning specific, highly effective speech that helped Bay Area blacks fight discrimination in public accommodations and hiring. That gave added significance—and energy—to our fight for free speech. It also determined what we could and could not accept, all the more as we came to understand the legal ins and outs of First Amendment thinking. Many brilliant, well-meaning professors never did understand why free speech had to include the right to advocate illegal activity. For the civil rights veterans in FSM, the reason became increasingly obvious. In recruiting for off-campus civil rights protests, student activists often advocated breaking the law in nonviolent civil disobedience. Supreme Court rulings backed our reading of the First Amendment, but even if they had not, we would have taken the same stand.

Were we intransigent? Absolutely. It was the only way to win what we were fighting for. Yet, through it all, we were rarely intolerant. Meetings of FSM's Executive Committee and Graduate Coordinating Committee (GCC), both of which I came to chair, encouraged vigorous, often rollicking debate. We even opened the floor to those in our midst who were conniving with administration envoys to scuttle the movement.

Compare this with the attitude of administrators and faculty who tried to keep me from speaking at the graduate school meeting in Pauley Ballroom in November, then used campus police to haul Mario away at the Greek Theatre on December 7. To borrow from William Burroughs in *Naked Lunch*, I'm afraid that our would-be mentors were tight-assed control freaks and, in their own way, a bit Stalinesque.

FSM's greatest accomplishment, in my view, grew directly out of our libertarian bent, capping the efforts of SNCC, SDS, and an earlier generation of Berkeley activists featured in another epic film, HUAC's *Operation Abolition*. If HUAC only knew how many of us first thought of coming to Berkeley after seeing that film.

Much as HUAC had warned, our victory helped cripple anticommunism as an effective weapon against social and political change. By anticommunism, I don't mean opposing either the Soviet Union or small Leninist vanguards acting in the name of "the masses." As it happens, I never liked the Soviets and always thought the masses did better acting for themselves. But anticommunism as we came to understand it had little to do with communism or any real Communist threat. It was much more about smearing Martin Luther King to stop integration, red-baiting Claude Pepper to quash universal health care, investigating "Communist influence" to smash unions, and hyping the Red Menace to sell tanks, planes, and U.S. intervention everywhere from Guatemala to Vietnam. Anticommunism was an ideological virus that infected the entire culture, especially when liberals and social democrats embraced the Cold War abroad and at home, falling all over themselves to deny they were ever Communists, to denounce those who were, and to drive every suspected radical from any movement for reform.

Our response was different: we just said "no."

Take FSM's decision to include Bettina Aptheker in the leadership. The daughter of a highly visible American Communist, she made a statement just by being there, not to mention her personal contribution in smoothing ruffled edges and bringing opposing groups together. With Bettina on the Steering Committee, FSM told the world that free speech had to be for everyone, including Communists, and that red-baiting would never dissuade, divert, or divide us.

Did that stop the smears? Not at first, and the worst came from our liberal and social-democratic friends. Within our supposedly united front, the Young Democrats and Young People's Socialist League never stopped warning of Communist militancy, manipulation, and domination. Tirelessly, they spread their scare stories to faculty, administrators, and even Governor Pat Brown. Beyond campus, there were always willing journalists, some of whom we assumed to be speaking for University president Clark Kerr, whom we saw as the source for the most outrageous attacks. One notorious column charged that 49 percent of FSM leaders were Maoists or Castroites. For whatever reason, I was picked to rebut the attack in a local television interview. It seemed the perfect opportunity for a send-up. Carefully dressed in my Joe College rowing sweater, I put on a completely straight face and told the reporter, "No, I believe the figure is closer to 58 percent."

Not content, I went looking for trouble. Chairing a noontime rally on Sproul Hall steps following the abortive sit-in of November 23, I explained that the massive screwup wasn't really our fault. Soviet premier Nikita Khrushchev had just been deposed, and we didn't have the phone numbers of the new guys in the Kremlin to get our daily instructions. Everyone in the plaza laughed, but I'm told that my stupid joke made the pages of a California state senate report naming me as one of the FSM's top Commies. Who cared? I could always drive a truck.

Few of my fellow students were quite so reckless, but most learned to inoculate themselves against the anti-Communist disease with small doses of courage and large dollops of laughter. By the following spring, red-baiting had almost no effect on our antiwar protests.

At the time, I was traveling to dozens of southern campuses, spreading fear of Berkeley among college administrators and building student support for SDS's antiwar March on Washington. Even at the smallest, most remote schools, I found a similar, if less pronounced, weakening of the anti-Communist virus, in part because of the media-driven impact of what we had done at Berkeley, but far more, I suspect, from a youthful skepticism "blowing in the wind." How many times could anti-Communists scare people with the Bolshevik bogeyman before they just had to laugh in their faces?

Whatever its cause, the weakening of anticommunism had enormous impact. Without it the antiwar movement could well have been crushed or turned in on itself, civil rights leaders like King would have found it even harder to come out publicly against the war, and as General Curtis LeMay suggested, America might well have bombed Vietnam into the Stone Age, then repaved it as a parking lot.

Paradoxically, the activists at Berkeley least responsible for the success of our anti-anticommunism were the Communists, and for good reason. Many of them came from families who knew firsthand the blacklists, beatings, and jailings of the late 1940s and early 1950s. Poor Bettina wouldn't even admit she was a member of the party until many months later, and we all understood her reluctance. Most of us just didn't share it. Sons and daughters of middle-class America, we felt bullet proof.

One sad result of the Communists' fear was that, except for Bettina, they never got the kudos they deserved. I remember meeting the educator Christopher Jencks socially right after he did staff work for the Byrne Report on FSM. "The report's finished," he told me in a conspiratorial tone. "I just want to know for myself—how important were the Communists in the FSM?"

"Very," I said.

"Through Bettina?" he asked.

"Not really," I smiled. "Mostly through me."

I was only half joking. One of my closest friends in FSM was a fellow history grad named Bob Kauffman, a former Freedom Rider in the South and a leading light in the Northern California Communist Party. Bob was one of the warmest, brightest, most sensible people I had met at Berkeley, and he played a leading role in both the GCC and the FSM Executive Committee. Whenever he thought those of us on the Steering Committee were racing ahead too fast for the rest of the movement, he'd sit me down and set me straight. Nasty old red that he was, Bob's advice was always rather moderate and often right on the mark.

No one I knew in the Communist Party at the time understood better than Bob how battle-scarred and gun-shy the Old Left had become, and how much this older generation of radicals had to learn from the energy, imagination, and daring of the New Left. He once joked that the Los Angeles smog really started when all the scared old Commies in Southern California raced out to their backyards to burn their Marx and Lenin. Bob died a few years after the FSM without ever getting credit for his role in keeping the movement on course. In many ways, he epitomized the role the graduate leaders played, a role that Mario Savio, Jack Weinberg, and many undergraduates never seemed to grasp. Perhaps we looked too close to thirty, or close to our professors, in whose sleepy footsteps the action faction expected us to falter.

The graduate strategy, as we came to see it, was to build within the FSM a mass movement of grad students committed to fight for free speech in the way we defined it. Like SNCC field secretaries or Marcello Mastroianni's anarcho-syndicalist, we saw ourselves as organizers above all else, working every day in most of the graduate departments to explain our positions, cajole our fellow grads, defend Mario and the movement, and create departmental action groups, which some of us laughingly called "soviets."

Grad student leaders also favored direct action, and only once broke with Jack and Mario on using it. This was over the abortive sit-in of November 23, which we felt lacked sufficient support. I still remember the heat I took personally for publicly speaking out against the sit-in, violating some unwritten rule of democratic centralism that I never would have agreed to follow. As it happened, having some of the Steering Committee visibly opposed to the sit-in made it far easier to reunite the FSM after the sit-in petered out.

Why did this sit-in lack support when two weeks later we could mobilize nearly fifteen hundred students to put their bodies on the line? The answer is easy. In November the FSM seemed to be escalating the conflict on its own initiative. In December we were responding to an atrocity—the administration's move to expel Mario and others and to throw several groups off campus. That move went against our American grain, and, as was true throughout the sixties, to build support for a major direct action, we often did better reacting to atrocities than acting on our own.

In planning the abortive sit-in, no one on the Steering Committee was thinking clearly. Only days before, the Regents had publicly announced that they intended to press ahead with disciplinary proceedings. But our direct action faction was in no mood to wait, and in the mad rush of the moment, none of us ever recalled the Regents' announcement.

Apart from this one sit-in, the grad organizers generally viewed direct action as a great tool to wake people up, force them off the fence, build their commitment, and—when properly deployed—to escalate the conflict, which we had to do if we wanted to win. But, in our view, direct action alone would never force the administration to give in, not even a massive sit-in with hundreds of arrests. What would? For starters, a strike led by the TAs, the underpaid, overworked teaching assistants who taught so many of the undergrad courses. TAs were central to all our organizing and the key to victory as we saw it.

We had talked about a strike since October, when Benson Brown and others in the math department first raised it as a serious possibility. The idea gained strength as worried faculty began prematurely threatening retaliation. Besides bringing more TAs to our side, these threats helped convince us that maybe, just maybe, a strike could work.

On November 28 the administration sent disciplinary letters to Mario and the others, and the FSM Steering Committee began planning a sit-in for December 2. On the Thursday or Friday before the big day, a jam-packed meeting of the GCC overwhelmingly called for a strike the following week "if conditions warrant." For Mario, the sit-in would be an existential cry. For the grad organizers, it was more of a trigger to further action.

The sit-in itself was fabulous, truly "a festival of the oppressed." But, in the interest of historical accuracy, let me clear up two minor misperceptions. Our "Free University of California," at which grad students taught freedom courses during the sit-in, echoed an SDS slogan, "A Free University in a Free Society." But we picked the name primarily because we liked the initials "FUC." Who made that decision? I did, along with several similarly salacious fellow students.

Of even less importance, nobody ordered me to sneak out the window and climb down the rope to run the strike. The GCC had already named a strike committee headed by Brian Mulloney and Susan Stein, and they hardly needed me. What happened was more chaotic. Just as the police were closing in, someone yelled that I should leave so we would have a Steering Committee member on campus and not in jail. I don't think I ever knew who made the decision, though I'm sure I would have taken their name in vain when I found myself dangling from a rope with very little idea of what to do next.

Spurred by the image of cops on campus arresting fellow students, our strike succeeded better than we ever expected, closing down most University departments. But the grad organizers still had major work to do. We had decided that the best way to insure victory was to win over a majority of the professors, then get the administration to give in to them. This would allow the administrators to save face, though probably not their jobs, and we didn't really care whether the FSM or the faculty had the honor of accepting their surrender.

Grad students had begun talking to professors from the moment the police car came on campus, well before we formed the GCC. But as we became increasingly convinced that free speech had to include the right to advocate illegal acts, we were continually astounded by how little the faculty knew about First Amendment law. Most just wanted to defuse the conflict and could not grasp why we wouldn't soften our stand. I remember personally telling some rather sympathetic profs that we'd rather have two of them support our position publicly than two hundred trying to work out an inadequate compromise. I'm sure they found me utterly unreasonable.

The sit-in and arrests, the strike and the campus police dragging Mario off-stage at the Greek Theatre dramatically changed the conversation, forcing increasing numbers of the faculty to think through what we were saying. In every department, our grad organizers spent those final days talking to every professor in sight. Many of them came to agree with us, finding our arguments persuasive once they took time to listen. But even at this distance, I suspect that we finally won our majority in the Academic Senate largely because the professors feared what we might do next.

The funny thing is that none of us had the slightest idea. Happily, it never mattered. Our endgame worked, and just as the grad organizers had planned, the administration gave in to the faculty, securing a famous victory for the Berkeley FSM.

A View from the Margins

David A. Hollinger

The story of the Free Speech Movement is usually told from the perspective of its recognized leaders and of persons who have volunteered to serve as the historic voices of the FSM decade after decade. Their constructions dominate our picture of the FSM, as well they should. There is no substitute for top-down history. The men and women who did the most to define the movement at the time and whose later lives have been the most obviously caught up in its legacy are rightly the center of our historical gaze. But additional dimensions of the FSM may come into view if we supplement these familiar accounts with the testimony of another class of persons: those who were moved and influenced by the experience of the FSM as students and then went their various ways. The testimony of these rank-and-file participants might expand our understanding of the movement and its consequences for those touched by it.

The people I have in mind generally made no effort to conceal their sixties experiences, but they wrote no memoirs about them. Their indisposition to talk more than they do about the FSM might reflect, in some cases, a realistic sense that, in the larger scheme of things, the FSM was not such a big deal—at least not when compared to the risking of one's life in a voter registration drive in Mississippi, which some, including Mario Savio, did during the summer preceding the FSM. The rank-and-file FSM participants to whom I refer have done little boasting and apologizing about the FSM and have been content to leave the debate about the meaning of "the sixties" largely to those whose lives continued to revolve around what they did way back then. Their friends are often only vaguely aware, if at all, of this phase of their lives ("Oh, so you were at Berkeley in the sixties; did you know Mario Savio, whose death I read about recently?"). These inconspicuous veterans of the FSM, who have long since moved on to other things, are scattered here and there in any number of vocations, including academia.

I am one of these people. I exercised no leadership in the FSM. I was not arrested. I never spoke from the Sproul Hall steps. These nonactions I share with countless others. Our modest contributions to the movement were limited by and large to carrying a sign during demonstrations and attending meetings at which principles and strategies were debated at exhausting length. But if our impact on the movement was slight, the movement's impact on us was sometimes substantial. I do not want to imply that most of the others in this category would bear witness to the same features of the experience that seem the most important to me. No doubt each of us has his or her own sixties, which overlaps only in part with that of our generational peers. The more deeply marked one is by an experience, some would say, the more distinctively individual is the mark it leaves. In any event, I pretend to no overall interpretation. I offer here a view from the margins without supposing that the particular margins on which I stood are the only interesting ones. The FSM had a prodigious circumference. Its margins were many and extensive. Perhaps that in itself is a point of historical significance not always registered in the memoirs of the movement's leaders.

An indicator of my own marginality is the fact that one of my most vivid recollections of the year of the FSM concerns an incident showing the cordial relationship between Mario Savio and the philosophy professor Joseph Tussman. I was present when Savio gave a speech at Sproul Plaza during which he warned that what was then known as the "Tussman plan"—a pilot program for an alternative structure for undergraduate liberal arts education along the lines of the intensive, rigorous study of Great Books—was in the process of being "shelved." Savio was appalled at this and sought to enlist student support for Tussman in what was widely seen as Tussman's righteous battle against defenders of the status quo among the faculty and administration. Tussman himself was in the audience that day and rushed up to Savio and whispered in his ear for a few seconds. Savio then returned to the microphone and explained to a silent and expectant crowd that the Academic Senate might still back Tussman, so all was not over with the Tussman plan. Then Savio vehemently reasserted his support for Tussman's effort to reform undergraduate education.

This tiny incident tells us something about the cultural diversity of the FSM that is often missed in its popular representations. Some student supporters of the FSM were sufficiently engaged by intellectual issues and sufficiently concerned about the state of higher education that they could take an interest in the faculty's debate over the Tussman plan. Michael Rossman, another person who, like Savio, was prominently identified with the

FSM, was actually hired by Tussman to teach in the program. This particular combination did not work, and Rossman was soon separated from the Tussman program. But several years later while at the State University of New York at Buffalo, I, along with several other newly minted assistant professors in humanistic and social scientific disciplines, helped to found a teaching unit modeled on the Tussman program. I invoke my involvement with "Vico College," as we Buffalonians of 1970 called our version of the Tussman plan, to underscore the fact that the FSM was commodious enough to have room for a respectful attitude toward the highly classical, unapologetically canonical, aggressively Socratic approach to education defended by Tussman.

If Clark Kerr was Berkeley's Bentham in the 1960s, Tussman was its Coleridge. Kerr's frankly utilitarian approach to higher education, as displayed in his *Uses of the University*, contrasted with the concern for the mind's interior that was manifest in Tussman's experiment. The analogy to Bentham and Coleridge may seem strained, but it was compelling to me in the context of John Stuart Mill's essays on Bentham and Coleridge, which many of us at Berkeley in those years read under the tutelage of one of the campus's greatest teachers, Carl Schorske.

The FSM had within it some decidedly "Coleridgean tendencies." Or, to put the point more precisely, some people drawn to the FSM possessed what I am calling Coleridgean tendencies and did not feel them to be in tension with their allegiance to the FSM. This way of putting it intentionally begs the question of what properties help constitute a movement and what properties are carried by some of its adherents without being salient to the movement's essence. Just what that essence was I will leave to others to debate. But whatever else the FSM may have been, it was a means by which some of us addressed, however awkwardly, our concerns about the nature of universities and their role in society.

Of the Coleridgean tendencies I recall so vividly and of which I partook, there is little trace in the voice David Lance Goines brings to the telling of the FSM story in his book of 1993, *The Free Speech Movement: Coming of Age in the 1960s*. Goines mentions Tussman only in the latter's capacity as a faculty politician, not in his capacity as an educational reformer whose specific reforms were appreciated by at least some students in the FSM. Some of the sources Goines reprints do convey something of the diversity of moods manifest within the FSM, but the distinctive feature of Goines's book is its authorial voice, which affirms what are to me the FSM's least attractive and least defensible aspects. Flippant, uninterested in institutions, ungenerous in representing the motives and character of folks who felt differently than he did about the issues, Goines gives us the FSM at its most giddy and self-absorbed. But in displaying this sensibility, Goines has performed a valuable service. His book is an ideal corrective to the picture of the FSM that might emerge if all one had to go on was the testimony of people like me. Goines, so far as I can discern from his book, cared not one whit for academic culture and never pretended to. For me and those to whom I was the closest in 1964–1965, the FSM was always bound up with the relation of academic values to social justice. But Goines's I'm-in-it-mostly-for-fun voice is absolutely authentic. In that voice, his book recounts many incidents that I remember much as he does. He is not making it all up. The sensibility Goines expresses was indisputably manifest in the FSM; indeed, that sensibility is surely more representative than my own, perhaps many times over.

Another virtue of Goines's joyride mentality is that it shares with Savio's earnest, intellectual, pensive side a certain capacity to confuse, if not to disrupt, some of the standard narratives of campus politics in the 1960s. Those narratives are often generated by two parties to the cultural wars of the last quarter century. The one party is eager to see the campus radicalism of that decade as a healthy and progressive moment in human liberation, in the manner of Mark Kitchell's documentary film *Berkeley in the '60s*. The other side is eager to discredit the whole thing as decadent and dangerous, in the manner of George Will and Newt Gingrich and Alan Bloom. Both of these parties are inclined to hold the FSM—when they refer to it at all—hostage to whatever they wish to claim about the history of the 1960s as a whole and the pernicious, or virtuous, effects of campus radicalism on the culture, society, and politics of the United States. The idealizers and the trashers each have their uses of "the sixties."

Neither party is well served by Goines's glib, almost principled immaturity nor by Savio's sober and brooding Coleridgean aspect. The trashers can make some use of Goines, but his voice is too fun loving and upbeat—too charming!—to be of wide-ranging polemical utility. Besides, Goines himself has inconveniently gone on to become neither a murderer nor a dropout but a disciplined and creative artist whose tasteful posters for Chez Panisse and other Bay Area commercial and nonprofit enterprises hang from the walls of many homes to which the Wall Street Journal is delivered daily.

For Savio's engagement with Tussman the trashers have no use at all. When reminded of it they sometimes deny its reality. It is too threatening. When I called attention to the Tussman-Savio connection in a 1994 symposium marking the FSM's thirtieth anniversary, I was angrily accused of distorting history. The trashers thus tend to overlook the FSM or to shoehorn it into a generic vision of sixties radicalism that derives what legitimacy it has from events that took place after 1967. The trashers are better served by the bombing of ROTC buildings and by the praise the Weather Underground's Bernadine Dohrn awarded to the Charlie Manson family for "offing the pigs." That's *their* 1960s.

The idealizers, on the other hand, are more likely than the trashers to refer to the FSM. But the idealizers usually care less about the distinctive features and diverse constituency of the FSM than about those of its generic aspects that enable one to make the entire episode of sixties campus radicalism look good today. An exception to this rule is indeed *Berkeley in the '6os,* which does an unusually scrupulous job of indicating the differences between the FSM and later movements at Berkeley. The idealizers do not get much help from Goines because his approach does not yield the broader political engagements and accomplishments on which the idealizers want to concentrate. Moreover, too much of what Goines reports can now seem silly, the antics of a lot of college kids trying to grow up but largely failing.

Yet the idealizers cannot get much mileage out of the T. S. Eliot–quoting and Tussman-appreciating side of Savio, either. Such respect for the old European canon is too conservative educationally and makes the FSM sound more like the last gasp of "the fifties" than anything relevant to a conversation about "the sixties." Moreover, Savio's Coleridgean impulses, like Goines's joyride, can come across as insufficiently politicized. So it is that we hear quoted over and over again Savio's speech about the odiousness of the machine and the need to stop it by putting our bodies on its levers. That's the side of Mario Savio that remains the most useful to the idealizers. Insofar as the FSM fits into *their* 1960s, that's where the fit is the most comfortable.

It would be inaccurate to depict the FSM as exclusively, or even predominantly, a movement of relentlessly serious intellectuals concerned about liberal values, social justice, and the relation of higher education to politics. Goines's book can serve as a reminder of how mistaken this depiction would be. For me personally, however, the FSM was mostly just that. What made it so was not only the reality of the threat to the classical liberal value of free speech, as my friends and I understood the specific points at issue between the FSM and the campus administration. Nor was it simply the close connection between the FSM and the Civil Rights Movement, vital as this connection was to the moral claims of the FSM. Nor was the character of the FSM experience for me defined by these two things even when combined with the imperative to protect the University's honor from vested interests in California eager to stifle the University's critical potential, although this mattered enormously to me and many of the other graduate students with whom I discussed the campus situation constantly. Beyond all that was another cluster of engagements that became indissolubly bound up with these three.

During the late November–early December weeks of 1964, when I was the most involved in the FSM, I was simultaneously reading Perry Miller's books on colonial New England for a graduate seminar. The moral intensity of Miller, of his Puritan subjects, and of the FSM's advocacy of free speech was a formidable combination. The subject matter I was studying, the scholar through whose eyes I was studying that subject matter, and the immediate political and social environment in which I was living all reinforced one another in a kind of spiral of moral seriousness. My immediate circle was made up of graduate students who were trying to figure out what they believed about academic professionalism generally and about the historian's calling in particular. Not everyone came to the same conclusions or held in later years to the particular position they developed during that era of fervency. But the atmosphere was one of deep searching, one in which the behavior of individuals and groups within the administration, the faculty, and the political elites of California was felt to be highly relevant to one's assessment of the role of scholars and scientists in society. My friends and I constantly scrutinized and evaluated the behavior of ourselves and of the major actors in the drama, especially the faculty's Academic Senate.

We attended carefully to reports of the activities of the various groups within the Senate, above all one known as the "Committee of 200." Historians were prominent in this collection of faculty sympathetic with the FSM, which also included two professors of English much appreciated in my circle, Henry Nash Smith and Charles Muscatine. The latter was known for having refused to sign the notorious loyalty oath imposed by the Regents during another campus crisis fifteen years before. During those several weeks, life outside of class seemed to have become an all-day, half-the-night informal seminar involving everyone I knew discussing the meaning of the university and of the life of the mind in relation to the rest of the world. Although I had yet to read Max Weber's essays on the vocation of science and on the vocation of politics, graduate students from political theory and sociology quoted them regularly, and skeptically. Many of these freewheeling discussions took place on the Terrace, a section of what is now the Cesar Chavez building that was then a gathering place for graduate students. There, I alternated between reading chapters of Miller's *Jonathan Edwards* and joining in debates of campus issues at nearby tables. Yet I admired the strict professionalism of Robert Middlekauff, in whose course Miller's works were being addressed. Middlekauff's personal sympathies for the FSM were undisguised, but when we went to his classroom in Haviland Hall we knew we were there to talk about Puritanism, and we did.

When the Senate approved by an 8-1 margin the December 8 resolutions to support the key demands of the FSM, this seemed to me and to most others I knew to be a reassuring vindication of academia. The faculty had met its responsibility after all; it had addressed the crisis head-on and saved the honor of the University. I personally was greatly strengthened in my resolve to pursue an academic calling. And I formed a view of the potential importance of faculty senates. My own determination always to be involved in faculty governance dates from December 8, 1964.

Hence the particular margins of the FSM to which I can bear witness are decidedly academic. And it is from these particular margins that I want to address, in closing, the character of Mario Savio.

The word most often attached to Mario Savio in countless press accounts, from the fall of 1964 until his recent death, is *fiery*. This adjective, at least as applied to Savio, invites some commentary. If Savio spoke with passion and was capable of volatility, and was thus fiery in this familiar sense of the term, he was also fiery in another sense: he carried the torch of rational analysis. His speeches often included detailed arguments about the implications of this or that principle; he made distinctions; he was an Enlightenment-style demystifier who brought inherited institutions and practices under rigorous scrutiny. In later life he proved to be, after all, a gifted teacher of science, a calling that did not surprise me in the least as I found it fully compatible with the qualities that in the 1960s distinguished Savio from many other, less reason-centered speakers to whom I listened throughout that decade. Mario Savio brought to the debates of public meetings—arenas so often for demagoguery, manipulation, and ego tripping—an intense commitment to real discussion, to open debate. He wanted people to be persuaded, through honest and fair dialogue, that a given course of action was the right one. Savio also turned the torch of demystification on himself; he interrogated himself rigorously; he was visibly capable of self-doubt. That's why he, alone of the Berkeley students who gave themselves to the movement in those years, is an emblem for "my" 1960s.

It is somewhat misleading that the one speech of Savio most often quoted is the one about laying one's body on the levers of the machine. I complain of this by way not of diminishing the significance of that speech but of insisting that, had somebody else said those exact words, they would not have had the same effect on the same people. That legendary utterance, so often taken as the greatest example of Savio's "fire," was given credibility by the kinds of things he had been saying for the previous two months, by the genuine effort he had made to bring intellect to the issues before the movement, by the fire of his reason.

So, that's *my* 1960s; not Woodstock, not the slogans and the chants, not the gratuitous personal cruelties inflicted in the name of honest relationships, but the sincere if inadequate effort to unite reason and affection, to render intimate the flame of learning and the flower of love, to enact in secular time T. S. Eliot's Christian prophecy of a moment when the "tongues of flame are enfolded into the crowned knot of fire, and the fire and rose are one." As long as the Campanile stands in Berkeley, let the memory of Mario Savio stand there, too, as a column of fire.

Dressing for the Revolution

Kate Coleman

There were plenty of red-diaper babies—children of Commie parents—in lefty politics at Berkeley, but I was not among them. I was a Valley Girl from Encino, California. John Wayne lived on my corner. Patty Andrews, one of the Andrews Sisters, lived across the street. My parents were divorced when I was ten years old. My mother was blind from the time I was three and had additional health problems that prevented her from a working life or even participating fully as a parent. We lived in my rich uncle's discarded old house in Los Angeles. He'd moved on to Beverly Hills. You could say I was bourgeois, given my neighbors and address, but I suffered from a Cinderella complex, in part because we were poor relations and my mother couldn't see to dress me. I worried a lot about being presentable. I preface my treatise with this personal history because it perhaps explains my desire to appear normal no matter what the circumstances, even within the parameters of my growing disaffection with authority at Berkeley.

My rebel-versus-Valley-Girl tensions began in high school, foreshadowing the lefty I would become: I was sent to the principal's office, for example, for refusing to "drop" during a nuke "drop drill," telling my teacher I thought it was a stupid exercise in futility; and I wrote for a mimeographed poetry magazine that the school eventually banned because of one bard's poem about kissing a breast. And, more to the sartorial point, I dressed like a beatnik, but a neat one, in black skirt, tights, and, my favorite, a little plaid corduroy vest. My black hair and long bangs completed the picture.

Such high-school nonconformity was a prelude for Berkeley, and I went gaga when I got here, hooking up with SLATE, the on-campus issues-oriented political party that called for no ROTC on campus, an end to capital punishment and nuclear testing, and free birth control on demand. SLATE stood for a "slate" of candidates, a lefty rival to the frat rats, and it had in its membership then a rather large pool of very smart, very lefty grad students—mostly male—whom I, quite frankly, worshipped and sought to emulate politically and intellectually. They had beards, wore blue work shirts and lots of baggy corduroys.

The tonic for my inchoate lefty yearnings and unformed ideology came my first semester, in the spring of 1960, when the House Un-American Activities Committee came to San Francisco. The Commie-hunting committee subpoenaed Doug Wachter, a Cal student, along with Archie Brown, the fiery ILWU labor leader, to name just a couple. The protest that exploded down the steps of city hall, the picket lines, the pitched battle that marked the first northern student activism (to balance the earliest civil rights demonstrations beginning in the South)—it was a heady brew, imbibed by this coed in huge gulps.

Zap! I came over to the "dark side," happily pitching myself under the aegis of student leftyism. Of course, along with my commitments to civil liberties and civil rights came an attendant discarding of the virgin fetish. A sympathetic Berkeley physician prescribed diaphragms for Cal coeds, and sometime after I'd lost my hymen, I finally got one. Talk about dressing for any circumstance: I was so horrified by the thought of getting pregnant— I'd previously gone unprotected—that I wore my diaphragm everywhere, even to the market. After all, you never knew when you'd be jumped. (A scant two years later the pill came out and revolutionized everything, but that's another story.)

In between HUAC and the FSM, there were a couple of years of militant civil rights demos calling for an end to Jim Crow in hiring. I missed the big Sheraton Palace sit-in, but I marched at Jack London Square and messed with Lucky Supermarkets. The shop-in at Lucky's was a devilish tactic of loading up carts, bringing them to the counter, and then not buying, forcing them to restock the mess. When local black youth, CORE members from Oakland, threw fresh produce around the store, I was horrified. But one day a little old Berkeley lady rammed her shopping cart into my Achilles heel and I buckled to the floor. "Why did you do that?," I wailed painfully. "I used to be for CORE," she hissed, "but not any more." That got me over the property thing. I started throwing cabbages myself.

So I was radicalized in my five years at Cal culminating in the Free Speech Movement, which took place in my senior year. After all these years of being a student activist, I had noticed one thing about the world beyond the campus: they were always categorizing us as dirty beatniks, filthy students, and the like. I was dismayed by these descriptions in press and television accounts, since I, for one, was fastidious and always conscious of my appearance, as I stated earlier. This daughter of a blind woman cared very much about being tidy, especially since as a kid, if I tore a hem or ripped a lining, I was the safety-pin queen well before punk style had made that particular mode de rigueur.

And so it was that on the eve of December 2, 1964, contemplating the culminating sit-in in Sproul Hall that night, I was wracked with indecision. How was I going to dress for the revolution in such a way that I would reflect well upon the aesthetics of a movement about which I was very passionate?

I had just the outfit, I was sure: crimson print Swedish ski sweater (tight weave), black shiny tight pants that looked like patent leather but were really cheap-chic rubber through and through, and a pair of matching shiny faux-leather black rubber boots up to the knee. I'd be slick, cutting edge, warm, and encased in protective RUBBER! Was I out of my mind!

I thought I'd be in Siberia. I was wrong. For most of the sit-in upstairs, side-by-side with folk singer Joanie Baez, we smeared peanut butter on white bread to give out to the hungry hordes of fellow demonstrators. We were jammed, body to body, on the second, then the third floor. No, I didn't break into any of the offices—I was a Valley Girl, remember? But I was angry nonetheless at reading contracts with big Central Valley growers and other damning information on UC's administration. (And they were coming down on us for our off-campus agitation. What about their collusion with big growers and industry?)

Did I tell you it was HOT up there?

At some point in those wee hours, the cops charged in wedge formation and grabbed recognizable leaders out of the crowd and carted them off. It was selective arrest. I recall that shortly thereafter, a naive fellow demonstrator stood up and yelled, "Now that they've got the leadership, we might as well cooperate in our arrests."

NO WAY! With my booming voice I urged everyone to stay seated, stay limp, and to resist passively and not at all "cooperate" with the arrest.

I then heard the officiating cop yell and point in my direction: "Get her!" They waded through others, grabbed me, and dragged me off, twisting my arms upright to keep me erect, as it were. I felt my arms were going to be ripped out of their sockets. I was vaguely aware of sweating more in fear than from the very real physical anguish I was feeling—especially when they flung me into an elevator to the floor. I lay in a heap of bodies as we went down, down to the basement of Sproul where they had set up a temporary processing center. I was photographed and fingerprinted on the spot.

And then a police matron ushered me into a teeny, closet-sized room and closed the door. There was barely room for the both of us. She ordered me to strip to my underwear and remove my boots.

It was a struggle in that confined space to peel down my wet rubber pants, to tug at my tight boots, which encased my feet like a sauna. As I detached each article of clothing from my sweaty body, yet another emanation filled the cubby with a rank odor.

I was dying there in a puddle of embarrassment and humiliation while the matron remained adamantine and severe. She ran her hands under my bra for hidden—what? razor blades? soap? Oh, a girl could dream. And she repeated it along the waist and leg bands of my underpants. Oh, the horror! as Joseph Conrad would have said, I'm sure, had he caught a whiff of my stewing body juices.

With difficulty, I tried unsuccessfully to resist my own exploration of what she must be thinking of me at that moment. To her I must be the cesspool of the Free Speech Movement. But so mortified was I that something in my thinking began to shift. It was not my fault that they were arresting me; it was theirs—no, hers. For she was there every bit as voluntarily as I. And if she chose to frisk me in a closet after I had sat-in all night in a dubious outfit better designed for the North Sea, then that was her choice. "Fuck her if she can't take the smell!" was my next thought.

Somehow I lived through the search. At the end, I had managed to transform my humiliation into a triumph of smell-o-rama weaponry. I wore my odors now as a badge, a rite of passage, and did so all though my succeeding stints at the Oakland city jail drunk tank, followed by the San Leandro armory, and finally the Santa Rita jail, where I remained until I was bailed out, I believe, two days later.

I arrived home exhausted and undressed. Even with the windows open in my tiny bedroom it was too much. I tossed the pants and rubber boots out on the roof outside and shut the window. After a shower and long sleep I awoke the next morning resolved to take the offending clothing directly to the trash. But it was gone, covertly whisked to Washington, D.C., I believe to this day, by the secret sniff squad of the FBI.

Of the many lessons I learned for the revolution during the FSM, not the least of them was what to wear to the revolution: Wear cotton. Wear open shoes. They breathe. We might even say, they breathe freely. Which was, after all, what the FSM was all about.

The "Rossman Report"

A Memoir of Making History[1]

Michael Rossman

For Mario, who loved a good read and efforts at honesty

In the episode of the Free Speech Movement, I think we were inhabited by spirits larger than ourselves, somewhere between ancestral and primordial in nature. We had no cultural vision with which to recognize them as such, nor language to speak of being the vehicles of what flowed through us. All we could say of "the spirit of Democracy" was that this was a metaphor. And all we knew was that the mundane world, in which our ordinary selves felt their ways through the common crisis, had become charged with an extraordinary energy—a luminosity at times almost tangible, yet invisible to the eye, that made each occasion, each decision, each act no more than what it funkily was, yet ever so much so, resonant in its significances.

Such a frame seems pertinent to the story of the report that came informally to bear my name, for I have always thought that vital dimensions of the FSM episode have escaped historical recognition and examination. Though I alluded to them long ago,[2] until recently I hardly connected them with my personal experience of organizing the "Rossman Report." I saw the Report's story simply as an illustration of the FSM's participatory energy and spirit, in the usual metaphorical sense. Readers concerned only with what can be stated precisely may well take it simply as such, as an exemplar of the FSM's organizing process, and be satisfied with its face value.

Yet I have come lately to think there may be more to it than this. In 1998, working on the website of the newly incorporated Free Speech Movement Archives, I had a curious experience as I prepared the 1964 text of *Administrative Pressures and Student Political Activity at the University of California: A Preliminary Report* for online republication. While writing an introduction telling how the Report came to be, I came to see with a detached eye how remarkably driven its organizer had been and to grasp that my personal story might be more crucial to the social phenomenon than I had realized or could understand. Given such uncertainty, how can one know what may seem germane to those who come to see more clearly? In my account here, I have put some personal data that may bear on the case.

For thirty-odd years, with bashful modesty that I believed completely, I discounted my role in organizing the Report: "Yeah, that's how I got the reputation as a wizard organizer that put me on the FSM Steering Committee. But I hardly did anything; I just started asking for help, and a bunch of folks responded and did it." Looking now at the project's internal documents, one might conclude instead that it was planned and directed in cold rigor and confidence by someone wearing a verbal costume of confusion and disorganization. If the disjunction between these views does not testify simply to my private dissociation, it may also be an artifact of an experience of *possession*—for such spirits as worked through us imbue their conduits with senses of responsibility both deeply grasped and hardly to be grasped as personal.

THE REPORT'S ORGANIZER: HIS BACKGROUND AND STATE OF MIND

When the FSM began I had been at Berkeley for six years, having transferred in fall 1958 as a junior from the University of Chicago, where I had been coleader of a brief movement of educational reform whose themes, though tame in comparison, in some regards prefigured the FSM's.[3] Beyond helping organize the senior skit in high school, this was my only direct experience as an organizer before the FSM. I came here in part because friends' letters reported a tantalizing awakening of political concern. By the time I arrived, TASC (Towards an Active Student Community) had metamorphosed into SLATE, the first umbrella organization sheltering the diverse buds of a new activism. Though never a member, as I am not a joiner, I was a fellow traveler and came shyly to know some of SLATE's people and stories in the early, small civil rights pickets and peace demonstrations. By 1960, when the swell of activism brought hundreds of Berkeley students to demonstrate against HUAC and Chessman's execution, in the public birth cry of the New Left, I was deeply involved in both affairs as a supporting journalist as well as a body on the line and picket captain.[4]

Disoriented by conflicting tugs of life, I dropped out and worked for twenty months as a laborer on campus. I remained on staff at the campus literary magazine, where my early essay on the character of the New Left was published,[5] and served as recording secretary for the Bay Area Student Committee for Abolition of HUAC while our tense little band sent literature and speakers to support groups nationwide. The experience was draining and alienated me from activist organizing. I was further disheartened when, in functional retaliation for its role in the anti-HUAC demonstrations,

SLATE was banned from using campus facilities and all our protests proved futile.

By the time I reentered school, in the depressed aftermath of the Cuban missile crisis, I was hot for study. I undertook graduate work in mathematics so devotedly that I went to only a handful of demonstrations over the next two years, while the local tide of civil rights activism was swelling to epic proportions. I kept in touch through friends and occasional SLATE parties, wrote political poems, and thought actively about what was unfolding. But as an actor, I had reduced myself to just another occasional body on the line, well back from the front where hundreds by then were being arrested. By fall 1964 I was so removed from campus action that I didn't pay much attention to the latest rule tightening until the gathering protest was in its second week. I went to check out the novel midnight vigil on Sproul Steps, but the kids there seemed so young and so inappropriately rowdy with their guitars, that I felt quite alienated and went back home to study more topology.

In sum, on the eve of my mobilization as an organizer in the FSM, I had lived through nearly the whole history of local activism leading to this episode as a reflective participant—in effect, preparing myself to serve as an elder (at twenty-four) within the new movement. Though by then I had various activist credentials, most were dated and I wasn't seeking to extend them. My bent was more literary, to be a political writer, as I became in earnest after the FSM.[6] I had no training, ambitions, or pretensions as a historian. At most, I saw myself as a participant journalist recording and interpreting a story unfolding in our lives.

It is pertinent also that by fall 1964 I had been smoking marijuana for eighteen months. That summer, I had had my first experiences with LSD. Such experiences, in the context of that time, were related to mobilizations of perception and energy at deep levels for many in the FSM—how many no one knows—for deeply political aversions still inhibit inquiry into such connections, in fields that lack theory to explain them.

THE REPORT'S GENESIS IN A CRUCIBLE OF PUBLIC DIALOGUE

Shortly before noon on October 2, I joined friends on the Terrace to await the promised confrontation, as groups of the "United Front" set up tables again in Sproul Plaza to defy the ban on political expression. The air was already electric with blank expectation when the sudden arrival of the police car brought us to our feet and shocked me to the core. Soon enough, cops on campus would become commonplace throughout the land; but in this first instant of transgression, something even deeper than a hallowed academic tradition was violated and rang me with despair. It was so unfair! As we hurried over, I felt the whole lonely, demoralizing burden of six years of striving for a campus toehold against the administration's hostility rise in me like bile. By the time we got there they were loading someone they'd arrested, awkward with his limpness, into the car.

A hundred people will tell you they were the first to sit down to keep the car from taking him away. No matter what the news clips show, each is telling a truth; for it was a moment of collective impulse—not the first, but the most immediate and dramatic—in which we moved as one while acting independently. My own move had been rehearsed four years earlier when we sprang to block a press car at the gate to San Quentin during Chessman's execution. We were too few then; they just kicked us out of the way. But now we were more—thirty, a hundred fore and aft, then more on the sides, until our seated encirclement stretched ten yards in every direction. As someone climbed on the car and someone else went to fetch a megaphone, I let go of the bumper and settled myself beside a wheel to wait. Ordinary time stood suspended; we had stopped the Authorities in the act of transgression, and the instant of impossibility and possibility stretched on, unresolved. I didn't know who we were—looking round, I saw some friends and others I recognized, but they were swamped in strangers. All I knew was that we had to keep the car, had to keep the open instant from closing into jail, for it was the first thing we had won on campus from all the years of struggle and loss.

In this state, transfixed more by the enormity of our response than by the crime of our governors, our conversation began. It went on for twenty-seven hours, not counting a break for sleep. Recordings testify to how funky and utterly mundane it was, in each stumbling burst of passion or strategic analysis, each academic note, each play of wit or vow, the passages of fear. But nothing can convey the way the whole was transcendent. Sitting there responding to each speaker with my mind and heart, somewhere even deeper within I grew utterly amazed as I realized I was involved in the first public dialogue I had witnessed in my life.

Though transcribable as such, this was not an intellectual perception, but a sensate apprehension through my whole being of an existential condition, before words could form to describe it. All I can compare it to, thirty-six years later, is a psychedelic experience of a transcendent spiritual state—less because I am frozen in retrospect than because I have no other model to describe a radically altered state of consciousness in which one perceives nothing as altered save in its revelation of its depths of being. In our case, this change of state was hard to recognize as such, for we didn't have a drug conveniently identified as its agent or a cultural background to grasp that such transformation could occur as a secular phenomenon, and its effects were easily mistaken for mere inflammation of political (or baser) passions. Yet even so, evidence of a radical alteration of our state remained. For in the long, suspended moment of that dialogue, what had been largely an atomized mass of us became a true *public*, a participatory polity.

The circumstance of this occurrence was extraordinary. We were engaged together in an unprecedented defiance to affirm core values. All knew, in varying degree, that our careers were at risk, and our bodies too. We couldn't see the six hundred cops arming behind Sproul Hall with orders to beat us into the ground if we resisted, but our premonitions were tangible. In such circumstance, it's only natural that we came to feel bonded—yet something deeper happened among us. I think we created ourselves as a *public* through our deliberative dialogue, created ourselves as citizens in an existential commonweal, pledged together, uncertainly dependent upon each other. In the months that followed, as we worked out our roles in the drama, we were proud to be recognized by sympathizers as bearers of the spirits of Liberty and Democracy and deeply reassured to see ourselves so—less because any inner doubts were stilled, I reckon, than because we were so certain that this description was merely a metaphor. To be bearers-on of precious tradition in a vital circumstance, to be *citizens*, was already so real and rich and strange a role or state that we could hardly grasp it fully or be moved to wonder further as we clung to its familiarities. Even so, a glow I could not see persisted in my perception, and with it a sense of the uncanny, from the moment I realized what was happening in our dialogue.

However one parses that collective experience, I felt myself in an altered state that extended among us and found myself simultaneously thrilled, terrified, and nonchalant in the condition. I can hardly express the strangeness of feelings, as gossamer as they were dramatic, the utter mingling of the sacred and profane. The dialogue was holy; my heart opened as I recognized its miracle; I hung on every word I heard. And also I picked my nose, chatted with friends, and flirted with a cute stranger. By 3:00 P.M. or so, though reluctant to leave its enthralling embrace, I went off with two hundred others to the second floor of Sproul to blockade the office of the dean of men until he or some higher administrator would meet with us.

As we jammed the broad public corridor, our dialogue flared again. Here its focus was narrower, on the tactical situation—on whom to let enter or leave, whom to bar, what to demand if ever they'd talk with us—though as deeply engaged with the moral issue. Thrilled to find myself again in the presence I had left, the glow, I listened as the talk ran on and on. As all had claim to speak, we could rag a point endlessly, but were sensible enough to make slow progress. We were at it for two hours before the distinguished faculty group arrived to convince us to leave the building, give up the car. Gingerly they explained how they were trying to mediate the situation, negotiate with the administration "on your behalf." Many faculty would support "a reasonable degree of freedom," they said. But nothing could proceed while we held a knife to the administration's throat, creating chaos, making it impossible for them to do anything.

I joined the dialogue then, as a child asking naively *why* it was impossible. They explained over and over, dodging spirited interjections, until something cracked open in me. I stood up and simply raved at them for the depth of their betrayal, their impotence. Where had they been the past two weeks, the past six years? Why were the men who should have led us in defense of shared values trailing us instead, pushing us to back down? Really, I was quite beside myself, out of control, watching myself raving like a man possessed until I slumped down hoarse, still trembling with that blast of raw emotion.

Or so I had remembered until checking the transcript yesterday. It seems I did scream at one point as I taxed them for betrayal. Yet the content of my rave was surprisingly academic and coherent. "You are treating this as if it were two weeks old," I said. "This is not two weeks old, it is . . . six years old. . . . We have been driven to the first civil disobedience on campus . . . after a period of six years of having our liberties chopped away one by one. Of petitioning nicely, of discussing nicely. WHERE HAS THE FACULTY BEEN DURING ALL THIS?" And I told them where, ticking off the few, ineffectual highlights of their intervention in our punishments and in their own—including the firing of the only professor (of history, Richard Drinnon) who had stood with us at the lonely gates of San Quentin.

Since we refused to budge before direct negotiations with the administration began, the professors withdrew, and our talk resumed until campus police arrived to close Sproul Hall early, breaking another tradition. We rushed downstairs to jam the doorway and held it open until the cops tired of wrenching us apart. Soon after, we voted to leave anyway, as they had sealed off the upper floors; and we rejoined our comrades around the podium of the car in the glow of public dialogue.

Years later I came to write about the peculiar properties of such open circles of testament and decision, in which all may speak with equal authority and everything pertinent may be considered.[7] To identify them simply as democratic forms is misleading, for their characteristic textures and dynamics are quite different from usual forms of democratic discussion structured by moderation and linear argument. So too are the effects on their participants, in ways verging toward the transpersonal in at least a metaphorical sense. When they work, from a disorderly anarchy a self-organizing coherence emerges, both in content and in persons, too multidimensional to describe simply.

Such forums were vital to the FSM from then on. Indeed, the experience of this one was so vivid and compelling that it set the tone of the movement that emerged and began a tradition of "open microphone" that distinguished crisis politics and organizational workings in Berkeley for decades thereafter. Yet surely this occasion was unique in the sheer novelty of the experience of direct democracy, as in the surreal theater of our encampment, the heightened sense of danger and meaning.

And so I found myself among a spontaneous polity engaged in the raw act of self-governance, of self-creation, crystallizing through its open dialogue. Periodically we paused to vote on this or that, as a thousand informed and independent minds, in what the media, administrators, and even our professors could recognize only as a "mob scene." And then we resumed, as the long moment without resolution stretched on with no sign of when or if they'd talk with us or when the cops would descend. In an existential daze of adrenaline and wonder, I listened as speaker after speaker mounted the car to extend the dialogue with perspectives of constitutional law, mythology, local politics, of hope and fear. And running through all this were bits and threads of our history.

Ours was a living history, too recent and marginal and local to be well recorded, born mainly in oral tradition, in the patchwork of stories our veterans remembered and retold—about the rebirth of social activism at Berkeley after the despair of the fifties and how the University administration had tried to contain and abort it. Though thousands of students had woven themselves recently into this history in civil rights demonstrations, the inner story of struggle for civil liberty remained almost the private memory of a handful of veterans until we began to share it from atop the car. Our history became our property in a newly public way, for a larger we, as we began to retell the stories and bring them up-to-date. As much as our sharing of ideas and the urgencies of the moment, I think this sharing of history—and the very consciousness of history—helped to knit us into community and polity.

Little beyond the very recent was shared that day or the next, as our focus was so immediate. The effect was mainly to make the newly inducted aware there was a history that they were extending. And even this sense dissolved in the moment, as midnight passed and we focused on crises within the crisis. Hundreds of drunken fraternity boys had joined the surrounding throng to shower lit cigarettes on our jammed, seated ranks, Jew-bait the student-body vice president, and chant for our blood as the blue goons of the sheriff's department egged them on. For me as for many, to watch Mario hoarsely appealing to reason from atop the car was both to witness heart-rending futility and to expand with awe in the presence of an archetype taking substance in funky reality. The memory will burn until I die. The surge of threat did not recede until a priest climbed the car to tell them that so much hate leads to murder and to go home. The small rain of fire faded out as we sat silent half an hour until they left. And then our dialogue resumed.

I don't recall if it was soon before this or after that I removed my shoes to take my own turn atop the car. Surely the need to offer whatever I could throbbed in me as in so many there and later. But perhaps it was merely private ego that led me to put my name on the speakers' list. "This didn't begin two weeks ago," I said, mainly to my juniors there, concerned that they understand our pent justification in protesting and how badly the deck was stacked against us. "There's a history; it's been going on for six years and more." And I went on to note as many highlights as I could of the long assault on our civil liberty before my five minutes were up and I stepped down, with so much unsaid still inside. Soon after, I ducked away to fetch my sleeping bag from home and returned to listen until the dialogue suspended and I fell into brief sleep.

.   .   .

I have written elsewhere of the next day.[8] From dawn to dusk our dialogue proceeded in that phantasmagorical theater as we waited for word of negotiation while thousands of spectators gathered round us and cops from ten jurisdictions converged. It was Indian summer; we were sweltering, spacey. As light blazed from the Greek columns of Sproul's facade, the Plaza shimmered and we found ourselves in the agora of Athens, huddled in the cradle of democracy, riveted on every word. Yet all we could see was our familiar selves, sweating, stuttering, with no language but metaphor to grasp what was coursing through us.

Years earlier, after the HUAC demonstrations, I had written, "It is one thing to say that we are living in the middle of history; everyone is aware of this. It is quite another to *know* that this is so, to participate in actions that one knows are in the growing-bud of the historical tree."[9] This time the feeling was even more so—again, a sensate apprehension rather than an intellectual perception, forming so deeply before words that I had no sense of history as such but only of the extraordinary moment of *now* stretching on and on through our dialogue, until word came that the cops were gearing to descend. Doubtless, many references were made that day to our history, but I imagine I gave them no more note than any others, for all were vital, surcharged. In the deepening twilight as we prepared for the attack, I felt hope and despair flicker in wild oscillation. I thought someone would be killed; I trusted it wouldn't be me. At what seemed the last moment, Mario, conscience stricken because we hadn't yet been given the chance to approve its terms, mounted the car to announce the apparent compromise reached with President Kerr. We'd give up the car, Jack would be released, the suspensions of our leaders would be put to fair tribunal, and a tripartite committee would study the issue of regulation of student political activity to make recommendations to the administration. Though many besides myself were so torn by mistrust of the offered process that they would have stayed on, together we accepted this as enough for now and voted to leave, dispersing exhausted, glowing, charged.

Though the moment's peril had dissolved, nothing had been resolved. Whatever energy had possessed us in that crucible, its signature and momentum were full-fledged. From that point on, the entire drama of the FSM unfolded with the sense of Greek inexorability remarked on by so many of its literate participants. I couldn't tell how many others felt with me like characters in an Attic tragedy, playing our free parts, as only our uncertain selves, in a mythic script that we already knew by heart. Soon after the climax, I ventured that we had committed ourselves around the car not simply to a cause but to the creation and completion of an Event whose dimensions we could scarcely understand; and argued that every theme and dynamic of the long conflict were already preconfigured in this opening act.[10] I still have no language for that mind-wrenching simultaneity of destiny and free will. But no account of contingent history, howsoever convincing, will explain the origin of the feeling or why it persisted through the whole episode.

THE PRIVATE PROCESS OF THE REPORT

Hardly an hour before the end, Karen threaded her way through fear to join me beside the car. I had seen her only off and on since we broke up the previous year and was as startled as grateful, since she was so distant from activism that she wouldn't even walk a picket line. After the anticlimax, she steered me in silence through nightfall to my apartment, holding shaky hands, plunked me on the bed, made tea, and pleaded, "What's going on? Tell me what's happening," fierce and forlorn. I opened my mouth and broke down sobbing, gasped to recover, and sobbed again. How to explain what had been going on and where it had come to? Still I tried, in clots of coherence between the tears. She listened, eyes wide as mine, trying to grasp the sense. I went on and on till Aphrodite took pity and Karen folded me in her arms, and we made love and sank into the well of dream.

By noon she left. Across town, my old and new comrades were gathering to work out the formal structure of the movement of our desire, mechanisms to harness direct democracy to its task. I ached to join them, but I was beside myself, torn open, bursting with all that had crystallized around the car, the energy, the history, our extraordinary presence. After making an outline, I turned on the tape recorder. "I'm making this tape because some participant journalism is needed, of a kind we've never had," I began and went on for an hour and a half.

Given that I was a young man wildly excited, setting out to describe the amazing event he had just been through, the result was rather academic in content if not in its textures of feeling. Reaching back to the fifties, I recalled our movement's struggle for civil liberty, touching on as many key events and dynamics as systematically as I could. Though the earlier parts of the tape transcript were most heavily edited before its later publication, enough detail remains to show how fully my account prefigured the agenda of the Report that was to come.[11]

That next week, the campus was abuzz with people looking to connect and be useful, in between trying to reconnect with ordinary life. The weekend convention that named our movement had already mapped some of its channels. After Monday classes, I went to the TAs' caucus forming in the statistics department and was elected as a representative to the newly organizing Graduate Coordinating Committee. In the GCC's early meetings, besides arguing for militancy, I proposed that we research and publish the conflict's fuller history. Thousands had been energized by the confrontation; to inform them was to make them more fully ours. The coherent record of our repression was crucial evidence to place upon the table and to show the world. What could be clearer? Surely a caucus in the history department could take it on?

Though sympathy may have been wider than I recognized, I might as well have proposed to a wall, for everyone was already committed to affairs of more immediate consequence. Disappointed, I faced the stern dictum that ruled throughout the FSM—*if you think it's worth doing, get to it yourself*— and went home to begin. For a week or more I toiled alone, locked in my room, breaking only to tend my classes as a TA and to check with friends and the *Daily Cal* about what was happening. It was agonizing to wrench myself away from the immediacy and urgency of the present, the replenishment of comradeship, to engage the ghostly past. But I couldn't help it. Wired with late caffeine and whatever else, I was burning not simply with a line of argument but with the staggering richness and complexity of the whole history it ran through.

Faced with the problem of how to argue the case beyond our partisan crowd, I fumbled my way towards a functional analysis through which one could understand not only the administration's occasional dramatic edicts and tampering but its entire pattern of student governance by mostly well-meaning and liberal administrators, as a methodical repression of the New Left's burgeoning activism. I say "fumbled towards," yet it's clear that the bones of this analysis were already fully formed in my taped account, and they may well have been stated as I spoke atop the car. This perspective became the basis of the public bulletins I later wrote to recruit and orient volunteers for the Report project and of internal guides for researchers in several areas. It remained the basis for my covering essay in the Report as well as for the selection of the included studies.

By the time I made my last outline, ten days into the public project, it ran for fourteen pages in tiny script, setting out the developmental history and character of what had been repressed, and a defensible perspective, before turning to methodical survey of the history and effect of administrative regulation on each separate strand of our activity. But well before the outline got to this stage, the task blew me away. On October 16 I looked in despair at the disorderly sheaf of typescript in single-spaced elite type on cockle bond, the maze of beginnings I'd made to explain this theme, that progression, this crux. Too much! I just couldn't! The clock was ticking, the reconstituted Committee on Campus Political Activity (CCPA) was preparing to meet. I gave up and went to ask for help.

Nineteen days later, a group of over two hundred volunteers had researched and published *Administrative Pressures and Student Political Activity at the University of California: A Preliminary Report*—amounting to 145 pages and some sixty-five thousand words, including twenty of the forty-three studies brought to first completion—and submitted it to the CCPA as the FSM's brief. Almost overnight, our case had acquired a broad historical context and grounding—and I had acquired a reputation as an inspired organizer, which helped move me quickly through the FSM's organizational structure to its Steering Committee.

THE PUBLIC PROCESS OF THE REPORT

Seeking help, I turned first to old comrades, my political peers and elders. They were mostly from SLATE, the small umbrella that had sheltered most of our activism before 1961, when the administration severed its campus ties. They remembered much more about this and earlier travails than I did. But of course almost all were either off campus in other lives or too busy already in the conflict to attend to old history. So I turned for help mostly to younger people who knew less and found them prepared to learn and do more. The cop-car siege had galvanized the campus; there were hundreds, perhaps thousands, looking for ways to participate, to belong by the gift of purposeful work to what was happening—which was not simply a "civil liberties protest," but something involving our deeper senses of autonomy, identity, and purpose. What was striking was not how many had already been activists but how many had not been. The FSM was remarkable in providing so many with a chance and vehicle for active participation.

This agitated mixture of the already active and the newly activated was the raw material, the resource pool, from which emerged the dozens of autonomous work groups that formed the movement's functional structure. In this climate of awakened commitment, wherever needs were recognized people gathered to try to meet them, forming Legal Central, Press

Correction Central, the Newsletter Committee, departmental caucuses—and off in another corner, for seventeen frantic days, the "repression report committee," or whatever it was called, for we had no time to choose a name.

After checking out the old guard, I kept asking for help. I asked my sister, Devora, my "apolitical" friends, grad students in my department, fellow poets around the literary magazine, strangers in the cafeteria. Sometimes I asked them to ask their friends, to think of others who might want to get involved; but usually I didn't need to, for their thoughts were ahead of mine. I went also to promising public venues—GCC meetings, the gathering where unaffiliated students were organizing as Independents. All I recall saying each time was, *This needs doing, do you want to help?* But surely I must have talked a blue streak.

The need was as uncertain as it was clear. Our present struggle had a background that should be made explicit, as one prerequisite to conducting responsible political business in what we still thought of as an intellectual community rather than a managerial slum where force ruled. If the Report could be completed in time, it might strengthen the FSM's case in the CCPA's proceedings—though of course the CCPA was only advisory to the real rule makers.

People responded to this long shot as they did to opportunity all through the FSM. On the Steering Committee, sometimes when something needed doing we'd go to campus to find people with FSM buttons, explaining what and why. If they didn't agree or it didn't suit their fancy—well, tough; the FSM wasn't a membership organization; we had no power to direct anyone. But if they did agree, they would not simply "do the job" but would transform the task, reshaping it as their own, often in ways we'd never anticipated. And so it was with the Report. Like every other work of the FSM, it was a collective task freely organized by its participants. Each did what she chose, bit off her own piece of the task, a piece she hoped would be to her taste and no more than she could handle or get help with. For there was so much to do: deciding what to report and who would take it on, finding information through print and people, writing and editing each report, keeping track of who was doing what and when, squirreling stencils away for the printing job, bringing beer to the collating party.

Early on, at the Independents' meeting, Lynne Hollander, a senior in English at twenty-three with no relevant preparation, joined me to take on the Herculean task of editorial coordination among a dispersed network of researchers that soon involved ninety people. She recruited her former lover to report on the disenfranchisement of the graduate students, and he recruited his; and so it went, as impulse propagated in chain reaction and folks we'd never heard of started calling in.

On October 18 I went to the FSM Executive Committee to announce the project and ask for help in publishing the Report. Since representatives of every organization involved were there, two days later thousands must have known that some group had taken on the project. The effect was less to bring an avalanche of volunteers than to affirm and deepen the movement's collective sense of purpose, dignity, and justification—and of history itself in the making.

By then the FSM's communication needs had spawned a ragtag publishing empire in a basement, with the donated mimeograph and letterpress machines that cranked out four million pages of leaflets and newsletters in constant, last-minute production. Press Central's story was as rich and idiosyncratic as the story of this report. There I met Thom Irwin and Marston Schultz—students in landscape architecture and architecture at twenty-three, though Thom had dropped out to study via University Extension—who began organizing others for the task of rush publication, or rather for the travail, for our mechanisms of publishing were so primitive and laborious in that era.[12]

By the next evening, Press Central had printed the first "Confused Poop Sheet for Research on Repression at Berkeley"—three single-spaced, tight-margined mimeo pages, an invitation sketching the project's scope and guidelines, listing fifteen topics with ten coordinators to call. By its second edition "Confused Poop" had become "Information" and had doubled in length and density, listing forty-one topics and two dozen coordinators, pleading for others to take on the rest. The third bulletin skipped the rhetoric to focus on organization and coordination, added twenty-four topics, and announced a general meeting for that night, October 22, hoping it would draw more volunteers.

That gathering was a carnival, the first time more than three or four of us had met face-to-face. You can imagine what we all felt on looking around the crowded room to grasp the funky substance and reality of our venture together, of others on whom we could depend. The room buzzed with enough energies to carry and blur any sense of the uncanny; I recall only my feelings of gratitude and hope. In two hours we whipped through information, problems, and connections and then dispersed, since the deadline loomed. A few did full-time labor, but most fit what they could into as much or little of the rest of life as they managed to maintain—leaving Lynne to keep track of their living maze, nag the tardy, and counsel those with writer's block; and leaving me, with her assistance, to digest what started coming in.

Beyond responding to scattered calls for advice or connections, I had no contact with researchers or writers in the field. Collectively, they must have worked like dogs, an anarchic sledge team. By ten days later most of what we'd get had arrived, some through relays of editors. The heap totaled some seventy documents in six hundred pages—ranging in size from a brief affidavit of what several heard the chancellor say to a fifty-nine-page treatment of the local civil rights movement; in character from dense source interviews with SLATEniks to clumsy summaries of secondary accounts; in quality from these to competent study of the campaign against compulsory military training; reaching back to the loyalty oath controversy and afield to the University's suppression of research on its relation with agribusiness and its collusion in siting a nuclear reactor on an earthquake fault.

All had been authorized by our "central committee," that is, by me and/or Lynne and whomever else was around when people came with proposals. In practice, we approved everything, saying, "Fine, go to it," offering whatever we could to help shape or refine it—for every time someone said, "This needs doing and I'm willing," the topic was indeed worth pursuing. We had to trust that folks could carry through, and most managed a decent approximation. Had we had more time, we might have better prioritized their work and done more editing. Only a fraction of the full terrain was covered. But it was time to punt or throw our pass.

I sorted through the heap with Lynne, triaging competence and pertinence against constraints of size. For a week, I'd been drafting the overview essay from my earlier work, summarizing the detailed logic of our historical case with specific references, redrafting as more contributions arrived. Finally our triaging and my draft converged in sixty footnotes tying the draft to a supporting text of twenty reports, and we sent this too to the printers on November 2.

From our standpoint it was magical: Couriers were called to take the raw, edit-scrawled manuscripts to Press Central, and neat piles of pages appeared at the collating party two days later. Long after, Thom told me what that entailed. He and Marston had recruited an on-call force of forty typists, forty couriers, and as many others to staff round-the-clock shifts. As the typed masters came in, they went out again to yet others standing ready at hand-cranked ditto machines, phoning in when they were free for use. Since these were more common and accessible on campus than mimeos, it's not clear that our choice of this medium made printing more difficult. But certainly the process was dramatic, with people diving out of office windows to huddle and return, dodging the campus cops.

As published by the only means at our disposal—manual typewriters and secretarial Selectrics and the ditto machines used for routine departmental bulletins, lent to us by sympathetic staff—the Report's supporting texts amounted to 137 pages of single-spaced typescript with narrow margins in motley typefaces, often changing within a document, all printed in the pale violet ink of ditto transfer, legible but taxing to read. Only the seven-page overview essay was sharply clear, printed in competent offset on the FSM's own press.

By late morning on November 4 the collating party began. Our exuberant crew punched holes in thirty thousand sheets, collated them page by page, and bound the sheaves in manila folders with pockets, securing each with three bright brass clips after the overview essay was laid in. Having stretched the ditto masters to their max, we distributed the faintest sheets as fairly as we could—after reserving the best for ten presentation copies— and wound up with about two hundred copies of the whole. Two went to each of the forty-three organizations represented on the FSM's Executive Committee. Most of the rest went to sympathetic faculty in key departments and to various campus libraries; a few to the outside world as to the administration, including copies to President Kerr and the Regents. The overview essay was distributed much more widely; we must have sold two thousand copies for a quarter each at the FSM's tables and given away half again as many, blanketing professors' mailboxes in every department and our own constituency as well as we could.

Late that afternoon we brought ten copies of the Report to the FSM's representatives, just in time to present at the CCPA's fifth meeting. As each copy weighed nearly two pounds, we imagined their satisfying *thump!* on the conference table. In the minutes of that intensely focused discussion no mention of the Report appears. Three days later the committee deadlocked and was dissolved by the chancellor, as the FSM began direct action again.

THE EFFECTS OF THE REPORT

So what did all our effort come to? I doubt that anyone besides myself read the entire Report that fall, if ever. Indeed, I doubt that anyone besides Lynne and one unfortunate aide to President Kerr read very much of it then, and not simply because copies were scarce and faint. Surely some hundreds of young activists read portions of those that passed into organizations, eager to catch up on certain issues; and probably some faculty and administrators browsed theirs to check the texture and content of our evidence. But who had time and motivation for more than this— and reading its brief overview—while events were sweeping us on so dramatically?

After the FSM climaxed, the Report became even more dated and incomplete, an academic curiosity almost lost to history's archaeology. Most copies probably still survive tucked away in personal archives, long unseen. A few persisted in libraries, hardly accessible even there, their content becoming of piecemeal interest only to a few specialized scholars. Perhaps these were occasionally consulted, but I have seen no evidence in print more specific than three token citations in exhaustive source lists.[13] Indeed, the very fact of the Report project essentially vanished from historical recall. So far as I know, only two laconic references have appeared in all that has been published about the FSM—each two sentences long, noting simply that a group following my lead had been at work on a "massively documented" report whose overview was widely distributed.[14]

Only since 1999 has the Report's content become more publicly available, shared on the Web in a joint project by the Free Speech Movement Archives and the University's Bancroft Library, assisted crucially by a gift from Stephen Silberstein—in an edition augmented by all the other, unpublished material prepared by our working group, including its bulletins and internal papers, and the commentary of this memoir. Indeed, since we called the Report "preliminary" in part because we had begun to include the FSM's unfolding history in it, the entire suite of documents pertaining to the FSM, placed on the Web by the joint FSM Archives/ Bancroft project, may be understood as the Report's extension.

From the black hole of University administration, there survives only one document concerning the original Report, so far as I know: a response to Kerr's request that it be reviewed "to determine the historical accuracy of its assertions."[15] The author was quite scornful, sputtering with adjectives: "poorly edited . . . outdated . . . uneven in quality . . . some prepared by freshmen . . . [not] reliable or thorough . . . secondary sources . . . misstatements of fact . . . omissions, misinterpretations, and inadequately supported generalizations." Need I say I'm grinning? All this was true enough except the last, and I could cheerfully add a dozen more, evident to us from the beginning; for our production was as slapdash and amateurish as one can imagine, the awkward form of instantiated love, of Eros, of passion for the truth of history.

Surely its face was pimpled. Yet it's not enough to say, "Hey, give us a break; we pulled off a practical miracle, doing it as best we could." For also we were talented, thoughtful, and competent, as well as inspired, and we did a decent job, leaving a body of material that will long be of value to scholars and, through them, perhaps to others—a rich slice of a history too complex for any work to encompass, as democratic as its subject, bearing some sense of the whole. As for our purpose then, it is notable that Kerr's reviewer, despite his adjectives, completely dodged the issue of our accuracy, while acknowledging the problem tacitly by noting that at least nine of the Report's studies had been farmed out for further research. The real problem was perhaps more visible in his conclusion that "even a comprehensive commentary . . . would only stimulate a continuing, endless, and ultimately unsatisfactory dialogue," which was of course the attitude that infuriated us.

Yet others then were more attentive, if closely only to the Report's overview. For to this day, that brief summary remains as forceful and sound as our grasp then of the affair, and as compact—dry as dust almost, marshaling fact after fact to document the University's stifling of our social dissent, and of dissent against its policies of governance, coming even then to climax. The five thousand copies we published were read by probably twice that number within a week, being scarcely longer than three ordinary FSM leaflets together and much better printed. I don't know that this changed many students' minds or added much to their sense of local history and justification; but many learned more clearly about how power works in our bureaucratized world.

Beyond them, the overview's reception varied. The police-car dialogue had already made students widely aware that a long history of grievance underlay the struggle for political expression. Though a few (lower) administrators had understood this sympathetically, most had heard the radicals' perennial complaints of oppression as ungrateful noise confusing the progress of true liberalization, if not as something more pernicious, and had little interest in a corrective text. The faculty were still so insulated even from concern for student activism, let alone from knowledge of the actual textures of our institutional experience, that few had more than an inkling that a historical case might be made for our stance. That many read the overview left in their mailboxes and found it coherent may have contributed modestly towards the overwhelming majority in our favor in the Academic Senate vote a month later, though the drama of injustice by then assured this.

Yet such assessments understate the Report's accomplishment, for its main import and consequence were symbolic. From the time rumor spread that someone had taken on this project, it filled an ache in consciousness among us. The ache was in part to know that others had covered each vital base and that others like oneself were so empowered, for this promised one's own power for good. In this respect, the instant legend of our accomplishment—*the whole history from an army, almost overnight!*—lent strength to many and to our whole. Beyond this, the ache was specific. We ached for our history not only as ammunition, nor merely because we were intellectuals still, howsoever inflamed, bound to testify to the importance of its inquiry. We ached for it because it helped make us whole, as citizens and in our selves. To know, even distantly, that the massive, historical substance of our grievance *had* been recorded and made public by our collectivity did more than strengthen our senses of justification and power: it helped restore us to our selves, in polity and person. In such unmeasurable senses, I think the Report was at least well worth our effort, if not a symbolic triumph.

OF MY FURTHER TRAJECTORY IN THE FSM

Soon after the Report's publication, Lynne and I were given nonvoting seats on the FSM Executive Committee in tribute to the Report's perceived importance and its large workforce. On November 14 I was elected from there to the Steering Committee in its final reconstitution, in part because I stood somewhat outside a current polarization. But the process of my induction onto the Steering Committee had begun well before, on my initiative. I was itching for the Report to be done so that I could offer whatever else I could to our goings-on. All I had to give, beyond my body and wit, was my skill as a writer. Bothered by the strident tones of the FSM's leaflets, I volunteered to rewrite them before they went out and, after one trial, was invited to continue. Naturally, I had to sit through the long meetings to grasp what I was to digest. There I found myself accepted as an equal in an intense collective dialogue, selectively indifferent to formal bounds. In similar fashion, several others—most notably, the young Protestant theologian Walt Herbert—were effectively drafted onto the FSM's vanguard body by a process at once quite undemocratic and quite consensual. Of course the formalities were observed: the Steering Committee was entitled to host consultants, and we had no vote. But in practice, the distinction was nearly trivial in a dialogue that decided by consensus. And soon enough it vanished for me.

And thus I came to be the main writer of the FSM's official propaganda, or at least its leaflets, for the conflict's five final weeks. In this employ, I learned more about how much power he has who writes the final draft at 4:00 A.M. Yet I swear I spoke for us all, as well as I was able: my phrasings were rarely rebuked by my comrades, though sometimes sharpened. As for what other role I played, only its public face was apparent in the few speeches I gave at rallies. My inner role remains an elusive elephant, limned by a few nearby commentators as sighted and blind as I. One accounts me a moralist, another a clown, another a romantic nihilist, another merely a crashing bore, and others simply as minor. I'm sure I was all of those and more, as was the Report; and perhaps the group's chief mystic too, though one other among us might qualify. If so, it can hardly be blamed on psychedelics alone, since at least five of our elected dozen had used marijuana and at least one other LSD by then. Such uses, as I suggest earlier, had some influence within what actually happened in that intense company, as in our larger ensemble, as well as on my perception of these.

All I know for sure, even now, is that our radically diverse personalities and perspectives were fused for a long moment in a transcendent harmony that left us fully our selves as its use made us more deeply so. It was real—there was discord, misunderstanding, and bitterness among us as well as love; and it was also magical, in the true spirit of Democracy.

Of this, just one thing more. I've made my progression to the Steering Committee seem quite natural and logical. Perhaps it testifies only to my ego and drive for power and stature, though I've hardly lived life that way. Yet what drove me, though selfish enough, was a deeper hunger almost beyond words. Around the car I had felt a *glow* of a distinct species of energy. I would not come to be able to speak even so vaguely of the feeling for some years, until I met its circumstances again and again; but even then it was clear and called me. After we dispersed, I felt like a blind worm seeking the touch of light and burrowed with all my being towards where I felt it most strongly, in the collective crucible that Mario stirred. Of my experience there I hope some day to grasp and write more. Till then, this will remain my overriding sense of the journey.

OF MAKING HISTORY

Later, when I came to speak of the project, almost all I could (or chose to) recall was the amazing concentrated blaze of collective effort that produced the Report. This is how I recorded the story, two and then three decades later in unfinished memoirs, as a miniature of the FSM minus only the infighting. Focusing on the sociology of the process, I reduced the complexity of my earlier role to a dozen lines of almost perfunctory summary, as if I had been simply an accidental catalyst, and treated my role thereafter in hardly more detail or emphasis, as largely titular.

In such forgetfulness or deception I was moved by what might be called a political commitment, if not a counternarcissistic drive, of a kind that led political poster artists from the mid-sixties long onward to issue their work unsigned. The drive is not simply to repress unseemly display of personal ego and pride but to testify to transcendent reality, the vital power of democratic collectivity. It is easy to mock the idea of "the spirit of the collective," but no language yet serves to express what the phrasings grope at, the peculiar state in which one finds oneself both actor and agent, wholly and only oneself yet simultaneously *selfless*, a vehicle of common, "higher" will. Even to call it "collective" is already half to lie, but we keep trying. All we can grasp clearly is the practical, life-furthering power of *collective* action, and even this we confuse with *mass* as we push the idea.

And so I came, nearly consciously, to deform the history I wrote, to serve a well-meant political agenda and urge. As nearly as I could without lying outright, I found myself straining to present the Report's effort as collective, not only in its outer mechanics but to the core, and was somewhat pleased by the result, as by the memory. I pardoned the slanting I recognized because it testified to deeper truth, for the experiences that sandwiched this one—the days around the car, my month in the intense dialogue of the Steering Committee, the FSM itself—were supernally collective. Yet even so, I was also lying, not least to myself.

When the editors of this volume invited me to contribute, of course I chose this story. Since I thought that this memoir was already nearly complete, I expected to spend only a few days tidying it up, but conscience intervened. As an editor myself, I had recently recognized how remarkably driven the Report's key organizer had been, but scarcely more than this. Even so, the point seemed important to the account, and I sat back to explore it—focusing on my own history, feelings, and perceptions, including some I have long fumbled to express. I was surprised to recognize how early I put forth the Report's agenda, how long I'd been preparing, how thoroughly I dominated its production, how unerring and uncanny was the bolt of energy that drove me. Standing now with the specificity of my role so fully exposed, I feel almost foolish. Who was I kidding? Would there have been a "Rossman Report" without Rossman? Who was this "selfless" fool?

For decades the historian Reggie Zelnik and I have argued politely about contingent history. Would there have been an FSM without Mario? There would surely have been something. Reggie thinks it would have been quite different and likely much less effective. I have thought that not even Mario nor the ravaged Chancellor Strong was irreplaceable once the affair began—that given the tensions and energies represented so widely and deeply on all sides, something of equivalent kind and consequence was bound to result, as if in fated theater.

In this view, moved by the same political agenda and spirit, I have less stood aside than leaned outward from my certain knowledge of Mario's uniqueness and importance to the FSM. From the moment I witnessed him speak from the car, I knew him as an extraordinary presence within our extraordinary presence, in a way that went to the heart and only deepened as that drama climaxed, as he went on in public blaze, as we talked together for endless hours in Steering Committee, in jail, in our sporadic, intense friendship till his death. There are real saints, and he was one in his quirky, tortured humanity. In terms pregnant in this memoir, Mario was an *avatar* embodying a transcendental signature and force. Insofar as the spirits of Democracy and Liberty flowed through us, he was their brightest conduit, our crooked lightning rod, and everyone knew it. How can what happened be imagined without him? Yet in my leaning so, I am moved by an equal truth, with which Mario agreed.

For from the first, I was swept with visceral revulsion and grief at the way the media hastened to identify and focus on a Leader, transmuting the FSM from an awakened public to a led mass in a way that endures to this day in popular legend, reinforced recently by national recognition of Mario's death. Though one might wish professional historians to be wiser than this caricature, it persists more subtly in even the most compassionate treatments of our movement, perhaps emphasized by this very volume and even by these reflections. Yet in the largest dramas of the FSM as in the most intimate, we were cast into an existential democracy in which the contribution of each person, no matter how "trivial"—including the moderates who "betrayed" the movement—was vital to the whole. Though putting it so be romantic, this reality was attested by the hundreds of practical heroes and heroines who emerged, at innumerable junctures, and by the FSM's subsequent reputation as the most participant-democratic movement of its era. To have this be its leading memory and legend, rather than the image of Mario as Leader (or even as Avatar), seems more nearly true in fact as well as spirit and more healthy in its teaching. May he remain as he was, the brightest star in our bright constellation.

As for the Report, the argument here for contingent history is even stronger than in Mario's case, and simpler. It seems that I dreamed the whole thing up after spending my adult lifetime preparing, clapped my hands, and watched an army spring forth to materialize my fantasy—or less grandly, that I was a uniquely qualified and driven organizer, mildly charismatic if not divinely inspired. How could the Report have been without me?

Having put Reggie's case so strongly, I am reduced to metaphor for reply, beyond the clarity of certain background facts. There were probably forty SLATE veterans around with more extensive and intimate experience of our history, many more disposed by academic training than I to take on such a task. Nor was one so qualified necessary, given the broader pool of people with such bents, for the history was essentially as I found it rather than as I construed it, and was generally accessible in a community newly opened to connection. Had anyone else of even moderate capacity, drive, and friendships engaged it, she or he would as readily have found partners for so meaningful a task among so many aching to be useful and traced the same terrain. My guiding list of topics was merely a first draft of common knowledge and assessment, soon fleshed out by others' suggestions, as would have happened with anyone as partisan as I starting to inquire. As for the analytical framework sprung like Minerva from my brow, and the Report's attempted tones of reason, method, and dispassion, I can only say that the analysis was primitive, primal, involving no more than the kind of practical understanding that any serious inquiry would duplicate; and that the tones were shaped in deference to the common manners and ideals of our larger community. If no one griped about the slants, tones, and contents of my directives, this was less because I was inspired or dictatorial than because these did indeed represent our common understanding. In such senses, the Report project was even more collective and my role even more selfless than I had portrayed. The most I can claim to be my own is the prose style of its covering essay, though the tone's so dry it hardly sounds like me.

In sum, I see no way to claim that I was essential to the Report save to posit that no one would have taken it on if I had not. Lord knows that's how I felt, as did hundreds of others at their self-chosen tasks. Yet this contention is hardly credible, at best unlikely, given the wide, instant recognition of the project's importance among so many talented, imaginative people seeking to be useful.[16] Had any other been Clio's catalyst in this affair, the idiosyncratic history of their preparation would in retrospect have seemed as logical and compelling as mine. Yet even so, I was vital, in all my specificity. How can this be, to be vital and not be? Was even Mario so?

When the great charges gather in the clouds, they find their way to ground. The path of lightning is always specific and contingent, depending irreproducibly upon the actual history and subtle properties of each molecule it inflames. Sometimes it's a sure bet where and when it will strike, the question remaining as to the precise moment and which tree will kindle first—the tallest being the most likely; without it the next tallest, a little less so.

History is always contingent—contingent as Kennedy's assassination, contingent as lightning, the irreproducible logic of each happenstance turning visible in retrospect, realizing the inexorable logic of its path to ground, the kindled fire. The tension between these historical logics is a matter of scale of view, an artifact of single mind; we cannot grasp fully what works through us and how, though we give it the names of our age and try. Had Rosa Parks not sat on the bus nor I undertaken the Report, would not someone have done something kindred taken by so many to mean as much? Absent Mario and our FSM, as a common tide rose in the campuses of this land of conflicted freedom, would there really not have been some spark as bright to signal that student youth were entitled and empowered to exercise civil liberty? That World War I hinged on an assassination has been debunked, but the trauma of Martin Luther King's murder still blurs insight. Though the Black Plague and Hiroshima seem ever so contingent, ecology and Mars teach us: *If not this way then that, lightning comes to ground.*

AFTERWORD: THE BETRAYAL OF LENNY GLASER

As background to this story of betrayal, one should understand the role of Lenny Glaser (later known as Lenni Brenner) in the political culture of the Berkeley campus during the era leading to the FSM. If one can summarize six rich years of history by saying that SLATE was the key organizer of students' increasing expression of civil liberties, one might say on the same scale that Glaser was the individual exemplar of free speech.

For years, his thoughtful and passionate tirades greeted students on cold mornings, assailed them at noon as they hurried past the pedestal at Bancroft and Telegraph where he perched, eyes gleaming as he criticized Kennedy during the Cuban missile crisis, mocked the Pope's stand on birth control, told us marijuana wouldn't make us crazy. One must understand the era's context, still shadowed with McCarthyism's chill, to grasp how aberrant his act seemed; and one must understand the subtext of collective feelings, gathering to erupt in the later 1960s, to grasp the shameful fascination of his lingering words and example for many who hurried past, averting their eyes from that crazy guy. In the annals of campus political history, the laurel for solitary courage is often credited to Fred Moore for his 1961 fast on the Sproul Steps in protest of compulsory military training. Yet to my mind, the courage of Glaser's lonely example was as vivid and long sustained and more fertile in influencing the emerging culture of political expression.

Of course, Glaser's act drew the attention of campus administrators and police. That these authorities were not friendly then to such liberty of speech is well-known, but one must appreciate the particular structure of their hostility, which led them to view Glaser as more than an individual nut. From 1958 on, campus administrators had been called on not simply to deal with the consequences of an increasingly active political movement but to understand the dynamics of its development among a student mass that had seemed quite tractable. During 1960–1961 I participated in a liberal salient of their inquiry in meetings convened by Dean of Men Arleigh Williams. But their political perspectives were divided, and the views of Vice Chancellor Sherriffs came instead to govern administrative perceptions, applying a theory of malignancy to describe our troublesome development as driven by the infectious agency of Red-stained "non-student agitators."

At this distance, the paranoia of the administration's analysis is clearly visible as a relic of early Cold War culture, remarkable in its persistence. Gathering momentum continually, this view did not reach the apex of its folly until after the antiwar movement's escalation in 1967. But its thorough entrenchment by 1964 was reflected in President Kerr's incautious assertion that 49 percent of the FSM demonstrators were "followers of the Mao-Castro line," and his subsequent "correction" allowing that only a small minority were Red provocateurs. The gulf of understanding thus demonstrated was essential to the campus administration's provocation and subsequent mismanagement of the free speech crisis and to its extraordinary intervention in Glaser's legal case.

To account for this impropriety one must also understand the state of mind of the administrators involved. The rising, fractious tide of student dissent had suddenly come home, as protest against the decree banning political tables escalated out of control. The unprecedented sit-ins and police-car blockade of September 30 and October 1–2 left ranking administrators in a hysterical state, seeking external agencies to blame for the disturbance and means to quell it. By October 8 University officials filed a petition to revoke Glaser's probation on grounds (as later summarized by the appeals judge) that he "had been creating a disturbance and interfering with an officer in the performance of his duties" on September 30 and October 1.[17]

During a prior series of arrests for civil rights activity, Glaser had been cited also for possession of a marijuana roach. Although conviction on this count threatened a prison term of one to ten years, he had been granted probation. In that era, considerations of due process did not extend to revocation hearings, since probation and revocation were still seen as discretionary gestures by judges. The University sent a representative to the probation hearing to testify against Glaser, who was not allowed to present witnesses on his own behalf. His probation was revoked, leaving him to serve thirty-nine months in the state prison in San Luis Obispo.

At the time, such details of the University's intervention were unknown to the FSM political community. All we knew, vaguely and somewhat inaccurately, was that campus police had caused Glaser's arrest for possession of a roach and that he had vanished. But it was clear that he had been specially targeted as a political troublemaker, that the marijuana charge was a pretext for his removal from the scene of ongoing protest, and that he needed and merited our support.

To our shame, I must record that we lifted barely a voice and not one finger in his behalf. A few spoke for him at the Executive Committee meeting of October 18, where it was decided that some would study the matter and report back; I doubt that they did. I think we may even have considered his defense at a Steering Committee meeting and decided against it. The injustice of his case was glaring and closely linked to the one we were protesting. But our response was paralyzed, as much by inner conflict as by outward considerations.

In retrospect, it may seem simply prudent for us to have averted our attention from Glaser's predicament. Beside having so much else on our hands, we had strong reason to distance our movement from his case. Desperate for public support in a climate where newspapers were contending to publicize the Commie agitators responsible for our rebellion, we could ill afford to have the FSM identified also with drug use by supporting a pot-smoking Trotskyist sure to be spotlighted, accurately, as a crusader against drug laws. So we backed off from this hot potato, so quickly that we may scarcely be said to have encountered it—savoring our senses of being prudent protectors of our movement, to mitigate the sense of shame some also felt at abandoning Glaser and the issues he represented.

For by then many of us had come not only to understand that marijuana use should not be construed as a crime but to recognize the very issue of regulation of such consciousness-affecting agents as a key frontier of civil liberties, extending protection of freedom of thought and expression. In this light, Glaser's years of campus preachment had been entirely political, rather than divided embarrassingly between politics and drugs, as many activists of traditional political mind had viewed them; and the roach was not just a pretext for arrest but integral to his case. The FSM could hardly have supported him properly without expanding its consciousness of its own cause. What wonder that we shirked the theoretical and practical complications involved!

This story of injustice and cowardice—of the University's extraordinary, unconscionable persecution of a political agitator and the FSM's failure to contest it—is part of the buried history of the FSM and of the peculiar war against marijuana continuing to this day.[18]

NOTES

1. A substantially extended version of this memoir will appear in the author's forthcoming book on the FSM.

2. Michael Rossman, "Barefoot in a Marshmallow World," *Ramparts* 4 (Jan. 1966), included in Rossman, *The Wedding Within the War* (Garden City, N.Y.: Doubleday, 1971), 124–36; and idem, "Looking Back at the FSM," in *New Age Blues* (New York: E. P. Dutton, 1979); see also within "Ten Years Later: Inside the FSM," *California Monthly* 85 (Dec. 1974): 10, 12.

3. In particular, the Committee for Liberal Education tried to publicize processes of administrative decision that affected students vitally yet were beyond our influence.

4. See Rossman, "The Vigil at Chessman's Execution," *DC*, 4 May 1960, and "The Protest against HUAC," both in *Wedding*, 33–45, 47–71.

5. "New Faces on the Picket Line," *Occident* (fall 1961): 5–14.

6. Though this characterization is life-long, my experience in the FSM restored and focused my appetite for social organizing, leading me during 1966–1972 to be among the principal organizers of the national movement of student-initiated reform in higher education.

7. See Rossman, "The FSM and the Open Circle Model," in *On Learning and Social Change* (New York: Random House, 1972), esp. 71–72, 76–79; and idem, "Open Circle Processes," in "Learning Games" (manuscript in author's possession, c. 1976), 52–60.

8. Rossman, "The Birth of the Free Speech Movement" in *Wedding*, 92–120.

9. Rossman, "The Protest against HUAC," in ibid., 68–69.

10. Rossman, "Barefoot in a Marshmallow World."

11. Rossman, "The Birth of the Free Speech Movement."

12. Beside expediting the Report, Schultz had already begun independently to gather the documents of the conflict, assembling the core of the FSM's archival legacy, now in the Bancroft Library. As a Report volunteer Laura Murra set out to gather the emerging literature about the FSM, preparing her distinguished role as Laura X, the magpie archivist of the early years of the emerging feminist movement.

13. In the 1965 Byrne Report ("Byrne Report to the Forbes Committee of the Board of Regents," 7 May 1965 [copy available in University Archives, Bancroft Library, University of California at Berkeley]) and in two books: W. J. Rorabaugh, *Berkeley at War* (New York: Oxford University Press, 1989), and David Lance Goines, *The Free Speech Movement: Coming of Age in the 1960s* (Berkeley: Ten Speed Press, 1993).

14. See Robert Starobin, "Graduate Students and the Free Speech Movement," *Graduate Student Journal I,* 4 (spring 1965): 19; Max Heirich, *The Spiral of Conflict: Berkeley 1964* (New York: Columbia University Press, 1971), 243; Goines, 310n. Starobin's article notes that it was intended for the "final" edition of the Report. Heirich confuses the Report with its overview in saying thousands of copies were distributed. Goines repeats Starobin's reference, adding only the names of Hollander, Schultz, and Irwin as responsibles.

15. This was a typed letter from Robert S. Johnson to President Kerr, 24 Nov. 1964 (copy in author's possession).

16. I can hardly have been the only one to imagine our history's value as a tool of organizing and negotiating. That no word surfaced of others beginning independently isn't surprising, since my own activity affected the field situation. Atop the cop car, I had identified myself publicly by my concern for our history's pertinence. During the next week I made myself visible in the main public venue (the forming GCC) as the one concerned with such a project and left an impression that I was off to engage it. After October 16 everyone knew that a group had undertaken the project. At any stage, anyone who'd begun tentatively might well have thought the matter in better hands, which is surely why no competitors emerged and why the potential post would have called other candidates more actively if I had not appeared to fill it.

17. In *Spiral of Conflict* (150) Heirich dubiously cites a professor's impression that Glaser was the first to throw himself before the police car to entrap it. In *Berkeley at War*, Rorabaugh repeats this claim (130), drawing on a 24 Jan. 1968 *San Francisco Express-Times* story on Glaser's release from prison. As I suggest elsewhere, though the claim may be slightly false in fact, it is true in spirit. Glaser was among the first to try to stop the car and likely the loudest to yell for help; and he was almost certainly the one most recognizable to campus police, who may indeed have mistaken him as the chief instigator of our novel defiance, given their mindset of infectious "non-student" agents and their prior assessment of him as among the worst. Lacking sufficient documentation, I cannot say with certainty whether the impulse to put Glaser away originated with the campus police or the administration. But surely his prominent role was soon brought to the attention of key administrators, most notably Sherriffs, who were scrambling to understand what had happened, and surely the action against him proceeded with their oversight and blessing.

18. In *The Free Speech Movement* (184–185n) Goines quotes Rorabaugh's indirectly derived version of this story and adds an alternative account of Glaser's jailing. Though each version is as plausible as the rumors that reached us then, neither is accurate about the process, and neither recognizes the administration's aggressive role in Glaser's imprisonment. Goines mentions "the Executive Committee meeting where both Mario and I made impassioned speeches about solidarity and not letting [Glaser] fry all alone," and notes that nothing came of this but doesn't discuss why.

The FSM and the Vision
of a New Left

Jeff Lustig

It's hard to know what to make of the sixties. It resists comprehension in a way other periods do not. Looking back from the vantage of 1964 the meaning of the thirties or the forties seemed clear. Looking back, however, from the longer vantage of the present, the verdict on the sixties is still out. We have yet to agree on its meaning.

We have yet, in particular, to understand Berkeley's Free Speech Movement, an early struggle and an eventual catalyst of the largest mass student arrest in the nation's history. The problem is not with understanding what the FSM accomplished. It ran the writ of the First Amendment to the Berkeley campus and changed the identity of American college students in the process. It burned off the fog of Cold War repression. It lay the grounds for later antiwar protests. But what was the movement that did these things? A traditional reform campaign? A generational rebellion? A balked revolution? None of the terms seems quite right. The event defies the familiar categories as successfully as students in 1964 dodged the plans University administrators carefully laid for them.

The reason the FSM and other early sixties' movements—SDS in the East and SNCC in the South—elude our usual categories is that they were crucibles of a new kind of radicalism, seedbeds of a new Left. The Left that would emerge out of the bases they prepared would be a curious one, lacking a manifesto, a party, and even a unified theory. It would differ from what had preceded it and would often perplex veterans of the previous struggles. (Italian filmmaker Michelangelo Antonioni, researching *Zabriskie Point* in the Bay Area, grew perturbed by its activists' inability to name their party or present their overall program.) Its activists would invite the charge that they lacked "the convictions of [their] courage."[1]

But the early, relatively brief struggle in Berkeley still continues to generate interest and excite debate. Why? Because of the specific nature of its radicalism, I propose, and the new politics it already exemplified. The FSM in fact reveals something important about the sixties as a whole—that it was "radical" *before* it was left. The nature of its early radicalism is what made the later left "new." In the current period, amidst the confusion generated by the collapse of the theory and expectations that guided leftist thought for a century, much may be gained from looking back at the actions of people who already saw beyond the contending myths of the Cold War. They were people who had arrived early at the end of history.

IN THE BEGINNING WAS THE ACT

To understand this early period it is necessary to overcome an initial obstacle. The obstacle is raised by the fact that we know something that no one knew at the time—namely, that there *was* a "sixties." Everyone today from the most innocent freshman to the most cosmopolitan scholar knows that young people in those days scorned authority, broke rules, picketed businesses, and sat in because it was "the sixties." That's what people did. Embracing this notion, however, prevents us from understanding precisely what we need to explain.

No one who confronted authorities and risked arrest in 1963 or 1964 knew that there would be a "sixties." They could not explain their rebellion or anchor their identities with reference to a decade that had yet to be created. The problem is to explain their initial willingness to act without this reference, to retrieve their vital moments of decision from beneath the appearance of inevitability where they have been buried for many years now.[2] What exactly did the early protesters think they were doing?

The first place to go for an answer to this question is their own words. And the best distillation of those words as they appeared in a multitude of addresses, leaflets, and conversations is in the lucid speeches of one of their leaders, Mario Savio, particularly in his justly remembered summons to the Sproul Hall sit-in, December 2, 1964: "There is a time when the operation of the machine becomes so odious," he declared, "makes you so sick at heart, that you can't take part, can't even tacitly take part; and you've got to put your bodies upon the gears and upon the wheels, upon the levers, upon all the apparatus, and you've got to make it stop. And you've got to indicate to the people who run it, to the people who own it, that unless you're free, the machine will be prevented from working at all!"[3]

This was an extraordinary appeal in the vocabulary of American politics, rare in its cogency and striking in its resort to the evidence of his listeners' hearts and bodies. It declined the familiar tropes of American reform and eschewed the appeals of the established left. Savio promised to bargain no interests, delineated no class forces, and depicted no inevitable contradictions. (Having just returned from a trip to Cuba, I was struck by this at the time.) He even declined to assure anyone of ultimate victory, a standard element of most calls to action. Taken literally, indeed, his central metaphor hinted otherwise. The effect of bodies on gears is obvious, but so, unfortunately, is that of gears on bodies.

What he did do was to capture the existential posture of his listeners, the personal sentiments of the students gathered in Sproul Plaza, with remarkable precision. His language was radical in the etymological sense; it cut through stock phrases and conventional clichés to the *roots* of people's personal convictions. We Berkeley students had indeed come to feel that the knowledge industry celebrated by UC's president, Clark Kerr, was odious. The administrators' attempts to manipulate and deceive us did, in fact, make us sick at heart. We did feel ourselves faced by a machine that threatened the intellectual and political autonomy we came to the University to develop. But as products of the fifties ideology of a seamless, inescapable modernity, we had little real hope of beating the system. Confidence in victory was not one of our inspirations to action.

Beyond this special diction, Savio's statement gave voice to three themes that together explain the early decisions to act and the distinctive politics they forged. The first was the indictment of the University's practices on the basis of the society's professed values: free speech, civil rights, the necessity of education for democratic citizenship. It was the civil rights struggle that originally gave birth to the Berkeley struggle. And it was stubborn fidelity to free speech that ultimately transformed American college students from wards of random deans and coaches acting in loco parentis to young adults intent on following their own thoughts into action.

The last of these values, the commitment to a liberal education, developed in the course of the struggle itself. It was intimated from the start in calls for educational reform, especially in the publications of the student organization SLATE.[4] But Savio invoked it directly in indicating *why* the machine had to be stopped, revealing that his listeners had come to a sophisticated understanding of the historical choice facing American higher education. He spoke from within the controversy sparked by Kerr's recently published *Uses of the University* and in reaction to corporate analogies increasingly in vogue on the campus. "I ask you to consider: if this is a firm, and if the Board of Regents are the board of directors, and if President Kerr in fact is the manager, then . . . we're the raw material! But we're a bunch of raw material that don't mean to . . . be made into any product, don't mean to end up being bought by some clients of the university."[5] It was the prospect of being made into products by the knowledge factory rather than educated to be independent thinkers that galled students and forced them to explicate why they had come to the University in the first place. It was in defense of their original intentions that they put the instructions from the ubiquitous IBM cards on their own buttons and picket signs: "Do not bend, fold, spindle, or mutilate."

In the course of the struggle we students began to affirm a different purpose for public higher education from the industrial service model proposed by Kerr. We began to insist that the original and still primary purpose of public higher education was political, in the broadest sense, not economic. It was to prepare people for democratic citizenship. Students were entitled to full rights of free speech and advocacy and entitled to discuss policies, debate positions, and prepare for off-campus actions (e.g., against segregated businesses) because they were citizens-in-training preparing to be members of a democratic public. Moving at this point beyond traditional ideas, FSMers forged a new understanding of the concept of a public along lines prepared by thinkers like John Dewey, C. Wright Mills, and Paul Goodman. We urged that the *public* in "public education" referred to more than a funding source, and we identified the overarching purpose of the whole enterprise: to prepare people to be members of democratic publics. Such publics would also, we hoped, revitalize democracy in an increasingly bureaucratized society. Disseminating political information and preparing for action through debate was not a distraction from higher education thus conceived but an essential part of it.[6]

The second notable feature of Savio's speech was its emphasis on action: action as the expression of belief and test of belief, and direct action also as the test of larger institutional realities. Savio's words themselves constituted an action moving others to act. The underlying point that the FSM had demonstrated from the beginning was that the essence of protest politics, beyond petitioning and meeting and issuing reports, was the taking of physical action. This will to act, this emphasis on taking a stand, had also been at the heart of the civil rights struggle in which Savio and others had participated. You "put your body on the line" in this tradition not because you were sure of success or historical vindication but out of a conviction that something that was deeply wrong had to be disrupted.

If the history of sit-downs and sit-ins runs back to the CIO of the late thirties, the history of public disaffiliation runs back to abolitionism and early dissenting churches. It is the tradition of moral witness emphasizing that one must, when faced with deep injustice, go beyond simply speaking one's mind or voting one's conscience. One must bear public witness, affirming that what is being done *is* an injustice and standing for the truth that is being denied. The decision to participate in direct action of this sort rarely claims epistemological certainty or strategic efficacy. It emerges on the far side of familiar phrases and strategies and constitutes a search for fresh words and explanations. Its intellectual method is that of the searcher and has more in common with Walt Whitman's or Jack Kerouac's man on the open road than with that of confident liberals and "scientific" socialists.[7] It is firm only in the knowledge that some things will not be suffered further.

Henry David Thoreau had provided Savio with his central metaphor (Thoreau: "All machines have their friction. . . . But when the friction has its machine . . . let your life be a counter-friction to stop the machine"). And Thoreau may also have provided the best case for this kind of action. Anticipating the existentialists by a century, he urged that action proved not only belief but also who one was as a person. It was intrinsically "radical." "Action from principle, . . . the performance of right, changes things and relations; it is essentially revolutionary. [It] not only divides States and churches . . . ay, it divides the *individual,* separating the diabolical in him from the divine."[8]

This performance of right, this decision to reach deep into one's innermost convictions and then to act on them publicly, takes courage. It took staunchness in the wake of McCarthyism to risk blacklist and censure from the society and staunchness to confront an institution that held the keys to one's future. It also took intellectual courage to insist on finding one's own terms for the effort rather than retreating to the protective verbiage of others' struggles. In Berkeley there was a history of this courage that helped embolden the protesters, running from UC's loyalty-oath resistors of 1949–1950, to Fred Moore's lone anti-ROTC vigil in 1959, and up through the first soapbox speakers who defied UC's ban on political advocacy in the early sixties.

The tradition of moral witness was not the only tradition apparent in the FSM. We were also the beneficiaries of a group of skillful strategists sensitive to the demands of practical politics. "We were playing to win," another leader, Jack Weinberg, later put it.[9] And these leaders were capable of making the difficult but canny tactical judgments necessary to achieve that goal. The two approaches shaped and influenced each other, and both were necessary for the FSM's victory. But without the initial commitment to moral action, the early politics would not have achieved the distinctiveness it did, nor sparked the unexpected actions that repeatedly expanded the FSM's ranks and extended a sense of involvement within them.

PARTICIPATORY DEMOCRACY

The third theme of Savio's speech, consistent with the concern for a new kind of public and manifested by the rally he addressed, was its dedication to participatory politics. Americans tend to think of politics as a conflict of private interests for preexisting goods, waged by representatives in remote legislatures. The people in Sproul Plaza, by contrast, had come to regard politics as an affair of the assembled movement seeking "goods" that were only then being created. Where most Americans feel that politics affects only distant affairs, the student protesters had come to see its effects as close and palpable. "The issues of free speech and the factory, of politics and education . . . are inseparable" an FSM leaflet declared.[10]

Underlying this approach was a belief in the movement as a community rather than an interest group or reform association or even a centralized party. The same idea of "the beloved community" informed the struggle in the South and was explicit in SDS's *Port Huron Statement* of 1962.[11] "Although our issue has been free speech, our theme has been solidarity," a Berkeley leaflet issued in January 1965 announced. "We have joined together as a community. . . . By being willing to stand up for others, and knowing others are willing to stand up for us, we have gained more than political power; we have gained personal strength."[12] Whereas prevailing liberal assumptions pitted individual against community, this view recognized community as providing support for individuality and, indeed, providing the context for developing real, effective individuality.

These premises led to the conclusion that any democracy worth the name was a participatory democracy. It was a politics *by* the community and not simply for it.[13] The Berkeley activists broke with the age-old American fixation on representation as the essence of democracy and considered the exclusive reliance on representation to be an experiment that failed. They felt that the socialist experiment had failed, too; no party could presume to represent a class. Both Madisonian and Leninist traditions were seen as centralizing the means of making history and pointing in bureaucratic directions, making people objects rather than active agents of political affairs. This participatory approach generated a remarkably creative sense of politics in a few short years and also produced a number of new forms of mutuality. Politics seemed to be at once an expression of the common interest and a means for self-expression, something fun and rewarding rather than alienating. The commitment to participatory publics, finally, caused many activists to cease looking to the state as the preferred agent of democratic reform and even as the authentic voice of the public's interest, distancing them from a central tenet of Democratic and Old Left politics.[14]

RADICALS BEFORE LEFTISTS

The commitments to civil rights and liberties, moral action, and participatory democracy together defined a new vision of radical politics and gave rise to a bold, creative, and combative activism. Later, as many FSMers and veterans of SNCC and early SDS moved on to antiwar and Third World struggles and confronted the deeper realities of American politics, they also moved more consciously to the left. They developed the class perceptions that had been anticipated in their critiques of the knowledge industry, and a sensitivity to other forms of social domination, like race and gender. They came to understand that the contradictions they were attacking ran deep and that the interests they confronted were linked to a larger system of capital.

As they moved leftward the insights and commitments of the early years went with them. The commitment to direct action and large-scale public demonstrations remained distinctive of sixties protests. The activists' impulse to take their cues from their own subjective convictions rather than from "objective conditions" remained. And the desire for participation and forms of organization that would "prefigure" the desired future remained, anticipating the later emergence of non-Leninist forms of Marxism.[15]

A few observers sensed at the time that the student protesters had broken the established molds. In an unexpected descent into McCarthyism, UC's President Kerr was quoted in a newspaper interview as charging that "forty-nine percent of the [FSM's] hard-core group are followers of the Castro-Mao line."[16] The bizarre claim won him few supporters, but did capture the truth in a roundabout way. Kerr discerned that our vision was different. For those who understood the coded vocabulary of the times, the charge acknowledged what we were *not*—namely, Stalinists. We were not the Designated Enemy. Our presence was *totally* unauthorized, the worst thing imaginable from a manager's point of view.

Some more-recent accounts miss the distinctiveness of the period altogether. One familiar view sees the protesters as simply well-meaning reformers inspired by the Civil Rights Movement to become a "political force" and extend constitutional protections to those who lacked them. Theirs was simply another chapter in the unfolding chronicle of American democracy. This view, put best by Todd Gitlin and the *Berkeley in the '60s* documentary (and expressed in parts of the present volume), sees the early activists as having been most effective when they joined in "peaceable assemblies, striving for the utmost legality, accepting the rules laid down by the authorities." It judges them, however, as having thrown it all away when they shifted to the left, adopted a politics of resistance, abandoned pacifism, confused "strategy and identity," and squandered the moral capital they previously had accumulated. Becoming more extremist, they fell in with a bad lot (the Black Panthers) and finally forfeited larger public support.[17]

This interpretation makes a few valuable insights but fails as a summary overview. It charges the activists with later marginalizing themselves at exactly the same time it also credits them with retaining the ability to build the antiwar movement.[18] More to our present point, it fails again to explain why the early protesters engaged in the bold actions they did. People do not wrench themselves out of prepared life-paths and risk arrest simply because of well-meaning constitutional abstractions or because they decide first to pursue a vocation of reform and then try to figure out the best way to do it. Utilitarians don't make rebellions.

People are moved to protest only when they feel a deep sense of wrong and when they are convinced that much will be lost if they do *not* act. They protest radically only when they no longer feel that existing wrongs will be remedied through the available channels. The issue *was* free speech, but that did not mean what is often assumed. It did not mean, for example, that their primary commitment was a procedural one. Theirs was initially a substantive commitment to civil rights. More broadly, a call for First Amendment protections in the context of the times was less a commitment to American rule of law than a protest against it. By the late fifties in the Bay Area such a call was redolent with the promise of disruption. It summoned specters of atheism and communism, allegedly pornographic poets and irreverent stand-up comics. A "free speech movement" was not something meant to reaffirm the American way but to shake it up. Many FSMers already felt deeply alienated from the American way and betrayed by its politics and were already seeking something different. They did not, again, have to wait till later years for their radicalism.

Things did change after 1964. The social context in which the FSM had arisen, with its distinctive mix of innocence and passion, disappeared. The increasing ferocity of the war, stunning failure of constitutional remedies, and escalating penalties for dissent destroyed the moral and political ecology of the early years. The civility many have noted could hardly survive when the authorities themselves broke the rules in murderous response to exploding ghettos at home and the Vietnamese abroad. The stakes of the game changed. Most activists, learning in the process, changed with them. That they would do so was determined not by a confusion of "strategy and identity" but by their sustained belief that action, in the context of community, was still the test of political commitment. This was not an apostasy but an evolution from their early politics.

Against this interpretation it has sometimes been charged that we early protesters could hardly have been radicals and harbingers of a New Left, because we were largely middle class in origins. We were not sons and daughters of blue-collar workers. We had not tasted the bitter fruits of toil and were, indeed, mostly beneficiaries of the American dream. This demographic point is certainly true; but the conclusion drawn from it is not.

The fact of the matter is that it was precisely because we were familiar with the American dream and knew its superficialities, deceptions, and hidden costs, that we beneficiaries were the ones most likely to become estranged from it. This may have been an unpredicted route to radicalism according to the canons of socialist orthodoxy. But it was youth who were well acquainted with American middle-class existence who challenged its hegemony and sought to develop qualitative alternatives to it, rather than spending their efforts trying to open avenues to it. They were no longer seduced by the ideas that external show could trump internal authenticity and that material acquisitions could make up for unfulfilling lives and work. The search for new ways was clear in their choice of heroes. SNCC writer Julius Lester wrote that in the late fifties we suddenly discovered alternatives to "catatonia" and Levittown. "While Fidel liberated the Sierra Maestra, the beat generation created a liberated zone . . . in San Francisco."[19] What linked Castro and the beatniks despite the vast differences in their personal and historical importance was that both had taken up residence outside the American dream. Both established liberated zones outside the presumably inevitable Brave New World.

So if the later battles provided "a poor training ground for practical politics,"[20] it was because the activists had never much cared about those politics in the first place. Many, influenced by the insights of the beatniks across the Bay and Sierra-bound dropouts in town, worried that even protest politics was a sellout. They were already attracted to Herbert Marcuse's "global refusal." For those who had checked out, the FSM was an acceptable reentry only because it promised aspects of an outsider's politics and something beyond the insider game.

MARIO SAVIO'S LEADERSHIP AND LEGACY

Standing next to me at one of the rallies in Sproul Plaza in fall 1964, Professor Norman Jacobson chuckled and offered a prediction. Despite all the fuss, he proposed, we protesters would be running the University in twenty years. He based his forecast on his own experience at CCNY and the example of Clark Kerr, who had come to Berkeley to do graduate work and support farmworker strikers in 1933 and stayed on to become UC president.[21] Apostasy was inevitable. I feared Jacobson might be right.

But he was not. Not even close. The people who were active in those years and went on to live in the nation's cities and towns, to work in public services and private offices, would later testify to the incapacitating effects of the early struggle for later business as usual. It left them with a permanent tic, an occupational disability when faced with standard operating procedures. Many would remain active, but in grassroots, offbeat ways. Something about the experience continued to clog the normal channels. Mario Savio himself died in 1996, at 53, doing almost exactly what he had been doing in his early years. He was teaching, drafting leaflets, living a barely secure existence on a lecturer's salary, calling meetings to which too few people came, calling them again, engaging the issues at hand. He publicly debated his campus president the day before his heart attack, opposing changes in the California State University system being forced, appropriately, by a protégé of Kerr.[22]

It was because of a rare combination of talents that Mario was a leader—became a leader—of a movement so skeptical of leadership. On one hand he was possessed of a unique eloquence, one that elicited not adulation or ardor but understanding and appreciation. He found the words to say what people felt but had not found the words to say, and with an accuracy and dignity that made them proud of their inchoate convictions. On the other hand, he was possessed of a formidable talent for sound, logical analysis. He was dogged in his study of documents, exact in his memory of details, and skillful in his explication of complex situations. Even hostile administrators came to rely on his construction of events. His were large gifts, and when you add to them a keen moral sensitivity and a private life more painful than most, the outlines of an exceptional person begin to emerge: impassioned but thorough, self-effacing but assertive, emotionally variable though morally fixed. He helped more than one generation find and keep their moral bearings.

Mario threw himself back into intensive political activity after the FSM reunion in 1994, when he saw the anti-immigrant, anti–affirmative action forces in California "threatening everything we ever fought for." If we sat back now, he asked, "what do our earlier efforts count for?" He and his wife, Lynn Hollander, had discussed it and concluded that, "if we're in for the lamb, we're in for the sheep," a Sicilian adage meaning that, if one were to be hanged, it might as well be for the full offense—a troubling remark from someone in visibly poor health.[23]

Speaking at FSM's thirty-year reunion, Mario explained why he never embraced formal Marxism and gave a good sketch of the sclerotized form of it that prevailed in the late fifties. Earlier the same day he had urged that NAFTA and GATT did not make overseas workers our enemies but *did* raise questions about the distribution of wealth at home. At the reunion ten years earlier, he had declared (with reference to Freedom Summer, 1964), "Either we succeed making [Nicaragua] the Mississippi of this generation or it will be the Vietnam of this generation."[24] And in a pamphlet he wrote with his son shortly before his death, he called for "an end to the disgrace of a massive 'underclass.'"[25] With class-conscious Thoreauvians like this, one hardly needs Marxists.

Quoting Yeats, he concluded one of his talks at the 1994 reunion urging that the poet had to have been wrong when he wrote that "the best lack all conviction, while the worst / Are full of passionate intensity." He insisted that it was the best who were passionate, or rather, he proposed, compassionate.[26] Displaying his convictions as fervently as he did, Mario was his own best argument.

I have not meant to romanticize the FSM or deny its shortcomings. A disposition to moral witness alone cannot sustain a movement, and a politics of authenticity may in time breed its own deceptions. The New Left would fail in the brief span allotted it to develop theories and forms of organization capable of sustaining the early vision. But the early FSM, though limited, was also seminal. Seminal because its method of action cut through clichéd rhetoric and deadened habits to awaken participants' sense of commitment. Seminal because it pointed the way to a more ennobling idea of politics than that with which we were familiar. And seminal because it began to frame a vocabulary for identifying the oppressions distinctive of our era and to develop forms of organization capable of helping us fight them together. The legacy of the FSM is the legacy of people who saw what was at stake and took a stand.

NOTES

1. David Lance Goines, *The Free Speech Movement: Coming of Age in the 1960s* (Berkeley: Ten Speed Press, 1993), 137.

2. Frank Bardacke notes the shift of perspective that occurs between a moment of decision and later reflection about it: "Before something happens it is impossible to predict. Immediately after it happens, it's 'easy to explain.' Within twenty years it has become inevitable" (personal communication).

3. Savio quoted in Goines, 361.

4. See Richard Fallenbaum, "University Abdicates Social Responsibility," *Cal Reporter,* 13 May 1963, in Seymour Martin Lipset and Sheldon S. Wolin, eds., *The Berkeley Student Revolt: Facts and Interpretations* (Garden City, N.Y.: Doubleday, 1965), 64; and Bradford Cleaveland, "A Letter to Undergraduates," *SLATE Supplement Report* 1 (Sept. 1964), in ibid., 66.

5. Savio quoted in Goines, 361.

6. This view actually retrieved the older theory that universities are necessary for republican governance and that the primary value of higher education is political because it prepares people for democratic citizenship. See John A. Douglass, *The California Idea and American Higher Education: 1850s to the 1960 Master Plan* (Stanford, Calif.: Stanford University Press, 2000), 20 ff., 44; and Bruce Kimball, *Orators and Philosophers: A History of the Idea of Liberal Education* (New York: College Board, 1995).

7. Savio prefaced the famous passage of his speech with an invitation—"I ask you to consider"—and not with an injunction or declaration. (I am indebted to Greil Marcus for this observation.) The suspicion of grand theory was a product of the fact that most who became leftists in the sixties had already become familiar with the failures and oversights of mechanistic and determinist Marxism from reading people like Isaac Deutscher, Albert Camus, and Jean-Paul Sartre.

8. Thoreau, "Civil Disobedience," in *The Portable Thoreau,* ed. C. Bode (New York: Viking Press, 1947), 113, 119.

9. Jack Weinberg speech at FSM reunion, Berkeley, 1 Dec. 1994 (notes on speech in author's possession).

10. "We Want a University" (FSM leaflet of 4 Jan. 1965), in Lipset and Wolin, 211.

11. *The Port Huron Statement* called for a new "kind of independence [that] does not mean egoistic individualism" and is founded on "fraternity and honesty"

(quoted in Paul Jacobs and Saul Landau, eds., *The New Radicals* [New York: Vintage Books, 1966], 155).

12. "We have tried, in the context of a mass movement, to act politically with moral justification. We have tried to be sensitive to each of our supporters and the individual morality he has brought to the movement. . . . The concept of living cannot be separate from the concept of other people" ("We Want a University," 208–09).

13. Hannah Pitkin and Sara Shumer, "On Participation," *Democracy II* 4 (fall 1982): 43–54.

14. This view also distinguished theirs from the Port Huron approach, which, though participatory, still looked to the government, political parties, and Americans for Democratic Action. The new politics was so novel compared to the old that both Savio and Weinberg sometimes denied it was politics at all (Goines, 93, 99.)

15. On prefigurative politics see Wini Breines, *Community and Organization in The New Left, 1962–1968: The Great Refusal* (South Hadley, Mass.: J. F. Bergin, 1982). Coincident with non-Leninist experiments, many New Left veterans in the seventies and early eighties also reembraced moribund forms of Marxism-Leninism. See Jeff Lustig, "On Organization: The Question of the Leninist Party," *Politics and Society* 7 no. 1 (Nov., 1977): 27–67.

16. For one version of Kerr's statement, see Hal Draper, *Berkeley: The New Student Revolt*, 59. On the controversy over precisely what Kerr said, see Addendum to Cohen's Introduction to the present volume.

17. Gitlin, *The Sixties: Years of Hope, Days of Rage* (New York: Bantam Books, 1987), 83, 292, 296; Mark Kitchell, *Berkeley in the '60s* (New York: First Run Features, 1990), documentary film.

18. Gitlin, 409, 411, and (his conclusions) 435, 438.

19. Lester, *Search for a New Land: History as Subjective Experience* (New York: Dial Press, 1969), 30–31.

20. Gitlin, 437.

21. Actually Kerr attended the famous Tagus strike of 1933 not as a supporter but as a "neutral" observer, a stance consistent with the later role he assumed. Anne Loftis, *Witnesses to the Struggle: Imaging the 1930s California Labor Movement* (Reno: University of Nevada Press, 1998), 30 ff.

22. On Savio's work at Sonoma State University, see Jonah Raskin's essay in this volume.

23. Savio remarks at the meeting that launched the Campus Coalition for Human Rights and Social Justice, Berkeley, 2 Apr. 1995 (notes on speech in author's possession).

24. Quoted in Robert Cohen, "The FSM and Beyond: Berkeley Student Protest and Social Change in the 1960s" (unpublished manuscript, Berkeley, 1994, available in Bancroft Library, University of California at Berkeley), 55.

25. Mario Savio and Nadav Savio, *In Defense of Affirmative Action: The Case against Prop 209* (Oakland, Calif.: Campus Coalition for Human Rights and Social Justice, 1996), i.

26. "That's what we have to convey to people. Not the message of immiseration, but the message of commiseration, of compassion" (author's notes, 3 Dec. 1994).

1

Campus administrators take the names of student rules violators, late September 1964.

2

One of the "illegal" advocacy tables, late September 1964.

3

Student demonstrator displaying an "illegal" sign.

4

Dean Arleigh Williams with a campus policeman at the outset of the conflict.

5a

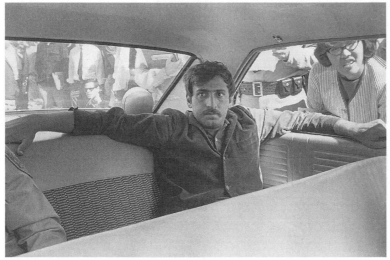

5b

Jack Weinberg held in police car, October 1 or 2.

6a

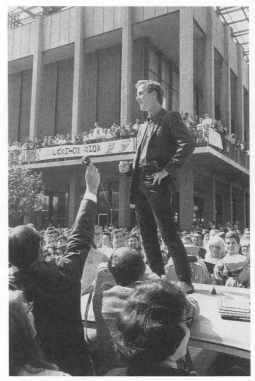

6b

(Left) **Mario Savio speaking from atop the police car.**

(Right) **Brian Turner speaking from atop the police car.**

7

Savio helps ASUC president Charles Powell to mount the police car.

8

Graduate student demonstrator.

9

CCPA board meeting, student delegates (left to right): Sid Stapleton, Suzanne Goldberg, Bettina Aptheker, Mario Savio, Charles Powell.

A view of Sproul Plaza from the student union roof.

11

12

(Top) **March on campus on November 20, 1964, the day of the Regents' meeting; three faculty members and a student carry a banner: professors John Leggett, Morton Paley, and John Searle and FSM leader Michael Rossman (left to right).**
(Below) **GCC leader Steve Weissman addresses a campus crowd.**

13

Mario Savio at his desk, early December 1964.

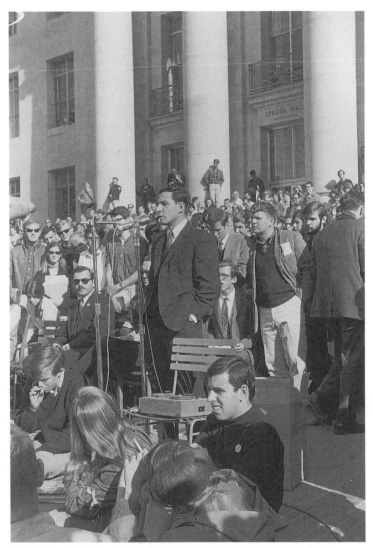

14

Professor John Searle addressing a crowd on Sproul Plaza shortly before the December 2 sit-in.

15

Joan Baez singing to FSM demonstrators near University Hall.

16

Demonstrators file up a Sproul Hall stairway, December 2.

17

Mario Savio and Martin Roysher in Sproul Hall, December 2. The _S_ on Roysher's armband is part of "FSM."

Savio addressing students during the December sit-in.

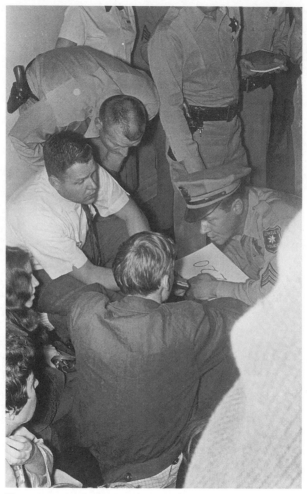

19

Arrest of a demonstrator in Sproul Hall, December 3.

20

Police dragging a demonstrator from Sproul Hall.

21

Arrest of FSM leader Jackie Goldberg, arrestee No. 133.

22

23

(Left) **Savio being interviewed shortly after his release from county jail.**
(Right) **President Clark Kerr addressing the convocation at the Greek Theatre, December 7.**

24

25

(Top) **Bettina Aptheker addressing a rally during the "filthy speech" conflict, spring 1965.**
(Below) **Professor Reginald Zelnik chairing the Vietnam debate in Harmon Gym, spring 1966 (see the essay in this volume by Leon Wofsy).**

26

27

(Top) **Professor Leo Lowenthal, faculty "Committee of 200" leader (photo taken in 1986).**
(Below) **Mario Savio in the 1980s (photo taken at Zelnik home).**

28

Official plaque dedicating the "Mario Savio Steps," erected in 1997 in front of Sproul Hall.

This Was *Their* Fight and *They* Had to Fight It

The FSM's Nonradical Rank and File

Robert Cohen

The most well remembered images from the Free Speech Movement are radical. The first famous FSM images were of the mass sit-in around the police car on Sproul Plaza that helped launch the Berkeley student rebellion. Equally memorable was the December student takeover of Sproul Hall, the UC administration building, which occasioned the largest mass arrest of students in American history, yielding news photos and TV shots of student protesters being dragged off to jail. These hundreds of arrests sparked yet more photogenic militancy as thousands of Berkeley students staged a strike to protest the use of police to crush the Sproul Hall sit-in. Such visual images of militancy were reinforced by the sound bites that dominated media coverage of the FSM. A key source of these sound bites was FSM student leader Mario Savio, an eloquent veteran of both Bay Area civil rights protests and Mississippi Freedom Summer whose anger at the sins of the multiversity burned almost as bright as his loathing for racism. The quote most often associated with the FSM comes from Savio, when he was beckoning students to join the movement's final Sproul Hall sit-in. Savio's words in this speech had a syndicalist ring to them, as he likened the University first to a business corporation and then to a heartless machine and spoke of a time "when the operation of the machine becomes so odious, makes you so sick at heart, that you can't take part . . . and you have to put your bodies upon the gears and upon the wheels, upon the levers, upon all the apparatus and you've got to make it stop."[1]

Historians of the 1960s have tended to cast the FSM as an unequivocally radical event, the complete embodiment of a new student left. Ideologically, the FSM is portrayed as a revolt against "the corporate liberalism of the modern university"; though FSMers "began with the liberal agenda of free speech . . . their liberalism led them quickly to radicalism, as the Free

Speech Movement exposed connections between political expression and other campus issues—parietal hours, pedagogy, and the purposes of the university." Tactically, the Berkeley rebellion is represented as a major step in the evolution of the New Left, as students began to take the civil disobedience popularized by the Civil Rights Movement and use it to build their protests on campus.[2] Militant rhetoric, building takeovers, and polarized politics were brought to campuses by students who followed the insurgency model ("the Berkeley invention," according to the President's Commission on Campus Unrest) pioneered by the FSM.[3] This view of the FSM, buttressed by the historical photos of mass protest and the famous quotes from Savio, has left the Berkeley rebellion with a secure and central place in the history of sixties radicalism and the New Left. Open up any textbook that mentions the FSM, and it is this radical context into which that campus revolt will be set.

This view of a "radical" FSM is not wrong, but it is incomplete. Savio did make some extremely militant speeches. Masses of Berkeley students did commit civil disobedience. Berkeley did inspire radical protests on other campuses. Yet there were many students in the FSM's rank and file who were not radicals.[4] The campus restrictions on free speech that initially sparked mass activism at Berkeley offended not only students affiliated with the left but those in the center and on the right and even those with no political affiliation at all.[5] Although this point is not new to historians of the movement, its implications have never been fully explored in the historiography. Nonradical students joined the FSM, and some even participated in its major acts of civil disobedience. As one FSM Central staffer observed, the FSM enjoyed "amazing support" from "'non-political' [that is, nonradical] types [who] felt that this was *their* fight and *they* had to fight it."[6] Yet the story of these students has for too long since been subordinated to the radical imagery, the Savio sound bites, and the tendency to depict the FSM as simply a chapter in the history of the New Left. Thanks to the work of the Bancroft Library, sources have recently surfaced that should enable us to begin seeing the FSM from the perspective of its nonradical rank and file.

The sources in question are statements that FSM defendants made in July 1965 near the end of the trial that grew out of the Sproul Hall sit-in of December 2–3, 1964. At this mass trial, FSM activists faced charges of trespassing and resisting arrest. Judge Rupert Crittenden, having found the defendants guilty, and on the eve of determining their sentences asked them to submit statements explaining why they had chosen to participate in the sit-in. These statements were left out of the official record of the trial; they were assumed lost but became accessible to scholars in 1999, when copies surfaced among the papers that FSM attorney Malcolm Burnstein donated to the Bancroft Library.[7] At least 515 of the 773 Sproul Hall arrestees chose to submit such statements to the judge. Taken together, these statements constitute arguably the richest collection of first-person testimony by FSM activists.[8] The collection is all the more unusual in that it is dominated by the rank-and-file activists rather than the much more widely publicized FSM leaders. In part this reflects the fact that the leadership was treated differently from the rank and file by the court. Sixty FSMers, including leaders and others with previous arrests (primarily for prior acts of civil disobedience in civil rights protests), were the only defendants assigned probation officers. The officers, in turn, were sometimes careless with or indifferent to the statements that their defendants had written to the judge and seem to have lost, omitted, or severely abridged eighteen of them.[9] There is also evidence that some FSM leaders never wrote such statements, refusing to do so as a form of protest against the legal proceedings and as a way of expressing group solidarity with the other defendants, who wanted to be judged not as individuals but as part of a movement. Some radicals, as defendant Marvin Garson put it, viewed the court's request for such a statement as "a final indignity. . . . We had always taken pride in standing together [throughout the semester of campus protest] rather than pleading for individual mercy." In refusing to give his probation officer a statement explaining his actions, a defiant Garson asserted that his thinking was "not the business of the state or of the courts in a country where men are not supposed to be punished for their ideas."[10] For all these reasons, then, some key FSM leaders are not represented in the collection of defendant statements. In contrast to the typical press and historical accounts, in which leaders are overrepresented, in this collection they are if anything underrepresented, leaving us with a rare opportunity to view the movement from the bottom up.[11]

In other kinds of cases such statements to a judge on the eve of sentencing might be more problematic as historical sources. Had this been a violent crime or one for which the defendants were apologetic or embarrassed, their statements might be poorly suited to gauging their state of mind at the time of the "crime." Such defendants would be naturally inclined to demonstrate repentance so as to secure more lenient sentences. But in the case of the FSM virtually none of the defendants seemed apologetic or embarrassed, and many in fact did not regard their nonviolent sit-in as even the minor infraction that it was alleged to represent—trespassing. They felt they were standing up for the First Amendment and were anxious to explain their motivations rather than distort or sugarcoat their stories in a self-serving manner. As Jo Freeman, author of one of the statements, recalled, she and her fellow protesters viewed themselves as entirely different from typical criminal defendants, who "commit criminal acts for personal gain in private in the hope of not getting caught." Those who went to jail and stood trial had, in Freeman's words, engaged in civil disobedience "for the public good in public; it was a public act not for personal gain. . . . The nature of [such an act of] civil disobedience precludes remorse."[12]

The statements to Judge Crittenden, however problematic they might seem as sources generated during a legal proceeding, often read like short, authentic political autobiographies whose authors sought to justify their political principles and commitment rather than engage in excuse making or blame shifting. The defendants did not use their statements to elicit leniency from the court or understanding from their parents by making apologies, airbrushing their motivations, or scapegoating the movement's radical leaders. They defied the rules of personal expediency by defending the FSM even at the risk of offending the trial judge. This is not to say, however, that all of the statements were uncritical of the FSM or its radical leaders. As we will see, there were nonradical FSMers who conceded that at times they had disagreed with the more militant actions and angry rhetoric of the movement's leaders. But even such disagreements were aired in a context of overall support for the FSM and seem to have honestly reflected the complexities and tensions of a politically diverse protest movement. Attesting to the veracity of the statements to Crittenden and their value as sources for understanding the FSM, Michael Rossman, a leading figure on the FSM Steering Committee, wrote in 1965 that these statements "moved me to tears. . . . They . . . are the only poetry of FSM in existence. With one exception in all that I read, they were gently but staunchly unrepentant. But more: they were a voice . . . of intellect welded to passion."[13]

The unrepentant character of the defendants' statements seems to explain why they never made it into the official record of the trial. According to Mal Burnstein, Judge Crittenden had requested these statements from the Sproul Hall occupation defendants in the hope that when confronted by fines and possible jail sentences they would become contrite. The judge apparently hoped for apologies and admissions of wrongdoing that would justify his anti-FSM rulings and verdicts. Since the statements were too defiant to serve his agenda, Crittenden apparently chose to omit them from the record, even though he had been the one who had solicited them.[14] The very candor of the statements, which made them so useless to Crittenden, render them invaluable to the historian seeking to understand the mind-set of FSM's rank and file, especially the nonradical majority, at the height of the FSM.[*]

---

[*]In donating these statements to the Bancroft Library, Burnstein, out of concern for the privacy of his former clients, included a provision against the use of the authors' names unless their permission was secured individually. Because of the logistical problems involved in tracking down the hundreds of authors in a timely manner, such permissions could not be pursued, so in the discussion that follows they are referred to via randomly selected letters (FSMer A,

To be sure, there *were* some radical rank-and-filers among the authors of these statements. But their numbers were small. Only 6 percent of those who wrote to the judge (31 of 515 authors) articulated anything resembling a radical critique of capitalism or the University, and fewer still even hinted at the need for continued campus militancy or a revolution in American higher education. Rare were the FSM activists who justified participation in the sit-in with anticapitalist rhetoric, as did A, a student active in CORE, who wrote that the "Bank of America and the grower-shipper agricultural interests of the state ran the university for their own interests, used bracero slave labor, paid unbelievably low wages, and most important, ran the University with disregard for the First Amendment's guarantees of civil liberties." Though acknowledging that technically he and his fellow protesters had broken the law, A contended that the laws they had violated were "the laws of the large industrialists and agricultural bosses. These men tried to kill the Civil Rights Movement. . . . As the I.W.W. has shown, the free speech fight is essential to radical change. The democracy I want includes free speech. The regents cannot tolerate it." Similarly, B, an equally radical student, indicated to the judge that he considered the sit-in too tame: "I would have been perfectly willing to see the movement progress further than it did, to the point of blocking doors, sitting on desks, etc."[15]

It is not, however, these few expressions of radicalism but rather the numerous statements by nonradical students that are the most striking, because they seem so unfamiliar. The rank and file represented in these statements emerge not as a New Left army, with hundreds of youths thinking and marching in lockstep, but as a loose political coalition that included many liberals (a strong majority, 399 of the 515 authors, or 77 percent) and a still more moderate minority (37 authors were moderates, while another 44 wrote statements that used one or two moderate arguments).[16] In employing the terms *moderate* and *liberal*, I mean to denote not fully formed ideologies but rather political tendencies and temperaments. Of these nonradicals, the students I call "moderates" expressed the most dissent and ambivalence about the militant tactics, rhetoric, and leadership that the FSM ultimately adopted; they seemed to come from either conservative, apolitical, or antipolitical backgrounds and had the most difficulty with the idea that they were part of a movement that defied University regulations and the law. Moderates tended to be highly individualistic and wary of mass protest; they would embrace such protest only as a last resort,

---

defendant B, student C, etc.). The editors did ask Burnstein to remove this restriction, since its practical effect is to bar from the historical record the names of rank-and-file FSMers, so neglected by historians. The full text of all the statements that I quote are available in Burnstein Papers, boxes 3 and 4.

and ambivalently. The students I term "liberals" were the largest group among the people who wrote statements; they seem to have entered the FSM predisposed to support reformist social movements, and though initially uncomfortable with civil disobedience, had—after some hesitation—come to accept this tactic. The liberals were less likely than the moderates to write critically about the FSM's militant leadership, but they also differed from that leadership in their high degree of idealism about the University and their disinclination to use class analysis or other radical rhetoric.[17]

Although a full-scale portrait of the FSM's nonradical rank and file would require a book-length study, it is possible here to explore their views on some central identifying issues and thereby at least offer a crude sketch of their mind-set. The FSM moderates may be readily identified as the movement's most reluctant activists. Unlike Savio and other veterans of the Civil Rights Movement, long accustomed to using civil disobedience as a political weapon, moderates were quite uncomfortable with breaking the law—even nonviolently. Some, in fact, though supportive of the Civil Rights Movement in principle, objected when that movement engaged in civil disobedience. C, for example, one of the few African American students arrested in the sit-in, had participated in lawful pickets with civil rights groups but never before engaged in civil disobedience; "when civil-righters have been arrested for civil disobedience," she wrote, "I felt they were infringing on the rights of others. . . . Someone may be morally wrong by discriminating, but I wouldn't be morally right by jeopardizing their rights (e.g. the Lucky shop-ins)."[18]

Believing that their cause was just, such moderates did not apologize for sitting in, but they explained that their decision to engage in civil disobedience had been painful and difficult and that they regretted that the UC administration's intransigence had left them no alternative. Embodying this moderate mind-set, student D stressed that his decision to sit in "was not taken lightly nor was I happy about it. Respect for the law has been an integral part of my upbringing. . . . We had no other way open to us to bring about . . . badly needed changes. . . . It is unfortunate that the price we had to pay to get the Administration to make such changes . . . is a criminal record which will follow us the rest of our lives." For FSMer E the decision to sit in had been excruciating because it "brought into conflict my loyalties to the University, to the state of California and its laws, and to the civil rights movement, so that silence would have been implicit partnership in injustice and the only available channel of protest was illegal." Some moderates, such as F, had spent weeks, even months on the fence, caught between the reverence for free speech that they shared with the FSM leadership and their reluctance to break the law:

> My decision to participate in the Sproul Hall sit-in was not an easy one and it
> took me quite a while. . . . From the beginning I deplored the action of the

Administration in abridging civil liberties. However, my concern was with the methods being used [by the FSM.] [I] never before participated in any protest action [and was initially] just a watchful bystander. [It] took me two and a half months of debating with myself. I felt our FSM had to succeed for if this kind of abridgment of rights could occur in an institution of learning . . . there was no telling where it could spread. Therefore I let myself be put under arrest, something I had wished to avoid, something I am sure that most of us were terribly, terribly unhappy about.[19]

In the most extreme cases, reluctance to engage in civil disobedience carried over until well into the day of the December sit-in. While the media focused on the seasoned political leaders, FSMer G represented a very different type of protester, one who almost missed the sit-in because of prolonged agonizing over the ethics of engaging in civil disobedience. G, who came from a conservative background, had been recruited into the FSM by her best friend, a Goldwater activist. Whereas the friend could not bring herself to join the sit-in because she feared her parents' reaction, G reluctantly took the plunge, although she did not enter Sproul Hall until 6:30 P.M., "after a day of very careful and worried thought."[20]

Some moderates, such as GB, tried to come up with lawful alternatives to sitting in. She proposed that the FSM instead conduct "a mass fast in front of Sproul." GB came up with this idea, according to her statement, because she saw the urgent need to protest "the unjust and arbitrary use of power by the administration" but disliked civil disobedience and "violation of the law." When her proposal was rejected by the FSM Steering Committee and the sit-in began, GB was "in an ambivalent attitude." But she then decided to enter the building "to stand up for what I believed in," yet was still "caught up in a conflict at the same time that I might have to be in violation of something else that I firmly believed in, the laws of our country as the limits and guarantees of our freedom. . . . In the conflict between my outraged sense of justice and the thought of being arrested for 'illegal assembly,' the scales tipped in favor of the former."

Having agonized so torturously over civil disobedience, moderates would never share the radicals' upbeat assessment of the sit-in as a moment of triumph. Radicals gloried in the fact that at Sproul the student movement had mounted one of the largest and most effective campus protests in history. Militants referred glowingly to the sit-in as an event that forged a spirit of camaraderie, a campus version of the beloved community.[21] It was a spirit that Berkeley radicals would seek to recreate throughout the sixties. But moderates like E came to and away from the sit-in in a much more somber mood. E wrote Crittenden, "I regretted and regret that all parties to the 'free speech' controversy acted as such fools that orderly procedure had collapsed by December. . . . The situation reflected the failure of us all, Administration and students, to keep the dialog alive." "It was with regret, not joy that I walked into Sproul Hall," wrote H, who had never been polit-ically active before; "I had hoped all along that some important person might say, 'You know, those students are people, human beings, and they have gripes. Maybe we should stop for a second and listen to them seri-ously.' But it hadn't happened." Other moderate students struck an equally somber note, including FSMer I, who wrote that he joined the sit-in "not with any joy (it was only afterwards on T.V. that Mario Savio's speech moved me), but with the feeling that I had been given no choice." FSMer I found it "tragic that for a semester students had been crying to be heard, admit-tedly sometimes rudely and rashly, and the only cognizance the Adminis-tration seemed to take of that cry was to attempt to quiet it down, never to listen to what was said on its merits." "To me the sit-in symbolized the fail-ure of *human* means for resolving the dispute," wrote J, "since it symbolized the breakdown of verbal communication. The mute piling of bodies as stones seemed as symbolically crude and unsophisticated a human endeavor as was possible." GB recalled the sit-in as "a nightmare of finger printing, mug shots, newspaper headlines, charges of 'Communist.'" Another mod-erate, though defending the sit-in as necessary to mobilize the faculty in defense of free speech, expressed regret that these events had "stained" the name of the University and that "students across the nation might suffer in their own common reputation" because of the Berkeley upheaval—which is why he expressed the "hope that there will never be a sequel to Decem-ber 2, 3; and that students and faculty will never again be so distant and mutually unintelligible."

Moderate students were aware that their political views and general lack of political affiliation or activist track record distinguished them from the leadership. They wore this separate identity almost as a badge of pride. Their statements find them justifying their decision to join the FSM's defense of free speech while maintaining a critical position on the move-ment's leaders. They were simultaneously affirming their solidarity with the movement and establishing their intellectual and political independence. K, for example, explained: "I was probably representative of most of my fellow arrestees and students in that I did not consider my actions prede-termined by any 'line' or group affiliation. I acted as an individual and, as such, was sometimes in the position of defending the Administration; urg-ing moderation; questioning the policy and tactics of the FSM Steering Committee."[22]

This sense of independence led a number of the moderates to dissent from some of Savio's more hard-edged rhetoric. L, who planned to become a college teacher, joined Savio in the sit-in but clearly disliked his words about stopping the University machine. He told the judge that he "went into Sproul in order to establish . . . communication" with the University administration—"not 'to bring the machine to a grinding halt'; quite the opposite. It was my belief that *in no other way* could the administration be convinced that communication was essential." Similarly, M insisted that "the sit-in was initiated with the intent of building a better university and not with the idea of destroying anything (despite Mr. Savio's oft quoted words)."

It is almost breathtaking to see just how far removed some of these moderates were from the defiant spirit of the sixties. In describing his state of mind on the eve of the sit-in, N wrote to the judge, "I thought that 'politics' was a dirty word. I believed that political activists *had* to be by *nature* scheming outsiders. . . . When handed a leaflet by a 'true believer' I chuckled inwardly and walked by." Such thoughts had more in common with the "silent generation" of the orderly 1950s than with the dominant image of student activists in the turbulent 1960s. In the same vein, some of these moderates had initially been reluctant to join the movement because, however just its demands, the FSM was a rebellion, destructive of good order and stability. Along these lines, FSMer O wrote, "I must admit that in the early months of the dispute . . . my first reaction was that order must be preserved—at all costs."

As these words suggest, students who, in a sense, still maintained a 1950s state of mind at the beginning of the school year refused initially to endorse the FSM (or at least its earliest acts of civil disobedience) because their first impulse was to back the authorities. A striking example of this initial resistance to the FSM's rebellious message came from P, a graduate student. Though arrested in December, during the early days of the FSM he had refused to engage in civil disobedience and spoke up publicly against such militant action. Present at the October blockade of the police car, he had addressed "the crowd from the Sheriff's car. . . . Never having dealt with the University Administration before, I deplored the harsh statements that were being made against it by the students." And even when this kind of student did engage in a seemingly radical act—occupying the administration building—he or she would stress its nonradical goals. O, for instance, insisted that "my protest was motivated . . . not by a desire for radical change, but rather a desire to return to already agreed to principles of public rights [to] preserve basic rights. I felt my duty to be one of *preservation.*"

What is remarkable about this moderate minority is that it actually shared some of the assumptions of faculty critics of the FSM such as Nathan Glazer, who had come down hard against the very idea of using civil disobedience on a college campus. Glazer derided the Sproul sit-in as coercive, a use of force that pressured the administration into meeting movement demands and short-circuited rational dialogue.[23] Like Glazer, FSM moderates disliked campus civil disobedience and recognized the dangerous potential of its coercive power. But unlike Glazer, they came around to the position that it could be used as a very last resort, and they conceded—reluctantly, to be sure—that the administration's behavior had proved that the University's bureaucracy would not engage in meaningful dialogue unless prodded to do so via civil disobedience. The essential difference between Glazer and these moderates was not ideological; both shared a reverence for the law and deep concern about the use of unlawful tactics on campus. But these students had experienced or, more to the point, had endured a kind of powerlessness that Glazer as a prominent faculty member was unable to grasp, and by December 2, the only way they could find to overcome that powerlessness and to have their simple demands for free speech acknowledged was by sitting in.

.   .   .

To judge from their statements to Crittenden, liberal student arrestees were far more numerous than their moderate counterparts and more upbeat about their political activism. Liberals tended to have agonized less than moderates in deciding to engage in civil disobedience; they also looked back on the sit-in with less regret and greater pride. In this vein, Q wrote that his participation in the sit-in was "one of the high points of my socially responsible life—far greater than my participation as a Naval Officer in the 'Formosa Strait' Emergency of 1958." "I feel pride in . . . maintaining my convictions. For in later life I fear the responsibilities of family and the dollar bill will be placed above my ideals," wrote R of his arrest in Sproul. FSMer S looked back upon the sit-in as the moment when "I personally learned to fight for my ideals in the face of overwhelming hostility. This I will never forget." T found "irony in the accusation by some" that the sit-in had been "un-American," since she viewed her work in the FSM on behalf of freedom as "the most expressly *American* behavior I have exhibited in my life."

Such expressions of pride had much to do with the language of rights in which the FSM's liberal majority thought and spoke. Most did not agonize about either joining the FSM or sitting in, because for them it seemed self-evident that constitutional rights they cherished, free speech and due process, had been trampled by the campus administration. The more eloquent among the FSM rank and file specifically cited the First and Fourteenth Amendments. But even in the absence of constitutional citations, defendants who were part of their movement's liberal majority almost always premised their pro-FSM essays on their inalienable rights to speak, organize politically, and be free from arbitrary punishment when they mobilized against an administration that had sought to deny them these rights. These students argued with confidence that they were in the right, that administration abuses had to be stopped, even if it took civil disobedience to achieve this.[24]

Convinced of the justness of their cause, liberal FSMers often looked to the past to strengthen their arguments on behalf of the rebellion, and they found many historical precedents and political authorities to legitimate the use of civil disobedience. These precedents affirmed the students' sense that their protests were in accord with the highest values of a democratic society. Among these precedents was the American Revolution, which students saw as a parallel conflict in which liberty-loving citizens resisted unjust authority—using both lawful and unlawful means of dissent. This is what defendant U had in mind when he explained that his participation in the sit-in had been sparked by "serious infringements of my constitutional rights. . . . All channels of communication had been blocked. . . . I felt strongly about my rights, just as those who threw tea into Boston Harbor almost two hundred years ago felt strongly about their rights. . . . I walked into Sproul on December 2, 1964 in order to secure my birthright." Invoking Patrick Henry, student V wrote that she saw the Sproul sit-in as similar "to many instances in history" in which "citizens have committed civil disobedience against the state in order to have certain distasteful laws removed. . . . We are taught to admire the reasons for the American Revolution. Is the Sproul Hall incident so different? Where is OUR representation?"[25]

Student W also began her defense of the Berkeley revolt by citing the Revolution, stressing that the FSM shared with "the Framers of the Constitution a belief . . . that the American society and government would become greater if an atmosphere prevailed which encouraged all points of view to be freely expressed." Claiming that she went into Sproul "to make the ideals of freedom of speech an actuality, at least on this campus, and not mere platitude," W went on to link the FSM with the classic defense of liberty by John Stuart Mill, implying that the sit-in embodied the libertarian spirit of Mill when he wrote that "the peculiar evil of silencing the expression of an opinion is that it is robbing the human race, posterity, as well as the existing generation—those who dissent from the opinion, still more than those who hold it. If the opinion is right, they are deprived of the opportunity of exchanging error for truth; if wrong, they lose, what is almost as great a benefit, the clearer perception and livelier impression of truth by its collision with error."

The list of authorities invoked in defense of the FSM reads like a hall of fame of liberal icons. In addition to Mill, FSMers invoked Gandhi and Thoreau, Justices Jackson, Douglas, and Holmes, historian Henry Steele Commager, writers Albert Camus and James Baldwin, and, of course, Martin Luther King, Jr. At times the statements read like political theory papers, with their authors almost self-consciously citing political figures and offering extensive quotations from them in a manner that sometimes seems overdone. But what these reflect is the desire of their young authors not to be stereotyped as mindless rioters; they wanted to have themselves and their ideas taken seriously—and not have their free speech movement seen as some kind of frivolous youthful exercise, a panty raid. This is what FSMer X had in mind when she wrote, "What we have done was done in the spirit of Jefferson and Thoreau, not in a spirit of violence or mere youthful rebellion."

Liberal FSMers saw in the tragedies of the past important lessons about the necessity for resisting evil—lessons which also served to legitimate the FSM. Most prominent among these was the case of Nazi Germany. For student Y the lesson was that "people only deserve the civil liberties they utilize and are willing to fight for. Hitler marched into Germany and took away civil liberties and few protested. If we are to criticize the Germans for being afraid to resist we ourselves must not be afraid." Invoking Hannah Arendt's *Eichmann in Jerusalem*, Z, a Lutheran theology student and history graduate student, argued that unlike Eichmann, that "classic obedient man," his fellow FSMers had recognized "the perils of silent obedience" and in so doing had stood up for "one of the great moral issues of our century."[26] Citing a World War II–era moral atrocity that occurred in America, FSMer AA, explained that the Japanese American exclusion and internment camps had shaped his political consciousness, making him sensitive to any "unconstitutional . . . infringement on personal liberty." He stressed that this sensitivity, which led him to join the sit-in, had developed before he had ever heard of Chancellor Strong, President Kerr, or Mario Savio. The lesson he had learned from the history of America's internment of the Japanese Americans was "that a citizen should never under any circumstances, yield temporarily or give up permanently one fraction of the rights granted to every citizen under the U.S. constitution." McCarthyism was another powerful historical memory, invoked, for example, by BB, who thought that "period of repression and hysteria" was related to the Berkeley revolt in that both showed "civil liberties . . . could only be defended by their constant exercise and by people ready and willing to defend them."

Among the precedents cited for resorting to civil disobedience, however, none was more popular among liberal FSMers than the Civil Rights Movement. Most of them had not themselves been activists in that movement, but they admired it deeply, and some had followed it so closely that they felt themselves vicariously a part of the nonviolent struggle for racial equality and social justice.[27] "I and many other students consider the civil rights movement the most moral and decent activity in America today," wrote CC to the judge. The Civil Rights Movement had legitimated the sit-in tactic, demonstrating that "passive resistance was a dignified and practical way for me to act" against injustice, explained DD. As BB entered the final stage of her decision to join the sit-in, she had looked to the Civil Rights Movement for inspiration, wondering "how people arrested in Civil Rights demonstrations felt. . . . I wondered if one reached a point where there was no wavering: one was positive of the correctness and inevitability of one's actions so that one no longer weighed the significance and consequence of a possible arrest." There was for these students something comforting about being able to invoke the names of such civil rights heroes as James Farmer and Martin Luther King and to see that the risks they took to defend student political rights linked them—because UC's crackdown on campus political advocacy was widely seen as aimed primarily at civil rights activists—to the Civil Rights Movement that they so admired. Thus DD wrote, "I feel that the rights of advocacy which the FSM was fighting for was intimately connected with the civil rights movement in the South," which made her feel herself "a part of the civil rights movement." Similarly, Y recalled, "When I first came to Berkeley, I was proud to hear that Berkeley students contributed so much money to the civil rights movement. . . . The best way to help the movement if you were unable to go to the South yourself" was to join the FSM's struggle to stop the ban on campus political advocacy, since that ban had been "a direct blow against the civil rights movement."

This sympathy with the Civil Rights Movement was one of the key ways in which liberal students without an activist background linked up emotionally with Savio and other veteran civil rights activists in the FSM. Among such liberal students, a good deal of admiration was directed to those who, like Savio, had risked their lives in the southern freedom struggle. This admiration was visible in the moving statements of students such as EE, who paid tribute to the leading activists they "met and worked with [in the FSM,] . . . students who had been lauded for their work in Mississippi, who were committed to justice, and who had a strong feeling for individual integrity and the democratic process. They would speak to anyone who would listen, debate with anyone who wanted to argue, and listen to anyone with an idea."[28] This admiration for the radical veterans of the Civil Rights Movement was substantial, even though liberal students had not yet connected the struggle against racism with a larger and radically critical view of American society in general and the University in particular.

It is on this last point, their attitude toward the University, that the difference between the liberals and radicals was most evident. The radicals tended to see the University as a capitalist-dominated and impersonal knowledge factory, one that churned out unthinking technocrats for corporate America. Key FSM militants had picked up some of these unflattering notions about the University from Berkeley's resident socialist elder, Hal Draper, who denounced Kerr and the "multiversity" in an influential speech he gave in fall 1964, published as the polemical pamphlet *The Mind of Clark Kerr.*[29] FSM leader Jack Weinberg, for instance, had been using Draperian rhetoric indicting the University almost from the very start of the FSM. As far back as October 1, when he was being dragged away to the police car on Sproul Plaza, he railed against the University as a knowledge factory that gagged rebels because these "parts" were not deemed to be up to the factory lords' "specifications." "Factories are run in an authoritarian fashion—non-union factories, anyway—and that's the nearest parallel to the university," charged Mario Savio. In explaining the Berkeley rebellion to a *Life* magazine reporter, Savio depicted students as an "exploited class," subjected to "all the techniques of the factory methods: tight scheduling, speedups, rules of conduct they're expected to obey with little or no say so. At Cal you're little more than an IBM card. . . . The University is a vast public utility which turns out future workers in . . . the military-industrial complex." Savio argued that the UC knowledge factory was doing a poor job of encouraging students to think and blamed not only the University's repressive administration but a faculty so concerned with "producing nonsensical publications . . . that should never have been written and won't be read" that it lacked the time to teach well. "Two thirds of the lectures I've heard . . . shouldn't ever have been given, they're so bad." It was, in Savio's eyes, a university so huge that students did not benefit much even from its most famous faculty, "those Noble Prize winners. Maybe a couple of times during the undergraduate years . . . if you look carefully, if you bring along your opera glasses you see them 100 feet away at the front of a lecture hall in which 500 people are sitting." Thus at Harvard, when asked whether he was worried that the Berkeley rebellion might discourage good students and faculty from coming to Cal, Savio replied that because the educational experience was so poor at Berkeley "we may be doing good if we get people not to go to the University of California."[30]

The FSM's liberal majority did not buy into this kind of rhetoric or the scathing critique of the University on which it rested. Liberal rank-and-filers were much less likely to echo Draper and voice his alienation from the University. FF, for example, wrote to Crittenden, "I love the university, and my actions were my attempt to make it closer to what the ideal university should be." FSMer Margot Adler captured this fondness for the University when she noted that at Berkeley she felt "anything but alienated," and she even defended the large lecture format in her letters home. During her first year at Berkeley Adler "felt a new sense of freedom and an almost Edenic sense of bliss, and it was a bit hard to see myself as the soulless IBM card depicted in FSM leaflets." This positive outlook on the University was typical, moreover, of a majority not only of FSMers but of the larger Berkeley student body. Sociologist Robert H. Somers found that 82 percent of the Berkeley students he surveyed in November 1964 reported themselves "satisfied or very satisfied" with their education at Berkeley.[31]

Liberal activism in the FSM was on one level an outgrowth of idealism about the University—as students experienced a variety of emotions from surprise to anger and then often disillusionment when the FSM controversy revealed that the leaders of UC had not lived up to their idealized conception of the University. This idealization was visible, for example, in GG's letter to Crittenden, which praised UC Berkeley as "a great institution" and the "Athens of the West," a place so committed to the life of the mind that one would expect it to stand always for "free and open debate . . . of all political persuasions." That so great a university "should attempt to limit free speech (and therefore stifle the civil rights movement) was and still is shocking to me." "Pure amazement" was the way HH characterized her initial reaction to the ban on political advocacy: "It was unbelievable to my idealistic, naive head that the administration of a university so concerned with the development of the youth of America would degrade itself so."

In explaining their affection for the University, some liberal students cited "the depth of its faculty," but most saved their greatest words of praise for its tradition of political and intellectual freedom. S wrote that she had no choice but to protest the ban on political advocacy "since a large part of my pride in the quality of the Berkeley campus was based on the degree of freedom [with] which students could learn about, advocate, and support the whole spectrum of political and social ideas on campus . . . a very important part of the education a student received at Berkeley." For such students, that motley assemblage of political card tables at the southern entrance to the campus was as much a center of learning as the library. As FSMer II explained: "During my three years at Berkeley I had appreciated the information, the possibility to purchase buttons and stickers and to give donations which these tables afforded. I depended upon them as channels of communication between myself as a citizen and the outside world. To me their existence was a vital part of what made the Berkeley campus a great university." JJ, in explaining his path to Berkeley and the FSM wrote, "I originally entered Cal because I was so impressed by the political atmosphere which the students created [which] differed from the apathy of the university which I attended before Cal. It was a very beautiful thing to go to school at Cal and to see students who cared about things other than those which materially touched their lives. I was willing to do almost anything to help Cal keep that special atmosphere which the administration was attempting to strip." Similarly, KK wrote of having come to the intellectual and political freedom of Berkeley after "five years in a politically sterile and moribund community. Before I came to Cal I had always held liberal political views which I had never been able to express in a community which was chiefly populated by business executives and DAR [Daughters of the American Revolution] members. Coming to Cal was a breath of long needed fresh air. For the first time, I had the atmosphere, time, and facilities for practicing, advocating, and developing my political principles."

As such statements suggest, the liberal majority was not promoting a radical critique of the University, which they openly admired for what they saw as its long history of nurturing dissent. They clearly believed that it was not the student movement but the administration that had broken with the University's liberal tradition. According to these students, the administration, by kowtowing to off-campus "political and economic pressure," had not lived up to its responsibilities. For LL, the administration had not merely blundered; it had betrayed the great tradition of the University: "If the university is not involved in the dynamic process of social change the whole society will suffer. If the university's traditional concern for political liberties is allowed to lapse into so much academic cant, then its trust to the public is betrayed. And betrayed so much the worse because that academic community begins to believe that its cowardice and cant portrays real commitment. All of us forget that the concept of freedom *means* something." Similarly, MM accused the administration of discarding its traditional role as the guardian of campus freedoms. In imposing new "restrictions of political and social activity [the] administration acquiesced to [outside] influence out of a desire to improve the university's image. . . . The function of the university [is] to provide an environment where students can mature intellectually, where they may seek, without hindrance, the answers to the questions they feel need to be answered, where all points of view may be put forward and discussed." NN too used part of her letter to Crittenden to take the administration to task for "compromising its responsibility by not allowing the student body to be 'educated' in the most comprehensive sense of the word . . . a university must at all times allow all forms of controversy."

In the eyes of liberal FSMers, it was not enough merely to criticize the administration's failure to protect the University's tradition of freedom. The entire University community had an obligation to protect that freedom. "A university is the vanguard of society," wrote OO, "and therefore often seems suspicious or dangerous to those who don't understand its role; all the members of the university community, faculty, students, and administrators, should attempt to protect the university from attack by [outside pressure] groups rather than attempt to force the university to conform to patterns which are mediocre enough so that everybody can approve of them." In short, students had to come to the aid of their university, to protect the freedoms that the administration had suppressed, and to stand up to the outside pressures to which the administration had succumbed. This is what MM had in mind when he defended his decision to join the sit-in and traced his activism in the FSM to "my desire to protect the freedom of the university and to preserve its functions [as a center of intellectual growth and political freedom,] the nature of which is embodied in the school's motto, 'let there be light.'" "The university as I valued it was in great danger," wrote PP, "and it was my responsibility to do something about it. I wished to preserve the University not only as a place where I could study English literature . . . or mathematics . . . but as place where free and unbridled learning could go on in fields not covered in the classroom." UC's administrators had "acted irresponsibly," QQ argued. "They acted to destroy a great and productive university; I acted to preserve it." For liberal FSMers, then, their protests were designed not to remake the University in a new and radical way but rather to restore it to its liberal traditions.

·   ·   ·

Had the FSM been merely a leftist faction or an ideologically driven political sect, the distance between these rank and file and the radical leaders could be taken as a sign of weakness—since such organizations tend to value a kind of ideological coherence that was lacking in the FSM. But the FSM was not a faction; it was a mass movement whose political diversity was in fact one of its main strengths. That diversity may have made the movement's life contentious at times, but it did not disrupt the fundamental solidarity that nonradicals displayed with the movement and its fight for student rights. Indeed, nonradical students, recognizing that some of the FSM's more radical and visible leaders had put themselves at serious risk, were protective of them. FSM rank-and-filers—moderates and liberals as well as radicals—took it as their duty to shield the movement's leaders from being singled out for reprisals. This, as much as the free speech issue itself, was at the heart of the December 2 sit-in. Students of all political stripes were rallying to protect their leaders from just such reprisals after Chancellor Strong, during the 1964 Thanksgiving break, initiated new disciplinary proceedings against them.[32]

There were several dimensions to this solidarity. On one level, FSM rank-and-filers were reacting to what seemed to them the "petty, vengeful manner" in which the administration "singled out for punishment" leading activists whose defiance of the campus ban on political advocacy had been no different than that of hundreds of other students. It seemed arbitrary to scapegoat these leaders. Since the administration had disregarded the lenient recommendations of the faculty's "Heyman Committee," FSM rank-and-filers were convinced that the due process rights of the suspended students would be trampled in any new disciplinary hearings.[33]

These inducements were important enough for many students to join the sit-in. But there was an additional source of anger in the FSM rank and file that was evident in all parts of the movement's wide political spectrum and that tells us much about the movement's ideas about leadership. Historians have noted that Savio embodied the New Left's ambivalence about leadership, scorned the celebrity imposed upon him by the media, rejected the idea of a movement run by charismatic leaders, and embraced instead the ethos of participatory democracy and the model of a grassroots movement of self-organized equals.[34] But what has not been as well understood is that in addition to being moved by his own antielitist sensibility, Savio had little choice but to act democratically, because FSM rank-and-filers would surely have repudiated anyone who saw himself as the FSM's maximum leader. This was a movement whose rank and file had thought long and hard about leadership issues because of the way the press and the administration had behaved. Campus officials and hostile editors had sought to weaken the FSM by red-baiting its most prominent figures, depicting it as the brainchild of a small group of manipulative subversives and troublemakers rather than as a mass movement that reflected genuine grievances and mainstream student opinion.[35]

Seeing themselves and their movement so caricatured infuriated FSM rank-and-filers because it implied that they were puppets or dupes of leftist leaders rather than intelligent college students whose protests were motivated by careful thought about serious grievances. They were offended by the Thanksgiving suspensions, which seemed to embody this notion of dupes and leaders while highlighting the administration's belief that the movement could be decapitated through the punishment of a handful of instigators. This is what student RR had in mind when he wrote that the administration's "'get the ring leaders'" attitude was "insulting, as if people at the university level and even graduate students could not think for themselves." The suspensions had to be resisted, wrote SS, because they were an attempt to "dismiss the entire affair as inspired by a minority of 'radicals' who stirred up a number of 'unthinking followers.'" TT, in turn, was "angered at the condescension implicit in the reasoning that the elimination of student leaders would eliminate student demands for free speech." "Leaders," UU told the judge, "constitute not a separate breed of people, but simply the members of an opinion group or 'movement' who are especially capable in foresight, organization, or articulating the important common notions. . . . They are neither demigods nor criminals to any greater extent than the rest of us."

Despite this powerfully protective sense of solidarity with the FSM's leaders, many rank-and-file defendants made a point to assert that it was the cause of free speech and due process rather than the appeal of any particular FSM leader that was at the heart of their activism. "It was the principle, not the principals that motivated me," VV explained to her mother, while AA stressed that he had been guided "by a sensitive conscience and a strong belief in morality" and not "brainwashed" by any leaders. WW denied that her decision to sit in had been "an emotional act—sown, watered, and reaped by a few skillful leaders." XX, who "disliked group action" and was "not a joiner," though admitting that FSM leaders had sometimes been "stubborn" and that "arrogant intransigence" had been "too often the characteristic position taken by the FSM," had decided nonetheless that the "FSM was basically right" in its defense of free speech. YY admitted that she had been "strongly influenced" by the leaders, but stressed that her thinking rested "ultimately" on her "own analysis of the facts. I never trusted FSM leaders to do my thinking for me. I often disagreed with them, and sometimes felt they were making serious mistakes."

Because the press had harped on Savio's agitational eloquence and singer Joan Baez's alluring musical presence at the rally that preceded the December sit-in—as if together they had been the pied pipers who drew entranced students into the protest—some defendants made a special point of emphasizing that neither enchanting song nor crafty oratory had led them into Sproul. ZZ wrote, for example, that "to the best of my knowledge no 'silver tongued orators' were in control of my mind." BB assured Judge Crittenden that it was not Savio's oratory that induced him to enter Sproul Hall, while AAA joked that he had not entered the building "under the impression that I was attending an informal folk-music concert, though I admit to being a big fan of Miss Baez." This impulse to demonstrate that their participation in the sit-in was well reasoned and not a product of manipulation even affected some rank-and-file radicals, including SDS organizer BBB, who wrote to Crittenden that before she sat in "I did not hear Mario Savio's speeches, nor did I hear Joan Baez's song. I made the decision myself in my apartment—as rationally as possible—aware then as I am now of the possible consequences."

Sitting in, then, became more than a way of supporting the suspended students; it was an affirmation that the FSM was a genuine mass movement supported by thousands of students who shared its commitment to free speech and student rights. This was CCC's thinking as she—who "had never been an activist before"—entered Sproul: "if enough of us" joined the sit-in "we would finally be listened to and not be merely discounted as a minor left-wing group . . . it was time to stand up for what we believed." DDD expressed the same impulse, seeing the mass sit-in as proof that the FSM was not a "small group of malcontents, non-students, professional agitators, Communists, or whatever other term occurred to" the administration. "When a thousand students entered Sproul Hall at this point the administration could not possibly pretend that 'a few trouble makers' constituted its problem," explained EEE. "This point, although secondary to the 'free speech' or 'rules' issue, is central to the sit-in and to students' new found dignity and solidarity."[36]

One did not have to be a radical or even a liberal to resent administration and press red-baiting or to repudiate the "red leaders and dupes" view of the FSM that it promoted. If anything, the red-baiting appears to have backfired, drawing moderates closer to the movement and leaving them more sympathetic to militant leaders. Physics graduate student FFF explained that, whereas in the early fall he was "mildly opposed to the FSM," having viewed its actions as "too hasty and impatient," he gradually became "totally annoyed by the news media which continually branded the protests as the work of a 'handful' of 'outsiders' and 'communist agitators.'" While these nonviolent demonstrations by aggrieved students "received wide publicity as 'riots,'" he continued, "real riots by students at vacation spots received little notice, and were dismissed as pranks. I have never belonged to any extremist organization of the left or right and I am neither 'subversive' nor an agitator but 'politically pure.' I felt the presence in the FSM of myself and others like me would demonstrate support from citizens whose loyalty was not suspect." And P, a graduate student who had initially opposed the FSM, soon found himself wondering why the administration was "so consistently contemptuous of a patently fair student complaint" and why President Kerr "took every opportunity to malign the aggrieved students through the news media by labeling them as unclean fringe elements, anarchists, Maoists, or Castroites." "When I discovered that a sit-in was planned against these accumulated grievances," he wrote, "I felt it was my duty as a former Fulbright Scholar and Fellow of the National Science Foundation to join the other students in making it clear to the public eye that not just beatniks, Maoists, Castroites, and other weird mentals were outraged by administrative high-handedness in abridging constitutional rights." Similarly, Q, a premed student, vehemently denied that FSM activists were revolutionaries or rowdies: "I am an honor student. I have never been disciplined by the school. I have [prior to the sit-in] never been arrested, nor have I been a member of any campus organization. . . . I am not an irresponsible rowdy. I do believe in law and order. [Now] I see how the label Communist can be used to avoid an issue." GGG's statement included a scorching indictment of the administration for its effort "to discredit all attempts to get back political freedom by slandering me and fellow students as Maoist-Castroites and outside agitators." The administration's innuendoes, he declared, constituted "a refusal to permit honest dialogue."

The dominant note in these student reactions to the use of red-baiting was anger directed mostly at the UC administration. This was, however, only the tip of an iceberg of student disdain for the administration's behavior. Anger, disgust, incredulity, disappointment, bitterness about the overall way in which the campus and statewide administrations had handled the crisis were almost universal among the arrested students and were reflected in almost all their letters to Judge Crittenden. Whether radical, liberal, or moderate, whether movement veterans or political neophytes, whether admirers or detractors of the University, the defendants spoke with one voice when it came to expressing outrage at the alleged misdeeds of the chancellor and the president.

To get a sense of this pervasive outrage one merely has to sample some of the most telling phrases the arrested students used to indict the administration: "a semester of frustration and disillusionment in dealing with the university['s] . . . evasive tactics"; "disgusted with being treated as members of a 'panty raid' or a football rally"; "arbitrary administrative punishment"; "a complete lack of confidence in the administration"; "arbitrary and non-negotiable manner in which these prohibitions were imposed"; "ignore and insult significant percentages of their students"; "dealt with student dissent as a problem to be disposed of instead of something to be heard and considered"; "harassment of student leaders . . . broken promises, . . . arbitrary decisions;" "lost faith in the administration's fairness and impartiality"; "the hypocrisy with which the administration met sincere protest"; "violation of the spirit of past agreements"; "university administrators were not acting honorably"; "Kafka-like"; "self-appointed monarchs"; "[used] terrorism to frighten the many by hurting a few"; "ancien régime"; "monolithic bureaucracy indifferent to legitimate grievances of faculty and students"; "vindictive . . . capricious . . . condescending"; "deceit, mistrust, and disrespect for the rights and ideas of the community with which they must work"; "nearsighted"; "shoddy administration lies"; "made a mockery of the Bill of Rights"; "the chancellor had decided to abolish Reason as well as political activity"; "treats us like helpless and innocent children"; "high handed"; "ignored our petitions, granted us hearings before non-existent committees, carried out lengthy negotiations in which their policy was merely affirmed by President Kerr . . . mouthed libertarian principles, while helping bigots."

Despite the highly emotional tone of these words, they were no mere exercises in name-calling. The students' disdain for the administration rested on a narrative drawn from its response to the multichaptered free speech crisis that unfolded week by week during fall semester 1964. Only a few of the people who wrote to Crittenden had the patience to detail the long train of abuses for which they indicted the administration, but most of the letters alluded to at least a few. The list began, of course, with the ban on political advocacy itself, then proceeded to Dean Towle's claim—quickly retracted after protesting students offered to do a traffic study—that the ban had been issued because of a "traffic obstruction," followed, as RR wrote, by the arrest of Jack Weinberg "for soliciting funds for civil rights." According to RR, the agreement reached after the protest against Weinberg's arrest "wasn't carried out in good faith," by which he had in mind the one-sided composition of the CCPA, the committee that was supposed to reach an agreement about the new rules governing political advocacy. Similarly, FSMer V noted that the administration "loaded" this committee,

and "its representatives . . . claimed that anything agreed to in the committee wouldn't be binding on the administration. They were talks, then, not
negotiations. The administration later rejected its own Heyman committee
report" (in which a faculty committee had recommended leniency for a
group of suspended students). Like many others, V found that the most
"disheartening" experience was when the Regents, having met to decide on
new campus rules regarding free speech, "decided to ignore the 5000 people [in the FSM's silent vigil] on the lawn outside and their four representatives inside." And the sit-in itself added another piece to this narrative
of administration offenses as students, hoping that their act of nonviolent
civil disobedience might gain them the attention of administrators, instead
were answered with a slap in the face, the police unceremoniously hauling
them off to jail.

The details of the narrative are less important than the authority it commanded among the students, particularly the moderates and liberals. This
record of abuse and deception accelerated the movement of nonradical
students into an activist role in the FSM and insured that the overall FSM
dynamic would be—if only incrementally—leftward, as moderates and liberals began, at least on the issue of free speech and administration abuse of
power, to sound as angry as the militants. Many students who had never
demonstrated before were led by one or several perceived atrocities to
protest in coalition with radicals they had ignored in the past.[37] A case in
point is HHH, who in the early fall still had faith that "the problem of political activity could be settled amicably" and still viewed "the University as a
community of scholars dedicated to reasonable discussion" but who as the
semester wore on became increasingly upset by the administration's arrogance and intransigence: It "became apparent to me [that UC] was not a
community of scholars at all. [The] administration had total power, faculty
who retreated into research, and a student body . . . with no voice. . . . The
idea of a university seemed to be lost; the administration believed that students did not . . . need a voice in what happened to them."

In some cases, this move toward activism was a life-changing experience.
Old assumptions, long-standing patterns of deference to authority were,
for HHH and some of her classmates, coming undone. In one of the most
vivid descriptions of this process, the liberal FSMer GG wrote,

> [S]tanding in front of Sproul hall, I did not even hear Mario's exhortation or
> Baez's song. My roommate and boyfriend were not there. I had to make this
> decision alone. I had a furious battle with myself. . . . Sitting in was right, but
> what about being arrested, my parents. If I go to law school could I pass the
> bar with an arrest on my record? Then the battle stopped. A feeling I cannot
> describe came over me. I walked in scared of the consequences, but knowing
> that I had to sit-in. . . . This commitment was a big step for me. My first year of
> college had been a process of tearing down old values. I had come to college

completely success oriented. I would marry a doctor and be a lawyer. In college I learned about other values—personal integrity, social consciousness. Still I only knew them on an intellectual plane. During my freshman year I could not even bring myself to join a picket-line, let alone sit-in at the Sheraton Palace. [Because of the FSM] the old commitment to success for its own sake, a big house in the hills was gone. Sitting in was a step toward finding new commitment.

Had many stories like GG's appeared in the letters to Crittenden they would indeed represent dramatic evidence that the encounter with the UC bureaucracy had rendered porous the political lines outlined in this essay—converting moderates into liberals and the liberal majority into radicals. In some instances such conversions did occur. Among the statements sent to Crittenden were more than a handful by students who were so shocked by the deployment of police and their roughing up of students that the experience moved them into something resembling the radical camp. However, those who underwent thoroughgoing radicalization were few, and it would be a gross overstatement to speak of mass radicalization.[38] To judge from the letters, most of the rank and file neither echoed GG's tale of a dramatic value shift nor embraced radicalism. (Nor do we know how many went on to become active in the New Left.) As should be evident by now, a sizable number managed to compartmentalize the FSM experience, viewing their civil disobedience as an emergency tactic. The more moderate among them continued to view that tactic as unfortunate and interpreted the sit-in as symbolizing "a terrible failing of any democratic system," one that they hoped would never again be needed on the Berkeley campus. Their primary goal during and after the FSM was reformist—to win for students the right to political advocacy. With that right secured, they intended not to enter a new life of political action but to return to their studies. Moderates came away from the movement resentful of those who tried to read too much into the Berkeley revolt, who forgot that the FSM battled for limited goals, and who saw the FSM as part of a more general youth rebellion. As one defendant explained: "So many side issues of . . . existential rebellion, modern man's 'alienation,' and academic reform have been brought into the FSM issues as well as the subsequently childish 'filthy speech movement' that I don't know what has become of this main point of unjust and arbitrary use of power by the administration. It has been lost in the ensuing publishing and television 'free for all.'"

.   .   .

It is a truism that all historical sources reflect the biases of their authors and the political climate in which they were produced, and this is certainly true of the statements that FSM rank-and-filers wrote to Judge Crittenden.

There were historically bound limitations on how willing their authors were to fully explore their connections to Savio and other radical leaders. On this relationship the statements, if accepted uncritically, may be misleading. As we have seen, the repeated accusation that the FSM was little more than the handiwork of a few subversive leaders left many students disinclined to credit Savio (or *any* leader) with a decisive role in their decision to join the movement. This tendency to minimize the leaders' role had grown even stronger by the time the students wrote their letters, that is, in the wake of a trial in which the prosecution resuscitated the rank-and-file-duped-by-manipulative-leaders formula to discredit the FSM.[39] In short, rank-and-filers had strong inducements to respond to exaggerations of the role of leaders by going to the other extreme.

In assessing the rank and file's attitude toward Savio's politics, it is important to understand that, though surely much more radical than the average FSMer, Savio was not the kind of radical that J. Edgar Hoover hoped to find. Hoover's FBI probe of Savio could locate zero evidence of Communist beliefs or affiliations, so the FBI resorted to a sleazy form of guilt by association, making far too much of his friendship with the FSM Steering Committee's only Communist, Bettina Aptheker.[40] Savio's radicalism was of an independent variety. Through his activism in Mississippi, he had developed a strong sensitivity to America's social injustices and a militancy both in confronting those injustices and condemning the society that generated and tolerated them. His indictment of the University, as we have seen, used radical imagery and spotlighted what he saw as the destructive role of a moneyed Board of Regents. Savio also saw the two-party electoral system as politically bankrupt, and in an early speech suggested that Americans would be given no real choice on Election Day since both parties had gone along with the Tonkin Gulf Resolution.[41] If asked (to cite the words of Reggie Zelnik, who knew him well and for many years), Savio might have

> called himself a socialist then, but not a Marxist, and I don't think that Socialism with a big "S" was a central part of his identity, which was more of what some Russian Marxists used to call that of a "radical democrat." I do remember one particular gathering I attended [in early fall 1964], when Mario, whom I did not know well yet, said to the small group of people . . . that there was one Marxist whose writings he had recently discovered who he thought was really excellent. I guessed from something he had said that it was Herbert Marcuse, and he immediately affirmed that I was right. . . . Mario I believe never overcame his attraction to Marxism. There was a level at which he really wished he could be a Marxist, but just couldn't, just like certain people who cannot, still wished they could believe in God. . . . Like a lot of radicals his dislike of capitalism was a more powerful internal mechanism than his love of socialism.[42]

Savio was not the kind of radical who pontificated about world revolution or used Old Left verbiage about the proletariat. He thought that self-professed revolutionaries who spoke a language cluttered with ideological cant that was alien to ordinary Americans were doomed to political irrelevance. This was why, for example, he thought so little of President Kerr's lifting of the campus ban on Communist speakers, whose ideological message was so lacking in appeal. To Savio, political speech mattered most when it was "consequential," that is, when it led to some immediate action against social injustice. So if one urged an audience of students to picket a racially discriminatory store, this was far more meaningful than clamoring all day about the dictatorship of the proletariat. This stress on pragmatic activism and undogmatic, unclichéd discourse helped make Savio's oratory effective; he spoke in a democratic vernacular that liberal and even moderate students could find appealing.[43]

To get at the political dynamic between Savio and the rank and file, especially the liberal majority, one must move beyond an either-or framework for judging political change (that is, either radicalization or no left impact at all). If it is obviously incorrect to speak of widespread leftist conversion experiences, one *can* see signs of political change and radical *influence*. After a semester of conflicts with the administration, liberal FSMers were still liberals, but they were liberals who had grown more comfortable with civil disobedience, more critical of authority, more alienated from the University administration. Although the liberals did not buy into the Draper or Savio rhetoric indicting the University as a capitalist-run machine, they did assimilate some of the more positive ideas Savio and others had been discussing about the purposes of education. They rarely credited Savio for this, yet many of their statements echoed Savio's view that college education should have a political dimension, that it should go beyond the classroom and involve students in discussions of (and potentially action on) real social problems. This rejection of a pure ivory tower was forceful and clear and suggested that, whether they knew it or not, many liberal rank-and-filers were following a more radical path toward redefining the purposes of higher education.

Few commentators have adequately understood that Savio's heated denunciations of Kerr and his vision of the multiversity did not signify (as Kerr himself wrongly assumed) that the FSM leader loathed the University.[44] Savio's anger at UC was fueled in part by his belief that the University could play a noble and egalitarian role in society—helping the poor, promoting antiracist movements, and fostering learning untainted by commercialism—in place of what he saw as Kerr's more technocratic and elitist vision.[45] Savio did not share the liberal FSMers' assumption that UC had once lived up to this ideal, for like other radicals, he was all too aware of past practices of suppressing dissent at UC.[46] Yet the critical Savio rhetoric reflected a belief that the University *could become* something better, could become a center of political and intellectual freedom and innovation, if only it was liberated from the burden of its bureaucratic administrators and conservative Regents. This was an idealism of sorts, though a tempered one, and it left room for both Savio and less radical students to find some common ground.

One of Savio's gifts as both an orator and political thinker was that he could take an idea with radical implications and normalize it, making it sound more acceptable to nonradical students. Usually, he presented his academic alternative to the multiversity in a language that showed how wary he was of alienating nonradicals. He often made the ideal of an administration-less university sound like a return to an older tradition of academic self-government, and he painted Kerr as an enemy of that tradition. Addressing Harvard students in December 1964, Savio declared that, in contrast to Kerr, the FSM represented a "more traditional educational philosophy. We believe in a university of scholars and students . . . with inquiry as its defining characteristic and freedom as its fundamental tool. Kerr's university is the most efficient . . . the most worldly. It is a university plugged into the military and the industrial [order]—but not to truth."[47]

A comparison of the rank and file's letters to Crittenden with Savio's FSM speeches yields at least four other critical elements linking Savio to the rank and file: (1) anger, (2) an empirical and democratic approach to political leadership, (3) a strong commitment to the Constitution's protections of free speech, and (4) an ability to link the campus world and student self-interest to the larger world beyond the campus.

1. Savio's public references to the behavior of the administration were invariably marked by anger. One has to hear the speeches to get a full sense of this. When completing some description of administration acts he viewed as unresponsive, dishonest, or autocratic, Savio would usually raise his voice and tighten his tone, making it clear to listeners that he could barely contain his rage. There were moments when Savio's anger got the best of him. Just prior to the police car incident, when a student asked him whether activists at the political tables should show their registration cards to administrators upon demand, Savio, replying in the negative, referred to these campus officials as "animals." During the sit-in he spoke of hiring a sound truck so that the FSM could tell the community how the administration was "shitting all over us"; the administration, he thundered, was good at the "dirty work" of punishing dissenters.[48] If at first such anger did not sit well with moderate students, by December Savio's fury was widely shared, which made him, on at least this one level, a natural student spokesman.

2. But Berkeley's critically minded student body demanded more than simple emotion. Savio had an extraordinary facility for building logical arguments that rested on firm evidentiary foundations. His rhetorical presentations were almost always empirically grounded, his anger

usually spilling over only after a detailed analysis and well-reasoned argument had been made. A typical Savio phrase was "the answer we received was the following," followed by a concise narration of his encounter with a University official and concluding with a devastating critique of the official's actions or arguments.[49] This was effective in part because it bore witness to a democratic leadership style, one that said to students that his meetings with the powerful were never "closed door," that he would not take to himself the traditional leadership prerogative of confidentiality but would tell everyone everything that he had learned from those meetings. Also, his use of narrative connected with ordinary students, who—as we saw in the letters to Crittenden—were assembling their own narratives of administration deeds and misdeeds as they decided whether to join forces with the FSM.

3. Savio always spoke as a defender of the Constitution and its most liberal aspects. To be sure, in his most famous "machines and levers" speech, replete with all its fiery radical imagery, Savio used the phrase "well meaning liberal" as a term of derision. But that speech cannot erase the ways in which, in his many previous FSM speeches discussing the Constitution and the courts, Savio sounded like an ACLU liberal himself.[50] He had much to say on the value of the First Amendment, free speech, and due process throughout the months of crisis, and when he spoke on these subjects his demeanor was less that of a radical firebrand than of a liberal young law professor. Even the uncompromising position he took with regard to possible punishment for unprotected speech was quintessentially liberal: The power to adjudicate such cases should rest not with University officials but with the courts, with their higher standards of proof and greater due process rights (a position at odds with Marxist mistrust of capitalist courts). In this respect Savio came across as the most uncompromising of liberals, unwilling to negotiate away one inch of student rights. Here was a posture that could not help but appeal to the FSM's liberal majority, who revered the Bill of Rights and were willing to make sacrifices to protect it.[51]

4. A final area of connection between Savio and the rank and file was both substantive and symbolic. As a veteran of Mississippi Freedom Summer, Savio embodied a kind of benign connection between the campus and the larger struggle for egalitarian social change. As such, he had the authority to link the local issue of political recruiting at the Bancroft and Telegraph entrance to the epic battle against Jim Crow in the South. Savio repeatedly dwelled on the need for students to incorporate thought and action, to reject an ivory tower approach to education, to engage in socially consequential speech. Coming as it did in the wake of the racist violence in Birmingham, the murder of civil rights workers in Mississippi, the wave of civil rights sit-ins and shop-ins in the Bay Area,

and an unusually ideological presidential election campaign, this link-
age between the campus and the larger political world was one that was
eagerly embraced by many students, whom it helped to convince that
the battle for student rights at Berkeley was not some parochial dispute
but was of national, even global significance.[52]

We have to recognize these commonalities so that we can understand why
a radical such as Savio could serve as the spokesman of a movement whose
rank and file was not predominantly radical. In Savio we see the New Left at
its most creative, when it was young, undogmatic, and able to find common
ground with a nonradical constituency. That constituency is well represented in the letters to Crittenden, which have enabled us to take a modest
first step toward a bottom-up history of the FSM. We have not yet begun to
explore the personal biographies, the political and career trajectories, of
those who gave no speeches, led no marches, made no headlines on their
own, but whose commitment swelled the crowds at rallies, enlarged the sit-
ins, and gave rise to what was at that point the largest, most sustained campus revolt in American history. This is one of the key tasks confronting the
coming generation of historians of the 1960s, and until it is completed we
cannot have anything resembling a definitive history of the FSM.

NOTES

1. Max Heirich, *Spiral of Conflict: Berkeley 1964* (New York: Columbia University
Press, 1968), 271–72. On Savio and the media, see Todd Gitlin, *The Whole World Is
Watching: Mass Media in the Making and Unmaking of the New Left* (Berkeley and Los
Angeles: University of California Press, 1980), 177–78. Savio's prominence in
media coverage of the FSM was such that the *New York Times* featured him in its
"Man in the News" column of 9 Dec. 1964. See also "Savio on Stage," *Newsweek,* 21
Dec. 1964, 71; "When and Where to Speak," *Time,* 18 Dec. 1964, 68; *San Francisco
Examiner,* 9 Dec. 1964; *Berkeley Daily Gazette,* 3 Dec. 1964. The media tended to oversimplify FSM politics by making the FSM look like a disciplined unit that followed
the commands of its charismatic leader. In reality its leadership was far more collective and democratic than the media implied. An elected Steering Committee
headed the movement, in consultation with a larger Executive Committee composed of representatives of student organizations and unaffiliated students. However, though unusually open and inclusive, the FSM was neither leaderless nor anar-
chistic. Its key leaders were centered in the Steering Committee and did much to
set the movement's direction. As FSMer Steve Brier recalled, "There was in the FSM
a democratic ethos. . . . But I don't want to romanticize things too much. There was
a lot of give and take, but there was definitely leadership. . . . There were people
with more [political] experience . . . and they were accepted as leaders. How could
it be different? It's not something to apologize for or pretend didn't exist" (quoted
in Ronald Fraser, ed., *1968: An International Student Generation in Revolt* [New York:
Pantheon, 1988], 92).

2. James J. Farrell, *The Spirit of the Sixties: The Making of Postwar Radicalism* (New York: Routledge, 1997), 158–59. A problem with Farrell's formulation is that it does not distinguish leaders from the rank and file or radicals from liberals. His account makes it seem as if the FSM was a monolith that moved quickly from a liberal to a radical agenda. Actually, as Savio stated in 1965, he and other veterans of the Civil Rights Movement came into the FSM *already radical*, though he distinguished this pragmatic radicalism from the more ideological radicalism of the Old Left. Savio recalled that the FSM's "tone has been set by the civil rights activists [and] was founded in a new non-ideological radicalism which is expressed most clearly in SNCC. Those people who have been most effective have been those who have made their decisions from a very pragmatic point of view. An activist pragmatic radical view to be sure, but not an ideological point of view." Savio saw the FSM as drawing strength and mass appeal from its character as an "issue oriented rather than ideological" movement. He thought that pragmatic radicals such as him could best promote student radicalization by avoiding ideological pronouncements and instead subtly encouraging students to notice the array of social forces and interests that shaped the FSM crisis. "There was," he observed, "a very clear threat and a very clear aggression against the university community by the administration and we responded against the issue. We did not make it our business to show how this was clearly linked to the California and national establishment. We allowed the other side to do it for us and they did" (Savio, "Comments on Berkeley," *Free Student News*, no. 1 [1965]). As these words suggest, then, it is an oversimplification to speak of the FSM as a liberal entity morphing into a radical one; it was a movement that from beginning to end had radical and liberal activists, ideals, sensibilities, and goals that coexisted, sometimes clashed, and sometimes coalesced.

3. *Report of the President's Commission on Campus Unrest* (Washington, D.C.: U.S. Government Printing Office, 1970), 22–23. For other accounts that stress the FSM's radical implications and pivotal role in the New Left's evolution, see Wini Breines, *Community and Organization in the New Left, 1962–1968: The Great Refusal* (New Brunswick, N.J.: Rutgers University Press, 1989), 23–31; Brett Eynon, "Community in Motion: The Free Speech Movement, Civil Rights, and the Roots of the New Left," *Oral History Review* 17 (spring 1989), 39–69.

4. I am using terms such as *rank and file* (and its derivatives), *FSMer, FSM activist*, and so forth to refer to those who were participants but not leaders in the FSM, no matter how early or late they entered the movement. One could draw a distinction between core activists/rank-and-filers, who were involved from the start, and those who became activists in subsequent weeks and months. But this is not a distinction that will concern me here, as I am focusing less on the genesis of the FSM than on its final stages, when it was most politically effective as a mass movement. Those who joined the final Sproul sit-in, even if this was their first action, must surely be seen as FSM activists. In a different, more formal kind of political organization, such a definition of political affiliation/membership might seem too loose, but, as Michael Rossman has observed, conventional or formal notions of political membership are poorly suited to understanding so unconventional a movement as the FSM; for his elaboration of this point, see Rossman, *The Wedding Within the War* (Garden City, N.Y.: Doubleday, 1971), 133.

5. Hal Draper, *Berkeley: The New Student Revolt* (New York: Grove Press, 1965), 31–33.

6. The FSM Central staffer quote is from his statement to Judge Rupert Critten-den, n.d., Malcolm Burnstein papers, BANC MSS 99/294(c) (hereafter cited as Burnstein Papers), box 4, Bancroft Library, University of California at Berkeley.

7. Malcolm Burnstein interview with author, Berkeley, 13 July 1999, audiotape in author's possession.

8. The statements are available in boxes 3 and 4, Burnstein Papers. There are 481 statements in the two boxes. Another 34 statements appear in FSM defendant pro-bation reports, which are in carton 2, Burnstein Papers. Note that those that have been put online (where they are available at <lib.berkeley.edu/BANC/FSM> appear without the names of the statement authors, whereas the full collection of statements in the Bancroft Library includes all the names. Some were accompanied by letters from faculty and parents attesting to the defendant's good character. The letter ask-ing the FSM defendants to write their statements to the judge came from FSM attor-ney Burnstein. See Burnstein to defendants, 30 June 1965, box 4, Burnstein Papers. Thus, though some of the statements were undated, it is evident from the Burnstein letter and the trial schedule that almost all of them were written in July 1965.

9. Katherine Simon Frank to Jo Freeman, 29 Mar. 2000, copy of letter in author's possession; Marvin Garson, "Untitled Article on the Berkeley Free Speech Defendants," n.d., Free Speech Movement records, CU-309 (hereafter cited as FSM Records," University Archives, Bancroft Library, University of California at Berkeley, p. 10.

10. Garson, "Untitled Article," 10; Garson probation report, 14 July 1965, Burn-stein Papers. Garson's essay remains one of the most insightful accounts of the FSM trial and is especially effective in offering a radical critique of the defense strategy. However, Garson underestimates his fellow defendants, who did not, as he feared, use their statements to plead for individual mercy. Instead they authored moving individual statements of solidarity with the movement and the free speech princi-ples for which they had been arrested, as will be seen below.

11. Savio refused to provide his probation officer with a statement explaining his role in the sit-in, because "to do so would embody more than this report since it would be based on his philosophy of life" and also because he felt he had already explained his motives in the trial itself. See Savio probation report, 20 July 1965, Burnstein Papers. Among the other FSM leaders for whom either no statements or very truncated statements survive (or at least are available in the Bancroft Library's collections) were Michael Rossman, Jack Weinberg, Marvin Garson, and Brian Turner.

12. Freeman interview with the author, New York, 15 June 2000 (notes from interview in author's possession). This sense that the protesters had of having done nothing wrong or illegal was linked to the nature of the sit-in itself, which was not only nonviolent but also minimally disruptive; for example, aisles were kept clear so that employees could go to and from their offices. This was, in other words, neither a blockade nor a trashing of the building. Since they were seeking peacefully to pro-mote a dialogue with the administration by sitting in the corridors of a building on their own campus, many felt that they were not violating the law and certainly not trespassing, and therefore voiced shock and indignation at their arrest. See, for

example, Ronald Anastasia probation report, 15 July 1965; Michael Eisen probation report, 14 July 1965; Brenda Goodman probation report, 20 July 1965, all in
Burnstein Papers; also see arrested student questionnaires, carton 1, ibid.

13. Rossman, *Wedding*, 136.

14. See Burnstein, "The FSM: A Movement Lawyer's Perspective," in this volume.

15. In assessing the politics of the FSM's membership, it is useful to compare the
composition of the Crittenden statement group with contemporary survey data. A
December 1964 survey of students arrested in Sproul Hall, taken by Berkeley political science graduate students, suggests at first glance a startling similarity. About 6
percent of the Crittenden group was composed of radicals—a percentage close to
the 4.5 percent revealed by the survey. But the survey, done by students motivated
by a desire to rebut the press's red-baiting, did not carry their questioning beyond
formal group affiliation to ideological orientation. One could easily imagine radicals who were anticapitalist and highly critical of the University's structure *not*
belonging to any traditional left group and being instead either unaffiliated or, like
Savio, part of a group outside the Old Left. (Savio belonged to a militant civil rights
group, University Friends of SNCC.) Since no survey questions probed the ideological orientation of such students, they would be miscounted as nonradical. The
December survey counted the 25.6 percent of Sproul Hall occupiers who belonged
to civil rights groups as nonradicals, thereby missing out entirely on the fact that
radicals of the early 1960s were often critical of the Old Left and unwilling to affili-
ate with Old Left organizations. Though a crude measure, the true relationship
between nonradicals and radicals was probably closer to the figures that the survey
gave for prior participation in protests: 61 percent of the arrestees had never before
been in a demonstration, while 7 percent had been in only two, and 9.2 percent
three or more. See Fact Finding Committee of Graduate Political Scientists, *The
Berkeley Free Speech Movement (Preliminary Report)*, 13 Dec. 1964, p. 32, FSM Records.

Another point of comparison can be found in a study by Glenn Lyonns, who surveyed 618 participants in the October sit-in around the police car and found that,
as with the authors of statements to Crittenden, liberals were the largest group. But
in his sample, liberals constituted a plurality of 49 percent, whereas in the Crittenden group they were a huge 77 percent. The radical presence in Lyonns's sample
was far more pronounced: 26 percent described themselves as democratic socialists
and 10 percent as revolutionary socialists, while only 6 percent of the Crittenden
authors viewed themselves as radicals (Lyonns, "The Police Car Demonstration: A
Survey of Participants," in Seymour Martin Lipset and Sheldon S. Wolin, eds., *The
Berkeley Student Revolt: Facts and Interpretations* [Garden City, N.Y.: Doubleday, 1965],
521). The stronger left presence in Lyonns's sample may reflect the fact that the
police car sit-in occurred much earlier than the final Sproul sit-in. Radicals in October would have been more willing than mainstream students to engage in civil disobedience, whereas two months later, as the crisis wore on, civil disobedience no
longer seemed such a radical act.

It is noteworthy, in comparing liberals with nontraditional radicals, that Savio's
thinking in 1965 was quite similar to A's: "When you just talk about 'class' or 'the
power structure' or anything of that sort it has a very unreal quality to it, but that's
what we came into contact with. All those police on campus, throwing people down
stairs, kicking people, punching people. It's very hard to have an abstract dreamy

feeling for that aspect—the organized violence and organized sadism of the power structure"; Savio, "Comments on Berkeley," *Free Student News,* no. 1 (1965).

16. By "moderate arguments" I mean those expressing reservations about civil disobedience or about the militancy of FSM leaders. I also see a distinction between the thirty-seven moderate authors who were the most uncomfortable with (and slow to adopt) civil disobedience and another group of forty-four who, though generally liberal and proud of their role in the sit-in, did include one or two statements indicating dislike of civil disobedience and reservations about breaking the law.

17. Another distinction between radicals and liberals concerns the way some spoke about the centrality of the free speech issue to the FSM. In the FSM's aftermath, radical movement leaders such as Savio and Jack Weinberg at times denied the centrality of the free speech issue to the FSM, as part of their argument that something deeper and more radical than civil liberties concerns animated the Berkeley rebellion. Savio would write that "Free Speech was in some ways a pretext. . . . Around that issue people could gain a community they had formerly lacked" (Savio, "Comments on Berkeley"). One would search in vain among the hundreds of statements that liberal FSMers wrote to Crittenden to find anyone offering this kind or argument. The rank-and-file liberal majority saw student rights—free speech, academic freedom, due process—as the heart of the Berkeley rebellion and at most added to this expressions of solidarity with the Civil Rights Movement but almost never spoke of some underlying radical quest.

18. The "shop-in" to which C referred was a controversial form of protest activists used to fight racial discrimination in a Bay Area supermarket chain. To protest the lack of minority hiring, they would place groceries in shopping carts and leave them at the checkout counter.

19. To get a sense of the vast difference in political temperament separating moderates such as F from radicals such as Savio, one has only to compare their reactions to the sit-in. Whereas the moderates, as evidenced by the agonized statements quoted in this essay, were hesitant about breaking the law and ambivalent about the sit-in they had reluctantly supported, Savio was euphoric about the sit-in and was quoted as follows in the *New York Times* (4 Dec. 1964): "This [the sit-in] is wonderful—wonderful. We'll bring the university to our terms." Contrast this with, for example, the views of another student, who entered Sproul Hall "with a heavy heart. . . . You feel heartsick, sick to the core for yourself and your comrades, sick for those who oppose you and who can only be shown what's what by such extreme measures" (David Richardson probation report, 21 July 1965, Burnstein Papers).

20. The information on G's recruitment into the FSM by her friend the Goldwater worker comes from a letter that her parents wrote to Crittenden, 9 July 1965, box 3, Burnstein Papers. This letter is also fascinating in that it captures the way that some concerned anti-FSM parents reacted to what was for them the shocking news that their child had been arrested in a campus protest. Eager to blame someone for the illegal act of their child, G's parents cast some of the blame on the friend who had recruited her and some on the faculty, since "several of her teachers were pleased with the FSM" and had been exposing her to favorable views on civil disobedience. "Unfortunately, we believe, [in] one of her classes . . . at Cal [she] studied in detail a 'paperback' of Thoreau titled 'Civil Disobedience.'" The parents also blamed mob psychology, writing that "we believe that she was caught up in the mass

hysteria of the affair." It is significant, however, that—as the parents acknowledged in their letter—G herself disputed their blame shifting and their negative view of the FSM. She denied being swayed by a mob and told her parents that she had joined the protest to secure "the right of 'freedom of speech.'" Reluctant as she had been to sit in, she was convinced that she had served the cause of freedom. G, as her parents noted, had told them that, because of her stand for free speech, "she thought we would be proud of her action in the 'sit-in,' and instead we are appalled at the students' defiance of the law."

21. Rossman, *Wedding*, 122–23.

22. Note, however, that, though it was substantive, the kind of dissent K and other nonradical rank-and-filers voiced over the militant tactics adopted by the FSM leadership was mild compared to that of nonradical leaders such as Jo Freeman, whose conflicts with the militants were much more personal. Having challenged the leadership of the Steering Committee over its confrontational tactics and lost a tense power struggle with the militants, Freeman came away with some bitter memories. She recalled that "we felt that militants treated the moderates [who advocated negotiation rather than confrontation with the UC administration] the way the administration treated the students. We were irritants to be disposed of, not people to be taken seriously. They had the power and thought they were right. They would not engage us in a discussion about strategy and tactics, and dismissed us as ratfinks" (Freeman interview with the author, New York, 30 Mar. 2000). The bitterness continues to run in both directions. Reflecting the view of Steering Committee leadership, David Goines's recent memoir depicts Freeman as a betrayer of the FSM who had demonstrated her disloyalty in early November 1964 by seeking to negotiate a separate peace with President Kerr (David Lance Goines, *The Free Speech Movement: Coming of Age in the 1960s* [Berkeley: Ten Speed Press, 1993], 303–26).

23. Glazer, *Remembering the Answers: Essays on the American Student Revolt* (New York: Basic Books, 1970), 100–130.

24. On the liberal majority in the FSM, see W. J. Rorabaugh, *Berkeley at War* (New York: Oxford University Press, 1989), 33.

25. Although most of the liberal majority used secular arguments to justify their participation, a small yet articulate minority invoked religious ideals. One defendant linked her activism to having been "born and raised a Roman Catholic" and as a consequence having become "impressed by Christ's message of profound and all pervasive love." Her "personal ethic" was "built upon Christ's basic teaching . . . love your neighbor as yourself. . . . You cannot love God and hate your neighbor. Thus for me the current civil rights issue is a deeply moral one." Another FSMer who connected his participation with his Catholicism had become awakened to "sociopolitical evils" the previous summer while doing community work in rural Mexico. When he returned to Berkeley and saw "my rights being slowly undone and my fellows being treated unfairly I had to act . . . because I am a Catholic and have come to believe strongly in Pope John's teaching that as Christians we should involve ourselves deeply in the problems of the world." A Protestant wrote that she had joined the occupation of Sproul Hall "because I am a Christian. My understanding of the fundamental truths of the Christian faith compelled me to take a personal stand against what I believed to be a grave social injustice." FSMer III, who mocked herself as a "died in the wool chicken," answered the question of why she risked arrest

and physical harm at Sproul by citing not her faith—which had lapsed, she wrote—but her religious roots. She had been "brought up in a very religious, fundamentalist home, and though I can no longer even suffer God, the essential concepts of much of that upbringing have stayed with me. . . . I am my brother's keeper." It is striking, however, that while these Protestants and Catholics invoked religion on behalf of the FSM only one Jewish student did so.

26. Among FSMers who drew cautionary lessons from Nazi Germany was a visiting student from Germany who claimed that he joined the FSM in order to prevent the United States' universities from falling into a repressive state, analogous to what ruined German higher education during the Third Reich: "After the Nazi rise to power, one of their first things was to abolish traditional freedom in the universities. Though I see no obvious relation between the political structure of Germany then and the U.S. now, I still feel that a possibility of danger exists even in this country, and I considered it to be a duty to stand up and be counted; not as an American but as a member of a universal culture of students and professors."

27. Twenty percent of the liberal FSMers who submitted statements to Crittenden expressed in their statements solidarity with the Civil Rights Movement and linked the FSM to that movement.

28. Speaking of students' desire to identify with the Civil Rights Movement, Savio recalled that the moral attraction of the movement on the Berkeley campus extended far beyond the core of activists who had gone South or participated in Bay Area civil rights actions. "There was a desire to be part of it [the Civil Rights Movement]. It was the most real [moral] thing going on . . . and so while a good number of people from this campus . . . did take part in local demonstrations and others . . . went south, I would say there was a much larger part of the campus—maybe as much as 10 percent—that was sort of vicariously part of the civil rights movement"; Savio interview with Robert Cohen and David Pickell, Berkeley, 29 Sept. 1984, transcript available in FSM Records.

29. This pamphlet was reprinted as an appendix in Draper, 199–215.

30. UC Berkeley's Media Resource Center has placed online the radio station KPFA tapes of the FSM events of October 1, 1964, so that one can now hear over the Internet Weinberg's speech as he was being arrested. The speech is in "Car Top Rally," 1 Oct. tape, <lib.berkeley.edu/MRC/FSM.html>; Savio's remarks criticizing education at UC are from *Harvard Crimson*, 15 Dec. 1964; and *Life*, 26 Feb. 1965, 101.

31. Margot Adler, "My Life in the FSM," in this volume, pp. 115. Somers concluded that this 82 percent satisfaction rate "damaged" or "destroyed" the supposition that the Berkeley rebellion was sparked by "some general feeling of dissatisfaction with the university" (Somers, "The Mainsprings of the Rebellion: A Survey of Berkeley Students in November 1964," in Lipset and Wolin, 536). For the examples of two more rank-and-filers who saw the cause of educational reform as at best peripheral to the FSM, see Eynon, "Community in Motion," 59. Somers probably goes too far, however, in dismissing the issue of educational reform. However little the issue resonated initially with mainstream students, it certainly helped to inspire some of the radicals who played a leading role in the movement and who had been influenced by Draper's critique of Kerr and the multiversity. Indeed, Lyonns's poll of the students who surrounded the police car, among whom radicals figured so

prominently, found 40 percent expressing "dissatisfaction with courses, exams, professors, etc." (Lyonns, "Survey of Participants," 521, 523). Moreover, Berkeley radicals had long been critical of the impersonal and commercial nature of mass higher education at UC. As early as 1962, David Horowitz, in a book that sold some twenty-five thousand copies, had denounced Berkeley education as "an assembly line from lecture to lecture, from exam to exam . . . a 'factory,' . . . the River Rouge of the intellect." And just prior to the FSM, Brad Cleaveland had written a scathing indictment of education at Berkeley that was published by SLATE. See Horowitz, *Student* (New York: Ballantine Books, 1962), 13–15; Cleaveland, "Letter to Undergraduates," in Lipset and Wolin, 66–81. Although radicals clearly dominated the educational reform issue initially, it would also be simplistic to argue that they had a monopoly on such concerns, especially as the FSM evolved and spread. John Searle, for example, urges us to consider the educational reform issue not as a precipitant of the Berkeley rebellion but as its product. At the beginning of the FSM, he reminds us, a survey showed over 80 percent of students surveyed to be satisfied with their education. In the FSM "they did not so much become dissatisfied as they discovered . . . a dissatisfaction of which they had previously been unaware. What happened in the FSM was a kind of shock of recognition as people became aware that they no longer believed in the official beliefs that they had thought they believed in; and most surprisingly they found that thousands of others shared their new beliefs" (Searle, *The Campus War: A Sympathetic Look at the University in Agony* (New York: World Publishing, 69). Note, however, that Searle offers no documentation establishing that thousands of students evolved a more negative view of Berkeley education during the FSM; the statements to Crittenden reflect only very limited concern with changing the University in any fundamental way. It is also worth noting that Cleaveland would later complain that, despite all the rhetoric denouncing UC as a knowledge factory, "Free Speech was the only issue that FSM leaders allowed to be taken seriously" (Cleaveland, "Introduction to Letter to Undergraduates," in Robert Cohen, ed., "The FSM and Beyond: Berkeley Student Protest and Social Change in the 1960s" [unpublished manuscript, 1994; copy in FSM Records], 111). Savio himself would later complain that the student left—having generated a host of educational reform reports and experiments during the FSM—failed to follow up on this reform work (perhaps because for students the Vietnam War became a much larger issue than reforming education). See Savio's scathing criticism of the Berkeley student left for its lethargic response to the reformist report of the Student-Faculty Committee on University Governance, *Daily Californian*, 24 May 1968.

32. Heirich, *Spiral of Conflict*, 265–73.

33. On the Heyman Committee, see Heirich, *Spiral of Conflict*, 249–50, 253–54; and Reginald Zelnik's essay on the faculty in this volume.

34. Gitlin, *The Whole World Is Watching*, 177–78; Doug Rossinow, "Mario Savio and the Politics of Authenticity," in this volume.

35. For a robust attack on UC administration red-baiting of the FSM, see Draper, 58–61. On press red-baiting of the FSM, see Colin Miller, "The Press and the Student Revolt," in Michael V. Miller and Susan Gilmore, eds., *Revolution at Berkeley: The Crisis in Education* (New York: Dell, 1965), 313–48.

36. In the statement she gave to her probation officer, FSM newsletter editor Barbara Garson captured this resentment aptly when she asserted, "I was neither duped by leaders nor the leader of dupes. I find either implication equally distasteful" (Garson probation report, 20 July 1965, Burnstein Papers).

37. Lyonns's survey of the protesters who participated in the immobilizing of the police car found that 71 percent did not belong to a campus political or social action group and 48 percent had never participated in any demonstrations before (Lyonns, "Survey of Participants," 522).

38. Only nine of the statements to Crittenden spoke of the FSM as an event that had been radicalizing. This does serious damage to Savio's estimate of the impact that the FSM and especially the mass arrests at Sproul would have on liberal FSMers. Savio believed that in the aftermath of the violent police action, revealing "the organized force and organized sadism of the power structure," "it's very clear, and especially for the people who were in Sproul Hall and arrested under those circumstances . . . it will never be possible to be 'liberals again.'" (Savio, "Comments on Berkeley"). Although the data from the Crittenden statements belies Savio's assertion, his argument about radicalization should not be dismissed entirely, since, as was suggested earlier, radicals were probably underrepresented among the authors of these statements. And Savio is surely correct in seeing the FSM as having caused significant political change, altering perceptions about the University administration and tilting Berkeley student politics leftward. It also seems likely that radicalization progressed further as the Vietnam crisis and the antiwar movement grew.

39. This attack on the FSM leaders in court went beyond mere rhetoric. So convinced were prosecutors and judge that subversive leaders had "brainwashed other defendants into committing civil disobedience" that the court punished the leaders more heavily. While the vast majority of defendants only had to pay fines, "ten so-called leaders received 30 to 120 days in jail in addition to fines and probation" (Malcolm Burnstein, essay in this volume).

40. This is not to diminish the importance of Savio's friendship with Aptheker. But that friendship did not—as one might gather from the FBI reports—place him in the orbit of the CPUSA or in any way justify FBI surveillance of him. Typical of the FBI's outlook on Savio was a Bureau memorandum that characterized him as "the leader of the recent lawless demonstrat[ion] at the University of California which resulted in the arrest of 781 demonstrators. . . . Investigation of Savio to date has not developed any information indicating affiliation on his part with a subversive group. However, he has been extremely close and in frequent company of Bettina Aptheker, a current active leader in the Communist Party in San Francisco. . . . In view of the close association of Bettina Aptheker (daughter of Herbert Aptheker, member of the National Committee of the Communist Party, USA) with Savio, all offices have been instructed to intensify their coverage of Savio . . . and advise the Bureau of all pertinent information developed, particularly if there is any indication that Savio or his companions are in contact with subversive groups (J. F. Bland to W. C. Sullivan, 11 Dec. 1964, FBI file 100-443052, Subject Mario Savio [obtained under a Freedom of Information Act request]).

41. Savio's remarks came in rebuttal to Professor Thomas Barnes and can be heard in "Sproul Hall Sit-In," 30 Sept.–1 Oct. 1964, <lib.berkeley.edu/MRC/FSM .html>. Also see, Heirich, 133.

42. Zelnik e-mail to the author, 17 Mar. 2000 (correspondence in author's possession).

43. Savio, "Comments on Berkeley"; Savio interview with Cohen and Pickell. When asked in 1984 whether he considered himself radical in 1964, Savio replied, "Oh yes." Savio characterized his politics as that of a democratic socialist: "When the FSM began I considered myself a democrat with a small "d." Sort of modern day Jeffersonian. I realized that if we were to have an industrialized society, then the society's institutions had to be responsive to the people in some sort of democratic fashion. That is neither more nor less than socialism: economic and social decisions, as well as narrowly political decisions within the power of the people" (Ron Dellabough, "A Conversation with Mario Savio and Bettina Aptheker," *California Monthly*, Dec. 1984, 18, 20.

44. Kerr's belief that Savio loathed the university is reflected in Kerr, *The Gold and the Blue: A Personal Memoir of the University of California, 1949–1967*, vol. 2: *Political Turmoil* (Berkeley and Los Angeles: University of California Press, 2003), chap. 11.

45. Mario Savio, Introduction, and "An End to History," in Draper, 2, 181.

46. "Administrative Pressures and Student Political Activity at the University of California: A Preliminary Report" [1964], FSM Records.

47. *Harvard Crimson*, 15 Dec. 1964.

48. Savio advice to protesters and Savio speech, "Car Top Rally," 1 Oct. tape, <lib.berkeley.edu/MRC/FSM.html>.

49. Savio speech just prior to 2 Dec. Sproul Hall sit-in, quoted in Goines, 361.

50. Ibid.; Savio speech, "Car Top Rally." On Savio's invocation of the First and Fourteenth Amendments in defense of student rights, see also Arleigh Williams's description of his initial encounters with Savio in Goines, 134–35, 145–46.

51. Savio speech, "Car Top Rally"; Savio interview with Cohen and Pickell; Goines, 295, 297.

52. Savio, "An End to History," in Draper, 179, 182; see also Savio's rebuttal to Barnes, "Sproul Hall Sit-In," 30 Sept.–1 Oct 1964, <lib.berkeley.edu/MRC/FSM.html>.

On the Side of the Angels

The Berkeley Faculty and the FSM

Reginald E. Zelnik

Feelings of bewilderment, then of guilt and shame were shown by many Berkeley faculty members who had given student affairs short shrift on past occasions. Overcome by their own shortcomings, many set out to prove that they were after all on the "side of the angels" and joined students in blaming everything on an already bumbling administration.

KATHERINE TOWLE, *UC Berkeley dean of students, 1966*[1]

[Chancellor] Strong was, I think, at times convinced that faculty members were actually out there leading the demonstrations. I think this was seldom, if ever, the case.

LINCOLN CONSTANCE, *vice chancellor for academic affairs at the time of the FSM*[2]

[The faculty] want us to use their tactics. They think they are on our side; but they have an innate instinct for submission. They may think like men; but they act like rabbits.

FSM Newsletter, *17 Nov. 1964*

"Thank God for the faculty!" a co-ed wearing someone's fraternity pin commented, tears rolling down her face.

December 8, 1964, *quoted in* Daily Californian, *9 Dec. 1964*

No simple division of the Berkeley faculty into two polarized factions, "pro-" and "anti-" FSM, can do justice to the historical reality of the fall of 1964. During the days of the Free Speech Movement, I belonged to the loose, informal faculty group eventually known as the "Committee of 200" (or simply "the 200") and commonly described as "the pro-FSM faculty." Although in the broadest sense that designation is reasonable, it oversimplifies the complex reality of those troubled and uncertain times, a reality that I hope to illuminate in the present essay. In addition to recounting the story of the 200, I will be addressing the roles of other faculty participants, including some who cannot be neatly shoehorned into any easily definable group. It is my hope that the reader will emerge with a sense of the variety of attitudes present within the faculty, and of the shifting subjectivities that evolved over time as events outstripped the fixed positions of individuals and drove them to reassess their previous positions. This story cannot be understood unless one keeps in mind the role of the largest faculty group of all—the indifferent and inactive, or those who can be so described until the climactic events of early December 1964. By its very nature it was the group that left the fewest documentary traces, yet at the end of the story, the faculty meeting of December 8, it is the group whose belated decision to accept the validity, or at least the necessity, of the "pro-FSM" position made possible the movement's victory.

Overall, the day-to-day events of the FSM period were driven not by faculty but by students and administrators. They were the dynamic protagonists, while faculty tended to react to the scenarios these protagonists created, intervening at crucial moments but then withdrawing to a more passive role until a new challenge drew them back in. Just *how* various groups of faculty reacted to these challenges was, of course, of paramount importance. But for the most part it was student militants and key administrators who set the terms of the conflict. The most important role of faculty was as the elusive object of both the FSM's and the administration's attention. Many of the words and deeds of these two sets of players were designed to sway faculty opinion. By prevailing in the contest for the hearts and minds of faculty, the FSM emerged the victor.

Although the FSM emerged in the fall of 1964, the larger story of faculty involvement in "speech" and academic freedom issues at Berkeley dates back at least to the bitter loyalty oath controversy of 1949–1950, the echoes of which still resounded among the faculty in the 1960s.[3] Of more immediate consequence to the events of 1964 was faculty involvement in a series of controversies during the chancellorships of Glenn T. Seaborg (1958–1961) and Edward W. Strong (1961–1965). The Seaborg and early Strong chancellorships were a time when free speech controversies erupted periodically but did not yet generate mass protests. The disputes were largely confined to a smaller, less conspicuous arena located at the points of intersection of several bodies: the campus and statewide administrations; the ASUC senate's executive committee ("ex com"); the *Daily Californian (Daily Cal)*; the combative but usually well mannered student organization known as SLATE; and a small group of committed faculty, often operating outside the faculty's influential but sluggish representative body, the Academic Senate, sometimes in cooperation with the local branch of the AAUP.[4]

While the "Kerr Directives" and their attendant controversies are too large a topic for this essay, it is noteworthy that objections to aspects of these regulations governing the campus's "open forum" brought administrators into serious conflict with faculty, including the Academic Senate, and particularly with the Senate's prestigious Committee on Academic Freedom (CAF), then chaired by law professor Frank Newman (later a California

Supreme Court justice). In summer 1959, a few months before issuing the Directives, Kerr met his obligation to consult with faculty by submitting a draft copy of the document to CAF for its comments. Responding on September 1, CAF questioned the wisdom of two very controversial provisions. It recommended to Kerr that (1) an entire section delineating the administration's control over and prior approval of invitations to off-campus speakers be removed; and (2) student organizations that took positions on off-campus issues, a practice banned by the Directives, be allowed the same campus privileges as other student organizations. Though phrased in a neutral manner, both recommendations implied a criticism of the draft from a civil liberties point of view. Calling CAF's advice "most helpful," Kerr accepted some of its recommendations but not the ones just noted, which CAF later called "the essence" of its proposals. Then, on October 12, CAF recommended yet another liberalizing change, the elimination of the ban on the *ASUC's* taking positions on off-campus issues, only to see its suggestion rejected once again. When the Directives were published later that month, these were precisely the areas that generated the most vehement protest from SLATE, the *Daily Cal,* and the ASUC ex com; they were also areas that would contribute to the conflicts of the next few years.[5]

In spring 1960, for example, the administration clashed with the ASUC ex com and the *Daily Cal* over the widely discussed Koch "free love" case, involving a University of Illinois professor who was fired for his public statements on the social benefits of intercourse between unmarried partners. When the ex com voted to condemn the Illinois administration and defend the free speech rights of the professor, the Berkeley campus administration, citing the Kerr Directives, tried to pressure ex com to rescind its statement, asserting that UC policy enjoined student organizations from taking positions on such "off-campus" issues. Here some faculty entered the fray. In a statement published in the *Daily Cal,* a small faculty group, this time with no official standing, criticized the administration's decision and even congratulated the ASUC for its courage. In a characteristic trope of liberal faculty in such situations, the professors offered polite words about "constructive" aspects of the Kerr Directives and praised the intellectual vitality, free expression, and civic engagement that distinguished the Berkeley campus, attributes that "reassure us that ours is a great and true university." Less politely, the statement went on to regret the administration's "moral obtuseness" and, in a resounding if awkward turn of phrase, affirmed that "a great university manifests its true character most clearly by its willingness to risk such embarrassment [in its public relations] and to defend those who cause it against both public and internal censure." Among the signers whose names would resurface in 1964 were Charles Sellers (history), Kenneth Stampp (history), and Henry Rosovsky (economics and history).[6] In addition to the issue at hand, the anger of these men was fueled by continuing conflicts with the administration over the right of faculty to identify the University as their place of employment when taking positions on public issues. But the administration held firm and the ban on the ex com's advocacy rights remained in force.[7]

Another related case of faculty involvement foreshadowing the issues of 1964 was the report of the Bellquist Committee (or Special Committee on the Administration of the Regulations on Student Government, Student Organizations, and Use of University Facilities). In the considered opinion of Dean Katherine Towle, if the administration had taken this committee's recommendations to Chancellor Seaborg seriously, it might have averted the entire "FSM uprising, or at least altered its course."[8] What she had in mind was a report dated July 28, 1960, and signed by the committee chairman (Eric Bellquist, political science) and four other professors, including, once again, Frank Newman.[9] These recommendations were the committee's unanimous response to Seaborg's request to review the still troublesome Kerr Directives. Seaborg had asked the Academic Senate to appoint the committee in December 1959, at a time when the Directives were still being modified by Kerr, thanks in part to criticisms by SLATE. The committee began meeting on March 22, 1960, its meetings regularly attended by Vice Chancellor Alex Sherriffs and Dean of Students William Shepard. Although Seaborg claimed to be asking the committee for advice only on how to administer and enforce the policies, he had to know that the policies themselves were under fire from several quarters. In its letter to Seaborg the committee described its own understanding of its work as "not only to consider problems of interpretation that have arisen as to the President's directives, but also to concretize the variant policies that seem to inhere therein. . . . Our discussions have led us to unanimous agreement that the following modifications . . . would be desirable, and we list them so that you may advise the President if that seems appropriate."[10]

Towle would look back on three of the committee's recommendations as "particularly pertinent" to issues later raised by the FSM: (1) Existing restrictions on political recruiting and on supporting political candidates should be lifted; there was "no reason" why campus audiences "should be denied a full range of political discussion." (2) Restrictions on fund-raising should be liberalized. ("Why," the committee asked, "should political and other groups be denied the privilege of a collection?") (3) Current censorship of student-generated advocacy literature should be radically reduced. "Entirely apart from questions of free speech," the committee declared, partially anticipating by four years the FSM's "extreme" rhetoric with respect to the administration's role, "we believe that . . . *the University's only legitimate concern [in this sensitive area] relates to littering and other custodial matters*" (emphasis added). These criticisms manifested the same spirit as the CAF recommendations of the previous year.

The administration's response to these recommendations ranged from tepid to hostile. They were "startling, to say the least," Seaborg recalled and, in his view, far exceeded the committee's charge. When Vice Chancellor Sherriffs read the report aloud to Seaborg's "cabinet," the response, in Seaborg's words, was "uniformly negative."[11] With time, the Bellquist report was buried so deep that Towle was not even informed of it by her predecessor, Dean Shepard, when she took office. She learned about it accidentally, after the FSM was over, and it was her impression that even Chancellor Strong had not been briefed on the report when he succeeded Seaborg, a failure for which she also blamed Sherriffs. Her later thoughts on the consequences of this silence are remarkable: "Had I . . . known about it when I became Dean of Students in 1961, I certainly would have attempted to have the University regulations rewritten to incorporate all the points that it brings up, or at the very least brought them to EWS's [Strong's] attention. . . . We might have been saved much of our 1964–65 travail."[12]

The HUAC demonstrations of 1960 provoked another faculty intervention and introduced a new actor, philosophy professor John Searle, who in 1964 became the faculty's most well known partisan of the FSM. Berkeley students, organized in part by SLATE, had figured prominently in demonstrations when the Committee on Un-American Activities visited San Francisco that May.[13] With some thirty Berkeley students among the arrested demonstrators, this confrontation and the ensuing trials enlivened the campus political atmosphere. But even more invigorating was HUAC's decision to disseminate its "documentary" propaganda film, *Operation Abolition,* which purported to demonstrate that its student opponents were tools of the Communist Party. This patently absurd film proved to be a blessing to SLATE, since exposing its inaccuracies was an effective way of unmasking HUAC while simultaneously stimulating student political activity, an outcome that failed to delight the campus administration.

The faculty role in this affair began shortly after the HUAC demonstrations, when a small group of Berkeley professors came to the defense of arrested students widely seen as victims of police misconduct. Like Searle, several of these professors would figure prominently in the events of 1964, mainly as supporters of the FSM, for example, Phillip Selznick (sociology), Henry Nash Smith (English), and Kenneth Stampp. One, however, Lewis Feuer (philosophy), would become one of the FSM's most rancorous critics. Although the faculty group did not come into direct conflict with the University administration, it almost certainly would have done so had criminal charges against the students not been dropped, since the University had reserved the right to discipline the students if they were convicted.[14]

The dropping of the charges did not mark the end of faculty involvement in the HUAC affair. When a Sociology graduate student who was arrested at the demonstrations was told by a funding agency that she would lose her fellowship, she was supported (unsuccessfully) by the campus branch of AAUP. Another HUAC-related conflict, the one that first turned Searle into a campus figure, was connected with *Operation Abolition*. In fall 1960 Searle, a passionate foe of HUAC, was invited by Berkeley law students to be a commentator at a showing of that film. According to Searle, he was advised only an hour before the scheduled event that, because seven days notice had not been given (a violation of the chancellor's interpretation of the Kerr Directives), the event would be canceled unless the organizers added a pro-HUAC speaker to the program. The conflict was settled only when Searle agreed to deliver his critique off campus. The incident left a bitter legacy; this was the first time the Directives had been used to impede the speech of a professor, and Searle was not about to let it pass in silence. "What right do administrative officers have," he asked, "to forbid faculty members to address student groups?" And even more pointedly: "Was the [seven-day] rule invoked as a technicality to facilitate the silencing of a view considered uncongenial?" As Searle was quick to point out, there were many examples of the rule's being ignored by the administration when politically sensitive speech was not involved.[15] The following year the issue of the applicability of the Kerr Directives to faculty speakers was also pursued by the Berkeley AAUP, this time resulting in a directive from Kerr stating that it did *not*. While reaffirming the requirement for prior notification and approval by the chancellor, Kerr also noted that the seven-day notification period for off-campus speakers was *not* a statewide requirement.[16]

More faculty interventions on free speech issues occurred during the early years of Strong's chancellorship.[17] In June 1961 a small faculty group sought to reverse the suspension of SLATE, a group that continued to be a thorn in the side of administrators. (SLATE's latest "offense" was defiance of the administration's order to cease calling itself a "campus political party.")[18] Of the men who initiated this effort, at least six—Carl Schorske (history), Sellers, Selznick, Stampp, Smith, and the renowned sociologist Leo Lowenthal—would later have high profiles as "pro-FSM" faculty. On July 17, having gathered thirty-nine faculty signatures, the group submitted a long memorandum "for the consideration of the President and administrative officers of the University." In it they questioned excessive restrictions on student political activity and decried the lack of consultation with faculty on such policies. A separate memorandum signed by roughly the same group (this time with forty-one names) called for the reconsideration of SLATE's suspension. The result was a meeting on July 19 between Kerr and some of the signers, immediately followed by a memo to Kerr from eight of them suggesting disappointment with the meeting. Finally, in August, after meeting with other faculty, eight professors (later dubbed by Schorske the faculty's "civil libertarian left-wing"), including the six mentioned above, sent a long memo to Kerr and Strong again protesting SLATE's suspension.

Anticipating issues that would rock the campus three years later, they argued that the administration's reading of the California constitution as restricting student political activity was "questionable." As would be typical of even the most liberal faculty in 1964, their wording was cautious, characterized by a quest for reason and cooperation. They took pains to commend the administration's recent "liberalizing measures" and (partial) defense of the open forum from outside pressures, even conceding that SLATE merited "some kind of punitive action." The concluding paragraph illustrates the mood of certain faculty, animated by a liberal sense of mission yet anxious to keep conflict with administrators to a polite minimum: "We have no wish to magnify disagreements. As faculty members, we try to make ourselves available to the problems of students, and we hope that a dialogue with you, from time to time, will be welcomed as creative and enlightening."[19]

Some two years later, in 1963, at the request of SLATE (which recovered quite remarkably from its suspension), faculty of the history department, which Schorske now chaired, tried to convince the chancellor to allow Communist historian Herbert Aptheker to speak as part of the department's colloquium series. (This was only the latest of several conflicts in 1961–1963 over the proposed appearance of Communist speakers on UC campuses, the most celebrated conflict having taken place at Riverside.)[20] Despite the efforts of Schorske, Stampp, and others, Strong, citing Regents' policy, held firm.[21] The Aptheker talk did take place and was billed as a departmental function, but it had to be held off campus in the YMCA building. Later, in another controversy over a meeting with a Communist speaker (Albert "Mickey" Lima), Schorske was attacked for having chaired the meeting, though this time, the ban having since been lifted under the pressure of pending litigation of the Riverside case, Schorske's adversaries were not University officials but off-campus right-wing protesters. In fact, Schorske's handling of the affair was praised by both Strong and Kerr. (Kerr had been instrumental in convincing the Regents to lift the ban, though with a burdensome proviso that a tenured faculty moderator must always be present).[22]

The pattern of faculty involvement revealed by these examples is fairly straightforward. There was a small group of liberal professors with a strong commitment to free speech and civil liberties but little sign of strong left-wing affinities. Acting informally and not as an organized group, though sometimes represented by CAF and supported by the AAUP (to which some of them belonged), these men would react in earnest when they perceived an outrage, often called to their attention by students, against free speech or academic freedom. Although their statements were often public and they were sometimes willing to cooperate with student organizations and share their views with the *Daily Cal*, their preferred modus operandi was polite though pointed (and occasionally effective) correspondence with the offending administrators. The prospect of having to deal directly with a massive and militant student movement was not yet on their intellectual horizon when unexpected developments forced them to change course in fall semester 1964.

.   .   .

Except as individual bystanders, no faculty were involved in the initial confrontation over the "Bancroft strip" on September 14, 1964, when the dean of students announced that the strip would no longer function as a free-speech sanctuary. At the time of the announcement campus officials did not seem to grasp its possible consequences. According to Vice Chancellor Lincoln Constance, "It just looked like a little bit of tidy housekeeping that we had somehow neglected."[23] Nor were many faculty quick to react in the days that followed. During the tense confrontations of the next two weeks, however, leading up to the announced suspension of several students on September 30, sit-ins on the same and the next day, and the police car incident of October 1, a few faculty members began to make their presence felt. Although there may have been a dozen others, it is the now familiar names of Sellers and Searle that come most readily to mind, along with those of George Stocking (history), John Leggett (sociology), and Jackson Burgess and Thomas Parkinson (both English).

The interventions by these faculty took the form of intense exchanges with students and administrators and speaking out in favor of the protesters' still evolving positions (first formally articulated on September 17) while questioning the wisdom of the administration's "tidy housekeeping." Starting on October 1, these and other faculty began to denounce the administration's punitive measures taken against certain demonstrators. As early as September 22, as the protest movement was just emerging and when there was talk of finding a faculty member to debate Vice Chancellor Sherriffs, a staunch defender of the withdrawal of the strip, students advanced the names of Sellers, Stocking, and Burgess. They were named, no doubt, because they were among a small group of faculty who had marched with students in front of Sproul Hall on the previous day to protest the ban on political advocacy, fund-raising, and recruitment on the strip, or as Sellers described it, the administration's "harassment of political activity," "smothering freedom in the hope of appeasing outside pressures."[24] This was probably the first public act identifying any professor with the student cause, though it involved only a few, mainly junior, faculty. Nor was it a coordinated effort. Stocking, a young historian who joined student picket lines on the 21st and 22nd, called his participation an "independent action," not representative of any group: "Since I have chosen to devote my life to University teaching and research, I oppose these restrictions which are a flagrant violation of the idea of a University"; he also challenged the administration's claim that traffic congestion was germane to its decision.[25] Parkinson, who had headed the local AAUP during the storm over the Communist speaker ban, seems to have been a particular irritant to the chancellor, who believed—on what basis I cannot imagine—he was egging on the students who entered Sproul Hall on the 30th.[26]

A few days after the demonstrations in front of Sproul Hall another small (if less disorganized) group of faculty—most notably Arthur Ross (business administration, Institute of Industrial Relations [IIR]); Seymour Martin Lipset, Nathan Glazer, and William Peterson (all sociology); and Earl "Budd" Cheit (business)—entered the discussion more in the capacity of friendly advisors to and even semi-allies of the administration than as advocates of the demonstrators, though at first their attitude toward the students was fairly friendly. Attempting to exert a calming influence on both sides, they "thrust themselves into the situation as mediators" (Glazer's words)[27] and at times prodded administrators to be flexible. The events that heightened the conflict beginning on September 30—the defiant placement of "unauthorized" tables; a provocative statement by the governor; the suspension of eight students (including Mario Savio); a determined, at times aggressive, but mainly nondisruptive "sleep-in"; and, above all, the beginning of the notorious police car affair, including the near intervention of hundreds of police—all of this quickly magnified the role of these faculty figures. That Mario, even while denouncing the administration as "bastards," publicly and in a mood of hope referred to this faculty contingent as a group of "independent faculty members" reflected both the unsettled quality of faculty attitudes at this early stage and the artless uncertainty of student perceptions of the faculty.[28] Moreover, although none of the names just mentioned would later be associated with the "pro-FSM" faculty, on October 5 not only such open FSM sympathizers as Sellers and Leggett but even Glazer (cautiously, to be sure) took part in a Sproul Steps rally in a manner that lent credibility to the FSM position.[29]

By late afternoon of October 2, with the police car held at bay by a huge gathering of emotionally charged students and with pressure on the administration reaching peak proportions, the intervention of the "independent faculty members" began to bear fruit. At that time Vice Chancellor Constance met with an unofficial faculty delegation—later dubbed "the group of 15"—brought together at the initiative of Henry Rosovsky. It was a group of distinguished scholars, all of them well known to Kerr, who by this time had drafted proposals designed to resolve the conflict. In addition to Rosovsky, Glazer, and Petersen, they included Paul Seabury, Ernst Haas, and Robert Scalapino (all political science); William Kornhauser, Neil Smelser, and David Matza (all sociology); Roy Radner (economics); Schorske; and Joseph Tussman (philosophy), later described by the chancellor as "my good friend."[30] Again the continued fluidity of faculty attachments is noteworthy, as four of these negotiators—Kornhauser, Matza, Schorske, and Tussman—eventually came to be identified with the liberal 200, while most of the others would occupy positions closer to the administration, or at least to Kerr, who (much to the chancellor's chagrin) was about to become personally involved in the negotiations.

The group of 15 intervened in the conflict without the blessing of the chancellor, who viewed such faculty assertiveness as an expression of low confidence in him, even a usurpation of his authority. Constance, who was dealing with "the 15" because of Strong's calculated absence, confirms this in his recollection of the very strained meeting: "I remember the group of faculty. . . . They wanted to see the Chancellor to ask to go to the President, because they felt campus leadership had failed, that there was imminent disaster" (that is, massive police intervention). Constance also recalled the gist of his response: "I'm representing the Chancellor, and you're asking to go over his head. It must be very apparent to all of you that I couldn't possibly give you that permission. But you're all big boys now, and I assume that you'll probably do what you think you need to do." When the group then asked him if *he* would contact Kerr, bypassing the chancellor, Constance refused. The group then insisted on its "duty" to phone the president, and the call was placed from the chancellor's conference room by Rosovsky, who read the proposals to Kerr. Apparently Kerr's response was far from positive. Kerr was thought to be extremely depressed about the situation, believing that the proposals had come too late and "all of his work over the years was going down the drain." When the group began to ponder its next steps, Constance recalls, "I excused myself and left." His conclusion was that the intervention of "the 15" was improper: "The faculty were spinning their wheels."[31]

Spinning or not, within a couple of hours the group of 15, having conferred with Kerr and with leaders of the students, hammered out a provisional agreement in time to avert what might have been a catastrophe. This was the well-known pact of October 2, which bore the signatures of Kerr, Savio, and eight other demonstrators (Strong was a nonsigner). The agreement, which looked as if it might bring about an early end to the conflict, put some of the protesters in an upbeat mood. Savio greeted it as a substantial victory, declaring that "although the whole war is far from over, we have won the biggest battle."[32] On the next day a new coalition group, the FSM, was born in high hopes.

Faculty were supposed to play a central role in the putative settlement. Three key paragraphs, 2, 3, and 5, referred specifically to faculty: (2) A committee representing "students, faculty, and administration" was to investigate all aspects of political behavior on campus and make recommendations to the administration. (3) The chancellor was to appoint to the committee "four students, four faculty, and four administration representatives." (5) The cases of students who had been suspended indefinitely were to be submitted to the "Student Conduct Committee of the Academic Senate," which was to make a recommendation on the length of the suspensions. However, whereas paragraph 2 seemed to hold out the promise that the issues under dispute would be addressed by students, faculty, and administrators as equal participants, paragraph 3, by leaving the choice of faculty and student members to one of the parties, the chancellor, planted the seeds of future conflict.[33] Paragraph 5, as it turned out, would be equally controversial, for unbeknownst to most, perhaps all, of the negotiators, the only existing body resembling a *faculty* committee on student conduct was actually an administration committee, with no connection to the Academic Senate. Yet student negotiators had agreed to this provision precisely because of their trust in what they believed to be an independent faculty judicial body. And underlying all these problems was the question of whether *any* committee that emerged from this agreement, whether dealing with campus rules of political engagement or the fate of suspended students, would have final jurisdiction.

Almost immediately, the place of faculty on the two committees that featured in the agreement became a matter of dispute that centered on the role of the Academic Senate. The establishment of the committees was bound to bring the Senate, and with it that faculty body's latent claims to a greater share in University governance, into the picture. The first issue was the composition of the tripartite Study Committee on Political Freedom, later renamed the Campus Committee on Political Activity (CCPA).

On October 5 the chancellor, purporting to comply with the terms of the pact, announced the names of the CCPA members, including the four faculty. All faculty delegates named were senior, prestigious professors: Robley Williams (virology), who was named committee chairman, Joseph Garbarino (business), Theodore Vermeulen (chemical engineering), and Rosovsky. Of the four, only Rosovsky had belonged to the now defunct group that negotiated the pact. Williams, Garbarino, and Vermeulen were all chairmen of important Senate committees (Budget, CAF, and Educational Policy, respectively), a circumstance that may have partially offset the fact that they were not named by the Senate's Committee on Committees. But this was not enough of a connection with the Senate to satisfy FSM leaders that the faculty representatives were truly "representative." Displaying a touching degree of confidence that a representative faculty group would be more favorable to their cause than one appointed by the chancellor and, perhaps for strategic reasons, casting the faculty into a victim's role that paralleled their own, the FSM quickly added this shortcoming to other bitter complaints about the committee's structure and competence (the most salient being the underrepresentation of the FSM).

To help resolve these conflicts over the agreement and to deal with other pressing problems (for example, whether the FSM should be allowed to hold a rally to discuss the agreement itself and, if not, whether Savio should be arrested if he tried to speak), both campus and statewide administrators continued to rely on informal faculty intermediaries and advisors. The composition of these faculty groups was elastic and inconsistent, however, and the roles of intermediary and advisor were difficult to separate. Unclear too was the degree to which each major component of the administration—presidential and chancellorial—welcomed such faculty involvement. In retrospect it is evident that the chancellor did not. In Constance's words, Strong was beginning to believe that any faculty who became involved had "turned against him." Constance assured Strong that while many faculty were "probably doing more bad than good, . . . I don't think there's any reason for thinking they're not being involved for what they feel are the very best reasons. They're trying to dampen the thing."[34]

On October 5 an important meeting with one such faculty group took place in Strong's office. It was attended not by Strong but by his "faculty assistant," Allan Searcy (who became an administration delegate to the CCPA), Vice Chancellor Constance, and Savio. The meeting was also attended by five faculty, three of whom—Rosovsky, Scalapino, and Petersen—were already in the thick of things and two of whom—Owen Chamberlain (physics) and Selznick—were just beginning to get involved (though Selznick had once crossed swords with Strong over the SLATE suspension). News of the presence of the two new faculty was particularly galling to Strong, who instructed Constance that any question raised by the faculty group should be referred to his own advisors "for consideration and reply."[35] Here Strong's instinct was sound, for both Selznick and Chamberlain—who with other faculty had met with FSM leaders on October 4 in an effort to avert a conflict over a planned rally[36]—would soon identify with the cause of the FSM.

Increasingly, the CCPA's composition loomed as the major obstacle to fruitful negotiation. Because CCPA members were chosen by their adversary, FSM leaders deeply distrusted it and vigorously challenged its legitimacy, insisting that a special committee of the Academic Senate be created to choose the faculty delegates while "students should choose the student members."[37] In fact, there already was a Senate committee, the Committee on Committees, that was routinely tasked with the appointment of faculty to other Senate committees, be they standing or ad hoc. (I still recall how the odd-sounding, unfamiliar name of that committee became the butt of playful mockery by Savio and others.) The problem was that the chancellor, who, like the students, grasped the symbolic significance of his power to appoint the CCPA, and knowing that he was not violating the *letter* of the agreement, insisted on choosing the members. In response, on October 7 a preliminary meeting of the CCPA was aborted by defiant FSM Steering Committee members who, enraged that student and faculty representatives were chosen by the chancellor (a novel student role—protector of faculty independence), came to the meeting only to deny the CCPA's legitimacy.[38]

Another unofficial faculty group, having met with Strong and other campus officials, now "thrust" itself into the picture in a way that was expressly critical of the FSM. This group, headed by Scalapino (whose role was rapidly expanding), issued a statement that, though asserting its belief in "the importance of maximum freedom for peaceful student political action," chided the FSM for its "rigid and unreasonable position" on student representation and for jeopardizing the CCPA's prospects for success. Joining Scalapino in this statement were Glazer, Lipset, and Rosovsky (three of the original group of 15), Selznick and, for the first time, Stampp.[39] These would prove to be strange bedfellows, for within a few weeks they would find themselves on opposing sides of the faculty barricades. Once more we see the fluidity of faculty positions, neatly encapsulated by the signing of the statement by two sociology colleagues, Glazer and Selznick, whose positions would evolve so contrarily that a few months later they would be quarreling with each other about these events in the pages of national magazines.[40]

On the next day, October 8, another group of faculty, all parties to the earlier negotiations, issued a statement backing Kerr, praising him for having acted in good faith on October 2, and implying that the FSM was responsible for the impasse. "We renew our endorsement of President Kerr's action of that day, and we urge all student leaders to enter the dialogue concerning University policy on political action in a spirit of moderation and good will, using the proceedings that have been established under the agreement." These sentiments were shared by Charlie Powell, ASUC president.[41]

But the critical statements made by these faculty groups failed to alter the FSM's position; if anything they added to its bitterness. This is not to say that FSM students felt altogether abandoned by faculty. Acting as individuals, at least two professors, Leggett and Sellers, had joined with the FSM at its rally on October 5, thereby adding to the FSM's still unsettled legitimacy in the eyes of uncommitted students while provoking an angry denunciation of Sellers by conservative city councilman John DeBonis.[42] And other faculty, mainly from math and statistics, prepared a public statement announcing their shock at the "massing" of police on campus on October 2.[43] On the "official" side of the faculty, on October 7, the chairman of the Academic Senate, Richard Jennings (law), possibly stung by repeated assertions that the chancellor had ignored the Senate, announced that the Senate was contemplating a request to two of its most important committees,

CAF and Educational Policy, to take up the substantive questions of free speech policy. Since the chairs of both committees were already designated members of the CCPA, what was really at stake was not so much which individuals would examine which issues but to whom they would answer—the Senate or the chancellor. This was the first sign of direct, independent involvement by an official faculty body, though it was not enough to change the FSM's attitude toward the legitimacy of the CCPA.[44]

Pressure on a still skittish Academic Senate to become more engaged was on the rise. If the pressure had initially come from the FSM, by October 9 even the cautious *Daily Cal* was calling for more faculty involvement. Although still defending the administration against FSM charges that it had acted "in bad faith," correctly noting that student negotiators on October 2 had agreed to language that implied (though not emphasizing) that the administration would appoint the CCPA, the paper asked the chancellor to let the Senate appoint the faculty delegates. The CCPA itself added to the pressure for Senate action by announcing that it would hold a public meeting on October 13, the very day when, quite fortuitously, the Senate was already scheduled to meet.[45] On October 9, Garbarino, chairman of CAF (two of its five members, Stampp and Jacobus ten Broek, would prove to be among the more steadfast faculty supporters of the FSM's positions),[46] lobbed a warning shot across the bow of the CCPA by informing the chancellor that (in keeping with Jennings's earlier statement) CAF was undertaking its own examination of the issues.[47]

Parallel to the debate over the CCPA was the equally thorny question of just what "faculty" committee was to adjudicate the cases of the suspended students. Whatever the administration's intent on October 2, the fact that there was no *Senate* "committee on student conduct" but only an *administration* committee whose faculty members were chosen by the chancellor, lent credibility to FSM charges of bad faith, setting the stage for more recrimination. Although the administration, supported by the *Daily Cal,* defended itself against this charge by insisting that there had been an honest misunderstanding (one that may have originated with the faculty negotiators, characteristically innocent of the details of the Academic Senate's structure and functions), the FSM, displaying a fragile faith in faculty institutions, insisted that the Senate appoint its own committee with final authority to adjudicate the cases. Consequently, the suspended students (with support from the ACLU) refused to appear before the chancellor's committee, claiming with literal accuracy that the agreement had stipulated a committee of the Senate.[48] The students were adamant, telling Towle that they would agree only to a hearing by a committee responsible to the faculty.[49] This was an early expression of what would remain a constant goal of the FSM: to wean a hesitant faculty away from its tendency to identify with the administration and bring it over to the student side of the battle line. A battle was indeed brewing between two warring parties, and each was hungry for faculty allies. Although thus far the faculty as a body had been reluctant to take sides, the need for agreement on the disciplinary procedures was increasingly pressing as reciprocal threats of civil disobedience and disciplinary action escalated.

But disciplinary prerogatives were an issue on which Strong was not prepared to yield. Meeting on the morning of October 8 with his own preferred committee of faculty advisors, all of them deans or directors of institutes,[50] along with Senate Chairman Jennings, he contemplated what course to take on the disciplinary matter. Strong was still hoping that the FSM could be persuaded that referring the cases to a nonexistent committee was an honest error and that it would then recognize the authority of his Committee on Student Conduct.[51] But time was pressing in on him: the disciplinary hearing was supposed to take place within a week of October 2 (already impossible), the Senate was scheduled to meet in just five days, and the Regents were scheduled to meet three days later. By the following day, with the FSM still holding firm, Strong and his closest advisors had begun to consider the possibility of allowing the Senate to create its own ad hoc disciplinary committee, though the notion of granting that committee final authority does not seem to have been seriously contemplated.[52]

As the Senate meeting approached, the number of faculty expressing sympathy with the FSM, especially on the issue of suspensions, though still small, was growing. Anticipation of controversial Senate meetings usually tends to generate informal faculty caucuses and petitions, and this meeting was no exception. A petition calling for immediate reinstatement of the suspended students was submitted on the 12th, the eve of the meeting, with 88 signatures, to the Chancellor's Committee on Student Conduct. Anticipating future patterns, the most heavily represented departments were math (twenty) and history (seventeen). Among the signers, and soon to emerge as the FSM's most ardent faculty defender, was John Searle.[53]

When the Senate met, however, the main business on its agenda was not the FSM but a politically charged academic freedom controversy. It involved grave accusations that the chancellor had violated the academic freedom of Eli Katz, an acting assistant professor of German, by asking him improper questions about past connections with the Communist Party as a precondition for the "regularization" of his appointment. Misgivings about Strong's treatment of Katz meant that much of the faculty's emotional energy was absorbed by his case, resonant as it was with echoes of the loyalty oath. It inevitably displaced some of the attention the Senate might otherwise have devoted to the FSM, though at the same time, anger about the Katz case, which entailed the opening of old and painful wounds, may have also encouraged some faculty to extend their anger to Strong's handling of the free speech controversy.[54]

Although the Senate failed to take advantage of its October 13 meeting to resolve the substantive issues of campus advocacy, it did not ignore the free speech conflict. With 450 voting members in attendance, the Senate held what the *Daily Cal* termed a "hectic session," which included a reassuring speech by Strong and several unsuccessful motions and amendments on both sides of the issues. The body managed to pass two FSM-related resolutions.[55] The first, offered by Charles Muscatine (English), a veteran of the oath conflict, endorsed "maximum freedom for student political activity" and directed CAF to "inquire immediately into the recent University rulings on student political activity in the Bancroft-Telegraph area . . . and the larger problem of students' rights to the expression of political opinion on campus." It instructed CAF to report back "as quickly as possible what action on the part of the faculty may be advisable." An attempt by Petersen, fast becoming one of the FSM's leading critics, to amend the motion symbolically by adding "within the law" after "maximum freedom" went down to defeat.

Although the chancellor himself had claimed to favor an inquiry by CAF, Muscatine's motion, especially after the defeat of Petersen's amendment, has to be seen as a friendly if limited gesture toward the FSM. The resolution did contain some predictably cheery language about recent improvement of the University's "atmosphere of free inquiry," but passage of its main section suggested that many faculty doubted that the Strong-appointed CCPA could resolve the conflict without intervention by CAF. Yet at the same meeting, in seeming contradiction to its first motion, the Senate balanced its implicit criticism of the administration by passing a second motion, offered by Lipset and supported by Petersen, calling on "all parties" to "resolve the dispute in peaceful and orderly fashion and . . . to make full use of the joint faculty-student-administrative committee for that purpose." This amounted to a plea to the FSM to accept the legitimacy of CCPA *as currently constituted*.

The Senate debate prefigured in muted form some of the conflicts that would divide the faculty in the weeks ahead. Lipset and Petersen, for example, who had already been active as "intermediaries," expressed their fear that the unamended Muscatine motion would give *outsiders* the impression that the faculty condoned such conduct as the "trapping" of police cars. But Petersen's amendment, intended to vitiate that impression, *was* defeated, its opponents arguing that since the additional language was an implicit condemnation of the FSM, it would preempt the mission of CAF. Yet at the same time, a motion by David Rynin (philosophy) calling for the lifting of the suspensions failed to gain a majority. This still imprecise and labile division of faculty opinion—between those who feared looking permissive in the eyes of the *off-campus* world and those who, with greater solicitude for student opinion, were anxious not to burn the bridges between faculty and students—would remain in play until the events of December 2–3 began to overwhelm and then, by December 8, decisively reshape the contours of faculty sentiment.

Whereas the referral of the free speech issue to CAF was welcomed by the FSM, the resolution calling for FSM cooperation with CCPA fell mainly on deaf ears. This was made crystal clear that evening (October 13) at a CCPA meeting in Harmon Gymnasium, where members of the FSM and others (even a Young Republican!), with varying degrees of (im)politeness and (dis)respect, berated the administration and the committee, repeating the charge that it was improperly constituted and urging it to disband.[56] As tension mounted on campus, the CCPA seemed stillborn, the exhortations of the faculty, powerless.

Only two days later, however, there were new signs of possible conciliation. Kerr's new flexibility and the anticipated continuation of the Senate meeting on October 15 (the previous meeting having failed to complete its business) made it possible to (temporarily) resolve the outstanding *procedural* issues. Probably influenced by the Senate's actions at its first meeting, anticipation of action at its next, and the need for a calm campus during the coming Regents meeting at UC Davis, Kerr, bypassing Chancellor Strong once again (and thereby contributing to Strong's growing bitterness and political infirmity), made two groundbreaking concessions: he would expand the faculty contingent of CCPA to include two Academic Senate appointees (while adding two more students and two more administrators), and he would ask the Senate to create a new ad hoc committee to hear the cases of the suspended students, a concession that had the practical effect of nullifying the role of the chancellor's committee. Although it was not public knowledge at the time, these changes had been hammered out at Davis on the previous evening at a late-night meeting of Kerr, some Regents, and sixteen trusted faculty. Having met with the Regents in executive session, Kerr informed the chancellor of the concessions only on the morning of the 15th, when he asked for his agreement. Strong had little choice but to submit, but felt slighted and isolated. Driving back to Berkeley from the Regents meeting, he told his wife, "My trust in the President has been shaken. I don't know where I stand. I'm very uncertain and very uneasy, suddenly."[57]

Thanks to Kerr's concessions on the procedural issues, the faculty now was able, however briefly, to satisfy both the FSM and the president. At its meeting on the 15th (attended by some 475 members), the Senate listened to Arthur Ross announce the proposed changes on Kerr's behalf and read a statement wherein Kerr assured the faculty that Strong "joins me in the above statements." Since there was no apparent reason for the Senate to vote on the president's expansion of the CCPA, which no one challenged, Ross made only one formal motion: to establish a new "five-man *ad hoc* committee" to hear the cases of the suspended students. It passed without dissent.[58]

The CCPA now gained whatever legitimacy it would ever attain in the eyes of the FSM, as the Senate quickly submitted two new faculty names to an unenthusiastic chancellor. Strictly speaking, the CCPA *did* remain his creature—it was still *advisory* to him, and the new faculty representatives, though nominated by the Senate, were still appointed by him. But taken together with the shunting aside of the Committee on Student Conduct, these changes were sufficient to cause the *Daily Cal* to sing the praises of Kerr and the faculty, asserting with a premature sigh of relief that the immediate crisis was at long last resolved: "[I]f President Kerr and 15 faculty members had not stepped in at the eleventh hour two weeks ago, this University could have suffered incredible damage. The end to the Bancroft-Telegraph controversy has begun." As to the FSM, it saw the outcome of the Senate meeting as sufficiently positive to be called a "battle won." Speaking at a rally, Savio said of the new agreement: "I'm very happy about [it]. The [new] ground rules are completely acceptable."[59]

But the two procedural changes were hardly the initiatives of an independent faculty. Rather, they were the outcome of negotiations between FSM leaders, UC administrators, and faculty close to Kerr (most notably Ross[60]), with the Senate there only to give the agreement its blessing. True, the groundwork for creation of a faculty disciplinary committee was already in preparation behind the scenes a few days earlier, which docs suggest that faculty attitudes were taken into account by Kerr and his supporters. But it is only if faculty behavior on October 15 is understood as a rubber-stamping of compromises already reached that we can account for the meeting's near unanimity, Kerr's concessions having garnered the support of faculty whose sympathies were quite diverse. One could vote for the new faculty disciplinary committee convinced that this would satisfy the president, the FSM, or both. With the obvious exceptions of Strong and his closest aides, the outcome seemed to appease everyone.

That the Senate was not yet prepared to throw its weight behind the FSM was also revealed by another part of the October 15 proceedings. On the 13th, it will be recalled, Petersen had failed in his attempt to reassure the outside world of the faculty's "responsibility" by adding the words *within the law* to Muscatine's motion. But the defeat of that amendment had evidently left a significant number of faculty (not to mention administrators) extremely uncomfortable, for on the 15th, aware, no doubt, that the Regents were scheduled to meet the next day, Frank Newman, former chairman of CAF and long a "persistent champion of civil liberties,"[61] presented a motion explicitly intended to remove the specter of faculty permissiveness. Noting in a "Whereas" clause that the position taken two days earlier had been "widely misunderstood as condoning lawlessness,"

Newman called on the Senate to reaffirm "its conviction that force and violence have no place on this campus." After considerable debate and an unsuccessful attempt by Sellers to put through a substitute motion that would have softened the implied criticism of the FSM and abandoned the motion's defensive tone, the Newman motion was passed.[62] In its official capacity, the faculty continued to face Janus-like in two directions, while the conflict on campus was taking its still unsteady course.

.   .   .

Despite its troubled beginnings, ceaseless recriminations, and ultimate paralysis, the reconstituted CCPA did provide a controlled forum in which faculty, students, and administrators were at last able to exchange views and explore solutions. The committee now had eighteen members, six from each of its constituent groups, with the student contingent dominated by four representatives from the FSM (Aptheker, Savio, Sid Stapelton, Suzanne Goldberg). The two new faculty members, chosen by the Academic Senate's Committee on Committees, were Sanford Kadish (law) and Earl Cheit (business), who was identified earlier as a close consultant to the administration. Neither person substantially changed the "establishment" coloration of the faculty contingent, but both became important contributors to the discussions. It was agreed by all parties that there should be two or three public hearings a week, for a total of no more than three weeks. In fact there would be seven meetings, held over an eighteen-day period from October 21 to November 7, after which the CCPA would cease to function.[63]

The CCPA began by designing its own internal procedures. It broke itself into subcommittees, each including a representative from every constituent group. Substantive decisions were to be made by group consensus, not by counting individual votes. (Savio argued forcefully but unsuccessfully for application of the same system to procedural decisions.) Under this protocol, any substantive proposal could in effect be vetoed by a majority of any one group. But because an increasingly isolated campus administration desperately needed to show that it had faculty support and because the students continued to grasp the need to win over, or at least neutralize, faculty opinion, the faculty contingent became pivotal. Although a faculty member announced at the opening meeting that the faculty's role would be that of "arbitrator," in practice its role was more like that of an undecided juror in a nearly hung jury. Each of the adversaries needed to win it over, while hoping that the specter of a faculty joined together with its own side would soften the position of the other. But the faculty were also people with ongoing professional, personal, and psychological ties to the University's rotating administrators, who, when not serving in that capacity, doubled as their fellow professors, their once and future colleagues.[64] This meant that the students, if they indeed hoped for a student-faculty alliance, were faced with a tall order. Yet they were partially successful, at least until the last few meetings.

The CCPA's October 24 meeting was largely devoted to an issue in a gray area between procedure and substance: what campus rules should be in force pending the outcome of deliberations? Whereas the chancellor wished to keep enforcing the rules that obtained *after* the Bancroft strip was withdrawn, the FSM, so that fund-raising and recruiting not be completely interrupted, insisted on the status quo ante. But the faculty delegates joined with administration delegates in rejecting a student proposal to urge Strong to soften his position. This outcome did not break the truce of October 2, however, as the FSM continued to refrain from putting the administration to the test by violating the new rules. Nevertheless, the failure to reach consensus increased tensions in the committee.

The ensuing meetings were arduous, but they did provide a useful focal point for the attention of the campus, including faculty, and helped to narrow and sharpen the definition of the outstanding issues. By this time the truly contentious substantive issues had already been narrowed to two: (1) the right of students to *advocate* any political ideas on campus, *advocate* here meaning not only to argue in favor of a cause in principle (this had been conceded early on) but to urge the listeners to take specific *actions*, specifically *off-campus* actions; and (2) the closely related right to use the campus as a staging area for those off-campus actions, increasingly summed up in the debates by words such as *organizing, mounting*, and sometimes *implementing*.

Part of the narrowing process had already begun by September 21, when Dean Towle explicitly recognized the general validity of on-campus advocacy. It was continued on the 25th, when the Regents conceded the right of political speech, and on the 28th, when at a University meeting the chancellor said, "You may have advocacy on the campus."[65] But advocacy of *what?* and in what *form?* Strong had put his finger on the issue when, on the day before the CCPA resumed its meetings, he told the *Daily Cal* that the University now had free speech and an open forum, "but we have to draw a line between this freedom and the planning and implementing of political action."[66] But at this point Strong said nothing really specific about the nature of that action, made no distinction between action that was lawful and that which was not.

As the meetings progressed, the line that Strong insisted on drawing—essentially the line between advocating and mounting—became harder to maintain, as faculty delegates made increasingly clear their readiness to side with the FSM on this issue and support the right to advocacy that was action bent. It was becoming less and less comfortable for the administration delegates to stand alone in defense of Strong's position. Towle, for example, was pushed by Savio into the implausible position of having to suggest that, despite the ban on mounting, it might be permissible to say at a campus rally that joining a particular off-campus picket line "is a worthy cause and that I would hope you go"(session of October 28).

For a while, then, a student-faculty bloc actually seemed attainable, especially when the faculty introduced a set of proposals ("the Cheit Proposals") that was received by Savio and others with palpable enthusiasm. The faculty delegates, most likely with civil rights activities in mind, seemed to have reached a consensus that it was unacceptable to discipline students for urging other students to join, let us say, an off-campus picket line. Yet ironically, this very consensus forced into the open a new and fatal aspect of the advocacy-versus-mounting issue, an aspect that up to this point had received only passing and unfocused attention, even in statements by the FSM.

In effect, the new question was: Assuming the distinction between advocating and mounting were to be dropped, what should be the disposition of a case in which the off-campus action advocated on campus turned out or appeared to be *illegal?* It was this new point—*new* in the sense that, masked as it was by other arguments, it had not yet been at the center of debate—that soon proved the Achilles' heel of the negotiations. If the question of whether the off-campus action was legal had been touched on before, it had not been portrayed as a critical dividing line. Since the administration had refused to authorize *any* "mounting," the distinction had been of no apparent interest to it, at least not in its public pronouncements (though behind the scenes, as was later revealed in the *Daily Cal*, the issue of off-campus illegal action had indeed been a subject of discussion between Kerr and the Regents' counsel, as well as several UC chancellors).[67] As to the FSM itself, it was still resolutely focused on the goal of reversing the administration's *general* policy. Hence in a major statement issued as late as October 27, after the CCPA had already held two meetings, the FSM could still expound its *primary* demand, that the administration acknowledge the freedom to advocate "off-campus political and social action," with no reference at all to the administration's concerns about the legality of the particular action.[68]

By November 4, however, and again on the 5th and 7th (CCPA's final meeting), the issue of legality had become the fault line that divided the FSM from administrators. No campus official was prepared to tell the Regents, press, or local politicians that the campus could now be used to mount "illegal acts." But more to the point, the issue now produced new strains in relations between the CCPA's student and faculty members. For the closer faculty and students came to reaching a consensus on the right to advocate and mount off-campus actions, the more this near agreement would bring into sharp relief the issue of just what those actions might or might not be.

It was an administration delegate, Searcy, who at the CCPA's third meeting (October 28) introduced the question of legality, which then became the central issue at the remaining meetings.[69] Offering what was meant to be a concession on the advocacy issue, Searcy affirmed that "students should have the right to carry on legal activity." But, he hastened to add, "when they become involved in action which is *illegal*, difficulty arises. The university has a responsibility in this" (emphasis added). This was a view that, still unbeknownst to the student delegates on the 28th, closely followed sentiments expressed to Kerr in an abortive policy recommendation by the Regents' counsel two weeks earlier.

Attorney Malcolm Burnstein,[70] counsel to the FSM at the CCPA meetings, was quick to respond to Searcy's intervention. It was not a university's prerogative, he argued, to determine the legality of an off-campus political action. "If an action is illegal, provisions for deciding this are outside the university," by which he meant that they were vested in the judiciary. In other words, students should have the right to urge participation in an off-campus action—a sit-in, for example—without fear that the University would act against them.[71] With these two conflicting positions—Burnstein's and Searcy's—now on the table, the main substantive issue had finally been joined.

On November 10 the CCPA faculty issued their own authoritative report, a six-page document designed to explain the stalemate to the campus and justify their own role.[72] It included a verbatim text of the faculty's initial proposals for the liberalization of regulations (the Cheit Proposals), which in effect had become the CCPA's working document. The proposals were presented together with an explanation of the main areas of agreement and disagreement. The key passage called on the administration to drop the distinction between advocating and mounting and to allow complete freedom of expression, "subject only to restrictions necessary for normal conduct of University functions and business"—a subordinate clause that anticipated the limitation of such restrictions to considerations of time, place, and manner (the formula finally adopted by the Academic Senate on December 8). The same paragraph reduced the requirements for inviting off-campus speakers to minimal formalities, with no allusion to any restriction on the content of speech. There was only one reason, the report explained, why this pivotal paragraph had failed to produce a final agreement—indeed, had not even been brought to a vote. The unresolvable problem, the East Jerusalem of the committee's negotiations, was "how to deal with the question of the authority of the University to discipline [students] for on-campus conduct that results in off-campus law violation."

The CCPA faculty, then, had landed closer to the administration's position than to the students'. The student version rejected any distinction between legal and illegal off-campus acts and denied the administration any disciplinary authority "in the area of first amendment rights and civil liberties," an area in which students should be subject "only to the civil authorities." Thus if students on campus organized a sit-in at Lucky's and this was said by the district attorney to be unlawful, the on-campus organizers might by convicted by the courts but would retain their academic standing.

The administration's text conceded that students would be granted the right to advocate and organize a *legal* off-campus action, such as a peaceful picket line, but insisted that if the off-campus act proved to be "unlawful," the on-campus organizers would be subject to "such disciplinary action as is appropriate upon a fair hearing as to the appropriateness of the action taken." Hence, in addition to whatever punishment was meted out by a court, a student could also be punished—perhaps expelled, if "appropriate"—by the University. The nature of the "fair hearing" was not specified, nor was it clear from the language whether conviction in the courts was a prerequisite to University discipline or whether it was sufficient for the campus disciplinary committee (or other campus authorities) to determine that the off-campus action was unlawful, a much lower threshold. In the absence of clarity on this point, the FSM delegates were justified in assuming the more menacing scenario, which they (Savio in particular) loosely equated with "prior restraint"; either interpretation, however, was unacceptable to them.

The faculty version, though more succinct, was difficult to distinguish from the administration's: "If unlawful acts directly result from campus advocacy for which unlawful acts the speaker or his sponsoring organization can fairly be held accountable under prevailing legal principles, the University should be entitled, after a fair hearing, to impose appropriate discipline." This language had the same practical effect as the administration's and, if anything, was even clearer in its implication that a conviction in the courts was *not* a prerequisite to campus discipline. Little wonder, then, that FSM delegates felt outgunned and outmaneuvered, especially when, in a moment fraught with negative symbolism, faculty and administration voted together to reject the students' unambiguous wording. They of course had the option, as their legal advisors had encouraged them to do,[73] to emphasize the positive—that is, to declare "victory" by claiming the agreement to permit the unrestricted advocacy and mounting of *lawful* actions as a great accomplishment (which, if we count from the baseline of September 14, it *was*) and by announcing that they would then go to court to test the constitutionality of the residual restriction on *un*lawful advocacy.

In retrospect, however, one can see two persuasive arguments against that course of action.[74] (1) Outcome: Although, as Robert Post has explained, future court decisions would validate many aspects of the FSM's position, this was still a gray area at the time, and in 1964 one could imagine quite easily a judicial ruling that even under the First Amendment university administrations, in keeping with the special mission of academic institutions, had special rights, in certain circumstances, to impose restrictions that could not be applied, say, by cities or states.[75] Note also that even a ruling that upheld the University's constitutional *right* to punish students for this type of advocacy would not be a ruling that it *must*. Thus a debate over the *fairness* of such a policy could not be resolved by the courts alone. (2) Timing: Litigation in the courts could drag on for years. Meanwhile, local civil rights activity that was felt to be pressing had been held in abeyance since October 2. With extended litigation, either student activists would lose even more precious time or their activity would go on but at the cost of suspensions and expulsions, pending the results of appeals. These considerations, fueled, no doubt, by the adrenaline that was continually pumped by the excitement of combat, caused the FSM to reject the advice of its own attorney and to spurn the faculty delegates' proposal as long as it embraced the administration's view of the "legality question." From this time until the eve of the faculty turnabout of December 8, relations between militant members of the FSM leadership and what they too loosely dubbed "*the* faculty" became particularly tense. As one of the former saw it, overlooking how close to success the negotiations had come, "the professors had backed down from supporting free speech."[76]

Because the issues were now so complicated, many students who had supported the FSM had trouble appreciating the do-or-die significance of the unresolved questions or why the FSM was threatening a return to civil disobedience. In the words of David Goines, one of the suspended students, the matter of advocacy was "crystal clear" to FSM delegates to the CCPA but "was as clear as mud to everybody else, including the FSM membership."[77] As has been described elsewhere, there was even a serious split in the FSM Executive Committee at this time, with "moderates" sorely tempted to reach an accommodation along the lines of the Cheit Proposals and "radicals," including Savio, viewing the situation as an impasse that justified a return to mass civil disobedience lest the momentum of the movement be lost and the FSM be seen to back down. The radical position won, but it was a very close call.[78]

With the CCPA deadlocked and, as of November 9, with the FSM again openly flouting the rules by setting up tables, the faculty delegates sought additional ways to explain their position to the campus community—particularly to graduate students and TAs, whose support the FSM so desperately needed if a student strike was to figure in its coming strategy. Some days after CCPA's collapse, on November 18, seeking to provide the faculty delegates with a public forum, Sanford Elberg, the highly respected dean of the graduate division, convoked a campuswide meeting attended by some 450 employed graduate students. Only faculty were meant to speak, but under pressure from the graduate student arm of the FSM (the GCC) two graduate students, Steve Weissman (chairman of the GCC) and Suzanne Goldberg (a member of the CCPA), were permitted to address the audience. With student opinion in a state of flux and confusion, each party felt obliged to justify its own intransigence to the audience, but it was not the faculty speakers (Cheit and Rosovsky), awkward and ill at ease in the face of this unusual setting, but the students who rose to the occasion. Weissman spoke only briefly but was particularly effective in explicating the advocacy issues and moving his audience, whereas the faculty perspective, tainted as it was by its support of the chancellor on the illegality issue, was hard to convey and poorly received.[79] From this point on, many more TAs, acting under the aegis of the GCC, were ready to cooperate with the FSM. And as Ph.D. candidates and research assistants—junior partners, as it were, of their professors—they were bound to stimulate more faculty concern.

.   .   .

The other important outcome of the October 15 Senate meeting was the establishment of an ad hoc faculty committee to hear the case of the suspended students, as requested by Kerr under pressure from the FSM. For purposes of this case, the new committee, chaired by a young law professor, Ira Michael Heyman (it was soon known as the Heyman Committee)[80] supplanted the chancellor's Committee on Student Conduct—yet another sign of the continued erosion of his authority. To add insult to injury, on the very day of the Senate vote members of the chancellor's committee, unaware of what was happening, spent "eight long, hot hours" on the case before hearing a report that it had been removed from their jurisdiction. After concluding that it was up to the chancellor to decide if it should continue its inquiry, the committee then adjourned "until the report was confirmed."[81] In the case of the eight students, it never reconvened.

On October 21 the Heyman Committee presented its preliminary recommendation—that as a gesture of goodwill the chancellor temporarily reinstate the suspended students pending final disposition of the case. Five days later, as he struggled to maintain the dignity of his office, the chancellor, after conferring with Kerr and certain Regents, rejected this advice (against the better judgment of his own staff).[82]

The Heyman Committee began its public hearings on October 28, by which time the students had already been suspended for nearly a month. At the urging of the young attorney Peter Franck, head of the ACLU's Berkeley chapter and a founding member of SLATE, the ACLU represented the students. Campus sentiment seemed to run heavily in their favor, as reflected in a *Daily Cal* column calling for their reinstatement. The hearings, which ran for a total of some twenty hours, were well covered in the *Daily Cal,* where the campus could follow the attorneys' vigorous interrogations of various deans, especially on the key issue of selectivity of prosecution. With the FSM demanding a quick decision (while the otherwise sympathetic *Daily Cal* faulted FSM for its impatience), the last public hearing concluded on November 3, after which the committee began to deliberate in camera.[83] It reached its verdict on the 10th and released its detailed report to the public on the 12th, just three tense days after the collapse of the CCPA and resumption of civil disobedience.

Although it did not go as far as the FSM had urged, full reinstatement without prejudice, in both tone and substance the report was much more favorable to the students than to the administration, whose "shortcomings" it elaborated "with confidence that the University administration will be as desirous as we are of correcting them." The report spoke sympathetically of the students' high-minded motives and "understandable" behavior, while criticizing the administration for "gratuitously" singling out some students for "heavy penalties" that it "summarily imposed" in the hope of "making examples" of them, treating them "almost as hostages." It also noted the "vagueness" of many campus regulations. The committee called for full reinstatement of six of the students, retroactive to *the original date of the suspensions,* thereby absolving them, in effect, of any serious offense (their offenses "warrant[ing] only a minimum punishment"). Their suspensions were to be "expunged" from their records and replaced by the much less onerous penalty of "censure." The committee was slightly less generous to two other students, Savio and Art Goldberg, for whom it recommended six-week suspensions for their leadership roles in the Sproul Hall sit-in of September 30 (Savio) and in the obstruction of aisles on September 28 when Strong was addressing a University meeting (Goldberg). But since their "indefinite" suspensions had begun six weeks earlier, the committee was actually recommending the immediate termination of their suspensions, as well, thereby sentencing them to time already served, though with the suspensions remaining in their records. It is noteworthy that these two violations, the ones the committee took most seriously, amounted to interference with the normal functions of the University, the kind of charge whose legitimacy the FSM had never challenged in principle.[84]

Infuriated by the report, Strong was even angrier at the Heyman Committee's provocative decision to formally submit it not to him (he *was* sent a courtesy copy) but to its parent body, the Academic Senate. Equally upsetting was the committee's rejection of an invitation by Strong and Kerr to meet with them before submitting the report. These were surely calculated acts of defiance by a committee whose previous request to Strong for the students' temporary reinstatement had been ignored. In fact, Strong and Heyman had been wrestling over the question of jurisdiction for some time. (Strong: "Did this committee report first in the Academic Senate, or did it report to the Chancellor with a memo to the senate? . . . The question . . . became a matter of dispute between Mike Heyman and myself.") Much more than a "dispute," it was a local constitutional crisis, with Heyman arguing that a Senate committee reports in the first instance to the Senate while Strong insisted it submit its recommendations "to *me* for *action*."[85] If the Heyman Committee was not a strikingly liberal group of faculty overall, for the moment its members' deference to faculty institutions had trumped any inclination to accommodate a weakened chancellor. Faced with their defiance, on November 13 Strong declared more laconically than testily that he and Kerr "completely disagree with this procedure." But keeping his emotions in check, he went on to say (without apparent irony) that "out of respect for and courtesy to the Academic Senate" he would await its reaction to the report before commenting. A few days later, however, the committee backed down on the procedural issue, conceding that it should have addressed its report to Strong while filing a copy with the Senate. Perhaps it anticipated that the Regents, who were to meet in two or three days, would be more accommodating on the punishments if the committee looked less defiant about formalities.[86]

The FSM was generally satisfied with the committee's recommendations, which may have created something of a counterweight to the antifaculty sentiment generated a few days earlier by tensions in the CCPA. Savio, who read the Heyman report as a vindication of the FSM's position, found it "gratifying that the initial contentions of the students that the rules governing political activity were obscure and their reinforcement [*sic*] was arbitrary have been upheld by the faculty findings."[87] As it turned out, however, neither faculty nor chancellor but the Regents would decide the discipline issue, though Strong leaves little doubt that he intensely lobbied the Board to reject the committee's findings.[88] And he would get his way.

. . .

Well before the Regents met on November 20, even as tensions were mounting over the deliberations of the CCPA and the Heyman Committee, the efforts of informal faculty groups, first seen on October 2, continued. Though uneven and irregular, these efforts were never entirely absent. But the collapse of the CCPA revitalized them, especially among those faculty most open to the FSM's cause. While the administration struggled to build a consensus around the position of the CCPA faculty—that is, expansion of advocacy rights but discipline for "illegal" advocacy—those faculty inclined toward the FSM, spurred on after November 12 by Strong's dismissive treatment of the Heyman Committee, sought a different solution.

Some "pro-FSM" faculty were centered in the "Sellers circle," a term I use not because Sellers, an early supporter of the FSM, was its *leader* (there was none) but because it usually held its meetings in his Dwinelle Hall office, where his typewriter was often at work devising letters, petitions, and motions. I dwell on this group not only because, as a member, I have first-hand knowledge and some still vivid memories but also because a direct line can be drawn leading from it to the Committee of 200 that was born on December 6, and thence to the resolutions passed by the Academic Senate two days later.

The Sellers circle usually consisted of a dozen or so tenured professors and one very junior acting assistant professor—me. The senior men (there were, it need hardly be said, no women) were mainly in their forties, but to me, at twenty-eight, that seemed pretty old. Although others came on occasion, the most stable presences were Sellers, Schorske, Stampp, Selznick, Muscatine, ten Broek, Lowenthal, Sheldon Wolin and Herbert McClosky (both political science), William Kornhauser (sociology), Henry Nash Smith (English), and, the only "hard" science person in the cohort, a veteran of the battle of the loyalty oath and former president of the Berkeley chapter of the AAUP, Howard Schachman (molecular biology).[89] Schachman gave the group its confidence and resolve, while Lowenthal, the oldest and most famous member, gave it a dose of international gravitas. They all knew each other well, some as coconspirators in previous political skirmishes. Another common denominator, in addition to devotion to civil liberties and a high level of scholarly distinction, was that most had close academic relations with some of Berkeley's brightest graduate students, including students deeply involved in the FSM.

At first I felt awkward and out of place in the group and kept waiting to be asked to leave. To this day I am not quite certain just how I got there, but it surely had something to do with ongoing office and corridor conversations among a second liberal faculty group, a cohort of junior historians— colleagues and friends—including Larry Levine, Robert Middlekauff, Irv Scheiner, George Stocking, and me. We had been engaged in discussions of the FSM and related issues since sometime in October. Because Scheiner was personally close to Rosovsky, who held a joint appointment in economics and history, this group had access to a key player who, as we knew, had access to the administration, especially Kerr. We were all strong civil libertarians and civil rights supporters, and we shared various ideas about how to find a solution to the conflict that would secure free speech and advocacy, preferably without costing the administration a total loss of face. I don't think any of us was completely at ease with all aspects of the FSM's confrontational style, but our sympathies were generally on the FSM's side, and we were critical of what we perceived as the administration's stubborn postures and posturing; when the CCPA reached an impasse, we were disappointed that its faculty contingent had acceded so decisively to the administration's distinction between legal and illegal advocacy.

One of the ideas that had emerged from these discussions by late October, when the CCPA was still alive but growing ill, was forwarded to the CCPA and presumably to Kerr's office through the Scheiner-Rosovsky nexus. Although someone seems to have attached the proposal to my name as a shorthand device (Rosovsky, when testifying for the defense at the trial of FSM defendants in May 1965, called it "the Zelnik proposal"), neither I nor my friends ever did so, and for good reason: with respect to the many documents generated during these tumultuous days, up to and including the December 8 resolutions, single-person authorship was virtually nonexistent. (Later, not surprisingly, almost every participant had a different memory of the genesis of the many proposals of 1964, proposals that in fact took shape dialogically: someone would prepare a draft and show it to someone else who would criticize and revise it, but those revisions would then be only partially accepted, would be revised again, and so forth.)

Our proposal, which in its various incarnations we discussed with Savio, the FSM Steering Committee, and possibly its Executive Committee, was in part a response to the impasse reached in the CCPA. The essence of the proposal, which now looks pretty awkward to me but with which I was pleased at the time, was this: Whereas, consistent with the demands of the FSM, cases arising from the advocacy of illegal actions should be adjudicated in the courts, a campus judicial body would also be authorized to take up some of these cases, but with guarantees that accused students be granted every possible right to make the same constitutional claims before that body that they would be able to make in a criminal court. We saw this as a reasonable compromise that would safeguard the rights of students while allowing the administration to save face in the eyes of a public and of media that were then very hostile to the FSM. The University could claim that it had not abdicated all its responsibility for student conduct, but accused students would be assured that their rights were as fully recognized *on* campus as off.

I believed then as I do now that Mario and others took the proposal seriously, though no one can say with certainty that in the end they would have accepted it. But to be palatable to the FSM, it had to include such safeguards as full adversary proceedings and legal representation of the accused by counsel of their choice, with the authority of the judicial body, consisting (like the Heyman Committee) of faculty chosen by the Academic Senate, to be final. In at least one variant, I believe, the committee chairman was to be a member of the law faculty.

It is unclear whether the proposal ever reached the top echelons of the administration. At the FSM trial, Rosovsky recalled having turned it over to Kerr's staff while the CCPA was still in operation. But in May 1965 the president's office was surprised when it was alerted to Rosovsky's testimony, and Kerr himself has no memory of having explored the proposal.[90] My best guess is that the proposal did reach the administration at some level, but that once CCPA had collapsed and campus rule violations had resumed, the administration's attention was focused elsewhere.

After CCPA's collapse our history group continued to pursue its quest for a just solution. My own assumption at the time was that our proposal was circulating among top administrators and that its content would be reflected in the decisions of the Regents, scheduled to meet on November 20. We also knew that, thanks to the work of the Sellers circle, there would be an emergency meeting of the Academic Senate on November 24, which meant we would not have to await the scheduled meeting of December 8 to bring a new motion before that body. This seemed all the more plausible in that the Sellers circle was linked with the history group by virtue of the participation of Schorske, Sellers, and Stampp, our senior colleagues, who shared much of our outlook on what was happening and to whom some of us were personally close.

Having joined the faculty only two months earlier, I was less acquainted with these senior figures than were others. My best memory is that I wandered into one of their meetings at the request of one of them, possibly Schorske, to report on our proposal and perhaps to discuss the state of mind of the students. Though a faculty member, I was still a graduate student myself, having not yet finished my Stanford dissertation, and senior faculty may have taken this as an indication of insight into the students' thinking. I had not yet broken the "over thirty" barrier, but more to the point, in the course of our encounters I had developed a personal rapport with some key members of the FSM, including Mario, Steve Weissman (a history graduate student), and the undergraduate Martin Roysher, to some extent because we could, to various degrees, speak the same political language. In any case, I was invited to keep coming to the Sellers circle, or at least wasn't told to stay away. Although the two groups of liberal faculty had not yet commingled, a basis had been laid for closer (if never perfect) cooperation.

The pivotal importance of November 20 should not be underestimated. The Regents were to meet, and a restless campus tensely awaited their pronouncements. Some three thousand FSM supporters marched to the music of Joan Baez from Sproul Plaza to the large grass lawn at the western edge of the campus, across the street from University Hall, where the Regents were meeting. There, in a mass vigil, the crowd awaited the outcome of their deliberations. The Regents meeting was attended by Savio and four other representatives of the FSM, though their request to address the Regents and present them with a petition was denied. I too was waiting on the lawn, part of a small, apprehensive faculty contingent.[91]

Thirty-seven years later, it is hard to reconstruct the varied expectations of the assembled crowd. Speaking for myself but perhaps for other faculty as well, my best recollection is that I was rather pessimistic. I certainly did not expect the Regents to suddenly announce their readiness to tolerate the on-campus advocacy of potentially unlawful acts, but I did have some hope that they would endorse (1) the CCPA faculty's acceptance of the legitimacy of all *other* advocacy, a position that by then was essentially endorsed by Kerr and even Strong; (2) some version of our group's proposal for a genuine faculty committee to hear future disciplinary cases growing out of campus political activity, with a strong set of safeguards for constitutional rights; and (3) the Heyman Committee's disposition of the disputed disciplinary cases. It was (and is) my belief that, given the weariness of so many students and the desire of key FSMers for a fair solution even if it fell short of their full aspirations, a Regental decision that incorporated *all* of these elements would have ended the most stressful phase of the conflict. To be sure, there would have been fierce debate within the FSM. Some, understandably enough, would have called the solution a "sell-out," while others, just as understandably, would have seen it as a partial yet major, even historic, victory for student rights and free speech. But when one considers the weak response to calls for a sit-in the following Monday, when it was known that the Regents had conceded much *less* than these three points, it is easy to imagine that a robust display of Regental statesmanship would have significantly changed the terms of the conflict.

Such was not to be the case, however, for in Kerr's words, "The regents were in a bad mood."[92] Here is what they did: (1) following Kerr's advice, they responded positively on the first point—the right to advocate, organize, and mount *lawful* political actions. But they were silent on how and when the determination of "lawfulness" would be made, and though it is true that at a later news conference Kerr asserted that "*in the usual case* [my emphasis], you'd wait for the courts to decide," suggesting that (in keeping with CCPA faculty proposals) there would be no prior restraint, no such hope was offered by the Regents. (2) They flatly ignored our request for faculty authority in the adjudication of constitutionally sensitive disciplinary cases while pointedly upholding the authority of the chancellor's badly compromised "Faculty" committee, with no new procedural safeguards. (3) Though coming up with a fairly moderate formula of their own, they rejected the more generous recommendations of the Heyman Committee (for example, they placed Savio and Goldberg on academic probation for the rest of the semester), and, a still greater provocation (initially proposed by Strong and Kerr), they called for immediate disciplinary action against violators of campus rules in the period *after* September 30, the hearings to be conducted by the discredited "Faculty" committee. Although the number of new cases to be opened was unspecified, many students had been cited, especially in the past ten days.

Despite my fairly low expectations, my own reaction when the outcome was read over loudspeakers was one of shock and disbelief. (Mario told me

I turned pale.) My feeling was that our group had been working hard for weeks to develop a formula that was both principled and practical, had made some real progress in getting FSM leaders to take our ideas seriously, and had communicated these ideas through "proper channels" (opened up by Rosovsky) to the University's key decision makers, only to find ourselves slapped in the face.[93]

FSM leaders were at least as upset, in part because too many of their supporters, exhausted from weeks of turmoil and now facing ever greater risk of punishment, may have been confused by the Regents' language. Some may have been bewitched by the lure of a settlement that, after all, was not radically different from a proposal recently endorsed by the ASUC and transmitted to the Regents by Kerr.[94] When all was said and done, the punishments for the eight students were still fairly light, the right to advocate everything but illegal actions had been won in principle, and the threat of new disciplinary action, still vague, may not have been clearly communicated in the initial reports from the Regents meeting. To many, given the seeming finality of the Regents' pronouncements, this may have looked "as good as it gets." As Searle pointed out a little later, perhaps with slight exaggeration, after the Regents meeting the issues appeared "less polarizing." As the FSM's unrivaled faculty favorite at the time (and surely the most unreserved in his support), Searle himself was now convinced that "the FSM was dead and that the war was over, with the students winning a partial and ambiguous, but still substantial victory."[95] While Weissman and a few militants quickly called for direct action, Savio, Rossman, and others, people who seldom shied away from conflict, wisely grasped the difficulty of their present position and the perplexed state of mind of many students. They cautioned the assembled crowd to act with restraint, to spend the weekend thinking and talking, and to wait until Monday to decide on a course of action. Savio even suggested that the situation still left room for hope. I also addressed the crowd, in a similar vein, gathering up what I could find of my green faculty persona to remind the crowd that the Academic Senate had an emergency meeting set for Tuesday and suggesting, almost promising (somewhat recklessly, as it turned out), that something positive would result.[96]

To no one's surprise, on Sunday the chancellor publicly endorsed the Regents' decision to preclude the advocacy and organization of "unlawful" actions while allowing for "lawful" advocacy and organizing in select campus locations.[97] At noon on Monday, while faculty nervously prepared for Tuesday's Senate meeting, students gathered on Sproul Plaza to hear discouraged, disappointed, and divided FSM leaders debate the relative merits of a sit-in versus the more cautious approach of testing their position in the courts. Over the weekend there had been some shifting of positions, with Weissman, president of the influential GCC, now opposing a sit-in and

Savio speaking in its favor. The speakers *in favor*—Savio, Roysher, Weinberg, and others—held back from any claim that a sit-in was likely to lead to victory. Their emphasis instead was on the moral and existential nature of the act—"a plea, sort of an existential cry" (Weinberg), a matter of "individual conscience" (Savio), a personal gesture of "moral witness" (Roysher)—which is exactly what Weissman was rejecting. The dreary result was what Goines, who *favored* the action, has since described as "a muddled sit-in," with barely more than three hundred protesters entering Sproul Hall, many quite hesitantly. That move was followed by acrimonious argument inside the building about whether to leave at the 5:00 P.M. closing time or to risk trespassing charges. With Aptheker advocating prudence, the debate was ended by a 6–5 vote of the Steering Committee to vacate the building. Many threatened to ignore the majority decision, but most were convinced by a disheartened Savio, who, though he had strongly supported the minority, asked the crowd to respect the majority vote. "The split," in Goines's words, "left us with a feeling of deep discouragement."[98]

Many faculty were present at the debates that raged on the Sproul steps that afternoon. Few of us were enthusiasts for campus sit-ins, and those who harbored hopes for the Senate meeting saw a sit-in as a dangerous distraction. Now somewhat accustomed to speaking out at rallies, I joined with those who argued against a sit-in, pointing out to a student audience that was already wary of the action that the meeting scheduled for the next day was certain to be—and here my rhetoric was surely inflated—among the most important faculty meetings in the University's history (wrong, but off by just two weeks). I summarized the motion that our group planned to introduce and emphasized that one of its main points was to give faculty a decisive role in setting policy and resolving free speech controversies. I openly acknowledged that this was not the fully developed FSM position, which (except for "time, place, and manner") called for *no* University oversight of political activity in any form, although one part of the motion came close to that position. Students by now were hungry for faculty involvement, and my remarks were well received. Since my speech came right after Mario spoke to the crowd in a positive and gratified way about what faculty support had been forthcoming, my colleagues and I left the rally concerned about the sit-in but determined to accomplish something at the Senate meeting.[99]

In preparation for that meeting, on November 23 the history group drafted a preliminary version of what became our motion.[100] The draft, signed by Richard Abrams, Levine, Middlekauff, Robert Paxton, Sheldon Rothblatt, Scheiner, Sellers, Schorske, John M. Smith, and me, was then hastily circulated to the entire faculty. Of the original signers, only Schorske and Sellers, members of the Sellers circle, were tenured professors. Levine, who bravely accepted the onerous task of acting as our spokesman at the meeting, recalls his feeling of disappointment that more senior faculty, whose jobs were not in jeopardy, failed to "take the lead," leaving it to us greenhorns to carry the ball. My own possibly flawed recollection is somewhat more positive: we, Larry in particular, did indeed carry the ball, defending our motion in the face of opposition from skilled and seasoned adversaries, people who now supported and were supported by the administration and who knew all too well how to bend the intricacies of *Robert's Rules* to their advantage. Nevertheless, several of our more seasoned colleagues—Jerry Neilands (biochemistry), who seconded the motion, Sellers, and others—did speak in its behalf, and we of course could not have come as close as we did (232–205) to winning a key vote and would not have been able to actually *defeat* a hostile substitute motion by Arthur Ross (274–261) without scores of senior faculty on our side. But it *was* rough going, as we whispered frantically, passing notes back and forth in response to the amendments and procedural motions of those whom Larry calls the Senate's "doyens." Greeting our "out of order" motion "with amused contempt"—we had framed it as "the sense of the Berkeley Division" instead of as "the sense of the meeting"!—they "mangled and distorted it through parliamentary maneuvers and amendments," making it "almost unrecognizable" and causing Larry himself to urge the assembly to vote against the altered version.[101]

I cannot overemphasize how intimidating from our perspective the Senate atmosphere was on that day, how difficult it was then to speak up in the face of 525 (mainly senior) faculty members, at least half of them very impatient with our challenge. As a junior physics professor was later told by a friendly senior colleague, "a young faculty member speaking in the [Academic] senate creates a very bad impression,"[102] and there can be little doubt about the presence among untenured faculty, both then and later, of fear for one's job security. By now the Regents had pronounced their "final" word, as had the chancellor, and to many faculty that word seemed pretty reasonable. Speaking for Strong, Vice Chancellor Constance had begun the meeting with a carefully worded talk, filled with conciliatory language in which, claiming the moral support of CCPA faculty, he promised careful, sensitive implementation of the Regents' policies, while thanking and reaching out to concerned faculty ("we administrators are faculty members under the skin"), and calling for their support.[103] As the assembled faculty knew, the FSM itself may have been petering out, as witness the rather pathetic response to the previous day's sit-in. And finally, even many sympathetic faculty were now more focused on the Katz case, the original and primary purpose of this meeting, than on the FSM.[104] For all these reasons, the notion that we were making unnecessary trouble, were too impatient, was very much in the air. Our group was well aware that many senior faculty, including important figures such as Cheit, Ross, and our own department chair, Henry May, would speak against our motion.[105] Even Heyman, whose views had been spurned by the administration, now adopted a conciliatory tone. Since my "acting" status deprived me of the right to speak (technically I was not even supposed to attend, but this prohibition was not enforced before December 8), I was spared the ordeal, but those younger faculty who did take up the challenge, including (besides the history group) Morris Hirsch of math, deserve great credit. Although students at the time were well aware of the meeting, which to many was the last hope for vindication of the FSM position, at least on the discipline issue, I doubt they were aware of the rugged atmospherics. But later Bob Starobin, one of two history graduate representatives on the GCC, in an otherwise captious interview ("They got the thing on the floor but they bollixed it."), would say, "Levine was really the only guy that had the guts to get up and make the kind of resolution that he made."[106]

Much to its credit, the engaged faculty did not lose heart after the battering of November 24. If it is fair to say that our activities generally represented a mixture of civil libertarian principle and the urge to bring peace to the campus, the latter was hardly a consideration by the evening of the 24th, when there was little fight left in any of the dogs. The continued planning in Sellers's office had few incentives other than principle and the promise of yet another Senate meeting on the horizon. Although it dampened our mood, the recent voting had demonstrated that with proper preparation and attention to *Robert's Rules* (a copy of which Levine hastened to purchase after the meeting), there was a fighting chance to pass a decent resolution next time round. The same Senate meeting, after all, had voted overwhelmingly to condemn the administration in the Katz case for "its disregard of and contempt for the Academic Senate and its duly constituted Committee system."[107] Meanwhile, with Thanksgiving recess only two days away, the campus could look forward to a four-day lull.

But not the administration! On Saturday the 28th, while others were recovering from turkey dinners, Strong fulfilled the Regents' injunction to take action against post–September 30 rule violations. Notices were mailed to four of the FSM's most conspicuous figures—Savio, Brian Turner, and siblings Art and Jackie Goldberg, Jackie being one of the most moderate FSM leaders. Against the better judgment of deans Towle and Williams but with energetic support from Sherriffs, Strong charged the four with having violated rules on October 1 and 2 in connection with the police car incident; additional charges were leveled against Savio and Art Goldberg. Moreover, the four were told to appear before the suddenly resuscitated "Faculty" Committee on Student Conduct. I will not rehearse the argument made by virtually every commentator on the FSM saga that this vindictive act of folly had a radical effect on the course of events. Students whose interest had been ebbing were now compelled to face a stark choice: either

allow four comrades to risk potentially grave punishment or try to re-
vive their nearly exhausted protests. Nothing could have been more calculated to breathe new life into a flagging, some even said dying, FSM. In
Goines's words, "the administration had once again done the devil's work
for him."[108]

On Monday, with the campus abuzz with news of the chancellor's letter
and rumors of possible new citations (there were possibly hundreds of
potential cases between October 2 and the last sit-in), students and faculty
returned from vacation. By the following day, December 1, the FSM had
issued a twenty-four-hour ultimatum, and the words "strike" and "sit-in"
were heard repeatedly. The GCC, having opposed the recent sit-in, now
reverted to its former militancy and was again talking "strike." Many anticipated an action on the following day, most likely another sit-in.

That the dramatic events that would flow from the December 2 demonstration, especially the deployment of police, were a precondition to the
Academic Senate's pro-FSM vote of December 8 is undeniable. But it is no
less deniable that the faculty who would come to be known as "the 200"—
the losers of November 24 and eventual winners of December 8—were
preparing for the Senate meeting well before the sit-in. Our group intensified its work as the date of the meeting approached and especially after
learning of the retroactive discipline. On November 30, the day Strong's
statement became public, our typewriters were again feverishly at work as
we began drafting a motion that was to pick up where the defeated motion
of November 24 had left off.[109]

On December 2, still hours before the sit-in, members of the Sellers circle circulated an open letter "To Members of the Academic Senate" along
with a four-part "sense motion" they hoped to put to a vote on the 8th. The
signers included Schorske, Sellers, Kornhauser, and Wolin, as well as Mark
Schorer (English) and Steve Smale (math). Schorer, who was very close to
Henry Nash Smith, may have attended circle meetings on a few occasions;
Smale, though not part of the circle, was an eminent member of the
department whose faculty most consistently (and perhaps least critically)
supported the FSM. For strategic reasons, not all members of the Sellers
circle had signed the letter or endorsed the motion, but both statements
should be understood as blended products of the circle and the history
group, as may be seen by comparing the December 2 and November 30
drafts.[110]

Unaware of the chain of events about to unfold, though prophetically
anticipating that "continuation of the present situation may well lead
to police activity, a TA strike, and other serious disruptions of our educational program," the authors of the letter had been alerted to the fact that
CAF (two members of which belonged to the Sellers circle) had not yet
completed a thorough report for presentation to the Senate. Independent

faculty action had to be taken, they wrote, "because events have not waited on the careful and detailed report we expect from our Committee on Academic Freedom early in the coming semester."

In classical professorial fashion, the letter began on a note of fabricated harmony—a conciliatory gesture toward Strong aimed at attracting less committed faculty: "The policies announced by Chancellor Strong," it said, using words that could as easily have been used by those on the other side of the faculty divide, "take us a long way toward a happy solution." And the letter closed on a seemingly evenhanded note declaring the signers to be neither "condoning nor condemning the actions of any of the parties" and stressing the need "to turn away from past events and toward the task of restoring our University community." But the central paragraph, presenting the signers' position on "two substantive matters," belied both the buoyant tone of the opening and the neutral tone of the conclusion by getting to the heart of the conflict. The "matters" were, of course, advocacy and discipline, the most burning questions almost from the very outset.

On the "hotly disputed question of 'advocacy,'" the authors' approach was to seem to take the most liberal-sounding yet vague assertion of the Regents and the chancellor seriously and to provide it with their own more liberal "interpretation," one they hoped would prove "acceptable to all segments of the University community." This approach was embodied in paragraph 1 of their draft motion: "In keeping with the statement in the policies announced by the Chancellor, 'The advocacy of ideas and acts which is constitutionally protected off the campus should be protected on the campus,' the University should take action only against such on-campus advocacy as is constitutionally unprotected."

This language seemed to mimic a fundamental principle of the FSM, but not unlike the chancellor's statement, it still left room for the punishment of students for advocacy the *administration* deemed to be constitutionally *un*protected, to wit (though left unspecified), advocacy of illegal acts. That is why it is essential to read that paragraph in conjunction with the signers' treatment of the other "substantive matter," the structure of discipline. As stated in the covering letter, the proposal in this area was based on the belief that "only the Academic Senate can provide an adjudicatory body that would be sufficiently independent of ex parte influences in the controversial area of political activity." Essentially, this was a restatement of the Levine motion. Translated into more direct language, the last words would have read, "an adjudicatory body that could be trusted not to succumb to outside political pressures to suppress student activists." On this basis, the draft motion called for "an independent committee" appointed by the Academic Senate, instructed to adhere to the "basic principles of due process," with full jurisdiction over cases involving political "speech and activity"; a committee—and this point is crucial—whose decisions would be "final." In effect, the chancellor would be stripped of his power to discipline students for acts of "political speech and activity."

In sum, though under the December 2 draft motion a student might still be subjected to campus discipline for acts that were *not* constitutionally protected (the one important area in which the proposal still fell short of the FSM position), if the administration chose to press charges the student would at least have the robust protection of full due process administered by an independent faculty committee and responsive to the defense that the advocacy in dispute was protected by the First and Fourteenth Amendments. The draft also suggested that the sole basis for deciding that specific speech could "reasonably" be subject to University regulation was whether this was necessary in order to "prevent interference with other University activities," which amounted to a succinct way of stating the "time, place, and manner" principle that would be applied on December 8. Finally, it is of no small importance that the motion called upon the administration, pending the final CAF report, to "withhold further discipline against students accused of violations in the course of the recent controversy," that is, since October 1, while asking students, again pending CAF's report, to "observe existing regulations."

It may be of some value to ponder three significant counterfactual questions, suggested by the proposed motion: *If new discipline cases had not been announced and if as a consequence the sit-in and resulting arrests had not taken place,*

a. Would the Academic Senate have passed this motion on December 8, or something close to it?
b. Had it been passed, would students in general and the FSM in particular have then been satisfied?
c. Would the administration and/or the Regents then have accepted the terms of the motion?

Stated briefly, my own (informed, I hope) opinion is that:

a. The Senate would have passed the motion; it had, after all, come close to passing something similar on November 24, despite the parliamentary confusion and even before the chancellor's provocative announcement of retroactive discipline.
b. Though somewhat grudgingly and not unanimously, the FSM leaders would have gone along with the Academic Senate, leaving the remaining disputed issues to be tested in the courts, especially if the specific terms of "due process" were spelled out to its satisfaction. Based on my own conversations with them in November, I believe that Mario and others understood that with such safeguards the likelihood of any campus discipline for advocacy-related acts was virtually nil. And it is clear from

the divisions on November 23 that other members of the Steering Committee, not to mention the "rank and file" and of course "students in
general," would have been at least as open to this solution.

c. I fear that both the administration and the Regents would have been
reluctant to accept the December 2 draft motions without serious modification. Based on their past conduct, they would surely have insisted on
an unequivocal reference to the inadmissibility of mounting illegal
actions. And based on their future conduct, they almost certainly would
have insisted that disciplinary power remain with the administration,
as it had "traditionally" (a canard that would soon be corrected by the
research of two history professors; see note 162). Nevertheless, if the
motion had passed overwhelmingly and if the FSM had agreed to its
terms, then who can say that the Regents would not have found a face-
saving formula that allowed them to live with this solution, at least de
facto? The chances for such flexibility would certainly have been
enhanced if President Kerr had recommended it, something we can
never know for sure. End of counterfactual excursion!

.   .   .

Well, the sit-in *did* take place, followed by the summoning of police, arrests,
bookings, the clearing of the building, and the bussing of over eight hundred spirited demonstrators to the Alameda County jail—all of which
would soon create a radically new mood on campus, including among the
faculty. This is not to say that many, if any, faculty welcomed the decision to
sit in. Despite the chancellor's (and others') belief that faculty egged on
the students, I know of no faculty in my own circles who expressed enthusiasm for occupation of Sproul Hall. I think what we *did* have was a sense of
the sit-in's inevitability and a belief that the Regents' inflexibility and the
administration's vindictiveness had unleashed the coming storm. I know
with certainty of only one faculty member, Smale, who actually took part in
the sit-in, and he left before the arrests.[111] Like many faculty, I was on the
Plaza when the students, accompanied by the singing of Joan Baez, entered
Sproul Hall in a festive spirit.[112] If I found the moment emotionally exhilarating, like many others (including, I believe, many of the sitters-in), I
viewed it as yet another gesture of moral witness, with little hope of a positive outcome. I went to bed late that night knowing that hundreds were still
in the building but not knowing of course that they were soon to be
arrested and hauled away. Early in the morning, around 2 A.M., like many
other "friendly" faculty (and even a few who had remained aloof), I
received a frantic phone call from either a student or a professor urging
me to hurry to campus. There I found perhaps a dozen of my equally
bewildered colleagues, though except for Stampp (to whom police denied

access to Sproul Hall despite his membership on CAF) and Levine, I have no specific memory of whom I saw.[113] With time, while police were slowly clearing demonstrators from the building, more faculty arrived. Within a few hours, many had volunteered to contribute to a bail fund that eventually raised $85,000 and that by the following day had secured the release of all arrestees but one; many were fetched from the jail by up to fifty eager professors,[114] including some who had been lukewarm to the FSM. This was a measure of the transformational power of the sight and sounds of the mass arrests of students by a congeries of city, county, and state police.

With this turmoil in the background, concerned faculty struggled on December 3 to come up with a new plan of action. Students and TAs were responding positively to the FSM's call for a campuswide strike spearheaded by the GCC. As reported by the *Daily Cal*, "large groups of faculty members and graduate students met to determine their policy towards the strike," while "University and state leaders issued statements, some lambasting the administration and some the FSM."[115] Large numbers of faculty, whether or not they were "striking," now found it morally untenable to meet routinely with their classes;[116] but even pro-FSM faculty were mindful of their obligations to nonstriking students and therefore struggled to reconcile their conflicting loyalties. Some met their classes off campus to avoid crossing picket lines, many of which were manned by their own graduate students; others met on campus but devoted their classes to discussion of the crisis; a few dismissed classes outright as a symbol of their solidarity with the strikers. Thus Leon Litwack, then a visiting professor, famously released his U.S. history class with the declaration that it was inappropriate "to study, if not to celebrate, the rebels of the past while we seek to silence the rebels of the present," while Norman Jacobson challenged his political theory class with the words of Albert Camus: "by our own silence or by the stand we take, we too shall enter the fray." Jacobson, who had been witnessing "the astonishing scene at Sproul Hall" for many hours, continued: "as I have tried to absorb the significance of what was taking place before my eyes, it became clear to me that I simply was incapable of violating the palpable air of protest which today surrounds every building on this campus. There will be no class today." Searle was characteristically succinct: "For me to teach, would be a betrayal of those [arrested] students who cannot be present." Leo Lowenthal, vice chairman of sociology, now speaking for the heads of other social science departments, called for the temporary suspension of classes so that faculty might spend time resolving the crisis.[117] But probably the most typical reaction to the strike on the part of the FSM's more circumspect faculty sympathizers is captured in Stampp's recollections of his own state of mind:

> I had mixed feeling about faculty dismissing classes. If students wanted to go on strike, that's fine, that's their decision. But there were students who did not

sympathize with the strike, and several of them came and talked to me saying: "You can't make decisions for us. You must be there to lecture if we want to come to lectures." I missed one class. I didn't dismiss my class except once when the Committee on Academic Freedom was meeting, and some of my students were a little upset about that. I held a special class later on for those who wanted to come to make up for the class I missed. I really had very strong [positive] feelings about the Free Speech Movement. I sympathized with it, but also [was concerned] about our responsibilities as teachers here, and not making these decisions for students. If you dismiss your class, then you've made the decision for all of them, whether they sympathize with it or not.[118]

Under the new circumstances, in the words of Henry May, most faculty "felt they had to take a position."[119] My own recollection, somewhat hazy, is that late in the morning I was walking north across the campus, away from Sproul Plaza, in search of friendly faculty faces, when I ran into one of the original "group of 15," Glazer, whom I barely knew, looking more than a little frantic. (I may have looked just as frantic to him!) Although we know from his subsequent writings that he regretted Strong's decision to discipline the four students, which he saw as a breach of faith, by now Glazer had grown increasingly impatient with the FSM, especially with what he viewed as their stubborn insistence on the right to advocate and mount illegal actions.[120] But in spite (or perhaps because) of our differences, of which he must have been aware, he stopped to talk and seemed to value my opinion. He and some of his colleagues were thinking of calling a faculty meeting in Wheeler Auditorium (where he had a class scheduled early that afternoon), but he wasn't certain if it was the right move; what did I think? I of course encouraged him and then went on to contact my own colleagues to urge them to attend and to spread the word. Although I would not claim that no Wheeler meeting would have taken place absent my chance meeting with Glazer—other faculty were no doubt debating similar proposals—at the time I thought our encounter a great act of fate.

At one o'clock that afternoon, with arrests still under way, a standing-room-only crowd of over eight hundred faculty packed into Wheeler, where Glazer had canceled his class to make way for the gathering, which he chaired.[121] There were moments of confusion during the long debate that followed, but on the whole the meeting went amazingly smoothly. I was particularly excited because, whereas I had had to remain silent at the Senate meetings, confining myself to whispering and passing notes, this was an unofficial meeting, and at last I would be able to speak my mind before a large assemblage of faculty.

The first motion was introduced by May, the chairman of my department. May had kept his distance from the plottings of his more activist colleagues, and his proposal now was entirely his own. "In the middle of the night," he recalls, he had "dreamed up what came to be called the May Resolutions."[122] Then he crafted his proposals into an open letter to Kerr, Strong, and the *Daily Cal.* Signed by May as "Chairman, Department of History," it's opening words conveyed his sense of urgency: "In view of the desperate situation now confronting the University." This was followed by the declaration that "every effort must be made to restore the unity of our campus community and to end the series of provocation[s] and reprisals which has resulted in disaster." To those ends, the letter then called for three immediate "actions": (1) implementing the administration's "new and liberalized" rules, pending their further improvement; (2) dropping all disciplinary action for offenses occurring "before the present date"; (3) and forming an "*Academic Senate*" committee "to which students may appeal decisions of the administration regarding penalties for offenses arising from political actions, *and that decisions of this committee be final*" (emphasis added).[123]

This was essentially the motion May introduced at the "extralegal faculty meeting" in Wheeler Auditorium.[124] A few days earlier it might well have been viewed by many of us as a significant step in the right direction. Although his acclaim for the "new and liberalized rules" accorded well with the administration's position, May's call for so sweeping an amnesty was surely a giant stride in the direction of accommodation, a serious breakthrough coming from where it did. As to item 3, though disappointing insofar as it left discipline at the first instance in the chancellor's hands, it nonetheless contained a fresh and constructive notion—the right of appeal to a genuine faculty committee. I should add, however, that if the language reported the next day in the *Daily Cal* is correct, the motion omitted the important words about the finality of the committee's decisions that were in the original letter. The words *do* appear, however, in the version later reported in the authoritative account published in *California Monthly*.[125]

Be that as it may, if there was a serious flaw in May's motion, it was its failure to confront what was now the central issue: regulation of the content of on-campus advocacy as it related to possibly unlawful off-campus acts. However, this lacuna was soon filled by a motion made by a member of the Sellers circle, Herb McClosky, who proposed as an additional clause nothing less than the nullification of the Regents' decision that the University could punish students for such advocacy. (For further clarification, he also proposed a clause stating that no student could be punished by the University for participating in any off-campus activity.) Somehow, it was barely noticed that, though proposed as an *addition* to May's motion, McClosky's language was in logical contradiction to May's item 1. Such "technicalities," which would have absorbed many minutes of wrangling at a Senate meeting, were easily ignored at the gathering in Wheeler. The motion passed overwhelmingly.[126]

As further evidence of the degree to which the faculty mood had shifted in just a few hours, two more notable events took place at the meeting. First, Roger Stanier, an eminent professor of bacteriology, read aloud a telegram he planned to send to Governor Edmund Brown condemning his decision to send in police. It read in part: "Punitive action taken against hundreds of students cannot help to solve our current problems, and will aggravate the already serious situation. Only prompt release of the arrested students offers any prospect of restoring the unity of campus life and of a return to formal academic functions." The assembled faculty gave Stanier a prolonged standing ovation, after which some 360 people added their names to the telegram.[127]

Second, in an act that, though understandable, was hardly merciful, John Reynolds (physics), chairman of the Berkeley chapter of the AAUP, read a statement calling for Strong's resignation. (To the best of my knowledge, though our patience with the chancellor had long since run out, no one from the Sellers circle took part in the preparation of the statement.) Although the statement was greeted with loud applause, in the end Reynolds charitably refrained from offering it as a motion.[128]

The size of the Wheeler meeting, the strength of the motions passed, and the passion displayed by so many speakers inevitably alerted the administration to the change in faculty mood. With the strike growing and a Senate meeting just five days away, there was a clear danger that the faculty would pass an *official* resolution that paralleled the motions of December 3. The medical breakdown of a chancellor—he was hospitalized on December 5 with severe gall bladder problems[129]—already damaged by *political* infirmity was about to eliminate the local administration from the picture. But even before that happened the president, whose relations with the chancellor had reached an all-time low, was badly in need of an institutional counterweight to an increasingly refractory faculty. What he needed was a body that could offset the moral force of a faculty that threatened to give aid and comfort to a movement that, in Kerr's eyes, was forsaking democratic processes "in favor of anarchy."[130] He soon found this counterweight in a proposal by Chairman Scalapino, one of the original "15" of October 2 and by now a forceful critic of FSM intransigence. What Scalapino had in mind was the constitution of a special committee of departmental chairmen, a kind of council of elders to act in cooperation with the president and help him weather the crisis. But though department chairmen *were* certainly leading members of the faculty and in the public eye were powerful and influential, there was no statutory basis for their corporate existence; they were, in effect, an enlarged presidential emergency committee, a symptom, as it were, of the prevailing turmoil. According to May, one of the group's leading members, "The idea was that all other authority had pretty well broken down and this was a remaining kind of authority." The plan quickly received the blessing of Kerr, who from December 3 to 7 endeavored to run the campus with a select subgroup of these chairmen, a "working committee" of five, as his privy council. During those hectic days the group conducted "endless," sometimes all-night meetings as it endeavored to work out viable terms to present to the plenary group of chairmen, which was somewhat less united and more unpredictable than the smaller one (though even the smaller group was not always of one mind, including as it did Joseph Tussman, whose general bent had been favorable to the FSM). These "terms," according to May, who briefly became the chairmen's spokesman, were essentially his own earlier proposal "with a special emphasis on immediate amnesty."[131]

On Friday, December 4, May held a televised press conference. Although he has recently described the issue of whether he was speaking in behalf of the other chairmen as "a little ambiguous" (some were by his side), the opening of his statement noted that it had "the authorization of a group of department chairmen established yesterday in an effort to establish a platform for solution to the present crisis." May was bravely, if not desperately, trying to convey to the outside world—especially to those most inclined to condemn concessions to the FSM—why "many of the faculty members to some extent were sympathetic with the students" while also assuring the same audience that Berkeley faculty "do not approve of demands for a capitulation or of invasion of buildings." Though his argument was logically consistent, this was a hard circle to square. He tried to do it, in part, by justifying concessions to the FSM's key demand, to allow the campus to be used to organize off-campus political actions, by focusing on the most palatable examples, petitioning and fund-raising, while stressing that no violence or serious trouble had resulted from such activity in the past. He also explained why it was that, "understandably," students "felt tricked" by the administration's decision to renew its disciplinary plans and why that decision meant that "the faculty, with regret, has no choice but to be critical of the administration." Absent, however, was any exploration of the lawful-unlawful distinction, the issue covered by McClosky's "addition" to May's resolutions of the previous day. May's press conference revealed his controversial resolutions to the outside world, including their most far-reaching concessions (full amnesty and creation of a faculty appeals board), while projecting a faculty consensus in favor of enforcing of the rules announced by Strong after the Regents meeting. Much less controversial was his impeccable concluding sentence: "No settlement is possible which does not take account of the strong emotions now influencing our students and many of our faculty."[132]

The position projected at the press conference, which I would call "administration position on advocacy cum May position on amnesty," was soon adopted by the larger group of chairmen. May recalls that the strongest objections came from the right, presumably because of the amnesty element. "[T]he left of the faculty didn't support the line I took there, but they didn't go after me at the time."[133] This corresponds with my own recollection, but I would add that "the left" (presumably meaning the Sellers circle et al.) was not so much reluctant to criticize that "line" as it was preoccupied with preparations for the pending Senate meeting.

President Kerr put up some brief resistance to the call for amnesty, especially as it affected Savio and the other recently charged students. To drop these charges was seen by many outsiders as the ultimate capitulation, and to Strong himself, despite the earnest pleas of Dean Towle, it was nonnegotiable.[134] Late at night on December 4, Strong was summoned to the president's private residence, where the two officials met with a handful of chairmen, including Scalapino. There the chairmen tried in vain to convince Kerr and Strong to adopt their position on amnesty, but the charges against the four remained a stumbling block. When the meeting broke up at 2 A.M., Strong remained for some time to confer alone with Kerr. According to Strong, he then departed the residence with the distinct impression that he and Kerr saw eye to eye on refusing amnesty. After a few hours sleep, however, when he returned to his office early Saturday morning, an exhausted Strong was "astounded" to learn that Kerr was ready to accept the amnesty package in toto. At this point Strong viewed Kerr's capitulation as a sure sign that his remaining tenure as chancellor would be brief. Later that evening, immediately after a phone call from Scalapino to discuss the chairmen's proposals, Strong was hit by his gall bladder attack and hospitalized in San Francisco, where he remained for a week.[135]

By the following day, Sunday, the chairmen, some of whom had been working with Kerr and the Regents over the weekend, agreed that at 11:00 Monday morning an "extraordinary convocation" should take place in the campus's majestic Greek Theatre, where their proposal, or more accurately, their agreement with Kerr, would be publicly unveiled.[136] An announcement to this effect in Monday's *Daily Cal* informed the campus that an "almost unanimous" agreement had been reached on a proposal prepared by the chairmen's "working committee" with the "concurrence" of Kerr (who had consulted with the Regents and a key group of deans and chairmen at the Airport Hilton) and that the chairmen had unanimously approved the proposal "in its essential elements." The Regents having reluctantly given the plan their approval,[137] the terms were to be announced at the convocation, where Scalapino and Kerr would be featured speakers. In preparation for the event, all chairmen were to hold departmental meetings at 9:00 A.M., at which time classes would be dismissed until the convocation was over (followed by more discussions in the afternoon). The chairmen's announcement concluded: "All parties to this agreement are extremely optimistic that it will unite the great body of the

University, strengthen faculty-student relations, and inaugurate a new era of freedom under law."[138]

One possible basis for this optimism, whether genuine or not, was a series of statements by ASUC leaders, alumni, *Daily Cal* editors, and most important, prominent faculty expressing support for the administration and disapproval of the sit-in while implicitly criticizing the faculty meeting of December 3. To the applause of the *Daily Cal*, for example, nine political science professors issued a statement praising students "who continued to attend their classes," condemning the "illegal occupation" and "disruption" of University facilities, and advising striking students "to return to their classes and resume their studies forthwith." Invoking their expertise as "teachers of Government," they called students' attention to "the absolute necessity for pursuing orderly and legal processes in attempting, in good conscience, to correct any grievances." "Especially in a democratic society," they continued,

> students must recognize that the derogation of due process and the disruption of normal administration in the name of Freedom or Free Speech is demagoguery, not democracy. [The University] has now become a national and international model for higher education, scientific research and intellectual services of vast array, with crucial contractual relationships to other institutions and governments. . . . To hamper the work of such a world-renowned and world-committed institution and to engage in behavior which subjects it to obloquy, is not solely an injury to a single University campus but a threat to the attainment of the larger ideals of freedom, science, and service."[139]

Less verbosely and no doubt more effectively, on December 3 over two hundred faculty, including four Nobel laureates, telegraphed the governor: "During this time of turmoil and misunderstanding, we, the undersigned members of the faculty of the Berkeley campus, reaffirm our confidence in President Clark Kerr and Chancellor Edward W. Strong." This effort was coordinated by Professor E. L. Stokstad (nutrition) and included among the initial signers Robley Williams, former head of the CCPA.[140]

But such views would not command the allegiance of most faculty. While the chairmen worked tirelessly to design a position generous enough to calm the campus but cautious enough to win the president's approval, another faculty group was busy contriving language that would end the crisis on terms more congenial to the FSM. This group was an expanded edition of the Sellers circle, which for the first time now included the active participation of Searle. Closer to the FSM leadership than any other professor, perhaps for that very reason Searle had kept his distance from the Sellers circle, and it from him. Since the sit-in and arrests, however, this barrier, like many others, had fallen, which should have been a warning signal to the administration.

By Sunday, December 6, after a series of intense working sessions, the enlarged Sellers group had developed a rough set of resolutions that expanded on the motions of December 3, including, in contrast to the chairmen, the McClosky motion on advocacy. The time was now ripe to call another unofficial faculty meeting to gain approval of a single position for the Senate meeting. It was to be a unified alternative to whatever might be presented there by the chairmen but also to any well-meaning surprise proposals from like-minded faculty that might inadvertently cause confusion again on the Senate floor. Muscatine played a key role in organizing the hastily called meeting via his telephone tree ("twenty people each phoned two others who they thought would be sympathetic"),[141] and that evening, with Schachman presiding, some two hundred faculty gathered in Room 2003 of the Life Sciences Building, the number in attendance providing the group with its permanent name, the "Committee of 200." After protracted and serious discussion the meeting adopted a set of principles (sometimes known as Motions A, B, and C) that anticipated what would be passed by the Senate two days later. The close ties between the organizers of the December 6 meeting and Stampp and ten Broek, members of CAF who were also members of the Sellers circle, greatly facilitated the preparations. After conferring with a committee chosen by Schachman to refine the motions in cooperation with CAF, CAF would be the last body to vet and perfect that language prior to December 8. With some further editing, CAF adopted final language on the night of the 7th, when it voted to present the resolutions to the Senate as its own formal motion. The draft was then distributed to the faculty on the morning of the 8th. Although I believe he would agree that the December 8 resolutions had multiple parents and even multiple births and were not written by one set of authors at one sitting, Stampp is probably close to the mark when he credits ten Broek with being "the one person who had more input in working out these resolutions than anyone else."[142]

By the end of the meeting of the 200 the organizers believed that the stage was set for a successful Senate meeting; the resolutions had passed unanimously and with almost no challenges.[143] In Schorske's words, "we had the clarity of principle and the will to activate the Senate as an institution. [W]e had thought the thing through and we knew who we were."[144] Although some of us may have been a bit murkier in our thinking than these words suggest, we believed we were far ahead of any other faculty group, in part because we had been working on the problem for so long. As Glazer would observe two months later, his hostility not untinged with admiration, "For some days a substantial number of liberal faculty members had been preparing a resolution which asserted that political activity on campus should be regulated only as to 'time, place and manner' in order not to interfere with the functioning of the university, and they were rounding up support for its adoption."[145] This time they were also preparing a carefully honed Senate strategy, with contingency plans for politely thwarting any attempt to turn the chairmen's proposal into the main motion. For example, a brief motion, the "Stocking preamble," was kept in hand; in the event that some unanticipated motion were made, the Stocking preamble asked that it be tabled "until after the Berkeley Division has expressed itself on the substantive issues of the crisis," that is, until after the vote on the CAF resolutions.[146]

On Monday morning at 9:00 A.M., preconvocation departmental meetings began throughout the campus, with the chairmen having to bear the burden of presenting their own proposal to their faculty and graduate students. May has summarized his own experience at the history meeting: as soon as he appeared in the Dwinelle Hall meeting room, he understood that the assemblage was already aware of the contents of the agreement (hardly surprising given that a few chairmen, sympathetic with the FSM, had been reluctant signers and some had been speaking openly to colleagues from the 200; *at least* one chairman had attended the 200's meeting). As a result, May was now given "a pretty bad time." Indeed, except for the amnesty, the assemblage firmly rejected the terms of the agreement. Schorske, the most prominent "200" speaker present, "cast a little oil on the water," according to May, by moving to "thank the chairman for the amnesty, but not for the rest of it." In addition, speakers faulted the chairmen for ignoring the basic issues, and some even challenged the legitimacy of the chairmen's committee itself, accusing it of upholding the authority of the administration while usurping the statutory prerogatives of the Academic Senate. As a fulfillment of the aspirations of Kerr and his councilors, the history meeting was surely a failure.[147]

Comparable scenes were unfolding in other departments, though with considerable variation. Nothing resembling a complete set of records has been preserved, so I confine myself to a small and diverse sampling. At one extreme, a strong endorsement of the FSM position emerged in a letter adopted by the anthropology meeting. Referring to "the crusade for civil rights" as "one of the great social movements of our time," the letter contained the implication—one that was not visible in the more circumspect statements generated by the Sellers circle but was a common motif of the FSM itself—that to oppose the advocacy promoted by the FSM was to oppose the Civil Rights Movement itself and that "opposition to that movement can not be hidden by such phrases as 'off campus illegal activities.'" The letter asserted that the administration's statements "simply do not face the major issues" and that, notwithstanding recent concessions, the administration's actions "appear to penalize and discourage" participation in the Civil Rights Movement. The letter urged that political freedom on the campus "be interpreted in a way which is relevant to the present situation in the United States" and that "major efforts be made to establish communication between students, faculty, and administration." It also urged dropping of all charges against students, but by now, of course, that issue was not really in contention. In sum, the tone of the letter left no doubt on which side most anthropology faculty would be in the coming Senate debate.[148]

An equally pro-FSM statement was signed by twelve faculty of the College of Environmental Design. Calling the failure of faculty groups to resolve "student-Administration differences" the "most lamentable occurrence of these past two months," the statement asserted that "illegal acts [of advocacy] should be dealt with through the normal legal procedures of the public courts," unequivocally condemned the use of police, and asked that all pending disciplinary action be dropped. The statement was signed by a clear majority of the college faculty.[149]

At the other end of the spectrum, George Maslach, dean of the College of Engineering, seemed confident on that Monday morning that his faculty would strongly support the "extraordinary and unanimous group" of chairmen. He urged his colleagues to attend the Greek Theatre convocation, where "reserved seats for faculty will be maintained immediately in front of the stage." A full meeting of the engineering *faculty* (no mention of TAs or graduate students) was to be held that morning but would be restricted to fifty minutes, after which, Maslach continued, "I should like to have you start contacting and discussing this matter with students. . . . At 11 a.m., of course, your attendance at the Greek Theatre would be appreciated." In contrast to what transpired in the history department, there seemed to be little doubt that the dean would secure his colleagues' cooperation. There is no reason to believe that his confidence was misplaced.[150]

.   .   .

The dramatic events at the Greek Theatre have been recounted often, and for our purposes there are only two important points: (1) the sensational dénouement of the meeting—the dragging away of a limp Mario by campus police when he approached the microphone in defiance of a ruling by the meeting's chairman, Scalapino—marked the end of the brief authority of the chairmen's council, as well as of its fragile unity. (Right then and there, one chairman, Tussman, argued with another, Scalapino; Tussman wanted Mario immediately released from custody.)[151] In May's words, this moment "resulted in pandemonium and the complete and permanent collapse of anything like this compromise program that I'd been trying to promote."[152] (2) Pending the Senate meeting scheduled for the following day, the resulting vacuum of faculty authority was now filled by the 200. The initiative thus passed to those faculty who favored clear recognition of the students' right—at appropriate *times* and *places* and in a nondisruptive *manner*—to use campus facilities to organize off-campus political action; this was the only approach, they believed, that could put the University back on a steady course. There was no longer a serious rival to those who wished to pass a Senate resolution in this spirit, a goal that might have been thwarted if the Senate had convened in the face of the unanswered challenge of the chairmen's proposal issuing neatly from the convocation as a fait accompli.[153]

To be sure, the council of chairmen did not dissolve itself forthwith. Shortly after the convocation, there was a brief meeting in Scalapino's office—a negotiation in which the council no longer held any cards—between some chairmen, members of the 200, and Kerr. Although Kerr recalls that such a meeting was requested by members of the 200, I am still uncertain as to the identity of the faculty involved, though they certainly included a member of CAF and Kerr now recalls the presence of Stampp and Selznick. If the purpose of the meeting was to gain Kerr's assent to the 200's views, it was to no avail. Kerr recollects that he remained averse to any amnesty concession beyond those offered at the convocation, and he rejected at least one other crucial, by now nonnegotiable element of the 200's program—the removal of the lawful-unlawful distinction from any advocacy paragraph.[154] As already noted, CAF soon adopted the resolutions of the 200, fine-tuned but unchanged in any essential way.

.   .   .

When the Senate met in Wheeler Auditorium on December 8, the proposals of the chairmen were no longer in play, thanks in large part to the Greek Theatre fiasco. "The chairmen," as Strong would bitterly recall, "instead of getting up and defending their proposals, which had been adopted by the Regents, and urging that the senate not go beyond its [the chairmen's council's] recommendations, just folded."[155] And beyond its recommendations the Senate did go, adopting the resolutions of CAF without amendment by a landslide vote of 824–115.

No doubt there was much more individual variation, but for purposes of analysis one can point to three faculty motives for favoring the resolutions that were passed so overwhelmingly. Obviously 824 voters had not suddenly thought through the issues and come to exactly the same principled conclusion. Though some faculty acted out of pure conviction, their number is very hard to estimate. A very different and no doubt larger group were those who thought the resolutions essentially wrong but saw a "yes" vote as needed to save the campus. (There was at least one chairman in this group who had been "thoroughly . . . against what was going on" yet voted "yes" because he felt that "nothing else could bring peace to the University.")[156]

The numbers of such "practical" voters can be roughly calculated by subtracting the 115 who voted "no" on the main CAF resolutions from the 284 who voted "yes" when a vigorous symbolic effort was made by Lewis Feuer to amend those resolutions in a spirit hostile to the notion of unrestricted political advocacy (by raising the specter of violence, as discussed following). This leaves us with 169 who voted for the main resolutions, as it were, against their better judgment, strictly as a way to end the crisis. The remaining "yes" voters—let us say 650 persons—had to have included the 200, almost all of whom were strong advocates of some version of the CAF position, though even they, it should be remembered, had only recently proposed a solution to the advocacy issue that fell short of some of the FSM's desires. This leaves us with some 450 "yes" voters, a majority, whose positions may have been more equivocal, something along the lines of "The issues are complicated; CAF and other involved colleagues have offered us a solution; nothing else seems likely to work; besides, there is some fundamental way in which the FSM, whatever its faults, has been treated shabbily while pursuing generally worthy goals." Although such faculty were shocked by the spectacle of police dragging off nonviolent students, it is unlikely that many (if any) happily approved of the recent sit-in. Indeed, Glazer, who seconded the Feuer amendment, would write, notwithstanding all his criticisms of the 200, that "the great majority" of even that liberal group "had little sympathy for FSM tactics" (though unlike him, they believed "that its position on the rules was right").[157] His point may be overstated, since "sympathy" might simply mean a minimal recognition that without FSM militancy many faculty would not have taken even the initial step of *listening* to their story.[158] But such a restricted degree of sympathy hardly bespeaks a faculty that, as some would have it, was telling the students that "anything goes."

A close reading of the unofficial transcript of the Academic Senate discussion, the only Senate meeting that was tape-recorded, supports the foregoing analysis.[159] CAF's main resolution (also known as Motion A—see Appendix B, following) was introduced by its chairman, Joseph Garbarino. Since Garbarino was closely identified with neither the liberal left in general nor the 200 in particular, indeed had supported the lawful-unlawful distinction as a faculty delegate to CCPA, his appearance as the first speaker to the motion was a signal to the assembled senators that it enjoyed the support of mainstream faculty. The motion was then seconded and defended by Tussman, a further sign that even some members of the chairmen's group were squarely behind the liberal position, a point its supporters clearly meant to convey (Tussman began, "I'm Joseph Tussman. I am the chairman of the Department of Philosophy."). Whereas Garbarino's opening speech did not refer with any specificity to the "advocacy" aspects of the proposed resolution, Tussman spoke to those paragraphs directly and eloquently:

[Section 3] provides "that the content of speech or advocacy should not be restricted by the university. Off-campus student political activity shall not be subject to university regulation. On-campus advocacy or organization of such activity shall be subject only to such limitations as may be imposed under section 2." This . . . is a sensible rule, but I think we should regard it as more than just a sensible rule, as more than a way of avoiding tough administrative problems, and even as more than a rule which protects important rights. We should regard it and support it as symbolizing the fundamental commitment of the university to its own essential nature, for it expresses the conviction that ours is an institution whose proper mode of dealing with the mind is educational, not coercive. We are not the secular arm. If we have forgotten this, we should be grateful to those who are now reminding us. I hope the Senate will pass this motion, it is badly needed, it has been very carefully considered, it has the support of many members of the academic community.

To which Tussman then added with a touch of irony, "It is, I suppose, public knowledge that [the motion] is strongly supported by chairmen of departments; nevertheless, it is a good motion." His words were greeted with friendly and possibly nervous laughter.

Following a prearranged strategy, Tussman's speech was succeeded by a speech by Herb McClosky, maker of the advocacy motion of December 3. For anyone who had been following the events closely, McClosky was closely identified with the Sellers circle and the 200, but lest there be any doubt, he underlined this point, assuring his audience that the authors of the earlier draft ("Kornhauser, Lowenthal, et al.") stood fully behind the CAF version. This was clearly meant to preclude any "wildcat" motions or amendments from liberal faculty who had not been in the loop.

McClosky's speech was also illustrative of the degree to which members of the 200 blended their commitment to free speech principles with a concern for the University's well-being and a desire to return campus life to normal, a concern that was by no means a monopoly of the conservative faculty. He described the resolution he was supporting as "our best, perhaps now, our only hope"

> of settling what has been one of the most agonizing, shattering, and potentially destructive experiences that any American university has ever had to pass through. We believe that its adoption will bring us closer, perhaps safely through to a solution. No conflict of these proportions could take place without generating feelings of bitterness and disappointment, the desire to punish or to vindicate, but the time for recriminations, I think, has passed— who is wrong, or whether the greatest sins have been committed by the students, the administration, or the faculty. What matters now is how, by what means, we can survive. It is my hope, and I think I speak for all those who have worked to develop this resolution in its original form, that we can now put aside our differences and that we can all manage—students, faculty, University officials, and Regents—to strike an attitude of generosity and

magnanimity so that the damage might be repaired and so that we can all return to work.

When McClosky concluded Feuer took the floor to introduce his unfriendly amendment, which immediately became the center of debate. The key point was to add to the first sentence of CAF's third paragraph the words "provided that it [student speech] is directed to no immediate act of force or violence." This had the effect of carving out a seemingly self-evident area in which the content of advocacy would still be subject to University discipline. Of course nothing in the CAF resolution even hinted at tolerance for "immediate act[s] of force and violence" or at immunity from prosecution if such acts were planned on campus; nor did any speaker before or after Feuer make such a claim. Moreover, both Feuer's own language, with its emphasis on the word *immediate,* and the terms of the ensuing debate were on the face of it premised on the nightmare vision of particular acts of advocacy that presented a clear and present danger to persons or property, not advocacy in general, for example, of the right to use violence as a matter of principle. But such "clear and present danger" advocacy, as is well known, is not constitutionally protected, so that Feuer's suggestion that under the CAF resolution members of the campus KKK (if such there were) could with impunity urge a crowd to burn a synagogue or church and use the campus as a sanctuary was patently absurd, as was pointed out by opponents of the amendment. (Emotionally charged references to the KKK and to Nazi-infested German universities were invoked by several proponents of the amendment, as they were in previous and subsequent debate.) Someone urging such dangerous "immediate" action is always subject to arrest by campus or city police, without the need for any special provisions in campus rules. Moreover, section 2 of the resolution already provided for the University's right to protect itself from "interference" with its "normal functions," which meant there was no "immunity" for students who mounted an action that posed an immediate threat to those functions through "force and violence." Although in section 1 CAF *was* calling for an amnesty for *past* actions that might be construed as entailing the use of "force" (though hardly "violence"), there was no suggestion that the amnesty would extend into the future. In other words, logically speaking, insofar as Feuer's amendment was meant to refer to an immediate act of violence on campus, it was superfluous and, with one exception, added nothing that could not be reconciled with the main resolution. The exception was that Feuer did appear to reintroduce the possibility in some situations of having the *University,* not the courts, determine the degree to which the content of a speech act was protected, a point forcefully developed by ten Broek, who responded to the Feuer amendment for CAF.

The wording of the amendment did not specifically refer to the advocacy of off-campus acts. It even seemed to preclude that contingency by its emphasis on "immediate," a point reinforced by Glazer's seconding speech, which, though ambiguous, did present as Glazer's main concern a situation where "force and violence is directly organized on the campus." Given so narrow a construction of the amendment, it might well have been reasonable for CAF to simply accept it as "friendly," at least for the sake of a wider "yes" vote. But David Rynin, the first to speak from the floor in opposition to Feuer, addressed this question and explained in his own way why the amendment's intent was hostile:

> I find it very regrettable that we're putting ourselves in the position where we have to declare ourselves against force and violence. No one is in favor of force and violence. But if we . . . adopt this amendment . . . we should remember that we're not simply taking a position on force and violence. [The FSM] will understand this . . . as once again putting them in the position in which if they prepare boycotts or sit-ins or picketing against the outside community in the name of civil liberties and reserving and safeguarding the rights of minorities, that they are again subject to the same kind of punitive threats and actualities as has led to this miserable situation in the first place.

In other words, Rynin was arguing, not unreasonably given the absence of any actual *need* for a clause against *immediate* acts of violence, (1) that the amendment was meant to reopen the door to punishment for advocacy of off-campus civil disobedience and (2) that this reading of it would leave the larger conflict unresolved, thereby prolonging the campus wars.

To be sure, if one takes the amendment literally, especially the word *immediate,* Rynin's point looks off the mark. Superficially, the amendment *was* consistent with the notion that the adjudication of advocacy of off-campus civil disobedience, even if illegal, would be left to the civil authorities. But as the argument progressed, there was reason to share Rynin's anxiety. Feuer himself, in his allusions to the KKK and Germany, had actually illustrated his ominous scenarios with examples of actions that were not on the face of it "immediate," and other speakers did the same. For example, the venerable Carl Landauer, a man who could cite examples from Germany with the authority of his own painful experience, referenced campus organization of "lawless action in the [outside] community" when he spoke with passion in Feuer's behalf. In short, a fuzzy and at times almost invisible rhetorical line was drawn by the amendment's proponents between the position "we don't want force or violence on campus" (no one did, so why not say so?) and "we want the University to continue to discipline the on-campus organization of force or violence off campus." Despite the emphasis on the violence of racist groups, none of which was happening in the real world of Berkeley campus politics, this clearly looked to many like a slippery slope back to the containment of militant civil rights activities. And, apart from recognizing the secondary fuzziness of the line between "force" and "violence" (nonviolent yet coercive militant acts such as sit-ins and even picket lines could still be said to involve "force"), people like Rynin were legitimately worried that distrustful students, after months of conflict and betrayal, could not be disabused of their fear of that slippery slope regardless of Feuer's actual intent.

For making just that point, for taking into account how students might interpret the amendment, Rynin and other supporters of the main motion were accused of capitulating to "blackmail," the term used by Petersen, one of the original "15," the person who, supported by Lipset, had tried unsuccessfully to add the words *within the law* to Muscatine's motion of October 13. Asked by Feuer to give the closing argument for his amendment, Petersen said:

> We are threatened by a group which has found a mode of behavior that permits a group of irresponsible true believers to dictate what they want, and the solution that is offered by the opponents of this amendment is that this group is so powerful that if we offer even platitudinous opposition to their force and violence that we must expect as a result force and violence. I submit that this is blackmail. . . . I will not support a faculty which refuses to come out for the law in general against force and violence in general and moves from this position under the pressure of a bunch of rowdies into conspiring with the students to break other laws as well.

In effect, he was saying that to vote against the amendment was to condone the students' conduct, while to vote for it was to condemn it. When all was said and done, though telling points were scored on both sides, this is really what the debate over the amendment boiled down to. In a resolution aimed at ending the turmoil on the basis of high-minded principle and forgiveness of past offenses (including a conscious decision to refrain from any condemnation of the administration!), CAF and its supporters could not accept the addition of a clause that was meant to put the protesters down (and in any case, as happens in any legislative body, they were fearful of *any* amendments altering their carefully prepared language). A majority of those in attendance seemed to agree, as the amendment went down to defeat 737–284, surely a better indication of the actual division at the meeting than the vote of 824–115.[160]

.   .   .

At the conclusion of the Senate meeting thousands of students who had crowded into the empty spaces of Wheeler or gathered outside its doors to listen to the proceedings over a loudspeaker were in a state of incredible emotional elation. Tears of joy and relief flowed everywhere, many cries of somber delight could be heard. Denied admission to the auditorium because of my "acting" rank, I was listening and waiting among them, my physical location a kind of metaphor for my ambiguous status. I could actually feel the electric wave of excitement that passed through the crowd as the faculty, many of them uncomfortable yet no less elated than the students, emerged from the meeting and marched out of the building through aisles opened up for them by the waiting crowd.

Though most of us savored it while we could, this euphoria was not destined to last. Fault lines soon began to reappear not only between students and faculty but in the faculty majority itself. Some of the rifts were predictable, others less so. Among the more predictable were divisions already visible at the Senate meeting, where CAF had introduced a second resolution, Motion B, the goal of which was to give faculty an institutional role in the implementation of Motion A, which was yet to be accepted by the administration, let alone the Regents. Motion B called for the creation of an Emergency Executive Committee (EEC)—six elected members plus Richard Jennings, the Senate's chairman—to help secure the Regents' acceptance of the resolutions. As it turned out, however, this strategy backfired. The eventual winners of the election after two rounds of voting were faculty who, though moderates by most standards, had been much more critical of the FSM than the 200 and, more to the point, had chosen to run for the new offices because they were to various degrees impatient with the FSM's faculty friends. The losers were a slate of candidates promoted by the 200, including several members of the Sellers circle. To this outcome there was but one exception: Schorske, though finishing second on the first ballot, on the second ballot just managed to survive as sixth among the six elected members, the sole representative of our cohort to endure what can best be described as a faculty backlash, skillfully orchestrated mainly by faculty who had probably voted for the resolutions but were determined above all else to see to the restoration of "normality." At least two of the victors—Arthur Ross, who with the largest total of votes (both times) became the EEC's chairman, and Cheit (only number ten in the first vote)—were close to Kerr, both personally and academically. Ironically, the 200's effort to strike a blow for faculty autonomy had produced a committee that did not really represent its views, as many faculty with second thoughts about their own vote on December 8 now saw an opportunity to tip the scales in the other direction.[161] How many of the men elected had voted for Feuer's amendment I cannot say, but there can be little doubt that everyone who had voted for it also supported the less liberal slate, while others who had reluctantly voted against it must have done so as well. To the losers of the election, however, the 200, defeat did not mean an end to all activity. Sellers, Muscatine, Wolin, Hirsch, Henry Nash Smith, and others now devoted their time—with mixed success, to be sure—to writing circular letters and letters to newspapers publicizing and explaining the December 8 resolutions to the public and to their colleagues, including those at other campuses; circulating transcripts of the meeting (an "Academic Publicity Fund" was established for that purpose); and in some cases urging colleagues to flood the chairman of the Board of Regents with telegrams before the Board's December 18 meeting.[162]

As it turned out, within the limits of the EEC's *immediate* goal, to harness the Regents to the December 8 positions, Schorske, the 200's only link to the EEC, was able to cooperate quite effectively with the other members, and they with him, so that to a large extent it did accomplish that purpose. On December 18 the EEC won the Regents' acquiescence, however guarded and indirect, to much of the December 8 package, though not to section 4—faculty control of discipline. True, that acquiescence took the form not of positive endorsement of the resolutions but of a reluctance to repudiate them, along with the adoption of bland and ambiguous language that blurred some important distinctions in a manner that allowed the University administration to save face. Nevertheless, the language of the Regents failed to challenge the heart of the Senate's position, and they made no serious or overt attempt to roll back the right to advocate and organize off-campus actions, even "unlawful" ones. In its interim report of December 27, the EEC was able to say, *"As a practical matter, we can state that the actual operating situation* [when the campus reopens] *on January 4 will be substantially in conformance with the Senate's Resolution of December 8."*[163] And despite occasional flare-ups, such as the "filthy speech" crisis of the following spring (discussed following) and the "little free speech movement" of 1966,[164] and though no official language exists to this day that fully parallels the powerful words of the December 8 resolutions (though the existence of "time, place, and manner" rules implicitly confirms them), this basic arrangement has now held sway for over thirty-six years.

Yet despite this seemingly happy outcome and some would say *because* of it, the spring of 1965 marked the beginning of several years of unrelenting tension and intermittent explosions on the Berkeley campus. The escalating Vietnam War and, as a consequence, more ugly and bitter campus confrontations, added to these tensions and at times destroyed the delicate balance that had seemed to prevail in late December. Would these confrontations have had even more serious consequences if the advocacy issue had remained unresolved by the faculty? I believe they would have, though no one can answer this question with any degree of certainty.

EPILOGUE

Notwithstanding its superficial triviality, the so-called "filthy speech" episode of March 1965 put the faculty-student alliance of December 8 to a severe and rather unhappy test.[165] The crisis was brought on by the prominent and provocative display of the word FUCK on a sign carried on campus by a nonstudent and his subsequent arrest by campus police, followed by a series of "Obscenity Rallies" and several more arrests (including that of prominent FSMer Arthur Goldberg, who was soon expelled). These events precipitated the first rally on Sproul Steps that was called and organized specifically by faculty. The rally had as its primary purpose the efforts of liberal faculty to distance themselves from some FSMers' defense of the provocative, "obscene" contents of *Spider*, a new countercultural campus literary magazine, and of the right to freely shout or display "four letter" obscenities within the "time, place, and manner" rules, an issue that had never been seriously discussed by any of the contending parties in the fall. Subjected to severe criticism by the Regents and others for their alleged permissiveness, President Kerr and Acting Chancellor Martin Meyerson, a soft-spoken and humane liberal, offered to resign. But they were supported by the EEC and by the Academic Senate, which urged the Regents to reject the resignations. The resignations were withdrawn, but the post–December 8 wounds of the more conservative Regents had been opened and the atmosphere remained tense. Hoping to appease his critics, Meyerson placed a temporary ban on *Spider*, which had made it a point to print the "offensive" four-letter word (and others), thereby enhancing the prominence of the free speech issue and making it hard for Savio and other FSMers to keep their distance. They soon announced their refusal "to abdicate our commitment to all that we struggled for last semester."[166]

Although speakers at the faculty rally included professors such as Martin Malia, one of the organizers of the 200's electoral defeat, among the leading participants were also such strong and early friends of FSM as Sellers, Muscatine, and Parkinson, who rebuked the FSM for its misguided defense of childish self-indulgence and its rudeness to the (acting) chancellor and accused it of thereby debasing the cause of genuine free speech. (In fact Savio and others had been critical of some of the actions of the "offenders.") This time the controversy failed to capture the imagination of many students, but the faculty rally and subsequent faculty actions produced a state of shock among some FSM leaders, including Savio and Goldberg, and were a major factor in Mario's decision to leave the FSM on April 26. Among his bitter parting words on the next day: "Perhaps the saddest thing about this community is the continuing reluctance of faculty to defend the rights of students. . . . Berkeley students have been forced to desperate acts because their professors repeatedly have failed them."[167] One day later, on April 28, the FSM officially dissolved.

Seen in conjunction with the larger story told in my essay, the filthy speech episode should help us appreciate some of the structural, almost unavoidable aspects of the faculty role in campus political crises and faculty relations with student protesters and University officials. Faculty are men and women who, after years of training and apprenticeship, have worked their way into positions of prestige and authority, usually doing what they love most of all to do, research, write, and teach (the relative value placed on each, of course, varying). Though materially they are quite comfortable, their real vested interest is generally not in worldly goods but in the preservation of a climate in which they can pursue their work in relative calm, which should not be equated with the absence of intellectual excitement. When it comes to campus politics, they are truly a sleeping giant, with only a small handful of the highly committed wide awake unless and until aroused by a conflict initiated by others (usually a combination of heavy-handed administrative action and student militancy). Once aroused, however, they will form into distinguishable groups according to their preexisting political dispositions and relations with the administration, with a large, relatively apathetic and labile group hovering between the extremes, unpredictable in its leanings from moment to moment.

Under these circumstances, the most liberal and activist faculty are the ones on whom the attention of student activists will concentrate. Both for political reasons (student protesters certainly cannot win if they cannot attract the most liberal faculty) and for more emotional ones—and here I believe in the clichés about faculty functioning as father and elder-brother figures in the psyches of students, especially the younger and more sensitive ones—concentration on faculty can engender high levels of feeling, including incredible joy at blissful moments of cooperation (December 8) and incredible horror and dismay at times of rupture (as in the filthy speech affair). Either way the emotional investment can be enormous.

But even at the best of moments, the times of close alliance, the approaches of activist students and liberal faculty are almost never isomorphic. Even faculty who are critical of administrators will invariably have more invested in the institution, more of a tendency to rally to its leaders when they are under attack, more of an inclination to attack administrators with restraint and to couch their criticisms in language that is politic in their own eyes, hypocritical in the eyes of activists. Rare is the faculty liberal or, for that matter, even the faculty radical (for such there are) who will place himself or herself at risk of arrest or even of campus discipline. It is certainly no accident that no faculty were arrested in Sproul Hall on the night of December 3; and though naked fear of job loss may be a factor in explaining the reluctance of untenured faculty, a more hard-wired institutional inhibition based on something beyond political perspective as such, had to have been in play among the tenured. To be sure, with time and especially as the Vietnam War and war resistance produced a kind of "Vietnamization" of the Berkeley campus, one can find examples of faculty participation with students in on-campus civil disobedience.[168] (Not surprisingly, faculty participation in *off*-campus civil disobedience, though also not very common, is significantly more frequent.) The zenith of such action was the student- and faculty-run "Vietnam Commencement" of 1968, when nearly three hundred professors (with the old "200" well represented) stood on the Sproul Steps in defiance of the Board of Regents to announce their willingness to aid and abet student draft resisters. But this was a carefully planned, solemn, thoroughly thought-through event, with extraordinary student-faculty cooperation but also a clear division of labor between them (and, I hasten to add, opposition from the more extreme parts of the student left). It was certainly not the ordinary modus operandi and is never likely to be. From what I have seen, the story of faculty participation in campus movements will always entail tensions between faculty and student actors and especially between those who are closest to one another. As happened in the FSM, students, especially those who, though no "angels," conduct themselves with the intelligence, wit, and integrity of the FSMers, will always find their faculty allies and sometimes win the struggle with administrators for the faculty's hearts and minds, but the harmony will not be perfect, latent tensions will always reemerge, and some students will always manage to find their "rabbits."

APPENDIX A: THE ORIGINAL LEVINE MOTION

Source: *Academic Senate Minutes,* Meeting of November 24, 1964.

It is the sense of the Berkeley Division of the Academic Senate that a great university, dedicated to freedom of thought and responsible citizenship, cannot deny to its students the full exercise on campus of the rights guaranteed to citizens generally under the First and Fourteenth Amendments. The University's regulation of such activities should extend no further than is necessary to prevent undue interference with other University activities. Such regulations must be carefully drawn so that they cannot be used as an excuse for encroaching on the constitutionally protected scope of speech and political and social activity.

In enforcing such minimal and essential regulations by disciplinary action, the standards of due process must be maintained and penalties imposed solely and finally by an impartial body chosen by and responsible to the Academic Senate. The only alternative to such regulation by the University would be to leave all regulation to the courts.

APPENDIX B: MOTION A OF THE DECEMBER 8 RESOLUTIONS

Source: *Academic Senate Minutes,* Meeting of December 8, 1964.

In order to end the present crisis, to establish the confidence and trust essential to the restoration of normal University life, and to create a campus environment that encourages students to exercise free and responsible citizenship in the University and in the community at large, the Committee on Academic Freedom of the Berkeley Division of the Academic Senate moves the following propositions:

1. *That there shall be no University disciplinary measures against members or organizations of the University community for activities prior to December 8 connected with the current controversy over political speech and activity.*

2. *That the time, place, and manner of conducting political activity on the campus shall be subject to reasonable regulation to prevent interference with the normal functions of the University; that the regulations now in effect for this purpose shall remain in effect provisionally pending a future report of the Committee on Academic Freedom concerning the minimal regulations necessary.*

3. *That the content of speech or advocacy should not be restricted by the University. Off-campus student political activities shall not be subject to University regulation. On-campus advocacy or organization of such activities shall be subject only to such limitations as may be imposed under section 2.*

4. *That future disciplinary measures in the area of political activity shall be determined by a committee appointed by and responsible to the Berkeley Division of the Academic Senate.*

5. *That the Division urge the adoption of the foregoing policies and call on all members of the University community to join with the faculty in its efforts to restore the University to its normal functions.*

NOTES

1. *Journal of the Association of Women Deans*, 29 (spring 1966), reproduced in Katherine Towle, "Dean of Students, Administration and Leadership," interviewed in 1967 by Harriet Nathan, series director, University History Series, Bancroft Collection, University of California at Berkeley, 1970 (cited hereafter as Towle Oral History).

2. Lincoln Constance, "Versatile Berkeley Botanist: Plant Taxonomy and University Governance," oral history conducted in 1986 by Ann Lage, Regional Oral History Office, Bancroft Library, University of California at Berkeley, 1987 (cited hereafter as Constance Oral History), part XVII.

3. On the loyalty oath as seen and documented by one of the most renowned nonsigners, see Ernst H. Kantorowicz, *The Fundamental Issue: Documents and Marginal Notes on the University of California Loyalty Oath* (San Francisco: Parker Printing, 1950); also see David Gardner, *The California Oath Controversy* (Berkeley and Los Angeles: University of California Press, 1967); Angus E. Taylor, *The Academic Senate of the University of California: Its Role in the Shared Governance and Operation of the University of California* (Berkeley: Institute of Governmental Studies Press, 1998), 15–35. For a good overview of campus political conflicts in the three decades before the FSM, but one that has little specifically to say about the role of faculty, see Max Heirich and Sam Kaplan, "Yesterday's Discord," *California Monthly* (hereafter *CM*) 75 (Feb. 1965): 20–32.

4. For the sake of convenience, I will use "Academic Senate" as a shorthand for the Senate's Berkeley division. References to the *statewide* Academic Senate will be so designated. For a concise overview of the history of the Academic Senate, see Taylor; also, Jeff Hall, "The Berkeley Division of the Academic Senate: A Capsule History," available at <http://academic-senate.berkeley.edu/faq/links/history.html> (1995).

5. See "Three Changes in the Kerr Directives," p. 1, with copious quotes from the *Academic Senate Record* 6, no. 2, and the *Daily Californian* (hereafter *DC*), in "Administrative Pressures and Student Political Activity at the University of California: A Preliminary Report" (hereafter Rossman Report) [1964], Free Speech Movement records, CU-309 (hereafter FSM Records), University Archives, Bancroft Library, University of California at Berkeley). The criticisms did convince Kerr to change some of the language of the Directives: the requirement for the prior approval of off-campus speakers was replaced by the weaker requirement of prior notification, a substantial concession in the views of the CAF (ibid., 2). *Kerr Directives* was not an official name; Kerr himself preferred to describe them in the aggregate as the "open forum policy" (Verne A. Stadtman, *The University of California, 1868–1968* [New York: McGraw-Hill, 1970], 437), but we will defer to the more customary usage. On the heated conflict over the Directives between Kerr and SLATE, see *DC*, 15 and 16 Nov. 1961. The University later published the updated Directives and other related materials as a pamphlet: *University of California Policies Relating to Students and Student Organizations* (Sept. 1963, available in University Archives, Bancroft Library).

6. In Stampp's case a history of conflict with the administration dated back to the loyalty oath, when he was active in organizing support for the nonsigners. See Kenneth M. Stampp, "Historian of Slavery, the Civil War, and Reconstruction, University of California, Berkeley, 1946–1983," oral history conducted in 1996 by Ann Lage, Regional Oral History Office, Bancroft Library, University of California at Berkeley, 1998 (hereafter Stampp Oral History), 144–49, especially 146.

7. The Koch episode is described in Glenn T. Seaborg with Ray Colvig (hereafter Seaborg), *Chancellor at Berkeley* (Berkeley: Institute of Governmental Studies Press, 1994), 428–41; the faculty statement, cited from *DC*, 11 May 1960, is on pp. 437–38. The episode is also summarized in Chancellor Edward K. Strong, "Philosopher, Professor and Berkeley Chancellor, 1961–1965," oral history conducted in 1988 by Harriet Nathan, Regional Oral History Office, The Bancroft Library, University of California at Berkeley (hereafter Strong Oral History), part XII (tape 19, side B); unless otherwise indicated, all further citations from this source are from part XIV, which covers Sept.–Dec. 1964. See also Stadtman, 436.

8. Towle Oral History: "Bellquist Committee Recommendations—1960." A similar if more skeptical position is taken by President Kerr in his forthcoming memoir, *The Gold and the Blue: A Personal Memoir of the University of California, 1949–1967*, vol. 2: *Political Turmoil* (Berkeley and Los Angeles: University of California Press, 2003), chapt. 10, where he cites Towle's speculation with some sympathy. Towle was dean of women at the time, a year before she was named dean of students. Even as dean of students, "for some unknown reason," as she put it, Towle was never apprised of the Bellquist recommendations by Dean Shepard or Vice Chancellor Sherriffs, with whom the Bellquist Committee had consulted regularly before its report was, in Towle's words, "buried in the files"; she learned of its existence only in late spring 1965, from Bellquist himself. Towle politely ascribed the delay to administrative discontinuity.

9. In his memoir (443) Seaborg hints that he saw Newman as "principal author" of the report; though this may have been true, Bellquist had displayed a strong commitment to campus free speech at least as early as 1958 (ibid., 80–81). For the text of the Bellquist report, see Alex C. Sherriffs, "The University of California and the Free Speech Movement: Perspectives from a Faculty Member and an

Administrator," oral history conducted in 1978 by James H. Rowland, Regional Oral History Office, Bancroft Library, University of California at Berkeley, 1980 (hereafter Sherriffs Oral History), Appendix 2. Important sections are also included in Seaborg, 442, and Towle Oral History.

10. Bellquist report; Seaborg, 427ff.

11. Seaborg, 441, 443.

12. Towle quoted herself from her spring 1965 notes in Towle Oral History.

13. A Stanford graduate student at the time, I was present at one of the demonstrations. The most detailed, well-researched account of the HUAC affair and its repercussions at Berkeley is Alice Huberman and Jim Prickett, "HUAC: May 1960. The events; the aftermath," in Rossman Report. My account is based largely on that report.

14. Ibid., 6–7.

15. Ibid., 8–10 (quotes from Searle on pp. 9, 10). The article contains further information on the ripple effects on campus of the HUAC affair, emphasizing the administration's timidity in defending the rights of students, but none of the other incidents directly involved faculty.

16. Kerr's response to Berkeley AAUP Chairman Howard Schachman (28 July 1961), which includes a copy of his July 22 memo to "Chief Campus Officers" (i.e., chancellors), is reproduced in the AAUP's call to its meeting of 25 May 1962. A copy is in the private papers of Charles Sellers (hereafter Sellers Papers), now in my possession, but soon to be donated to the Bancroft Library's FSM Records at his request.

17. The main incidents are nicely summarized in Carl E. Schorske, "Intellectual Life, Civil Libertarian Issues, and the Student Movement at the University of California, Berkeley, 1960–1969," oral history conducted in 1996 and 1997 by Ann Lage, Regional Oral History Office, Bancroft Library, University of California at Berkeley, 2000 (hereafter Schorske Oral History), esp. 26–33; see also my introduction to that volume, where the pre-FSM events discussed below are summarized sequentially.

18. For a summary of SLATE's own account of this suspension, see "SLATE and Due Process: Abstract," in Rossman Report.

19. Memorandum of 23 Aug. 1961, appendix B, Schorske Oral History. The other signers were Hanan C. Selvin (sociology) and Van Dusen Kennedy (law), an active civil libertarian in his own right. Schorske's language describing the group is in his oral history, 27. Faculty statements cited in this paragraph are in the Sellers Papers. It is clear from a short note by Sellers that he and Schorske were the principal drafters of all the statements.

20. Stadtman, 437–38. The Regents' statewide ban on Communist speakers drew sharp criticism from the AAUP's Berkeley chapter (minutes of their meeting of 25 May 1962, Sellers Papers). Membership in the chapter was 248.

21. Strong was never comfortable with this position. In an address to the annual meeting of the AAUP in San Francisco, 26 Apr. 1963, he came very close to stating his principled opposition to the ban while defending his actions mainly on the grounds that he was obliged to implement Regental policy; Strong, "Shared Responsibility," 26 Apr. 1963, typed copy in Sellers Papers, 12–14.

22. On the Aptheker affair see Schorske to CAF, 13 Mar. 1963, appendix D, Schorske Oral History; Stampp Oral History, 230–31; Rossman Report, appendix A,

4; see also the ad protesting the banning of Aptheker placed in *DC,* 25 Feb. 1963, by nearly three hundred graduate students and faculty, but mainly students. On the Lima affair, see Schorske to W. J. Davis, 31 July 1963, appendix E, Schorske Oral History; Rossman Report, appendix A, 2. For background to the lifting of the Communist speaker ban and the role of the Riverside lawsuit (1962–1963), see Evan Alderson's fine summary in Rossman Report, appendix D, 1–2.

23. Constance Oral History, part XVII. When I say "no faculty" were involved, I exclude members of the faculty who held appointments in the administration, among whom of course was the chancellor, a professor in the philosophy department. Here and in what follows, such persons are portrayed in their function as administrators.

24. *San Francisco Chronicle,* 22 Sept. 1964. Sellers, one of the few tenured faculty involved at this stage, was also concerned that the administration's action would make the faculty into "hypocrites in the eyes of our students" (ibid.). Sellers's colleague Kenneth Stampp describes him as "probably the [history faculty's] most ardent" FSM supporter but then adds the name of Schorske; see Stampp Oral History, 240.

25. *DC,* 23 Sept. 1964.

26. According to Strong, on September 30 he planned to tell Parkinson that his name was "being used by the revolters [*sic*] as urging them on, and to explain the seriousness of the situation"; "Sit-In at Sproul Hall," tape 25, side A, Strong Oral History. (On Strong's suspicions regarding the faculty's agitational role, see also the epigraph citing Vice Chancellor Constance at this essay's opening.) Parkinson, a poet as well as a professor, had attracted public attention in January 1961 when he was shot in the face by a former student who considered him a Communist. Parkinson was wounded and the shots killed a student with whom he was talking (see Seaborg, 678–79).

27. Glazer, "What Happened at Berkeley," *Commentary,* Feb. 1965, reproduced in Seymour Martin Lipset and Sheldon S. Wolin, eds., *The Berkeley Student Revolt: Facts and Interpretations* (Garden City, N.Y.: Doubleday, 1965), 297.

28. Savio as quoted in *DC,* 2 Oct. 1964. The *DC* used the terms "sleep-in" and "lying-in" in its 1 Oct. report on the occupation of parts of Sproul Hall on 30 September; the action, which began as a *sit*-in, has also been called a "pack-in."

29. *San Francisco Chronicle,* 6 Oct. 1964; see also David Lance Goines, *The Free Speech Movement: Coming of Age in the 1960s* (Berkeley: Ten Speed Press, 1993), 283–84. Another example of the instability of faculty political identification at this early stage is the situation of Thomas Barnes. A fairly junior member of the history faculty, Barnes was also a part-time assistant to Dean of Men Arleigh Williams, aiding him in his sometimes heated discussions with protesting students; he was also faculty advisor to Campus CORE, one of the organizations whose unauthorized tables would be cited by the dean, soon leading to the arrest of Jack Weinberg. See Arleigh Williams, "Dean of Students Arleigh Williams: The Free Speech Movement and the Six Years' War, 1964–1970," oral history conducted in 1988 and 1989 by Germaine LaBerge, Regional Oral History Office, Bancroft Library, University of California at Berkeley, 1990 (hereafter Williams Oral History), tape 10, side B.

30. "Faculty Delegation: The Group of Fifteen (October 2)," Strong Oral History.

31. Constance Oral History, part XVII. The quote about Kerr's work going down the drain is Constance recalling Rosovsky's language. Kerr's own memory is consistent with the gist of Constance's account. According to Kerr, Strong was unwilling to cooperate with the faculty group, which then decided to contact Kerr directly by phoning him from Strong's conference room. Kerr notes in his memoir that he knew Rosovsky well, identifies him as leader of "the Rosovsky group" and calls its proposals "the Rosovsky proposals." Kerr also knew the group's other members (surely a factor in their decision to act collectively). Kerr, chapt. 11.

32. *DC,* 6 Oct. 1964.

33. Ironically, since paragraph 3 also stated that two of the four student members were to be chosen from among the members of the committee that had negotiated the agreement, students were given greater rights than faculty in choosing their representatives. The full text of the agreement is in *DC,* 5 Oct. 1964.

34. Constance Oral History, part XVII. Strong's distaste for faculty criticism of administrators was already visible in 1963 in his address to the annual meeting of the AAUP, where he warned of the danger that faculty would declare a "cold war" against the administration; "Shared Responsibility," 18 and passim.

35. "Savio's Status," tape 26, side A, Strong Oral History.

36. Max Heirich, *The Spiral of Conflict: Berkeley 1964* (New York: Columbia University Press, 1971), 218–19.

37. Candy Hughes, "Disagreement on Negotiation Group," *DC,* 7 Oct. 1964; "The Agreement," *FSM Newsletter* [8 or 9 Oct., 1964], esp. 4.

38. "Demonstrators Walk Out," *DC,* 8 Oct. 1964.

39. Stampp had been away from Berkeley during the first weeks of the crisis (Stampp Oral History, 234).

40. On the faculty statement see *DC,* 8 Oct. 1964, and minor correction on the next day. The later debate between Glazer and Selznick is in Lipset and Wolin. On the faculty group's meeting with Strong, see "Items from the Chancellor's Staff Meeting," tape 25, side B, Strong Oral History. Strong's identification of the six men coincides with that in *DC.* In late October Strong stated that all six signers were men who had been involved in the October 2 negotiations (Strong, "[To] Members of the Academic Senate" [circular letter, 26 Oct. 1964], p. 7, University Archives, Bancroft Library), but that could not have been true of Stampp, who was not in town. Lipset actually stood on the police car to tell the demonstrators that their actions were undemocratic and mimicked the tactics of the KKK. Glazer (and possibly Petersen) also spoke from atop the police car, urging students to lift the blockade; see Hal Draper, *Berkeley: The New Student Revolt* (New York: Grove Press, 1965), 47, 52. Other faculty who spoke from the car were Sellers and Leggett; Heirich, 167, 463n.

41. *DC,* 9 Oct. 1964. The statement was signed by two signers of the previous faculty statement (Glazer and Rosovsky), Petersen, and Frederick Reif (physics). Lewis Feuer (philosophy) was apparently involved at some point but was not a signatory.

42. DeBonis, as quoted in *DC,* 7 Oct. 1964: "Why should Sellers get out there? I pay him to teach classes, not be a rabble rouser [*sic*]. If that's what they are teaching God bless this country."

43. The announcement came in the form of an ad in *DC,* 20 Oct. 1964. It was signed by David Blackwell, Jacob Feldman, Henry Helson, Morris Hirsch, Lucien

LeCam, Stephen Smale, Aram Thomasian, and George Turin, all tenured professors. Several of them would later be identified with "the 200." Why the ad appeared three weeks after the incident it referenced remains unclear.

44. *DC,* 7 and 8 Oct. 1964.

45. *DC,* 9 Oct. 1964.

46. Stampp later described Garbarino as someone who "sympathized with FSM but was not an enthusiastic supporter," and himself and ten Broek as the members of the CAF "who were most supportive of it" (Stampp Oral History, 234).

47. "Senate Committee on Academic Freedom," tape 27, side B, Strong Oral History. In Strong's words, "[Garbarino] called me to say that his committee believed that it had the responsibility to study the free speech dispute. . . . Would I, therefore, assist the committee in its proposed review and evaluation by providing a summary of the background of the dispute, a review of actions taken prior to and in the course of the dispute, a citation of legislation and regulations and other material and information deemed by me to be relevant. Well, that was quite a package, and I said yes, I would do that expeditiously, and I did—my office did."

48. *DC,* 9 Oct. 1964.

49. "Responsibilities of the Dean of Women," Towle Oral History. In his 1965 account of these events, Draper (p. 67) makes a persuasive if inconclusive case that on October 2 some members of the faculty group of 15 had assured the student negotiators that charges would be dropped against the suspended students if the negotiators agreed to their terms. Be that as it may, the FSM never made the existence of such an assurance an issue, preferring to focus on the adjudicating committee's relation to the Academic Senate.

50. Martin Meyerson, dean of environmental design (who became acting chancellor after Strong's resignation); Frank Newman, dean of the law school; Sanford Elberg, dean of the graduate division and informal chair of the group; Arthur M. Ross, director of the IIR; and Joseph Lohman, dean of criminology, who had also been advising Strong on police- and crowd-related matters. Newman, to be sure, was an independent actor who, as we have seen, had a history of conflict with administrators.

51. "A Nonexistent Senate Committee on Student Conduct," tape 27, sides A and B, Strong Oral History.

52. Tape 27, side B, Strong Oral History.

53. Andrew L. Pierovich, "Chronology of Events: Three Months of Crisis," *CM* 75 (Feb. 1965): 47 (narrative of events of fall 1964 prepared by the managing editor of the California Alumni Association's magazine); "Faculty Petition," tape 27, side B, Strong Oral History. Among the other departments were psychology (eleven), statistics (eleven), molecular biology (seven), music (five), political science (five). Math and statistics would later merge into one department. Almost all eighty-eight names would figure among the faculty 200, discussed below.

54. The Katz case is summarized in *DC,* 13 Oct. 1964. See also *American Civil Liberties Union News,* Oct. 1964; the essay by Wofsy in the present volume; and the *DC* editorial of 14 Oct. 1964. The Chancellor's office clearly viewed Katz's appointment through a political lens. Note the language of then Vice Chancellor Lincoln Constance as he looked back on the case two decades later: "The University is always under pressure on these political things; while certainly an individual's political stance *should not be a major part of his appointment,* when it's as controversial as

this, it's only fair to give the administration a break" (Constance Oral History, part XVI [emphasis added]).

55. My account is based on *Academic Senate Minutes*, meetings of 13 and 15 Oct. 1964, University Archives, and *University Bulletin: A Weekly Bulletin for the Staff of the University of California*, 2 Nov. 1964, 65–67; see also Barry Bishin, "Academic Senate Amends," *DC*, 14 Oct. 1964. Though not permitted to vote or speak because of my "acting" status (I did not yet have a Ph.D., so my assistant professorship was not yet regularized), I was present at this and other Senate meetings that semester except the one on December 8.

56. *DC*, 14 Oct. 1964.

57. "Ad Hoc Senate Committee and Reporting (Oct. 15)," tape 28A, Strong Oral History.

58. *Academic Senate Minutes*, meetings of 13 and 15 Oct. 1964; *University Bulletin*, 2 Nov. 1964, 67.

59. *DC*, 16 and (Savio's statement) 19 Oct. 1964.

60. Goines (289, 291–92), who was present at an evening meeting between Ross and FSM leaders on Oct. 14, claims that the addition of two faculty members to the CCPA was already (tentatively) promised by Ross. On Ross's pivotal role in this story see also "Ad Hoc Senate Committee and Reporting," tape 28A, Strong Oral History; and Strong, "[To] Members of the Academic Senate," p. 7.

61. The quoted words are from Seaborg, 149; see also ibid., 59–60, and note 9, above.

62. *Academic Senate Minutes*, meetings of 13 and 15 Oct. 1964; *University Bulletin* 2 Nov. 1964, 67.

63. Unless otherwise noted, my discussion of the CCPA meetings is based on minutes on file in the FSM Records under the title "Committee on Campus Political Activity, Minutes of the Meeting," followed by the date. The committee met on 21, 24, 28, 29 Oct. and 4, 5, 7 Nov.

64. Strong was acutely aware of the symbiotic relationship between administrators and faculty based on the regular interchangeability of their roles and used it to buttress his at times desperate pleas for faculty support and understanding. See for example Strong, "Shared Responsibility," 6: "Have I and my fellow chief campus officers . . . become so separated from the selves we once were as faculty as to become self-alienated or, if not that, to become split personalities? I do not find either outcome to be evident."

65. As recalled by Towle in "Changing the Ban on Advocacy," Towle Oral History.

66. Helen Landfield, "Strong: More Disturbances," *DC*, 20 Oct. 1964.

67. Ann Lubar, "Kerr Refutes Letter Proof," *DC*, 5 Nov. 1964.

68. *DC*, 28 Oct. 1964.

69. For summaries of the tense debates at the 5 and 7 Nov. meetings, see Ann Lubar, "Comm. Tables Amended Motion," *DC*, 6 Nov., and (anonymous) "FSM to Lift Political Moratorium," *DC*, 9 Nov. 1964.

70. In addition to CCPA minutes for 28 Oct. and 4 Nov., see Burnstein's contribution to this volume.

71. In putting forth this argument Burnstein was not, I believe, invoking the legal concept of double jeopardy, although that notion was often used rhetorically

by the FSM in the weeks that followed. For an informed discussion of the issue, see Robert Post's essay in this volume.

72. "A Report on the Status of Deliberations of the Committee on Campus Political Activity as of November 7, 1964 by the Faculty Representatives on the Committee," FSM Records.

73. See Burnstein's essay in this volume.

74. For a succinct statement by an FSM militant of why he and others opposed turning to the courts for redress, see Brian Shannon's remarks in Goines, 277–78.

75. See Post's essay in this volume. Despite subsequent rulings favoring the kind of position taken by the FSM, courts continue to tolerate a limited array of university-imposed restrictions on free expression. Recently, for example, a U.S. Court of Appeals ruled in favor of a lawyer for the white-supremacist Nationalist Movement who sued the University of Mississippi for having barred spectators from waving Confederate flags at campus athletic events, in violation of the First Amendment. "The ruling upheld a decision last year [1999] from U.S. District Judge Neal Biggers Jr., who called the ban a reasonable limitation. The ban covers umbrellas, alcoholic beverages, flags, and all banners larger than 12 by 14 inches" (*San Francisco Chronicle*, 19 Aug. 2000).

76. Tom Miller, quoted in Goines, 306.

77. Ibid., 303.

78. For a well-documented (mainly from interviews conducted by Schultz) but controversial account of this split, see ibid., 303–26; see also Heirich, chapt. 11.

79. Robert Starobin, "Graduate Students in the FSM," *Graduate Student Journal*, no. 4 (spring 1965): 21; testimony of Starobin and Susan Stein in Goines, 399–402; *DC*, 19 Nov. 1964; Pierovich, "Chronology of Events," 56.

80. The full title was Ad Hoc Academic Senate Committee on Student Conduct. Other members were Robert Gordon (economics), Mason Haire (psychology, a researcher at the IIR), Richard Powell (chemistry chair), and Lloyd Ulman (economics, director of the IIR) (*DC*, 20 October 1964). These were conservative to moderate choices; at least two members enjoyed close relations with Kerr, who also belonged to the IIR.

81. Jim Branson, "Suspension Cases Taken from Student Conduct Comm.," *DC*, 16 Oct. 1964.

82. "Ad Hoc (Heyman) Committee's Request," tapes 28B and 29A, Strong Oral History. Strong recalled that on October 23 he discussed with Kerr the committee's request for provisional reinstatement of the students. He informed Kerr that "my Academic Advisory Committee and my Academic Administrative Council would, in [Dean] Sandy Elberg's judgment, recommend that we accede to the [committee's] requests." But on the 26th Strong told Heyman that he could not lift the suspensions without the Regents' and president's approval. His decision was reported in *DC*, 27 Oct. 1964.

83. Heyman Committee report, in "Documents," *CM* 75 (Feb. 1965): 82 (full report on 82–87); column by Eric Levine, *DC*, 27 Oct. 1964; coverage of hearings in *DC*, 28 Oct. and 4 Nov. 1964.

84. Heyman Committee report; Jim Branson, "FSM Protests to Continue," *DC*, 16 Nov. 1964. NB: Although Dean Williams was a principle witness against the students, the absence of vindictiveness on his part is clear from the report; in fact, in

reaching positive conclusions about the students' motives and conduct, the committee drew on Williams's testimony. Williams later praised the "wonderful committee," which "did a magnificent job" (Williams Oral History, tape 15B).

85. "Ad Hoc Senate Committee and Reporting," tape 28A, and "Summary," tape 30A, Strong Oral History.

86. For the committee's statement reversing itself on procedure, see Pierovich, "Chronology," 56; for Strong's full statement see ibid., 54 (see also *DC*, 16 Nov. 1964).

87. This does not mean, however, that the FSM now looked to the Academic Senate for deliverance, since FSM leaders, Art Goldberg in particular, insisted that Strong immediately accept the committee's recommendations and, at the very least, reinstate the six students with the lesser charges. For statements of Savio and Goldberg, see Pierovich, "Chronology," 54; also, *DC*, 16 Nov. 1964.

88. "Summary," tape 30A, Strong Oral History.

89. Somewhat later the group was joined by David Freedman (statistics) and, later still, Robert Cole (law).

90. Nor has his very able research associate, Marian Gade, been able to locate a copy in his papers. What she did find was a memo from the time of the trial saying that Rosovsky testified that "he had handed the Zelnick [*sic*] proposals to Mrs. Stephenson last October [1964] during the existence of CCPA, of which Mr. Rosovsky was a member." A staff person who was monitoring the trial for the president's office, anticipating that Kerr might be asked about it at the trial, had apparently alerted Kerr's office to Rosovsky's testimony. The memo, which was from "Mel" to Earl Bolton, vice president for University relations, goes on to say that "testimony by Rosovsky brought out [that] the FSM was ready to settle with administration on the basis of the Zelnick [*sic*] proposal and CCPA." Thanks to Ms. Gade for this information (e-mail communication, 13 July 2000). As I now interpret Rosovsky's words as reconstructed in this memo, what he meant was that when he was on the CCPA he believed the FSM would have been open to something like the Cheit Proposals, despite the retention of the legal-illegal distinction, provided all the due-process and other procedural safeguards of the "Zelnik proposal" were added. Note that the FSM's legal counsel had advocated acceptance of some version of the Cheit plan, even though it was *less* protective of the students than ours. However, CCPA minutes reveal no discussion of our plan. The subtext of Rosovsky's testimony for the defense was that the FSM was flexible and open to reasonable compromise. I testified along similar lines, and no one representing the FSM expressed unhappiness with this line of testimony, which was correctly seen as weakening the prosecution's case. Of course none of this "proves" that our plan was politically viable.

91. For a concise account of the events of November 20, including the Regents' statements and an important statement by Kerr, see the corresponding entry in Pierovich, "Chronology," 56–57. For two stylistically different yet basically consistent accounts of that day, see also Heirich, chapt. 12 (based in part on field notes taken at the event), and Goines, 337–41 (based in part on interviews).

92. Kerr, chapt. 11.

93. Heirich (256), who took notes, recalls that in addressing the crowd I said that the faculty had been slapped in the face by this decision. This paraphrase is close to my own recollection.

94. On the ASUC position, a modified version of the CCPA faculty's, see *DC*, 17 and 19 Nov. 1964, and Pierovich, "Chronology," 55–56. The ASUC position, like the Regents', preserved the chancellor's committee but provided for much more in the way of procedural safeguards.

95. John Searle, "The Faculty Resolution," in Michael V. Miller and Susan Gilmore, eds., *Revolution at Berkeley: The Crisis in American Education* (New York: Dell, 1965), 97.

96. Heirich, 256.

97. "Regents Set a New Policy (November 20)," tape 30A, Strong Oral History. Strong's position, now close to that of the CCPA faculty in most respects, was elaborated in a paid ad in *DC*, 24 Nov. 1964.

98. See the partially eyewitness accounts of these events in Goines, 343–47 (my quotes are from 343), and Heirich, 258–63.

99. Tapes of my speech, Mario's remarks, and other talks at the November 23 rally may be heard at the Moffitt Media Resources Center or on its website, at <http://lib.berkeley.edu/MRC/FSM.html>.

100. That draft is preserved in series 7, carton 3, folder 89, FSM Records.

101. See Levine's essay in this volume. His sense of our isolation from the rest of the faculty is corroborated in the essay by Leon Wofsy, also in this volume: "Though he [Levine] received some support in the Senate, he was treated as an upstart, his message rather rudely received and brushed aside by the majority." (Since the original Levine motion has been printed in full only in the *Academic Senate Minutes*, I include it here as Appendix A.) Later in the meeting a sense motion by Levine, this time confined to the issue of creating a permanent faculty disciplinary committee, was also defeated: "It is the sense of this meeting of the Academic Senate that a standing committee chosen by and responsible to the Senate should be appointed to deal with questions of student conduct arising with reference to political thought or action." See *Academic Senate Minutes*, meeting of 24 Nov. 1964, University Archives.

102. Sherwood Parker, citing the "exact words" of a senior colleague, quoted in Goines, 431.

103. Constance's speech is in *Academic Senate Minutes*, meeting of 24 Nov. 1964.

104. A strong motion on the Katz case passed overwhelmingly after the FSM part of the debate was over. One wonders, did anger at the chancellor over the Katz case help the FSM supporters at the meeting, or did it actually inhibit some faculty from supporting them lest it appear like "overkill"?

105. No one, however, doubted that May would treat us fairly, and despite our disagreements in the days that followed, he always did.

106. Interview with Schultz, in Goines, 350 (for Starobin's full account of the meeting, 350–52). The other history student on the GCC was Henry *Mayer* (mistakenly identified in ibid., 403, as Henry *May*).

107. *Academic Senate Minutes*, meeting of 24 Nov. 1964; the vote was 267–79.

108. Goines, 354–55.

109. Two drafts, both dated 30 Nov., are located in series 7, carton 3, folder 89, FSM Records. They are unsigned, but one is on history department stationary and the other bears my initials.

110. A copy of the letter and draft resolution is in folder 81, ibid. The signers were listed in alphabetical order.

111. There was, however, a *future* faculty member arrested in the sit-in—Richard Muller, now a Berkeley physics professor, then a TA (personal communication, 25 Sept. 2000). Without giving names, the *CM* spoke of "a few faculty members" in the sit-in but said that none was among the arrested ("Season of Discontent," *CM* 75 [Feb. 1965]: 13 [narrative of events of fall 1964 prepared by the editors of the California Alumni Association's magazine]). Despite their enthusiasm, even the very pro-FSM math faculty had trouble reaching a consensus about Sproul sit-ins. An undated, unsigned handwritten statement from this period, apparently drafted by Hirsch in collaboration with Smale and others, praises the local civil rights sit-ins but then both adds and crosses out these words: "Speaking for myself, I do not think a sit-in in Sproul Hall is justified at this time and I do not advocate it." To complicate matters, the words "at this time" are then crossed out within the crossed-out sentence (series 7, carton 3, folder 82, FSM Records).

112. The event was widely covered in the national press. See, for example, *New York Times*, 3 Dec. 1964.

113. Robert Cole (law) was one of the professors called to the campus (around 3 A.M.) who had not been previously involved but remained involved thereafter. Cole recalls as present at Sproul Steps (in addition to Stampp) Al Bendich and Fred Stripp (both speech department) and Joseph Tussman; see Cole's essay in the present volume.

114. *DC,* 4 and 7 Dec. 1964.

115. *DC,* 4 Dec. 1964.

116. Although he could be right, Searle does not document his assertion that "hundreds of professors" canceled classes (see his "Faculty Resolution," 99).

117. A copy of Jacobson's statement is in series 7, carton 3, folder 90, FSM Records; Searle and Lowenthal, as quoted in "Season of Discontent," 14; Litwack quoted in Miller and Gilmore, 330.

118. Stampp Oral History, 236.

119. May sees the "police on the campus" issue as one that "very many [faculty] felt strongly about." He also reminds us that there were still faculty who remained apart from the controversy "who never signed anything, never gave speeches, and went on teaching [and] were not molested" (Henry F. May, "Professor of American Intellectual History, University of California, Berkeley, 1952–1980," oral history conducted in 1998 by Ann Lage, Regional Oral History Office, Bancroft Library, 1999 [hereafter May Oral History], 121).

120. Glazer, 297–98.

121. This was more faculty than had ever shown up at an official Senate meeting (Searle, "Faculty Resolution," 99). My account of the meeting draws on *DC,* 4 Dec. 1964; Pierovich, "Chronology," 62–63 (includes the motions passed and other relevant texts); and my own recollection.

122. May Oral History, 122.

123. From the typescript in series 7, carton 3, folder 76, FSM Records; also in May Oral History, 123.

124. The phrase "extralegal faculty meeting" is used by May in ibid.

125. Pierovich, "Chronology," 63.

126. Ibid.; *DC,* 4 Dec. 1964.

127. Cooperating with Stanier in preparing the telegram was his colleague Leon Wofsy (see Wofsy's essay in this volume). The telegram to Brown and the Reynolds statement are in Pierovich, "Chronology," 63.

128. According to Strong, Reynolds later apologized to him for his "excessive zeal"; "Sproul Hall Sit-In," tape 30B, Strong Oral History.

129. *DC,* 7 Dec. 1964.

130. Kerr's statement of December 3 quoted in *DC,* 4 Dec. 1964.

131. May Oral History, 123–24. The precise sequence of events leading to the establishment of the chairmen's council remains somewhat hazy. May's recollection, that the idea came "mainly" from Scalapino, seems to suggest the possibility of a more complicated genealogy.

132. Ibid., 125. The full statement is in series 7, carton 3, folder 76, FSM Records; see also "Documents," *CM* (Feb. 1965): 88–89; *DC,* 5 Dec. 1964.

133. May Oral History, 126.

134. On December 5 Towle actually prepared a memo urging Strong not only to drop charges but to adopt the FSM's basic position on advocacy, but Sherriffs convinced her to delay submitting it until after the December 7 meeting at the Greek Theatre (see below), and it was never sent. The memo said, in part, that Strong should adopt the position that "the University should not and will not attempt to determine the constitutionality of advocacy: this is a matter for the courts." Towle argued that a "concise statement with respect to the meaning of 'unlawful action' would, we firmly believe, clear that air and give us all opportunity to return again to the continuing business of the University. In view of the Academic Senate's meeting on Tuesday, December 8, where this crucial matter is sure to engage much of the discussions, I urge most strongly that such a statement from the Chancellor and/or the President be issued. . . . We also recommend most earnestly that the University drop pending charges against the four students . . . since they have now subjected themselves to legal action by civil authority. For the University to continue to press charges would seem to serve no useful or helpful purpose in the current campus crisis. I, for one, wish to be on record as opposed to further action against these students. . . . Further, I urge immediate public announcement of the dropping of the charges." Towle was also speaking for others on her staff. For the full text see Sherriffs Oral History, appendix 6.

135. My account of the meeting at Kerr's home is based on Strong Oral History, tape 30B. Strong cites his own notes, written at the meeting, in support of his memory that Kerr opposed amnesty during the three-hour meeting. The meeting was also attended by a faculty member who was not a chairman—Paul Seabury (political science), who was close to Kerr. The most pro-FSM chairman who attended was Tussman. For Strong's account of his illness (including the call from Scalapino) and hospitalization, see ibid., tape 31A, where he also notes that while in the hospital he received a get-well card signed by each member of the FSM Steering Committee.

136. Without elaborating, the *CM* narrative refers to the chairmen's proposals as "of ambiguous origin," and suggests that the claim that they originated entirely among the chairmen was made "[i]n order to give them some legitimacy"; see "Season of Discontent," 15.

137. Details on the airport meeting were reported to Strong in person by Scalapino and others, who stopped by the hospital after the meeting. Strong, basing himself on the exchange in the hospital, is also the source of the information that the Regents' agreement to the proposals was "reluctant."

138. *DC*, 7 Dec. 1964. According to Kerr, seventy-three chairmen endorsed the agreement, and one abstained (Kerr, chapt. 11).

139. Ibid.; Pierovich, "Chronology," 66–67. Two of the signers, including the same Eric Bellquist who challenged the "Kerr Directives" during the Seaborg administration, were retired at the time.

140. Series 7, carton 3, folder 82, FSM Records; see also *DC*, 7 Dec. 1964.

141. Muscatine, as quoted in Goines, 433–34 (interview by Schultz).

142. Stampp Oral History, 237. (A key role in the drafting was also played by law professor Robert Cole.) For a portrayal of the atmosphere at the December 6 meeting, with an emphasis on the discussion's "high level of intelligence and rationality," see Searle, "Faculty Resolution," 100.

143. My only clear recollection of a dissenting voice is that of Martin Malia (history), who near the end of the meeting said that, though supporting the motions, he was worried about the direction things were taking.

144. Schorske Oral History, 92.

145. Glazer, 299.

146. The smaller committee representing "the 200" prepared for its internal use a set of "Recommendations on Tactics" for the Senate meeting, which included the Stocking preamble and the "Feldman resolution," "a 'non-controversial' statement of support for matters that everyone supports anyway," to be used if needed as a substitute motion for any "Law and Order" motion condemning the students, say, or "commending the action of Gov. Brown," if that motion could not be tabled. These documents are preserved in the Sellers Papers.

147. May Oral History, 126–27. Though surely present at the meeting, I have no recollection of it. Even Schorske, who spoke with so powerful a voice at the meeting, has little to say about it today, except that May "certainly chaired it pretty well"; more generally, he recalls that May was a very fair chairman during the crisis, which he was (Schorske Oral History, 99). A document that nicely illustrates May's efforts to be fair under great stress is the "notice for information" he circulated to the department on December 4, wherein he informed us of the chairmen's position that classes should continue "in a normal manner" but that if someone decided to dismiss a class it should be emphasized that the purpose was to make "a contribution to the solution of the crisis" (that is, dismissal of the class would not be construed as support of the strike). May added that he personally disapproved of the strike but expressed his "sympathy for the emotions that cause some members of the department and some teaching assistants to feel differently." In another circular (13 Nov.) during a strike action by TAs, though warning of possibly serious consequences of striking, May stated that he had written to the dean of the graduate division that the strikers were acting "on grounds of serious principle, and that it was important that the careers of individuals taking such action should not be damaged." Both documents are in series 7, carton 3, folder 76, FSM Records. (I cannot help but note that May's metaphor of Schorske's "casting oil on the water" has its counterpart in Schorske's oral history (p. 91), where he says (after praising Kerr for

his other accomplishments) that during the FSM Kerr's "initial rigidity . . . poured oil on the fire."

148. Letter dated 4 Dec. 1964, series 7, carton 3, folder 84, FSM Records.

149. Undated draft, folder 87, ibid.

150. Letter to members, faculty of the College of Engineering, 7 Dec. 1964, folder 86, ibid.

151. Another chairman, Robert Beloof (speech), shouted at Kerr, "You have to let him speak!" Both Beloof and Tussman addressed the enormous crowd that gathered on Sproul Plaza after the convocation and, in effect, disassociated themselves from the now defunct chairmen's plan (Draper, 124–25).

152. May Oral History, 127. Kerr categorically denies having agreed to the presence of police on stage, he and Scalapino having concluded that their presence would be provocative. Kerr believes that the campus police were there (with the approval of Vice President Bolton) because they feared disruption of the meeting and possible violence against him. He also believes that the story of possible violence had originated with Lipset, who in turn had heard it from students with whom he had political affinities (Kerr, chapt. 11). If the Lipset part is accurate, I suppose this should count as another example of faculty influence on the events of 1964.

153. The account in "Season of Discontent" (15) concluded that the chairmen's proposals, as approved by Kerr, "were intended to present a *fait accompli* to the meeting of the Academic Senate," a thought that many of us had at the time. An example of the kind of motion that might have come forth had the council of chairmen remained intact was prepared in the geology and geophysics department as late as December 8; it simply stated that the Senate "endorses the sense of the report submitted by the Council of Departmental Chairmen." Other motions prepared in the same department condemned in one breath both the "unwarranted" and "massive" use of police and the "extreme" and "lawless" actions of the students (series 7, carton 3, folder 88, FSM Records).

154. Kerr, chapt. 11; see also Heirich, 300–301. Kerr's recollection of the presence of Selznick and Stampp (and Scalapino) from personal e-mail communication, 27 Sept. 2000.

155. Strong Oral History, tape 31A.

156. The words of Sherwood Parker, referring to his chairman, as quoted in Goines, 430–31.

157. Glazer, 299.

158. This point is made by Selznick in his "Reply to Glazer," *Commentary*, Mar. 1965, in Lipset and Wolin, 303.

159. Transcript of December 8 meeting, audiotaped by Marston Schultz, transcribed by a group of students, printed on offset press, and distributed as a pamphlet titled *Academic Senate: Dec. 8, 1964* by Academic Publishing–Berkeley and other member groups of the Council of Campus Organizations (1964). It has been available online at the FSM website since 1999 at <http://www.fsm-a.org/stacks/ACSenate.html>. (For purposes of clarity, I have made a few minor changes in punctuation and capitalization.)

160. There was another (minor) attempt at amendment before the resolution was passed, a motion to substitute the word *policies* for *measures* in section 4; it was

easily defeated. In addition to the Dec. 8 transcript, see *Academic Senate Minutes,* meeting of 8 Dec. 1964.

161. Interestingly, on the first ballot, when no one received the required majority, members of "the 200" ran second through seventh (Academic Senate of UC, Berkeley Division, "Election of Emergency Executive Committee," circular of 12 Dec. 1964, University Archives). However, because on the first ballot votes for non-200 nominees had been distributed among a larger number of candidates, both moderate (e.g., Cheit) and outspokenly anti-FSM (e.g., Feuer), the runoff election, limited to the top twelve vote getters, produced very different results.

162. See especially the "Dear Colleague" circular letter of December 14, signed by Muscatine and six others, and the more handsome brochure "A Message on the Proposed Solution to the Free Speech Controversy," prepared for broad circulation by six members of the Sellers circle. These and other similar appeals are in the Sellers Papers, as are some interesting responses, both positive and hostile. The thrust of some of the hostile responses tended to be criticism of the Berkeley faculty for not taking a firm stand against the FSM's coercive tactics, a charge that Henry Nash Smith rebutted in a circular called "Why Has the Berkeley Faculty Failed to Condemn Violations of the Law by Students?" Among the positive responses, located in the Sellers Papers, was a unanimous vote by the academic senate of San Francisco State College on December 15 supporting the Berkeley Senate ("Summary of Minutes," Fall 1964, no. 9). Communications were also sent to the Regents by faculty who opposed the December 8 resolutions.

Also prepared at this time to bolster the EEC's case for faculty control of student discipline was a well-researched document by two Berkeley historians on the history of past faculty authority over discipline until it was voluntarily relinquished in 1921. See Irwin Scheiner and Robert Middlekauff, "A Note on the Academic Senate's Powers and Student Discipline," typed statement, copy in my possession.

163. EEC, "Interim Report," 27. Dec. 1964, p. 4, University Archives (emphasis in original). The Regents, meeting in Los Angeles, summarized their position in a four-point open letter to all UC faculty (18 Dec. 1964). Point 4 unanimously reaffirmed the Regents' "devotion to the 1st and 14th Amendments of the Constitution." A copy is on file in the Sellers Papers.

164. See Robert Cohen's article on the "little free speech movement" in this volume.

165. I have not undertaken separate research on the "filthy speech" crisis and do not purport to analyze it in any depth. Apart from my personal memory, my comments here are based on Andrew L. Pierovich's article, "Freedom and Campus Unity," *CM* 75 (May 1965): 10–13; see also Robert M. O'Neil and Sanford Kadish [UC law professors], "Freedom and Four Letter Words," loc. cit., 18–21; "Continuing Crisis at Berkeley," *CM* 75 (June 1965): 52–56; and Goines, 480–508.

166. "We've Been Confronted," statement released on March 19, copy in FSM Records.

167. Quoted in O'Neil and Kadish, "Continuing Crisis," 56.

168. I am thinking of the case of John Leggett, assistant professor of sociology, who was reprimanded by the administration for distributing material at the unauthorized table of a radical student organization in March 1966. See "Professor, Students Cited, Expelled from University," *CM* 76 (May 1966): 20.

From the Big Apple to Berkeley

Perspectives of a Junior Faculty Member

Lawrence W. Levine

When you are in the middle of a story it isn't a story at all, but only a confusion; a dark roaring, a blindness. . . . It's only afterwards that it becomes anything like a story at all. When you are telling it, to yourself or to someone else.
MARGARET ATWOOD, *Alias Grace*

When one looks back on the events in Berkeley during the 1960s, it is easy to fall into the trap of historical inevitability. It now seems logical that the political and cultural events on American university campuses that captured the attention of the nation in those years had to happen and that Berkeley, California, was the ideal stage for those events to first unfold.

At the time, however, none of what eventually took place seemed inevitable or, in fact, even likely. I arrived at the University of California at Berkeley in August 1962 to begin what turned out to be a thirty-two-year career there as a member of the department of history. I had been teaching at Princeton, within shouting distance—geographically at least—of New York, the only city I had ever lived in, and the decision to migrate to the Pacific frontier was fraught with a sense of adventure and deep feelings of anxiety. Not long after I arrived I was driving through the still unfamiliar streets around the campus and was suddenly surrounded by a howling mob of frenzied young men pressing forward toward a building where other male students were congregated, all of them peering upward. Unable to move my car, I stepped outside and looked up at the spectacle that captured the attention of my captors. There, leaning out of windows, were equally frenzied young women, many of whom were throwing out objects that floated gradually into the outstretched male hands that grabbed them eagerly. It was my first and only panty raid, and it led me to crawl back into my car to wait for the dispersal of the male mob and to contemplate in some despair what I was then convinced was the enormity of my mistake in voluntarily leaving the Big Apple for the provinces.

It was, of course, the reaction of the native New York chauvinist I was at that time, and nothing that happened in my first year completely dispelled the anxiety that had accompanied my departure from that city.

Nevertheless, I was soon to learn that the fraternity culture I had encountered during that incident did not define the entire Berkeley student culture. Indeed, there existed a left student culture that had surfaced in the anti–capital punishment protests against the execution of Caryl Chessman and against the House Un-American Activities Committee hearings in San Francisco, both of which occurred the year before I arrived in Berkeley, and that continued to manifest itself in the student organization SLATE, which was small but active in my first Berkeley years.

After settling into my new community, I resumed my civil rights activities by joining the Berkeley branch of the Congress of Racial Equality (CORE). Given that Berkeley was a college town housing a vast and complex university, there were surprisingly few students in Berkeley CORE, and most of those were graduate students. CORE focused during 1962, 1963, and 1964 on hiring and housing discrimination in Berkeley, documenting the segregation that marred even so putatively liberal a town as Berkeley. With regard to housing, our basic strategies were simple: typically, a European American like myself would enter a real estate office to inquire about an apartment or house to rent and emerge with several possibilities, whereas an African American colleague making a similar inquiry invariably would be told there were no vacancies. Or I would agree to rent an apartment, and before closing the deal I would bring my African American "wife" to see the place only to have the landlord or landlady "discover" that the residence was really not available. It would have been enormously helpful to have had the aid of Berkeley undergraduates in this endeavor, but few seemed interested.

In the summer of 1963 CORE staged a "live-in" around the rotunda of the state capitol in Sacramento in an ultimately successful effort to force a state senate committee to report out the Rumford Fair Housing Bill and allow the full senate to vote on it. We settled in with our sleeping bags for weeks on end, and a cautious Governor Pat Brown let us be to make our case to the tourists, legislators, and reporters who walked the capitol's halls. Again, Berkeley undergraduates were scarce. Building upon the success of our summer venture in Sacramento, we attempted during the 1963 Christmas season to stage a massive picket line against the many Berkeley stores that did not hire black employees. Although we were in a city with thirty thousand college students, we attracted too few picketers to realize our ambitious goals to picket all of the downtown area and were therefore forced to concentrate on one large pharmacy in a central location; ultimately we failed to effect any striking changes in hiring patterns.

None of these experiences prepared us for the outburst of student civil rights activity in 1964. During the winter and spring a young black woman, Tracy Sims, led mostly young protestors in a series of demonstrations against discriminatory hiring—picketing establishments on San Francisco's

Auto Row and staging sit-ins of as many as fifteen hundred demonstrators at San Francisco's Sheraton Palace Hotel and shop-ins at Bay Area Lucky's supermarkets, where demonstrators would fill their shopping carts to the brim, wheel them to the cashiers' stations, and leave them there. These demonstrations by the very students we had had trouble recruiting just months earlier took me totally by surprise and illustrated, to my satisfaction at least, how little I comprehended the dynamics of the world I lived in. It was to be only the first of a series of such surprises.

By the summer of 1964 the protests had spread to former U.S. senator William Knowland's *Oakland Tribune*. Busloads of Berkeley students, who had been recruited on campus, were transported to the *Tribune* building, where they picketed on behalf of fair hiring practices. Many of us were convinced that this act of encouraging Berkeley students to demonstrate against the business enterprise of so powerful a member of California's political establishment was the catalyst that led to the University's sudden withdrawal of the students' rights to maintain a handful of tables on the edge of the campus from which they handed out materials and organized activities advocating a wide variety of religious, social, and political causes. Four or five little tables at the juncture of Bancroft and Telegraph Avenues wasn't much of a free speech area but it was all that the University offered, and now it had disappeared.

With that disappearance the days of political lassitude were over, as were the days of my ambivalence concerning the move West. If you had told me that the sudden cancellation of the already meager rights of student political activity on campus would reveal the existence of a strikingly articulate and strategically savvy group of student leaders, I would have laughed. But there they were! If you had told me further that they would be able to touch and stimulate thousands of students and to change the face and the tone of the Berkeley campus forever, I would have shaken my head in disbelief. But they accomplished both of these feats, proving once again that the present can be at least as difficult to decipher as the ancient past.

In retrospect, I realize that I would have been less surprised had I paid closer attention to the fact that, beginning in the spring of 1961, a number of present and future Berkeley students had joined the Freedom Riders who went South to aid in the struggle for integration and African American constitutional rights and were part of the some one thousand white northern students who participated in the Mississippi Freedom Summer of 1964, where they helped to register black voters. From these endeavors such future student leaders as Mario Savio emerged with a heightened consciousness of freedom and civil rights, as well as a knowledge of the tactics of civil disobedience they would soon employ on the campuses to which they returned. What was unpredictable, of course, was how much these nascent student leaders would be aided by the striking ineptitude of the

Berkeley campus and University of California statewide administrations and by the aid of a varying group of faculty allies.

At first, those faculty came largely from the ranks of young, untenured professors like myself. In November several of us attempted to have the Academic Senate pass a resolution defending the students' rights of political activity on campus and calling for the establishment of a faculty committee with final jurisdiction over issues related to those rights. Although I had no parliamentary experience, the unwillingness of older, more experienced liberal colleagues to commit themselves publicly and take the lead vaulted me into the vacuum as the mover of and spokesperson for our resolution. It was an act of chutzpah that, on one vote at least, came close to succeeding but then ended badly. Our resolution was greeted by the amused contempt of the doyens of the Senate, who so mangled and distorted it through parliamentary maneuvers and amendments that in the end I myself not only voted against the almost unrecognizable "Levine Motion"—which a young professor of philosophy accurately characterized as "academic oatmeal"—but urged my colleagues to do the same. Thinking about it now, I find it remarkable that my junior colleagues and I did these things with no thought about whether or how our actions might impact our eventual tenure prospects. In a sense it was a testament not only to us but to our departments and to the University of California that we did what we did with no detriment to our careers. At the time of the Senate meeting, however, I was not elated by our freedom of action but depressed by our defeat and what I considered the myopia of our colleagues. I remember leaving that scene of futility and humiliation to walk down Telegraph Avenue to Cody's bookstore, where I purchased my first copy of *Robert's Rules of Order.* If I was going to engage in battle I needed the appropriate armor. That was one lesson learned.

Another was that the bulk of the faculty would be moved into action only by some drastic event. The inability or unwillingness of the president, the chancellor, and their aides to respond appropriately to what was happening on the campus helped to sow the seeds of that event. In the early hours of December 3, some eight hundred students sitting in at Sproul Hall were arrested. I was one of a small group of faculty present outside Sproul Hall throughout that chilly night while the arrests were being made. We were turned away in our attempts to enter the building as faculty observers to insure that the peaceful protestors were not being treated violently. (We had heard one young woman calling out through a window that the police were dragging the students down the stairs by their feet and allowing their heads to bounce on the steps—which turned out to be untrue.) We walked to Chancellor Strong's office and then his campus home, but he was at neither place; nor did we find President Kerr at his campus office. Feelings of futility were not new to us, but they were particularly strong during that long night. At dawn a small group of us resolved to hold an emergency meeting of faculty that would initiate a meeting of the Academic Senate. By noon that day the entire faculty received a call to action in their mailboxes, and about an hour later some eight hundred of us met to begin a discussion of the issues that would be dealt with in the Academic Senate meeting that was to be held on December 8. Not an easy task on that large campus with its vast faculty, but one we accomplished thanks to the efforts of a growing group of professors and graduate students. Only at this juncture did significant numbers of senior faculty get fully involved, and once they did, the junior faculty were unceremoniously shoved to the periphery. Another lesson learned.

Nevertheless, those of us who had been involved with the student movement had a vantage point from which to perceive and at times influence continuing events. What gradually struck me then and continues to impress me today is that what had begun as a political movement was having its greatest influence as a cultural movement. Certainly students' political gains, if not as monumental as their leaders' rhetoric promised, were substantial. The few tables at the edge of the campus multiplied into impressive rows of tables in Sproul Plaza through which thousands of members of the campus community strolled every day. Students won the right to hold rallies from Sproul Steps every weekday at noon. They won seats on, or at least a voice in, an array of departmental, college, and university committees. Most important, they won a political *presence* they had not enjoyed before.

As impressive as these achievements were, it was the *cultural* consequences of the Free Speech Movement and the many other movements it was allied with that changed the campus indelibly. I recall walking through the northern part of the campus one afternoon and coming upon a small group surrounding a male student who was delivering a harangue replete with filthy language. A young campus policeman pointed to a blond woman in the crowd and told the speaker to halt the flow of profanity because a "lady" was present. The young woman walked up to the cop, looked at him directly, and said, "Officer, fuck you!" The disbelief on the policeman's face was palpable. It wasn't primarily a question of language; it was the breaking down of paternalist protection and of imposed cultural roles. It was a symptom of something much larger. The formality that had characterized the campus when I first arrived in the early 1960s—from parietal rules to dress codes to relations between the various segments of the college community—did not survive the decade. A new looseness and openness in manner, dress, demeanor, language, personal relations became prevalent.

It is easy to dismiss this as mere window dressing, as Herbert Marcuse did in his notion of a one-dimensional America able to absorb and render meaningless all forms of behavioral dissent. But I would argue that in retrospect it's difficult to tell who was absorbing whom. I think it indisputable that the Berkeley campus became a freer, less hierarchical, more unpredictable, more diverse, and far more interesting place than it had been at the beginning of the 1960s. All of this may well have happened without the FSM, but that movement certainly expedited, shaped, and helped to spread these changes.

Have the more than thirty-five years since the FSM burst upon the scene alleviated some of the "confusion" and "blindness" that, the novelist Margaret Atwood argues, impair the vision of those who live through an event? Certainly! To give a single example, in one of his speeches Mario Savio prophesied that when the FSM won its struggle "real teaching" would take place on the Berkeley campus for the "first time." Though I admired Savio as a leader and liked him as a person, I remember reacting negatively to what I felt was the irresponsible rhetoric of that assertion. Berkeley had had its share of inspired teaching from the beginning, and I had not the slightest doubt that "real teaching" went on in my classroom and those of many of my colleagues. But in time I've come to realize that, if we consider how much freer faculty and students have now become to interact with and learn from each other, inside *and* outside the classroom, Savio's promise was not an empty one.

And yet, having told parts of my little story, I confess to some lingering uncertainty about the enduring impact of the FSM. All we can do, perhaps, is to adopt the long-range view of Mao Tse-tung, who, when asked if the French Revolution had influenced the Communist Revolution in China, replied that it was too soon to tell.

When the FSM Disturbed
the Faculty Peace

Leon Wofsy

I joined the faculty at Berkeley in August 1964, less than two months before the great free speech rebellion began. Coincidence? Not according to the Thirteenth Report of the (California) Senate Fact-Finding Subcommittee on Un-American Activities, June 1965.

I arrived on campus as a new associate professor in the department of bacteriology and immunology, but the Un-American Committee, headed by state senator Hugh Burns, saw my appointment as a subversive ruse. With vintage McCarthyite vision, it insisted that my Communist background and radical organizing experience as a youth were what really brought me here. So before I ever met Mario Savio or any of the student leaders who launched the FSM, the Burns committee gave me a major share of the credit for their remarkable success.

In fact, coming to Berkeley was for me almost like a dream come true. My field, immunology, was emerging as one of the most exciting areas of molecular and cell biology, and I was thrilled to be in the middle of it. UC Berkeley was clearly among the world's greatest universities, and in the forefront of rapidly advancing biological science. Also, our daughter Carla was beginning her senior year at UC Berkeley. When the invitation came to consider joining the Berkeley faculty, I phoned my wife and asked, Where would you most like to be? For both of us, the answer was the University of California at Berkeley.

Now, long after the FSM and I came to Berkeley, I'd like to look back a bit at how some of us on the faculty related to the FSM and, more generally, to the student upheavals of the sixties. That this has remained a largely untold story is strange in a way, since the UC faculty was a prime target during those years for the finger-pointing press and politicians, especially when Ronald Reagan took over as governor. Still, the story of the sixties is youth's rebellion, and many of the histories of that period were written by members of the generation that coined the phrase "Don't trust anyone over thirty."

From the beginning on October 1, 1964, when the University police car was surrounded by students on Sproul Plaza, a few faculty members were immediately sympathetic to the students. They were upset at the spectacle of a police action ordered by chancellor Edward Strong to prevent political speech and activity on Sproul Plaza. Philosophy professor John Searle went right to the scene of the incident and spoke up against the administration's restriction of free speech. In the following weeks, as the impasse with Chancellor Strong continued and faculty concern began to grow, Searle was joined by other faculty members in frequent consultations. Among the most involved were two young assistant professors in the history department, Reginald Zelnik and Lawrence Levine. I was introduced to Reggie and Larry by another faculty member and fellow immunologist, David Weiss, and we soon became friends. Although a newcomer to the Academic Senate, Levine was the first member to speak up and call on the faculty to intervene in favor of a more democratic policy toward student activities. Though he received some support in the Senate, he was treated as an upstart, his message rather rudely received and brushed aside by the majority.

During this initial period, I paid a lot of attention to the crisis and was intensely involved in discussion with faculty colleagues as well as with graduate students in my department who were participants in the actions of the FSM. I avoided a more participatory role because I was so new to the faculty. I tried hard not to be distracted from the urgent pressure to set up my new laboratory and get grant support for my research. I also had been conditioned by past experience to be wary of allowing my own radical history to provide fuel for those seeking to red-bait the student movement. (One of the contributions of the New Left in the sixties was to sweep away that kind of self-conscious adjustment to the atmosphere of McCarthyism in the fifties.)

The faculty as a whole did not respond assertively to what was happening until the sit-in and mass arrests at Sproul Hall on December 2–3. Outrage over the administration's resort to massive police intervention and the chancellor's unwillingness to concede on elementary issues of civil liberties brought some eight hundred faculty members together in an emergency meeting on the afternoon of December 3, the day that dawned with the student arrests. At that meeting, Roger Stanier, professor of bacteriology and immunology, read a telegram to Governor Edmond Brown protesting the arrests; the telegram was endorsed in a motion passed by acclamation.

Later that evening, there was a meeting of faculty who came to be known unofficially as the Committee of 200. Here it was agreed to draft a resolution for submission to the Academic Senate embodying the essential free speech demands of the students. For the next several years, although the Committee of 200 had no formal existence as an organization, faculty who took part in that initial effort continued to cooperate and became a kind of informal caucus, perhaps the most influential single group in the Berkeley division of the Academic Senate.

Even after the sit-in arrests, most faculty expected that President Clark Kerr would be able to accomplish what Chancellor Strong would not. The faculty had great respect for Kerr's credentials as a liberal highly skilled in educational diplomacy and the art of compromise. However, the illusion that Kerr could bring about a return to normalcy died in the Greek Theatre fiasco of December 7, when Mario Savio's attempt to speak in reply to Kerr was interrupted forcibly by police who dragged him off the platform. On the next day, December 8, the Academic Senate rebuffed the administration and passed what was essentially the resolution of the Committee of 200 by an astonishing vote of 824–115.

I have a very personal recollection of December 7 and 8. A short time after the Greek Theatre episode, I got an urgent message from a veteran faculty member who was very close to the administration. I was to go at once to see the acting chancellor, who had been asked by Kerr to seek my advice. Strong was no longer functioning as chancellor, although this was a secret even to the faculty, as was the identity of his temporary replacement. Whenever I think back to my memorable interview with the acting chancellor, Lincoln Constance, I am amused and embarrassed. I felt flattered and so hopeful as I gave my advice for transmission to Kerr. After the Greek Theatre, I thought, the administration is at last opening its mind to the need for reaching a serious agreement with the students. My advice was that the administration should make an unequivocal act of good faith by supporting the resolution of the Committee of 200 at the next day's Academic Senate meeting. That night my wife and I dropped in on the faculty member who had asked me to meet with the acting chancellor so that we could give him the good news. His mood was in somber contrast to my elation. "Leon," he said, "you have disappointed us." He explained that I had been called in because "we" (the administration) lacked the experience for coping with Mario Savio and his friends, who "talk the language of the gutter"; "we thought, Leon, that with your background, you would know how to handle them." My wife and I, mortified and angry, turned around and walked out.[1]

Far from sharing the administration's hostility toward the FSM leaders, many faculty saw something admirable in the new students of the sixties. Although often discomfited by the unprecedented disruption of the norms of academia, faculty sympathetic to the FSM were struck by the idealism and honesty of a new generation that got its inspiration through direct participation in the historic Civil Rights Movement. They found Mario Savio an especially attractive representative of the new student, so different from the "silent generation" of the fifties. His speech was forthright and fresh, without the clichés that would have permitted smug academics to dismiss him as an "ideologue." He and other FSM leaders were perceptive and devastatingly candid about the platitudes and hypocrisy that are part of standard operating procedure in all big establishments, including the university. To be sure, much of the rhetoric swirling in and around Sproul Plaza was less lofty and rational. The antiestablishment rage of student activists was more than occasionally indiscriminate. Regarding the faculty with suspicion and contempt, some viewed all liberals and the University itself as the enemy.

A number of the faculty 200 had themselves taken part in civil rights actions, for example in San Francisco's Auto Row. The bond for others was a strong commitment to civil liberties and academic freedom, expressed earlier in their refusal to submit to the loyalty oath imposed on the University during the years of McCarthyism.

In fact, in the fall of 1964 a very major academic freedom fight was going forward against the firing of assistant professor of German Eli Katz for his refusal to answer questions before the House Committee on Un-American Activities (HUAC). In November 1964, the Academic Senate voted 267–79 to insist that Katz be reinstated. That fight, which eventually was won, was led by Professor Howard Schachman of molecular biology, who became one of the most effective leaders of "the 200," and by the late Jacobus ten Broek of political science, justly celebrated for his brilliant legal analysis of violations of the U.S. Constitution involved in the internment of Japanese Americans during World War II.

CONNECTING WITH THE FSM

My own relationship to the FSM and what followed was shaped by several factors. As my FBI files reveal, my past, especially as national leader of the Labor Youth League from 1949 to 1956, made me a prime target for one of the FBI's "COINTELPRO" (counterintelligence program) campaigns. Before I taught my first class in immunology, the FBI warned Governor Brown of my presence. While I was overwhelmed with the normal jitters of setting up teaching and research programs in a new and, to me, rather awe-inspiring faculty position, the FBI was feeding material to a Birch Society journal called *Tocsin* and to then Congressman Mulford in order to "discredit" me. Actually it was the Burns (Un-American Committee) report, published eight months after the birth of the FSM, that led to my first acquaintance with any of the major student leaders. A few individuals were impressed by my response to the committee, published in the *San Francisco Chronicle* (June 23, 1965) and sought me out to express their support. Bettina Aptheker became a friend, as did, later still, Mario Savio and quite a few other student activists. The friendship with Bettina, well known as a student Communist, was at once warm and trusting, even though I had left the party more than nine years earlier and was anathema to party chief Gus Hall. With Mario, friendship grew over the years following the FSM and became closer still near the end of his life, when we worked together with others for immigrant rights, against Proposition 187, and for affirmative action, against Proposition 209.

From the beginning, I was very interested in the reactions of faculty and administration to the student "unrest." As of December 3, I put aside my initial hesitations, coauthored with Roger Stanier the emergency faculty telegram to Governor Brown, and helped initiate the meeting of "the 200." My strong predisposition was that the students should be heard and treated with respect. Like many of my colleagues, I was totally opposed to all attempts to meet the demands and concerns of the students with ultimata or police force. Even though I was still new to the club, I could not refrain from taking the floor at Academic Senate meetings, especially as patterns of police action and, eventually, National Guard intervention became more frequent through those turbulent times.

Some of the Senate meetings were memorable, especially those called in emergencies. There is such a thing as an academic style, albeit the forms are diverse, which I often admired but never could claim for myself. I remember the wry humor of English professor Tom Parkinson, the satirical quality of David Krech of psychology, the parliamentary astuteness of Frank Newman of law and Charles Sellers of history. I felt somehow like an immigrant in a new world when I spoke directly and with some passion, which was true to my own background and values, but may have sounded quite strange in the company of scholars. The difference was more of spirit than substance, however, since many other colleagues felt the issues of the time as deeply as I did.

Among the many facets of the FSM story, relived and analyzed by the contributors to this volume, there are two questions that I want to reflect on partly through my own experiences: (1) the intersection of the Regents' anti-Communist policy with its attempted suppression of the FSM, and (2) the continuing influence of the FSM upheaval on UC faculty beyond the FSM period, academic year 1964–1965.

THE REGENTS' ANTI-COMMUNIST BAN

The gulf between the FSM's New Left and the traditional Old Left was apparent to all except perhaps the majority of Regents and the Republican right. However, that distinction failed to discourage efforts to red-bait the FSM and link it to a supposed "Communist conspiracy." I have already referred to the Burns report and *Tocsin,* but the Regents and the UC administration also contributed to this McCarthy-style atmosphere.

Just as the University authorities sought to ban political speech and action by students, they were zealous in applying an official anti-Communist ban intended to keep "reds" off the faculty. This policy was in place long before the FSM and even before the loyalty oath controversy. During the 1960s it assumed renewed importance to the Regents and the UC administration. During this period the Regents claimed veto power, since then formally relinquished, over faculty appointments and promotions. Inevitably, the ban on "Communist" faculty was the excuse for subjecting "suspects" to inquisition by chancellors and undertaking discriminatory measures against perceived troublemakers. When Professor Katz was fired in 1964, the grounds were his refusal to justify to the chancellor his unwillingness to answer questions before HUAC. Similarly, the Regents held up my faculty appointment in July 1964 pending an interview with Chancellor Strong, who was to inform me officially of the anti-Communist ban. (Curiously, when I told Strong that I opposed the ban and would not engage in an examination of my political ideas as a condition for faculty appointment, he was apologetic, regretting that he had to obey the Regents' order even though he shared my viewpoint.) When the Burns committee charged a Communist plot in connection with the FSM, the University's prompt response was to dismiss nonfaculty staff, who were cited in the July 1965 report, and to reaffirm the application of the anti-Communist prohibition to faculty. Predictably, a few years later, some Regents tried to move more broadly to punish faculty members supportive of the FSM and active in opposition to the Vietnam War: the promotions to tenure of Zelnik and Jack Kirsch (biochemistry), having been approved at all levels of the campus review process, were held up by a minority of conservative Regents until strong protests from Chancellor Heyns and Berkeley faculty convinced the Regents to accede.

FACULTY ACTIVATED BY THE FSM

Whereas the FSM focused on student rights and the need for educational reform, attention was turned increasingly beyond the University to society as a whole. After 1964 the antiestablishment mood of the FSM erupted into broader arenas of challenge: to the Vietnam War, to prevailing cultural norms and social institutions, to oppression of racial minorities and people of the Third World. Over the next several years, the chain of student and youth rebellions initiated in Berkeley extended to virtually every U.S. campus, as well as to Paris, Rome, Tokyo, Prague, and numerous other world centers. Although FSM had a rather short life span as an organized entity, the energy it set free soon transformed the Berkeley campus into the foremost center of antiwar protest.

Within the Berkeley faculty, effects from the FSM encounters of 1964–1965 were felt at least through the early 1970s. A few faculty who had supported the FSM's demands were drawn into the administration of Chancellor Heyns and soon found themselves pitted unhappily against student antiwar protestors. In 1966 police were called to arrest students, including Mario Savio, for blocking the activity of Navy recruiters on campus. But many faculty drawn together through the FSM crisis themselves became antiwar activists. The FSM had awakened more than a few faculty to a strong sense of social responsibility and an appreciation of newly formed collegial ties across the boundaries of academic disciplines.

Examination of the FSM's ripple effect on the many social movements that emerged in the latter 1960s and 1970s would be outside the range of this volume's focus. Yet for me, a personal legacy of the FSM was the continuing association in social action with faculty and graduate students first brought together during the FSM. Even before the FSM itself disbanded, the first faculty-sponsored teach-ins on Vietnam were held despite an attempted ban by the Alameda County Board of Supervisors. In 1965 the Faculty Peace Committee (FPC) was formed. That committee met almost weekly when the University was in session and was active through the remaining years of the Vietnam War. Franz Schurmann of sociology and history, Peter Dale Scott of English, and Zelnik wrote *The Politics of Escalation*, one of the first and most convincing books indicting U.S. policy in Vietnam.[2]

The FPC was a unique outfit by the standards of the sixties. It was nonparochial in its interests, pluralistic in its encouragement of the different, sometimes competing approaches to developing peace movements and strategies. Its weekly bull sessions were exchanges of opinion and analysis of world events and local issues. It developed its own projects, supported participation in many others, and, although critical of some of the more extreme tactics of the Vietnam Day Committee, generally avoided issuing pronouncements on the "rights" and "wrongs" of the approaches of other peace groups. As a result, it was essentially free of the kinds of pulling and tearing that grew with the mounting frustrations of the peace movement as the Vietnam War wore on.

Of course there was no escaping some of the skirmishes on the left. Some of us who took part in the big antiwar marches joined with student leaders to defeat Jerry Rubin's dangerous proposal to crash the police lines that barred entry to Oakland. Several of our major projects were in turn attacked by some as "liberal" diversions from more militant encounters.

One FPC highlight was the great public debate on the Vietnam War between Arthur Goldberg, U.S. Ambassador to the United Nations, and Franz Schurmann, representing the FPC. It was held on March 25, 1966, before thousands of excited students in a packed Harmon Gym, with loud-speakers set up outside for the large overflow crowd. Goldberg had been invited to receive an honorary degree on Charter Day, which aroused strong campus protest. The debate, unprecedented in that it directly involved a high-level spokesman of the Johnson administration, completely overshad-owed the degree-granting ritual performed earlier in the Greek Theatre. Despite the tension surrounding the event and the provocative quality of the ambassador's argument in defense of the war, the huge crowd held back its response, maintaining a remarkable silence, until after the vote that Reggie Zelnik, who presided, promised would take place at the debate's conclusion. Then Goldberg was given a message to take back to Johnson: a loud and dramatic vote by the assemblage of about seven thousand, with barely more than a score on the other side, to condemn the war and gov-ernment policy in Vietnam.

The Vietnam Commencement, convened on May 17, 1968, by a student-faculty group known as the Campus Draft Opposition, was as large and impressive a ceremony as the Berkeley campus has seen. At the event, which I chaired, 773 draft-eligible students, many of them graduating seniors, took a public oath declaring, "Our war in Vietnam is unjust and immoral. As long as the United States is involved in this war I will not serve in the Armed Forces." About eight thousand students and faculty gathered in Sproul Plaza to honor and support them in the face of a Regents' ban on the observance. On the eve of the "illegal" gathering, Governor Reagan demanded that dis-ciplinary action be instituted against any faculty who participated. The response of three hundred members of the faculty was to publicly endorse the ceremony and to stand together on the steps of Sproul Hall during the proceedings. This was one of the rare occasions when Reagan and the Regents backed down, and no punitive action followed.

MEETING GOVERNOR REAGAN

I will not try to describe faculty involvement with students in projects of which I was not a part. Quite a few faculty were enthusiastic backers of Peo-ple's Park, which was created on an unused, run-down plot of UC-owned land taken over by student and community activists. While not unsympa-thetic to those who in the late sixties tried to create islands of freedom from dominant cultural and institutional controls, I was not swept up in the excitement and symbolism of People's Park.

In the end, however, no one on the campus could escape the ramifica-tions of People's Park. Buckshot fired by massed police, tear gas released from swooping helicopters, National Guard bayonets surrounding the cam-pus on orders of Governor Reagan, all of this left no sanctuary for a passive observer. One person was killed and another blinded by police fire. With the National Guard out in full force, Berkeley was close to becoming what

Kent State became one year later. In this setting, on May 21, 1969, seventeen professors took off for Sacramento to see if we could prevail on legislators to use their influence to call off the Guard and reduce the risk of greater tragedy. We took our mission very seriously, did not seek publicity that might jeopardize our effort, and did not ask to see the Governor, so as not to risk an inflammatory confrontation.

Governor Reagan, however, had a different agenda. As we talked with individual legislators and felt we were making headway, a message came that he wanted to see us. At the small auditorium to which we were summoned, we entered into a media event. Television cameras from all of the networks and dozens of reporters were there. Then Reagan came in and strode to the podium as the cameras flashed.

Nobel laureate Owen Chamberlain spoke for us and quietly began to tell the governor why we had come. He got no further than a sentence or two when the governor took over. Waving a pointed finger at us, he declared that "you professors" are responsible for all the violence, "you" told your students that they could break the law. Reagan went on, lecturing and accusing the eggheads for the benefit of the evening TV news and the morning headlines.

Here my story of that day becomes more personal. Fearing that our mission was ending in a disastrous propaganda coup for the governor, I interrupted his monologue and said something like, "That's a fine political speech, Governor, but we came here to talk reason, to see what can be done to avoid further violence." I will not try to reproduce the back and forth debate of the next fifteen or so minutes. Thanks to the governor, it was all captured on TV by eager crews who were unabashedly delighted by the rare unstaged drama. Reagan demanded at once to know "who are you?" then said he knew my name well and wouldn't be surprised at anything I said. When I said that the governor was responsible for the atmosphere of intimidation, for trying to run the campus by bayonet, for firing and threatening to fire any University administrator who might be willing to negotiate, he exploded with rage and shouted "liar."

That whole scene inevitably received a great deal of publicity, worldwide, most of it favorable to our faculty plea. My instant notoriety brought me a flood of letters, about half of them congratulatory. The other half was hate mail full of anti-Semitic and other racist vulgarity. There were death threats, including a funeral wreath. A paramilitary group wrote that it voted by a slim margin to permit me to finish out the semester, after which I would be terminated if I ever tried to teach again.

FACULTY-STUDENT INTERACTIONS

One campus crisis followed another in the aftermath of the FSM, reaching to crescendos of antagonism over People's Park and, earlier in 1969, the

Third World Strike. Hostility to student activism became more pronounced within the faculty as issues and grievances became more diverse, as the campus became more chaotic, and as the University came under intense economic and political fire especially from the governor.

The Third World Strike and its demands for a college or school of Third World studies probably aroused deeper feelings of opposition among faculty than any other campus movement of the time. Nor did it receive impressive support from most of the student body. The intensity of faculty hostility to the strike is explained only in part by its militancy and the fact that "trashing" sorties around campus, involving physical damage, were becoming a new fashion. Charges of racism against the faculty were rampant, and this was hard to take. A small but highly accomplished number of faculty were justly proud of their academic contributions in areas of history and sociology relevant to the experience of African Americans and other minorities. A sizable segment of the faculty, secure in its elite self-image, feared that opening the door to ethnic studies and corresponding new faculty appointments implied the erosion of "academic excellence." The campus administration was actually more sensitive than the faculty to the need for positive measures to meet legitimate criticism of the University's de facto exclusionary stance toward aspiring students and faculty of color.

Beyond free speech, the thrust of the FSM—at least for Mario Savio and many other participants—was educational reform. The idea was to change the university, to humanize it and make it more democratic. A recurrent theme in Mario's speeches was the need to expand and elevate the faculty-student interaction while reducing the role of administration. Many students were very critical of faculty, their perceived lack of interest in teaching, their political timidity and educational conservatism. Yet with time, some faculty and students were able to form a very productive and warm relationship while devising serious programs for educational reform to recommend to the Academic Senate. The most significant contribution was the report *The Culture of the University*, produced by a joint student and faculty Study Commission on University Governance, co-chaired by Law Professor Caleb Foote and a History graduate student, the late Henry Mayer.[3] The general mood of the faculty, however, was less and less favorable to reform as turbulence continued to shake the campus. One last big movement for change erupted at the end of 1972 when the University was "reconstituted" for a few days in the wake of President Nixon's bombing of Cambodia. Impatience with the University and anger over its service to the military-industrial complex merged with outrage over the expanding war. Once again, many thousands of students brought "business as usual" to a dramatic halt. A minority of faculty, with Sheldon Wolin of political science in the lead, worked with student leaders to develop constructive educational models that would make the University more vital in those difficult times.

However, the symbolic "reconstitution" was short-lived. Its aftermath was a determined and ultimately successful effort to restore faculty control to a traditionalist establishment. The Academic Senate was gutted by the formation of a so-called Representative Assembly, which excluded direct participation by most faculty. The Assembly, which lasted only a few years, was ineffectual except for its "dog in the manger" role, replacing general meetings of the faculty where significant debates and action had once occurred.

WHAT DID THE FSM ACHIEVE?

The legacy of the FSM is not to be found in an altered University, one whose basic character became significantly more humane and democratic. True, the embarrassingly crude restrictions on free speech that triggered the rebellion were scrapped, and there is now on the Berkeley campus more concern and respect for students than was evident in 1964. But in the late 1990s, with the Regents dominated by then governor Pete Wilson and Ward Connerly, UC was pressured more than ever to buckle under to political demands that distort its educational mission. With the explosion of new technologies, the University is involved with and beholden to outside corporate interests on a level that could hardly be imagined in 1964.[4]

The real successes of the FSM are larger than might appear from any analysis of educational reform. Like the Civil Rights Movement, the FSM broke the pattern of passivity toward injustice at a very critical time in our national history, on the eve of the crisis over the Vietnam War. Its spirit of challenge to authority grew into a generational refusal to conform to society's more arbitrary, often hypocritical norms of behavior and human relationships. Although the youth movements of the sixties did not themselves overcome patterns of sexism, they provided impetus for the feminist groundswell that followed. Similarly, though the FSM reflected the lack of racial and ethnic diversity of the University, its spirit catalyzed subsequent struggles to expand access and establish departments of African American, Chicano, and other ethnic studies.

When some look back at the sixties, they tend to remember disorder, emotionalism, and educational chaos. But Berkeley was in significant ways more, not less, of a university at that time. Whatever confusion and even nonsense was in the air, we engaged issues, dealt with ideas and with each other as people across the territorial confines of particular academic disciplines.

Universities provide educational and leadership continuity that keeps the wheels of society turning. But learning produces questioning of established ways. Moreover, the university functions by the continuous flow into its midst of new generations, those who are most prone to challenge the old and, periodically, to kick over the traces. Contrary to academia's "ivory tower" image, faculty are not insulated from society's expectations, nor from its positive inducements, nor from its negative pressures. The challenge of youth, however, exerts its own pressure, sometimes pushing ideas from strictly intellectual to moral ground as well. That can infect faculty, and that's what the FSM did for a time for some of us.

The FSM is history, but the phenomenon will show up again not as pale repetition but in the language and style of another generation that refuses to believe there is nothing new under the sun.

NOTES

1. The sequel to this little story came years later, when I got some of my FBI files under the Freedom of Information Act. Although only the acting chancellor and I had been in the room during our conversation on December 7, an FBI file carried the report of that encounter, taking note of my very unwelcome advice. Was President Kerr's office in regular liaison with the FBI, or was this a special function of the FSM emergency?

2. Franz Schurmann, Peter Dale Scott, and Reginald Zelnik, *The Politics of Escalation in Vietnam: A Citizen's White Paper,* with a forward by Arthur Schlesinger, Jr., and a summary and conclusions by Carl E. Schorske (Boston: Beacon Press, 1966).

3. Caleb Foote, Henry Mayer, and Associates, *The Culture of the University: Governance and Education* (San Francisco: Jossey-Bass, 1968).

4. Eyal Press and Jennifer Washburn, "The Kept University," *Atlantic Monthly,* Mar. 2000, 39–54.

The Berkeley Free Speech Movement and the Campus Ministry

Keith Chamberlain

When asked whether I could make a contribution to this volume on the Free Speech Movement, my first reaction was to say, "Under no circumstances." The episode was too remote from my present existence. And what could I say after thirty-five years had elapsed, especially since I had spent almost all that time in Europe, far from Berkeley and the United States? However, after looking at the scarce written material I could find in my still-to-be-resorted stacks from my last move, from Bad Vilbel back to Frankfurt, I reconsidered. Whether my selective memory will do justice to colleagues, friends, opponents, and the events themselves is of course uncertain. But was my selective judgment back then, when I wrote one report after another about the unfolding events, necessarily more reliable?

In 1964–1965 the Berkeley campus was generously endowed with people—not all of them clergy—working in the campus ministries (generously, that is, if we compare the numbers to the leaner years that followed). It is my recollection that, when the free speech controversy began, there was a general sense of sympathy for the protesting students and their cause among these campus ministry people. I can remember only two colleagues who strongly dissented. At the monthly meetings of the Campus Ecumenical Council we were always confronted with hot news and new crises. For us it was a time of good feeling and interesting problems. I particularly remember our close communication and cooperation with the rabbi Joe Gumbiner and the Roman Catholic priest Jim Fisher.

Some of us were more directly involved with the FSM than others. I was particularly close to the conflict because the FSM Executive Committee frequently met at Westminster House, the campus ministry center of the Presbyterian Church. I was substituting there that year for the regular University pastor, John Hadsell, who was on sabbatical year in Nigeria. I therefore enjoyed more institutional independence and flexibility than some of my colleagues, who were more closely tied to routine duties and long-term projects. It was also my good fortune to have a number of close contacts among young Berkeley faculty members, particularly in the history department.

Although church-related students were not prominent in the FSM leadership, they were quite active in the movement, and a fairly high percentage of those arrested in Sproul Hall on December 3 were members of campus religious organizations. In my own contacts with FSM movers and shakers I almost never encountered any significant antichurch prejudices. Some were pleasantly surprised by our openness to their position; others took it for granted, being fully aware of our common experience in the Civil Rights Movement. I remember a number of late-night conversations with FSM leaders following their intense meetings on matters of content, strategy, and tactics. To be sure, nobody sought any pastoral counseling from me, but many were interested in talking and sharing. This was particularly true of Mario Savio and Steve Weissman, two leading members of the FSM Steering Committee, and I can remember many other conversations with FSMers in other circumstance as well.

In cooperation with my colleague Joan Nash Eakin (recently deceased), I was also responsible for a weekly program with thirty students who lived in the Westminster House dorm. Usually we considered theological or ethical questions, and we naturally talked about the campus struggles. All these students were at least tolerant of the FSM, many were supportive, and a handful became FSM activists. With fierce loyalty, Joan (who was a permanent staff person) defended me from critics who felt that I was spending too much of my time with rebellious students. I shall always remain grateful for her support.

At the time, there were others in the campus ministry doing creative work with the involved students, faculty, and members of the University administration. Because I knew too little about their work, I will not attempt to describe their specific roles here; but what we all had in common was, I think, a desire to enable some students and faculty members to meet, plan, and organize, a willingness to make our facilities available to them. At the same time, we took on the task of interpreting the unfolding campus events to our church constituencies, who were, for the most part, dependent on hostile media for their information on the FSM and its activities.

In fact, my own sympathy for the FSM owed much to its outrageous treatment at the hands of the media. Endlessly repeated disparaging terms such as "the *so-called* Free Speech Movement," "the mob," and "Berkeley's Red Square" were characteristic of much of the polemical and mindless reporting. With all their faults, the student protesters were still the unfairly treated underdogs. (Incidentally, one annoying example of these faults was the habit some students had of putting out their cigarettes on our hardwood floors in Westminster House's large meeting hall. I became very tired of passing out ashtrays and admonishing students to use them and not the floor.)

In retrospect, I would characterize my own position toward the FSM as one of critical solidarity (a way of describing my work I learned to use some years later). This solidarity was only in part a result of the students' unfair treatment at the hands of the media (and others), noted above. The claim they put forth for the freedom to express oneself in a university context seemed to me to be both important and legitimate, but even more basic was the students' commitment to social justice, however diffuse or (frequently) tainted by arrogance it may have been.

The task of interpreting the controversy to my own church was crucial for my ministry, and I think, in retrospect, that I was fairly successful. Those in positions of authority read my reports and articles and were generally supportive. Many were grateful to ascertain that the representatives of our church were not totally irrelevant to the dramatic developments on campus. Extremely hostile reactions came from some (usually older) men in local congregations, who neither read my reports nor showed any interest in my attempts to describe and analyze the conflict. These tended to be the same folks who were uneasy and distressed by the church's role in the Civil Rights and emerging anti–Vietnam War movements.

At the end of academic year 1964–1965, after a summer with the Delta Ministry in Greenwood, Mississippi, I moved to Berlin to work with the German Christian Student Movement (Evangelische Studentengemeinde) and the World Student Christian Federation. Moving from Berkeley to Berlin was somewhat like jumping from the frying pan into the frying pan. The Berlin student rebellion against a hierarchically organized university that showed little interest in the consequences of its teaching and research was approaching full bloom. It was encouraged by a militant and surprisingly well informed movement against U.S. intervention in Vietnam and the German government's support for that intervention.

The revolt in the German universities was less spontaneous than the one in Berkeley. It was largely a product of intense political education by the German SDS (Sozialistische Deutsche Studentenbund), which had once been the student arm of the Social Democratic Party (SPD). This group had moved to a much more radical critique of postwar European society than the SPD and had adopted or rediscovered a Marxist mode of thinking. This neo-Marxist renaissance was a new phenomenon in postwar Germany and was instrumental in mobilizing impressive student movements in France and Italy as well. The whole development came to an explosive culmination in 1968, when the May events in Paris in particular expressed the depth and breadth of the new consciousness and the new ways of addressing the glaring contradictions in Western European societies. Nor was the German SDS the only campus organization in that country to radicalize students during this period. Had that been the case, the 1968 Vietnam Congress in Berlin, attended by thousands of students, would have been a more lonely affair.

I had the good fortune to become acquainted with two charismatic figures in their respective movements—Mario Savio in Berkeley and Rudi Dutschke in Berlin. It may be worth noting a few similarities and differences, a comparison that should give us a clue to understanding their separate historical contexts. (I hasten to add that I do not identify these two figures with the totality of the broad and complex movements that they represented.) Both Mario and Rudi were highly intelligent, courageous young men, uniquely able to articulate the feelings of students and others at mass gatherings. Both are now gone. Rudi died in 1980 of the delayed effects of a 1968 assassination attempt; Mario suffered a fatal heart attack in 1996. Mario, on one hand, was deeply and actively committed to the struggle for social justice. He had participated in projects with poor people and with those engaged in the struggle for their civil and human rights. It seems significant to me that it was he, and not some experienced representative of a traditional political organization, who became the principal public spokesman for the FSM.

Rudi, on the other hand, was a more academic and structured speaker. For years in the early sixties he had been involved in the intensive (German) SDS debates and deliberations. His choice of words reflected the theoretical language that characterized the social and economic analysis of SDS. But he was very able to communicate with others and, indeed, became the best-known articulator of the ideas of the German student movement—and, by the same token, the figure most hated by that movement's enemies.

Both Mario and Rudi were characterized by a highly moral sensitivity. Both were interested in the religious dimensions of history and society (Rudi was married to an American theology student), and both, in spite of their strongly differing languages and biographies, represented the open-ended, nondogmatic, radical stance of the sixties. Sadly, this morally motivated movement deteriorated in the ensuing years in both countries. Political sectarianism gained ground, mutual mistrust grew, and the "more correct than thou" groups became enormously influential in the declining and ever more fragmented political movements.

Must we then conclude that the freshness of the undogmatic political radicalism of the mid-sixties, as exemplified by the FSM, was only a straw in the wind? inevitably destined to end up in the garbage heap of history? I doubt this. Nor should the FSM phenomenon be seen as unrelated to other creative historical episodes, such as the Paris Commune, the Prague

Spring, the peace movements of the eighties. Taken together, these histori-cal experiences form a body of tradition, one on which we can and must draw if we are to work effectively to accomplish the task described by the World Council of Churches as "Justice, Peace and the Integrity of Cre-ation." In drawing hope and wisdom from these traditions (including all their shades of gray), we would do well to remember these words of the French socialist Jean Jaurès: "To be loyal to a tradition means to be loyal to the flames and not to the ashes."

Fall of 1964 at Berkeley

Confrontation Yields to Reconciliation

Clark Kerr

As the Boeing rose from the Narita airport on its long flight from Tokyo to San Francisco in mid-September 1964, I began to think again in an organized way about the University of California. I had been gone for nearly two months. I had left word not to interfere with my trip except for real emergencies. I had heard nothing from or about the University. Vice President Harry Wellman was in charge, and I had total confidence in his good judgment. I had seen an occasional *Herald Tribune* out of Paris left lying around on benches by American tourists, and I knew that there had been a long, hot summer in the South over civil rights. Otherwise I had been fully engaged by my trip, which had included a short vacation in the Greek Islands with my family and the family of a college friend. Then I had participated in a series of seminars in Yugoslavia, Czechoslovakia, Poland, and Moscow, discussing the apparent disintegration of the Communist system. The other Americans in these seminars were my colleagues in a project on the evolution of labor-management relations as the industrial system spread worldwide.[1] We thought we saw an ongoing process of convergence on "best practice." The best practice we thought we saw emerging out of worldwide industrialization was democracy in politics and welfare capitalism in economics. We observed the monolithic governance systems and monopolistic economic production systems, combined under overwhelming communist centralized power, decaying. As it turned out, we were twenty years ahead of actual events. At the end of the trip, I spent an intense week in Hong Kong and then an equally intense week in Tokyo as we opened new University of California Study Abroad programs.

As the airplane gained altitude, I began reviewing where the University of California stood. Everything looked good to me: that spring Berkeley had been rated as "the best balanced distinguished university" in the

United States, ahead of Harvard—a great triumph and a mild surprise—April 1964. As president of the University, along with the Board of Regents, I had been awarded the Alexander Meiklejohn Award for contributions to academic freedom by the American Association of University Professors (AAUP). A few years earlier the university had been on the AAUP's "blacklist" for the loyalty oath imposed by the Board of Regents. The Meiklejohn Award was another great triumph—April 1964. Three new campuses (San Diego, Irvine, Santa Cruz) were on schedule to open in fall 1965, all on spectacular sites. The Santa Barbara, Riverside, Davis, and San Francisco campuses were being reoriented and increasing their status within the University and within American higher education. Four years earlier, in 1960, the state legislature had endorsed the Master Plan for Higher Education by a vote of 119–1 (senate and assembly combined). The Master Plan was a major event initiating a worldwide movement toward universal access to higher education, guaranteeing for the first time in history that there would be a place in higher education for every high school graduate and persons otherwise qualified. It had also settled the assignments of missions and students to the University, state colleges, and community colleges; and the University had kept its sole possession of the most advanced degrees. The management of the University had been decentralized following my recommendations. Administrative authority had been mostly delegated to the chancellors, who were in reality now the executive heads of their campuses. The size of the president's staff had been cut by three-quarters. This had been the largest structural change in the whole history of the University. Faculty members had been granted continuous tenure for the first time. Lack of such tenure had made possible the loyalty oath controversy of 1949–1952 and the dismissal of faculty members. The University fully enjoyed free speech, as we then understood it to be defined by the courts. The University now permitted Communist speakers on its campuses for the first time in history—a very controversial action during that McCarthyite period. The courts, however, were in the early process of extending free speech to include other forms of expression, but we in the administration and on the Board of Regents were not yet aware of this. ROTC had been made voluntary, as students had long demanded. The University of California led the nation in making this change. A small "equality of opportunity" outreach program had been introduced (1963) to encourage greater attendance by minority students. Fraternities and sororities were being required to open their memberships to previously excluded groups. The University was as ready as it could be to face the oncoming tidal wave of students that had been my overwhelming concern for the past six years.

So I sat there in my airplane seat thinking that my initial six years as president had been well spent and that all was for the best (but still not perfect) for the University of California in what was not the best of all possible worlds, that all the battles I had fought had been worthwhile, and that easier times were ahead. The oncoming year, 1964–1965, should be a good one and certainly easier than the years that had gone before it—both the University and I deserved a less strenuous year, a time to relax.

However, I knew that I had one big task ahead: to do everything I could to ensure victory for the state bond issue on the ballot that fall. The $380 million bond issue included money to help the new campuses prepare to open and to assure that the existing campuses were equipped to accept vast numbers of new students. The passage of that bond issue was the greatest imperative. I knew I would have to travel the state, under conditions of increasing exhaustion, to carry the heaviest burden of this campaign. But I believed in it completely and was ready to endure the rigors of it—all those prospective students waiting to be served! (The bond issue of 1964 was carried, under what turned out to be very difficult circumstances, by a 64.8 percent majority.)

The University would continue "spreading light and goodness over all the West," as its alma mater promised. These were my reflections and my dreams as the Boeing crossed the Pacific Ocean.

I stopped intermittently dozing and thinking about what a good year we had ahead as the airplane landed at San Francisco Airport. And soon began the reality of the fall of 1964—the time of my greatest troubles.

. . .

The emphasis of this essay is on conciliation. This is not to suggest that confrontation, the major theme of most of the essays in this volume, was not important. It was important to setting the agenda. But it was conciliation that was essential to working out the solutions.

I consider this essay a "sketch" because it covers in abbreviated form a complicated and multifaceted series of events. No short and simple outline can do them justice. Those who wish to read a more extensive treatment of these events should see *The Gold and the Blue*, volume 2, which includes my account of the Free Speech Movement (FSM) as I saw it unfold in the fall of 1964.[2] Here I shall confine myself mostly to some concluding observations about that period from the point of view of a participant looking back more than thirty-five years later.

My major themes in this essay are:

(1) The basic frontstage issue: advocacy. There was a central issue of policy: should the university permit on its property political "advocacy" activities in addition to the already protected free speech as it was then narrowly defined? "Advocacy" included raising money and recruiting participants for off-campus activities—some of them potentially and even knowingly

illegal, as part of the Civil Rights Movement. In the end this issue was settled in the affirmative, as the FSM demanded, but with restrictions important to the University—restrictions with one of which, however, some leaders of the FSM strongly disagreed. These restrictions were "time, place, and
manner" rules, retention of control over student discipline by the Board of
Regents and the administration, and the continuation of the standard limitations on free speech as the courts had sanctioned them in applying the
First Amendment. It was the second of these with which the FSM disagreed.

The administration and Regents at that time made a distinction between
advocacy and the free speech we thought we had assured at great cost,
including enduring attacks by the state legislature's Committee on Un-
American Activities, which charged that I had opened up the University
to Communism.[3] We made exactly the same distinction between political
speech and advocacy as had long been made between discussion of
the impact of religious movements and beliefs in academic courses, on
one hand, and on-campus evangelism—that is, recruitment of religious
converts—on the other. However, I know of no serious debate prior
to 1964 over the fine points of free speech policy at the University. The
historic policy, as far as I can understand it, was to keep the University
out of political controversy, lest such controversy disrupt both external
political and internal academic relations. The central theme was neutrality
in politics.

Whereas the University was trying to protect itself from internal and
external disruptions of its academic missions, this effort was interpreted by
politically active students and faculty as an effort to stifle the Civil Rights
Movement. This it was not. In fact, the University was engaged in other
activities to advance civil rights: the inauguration of outreach programs for
minorities, the demand that fraternities and sororities reject discrimination in their admission policies, the opening up of opportunities in higher
education for all high school graduates, and the policy of refusal to penalize students for their off-campus civil rights activities, as some powerful
forces were demanding. The University was pro civil rights but it was anti
use of its facilities for external political purposes.

The distinction between speech and advocacy was long-standing in University policy. It dated back at least to February 15, 1935, when Regulation
5 by President Sproul was first published. This regulation said that "the
University assumes the right to prevent exploitation of its prestige . . . by
those who would use it as a platform for propaganda." It went on to say
"that its members, as individuals and as citizens, shall likewise always
respect—and not exploit, their University connection," and that "the University expects the State, in return, and to its own great gain, to protect this
indispensable freedom" of the University. The phrase "in return" indicated
an implied contract of reciprocal rights and responsibilities.

Before 1964 University authorities had not carefully thought through the distinction between speech and advocacy. When they finally did so, under great pressure, they ended up reluctantly changing University policy—and this was *before* the U.S. Supreme Court decisions, beginning in 1968, that clearly associated a broader notion of "free expression" with free speech. In late 1964, the University thus adopted a policy that was, for at least three years, more liberal than the rulings of the Supreme Court. However, we had been more concerned just prior to that time with clearing up the older and more repressive policies toward "free speech" of the Sproul years than with opening our minds to an expansion of opportunities for "free expression." We were oriented backward, not forward.

The implicit contract of 1935 was that the state would respect the academic freedom of the University and the University, in turn, would not allow its facilities to be used as a "platform for propaganda." The University was a place to "give play to intellect rather than to passion"—an ivory tower uncontaminated by the emotions of social conflict.

This was, to be sure, an antiseptic view of the University that worked well as long as no one vigorously challenged it, which was for a considerable period of time. It was, however, a point of potential vulnerability that was not properly anticipated. The message was that the University was not to be used to promote political or religious causes. Regulation 5 also said that "the University of California is the creature of the State and its loyalty to the State will never waver."

The president and Regents at the start of fall 1964 favored free intellectual discussion of political issues but did not want the University turned into a fortress from which students could set forth, often with illegal intent, to attack selected elements of society by raising money and recruiting participants on campus for off-campus political actions. It was believed, and with good reason, that this would politicize the University both in its academic life and in its relations with society. The University was an educational institution, not a political party or a church.

We thus looked on the "Free *Speech* Movement" as the "Free *Advocacy* Movement," which in fact it was, with the internal and external results we envisaged.

My reasons for disagreement with the policy on advocacy after the September 14 edict were that historically it was accompanied by the Sather Gate arrangement, which had by now been taken away, and that to try to enforce it on campus against stubborn resistance would create a police state atmosphere.

Among many other things, the controversy between UC and the FSM obscured the University's recent major contributions to free speech, including accepting Communists as speakers on campus, authorizing a wide spectrum of student groups to invite speakers of their own choosing, and assuring students that we would not punish them for political activities off campus as had been possible in earlier times. Our campaign to extend free speech as we then understood it was being appropriated by persons who had not fought the earlier battles or endured the consequences. By changing the definition of free speech to include advocacy, they were engaged, with great success, in transforming me overnight from a courageous and successful defender of free speech and winner of academe's most prestigious award into a reactionary opponent of free advocacy. I thought I had been the true leader of free speech within the University of California, as attested by the AAUP, and not the enemy of free speech.

(2) The secondary backstage issue: confrontation versus conciliation. There was a second issue relating to tactics: would the differing parties follow tactics of confrontation or conciliation? This came to involve three subsidiary conflicts: (a) within the administration (defined as the Regents and the top campus and University administrators), (b) within the faculty, and (c) within the groups of activist students. The conciliatory factions won out within the administration and faculty while the confrontational faction won out narrowly among the students until it eventually faded away, but something resembling that confrontational group was shortly resurrected in protests against the Vietnam War.

To settle the frontstage conflict over policy, it was essential to work out the three backstage conflicts over tactics in the way they actually were resolved— with conciliation victorious in two of them and the third withering away. The public saw the frontstage and front-page conflict, while the participants were mostly waging their intense backstage conflicts among themselves. It was a four-ring circus, and one had to watch what was going on in all four rings to understand the total situation.

I define *confrontation* as including aggressive speech and actions, hostile behavior, antagonistic allegations; and *conciliation* as actions and speech to encourage goodwill, to narrow differences, to promote agreement. Within confrontation, there are options over whether to rely on persuasive tactics, including mass assemblies, petitions, and consultations, or more coercive tactics, such as disturbing public meetings, obstructing the use of university facilities, and capturing a police car. Thus there was not only a choice to be made between conciliatory and confrontational approaches but, within confrontation tactics, between more persuasive methods, such as aggressive consultations, and more coercive ones, such as capture of a police car (by radical students) and use of external police (by campus authorities). There is a similar range of choices within the rubric of conciliation. It is a long continuum from all-out conciliation to all-out confrontation, with many choices to be made. A choice by one player of course affects the choice by the opponent.

WHY THEN?

The 1960s were the most likely decade for a student revolt in all of American history: The civil rights conflict was the most painful internal dispute in the United States since the Civil War; the Vietnam War, which took place in the same decade, was the most bitter controversy over external affairs since the War of Independence from Britain. The situation of undergraduates at the big American research universities had deteriorated after World War II during the rise of what I have elsewhere called the "federal grant university."[4] Many faculty had come to concentrate narrowly on their research and on their graduate students as billions of federal dollars were poured into university research. Berkeley was rated in 1964 as the "best balanced distinguished university" in the country, ahead of Harvard, a rating based mainly on its research accomplishments. Senior faculty members also became more involved in off-campus consultations, and more and more student contacts were turned over to teaching assistants and non-tenured faculty. Many students who came to the University with "romantic" expectations for a nurturing undergraduate environment were disappointed.[5]

Though often cited as the main reason, however, academic dissatisfaction was not really central to the "student revolt" in 1964, as I had wrongly predicted it would be in my 1963 Godkin Lectures at Harvard.[6] The revolt of 1964 was basically about dissatisfactions with off-campus conditions involving civil rights and lack of on-campus opportunities to oppose them. Students were also troubled over the recent assassination of President Kennedy, the new nuclear threats to world peace and even survival, and U.S. policy toward Cuba. To them, the world they were inheriting seemed to be going downhill fast. Academic dissatisfactions were background music, but activist students mostly were upset by developments in the surrounding society in relation to civil rights. At the same time they decried the limited scope on the campus itself for their oppositional activities.

Students around the world were taking part in national affairs as never before. After World War II there were anticolonial insurrections all around the planet, many of them student led. Most recently, student revolts had taken place in Cuba and Japan. Also, there were many more university students concentrated into larger institutions. Student power was a new force on the world map. It would explode throughout much of the industrialized world in 1968.

WHY BERKELEY?

Berkeley was big and thus had a large recruiting pool for political activists; it was located in a geographical area of left-wing political activity; it was academically elite and thus had a great many very bright, alert, self-confident, and sometimes even arrogant students willing and able to take leadership.

As a public university, it was subject to direct gubernatorial and legislative interferences and had a board of trustees who were more often political appointees than alumni and friends of the University, as at private institutions. Berkeley also had a historical ambiance of a liberal-radical flavor that attracted sympathetic students and faculty members. In this respect, it was part of a small group of politically active campuses that included the University of Wisconsin at Madison and City College of New York. The Berkeley campus was also encrusted with an unusual layer of restrictive rules limiting student political activities—beginning with Regulation 5 (1935). A staff study I initiated in fall 1964 revealed that no other Bay Area campus had such restrictive rules on student political activity or any rules at all.[7]

Berkeley was also crowded. It had 27,500 students in fall 1964 on a campus built for 15,000. This led to more impersonal responses to students. Once devoted to agriculture, engineering, and science, the campus was now completing a process of adding strength in the social sciences and humanities, whence came most of the student and faculty political activists. And as we built University-owned residence halls and assisted the growth of cooperative housing, we vastly increased the number of students living on or near the campus as compared to the numbers of traditional commuters scattered and living under home influences. Residence hall development also reduced the influence in student life of the more politically moderate fraternities and sororities.

Berkeley is in the San Francisco Bay area, home to Henry George, Jack London, the IWW ("Wobblies"), the San Francisco General Strike of 1934, the ILWU (the International Longshoremen's and Warehousemen's Union of Harry Bridges), Henry Miller and other avant-garde writers, and, more recently, the loyalty oath controversy of 1949 and HUAC disturbances of 1960. It was an exciting place for artists, intellectuals, and dissidents as well as for faculty and students. It was the Left Bank of the Paris of the Far West.

The University was in the midst of a fundamental historical change. It had been a one-campus university until 1919, when UCLA (then the "Southern Branch") was added. It was now becoming a nine-campus university, expanding academic missions at Davis, Santa Barbara, Riverside, and San Francisco, and creating new campuses at Santa Cruz, Irvine, and San Diego. These developments had major effects on Berkeley, no longer one of one but one of *nine* campuses, part of a larger system. Berkeley lost its dominance and became subject to control by and competition with others. Consequent resentment within the Berkeley faculty reached a peak when it was required in the mid-1960s, as part of a universitywide regental policy, to move temporarily to year-round operations. Thus, when the student revolt began in September 1964, much of the faculty was already in a contentious mood, exacerbated by some professors' growing dissatisfaction with Chancellor Edward Strong, particularly with his hard line in the Katz case.[8]

Another consequence of the University's growth was the decentralization of its administration. Historically, a single president with great ability and a huge staff had micromanaged all parts of the University, still primarily Berkeley, as though it were a single campus. Chancellors, first appointed at Berkeley and Los Angeles (1952), were first given wide authority, particularly in the area of student affairs, when I became president in 1958. With authority now divided, separate campus and universitywide policies might conflict with one another, as happened in the fall of 1964 when the president and the Berkeley chancellor came into contention over the conduct of student affairs. At least three chancellors, including Strong, tried to assert their authority against the president and even the Regents. Some chancellors were testing the limits of their power, acting as if they were heads of independent institutions like Harvard or Stanford, with no one above them except their own trustees.

Decentralization made it necessary to codify past regental and presidential practices in order to guide campus administrators, including in the area of student affairs. What actually occurred in this area was that President Sproul's past practices were assembled and recorded by members of my staff, a codification that was popularly identified as the "Kerr Directives" (1959). They were interpreted by activists as if they were a new and heavy burden of rules. In fact, the only changes made were liberalizing ones, as some activist opponents ultimately conceded.[9]

During decentralization, the old rules on student political involvement were greatly liberalized. For example: (a) Student organizations were allowed to invite outside speakers on their own, including on political issues; this was the "open forum." (b) In this period of the Cold War, even pro-Soviet Communists were allowed to speak on campus for the first time in University history. (c) An area (the famous 26-by-40-foot strip of public sidewalk on Bancroft Way) was set aside by the Board of Regents at the edge of the Berkeley campus for "advocacy" activities (raising money and recruiting participants for off-campus projects) as the campus border moved south to Bancroft Way, displacing the old Sather Gate free advocacy area, which had also been on city property.

These liberalizations alarmed the Burns Committee on Un-American Activities of the California state senate. I was accused of "opening the campus to communist officials." I was even at one point personally charged by Senator Burns with serving as a Communist agent!—an important background factor in my later dismissal as president of the University.[10]

On the liberal side, but with no apparent favorable consequences on campus, in the spring of 1964 the AAUP bestowed on me and the Board of Regents the Alexander Meiklejohn Award for contributions to academic freedom. A few years earlier the University had been blacklisted by the AAUP because of the loyalty oath. So the AAUP was now recognizing that a huge reorientation in outlook had taken place. Whereas in 1952 and 1956 Adlai Stevenson, candidate for president of the United States, was not allowed to speak on the Berkeley campus, in July 1963 A. J. (Mickey) Lima, an official of the Communist Party, was allowed to speak—an enormous policy change. I invited Stevenson to be the Charter Day speaker at Berkeley in 1964—a great occasion, intended and accepted as an apology for his exclusion in 1952 and 1956.

These, then, were key elements of the situation on the Berkeley campus as of September 1, 1964: the campus had total "free speech" as we then understood it to be narrowly defined by the courts and by the Regents—as *talk*. Advocacy activities were permitted on the 26-by-40-foot strip that the Regents had agreed (in 1959) to set aside on my and then Chancellor Seaborg's recommendation, by offering it to the city of Berkeley for such purposes. I thought the University had only one major disagreement with politically active students. Although it allowed officers of the Associated Students of the University of California (ASUC) to take political positions in their own names, using their official titles, it did not allow them to claim to speak in the name of the student body as a whole. Student leaders complained that this kept them penned into a "sandbox" when they wanted to participate in national and world affairs, but it was actually a very big "sandbox," the only limitation being that they could not claim to represent the entire student body. The Regents were not willing to force all students to belong to and pay dues to a partisan political organization, nor was I. We offered to let the ASUC become voluntary, but this was not acceptable to the activists.

This issue has now been partially settled by the U.S. Supreme Court in a case involving the University of Wisconsin.[11] The Court's decision allows student governments to use mandatory fees to fund groups that take political positions, provided that the funded advocacy activities are made available to the entire student body in a "neutral" fashion, with the meaning of "neutrality" still to be clarified. (As of this writing, a lower court has found that the University of Wisconsin was not, in fact, exercising the required "viewpoint neutrality.") Allowing funding of political action groups on a neutral basis is, however, different from allowing elected student officers to speak on behalf of a compulsory total student body on political issues.

Overall, as of September 1, 1964, the University of California found itself in open conflict with the California state senate Committee on Un-American Activities and with at least two chancellors (at UCLA and San Diego[12]) over independent campus control of campus affairs, a dispute that would soon include the Berkeley chancellor, and in open conflict over the "sandbox" status of the Associated Students.[13] Then, in September

1964, this combustible mixture was set aflame by an action of the Berkeley campus administration. The campus was bound to have had student troubles in the 1960s, but it was not bound to be among the first and one of the most notorious. This happened only because of what the politically active students considered to be an "atrocity" and I considered to be a major blunder.

TWO BLUNDERS

On September 14, 1964, the dean of students, under orders from the Berkeley chancellor, withdrew the 26-by-40-foot strip as a site for political advocacy. This was done without consultation with student leaders, Academic Senate committees, the office of the president, city authorities, or the Board of Regents, which had set aside the area for these purposes, and in opposition to the advice of the dean of students. In other words, it was done without going through the appropriate consultation procedures—or, in industrial relations parlance, without "clean hands." (Hence I use the word *blunder*, which I define as a mistake compounded of ignorance of consequences, prejudice, overconfidence, and lack of careful advance consideration.) This action did away with the long-standing Sather Gate Tradition that provided for an advocacy area on adjacent city property, the most precious tradition for politically active students. Moreover, this order came just when the Civil Rights Movement was coming to California and at a time of hotly contested state and national elections. Activist students had made plans for their fall campaigns on that very strip. Suddenly, they were confronted with a total prohibition—a wall of opposition—and with no warning.

In the late afternoon of the day after this order was announced, I returned home from Hong Kong and Tokyo. I learned about the order the next morning, September 16. When I heard the news from a staff assistant, I was absolutely stunned. I saw the whole record of easing campus restrictions on political activism being undermined. I anticipated an immediate student protest. (What I did not foresee, however, was that the order would ultimately result in the election of Ronald Reagan as governor and my dismissal as president.) I was deeply depressed. Why had this happened?

The Regents had set aside the advocacy area in September 1959, after careful consideration and with some opposition. Chancellor Seaborg had joined me in recommending this action, and Strong, Seaborg's successor, had no authority to overrule the Regents or the president. In addition, at a meeting of the Association of American Universities the previous spring (1964), we had been told by three of the university presidents that there were plans afoot in the Civil Rights Movement to target major universities for political action that fall. I had repeated this warning to all chancellors before I went abroad in July, as I had earlier in March, and urged them to be very cautious and not to do anything that would inflame the situation. Strong's order was the worst possible inflammatory action, including arousing the Young Republicans for Goldwater.

When I first heard about it, I sat there speculating about why Strong had done it. I knew that his vice chancellor for student affairs, Alex Sherriffs, was under attack from activist students and that he resented it. I knew that Strong was under attack from many faculty and that he resented it, but such attacks are part of the job. I also knew that Strong took his title of chancellor very seriously. He did not inform me about what was happening on campus or tell me of his major proposed actions, as Seaborg had always done. His attitude was, "I am in charge." Was he declaring his autonomy? Or was he just insensitive with no idea of the repercussions of his action? Was he really so alarmed by what turned out to be a nonexistent local Communist menace?[14] And why had he acted just as I was flying back from Tokyo? Was it an act of rebellion? Was he taking preemptive action before I got back? Was it sabotage? I was astounded.

So I went on campus that afternoon to talk with him and those he assembled: Sheriffs, Dean Towle, Strong's office manager, and his press officer. This was the only time I ever went on a campus to tell a chancellor I thought he had made a mistake and he better take it back. To Strong this was a slap in the face, a challenge to his authority over student affairs, which had been delegated to the campus level, though delegated within the policies of the Board of Regents, who themselves had set aside the 26-by-40-foot advocacy area.

The chancellor said that he had good reasons to do what he had done, for example:

1. The area was crowded with tables and chairs that interfered with heavy foot traffic. The ground was covered with litter, a disgrace at the entrance to a great academic institution. He was, he said, doing some badly needed "housecleaning" on what he thought of as "my" campus.
2. Vice Chancellor Sherriffs had just informed me about "a series of planned moves which would end up in civil disobedience demonstrations on the Berkeley campus with the purpose of removing you and Chancellor Strong from office"—as he put it, "a call for revolution."[15]
3. The *Oakland Tribune* had discovered that the Bancroft strip technically still belonged to the campus and not to the city of Berkeley. Strong feared that the *Tribune* might make this public or at least inform the Regents that campus rules were not being enforced on campus property and that he would be held responsible, since he knew of the failed transfer of the property to the city. The person in charge of the transfer, the Regents' land agent, Robert Underhill, had not followed through on the Regents' decision, and neither I nor the Regents had been told, though the chancellor clearly knew.

On reflection, I have concluded that the major reasons for the order of September 14 were housekeeping, fear that the *Tribune* might blow the whistle (it never did), concern that a "plot" was under way (as Strong then told me), and Strong's felt need to assert his authority.

Dean Towle was present at my meeting with the chancellor, but she kept totally silent. Only later did I learn that she agreed with me,[16] as did her assistant, Arleigh Williams. I assumed that her silence meant that she concurred with the chancellor, and I had great respect for her judgment. In any event, to my surprise Strong rejected my advice to withdraw the edict. He acted as if he expected my opposition and had decided in advance to fight it. He did not even say he would like to think about it. He just said "no" and stood fast. And he had brought along witnesses to his defiance, whereas I had expected a person-to-person discussion, with perhaps a request for time to think it over.

Chancellor Strong went ahead with what I believe was one of the worst administrative blunders in the history of the University. (Looking back over that history, another administrative blunder, in my judgment, was when President Sproul proposed a faculty loyalty oath in 1949.)

I then made another great administrative blunder. I did not order Strong to withdraw the order or declare, as an alternative, that as president I would rule the action to be null and void pending the meeting of the Regents the following week. Why did I make this historic blunder? Some of the concerns that went through my mind at the time, but not in a well-thought-out way and jumbled together in the process of responding to a sudden crisis, were that

1. I thought I was confronted by a united front of the chancellor, vice chancellor, and dean of students.
2. I was still dead tired from my overnight flight and, on my return, from trying to contend in a long night's work with a full desk, including preparation for the upcoming meeting with the Regents.
3. I was not prepared for a rejection of my advice and had not thought of applying the "null and void" solution.
4. As the main author of the policy of decentralization of the University, I did not want to reverse course as soon as I disagreed with some action.
5. I was concerned that the faculty might rally around the chancellor in his assertion of campus authority—then a hot topic at Berkeley—and I was certain that at least two other chancellors would vociferously support the cause of campus autonomy, as they did.
6. I habitually recoiled from issuing orders. I was not the "omnipotent" president my predecessor had been.
7. I thought there was time to work out solutions without a public controversy with the chancellor. I had not been in the country that "long hot

summer" and did not realize that there was little or no time to canvass opinions and consider alternative solutions.

Two blunders, then, one of commission and one of omission, and both by administrators, set on course the confrontation with activist students. I was thus committed by my *in*action to going along with the action of the chancellor while trying to find gradual ways to ameliorate it. I have regretted my blunder now for over thirty-five years and always will. But it took one other factor to create the FSM revolt: the existence of potentially significant cooperative groups of student and faculty political activists.

THE STUDENT-FACULTY COALITION

The events of the fall of 1964 can be properly understood only as a student-faculty uprising. It looked to the public like a student escapade, but the activist students could not have pulled it off alone. Theirs was only half of the story; faculty participation was the other half.

Both students and faculty had their political activists with their grievances. Common grievances included the University's failure to respect the activists' interpretation of the First Amendment and to apply this understanding to the University. The University said the rebellion was about free advocacy and not free speech, which both Regents and administrators believed they already provided. Activists claimed that the First Amendment also covered "free expression," including what they called "direct action" activities of raising money and recruiting participants for off-campus political action.

A second common student-faculty grievance soon arose: the unwillingness of the University to accept as legitimate the coercive civil disobedience that constituted the main tactics of the Civil Rights Movement, including sit-ins and physical disturbances of University functions and operations. Here I distinguish between the "persuasive" civil disobedience tactics of a Gandhi, concentrating on self-sacrificing activities, such as fasting or income loss in strikes, to assert one's moral commitments, and the "coercive" tactics of the FSM, intended to impose one's will physically rather than through moral persuasion. Let me note in passing that the "coercive" approach is more likely than the "persuasive" to result in a backlash, as happened in California in the 1960s, and is one reason that the Gandhi-inspired activists in India preferred persuasive methods.

The faculty, in addition, had a continuing grievance over the Regents' dismissal of the nonsigners of the loyalty oath (1949–1952) and, more recently, over the planned introduction of year-round operations with its changes in the academic calendar, among other grievances. For their part, activist current and former students still resented the behavior of police during the HUAC disturbances of 1960. There were other stimulants, but it was the loyalty oath controversy and the HUAC disturbances that had drawn a few faculty and many student activists to Berkeley from other college campuses and aroused others already there. It was an attractive battlefield for activists to enter.

Also, many students were already organized in SLATE, a group that was challenging the domination of student politics by fraternities and sororities and was organizing civil rights protests in San Francisco. And the liberal wing of the faculty also had organized a "Committee of 200" during the loyalty oath controversy, a coalition that still existed informally in interpersonal contacts.*

The student-faculty coalition was a kind of "popular front," but free of communist control. There was no single coalescing ideology, certainly not communism, although Chancellor Strong declared there was "a Communist-core and Communist-direction of the FSM revolt."[17] If anything, the common thread was the anarcho-syndicalism of "participatory democracy" and "direct action." There were few, *very* few, Communists involved. And communism, at that time, came in several antagonistic varieties: Stalinists, Trotskyites, Castroites, and Maoists, among others. I knew this situation well because of my work in industrial relations. There were almost no Stalinists in the FSM. And Stalinists really looked on the student movement as a renegade outfit pushing them out of their historic leadership of the left and handicapped by "infantile" inclinations.[18] The one acknowledged pro-Soviet communist, Bettina Aptheker, was of a reformist persuasion and a voice of experience and moderation within the FSM leadership. There was no Communist-led revolt, as the Berkeley vice chancellor and ultimately the chancellor said they believed. What did exist, however, was adherence by both some student and some faculty activists to the anarchist doctrine of "by any means necessary" and resort to the Blanquist or Leninist tactics of taking actions that would force the authorities to take repressive reactions such as calling in the police. I was concerned not to fall into this trap.

I saw a coming together of many individuals in a rather unruly mass, reacting ad hoc to actions by the campus administration—no overall plan, no plot, no off-campus coordination—just spur-of-the-moment reactions, but also a general inclination to cause trouble and to enjoy and even glory in it. And a small percentage of the student body could create a massive action group. Ten percent of thirty thousand was three thousand; then add former students, street people, high school students, and adult participant-observers, and you had five thousand, which media reporters could easily

*Editors' note: This group should not be confused with the Committee of 200 that formed in 1964 on the eve of the December 8 Academic Senate meeting; see Zelnik, "On the Side of the Angels," in this volume.

double in their estimates in order to capture headlines, even if 90 percent of the students were going about their usual business.

At the national level, the Students for a Democratic Society (SDS), founded at the University of Michigan, had started to operate in 1962. It was never much of a force at Berkeley, however, although the activist leaders there were part of the "New Left" that SDS represented nationally. What was later called "the movement" had at least two quite separate themes: (1) political action, which was grounded in civil rights and, later, protest against the Vietnam War, and (2) cultural rebellion, oriented around the counter-cultural themes of new styles of sex, music, dress, language, and the use of drugs, in opposition to the existing middle-class morality. The Berkeley movement in 1964 was mostly about political activism, whereas later on at the Santa Cruz campus the theme was more countercultural. The Berkeley movement was a swirling mass of people, of grievances, of responses to ill-advised administrative actions. It was spontaneous and reactive. It disappeared when the hard-line core of campus administrators was replaced and a softer-line group took over under chancellors Martin Meyerson and Roger Heyns, but it was soon reactivated by students under different leadership when the Vietnam War became the great issue.

In the end, the original Berkeley movement, the FSM, did gain something significant: political advocacy rights on campus. It is important to note, however, that these rights remained somewhat restricted. They were restricted by "time, place, and manner" rules, to which the FSM did not object; retention of disciplinary powers by the Regents, to which the FSM greatly objected; and continued regental authority to control speech on campus in accordance with Supreme Court rulings that went beyond the "no control" policy supported by the Academic Senate and its Committee on Academic Freedom (CAF) on December 8, 1964, a policy that even the FSM had not demanded. The FSM also led to further relaxation of the administration's in loco parentis attitudes and precipitated the final overthrow of fraternity-sorority domination of campus social and political life. It also brought the old, narrow "advocacy strip" right onto the central campus, where it exists to this day. And finally, the FSM was also significantly, but by no means solely, responsible for a major public backlash culminating in Ronald Reagan's 1966 election as governor of California and my resultant dismissal as president of the University.

Why such a significant movement? There were plenty of grievances around, both national and local. And the campus administration continued to create new grievances that constantly gave the movement new life. The leaders of the FSM were uncommonly gifted in assessing and guiding mass sentiments. Mario Savio, in particular, was a genius at understanding mass psychology and leading the masses with a great gift of oratory. The faculty activists also had some very bright, committed, and experienced leaders. The administration, in contrast, was split between the strict enforcers and the soft negotiators and was led on both sides by novices in political internecine warfare. The soft-line administrative leadership won out in the end, however, and the protest movement temporarily lost its momentum until Vietnam came along. In the meantime, there were three months of turmoil.

THE FOUR-RING CIRCUS

During these months, as already noted, there were four different conflicts going on at once: frontstage, and the only one the public or the media saw, was the conflict between FSM students and the administration; a second conflict, backstage, was within the administration and within the Regents— hard-line versus soft-line; a third, also backstage, was within the FSM—coercive versus persuasive civil disobedience; and a fourth, also backstage, was between "pro-cause/pro-University" faculty (advocates of civil rights and the First Amendment) on one hand, and on the other, a more unambivalent "pro-University" faculty (keep the University functioning in its normal way and avoid its involvement in external political causes and confrontational tactics).

"Pro-cause/pro-university"—I use this somewhat awkward locution because most of the activist faculty were both "pro-cause" (supportive of civil rights and free expression) *and* "pro-University" (they aimed to solve the problem with the FSM and commit the University to high moral principles, including no limitations on free speech or free expression). Some, of course, were more pro-cause, others more pro-University. At the end of the three months' turmoil, these faculty members thought that their Senate actions of December 8 had helped save the University, and they went along with the solutions of the Regents on December 18 to assist the same high goal, as I shall recount later.

I have carefully chosen my designation of these two groups. However, from the members of the activist faculty group I read and heard at the time only about the moral sanctity of their causes and how these causes were so important that they justified the students' resort to unusual tactics. I read and heard nothing about the wisdom or lack thereof of antagonizing the governor, the legislature, and the public of California and jeopardizing support for the University, or of fomenting political antagonisms within the faculty.

That fall I was traveling the state to encourage votes for a bond issue that would greatly benefit the University. At the time, we thought that the big concern for the University was the bond issue, not the FSM, a mere annoyance. How wrong we were! As I went around the state, I was bombarded by shouts: "What are your students doing?" I would reply: "Are you also asking what are your children doing?" To demands that I shoot the student activists off Sproul Plaza, I would remark that "Hell hath no wrath like that of a noncombatant."

I know that to the academic mind considerations of public opinion are off limits, below contempt, but those same academics were counting on me to bring home the bacon and would complain if I did not. I had to take public opinion into account even if they did not. And faculty members judged me, in large part, on how successful I was in assembling the University's financial resources. They might think they could live by high principles alone, but I had to live with political realities as well. I thought it somewhat unfair to hold me personally responsible for public support while they stood on high ground, denying its significance to academic decisions.

I also never read nor heard from pro-cause supporters about the morality of using educational facilities for political purposes. Suppose the dissidents had been supporting the Ku Klux Klan? Nor did I read or hear discussed the possibility of activist students using, instead, the many religious facilities nestled around the campus and devoted to the advancement of causes, or of their renting off-campus space. Convenience of access to a large audience was raised to the level of a great moral issue—only the use of Sproul Plaza was acceptable! Nor did I read or hear any discussion about the morality in a democracy of using illegal methods to secure results when legal methods had not been exhausted. I did, however, hear and read quite a bit—particularly from leaders of Stiles Hall and other religious centers—about whether it was wiser and more moral to use persuasive instead of coercive means of civil disobedience.

When dealing with anything as precious and vulnerable as the autonomy of the University and academic freedom within the University, the use of its name and facilities deserves careful consideration. Nevertheless, I am persuaded that most members of what I have called pro-cause/pro-University faculty really were pro-University as well as pro-cause. They saw themselves as guardians of the long-run welfare of their institution. But they did oppose limitations on student protests on campus even when reasonable alternative locations were possible.

Moreover, pro-cause faculty might have given more consideration to my record of accomplishments. What other university president in California or elsewhere had fought for and won all or any of the following: continuous tenure for the faculty, voluntary ROTC, permission for pro-Soviet Communists to speak on campus even at the height of the Cold War, a Master Plan for Higher Education with guarantees of universal access, and outreach programs for minorities. To this list should surely be added my all-out confrontations with a powerful legislative Committee on Un-American Activities as well as my battles against discrimination by fraternities and sororities, often supported by their powerful alumni.

What other university president? The answer is no one, not in the University of California and possibly not anywhere else. I thought that, given the time and the commitment of others to cooperate, I had accomplished a lot; but now I was being given neither time nor an atmosphere conducive to working out the problems. Yet, within a tumultuous three months in fall 1964, some conciliatory decisions were made. I realize, of course, that the above accomplishments were mostly not of interest to the Civil Rights Movement, but they were relevant to an evaluation of my behavior by the faculty.

REALITIES OF SOCIAL CONFLICT

It is fundamental to any serious understanding of the events of fall semester 1964 to be cognizant of all four conflicts that I summarized earlier. It is frequently true of social conflicts that there are several ongoing battles, not only the frontstage one between the two major disputing parties but also the one within each party—the iron law of internal disunity. This is one of the most universal rules about social conflict: Seldom are both sides unified internally. Those who talk most about unity and solidarity are often the most disunited. Another fundamental fact is that the internal fights within each side are likely to be more fierce, more hateful, more passionate than those between the two frontstage parties. They are more of the fingernail-scratching, hair-pulling, sharp elbowing variety, more personal and less considerate than are the major parties' cool preparations of manifestos for consumption by the general public.

Another side of social conflict is the tendency to view the other party as more monolithic, more calculating in its behavior, and more motivated by evil than it really is. The tendency is to assume the worst possible motives and the most Machiavellian tactics on the opposition's part. Each party desires unity and suffers disunity, but each assumes that the other is unified. Each has "good" and "bad" motives but assumes that the other has only bad motives. Each has disputes over tactics but assumes that the other will always be united in choosing evil tactics. As there were many misperceptions, so also at Berkeley in fall 1964 there was universal paranoia.

Thus, to settle the one "public" conflict it was first necessary to settle the three "private" conflicts. This meant that the soft-line administrators and Regents had to become dominant, that the pro-University faculty had to take over from the pro-cause/pro-University faculty, and that the faction within the FSM most able to accept a solution and make it stick had to be in charge. With respect to the last conflict I had two offers, one on the political left of the FSM and one on its right, to seize control from the Savio faction and make a settlement.[19] I did not accept either, in part because I did not think either group had enough control to make a settlement stick—only the Savio faction could do that. The three backstage conflicts were eventually worked out, and the central and publicly recognized conflict was then terminated, but all this took time—three months.

I was accused by some of "mediating" with the hard-line FSM leaders and making concessions to them. Actually I was mostly engaged in "conciliation" with the soft-line Regents and with the pro-University faculty in order to ensure their support. I did not think it possible for the University and the hard-line FSM and its most radical faculty supporters to agree on a solution, but I believed we might find a solution that the FSM would have to accept once it lost majority faculty support and that would also be acceptable to soft-line Regents. This is how it eventually worked out; and the FSM dissolved with Savio's resignation as its leader.

CALENDAR OF 1964 EVENTS, WITH COMMENTS

September 14. The proclamation from the dean of students, under orders from the chancellor and vice chancellor, ended the Sather Gate Tradition that provided an advocacy area on city property. This administrative blunder reversed the historic policy followed by President Sproul and myself and endorsed by the Regents.

September 16. Having been informed of this order after the fact, I met with the chancellor and others and urged them to rescind it. The chancellor refused, and I did not overrule him.

September 28. Activist students disrupted a University meeting by marching around and shouting. They substantially interfered with a speech by the chancellor.

September 30. Advocacy tables were set up on Sproul Plaza in violation of campus rules. Representatives of the dean of students began citing the violators. This led to a "pack-in" in Sproul Hall that severely interfered with University functions. The campus administration wanted to use the police to clear out the protesters, but I persuaded it not to do so. Sproul Hall was voluntarily evacuated that night.

October 1 and 2. Tables were put up again. One table occupant, a former student, was arrested. (Many former students were quite influentially involved, some of them FSM leaders.) When this man went limp, a police car was brought onto the plaza to take him away. A crowd surrounded the car and it could not move. There was a huge cry of anger from Regents, legislators, alumni, police officials, and many others at this attack on law and order. The car was held captive for thirty-two hours. The chancellor decided to have the police take measures to release it at 5:00 P.M., October 2. This was announced well in advance and attracted media people from the whole Bay Area as well as a crowd of students. I was fearful of violence if the police were involved. One bad judgment under high tension and a whole situation can blow up. (Arleigh Williams, associate dean of students, later said he thought there would have been "multiple killings" if I had not intervened.)[20] I had two phone calls: one from a faculty group with the same concern and a proposal for a solution,[21] and one from Governor Brown saying he feared violence and asking me, really *ordering* me, to step in and obtain a peaceful solution. I then met with representatives of the student activists and others. A solution was reached that the chancellor did not sign. Strong had been in and out of the room and was not present when the agreement was signed. When he returned, I gave him the agreement, which he then read; shaking his head, he passed it back to me unsigned. The police car was released.

I did not realize how totally antagonized the chancellor and vice chancellor were at my intervention (they seemed at the time to be relieved at the solution), nor did I tell them how antagonized I was at their creating a fait accompli the day before I returned from Tokyo. Mutual trust and friendship were destroyed and never restored.

October 2–November 8. After considerable conflict over procedure, discipline and several policy issues were referred, respectively, to (1) a special faculty committee on student conduct and (2) a joint student-faculty-administration committee on rules for political activity—"the Study Committee" (or the Committee on Campus Political Activity [CCPA]). During this period student activists complied with the October 2 agreement and refrained from advocacy activities on campus, although some of them were becoming restive.

November 9. With an apparent impasse in the deliberations of the CCPA, the FSM decided to abandon negotiations and return to direct action on November 9. This decision followed a split within the FSM Executive Committee. The vote for return to direct action has been variously described as 27–19 and 21–20.[22] The majority included representatives of civil rights groups, particularly SNCC and CORE. The minority that wanted to continue negotiations and avoid resumption of direct action included representatives of Young Democrats, Young Republicans, and Young Socialists.

The campus administration was irate at the repudiation of the October 2 agreement. So was I. So were the Regents. Student support for the FSM majority declined rapidly but temporarily.

November 12. The ad hoc faculty Committee on Student Conduct (Heyman Committee) issued its report on the discipline of students involved in actions up to and including September 30, which included the disruption of a University meeting and the pack-in of Sproul Hall. The committee recommended, in effect, no continuing penalties—in reality, no effective penalties at all. The FSM viewed this as a great triumph: the faculty would not support discipline for coercive civil disobedience on campus aimed at the administration, which is what some faculty members had earlier publicly assured the FSM.

The administration, the Regents, and some faculty reacted with dismay. So did I. I thought that the committee would at least issue some cautions about coercive civil disobedience on campus and possibly place some leaders on probation as a warning to be more respectful of the University in the future. Instead, it acted as though the University was on trial, not the students; and in fact, it was.

November 20. Meeting in Berkeley, the Board of Regents did not accept the Heyman Committee report in full and instead endorsed possible discipline for political actions after September 30, which included capture of the police car. It did this, in part because it concluded that the faculty on its own could not be counted on to support administrative efforts to maintain law and order. On my recommendation, however, the Board also changed the rules to allow the political advocacy on campus of *legal* off-campus actions. (Chancellor Strong did not join me in this recommendation.) I was still trying to retreat from the September 14 proclamation. This meant that only those students who advocated off-campus *illegal* actions still had a complaint. The Regents had made an important concession, but one that was totally ignored by activist students.

This, however, did not end the controversy, although the FSM coalition continued to fall apart. The big issue now shifted to whether there should be University discipline for past violations of campus rules. Activist students rallied around their leaders, opposing their being singled out for discipline. Over the Thanksgiving holiday, the chancellor, without consulting or informing me, but following regental instructions at their November meeting—instructions that the Chancellor had strongly encouraged them to give—sent out letters of discipline to four leaders, including Savio. This action quickly resurrected the movement. Had the action of the Regents at their November meeting stood by itself, the FSM, I think, would have crumbled.

December 2–6. The stage was set for the final act. Some one thousand students and other FSM supporters conducted a mass sit-in in Sproul Hall on December 2. The chancellor wanted to call in police to clear the building. Again I opposed this action and persuaded the governor that no action should be taken that night but that he and I should together enter Sproul Hall in the morning and try to persuade the students to leave. Among other things, I argued that these were "our" students and should not be treated like common criminals. Later that night the governor changed his mind and ordered the police to take immediate action. He telephoned me to say what he had done and that he expected my cooperation, and then abruptly hung up. Hundreds of students and nonstudents were arrested. The movement was greatly energized, and I was left with the charge before public opinion that I had opposed law and order. What I had done was oppose police action without trying persuasion first. I had long experience observing the use of police to quell industrial disputes and had seen how uncontrolled this instrument could become. The campus, including many faculty, was outraged by the arrests. A student strike began, supported by many teaching assistants, many students, and some faculty.

December 7. I called a University meeting in the Greek Theatre and stated that there would be no University discipline for past behavior, since, following the Sproul Hall arrests, the courts were now involved. I did this with the informal support of the Regents. Because this disposed of the remaining issue of University discipline, I thought the controversy had been concluded. However, after I finished speaking, Mario Savio seized the microphone. He clearly wanted to keep the controversy going. He was immediately dragged off the stage by campus police, whom I had explicitly asked Vice President Earl Bolton, who was working with campus officials, to exclude from the event. All hell broke loose. The police, without my knowledge, had been stationed backstage because of a rumor of a possible physical attack on me. The explosive atmosphere of the meeting had been created, in part, by FSM leaders using walkie-talkies to coordinate crowd responses to developments via messages sent to recipients stationed strategically throughout the crowd. Very professional.

December 8. The Berkeley division of the Academic Senate met and passed a resolution by a vote of 824–115 that generally supported the FSM's position. More specifically the Senate said: (1) As recommended by its Committee on Academic Freedom, there should be no University control over the content of speech—not even the standard prohibitions of immediate threat of "clear and present danger" or of obscenity, defamation, or conspiracy. The Senate voted down (737–284) an amendment that conceded no University control of the content of speech "provided that it is directed to no immediate act of force or violence"; here the FSM was actually given more than it had asked for, which was only the same degree of freedom of speech on campus as off campus. (2) "Disciplinary measures in the area of political activity shall be determined by a committee appointed by and responsible to the Academic Senate." (3) There should be "time, place, and manner" rules governing political activity on campus. Additionally, the Senate established an Emergency Executive Committee (EEC) to represent it "in dealing with problems arising out of the present crisis."[†]

In the next few days the Senate elected the EEC by secret ballot. It rejected members of a list presented by the activist faculty's Committee of 200, which had produced the December 8 resolution, except for one faculty member, Carl Schorske of history, who was perhaps the most academically respected and moderate member on that list. The rest of the committee (as elected) was drawn from more traditional leaders of the Senate. The Committee of 200 list was repudiated just one week after its program was adopted, an action of fundamental importance. My explanation of this seeming anomaly is that the Senate was being consistent. It was really voting for peace on December 8, and again on December 14 (when it elected the EEC), and then again when it quietly accepted the December 18 actions of the Board of Regents. The faculty majority wanted to end the conflict and return to academic affairs. At each opportunity it adopted what looked like the best route back to stability.

December 17–18. The Regents met in Los Angeles on December 17 and 18, with members of the EEC and the Academic Council of the statewide Academic Senate in attendance. The Board acted favorably on all of my recommendations:

1. It accepted the idea of "time, place, and manner" rules as presented to the Berkeley Senate by the CAF and endorsed by the Senate on December 8. I correctly assumed that this provision would ensure that political activities would not be allowed to interfere with strictly academic functions. This action was fully consistent with the Committee of 200 proposal of December 6.
2. It retained control of student discipline by the administration and Regents, against the Committee of 200 proposal of December 6.
3. It endorsed compliance with the First Amendment on campus as then interpreted by the courts. This meant that content of speech could be limited in certain areas: "clear and present danger," defamation, conspiracy, and obscenity. The Senate, under the Committee of 200's leadership, had sought to reject these standard limitations on December 8. The Board of Regents refused this.

[†]Editors' note: For the relevant text of the December 8 resolutions see Zelnik, "On the Side of the Angels," Appendix B.

This set of actions was acceptable to the EEC and to the universitywide Academic Council, and it proved to be acceptable to the faculty at large. Political advocacy on campus as demanded by the FSM was finally to be permitted but subject to important restrictions, as noted above. In practice, the "time, place, and manner" restrictions have worked very well.

The Board of Regents, strictly on its own, also asked that a replacement be found for Chancellor Strong. I accepted but did not recommend this.

I was very pleased with the Regents for their willingness to make reasonable accommodations and to reject vindictiveness, and with the Academic Senate for helping to develop and supporting reasonable solutions. A spokesperson for the FSM called the Regents' actions "horrendous," but the FSM quickly ceased to dominate activity on campus.[23] It finally went out of business on April 29, 1965, with Mario Savio saying, *though his reference was to a very specific post-FSM situation,* "perhaps the saddest thing about this community is the continuing reluctance of faculty to defend the rights of students."[24] Savio acknowledged disappointed hopes but blamed this result on the faculty. The new rules survived the period of intense protest against the war in Vietnam and continue basically unchanged to this day.

Only Savio had the respect and influence to conclude the episodes of FSM confrontations. He did so in sadness, however, not in triumph. Nevertheless, the FSM had won its specific grievance on the right of advocacy, though to the extent it wanted to change the University and the society more fundamentally, it did not succeed. There was no "thoroughgoing rebellion on this campus," as the SLATE supplement of September 10, 1964, had called for, particularly not against its academic programs.[25]

CHANCELLOR STRONG'S ALTERNATIVE

The FSM had a substantial but partial victory, and the pro-University faculty a total victory. Strong, however, met total defeat. Yet he had had much influential support: the *Oakland Tribune* and the Hearst press, much of the legislature and the general public, his friends in the faculty and particularly in the radiation lab, and the right wing of the Board of Regents—a powerful combination. And on reflection, I must confess, his policy of strict enforcement of existing rules might have worked. It turned out that student activists were really threatened by the prospect of dismissal, as evidenced by how hard they fought against academic penalties. And at the University of Chicago, a heavy dose of suspensions and dismissals totally suppressed the student revolt.[26] But if a policy of strict discipline and use of police might have worked, it might equally have resulted in a Kent State or Jackson State. Later, the hard-line policy of Governor Reagan would have disastrous consequences in the People's Park episode of 1969, where one person was killed and several wounded. That policy ran a big risk of horrendous consequences. Who knows? I do not. The Strong policy, given faculty support as at Chicago, might have brought a quick solution. But such support was not available at Berkeley.

SOME OBSERVATIONS

As of 1964, Berkeley was also developing a national reputation as a rising center for the social sciences and a regional reputation for advances in the arts: it had already become a world center for scientific research. It was designated, as noted earlier, in a 1964 survey as the "best balanced distinguished university" in the United States and possibly in the world—a position it held for the remainder of the twentieth century with ascending acclaim. The academic reputation of the campus has steadily increased since 1964, while the political has slowly decreased despite many efforts to perpetuate it, and decreased thus far more among students than faculty at Berkeley.

FSM leaders and their faculty supporters had a rather extreme definition of "free speech." It included (a) "advocacy" actions, such as raising money and recruiting participants for "direct action," before the Supreme Court had clearly included them as meeting the intent of the First Amendment; (b) no control by University authorities over the content of speech, including over "clear and present danger," defamation, obscenity, and conspiracy—all exempted in court decisions interpreting the First Amendment; (c) access of speakers to the maximum audience not only of adherents but also of passersby, and thus to a captive audience;[27] (d) full electronic amplification of speeches; (e) except for violations of reasonable "time, place, and manner" rules, no discipline for actions associated with political speech or expression. The FSM sought to acknowledge the December 8 action of the Senate as the effective University policy, rather than the December 18 action of the Regents. Overall, the FSM program sought to turn the campus into a wide-open staging ground for political activity beyond anything existing elsewhere in the United States.

The courts played a large part in the evolving dispute. As noted earlier, traditionally they had interpreted the First Amendment narrowly, as covering "freedom of speech," not freedom of expression as in "advocacy" activities. By 1964, however, the courts were already expanding the definition of *speech* to include other forms of expression, for example, some symbolic forms of action such as wearing armbands.

By November 1964, however, the general counsel, for reasons still not fully clear, reversed his position and told the Board that it was uncertain that its ban on advocacy could be constitutionally sustained.[28] The Board was shocked by this new advice, but it was eventually willing, though reluctant, to consider a broader approach to the problem. It accepted my advice in November that our policy should be modified to accept advocacy of "legal" actions, as noted above. A further change was made in 1965, when the Regents omitted from the new student rules any ban on advocacy of illegal off-campus actions. The 1965 action was not based on the situation in the courts, which was still uncertain, but on other considerations that were the bases of my arguments: that the University had long supported a convenient place, off campus, for advocacy actions, and it had been unwise to take this place away, especially without advance consultation; and that to enforce an antiadvocacy position effectively in the face of aggressive student opposition it would be necessary to police the whole campus to search out violations, thus creating a police-state atmosphere. The Regents' November decision accepting on-campus advocacy of "legal" off-campus actions was expanded in 1965 to remove the word *legal* but to rely particularly on "time, place, and manner" rules, as recommended by the Berkeley Senate. This was all well ahead of new and expanding interpretations of the First Amendment by the Supreme Court in a series of cases in the late 1960s that gave constitutional protection to some forms of "symbolic speech."[29]

The courts were also moving in two other related directions. One was to give university administrations less freedom to govern their campuses, less autonomy, by giving more oversight to the courts themselves, as later transpired, for example, in the areas of affirmative action and sexual harassment. The other was to treat a public university campus less as a protected enclave under its own rules and more as public property such as streets and parks.

The University was caught in the throes of these changing legal contexts. It was not sufficiently agile to escape unscathed. To what extent the courts were making political decisions is subject to controversy. But they did adapt to the new civil rights rebellion, with its reliance on civil disobedience with new interpretations of the Constitution. The University was behind this curve of interpretations, while the FSM and its faculty supporters were well ahead of it. Actually, given how big and unwieldy was the University, it was remarkable how fast it did move even in the face of inconclusive evidence of a changing court opinion.

Devoted to the decentralization of University administration (although decentralization cut me off from student and faculty life), I was reluctant to overturn chancellors' decisions, as in the case of Strong's edict of September 14.

I followed Academic Senate advice with only two exceptions: first, I joined the Regents in opposing the full recommendations of the student conduct committee report of November 12; and second, I joined in amending the advice of the Berkeley Senate of December 8. But I did not act so agreeably with the Board of Regents; I pushed it as far as I could without losing all influence, which, however, I ultimately did.[30]

Although I did not like confrontations, I did confront the state Un-American Activities Committee head on, as no one else ever did in all of California which led, in part, to its dissolution.[31]

There were still other orientations that affected my reactions to the events of the fall of 1964, thoughts that swirled around in my head at the time and were not carefully analyzed in a rational way. One was that I was anxious to protect the University from political interference. I had seen the internal and external political interferences that had undermined the academic life of universities in Latin America and Germany, and I was seeing them at work again in China. I was fearful of politicization of the American university interfering with its academic functions—and properly so in light of later developments. My experiences abroad had heightened my anxieties about the politicization of university life. In 1936 and 1939 my wife Kay and I had spent several summer months in Germany and Austria. There we were in direct contact with representatives of the American Friends Service Committee engaged in securing passage to the United States for Jewish refugees. It was then quite obvious that horrible developments were under way. We also learned how the Nazis had succeeded in dominating student and faculty life in German universities. I learned even more when I was a short-term adviser to the U.S. Occupation Forces in Germany after World War II.

I also spent several years in the 1950s and 1960s as a member of the Conference on Higher Education in the American Republics, which entailed several visits to Latin America. I visited universities in all the major Latin American countries and saw firsthand how politicized some of their institutions had become and how dysfunctional. I was disgusted with these perversions of academic life I saw there. I was also a founding member of the board of trustees of the Chinese University of Hong Kong, which gave me a chance to observe the beginnings of the political takeover of mainland Chinese universities—the "let a hundred flowers bloom" campaign. The flowers bloomed and then their heads were chopped off.

I thus became very concerned with the effects of the politicization of academic life and very fearful of similar developments in the United States. My fears were excessive, as it turned out, because I did not give full consideration to the enormous differences between the situations of Germany, Latin America, and China and that of the United States.

Equally important, I was impressed by President Sproul's political knowledge and was reluctant to reverse his policies. Sproul knew the political geography of California far better than I did. He had fully committed the University to a policy of no political advocacy on campus, combined with support for a convenient location off campus—the Sather Gate Tradition. I did not agree, however, with his sensitivity about outside speakers nor with his support for a loyalty oath for the faculty. But I had supported his "no advocacy" policy, although I did abandon it, somewhat reluctantly, in

November and December 1964. The University was an educational institution, not an evangelical institution, either religious or political.

I also brought to the events of fall 1964 my belief in the three rules of conduct I learned in the industrial relations arena: (a) Keep your contracts. The FSM unilaterally abandoned the October 2 agreement by returning to "direct action" on November 9. (b) Consider the total situation. The FSM and its faculty supporters paid no attention to possible negative public consequences of their actions on the University and its academic functions. (c) Never personally attack the people with whom you deal—they are the ones with whom you must work out a settlement and rely upon to make it succeed.

Above all, the University of California favored civil rights. In 1959 the Regents declared that all recognized student organizations, including fraternities and sororities, must be open to students of all races and religions. In 1960 the University was a key player in the negotiation of the Master Plan for Higher Education in California, which guaranteed a place in higher education for every high school graduate who wished to attend, regardless of race or gender. In 1963 the Regents adopted an outreach program to encourage minority students to take advantage of access opportunities, and over the years the program has expanded enormously. And in 1964, in my capacity as president, I said that the University would not punish students for their off-campus political activities, legal or illegal.

But the issue in fall 1964 was not civil rights as such but what on-campus activities in support of civil rights would be permitted: mass meetings, petitions, strikes, negotiations—always; political advocacy actions—not at first, but permitted beginning in November and December; disruption of University functions, seizure of property—no.

A FLOOD OF FALSE ALLEGATIONS—THE BIG MYTHS

The FSM and some members of its leadership attacked me personally and quite unfairly. They asserted that the Kerr Directives took away historical rights of students. They did not. They codified preexisting policies and practices. Where they made changes, they were always in a liberalizing direction.[32] The *Daily Cal* called this accusation "The Big Lie,"[33] the first of many. The FSM also claimed I said the University was a "factory."[34] I never said or wrote this. I did call the University a "city of intellect" with many types of activities within it.

I was labeled a "proto-fascist ideologue."[35] This was at a time when many anti-Communist socialists (such as Norman Thomas) and liberals were being called "social fascists" by the very far left. I was actually a New Deal liberal, and a Keynesian as an economist. Although the author of this claim, Hal Draper, did say that he himself did not believe this charge, he said that "by adding a single sentence" to one of my works, it would be true; he never said what that sentence was. Others, however, failed to note his rejection of the "proto-fascist" label, and "proto-fascist" got shortened to "fascist" as the charge was repeated over and over. Another label was "Eichmann-like"[36]—following orders regardless of how reprehensible. Actually my record was one of opposing governors, of fighting the state Committee on Un-American Activities, of arguing before the Board of Regents—a record which resulted eventually in my being dismissed as president of the University of California. I was too combative with superior authority—not too supine.

It was said that I ordered Dean Towle to issue the September 14 proclamation[37] (I did not) and that William Knowland of the *Oakland Tribune* had ordered me to clean up the situation at Berkeley. He never did this in any fashion, direct or indirect, and, in any event, I would not have followed such orders.[38] Where was the proof? Jackie Goldberg said with reference to the October 2 incident, "Kerr then calls the Oakland police" against the students.[39] I never called in the Oakland police nor asked anyone else to do so on my behalf. Years later, historian Garry Wills, echoing this allegation, called me the "Bull Connor" "of the Berkeley confrontations," referring to the Alabama sheriff who had used police dogs against demonstrators in the long, hot summer.[40]

Martin Roysher in this volume claims that I was guilty of an "intervention with the president and chairman of the board of CBS" that "turned a balanced documentary into diverting vignettes of groovy hippies." The exact opposite is true. I knew nothing of the "documentary" until I saw it on TV. I was startled. It showed a motorcycle gang riding up and down the outside steps of Wheeler Hall and shots of students engaged in orgies of sex and drug abuse. This was not a fair picture of either Berkeley or the FSM. I wrote a note to Frank Stanton of CBS saying just that. It turned out that the top leadership of CBS had its own doubts but initially defended this depiction of life at Berkeley.[41] The program *was* staged—not a "balanced documentary," but staged by CBS, not by me. Roysher says (in the same essay) that I intervened with the editors of *Newsweek* to change a story about the FSM. I have no idea what this is all about. No evidence is offered.

I was accused of "red-baiting." I did once say that "some elements [active in the demonstrations] have been impressed with the tactics of Fidel Castro and Mao Tse-tung. There are very few of these, but there are some."[42] Hal Draper, the FSM's chief guru, agreed with me, writing that my statement was "literally true."[43] What I did not say was that these "elements" were leaders of the FSM or even students. At that time in America *Communist* usually meant a member of the *pro-Soviet* CPUSA. It would be fair to say that I wished to correct the press's and public's misperception that the student movement was Communist led. It was not. As Jeff Lustig says in this volume, my remark did capture the truth that "we were *not* . . . Stalinists. We were not the Designated Enemy."[44] But because I received constant critical questioning about "Communists" at the University as I traveled around the state that fall in support of our pending bond issue, I could not simply ignore the question. The fact was that there were very few pro-Soviet Communists in the FSM, and in any case such Communists were in steep decline in the United States after Khrushchev's 1956 revelations. Maoists and Castroites, to be sure, were in sharp ascent, but they were not what was then meant by "Communists" in public discourse. The sources of my alleged statement (the so-called "49 percent") used by the FSM and others to substantiate the red-baiting charge were very questionable.[45] If I were guilty of anything, it was of telling the simple truth: pro-Soviet Communists were not much involved; other types of small-*c* communists were present in supportive roles.

The above discussion illustrates how some of my critics have engaged in fictional accounts, to put it delicately, or in "character assassination," when viewed from a less charitable point of view, as Reginald Zelnik has noted of some latter-day leaders of a radical group at Berkeley.[46] Chancellor Strong was exempt from such attacks even though he ordered the September 14 proclamation, called in the police on at least two occasions, charged "Communist direction of the FSM revolt," and refused to sign the October 2 agreement or to join me in recommending the major concession of November 1964. But he was essential to the FSM revolt in creating "atrocities" that kept the movement alive. By contrast, my policy of conciliation threatened support for the FSM, and eventually resulted in its withering away.

I have often felt that a scarecrow, even a "tyrant," was being created out of pieces of prevarication and then identified with my name. Max Ways, a senior editor of *Fortune*, after spending considerable time at Berkeley in the fall of 1964, concluded, "Never did an educational institution less deserve the name of tyrant than the University of California."[47] I think this false appraisal came about, in part, from a distorted model of the University and of the establishment in general. This model asserts that the University establishment was *unitary*, with all parts thinking and acting in unison. But as previously noted, this was not true of Regents, administrators, or faculty, either in concert or even within their separate spheres. The model further sees the University as *run from the top*, whereas actually there were several sources of initiative at several levels, especially within the administration. Finally, this model views the University administration as *totally evil in its intent*, though historically and in the recent past it had accomplished many good things, thanks to which the University received repeated national acclaim.

This was a period of intense conflict and unfair allegations, and not just on the left. The state legislature's Committee on Un-American Activities (the Burns committee) created its own scarecrow or tyrant in its 1965 report, where it stated that despite the Regents' policy of excluding Communists from employment, "the administration welcomes Communist organizations, throws the portals open to Communist speakers, and exhibits an easy tolerance of Communist activists." The report implied that I was foisting communism upon a gullible Board of Regents: "When the present university administration took over, however, these restrictions were eased. The Regents were persuaded to rescind their long-standing prohibition against Communist lecturers; . . . radical student organizations were given official university recognition; . . . an atmosphere of easy tolerance of left-wing radical activities pervaded the campus at Berkeley." The report artfully cast doubt on my loyalty: "In endeavoring to make a determination of how the Berkeley Campus became vulnerable to student rebels, and how a minority of Communist leaders managed to bring this great educational institution to its knees, it is indispensable that we know something of the background of the man who was in command when the rebellion occurred."[48]

Then in its 1966 report the Burns committee stated that the Regents intended to exclude "both Communist Party members *and other persons with Communistic ideologies*" (emphasis in original) and noted that I insisted on "proof of Party membership." This I did. Regental policy and the policy of the Academic Senate specifically said *membership*. More important, expanding the policy to include "other persons with Communistic ideologies" would have introduced endless debate as to what this meant and possibilities of an endless witch hunt. The Burns committee argued: "Just as an unkempt and dirty applicant would be rejected by any school, college or university administrator, so also a proper concern for the applicant's demonstrated attitude toward morality and toward the democratic way of life should enter into the administrator's decision, and he should welcome the fullest information bearing on these traits. As Chancellor and President, Clark Kerr has avoided consideration of such information." And I did. The Burns committee condemned my "narrow and rigid interpretation," noting that the "Communist Party had gone underground" and proof of membership was "practically impossible to obtain." It said that I was "confusing the requirements for judgment in the hiring of teachers with those for conviction in a criminal trial"; that I was insisting on "substantiated evidence." This I did. The report concluded that the Berkeley campus "in recent years" had failed to impose security measures, adding that the campus under my chancellorship and the University under my presidency had been "opposed to such measures."[49] Yes, as defined by the Burns committee.

I was thus portrayed as the evil genie who had introduced communism and Communists into the University. The FSM and the Burns committee, it would seem, were alike in their creation of grossly distorted images of an all-powerful tyrant. However, one might expect a better quality of scholarship from faculty and students than from politicians and their staff assistants.

May I note that, in constructing the image of a "tyrant," FSM participants were also constructing their own images as courageous heroes—without a tyrant there were no heroes, and they wanted to be heroes. The Burns committee, in asserting that the University was being infiltrated by Communists, was building a case for its own importance and its continuing value to California society. Both extremes were self-serving in building these false images of right-wing tyrant and a left-wing subversive.

McCarthyism from the right and from the left—devastating aspersions without proof: these images still haunt me as I circulate among our students and alumni. I accept all this as inevitable under the circumstances and recognize that the times were not conducive to careful judgments. These images were generated by students whom some of our faculty called "our best, brightest and most moral." They were angry that I would not go along with their rather extreme definitions of "free speech," just as the Burns committee was angry that I insisted on proof of Communist Party membership before dismissing anyone. I have asked of both the Burns committee and the FSM: where is the proof?

CONCLUSION

There are at least two ways of looking at the fall of 1964. One is as a long series of successful confrontations, the other is as a long series of eventually successful efforts at conciliation. The first culminated in the capture of the police car in early October and the strike in early December. The second was highlighted by the conciliation of October 2 (which disintegrated with the return to direct action in November) and by further efforts at conciliation at the Regents meeting of December 17–18. On December 8, whatever else it did, the Academic Senate voted for peace with the FSM; then, with the election of a moderate EEC on December 14, it voted for peace with the administration; and with its acceptance of the Regents' actions of December 18, the faculty accepted peace with the Board of Regents. On the confrontational side, the administration leader who stood for confrontation tactics, Chancellor Strong, was dismissed by the Regents in December; the faculty Committee of 200 faded away; and the FSM ceased to exist with Savio's resignation in April 1965. The student body at large briefly returned to its academic pursuits, until protests again escalated during the Vietnam War. The frontstage conflict was over, but only because so too were the three backstage conflicts: soft-line administrators and Regents prevailed; "pro-University" faculty took command; the most militant grouping of students dissolved.

The story of the fall of 1964 is best understood as the ultimate triumph of conciliation. Conciliation did not win the battle of the headlines or the history books. Overall, however, I particularly salute the influence of the conciliators among faculty, Regents, and students over those who advocated confrontation.

In the end, my soft-line approach was accepted by the Regents and the faculty, and the FSM abandoned its confrontations. We ended up with solutions that met with general agreement or at least consent and that have met the test of time, and we avoided any serious physical injuries—no Kent State, no Jackson State, no Tiananmen Square, and no Peoples Park, the later outcome at Berkeley when Governor Reagan followed a policy of police coercion, with one person killed and many injured.

Conciliation is, I believe, the superior approach in the academic world. By its very nature, the campus is a place for consultation, persuasion, reason, consideration of the views of others, agreed-upon solutions. One party's offer of conciliation, to be successful, must of course be met by conciliation by the other party or parties; or the conciliation by the one party must be effective in creating conditions under which the other fades away. At Berkeley in 1964–1965 there was some of both developments but mostly the FSM faded away while the pro-cause/pro-University faculty responded in a conciliatory way.

To be sure, confrontation did place the issue of "free expression" far higher on the University's agenda. But by itself, confrontation did not and could not work out a solution without complete capitulation by the University, which was not a possibility, although complete suppression, including the ejection of all extreme activists, was. And, once free expression was on the agenda, it still took conciliation to work out a solution. Placing an item at the top of the agenda and keeping it there, as the FSM did, is quite an accomplishment. The transition from an agenda item to actual policy, however, is more important, and that could be achieved and was achieved only with the president of the University, along with others, acting as a conciliator. And it was I, in the end, who also paid one of the highest personal prices.

Although I would not go so far as Benjamin Franklin did in saying, "There was never a good war or a bad peace," that is indeed my inclination, and so also with confrontation and conciliation. With one major modification (not voiding the edict of September 14), I would follow the same conciliatory course of action if I had to do it over again: peace on campus, goodwill toward opponents within the confines of reasonable rules of conduct.

In the end, the University of California at Berkeley was not made to "stop" because it was so "odious," as Savio proclaimed.[50] It has continued its operation, in peace and in progress, with voluntary and eagerly sought-after participation by faculty and students, thanks, in at least small part, to policies of conciliation by all the parties at the time of a crucial period in the historic fall of 1964.

NOTES

1. Clark Kerr, John T. Dunlop, Frederick H. Harbison, and Charles A. Myers, *Industrialism and Industrial Man: The Problems of Labor and Management in Economic Growth* (Cambridge: Harvard University Press, 1960); see also *Industrialism and Industrial Man Reconsidered: Some Perspectives on a Study over Two Decades of the Problems of Labor and Management in Economic Growth, Final Report of the Inter-University Study of Human Resources in National Development* (Princeton, N.J.: The Inter-University Study of Human Resources in National Development, 1975); Clark Kerr, *The Future of Industrial Societies—Convergence or Continuing Diversity?* (Cambridge, Mass.: Harvard University Press, 1983).

2. Kerr, *The Gold and the Blue: A Personal Memoir of the University of California, 1949–1967,* vol. 2: *Political Turmoil* (Berkeley and Los Angeles: University of California Press, 2003).

3. California Legislature, *Thirteenth Report of the Senate Factfinding Subcommittee on Un-American Activities, Senator Hugh M. Burns, Chair* (Sacramento: Senate of the State of California, 1965), 65.

4. Kerr, *The Uses of the University,* 4th ed. (Cambridge, Mass.: Harvard University Press, 1995 [1st ed., 1963]), chapt. 2.

5. Seymour Martin Lipset and Sheldon S. Wolin, eds., *The Berkeley Student Revolt: Facts and Interpretations* (Garden City, N.Y.: Doubleday, 1965), 208, 216.

6. Kerr, *Uses of the University,* chapt. 3.

7. "Student Rules Pertaining to On-Campus Solicitation of Funds and Membership," memo from David C. Fulton to Kerr and UC Regents, Nov. 1964 (in author's possession).

8. Strong believed that Katz, an acting professor, had lied when he signed the state oath affirming that he was not a Communist. Strong tried to block the renewal of Katz's appointment, based on the long-standing University policy of not employing members of the Communist Party, although he produced no proof of Katz's Communist affiliation. Some faculty members saw this as a violation of academic freedom. See Kerr, *Political Turmoil,* chapt. 10.

9. "In the last five years, great liberalizations have been made in the University's policies, especially in the area of making ideas available to students. SLATE has always been the first to commend these liberalizations" ("'The Big Myth' is Slate's Side of Kerr Letter," *Daily Californian* [hereafter cite as *DC*], 12 Dec. 1961).

10. For this and other citations to information regarding "un-American activities," see Kerr, *Political Turmoil,* chapt. 3.

11. *Board of Regents of the University of Wisconsin System v. Southworth,* no. 98-1189 (U.S. S. Ct., 22 Mar. 2000).

12. See Kerr, chapts. 23, "A Place in the Sun for UCLA," and 17, "Original Directions and Problems at the New Campuses," in *The Gold and the Blue,* vol. 1: *Academic Triumphs* (Berkeley and Los Angeles: University of California Press, 2001).

13. See Kerr, *Political Turmoil,* chapt. 9.

14. It should be noted that during World War II Strong had been manager of the radiation laboratory at Berkeley. The rad lab was involved in confronting first Hitler and then Stalin by developing new means of warfare. It was in the forefront of fighting first fascism and then communism. Several leaders of the lab were strongly opposed to the weak Communist threat internally as well as the strong threat externally.

15. Chancellor Edward W. Strong, "Philosopher, Professor and Berkeley Chancellor, 1961–1965," oral history conducted in 1988 by Harriet Nathan, Regional Oral History Office, Bancroft Library, University of California at Berkeley, 1992, 297.

16. In a *New York Times* story, Dean Towle is quoted as saying that she had "opposed the administrative actions that led to the creation of the Free Speech Movement" (14 Mar. 1965).

17. Strong memo to files (10 Dec. 1964), in Edward Strong Papers, vol. II, University Archives, Bancroft Library.

18. See Kerr, *Political Turmoil*, chapt. 4.

19. Ibid., chapt. 5.

20. Arleigh Williams, "Dean of Students Arleigh Williams: The Free Speech Movement and the Six Years' War, 1964–1970," oral history conducted in 1988 and 1989 by Germaine LaBerge, Regional Oral History Office, 1990, 96.

21. Led by Henry Rosovsky (history and economics), the group included William A. Kornhauser, William Petersen, Neil J. Smelser, David Matza, and Nathan Glazer, sociology; Paul Seabury, Robert A. Scalapino, and Ernst B. Haas, political science; Roy Radner, economics; Carl E. Schorske, history; and Joseph Tussman, philosophy.

22. Max Heirich, *The Spiral of Conflict: Berkeley 1964* (New York: Columbia University Press, 1971), 245. Reconstitution of the FSM Steering Committee and its vote to resume direct action took place on November 7, according to David Lance Goines, who also gives a slightly different account of the FSM Executive Committee's ratification of resumption of direct action. David Lance Goines, *The Free Speech Movement: Coming of Age in the 1960s* (Berkeley: Ten Speed Press, 1993), 304, 325.

23. Andrew L. Pierovich, "Chronology of Events," *California Monthly* 75 (Feb. 1965), 74.

24. Heirich, 375.

25. Ibid., 99.

26. Edward Shils, "Chronicle," *Minerva* 7, no. 4 (summer 1969).

27. See Robert Cohen's essay, "Mario Savio and Berkeley's 'Little Free Speech Movement' of 1966," in this volume.

28. Kerr, *Political Turmoil*, chapt. 8.

29. See, for example, *U.S. v. O'Brien*, 391 U.S. 367 (1968).

30. Kerr, *Political Turmoil*, chapt. 16.

31. UC Office of the President, *Analysis of the Thirteenth Report of the State Senate Factfinding Subcommittee on Un-American Activities, 1965* (Berkeley: UC Office of the President, 1965).

32. The *DC* editors wrote, "The Kerr regulations are far more liberal than the previous rules" (15 Nov. 1961). And even SLATE agreed that "great liberalizations have been made in the University's policies" (see note 9).

33. Ibid.

34. Jack Weinberg was quoted as saying at the time of the police car incident, "This is a knowledge factory. If you read Clark Kerr's books, these are his precise words" (see Heirich, 145).

35. Hal Draper, *Berkeley: The New Student Revolt* (New York: Grove Press, 1965), 212.

36. Bradford Cleaveland, "Education, Revolutions, and Citadels," in Lipset and Wolin, 91.

37. Jackie Goldberg, FSM Panel at University House (audiotape), 26 Sept. 1998, UC Berkeley (tape in author's possession).

38. "Whether it is true or not, all of us believed at the time, and many of us still do to this day, that he [Knowland] called up Clark Kerr and said, 'You've got to stop these shenanigans. The students are making too much trouble in Berkeley and Oakland, and in San Francisco, and we really want this stopped, so do something—because there's a bond issue coming up for state universities and I can editorially have at you.' We don't know if this is true or not; I believed it at the time. I think I probably still believe it now" (Goldberg, loc. cit.).

39. Ibid.

40. Garry Wills, *Certain Trumpets: The Call of Leaders* (New York: Simon and Schuster, 1994), 84.

41. See Bill Leonard, *In the Storm of the Eye* (New York: Putnam, 1987), 125. William Paley, chair of CBS, is quoted as saying he believed "part of it may have been staged."

42. Press conference, San Francisco, 2 Oct. 1964, as reported by James Benit in "Kerr Ruled Out Compromise," *San Francisco Chronicle,* 3 Oct. 1964. A few days later, referring to the relatively small crowd of people who surrounded the police car on the night of October 1, 1964, I also said, "In the estimates of experienced on-the-spot observers, the hard core group of demonstrators—those who continued as part of the demonstration through the night of October 1—contained at times as much as 40 percent off-campus elements. And within that off-campus group, there were persons identified as being sympathetic with the Communist Party and Communist causes" (press conference, Los Angeles, 6 Oct. 1964, as reported in *San Francisco Examiner,* 7 Oct. 1964).

43. Draper, 60.

44. See this volume, p. 221.

45. See Robert Cohen, "The Many Meanings of the FSM," in this volume.

46. The term *character assassination* was used by Zelnik in reference to the conduct of some radical leaders of the campus's Vietnam Day Committee in 1966 (see Cohen, "Mario Savio and Berkeley's 'Little Free Speech Movement,'" in this volume).

47. Max Ways, "On the Campus: A Troubled Reflection of the U.S.," *Fortune* 72, (Sept. 1965): 204.

48. California Legislature, 52, 65.

49. California Legislature, *Thirteenth Report Supplement on Un-American Activities, Senator Hugh M. Burns, Chair* (Sacramento: Senate of the State of California, 1966), 22, 23, 24.

50. Mario Savio, as quoted in Heirich, 271–72.

PART THREE

Legal and Constitutional Issues

Constitutionally Interpreting
the FSM Controversy

Robert Post

A glance at the FSM controversy of 1964 illustrates the remarkable rhetorical and cultural power of First Amendment freedoms. Struggles over these freedoms tend to assume a characteristic narrative form, with those seeking to liberate communication claiming the high ground of progress and emancipation against the retreating forces of conservative authority and censorship. Retrospective accounts of the FSM controversy display the customary earmarks of this narrative, pitting courageous students against a retrograde administration. But reconciling the First Amendment values expressed by this stark narrative to the domain of a public university is genuinely puzzling, for it is clear that universities legitimately and necessarily exercise the most pervasive discipline of communication.

Admission to universities, for example, typically requires evaluation of the written submissions of applicants. After admission, classroom discussion is strictly controlled: students must ordinarily restrict their comments to particular topics; they must express themselves in a civil manner; they must not speak unless recognized; they must obey severe time constraints. Student grades will largely depend upon an assessment of their writing. They will be penalized for poor grammar, illogical thinking, insufficient comprehension, outlandish ideas; they will be rewarded for clarity, elegance, innovation, intellectual mastery.

Faculty expression is also extensively regulated. Faculty are hired after close scrutiny of their writing. Their eventual tenure and promotions will turn on judgments concerning their scholarship. University distribution of grants, research support, and other discretionary resources ordinarily entails close review of faculty expression. Faculty teaching is tightly controlled as to its subject matter and carefully reviewed for its effects on students.

It is impossible to dismiss these regulations of speech as involving merely constraints of time, place, and manner. They instead entail judgments that are both content and viewpoint based. Faculty hired to teach astrophysics who insist instead upon teaching astrology are subject to discipline. Students required to write an examination on the behavior of whales risk failure if they write instead on the aesthetics of *Moby Dick*. Historians who advocate the view that the Holocaust never happened are unlikely to receive tenure. Chemistry students seeking to explain physical phenomena on the basis of phlogiston theory will assuredly suffer academic reversals.[1]

These examples illustrate only the most commonplace and routine instances of what must be regarded as a dense and comprehensive web of communicative regulation. It is clear both that such regulation is necessary for the continued existence of universities, at least as we know them, and that the state would be constitutionally barred from imposing analogous regulation upon speech generally. Yet public universities like UC Berkeley are subject to the First Amendment,[2] which explicitly prohibits "abridging the freedom of speech." Applying this prohibition to the daily functioning of a public university poses a real enigma, one that official pronouncements of the FSM era leave largely unelucidated.

Consider, for example, the famous resolution of the Berkeley Academic Senate on December 8, 1964, to the effect that "the content of speech or advocacy should not be restricted by the University."[3] Or consider the position in the FSM platform that "civil liberties and political freedoms which are constitutionally protected off campus must be equally protected on campus for all persons. . . . The Administration may not regulate the content of speech and political conduct."[4] Taken literally, neither position is compatible with the maintenance of a university.

The tendency to imagine that the First Amendment must mean the same thing on campus as off campus remains prevalent to this day. In recent times it has been invoked by conservative forces seeking to prevent the regulation of racist speech by "politically correct" university officials. This was the purpose of the so-called Leonard Law, passed by the California legislature in 1992, which prohibits private universities from making or enforcing "any rule subjecting any student to disciplinary sanctions solely on the basis of . . . communication that, when engaged in outside the campus, . . . is protected from governmental restriction by the First Amendment."[5]

On its face the law sets forth a rule that is absurd. If a citizen cannot constitutionally be penalized for advocating astrological determinism in the pages of the *New York Times*, does the California legislature mean to say that a physics student cannot be penalized for advocating this same view in the pages of her astronomy examination? Or that the student cannot be disciplined for disrupting classroom discussion by repeatedly advocating this view during a course on the French Revolution?

Of course it is highly unlikely that either participants in the FSM controversy or the California legislature meant for their words to be taken literally. Most probably they had in mind a more or less implicit picture of how universities distinctively regulate speech. In fact, if we closely examine the constitutional debates that were so vigorously pressed during the FSM, it becomes clear that they were more immediately concerned with the changing nature of this implicit picture than with any specifically legal analysis of the First Amendment. We can apprehend why this might be so if we somewhat sharpen our analysis of exactly how the First Amendment applies to state universities.

State universities are public organizations. Modern democratic states use public organizations to accomplish ends determined by democratic self-governance. A primary function of the First Amendment is to subject governmental ends to the perennial revision of a free and unconstrained public opinion. But public organizations could not function if their goals were ceaselessly unsettled in this way.

Within government organizations, therefore, objectives are taken as given; resources and persons are managed in order to achieve these objectives. The management of persons necessarily entails the management of their speech. For this reason the First Amendment has consistently been interpreted to permit the regulation of speech within state organizations where necessary to achieve legitimate organizational ends.[6] That is why the First Amendment does not prohibit the state from regulating communication within the military to preserve the national defense;[7] speech within the judicial system to attain the ends of justice;[8] employee speech within government bureaucracies to promote "the efficiency of the public services [that government] performs through its employees";[9] and so forth.[10]

First Amendment analysis of restrictions of speech within public universities follows this general logic. Public universities can regulate speech as is necessary to accomplish their goals. Of course universities have distinct and complex missions. One objective is the advancement of knowledge, which explains why the competence and achievements of faculty can constitutionally be assessed by reference to the professional standards of the scholarly disciplines that define knowledge. On this account, "the heart and soul of academic freedom lie not in free speech but in professional autonomy and collegial self-governance."[11] With respect to students, however, the paramount goal of universities is clearly education. The U.S. Supreme Court has thus held that because "a university's mission is education," the First Amendment does not prevent a university from imposing "reasonable regulations compatible with that mission upon the use of its campus and facilities."[12]

First Amendment assessments of university regulations of student speech accordingly always depend upon an account of a university's educational objectives. If university education is understood to aim at processes of socialization and cultural reproduction, so that "college authorities stand in loco parentis concerning the physical and moral welfare and mental training of the pupils,"[13] then student speech may be regulated as necessary to serve the end of ethical inculcation.[14] Some public universities have recently attempted to stress their role in the cultural reproduction of community norms to justify restrictions on hate speech.[15] By contrast, if university education is understood to be directed at the creation of autonomous and independent citizens prepared to engage in "our vigorous and free society,"[16] the First Amendment will impose quite different restrictions on campus regulations of speech.[17]

Interpreting the constitutional struggles of the FSM controversy, therefore, requires us carefully to attend to implicit disagreements about the educational mission of the university. We can see the outlines of such disagreement in Mario Savio's observation after the decisive faculty meeting of December 8 that the Academic Senate vote was a "direct attack on the doctrine of in loco parentis."[18] And we can see it in Jacobus ten Broek's defense of the Senate's vote on the grounds that the educational mission of the university entailed encouraging "students' commitment to the action and passion of our time."[19] This view of the role of university education is also implicit in FSM pronouncements: "Why do we teach history? Kerr would answer that the only reason . . . is for 'intellectual experience.' NONSENSE! One important reason we teach history is to learn from the experience of the past what to do for the present. Learning is not only for its own sake and thus as Chancellor Strong has said, 'The University is no ivory tower shut away from the world and from the needs and problems of society.'"[20]

This account of university education differs sharply from that which had been offered by University administrators. The University's official statement on academic freedom, originally articulated by President Sproul in 1934 but officially promulgated by him as University Regulation no. 5 in 1944, stated:

> The function of the university is to seek and to transmit knowledge and to train students in the processes whereby truth is to be made known. To convert, or to make converts, is alien and hostile to this dispassionate duty. Where it becomes necessary, in performing this function of a university, to consider political, social, or sectarian movements, they are dissected and examined—not taught, and the conclusion left, with no tipping of the scales, to the logic of the facts.
>
> The University is founded upon faith in intelligence and knowledge and it must defend their free operation. . . . Its obligation is to see that the conditions under which questions are examined are those which give play to intellect rather than to passion. . . .
>
> Its high function . . . the University will steadily continue to fulfill, serving the people by providing facilities for investigation and teaching free from

domination by parties, sects, or selfish interests. The University expects the State, in return, and to its own great gain, to protect this indispensable freedom, a freedom like the freedom of the press, that is the heritage and the right of a free people.[21]

In contrast to ten Broek and the FSM, Sproul conceptualized education as a matter of analysis rather than action, "intellect rather than ... passion." He therefore understood the educational process as requiring vigilant protection from the "domination" of political interests. University rules governing student speech reflected this view of educational mission. In 1938, for example, Sproul prohibited the use of University buildings "for the holding of partisan political ... exercises.... The University ... is a State educational institution and therefore cannot provide meeting places for these purposes."[22]

By 1964, immediately before the FSM controversy, these rules had at the Berkeley campus evolved into a complicated and messy set of regulations,[23] which were summarized on September 21 of that year by Dean of Students Katherine A. Towle:

> Briefly, these policies reserve the use of campus areas to registered students and staff of the Berkeley campus, prohibit solicitation of funds (including donations) "to aid projects not directly connected with some authorized activity of the University," specify the conditions for the appearance of speakers on campus, and for the distribution of handbills, pamphlets, circulars, and other forms of non-commercial literature.
>
> With respect to the latter, it is permissible to distribute materials presenting points of view for or against a proposition, a candidate, or with respect to a social or political issue. It is not permissible in materials distributed on University property to urge a specific vote, call for direct social or political action, or to seek to recruit individuals for such action.[24]

The FSM controversy erupted when the campus administration sought to apply these rules to a 26-foot strip of sidewalk at the entry to the campus at the intersection of Bancroft Way and Telegraph Avenue. For years this strip had been understood to belong to the city of Berkeley; students had accordingly used it to exercise normal First Amendment rights of partisan solicitation, recruitment, and advocacy. But in the fall of 1964 it was apparently discovered that this land actually belonged to the University, and Chancellor Edward W. Strong sought to terminate the exercise of these First Amendment rights by subordinating speech within the area to the University's educational mission as defined by its campus regulations. The yawning disparity between freedom of speech as enjoyed by citizens and freedom of speech as defined within the institutional confines of the University was thus starkly exposed.

The University's regulations were of course rendered instantly controversial. The University was pressed to explain why rights of partisan solicitation, recruitment, and advocacy were inconsistent with the achievement of its educational mission. One justification, implicit in Sproul's initial formulation of the issue, was that the University was responsible for inculcating the intellectual virtues of dispassion and disinterest, which could be accomplished only if students were insulated from the "domination" of partisan advocacy.

This justification was ultimately rooted in the tradition of in loco parentis; it assumed that the moral and intellectual development of students required their isolation from the contamination of the passion of political and social "movements." But by 1964 this justification carried little if any persuasive force. This was not because the distinction between intellectual engagement and partisan advocacy had lost its bite; in 1964, as today, the distinction could be used to evaluate the scholarly work of both students and faculty. Although some, like ten Broek and the FSM, sought to justify freedom of political advocacy by merging scholarship with activism, thus bringing partisan advocacy under the umbrella of academic freedom,[25] most took the opposite tack, arguing that political action was simply irrelevant to scholarship. Thus Carl Schorske: "The primary task of the University of California has always been and must always be teaching, learning, and research—not political activity. Our students, however, are citizens, and should enjoy the right to political expression and activity on the campus. That is all that the faculty resolution wishes to establish. Such is the proper division of authority for a university in a democratic society, whose youth are both students and citizens."[26]

By 1964 even Clark Kerr could explicitly acknowledge that "the current generation of students is well characterized as activist."[27] Students could and did engage in partisan activity just outside the boundaries of the campus, so that University regulations could not in fact isolate students from political action. The notion that the University could assume responsibility for the comprehensive moral and intellectual supervision of its students accordingly became less and less plausible.

Concomitantly with these developments, "the legal status of students in post-secondary institutions changed dramatically in the 1960s."[28] College students began to be seen more like adults and less like minors subject to the moral guardianship of a university—a trend exemplified by the ratification of the Twenty-Sixth Amendment in 1971, which lowered the voting age to 18.

Perhaps as a result of these developments, campus administrators in the fall of 1964 were not prepared to defend University restrictions on partisan activism as necessary to ensure the full moral and intellectual development of their students. Instead they articulated a quite different rationale. Sproul's original statement on academic freedom had postulated a bargain between the University and the state in which the University would provide "facilities for investigation and teaching free from domination by parties, sects, or selfish interests" and the state, in return, would respect the academic freedom and independence of the University. University officials defended prohibitions on partisan activism on the grounds that they were necessary for the University to fulfill its obligations under this bargain.

Kerr had endorsed this position in his Charter Day address of May 5, 1964. Ironically, Kerr wished to use the University's bargain to defend against conservative demands that students convicted of illegal actions during off-campus civil rights demonstrations be disciplined by the University.[29] He argued that "the activities of students acting as private citizens off-campus on non-University matters are outside the sphere of the University." Such activities were the concern of the state, which governed students in their capacities as citizens. They did not involve the University, whose jurisdiction extended only to "areas of direct University concern." Kerr thus postulated a categorical distinction between the roles of citizen and student, and he employed the geographical boundaries of the campus as a criterion to separate one from the other. It followed from this argument, however, that individuals while on campus would have to forsake their roles as citizens and fully adopt the role of student, for which, as Sproul had suggested, partisan activism was irrelevant:

> Just as the University cannot and should not follow the student into . . . his activities as a citizen off the campus, so also the students . . . cannot take the name of the University with them as they move into . . . political or other non-University activities; nor should they or can they use University facilities in connection with such affairs. The University has resisted and will continued to resist such efforts by students, just as it has resisted and will continue to resist the suggestions of others that the University take on some of the functions of the state. The University is an independent educational institution. It is not a partisan political . . . institution; nor is it an enforcement arm of the state. It will not accede to pressures for either form of exploitation of its name, its facilities, its authority. The University will not allow students or others connected with it to use it to further their non-University political or social . . . causes nor will it allow those outside the University to use it for non-University purposes. The University will remain what it always has been— a University devoted to instruction, research and public service wherever knowledge can serve society.

Chancellor Strong embraced this same justification in defending University restrictions on partisan activism. On September 27 he had been presented with an ASUC senate petition seeking, as Strong put it, the freedom in specific geographical areas of the campus "1) to solicit political party membership, 2) to mount political and social action on the campus, 3) to solicit funds on campus for such action, and 4) to receive funds to aid projects not directly concerned with an authorized activity of the University."[30] Strong was uncompromising in his response: "University facilities are not to be used for any of these four purposes."[31]

Strong justified his conclusion by reasserting Kerr's position that the University needed to distinguish between the status of persons as citizens and their status as students.[32] Like Kerr, Strong used the geographical boundaries of the campus to mark this distinction. Citing Sproul's reference to the bargain between the state and the University, Strong argued that the quid pro quo for University independence was that students on campus lay aside their status as citizens and as a consequence abandon rights of partisan activism:

> On the one side, an individual as a student is held responsible by the University for compliance with rules and regulations. On the other side, when a student goes off-campus to participate in some social or political action, he does so on his own responsibility as a citizen. He has no right, acting as a citizen, to involve the University, either by using its name or by using any of its facilities, to further such an action. For, were the University to become involved, the consequence is clear. We ask and expect from the State an indispensable freedom residing in independence—independence that rests on fulfillment of a public trust, namely, that the University will never allow itself to be dominated by, nor used by parties, sects, or selfish interests. By honoring this public trust steadfastly, the University is enabled also to honor and defend the rights of its members to act freely in the public domain in their capacity as citizens. The consequence of defaulting on this public trust would be the erosion of the independence of the University and the destruction of the position maintained by the University respecting the responsibilities of an individual as a student in the University and respecting his rights and responsibilities as a citizen of the state.

The Kerr-Strong position deserves close analysis. A public university certainly does hold a "public trust," which can be compromised only on pain of losing its legitimacy as a public institution. Implicit in this trust are a variety of obligations that include, for example, requirements of neutrality. A public university would lose its legitimacy were it to become partisan, a supporter of one or another political party.[33] But although the Kerr-Strong position invokes the concept of the university's public trust, it does not ultimately express a vision of that trust.

The closest Kerr and Strong come to such a vision is to intimate that allowing partisan solicitation, recruitment, and advocacy on campus would be inconsistent with proper university neutrality because it could be understood as official endorsement of partisan activism. But this intimation is implausible, for a university no more endorses the content of all the speech on its premises than it endorses the content of all the books in its library. At the beginning of the 1964 school year, for example, Towle had explicitly stated that "it is permissible to distribute materials presenting points of view for or against a proposition, a candidate, or with respect to a social or political issue."[34] The University could scarcely authorize such speech if authorization were understood to imply endorsement.

If the Kerr-Strong position does not ultimately rest on an account of the public trust, neither does it express a theory of educational mission. The premise of the position is that geography determines status. This premise seems clearly false. Crimes committed by students on campus are subject to civil prosecution by the state, so that students cannot shed their status as citizens while within the geographical boundaries of the University. Similarly, students do not automatically lose their status as students when they leave the campus. If a student were systematically to intimidate fellow students or professors while off campus, university discipline would surely be appropriate. A serious theory of the university's educational mission, therefore, would not turn solely on the single parameter of geography.

In fact the Kerr-Strong position appears to rest on the notion that prohibitions of on-campus partisan solicitation, recruitment, and advocacy were necessary in order to placate politicians who might otherwise undermine the University's independence.[35] Kerr and Strong evidently believed that allowing on-campus calls for political action risked provoking state suppression of the academic freedom necessary for the University to pursue its mission. Political action was to be prohibited based upon a political calculation about the effects of such activism on the reputation and standing of the University. It is this calculation alone that explains the otherwise strange distinction drawn by Towle between "materials presenting points of view for or against a . . . social or political issue" and "materials distributed on University property to . . . call for direct social or political action."[36]

The suppression of First Amendment rights on the basis of a political calculation of this kind is certainly suspect. Although sometimes warranted by extraordinary circumstances, it is presumptively impermissible to deny First Amendment rights on the basis of anticipated adverse reactions.[37] More importantly, however, the University's interest in fostering political *support* for its legitimate mission does not stand on the same constitutional footing as its interest in the *exercise* of its legitimate mission. Whereas the latter unproblematically supports restrictions on speech that would not be permissible in the larger society, the former does not. It would almost certainly be unconstitutional for the University to seek to protect its political interests by suppressing the off-campus organization and speech of students who were effectively opposing a bond initiative legitimately and urgently needed by the University.[38] It is not clear why it would be any more justified for the University to protect these same political interests by suppressing the identical organization and speech on campus.

Because the Kerr-Strong position did not articulate a principled vision of university mission but instead advanced a political judgment about potentially adverse political consequences, its authority depended, at least in part, upon student perceptions of its good faith and wisdom.[39] It requires a fair degree of trust for persons to refrain from doing what they would otherwise have a right to do on the basis of a political calculation of this kind, which no doubt contributed to the way in which the FSM conflict later became so intensely personalized. The accuracy of the judgment underlying the Kerr-Strong position, moreover, was always open to question.[40] Certainly it is pertinent to observe that history has proved it demonstrably incorrect. Partisan solicitation, recruitment, and advocacy are now permitted on campus, but the independence of the University has not for this reason been compromised. We have not been forced to purchase our academic freedom at the price of a monastic asceticism.

Finally and most importantly, it is also relevant in assessing the Kerr-Strong position that it directly challenged the FSM to inaugurate a spiral of increasingly chaotic political instability. This is because practical political calculations like those advanced by Kerr and Strong are always sensitive to the costs of alternative courses of action. The FSM thus had every incentive to use its political strength to alter the terms of the administration's political calculus. By implacably increasing the price of maintaining restrictions on partisan activism, the FSM could seek to change the context of the administration's judgments, thereby forcing the administration to reconsider its political reckoning. Strong might with reason complain that this tactic constituted "defamation of authority duly exercised," which "undermines respect for high offices and demoralizes a society,"[41] but the logic of the tactic was dictated by the form of the justification offered by the administration.

In fact FSM tactics proved highly effective. As the costs of repressing speech mounted, University officials were forced to reevaluate their assessment of relative risks. They consequently began to offer concessions.[42] By November 20 the Regents, at Kerr's urging, changed University policy to permit "certain campus facilities, carefully selected and properly regulated," to be "used by students and staff for planning, implementing, raising funds or recruiting participants for lawful off-campus action, not for unlawful off-campus action."[43] The new policy, said Kerr, met the demands pressed by the ASUC senate back in September.[44] Strong announced to the Academic Senate that "students now do have maximum political freedom."[45]

But the spiral of confrontation, once initiated, could not be so easily quelled. University officials chose to distinguish on-campus advocacy of legal off-campus action from on-campus advocacy of illegal off-campus action. They strenuously insisted that the latter be prohibited.[46] This distinction, however, was never rooted in any careful articulation of the educational mission of the University, and it therefore appeared to reassert the same kind of political judgment as that underlying the University's original prohibitions of partisan activism.

A student who advocates on campus that the off-campus homes of minority students be torched so as to drive them from the campus merits university discipline because he directly interferes with the educational objectives of the university. But these same objectives are not impaired by the speech of a student who on campus advocates in favor of illegal demonstrations in Mississippi to protest segregation (or, for that matter, by the speech of a student who advocates on campus in favor of illegal demonstrations in Boston in opposition to school desegregation). By refusing to distinguish between these two quite distinct circumstances, administration officials invited the FSM to read their adamant proscription of all advocacy of illegal off-campus conduct as based upon an undifferentiated fear of provoking a political backlash against the University.

Faced with yet another political calculation, the FSM continued to press the administration to recalibrate its assessment of political risks by increasing the costs of maintaining the ban on advocacy of illegal off-campus action. Moreover, the FSM had by this time become so distrustful of University officials as to embrace the position that all University control over the content of speech on campus ought to be abolished. This is clear from the FSM platform, which was published in the *Daily Californian* on November 13:

> Civil liberties and political freedoms which are constitutionally protected off-campus must be equally protected on campus for all persons. Similarly, illegal speech or conduct should receive no greater protection on campus than off-campus. The Administration may not regulate the content of speech and political conduct, and must leave solely to the appropriate civil authorities the right of punishment for transgressions of the law. Regulations governing the time, place, and manner of exercising constitutional rights are necessary for the maintenance and proper operation of University functions, but they must not, either directly or indirectly, interfere with the rights of speech or the content of speech.[47]

The platform takes the extreme position that, with the exception of content-neutral "time, place and manner" regulations,[48] speech that is legal off campus ought not to be regulated by the University. This position is quite extravagant because, as we have already seen, no university could function under such a rule. Although it is probable that the FSM did not mean the literal import of its words, it is nevertheless significant that the FSM failed to acknowledge the myriad of ways in which universities pervasively and necessarily discipline the content of otherwise perfectly legal speech, as for example in the evaluation of scholarship and student work.

The very reasons that justify such discipline are also relevant to the assessment of university controls on partisan advocacy within specific campus geographical "Hyde Parks," like the Bancroft-Telegraph strip, which the FSM most certainly did have in mind. Universities have strong and legitimate interests in regulating "political" advocacy specifically designed to interfere with their educational objectives. From the perspective of both the First Amendment and common sense, a university ought to be able to discipline a student who advocates the rape of female students, whether or not as a matter of technical First Amendment doctrine the advocacy can be punished by the criminal law.[49]

Not content with severely constricting the kinds of speech that a university ought to be able to regulate, the FSM platform goes further and proposes the extraordinary proposition that the University "must leave solely to the appropriate civil authorities the right of punishment for transgressions of the law."[50] Evidently, the FSM believed that the University ought not to discipline even those minimal forms of communication that the FSM was prepared to concede might rightfully be punished by the state. This conclusion was justified on the grounds that "the FSM believes that the University is not a competent body to decide questions of civil liberties, especially since it is subject to strong political pressure. Because students' rights have great political impact as well as legal significance, the courts should be the only body to decide upon them."[51] The intense personalization of the controversy is evident from this justification, which does not so much invoke a defensible account of the University's educational mission as express a fundamental mistrust of University officials.[52]

Taken as a whole, therefore, the explicit provisions of the FSM platform sought to prohibit virtually all University regulation of communication, thereby disabling the University from articulating and enforcing the special disciplinary rules that would define and construct the University's own distinct, educational mission. It thus constituted a basic assault on the University's position as an independent organization holding interests different from those of the general public.[53] No organization could accept such an ultimatum without dismantling itself, which no doubt in part explains Strong's unequivocal response to the FSM demand: "Activities of students in disobedience of the laws of the state and community are punishable in their courts. The University maintains jurisdiction over violations of its rules including those which prohibit use of University facilities for planning and recruiting for actions found to be unlawful by the courts."[54]

The FSM and the administration thus faced each other over a seemingly impassable divide. As the administration continued to insist that its judgments about the best interests of the University be respected, the FSM grew increasingly determined to strip the University of any distinctive role with respect to the regulation of speech. The standoff was broken by the faculty at its famous meeting of December 8. By a resounding vote of 824–115, the faculty voted to uphold the FSM position, urging in the two central paragraphs of its resolution

> 2. That the time, place and manner of conducting political activity on the campus shall be subject to reasonable regulation to prevent interference with the normal functions of the University; . . .

3. That the content of speech or advocacy should not be restricted by the University. Off-campus student political activities shall not be subject to University regulation. On-campus advocacy or organization of such activities shall be subject only to such limitations as may be imposed under section 2.[55]

The faculty resolutions were of sweeping effect. Like Kerr in his Charter Day address, they used the geographical boundaries of the campus as a categorical measure of the University's educational mission; they essentially denied that any off-campus student "political activities" could interfere with that mission. Like the FSM platform, the faculty resolutions sought flatly to prohibit University control over the content of speech. They would thus prohibit University discipline even of on-campus advocacy that could constitutionally be subject to criminal prosecution,[56] as for example student advocacy of the imminent and likely destruction of University property.

Like the FSM platform, the faculty resolutions refused to acknowledge the relevance of any distinct University objectives in regulating political speech. Even if the resolutions are not read literally but interpreted as applying only to designated "Hyde Park" areas on campus, they are best understood as premised on the view, most concisely expressed by Joseph Tussman, that there was no need for the University to impose "more restrictions on its students in the area of political activity than exists in the community-at-large."[57]

For the reasons I have already articulated, however, it is not plausible to regard the university as an institution without specific interests in the regulation of communication and of its content that are distinct from those of the public at large. This is also true with regard to potentially "political" communication. The university stands in a different relationship to students advocating the intimidation of fellow students than does the public at large.

Because the faculty resolutions fundamentally denied the relevance of distinctive university objectives and because such a denial is not in the long run compatible with the maintenance of a university, the resolutions are perhaps most charitably interpreted as a political intervention designed to end the escalating spiral of campus confrontation. The faculty prefaced its resolutions with the hope that they would "end the present crisis" and "establish the confidence and trust essential to the restoration of normal University life,"[58] and the resolutions were successful in achieving these goals. In effect the faculty purchased peace by handing the FSM what the latter rightly regarded as "an unprecedented victory."[59]

It is fair to conclude, therefore, that all sides to the controversy ultimately staked out positions that were motivated more by the political exigencies of the crisis than by any focused account of the intersection between First Amendment rights and the institutional mission of the university. It is thus not surprising that the cogency of these positions has diminished as the exigencies of that time have faded. The distinction so tenaciously insisted upon by the administration between the advocacy of legal and the advocacy of illegal off-campus action, for example, has long since disappeared from the University's regulations. The distinction has vanished because it never truly expressed a defensible account of the University's distinct institutional objectives.

The FSM's urgent demand that the University not enforce its own rules regarding speech has also disappeared as a live political question. Contemporary University policy explicitly provides that "violation of University policies or campus regulations may subject a person to possible legal penalties; if the person is a student, faculty member, or staff member of the University, that person may also be subject to disciplinary action."[60] These disciplinary sanctions apply to the numerous University regulations that regulate communication.[61] Demands that the University repudiate its jurisdiction to enforce these regulations have entirely vanished, probably because it is recognized that such jurisdiction reflects basic prerogatives of self-definition and self-protection that necessarily attach to any competent organization.[62]

Finally, the central thrust of the faculty resolutions, embodied in their flat prohibition of content-based regulation and in their categorical determination that off-campus "political activities" be insulated from University discipline, has also lapsed as a pressing constitutional concern. University regulations do not today prohibit the University from restricting the content of speech, and in fact many contemporary disciplinary rules require a determination of communicative content.[63] These rules apply not only to communication that occurs on University property but also potentially to political activity that does not occur on University property,[64] if jurisdiction over the latter is deemed necessary to serve "the mission of the University."[65]

In the long run, therefore, the University's disciplinary policies with regard to communication have uncontroversially gravitated toward a more realistic and defensible protection of the University's educational objectives. This is true even if we focus precisely on the University's current controls over political speech within the open "Hyde Park" areas of the campus. Berkeley's regulations presently provide:

> The University has a special obligation to protect free inquiry and free expression. On University grounds open to the public generally, all persons may exercise the constitutionally protected rights of free expression, speech and assembly. Such activities must not, however, interfere with the right of the University to conduct its affairs in an orderly manner and to maintain its property, nor may they interfere with the University's obligation to protect

the rights of all to teach, study, and freely exchange ideas. These regulations purport to assure the right of free expression and advocacy on the Berkeley campus, to minimize conflict between the form of exercise of that right and the rights of others in the effective use of University facilities, and to minimize possible interference with the University's responsibilities as an educational institution.[66]

Although these regulations are hardly a model of clarity, they can fairly be interpreted to stress that First Amendment rights are precious and protected except when overridden by the compelling imperative of the University to fulfill its "responsibilities as an educational institution." It is true that the regulations do not offer much in the way of specific guidance about how this imperative is to be defined or to be reconciled with First Amendment rights, but at least the regulations accurately articulate the conflicting values that require resolution in this difficult area of the law. They are in this regard a significant advance over the competing formulations of the FSM era.

What must be kept firmly in mind, however, is that Berkeley's contemporary regulations have evolved from a remarkable history of contest and confrontation. Our current regulations would have been inconceivable under Sproul's image of the University as an isolated and ascetic community susceptible to disabling contamination from politics and passion. They would also have been inconceivable under the Faustian bargain which Kerr and Strong were prepared to strike with the state, in which University personnel accepted a technocratic and monastic withdrawal from politics in return for academic freedom and independence.

The perceptions of the University's role advanced by administrative officials during the FSM crisis now seem like quaint and ancient history. But they were abandoned only reluctantly and only as a direct result of the courage and persistence of the FSM. The legendary struggle of 1964 fundamentally altered the concept of the University, and such political freedoms as we now enjoy derive from that transformation. Even if contemporary University regulations of speech have assumed forms deeply incon-sistent with the literal demands of the FSM, we are nevertheless deeply in its debt.

NOTES

1. On viewpoint discrimination within universities, see my "Subsidized Speech," *Yale Law Journal* 106 (Oct. 1996): 151, 165–67.

2. See *Healy v. James,* 408 U.S. 169, 180 (1972): "At the outset we note that state colleges and universities are not enclaves immune from the sweep of the First Amendment."

3. Quoted in Andrew L. Pierovich (managing editor), *California Monthly* (hereafter, *CM*), "Chronology of Events: Three Months of Crisis," reproduced in Seymour

Martin Lipset and Sheldon S. Wolin, *The Berkeley Student Revolt* (Garden City, N.Y.: Doubleday, 1965), 181.

4. FSM platform, in *Daily Californian* (hereafter *DC*), 13 Nov. 1964.

5. California Education Code, sec. 94367(a). The law was used to strike down Stanford's effort to prohibit racist speech on campus. See *Corry v. The Leland Stanford Junior University*, Cal. Supr. Court, 27 Feb. 1995, case no. 740309.

6. For a general explication of this account of the relationship between the First Amendment and state organizations, see my *Constitutional Domains: Democracy, Community, Management* (Cambridge, Mass.: Harvard University Press, 1995).

7. *Brown v. Glines*, 444 U.S. 348, 354 (1980).

8. See my "The Management of Speech: Discretion and Rights," *Supreme Court Review* (1984): 169, 196–206.

9. *Connick v. Myers*, 261 U.S. 138, 142 (1983).

10. For a full discussion, see my "Between Management and Governance: The History and Theory of the Public Forum," *UCLA Law Review* 34 (June–Aug. 1987): 1713.

11. Thomas L. Haskell, "Justifying the Rights of Academic Freedom in the Era of Power/Knowledge," in Louis Menand, ed., *The Future of Academic Freedom* (Chicago: University of Chicago Press, 1996), 54. Also see, e.g., *Academic Personnel Manual of the University of California*, sec. 005.

12. *Widmar v. Vincent*, 454 U.S. 263, 267 n. 5, 268–69 (1981); compare *Hazelwood School Dist. v. Kuhlmeier*, 484 U.S. 260, 266 (1987) ("A school need not tolerate student speech that is inconsistent with its 'basic educational mission,' . . . even though the government could not censor similar speech outside the school."). On First Amendment rights within the context of a university, see my "Racist Speech, Democracy, and the First Amendment," *William and Mary Law Review* 32 (winter 1990): 267, 317–25.

13. *Gott v. Berea College*, 161 S.W. 204, 206 (Ky. 1913); see *John B. Stetson University v. Hunt*, 102 S. 637, 640 (Fla. 1924).

14. For a modern statement of this position, see *Papish v. University of Missouri Curators*, 410 U.S. 667, 672 (1973) (Burger, C.J., dissenting).

15. See Post, "Racist Speech," 319–21.

16. *Healy v. James*, 408 U.S. 169, 194 (1972).

17. See Post, "Racist Speech," 321–23.

18. Quoted in *DC*, 9 Dec. 1964.

19. Quoted in *DC*, 16 Dec. 1964.

20. *Free Speech Now*, pamphlet, n.d., Free Speech Movement records, CU-309 (hereafter cited as FSM Records), University Archives, Bancroft Library, University of California at Berkeley.

21. On file in the FSM Records. Sproul's statement remains the authoritative pronouncement of the University regarding academic freedom. See *Academic Personnel Manual*, sec. 010, University of California Archives, Bancroft Library. On the stormy context of its original articulation in 1934, see C. Michael Otten, *University Authority and the Student: The Berkeley Experience* (Berkeley and Los Angeles: University of California Press, 1970), 108–19; Robert Cohen, *When the Old Left Was Young* (New York: Oxford University Press, 1993), 118–33. In addressing the Academic Senate in 1934, Sproul began: "Day by day in these troubled times the position of

University administrative officers grows more difficult as they face questions involving academic freedom or the right of free speech. Both radicals and reactionaries would use the University as an agency of propaganda and each group attacks bitterly those who strive to preserve its integrity as an institution for the discovery and dissemination of knowledge. It seems to me desirable, therefore, to announce to this Senate and to the public the principles which guide the President in these matters and which may be said to be, in a certain sense, the policy of the University" (*Minutes of the Academic Senate,* 27 Aug. 1934, University Archives).

22. Orders of the President no. 17, 10 Feb. 1938, FSM Records.

23. They may be found in the pamphlet published by the office of the dean of students, "Information for Student Organizations, 1964–1965," FSM Records.

24. Towle, "Use of Campus Facilities, Including Entrance at Bancroft Way and Telegraph Avenue and 'Hyde Park' Areas," 21 Sept. 1964, FSM Records.

25. See Jacobus ten Broek, Norman Jacobson, and Sheldon S. Wolin, "Academic Freedom and Student Political Activity," in Lipset and Wolin, 443–48.

26. "A Message on the Proposed Solution to the Free Speech Controversy: Nine Distinguished Members of the Faculty State Their Views," n.d., FSM Records.

27. "A Message to Alumni from President Kerr," *CM* 75 (Feb. 1965): 94–96.

28. William A. Kaplin, *The Law of Higher Education: Legal Implications of Administrative Decision Making* (San Francisco: Jossey-Bass, 1978), 175–76.

29. Kerr, "The University: Civil Rights and Civic Responsibilities," 5 May 1964, FSM Records.

30. "Chancellor's Remarks, University Meeting," 28 Sept. 1964, FSM Records. The petition actually sought: "1) Permission to distribute printed material advocating student participation in political and social action; 2) Permission to distribute printed material soliciting political party membership, or supporting or opposing partisan candidates or propositions in local or national elections; 3) Permission to receive funds to aid projects not directly concerned with an authorized activity of our University" (*DC,* 28 Sept. 1964). It is noteworthy that the students did not request the freedom "to mount political and social action," a peculiar locution that took on increasing importance as the controversy developed. The petition did address the central premise of the Kerr position, asserting "that the granting of these same requests in no way sacrifices the administration of our University's affairs to any political and sectarian influence."

31. "Any student or group of students seeking to recruit members for social or political action, or to solicit funds for such action, is free to do so off-campus, but is prohibited from doing so on campus." "Chancellor's Remarks, University Meeting," 28 Sept. 1964. Interestingly, on September 29 the *Daily Californian* reported Strong's remarks as representing a "substantial concession" because it permitted the distribution of "campaign literature advocating 'yes' and 'no' votes on propositions and candidates, and campaign buttons and bumper strips" at designated campus locations, including the Bancroft-Telegraph entrance.

32. Like Kerr, Strong used this distinction to defend against calls to discipline students involved in illegal off-campus political activity. "The University prohibits the mounting of social and political action on campus by reason of the following considerations. If the University permitted its facilities to be used to recruit membership in political parties and to promote social or political demonstrations in a

surrounding community, the University could then no longer hold fast to a fundamental position on which it has insisted. The University respects the right of each
student as a citizen to participate as he sees fit in off-campus, non-University courses
of action. When an individual, in so participating, acts in a disorderly way or is in
violation of the law, he is answerable to the civil authorities for his conduct. Some
citizens demand further that the individual as a student also be disciplined by the
University, that is, that he be censured, suspended, or expelled. We answer such
demand by pointing out that we respect the right of our students to act in their
capacity as citizens in the public domain" ("Chancellor's Remarks, University Meeting," 28 Sept. 1964).

33. Thus we read in the *Report of the President's Commission on Campus Unrest*
(Washington, D.C.: U.S. Government Printing Office, 1970): "The frequent
assumption of political positions by universities as institutions reduces their ability
to pursue their central missions. As Professor Kenneth Keniston has stated: 'The
main task of the university is to maintain a climate in which, among other things,
the critical spirit can flourish. If individual universities as organizations were to
align themselves officially with specifically political positions, their ability to defend
the critical function would be undermined. Acting as a lobby or pressure group for
some particular judgment or proposal, a university in effect closes its doors to those
whose critical sense leads them to disagree.'" The *Report* goes on to observe (190)
that "political involvement of the members of universities is quite another matter, of
course. Students, faculty members, and administrators may participate as individuals in the full range of peaceful political activities."

34. Towle, "Use of Campus Facilities."

35. See, e.g., "Strong's Statement," *DC*, 1 Oct. 1964: "Some students demand
on-campus solicitation of funds and planning and recruitment of off-campus social
and political action. The University cannot allow its facilities to be so used without
endangering its future as an independent educational institution."

36. Towle, "Use of Campus Facilities."

37. See, e.g., *Forsyth County, Ga. v. Nationalist Movement*, 505 U.S. 123 (1992);
Terminiello v. Chicago, 337 U.S. 1 (1949). Compare *Feiner v. New York*, 340 U.S. 315
(1951).

38. See, e.g., *Pickering v. Board of Education*, 391 U.S. 563 (1968).

39. It is clear that some on campus were persuaded by the Kerr-Strong position.
For example, the editors of *DC* argued that the University had benefited "for
decades" by remaining "politically aloof" and that to change this course would
encourage external political forces "to dabble in the administration of the University and bring to an end this era of independence." The editorial accused the FSM
of failing to understand "that those individuals transporting political and social
activity from this campus to the surrounding communities will not be treading on
one-way streets, but rather two-way streets. Coming in the opposite direction,
sooner or later, will be state legislators, law enforcement agencies, and the public
itself" ("An Appeal to the Regents," *DC*, 9 Dec. 1964).

40. As Philip Selznick observed at the time, "It is interesting that the 'realist'
defense of the original policy, as necessary to the protection of the university from
conservative criticism, was given small weight by the administration when the need
to abandon untenable distinctions became apparent. This suggests that the basic

policy never had any good reason for being, even as a defensive tactic, and was a needless affront to the sensibilities of the students" ("Reply to Glazer," in Lipset and Wolin, 304).

41. Strong address to the Town and Gown Club, 2 Nov. 1964, quoted in Pierovich, 136.

42. See, e.g., motion of Frank Kidner, dean of educational relations, in the CCPA, 5 Nov. 1964: "We [the administration representatives to the committee] would vote for a language which would recommend to the Chancellor, and then to the President or the Regents, the text of a regulation which would in no way inhibit on the campus of the University of California advocacy of off-campus political action and social action, including recruiting for off-campus political and social action, and including raising funds for off-campus political and social action, provided that we can discover language which makes it explicit and public that no one has any intention at any time of undertaking unlawful action" (CCPA, minutes of the meeting, 5 Nov. 1964, FSM Records).

43. Jim Branson, "Regents Decide on Regulations," *DC*, 23 Nov. 1964.

44. Kerr, "Statement: To the Campus," 24 Nov. 1964, FSM Records.

45. Strong to Academic Senate, 24 Nov. 1964, FSM Records.

46. "The demand of the FSM that the University permit the mounting of unlawful action on the campus without any penalty by the University cannot and will not be granted" (statement of Strong, 22 Nov. 1964, FSM Records).

47. *DC*, 13 Nov. 1964.

48. On the requirement that "time, place and manner" regulations be content neutral, see my "Recuperating First Amendment Doctrine," *Stanford Law Review* 47 (July 1995): 1249.

49. On the constitutional test for whether the advocacy of illegal conduct may be subject to criminal punishment, see *Brandenburg v. Ohio*, 395 U.S. 444, 447 (1969), which provides that "the constitutional guarantees of free speech and free press do not permit a State to forbid or proscribe advocacy of the use of force or of law violation except where such advocacy is directed to inciting or producing imminent lawless action and is likely to incite or produce such action."

50. FSM representatives proposed the following rule during the deliberations of the CCPA: "In the area of first amendment rights and civil liberties the University may impose no disciplinary action against members of the University community and organizations. In this area members of the University Community and organizations are subject only to the civil authorities" (remarks of Bettina Aptheker, minutes of the CCPA, 7 Nov. 1964, FSM Records).

51. "FSM Statement," *DC*, 9 Nov. 1964. Occasionally the FSM justified the proposition on the grounds that discipline by the University, when added to prosecution in the courts, would constitute double jeopardy. See, e.g., FSM press release, 17 Nov. (P.M.) 1964; FSM, "Why the Committee Deadlocked," leaflet, n.d., FSM Records. As a matter of positive constitutional law, this argument from double jeopardy is without merit. See, e.g., *Helvering v. Mitchell*, 303 U.S. 391 (1938). The argument fares no better from the perspective of common sense. For the University to expel a student convicted of assaulting a fellow student would no more constitute double jeopardy than would a decision by the San Francisco police force to fire a patrolman convicted of assaulting civilians. Ironically, it was Kerr who first

introduced the concept of double jeopardy in his May 5, 1964, Charter Day address (see note 29, above). Kerr sought to use the concept to protect students from calls for University discipline based upon illegal off-campus activities: "The punishment, for students and citizens, should fit the crime. One punishment, not two, should fit one crime. A citizen because he is a student should not be penalized more than his fellow citizen who is not a student."

52. The FSM position essentially amounted to denying to the University an interest in enforcing the general laws of the state. This is not plausible, however, because any state institution holding jurisdiction over a discrete geographical area has a strong interest in enforcing certain of those laws. A university can legitimately prevent and discipline assaults on its own campus by members of the university community. The case would not seem to be any different with regard to criminal communications on its own campus by university members. This would indicate that the FSM position is better interpreted as aimed at the particular University administrators with whom they were in conflict than as expressing any careful account of a university. This interpretation is reinforced by the obvious point that any generic concern with "strong political pressure" would seem more appropriately directed at the politicians who direct the application of the criminal law than at university officials.

53. Professor Sanford Kadish articulated this point quite clearly during the internal debates of the CCPA: "In a case where a student comes through my office window at night and swipes examination questions, that is burglary. I think the University is entitled to take disciplinary action. It is indispensable that any community have the means at its disposal to maintain itself as an organization" (minutes of the CCPA, 7 Nov. 1964, FSM Records).

54. Edward W. Strong, "To the Campus," *DC*, 24 Nov. 1964.

55. *Academic Senate Minutes*, 8 Dec. 1964, University Archives.

56. *Brandenburg v. Ohio*, 395 U.S. 444, 447 (1969).

57. Joseph Tussman, quoted in Barry Bishin, "Regents Decide Next Week," *DC*, 9 Dec. 1964.

58. *Academic Senate Minutes*, 8 Dec. 1964.

59. FSM, "Happiness Is an Academic Senate Meeting," quoted in Pierovich, 182.

60. University of California Policies Applying to Campus Activities, Organizations, and Students, sec. 40.20, 15 Aug. 1994, University Archives.

61. Examples are listed in note 63, below.

62. I should add that, contrary to the FSM's position, contemporary University regulations also assert the University's interest and competence in enforcing the general laws of the state. They provide that "University properties shall be used only in accordance with Federal, State, and local laws, and shall not be used for the purpose of organizing or carrying out unlawful activity" (University of California Policies Applying to Campus Activities, Organizations, and Students, sec. 40.10, 15 Aug. 1994). Speech that is illegal is thus also rendered an infraction of University regulations.

63. For example, the Berkeley Campus Code of Student Conduct (July 1998) prohibits "forgery" (sec. III[A][1]), "verbal abuse, threats, intimidation, harassment" (sec. III[A][10]), "plagiarism" (sec. III[B][2]), "furnishing false information

in the context of an academic assignment" (sec. III[B][3]), and the "theft or damage of intellectual property" (sec. III[B][6], University Archives).

64. The Berkeley Campus Code of Student Conduct, sec. III(A)(7), prohibits the "obstruction or disruption of teaching, research, administration, student disciplinary procedures or other University activity."

65. University disciplinary regulations "apply to students while on University property or in connection with official University functions. If specified in implementing campus regulations, these standards of conduct may apply to conduct which occurs off campus and which would violate student conduct and discipline policies or regulations if the conduct occurred on campus" (University of California Policies Applying to Campus Activities, Organizations, and Students, sec. 101.00, 15 Aug. 1994). The Campus Code of Student Conduct, sec. II(F), specifically applies to off-campus conduct "where it 1) adversely affects the health, safety, or security of any member of the University community, or the mission of the University, or 2) involves academic work or any records, or documents of the University" (July 1998).

66. Ibid., sec. 311. Section 211 of the code provides: "The purpose of these regulations is to facilitate the effective use and enjoyment of the facilities and services of the Berkeley campus as an educational institution."

December 1964

Some Reflections and Recollections

Robert H. Cole

For a brief moment thirty-seven years ago, the Good, the True, and the Beautiful seemed to some of us both one and real. This moment came after the vote on the Academic Senate's December 8 resolution, when a thousand members of the faculty filed out of Wheeler Hall through a narrow path between packed crowds of applauding students. It was the culmination of a week that shook our world. Caught up in intense emotion, our normal routines in shambles, we had been in an unrelenting whirlwind: demonstrations, meetings, negotiations, drafting, arguing, historicizing. We knew we were part of something of great social and educational importance. But what exactly was the goal that justified this sense of historic importance, the intensity and commitment, and that sublime though fleeting feeling when we passed the resolution that was to end the protracted campus crisis?

Specifically, the issue by this time was the freedom of students to advocate and organize *on* the Berkeley campus actions that would take place *off* the campus and that would be *illegal,* that is, typically, subject to criminal penalty if and where they occurred. This was understood to be different from on-campus advocacy and organization of off-campus actions that would be *legal* off campus. For example, one could organize on the campus a rally at the state capitol, a *legal* off-campus action, but one could *not* organize on the campus a massive sit-in at, say, a supermarket that would close it down, an *illegal* off-campus action.

This distinction between illegal and legal off-campus actions had not been the issue, however, when the FSM began. In September 1964 the FSM was fighting for the freedom to advocate and organize off-campus actions that everyone assumed were legal or constitutionally protected, for the University had prohibited all such political activity without distinction. People's attention was not yet focused on the issue of off-campus legality. But as events developed over the fall, the participants understood the issues in increasingly refined terms, and the political processes narrowed them. When a policy statement by the Regents on November 20 conceded the freedom to advocate and organize *legal* off-campus actions, only the illegal off-campus actions remained in dispute. To be sure, the distinction between illegal and legal action is quite contingent. For one thing, the planned off-campus activity might not materialize at all. For another, it might be planned to be illegal but turn out to be legal (or vice versa); legality would depend on the particular facts at the time the off-campus activity occurred. Moreover, whether the on-campus organizing would even be treated by a court as legally responsible for the off-campus action would also depend on the factual context. Thus, this distinction, which the FSM and its faculty supporters fought so hard to eliminate, was an unusually narrow and fact-contingent one for such an important historical role. At first glance, it may hardly seem to embody an ultimate principle. The right to advocate and organize illegal off-campus actions as the bedrock meaning of free speech? Yet it was just that, I think, and we can see why when we recall the full context of December 8.

One part of that context was the general background of how free speech law had developed in the decades before the 1960s. It largely revolved around Justice Brandeis's and Justice Holmes's "clear and present danger test" to determine whether advocacy (in the sense of incitement) could be punished. The general idea was that advocacy could be punished only under very specific circumstances: an imminent threat of harm to a clearly defined, protectible interest in property; prevention of violence or bodily harm; protection of freedom of movement; and the like. It is the harm to these interests that would make the off-campus actions "illegal." The threat must be likely enough and the threatened harm to the particular interest, in light of its importance, sufficiently serious to justify suppression of speech. You can safely advocate these crimes if no one will act on your exhortations. The logic of this "test" applies to organizational activities as well as literal "advocacy." Applying the test requires a careful look at the particular fact situation in its whole context.

"Clear and present danger" was much in the air during the FSM. To a generation that considered this test crucial in the evolution of First Amendment protections, the FSM became an embodiment of that very principle. On-campus political activity could not be constitutionally punished for its off-campus results if it did not in fact *clearly* and *presently* threaten to produce specific serious societal harms off campus. This is equally true for activities that threatened *on-campus harms,* but that was not the issue at the time (although the decisive sit-in in Sproul Hall on December 2–3 was, of course, on campus).

So it is important to recall just what these potentially illegal off-campus actions would be—or perhaps more accurately, what it was assumed they would be. Throughout the fall, it probably was assumed that they would be akin to the sit-in tactics that were so effective in the South. Those sit-ins—at lunch counters, for instance—were designed to demonstrate peacefully and plainly that African Americans were asking nothing more or less than to be served on the same terms as whites. The protesters simply occupied seats at the lunch counter, waiting for service that never came; their action became a criminal trespass when the owners asked them to leave. In the 1960s the U.S. Supreme Court reversed, on one ground or another, every conviction for southern sit-ins that it considered (as well as other peaceful protests, apart from ones at a jail or military base), although the Court never did hold that a sit-in was flatly protected by the First Amendment.

In the North, at the time, popular support for the southern sit-ins and for the cause of racial desegregation in general was great, certainly among liberals and youth. Hence, it was crucial to its supporters that Berkeley's free speech controversy was centered specifically over protests against racial inequality. First Amendment principles do not, of course, depend on the particular cause, but in fact, the FSM could never have succeeded and probably could never have begun had it been about, say, organizing off-campus pro-LSD or even pro-Goldwater protests. Although it should have been quite clear that the off-campus illegal actions debated during the FSM conflict would not be such precisely tailored exposures of crude discrimination as were the southern lunch-counter sit-ins, the general atmosphere of approval still carried over to the other forms of action—trespass, minor nonviolent obstruction, consumer boycotts, and picketing—that seemed likely to occur around Berkeley.

A further part of the relevant context for the December 8 resolution was the kind of student practices that were understood by the words *on-campus political organization*. Basically, what was meant at the time was the holding of meetings on campus and the placing of tables on Sproul Plaza in order to raise funds, distribute literature, and sign up volunteers for a variety of off-campus protest activities. An integral part of motivating and enlisting people was the advocacy, in meetings, leaflets, and speeches, of such actions. Some of these actions were vaguely defined or were to take place in an indefinite future; others would take place in the South; but some would entail trespasses or picketing directed against local employers who were alleged to discriminate.

Finally, an important part of the context is how the battle lines were drawn over the course of the fall. Many faculty and some students remembered the Regents' loyalty oath of the early 1950s and the University's long-standing prohibitions of "controversial" or "partisan" extracurricular speech on campus. Although under President Clark Kerr these broad prohibitions had been officially repealed by 1964, the more specific attempts to prohibit organization and advocacy seemed to be a continuation of the University's unjustifiable habit of suppressing free speech.

The campus administration's sudden withdrawal of the Bancroft strip as a free speech area and its arbitrary and erratic pattern of using discipline to snatch defeat from the jaws of victory repeatedly revitalized the FSM and reinvigorated its support while alienating many of those faculty who only wanted the administration to keep the peace. By December 8 great emotions had been stirred by what seemed like unnecessarily harsh arrests of 773 students in Sproul Hall, by the December 7 fiasco in the Greek Theatre, and by the disorienting sight of thousands of striking students jamming Sproul Plaza for days on end. In short, the technical issues of "clear and present danger" were by this time overwhelmed by the larger ideological issues of freedom and discipline, as well as, for perhaps most faculty bystanders, by the loss of confidence in the chancellor and his administration.

There were also among the more activist faculty strong feelings of frustration and anger, a few long-standing antiadministration enmities, and some new embitterments over friends' and colleagues' recent political stances. Nevertheless, it was never my impression that a dominant feeling among faculty was that one's opponents were "evil." It was rather that one's own views had emerged from all this history of turmoil and disputation as good, true, beautiful, and very important. Commitment to principles had by now become part of a larger emotional system. In the end, then, it was not really the technical issue alone that so moved us on December 8. It was the accumulation over time of significant ideas and passionate feelings, together with our sense of the historic importance of these events.

This overall context explains what might in hindsight seem like mistakes or inconsistencies in the drafting and enactment of the faculty's December 8 resolution. For instance, if taken literally the (Lewis) Feuer amendment, which was overwhelmingly defeated at the faculty meeting, did little more than incorporate the "clear and present danger" test into the proposed resolution. But at this point "our side" had to win unequivocally, for it had to be unambiguously clear that the conflict had at last been resolved. This was a practical and not simply partisan consideration. It precluded any amendments—and certainly one as obviously symbolic to everyone as Feuer's—to a resolution that had been so carefully scrutinized by the politically engaged faculty by the time of the meeting.

Similarly, it is true that the December 8 resolution can be read literally—as Robert Post tells us in this volume—as if all of the substantive and qualitative regulation of speech and expression that is absolutely essential in a university classroom and in the evaluation of academic research was now to be disallowed. The resolution, after all, does contain a broad statement that the content of speech and advocacy should not be restricted by the University. But in the context, none of the drafters thought such self-evident matters as control of classroom content and evaluation of research (or Post's examples of threats to fellow members of the community) were at issue. Everyone was focused on the behavior that was in fact being contested, and everyone understood "the content of speech and advocacy" to be about the classic questions of regulating public political speech. That a nuanced resolution incorporating a full theory of speech regulation in a university could have been drafted, passed, or emotionally accepted at a meeting of a thousand faculty members seems highly improbable. In any case, it hardly occurred to anyone present that such a statement would be appropriate in the pressure-packed context of the December 8 faculty meeting, which was our one chance to end the actual conflict we were in.

The overall context also explains the resolution's strict disavowal of University discipline in the kind of cases under discussion. Some have seen the intent of this part of the resolution as the establishment of broader protection of on-campus political activity than would be afforded to students by the First Amendment off campus. I don't think so. Rather, I think this disavowal reflected the fact that the disciplining of student leaders, an issue that generates enormous sympathy among students, had been driving events for much of the fall. The point was to get the University entirely out of the business of imposing discipline for political activity (unless those actions interfered, under constitutional standards, with the University's normal day-to-day functions), both because of the faculty's loss of confidence in the campus administration and because of an emerging educational view that these issues should be left entirely in the hands of the civil authorities. This disavowal of discipline was part of a fresh approach toward secularizing student life, an approach that entailed a revision of the concept of a university community by limiting the university's interference with the student's role as citizen, and thereby interring outmoded notions of in loco parentis. The limits of speech were to be determined on a case-by-case basis, not by deans or university committees, but by courts. The substantive issue of organizing off-campus actions was itself part of this emerging view. The First Amendment was to apply to politics on the campus, as it does to political society elsewhere, and students were not to be viewed as making up a special kind of political subsociety for which there were different rules of free speech.

Indeed, the weightiest consequence of the FSM may have been its early, explosive part in the process of redefining the American university's relation to the larger society. That process is still going on, perhaps more urgently than ever, because the stakes that society has in research universities are so great. In some ways the present situation is the reverse of that acted out in the FSM. To oversimplify, the issue then was how much the university (through student activists, say) could change the society; now society is changing the university. Economic and technological issues now dominate, and the general tendency is more to incorporate society's interests and the norms of the market and of corporate-commercial enterprise into the university than it is to separate the university from society or project the consequences of campus activity on the outside world. In any event, the FSM made the relationship between university and society a clearer and more central issue.

Most Berkeley faculty did not become involved in the politics of the FSM until late in the fall. Most were probably apolitical and considered the controversy an unnecessary distraction from their real work. They may have discussed the daily happenings at lunch, formed opinions on the issues, and so on, but it was only the events of early December—the big sit-in, the strike and massive student rallies, and the December 7 Greek Theatre fiasco—that brought about the huge faculty turnout for the December 8 meeting. Like that of so many other faculty, my own involvement (with one exception) came very late in the fall, although perhaps for unusual reasons. The exception was that, together with two constitutional law colleagues, Bob O'Neil and Hans Linde (visiting from Oregon), I had been named to a "legal advisory committee" to the Berkeley Academic Senate's Committee on Academic Freedom (CAF); we met with CAF in mid-November to provide guidance on the legal issues arising out of the free speech controversy. Otherwise, although I was professionally dedicated to those issues and had been active in liberal causes since coming to Berkeley, I had shielded myself all semester from the wild events on the "lower campus" in an effort to complete a series of "tenure articles." I had finished the first one early in the fall, and it had just become the basis of my recommended promotion to tenure. I had barely finished the second at the end of November when, around 3:00 in the morning of December 3, I was awakened by a phone call from a student: "They are arresting us in Sproul Hall and it is terrible." This call radically changed not only the rest of my semester but also, since it led indirectly to a profoundly formative post-FSM tour of duty with Chancellor Roger Heyns, my whole career at Berkeley. For present purposes, it may be useful to summarize my experience in early December. At the risk of sounding self-serving and in spite of the genuine hazards of memory, this account may help convey the feelings and activities of perhaps many of the more involved faculty participants in that extraordinary week, the frenzy, the emotion, and the felt significance of unfolding events.

After that early morning phone call, I rushed off to Sproul Hall to see what could be done. Perhaps four or five other faculty members were there outside in the darkness. It is hazy, but I at least seem to remember Al

Bendich, Ken Stampp, and Fred Stripp. We were prevented by the police from going inside the building or having any contact with the students or any influence on the conduct of the huge arrest operation then in progress. The glass-enclosed south stairwell of Sproul had been entirely papered over so no one could see the students being taken down the stairs, but we could see them being hauled out of the building.

Later in the morning, when, as I recall, the arrests were mostly over, I hurried to the law school, intending to urge my colleagues to issue a statement condemning the governor's decision to order the arrests. Instead I found them already drafting a statement not protesting the arrests but supporting them. We were a very collegial law faculty, and, despite my junior status, my opposition to the planned statement precipitated what turned out to be an intense faculty meeting over the next two or three days, one that has become a legend in the law school. It ended with a neutral statement that preserved our collegiality and was sealed with a reconciling embrace between Adrian Kragen and myself, the main protagonists of the opposing points of view.

Personal relationships at the law school were genuinely warm; I did have allies, and one could say that my views had been heard and my opposition to a draconian statement had been successful. Nevertheless, I felt painfully isolated and embattled there. It was not a time of nicely calibrated, unemotional perspective. It seemed very important that those one cared about should share one's view of what was right. One tenured colleague told students I would surely be denied tenure by the Regents because of my political position; I dismissed this as improbable, but perhaps it had some emotional effect on me. At the same time, at meetings with senior faculty from other departments and seemingly influential outsiders, I felt that I was being taken seriously as a participant in efforts to resolve the crisis. All kinds of people, regardless of the practical importance of what they were doing, must have felt as if they were on similar roller coasters of emotion as they met, protested, argued, felt bolstered or betrayed. Yet I suspect most faculty tended to internalize their fluctuating emotions, experiencing the continuous intensity of feeling as private and isolating.

While those debates were continuing at the law school, much more was going on elsewhere. I bounced from our own meetings to numerous others—for example, one or two meetings at the home of Fred Balderston, who hoped to use his access to the governor's office. Different people participated in the excitement of this week at very different levels. There must have been hundreds of meetings at which people just wanted to share opinions, gain inside information, or use their academic expertise to assess the significance of what was happening. Other meetings were conceived as efforts to influence events. Students were on strike, many attending huge rallies. Historians of the FSM should appreciate how widespread and pervasive was the sense of involvement in great events, and they should also be skeptical of the revisionism and personal exaggeration that this sense of importance can generate.

For me the most important set of meetings involved the unofficial faculty "Committee of 200," informally chaired by Howard Schachman. Someone among them had identified me as a liberal constitutional law professor, and I then joined its steering committee, which had been meeting for some time, to help draft the language that eventually became the December 8 resolution. That small group, including some who moved in and out of it, was extraordinary in its intellectual talents and powers: David Freedman, Herb McClosky, Chuck Muscatine, Carl Schorske, John Searle, Charlie Sellers, Henry Nash Smith, Ken Stampp, Chick ten Broek, Sheldon Wolin, and Reggie Zelnik (my alphabetical list is probably incomplete). From those few days of intense discussion and mutual commitment on issues of real importance emerged friendships and insights that have mattered now for decades. More generally, one of the great serendipitous benefits of the FSM was that, in the Committee of 200 and other such alliances, it jump-started the development of interdisciplinary relationships among faculty from what had been isolated departments. This interaction across disciplinary lines is now one of Berkeley's great strengths.

A fresh openness to relationships of respect between faculty and students was also generated during the FSM. In my case, for instance, two extraordinary graduate student leaders of the FSM, Myra Jahlen and Carl Riskin, got in touch with me, and during this same week we worked together drafting an FSM platform.[1] Decades later we are still friends. Again more generally, the political respect and working cooperation between some students and some faculty during the FSM and the seriousness with which student concerns had then to be taken helped start a process of augmenting the role of students in education at Berkeley and the degree of faculty responsiveness.

The academic home of the FSM's leadership and most of its rank and file was the College of Letters and Science. Law school students overwhelmingly supported the goals of the FSM and, though less overwhelmingly, its tactics. They followed our extended faculty meeting and clearly supported those of us who opposed the arrests. But they were not notably active in the demonstrations and activities on the "lower campus." Only 8 of the 773 arrested in the big sit-in were law students, considerably less than their proportion of the total student population. Even the law students who had been undergraduate activists were relatively quiet during the FSM. Perhaps they felt they had moved into a new professional life or that a new group and generation of students had taken over, or perhaps the law school was too remote from the rest of the campus. As a whole, the law school student body in the early 1960s was quite traditional. The FSM, however, marked a great turning point toward a student body that would be more involved in public interest law, clinical legal education, and social activism.

Meanwhile, Bob O'Neil, Hans Linde, and I, the "legal advisory committee" for CAF, had to draft our formal analysis in support of the December 8 resolution. The plan was for the resolution to be introduced by Joe Garbarino as chair of CAF, who of course was not to speak on behalf of the Committee of 200, which lacked official standing, although it is a reflection of the politics of the situation that two members of the 200's steering committee, which prepared the preliminary draft, were also on CAF. Because the pressure of events must have overwhelmed the contemplated timetable, the legal advisory committee's published memorandum to CAF is dated December 15, but the views it expressed were relayed to the faculty on December 8 as part of CAF's oral report supporting the resolution.[2]

Sometime after December 8 I decided to write another memo, this one to the Regents. I asked O'Neil and Linde to join it, in part for the extra credibility this would have with the Regents, and they did. The memo, dated December 16, made a legal argument to the effect that the Regents' November 20 policy statement and the December 8 resolution were entirely consistent. The Regents' policy statement, it will be recalled, had permitted students to organize on campus "for lawful . . . not for unlawful off-campus action." The memo construed the full text of that policy statement to have prohibited only constitutionally punishable accessorial and conspiratorial crimes, not advocacy involving a significant claim of constitutional protection. In contrast the December 8 resolution dealt only with this potentially protected advocacy and not with accessorial crimes. Hence, the Regents' policy did not prevent the faculty from passing the resolution and would not prevent the administration from adopting it. Moreover, the inference from this analysis was that the Regents had already implicitly acknowledged on November 20 that the First Amendment applies to the campus. There was thus no reason for the Regents to act against the Senate resolution. On the contrary, there would be no loss of face if the Board would now simply make explicit its implicit policy that the First Amendment applies to the campus.

I asked Budd Cheit to bring the memo to the Regents' meeting of December 17–18. He had been elected to the Senate's Emergency Executive Committee (EEC), which had been created by a separate resolution introduced on December 8 by Henry Nash Smith, of the Committee of 200. The EEC's members, nominated and elected by mail ballot between December 9 and 14, were to meet with the Regents in Los Angeles. In all likelihood, EEC member Arthur Sherry, to whom the memo was formally addressed because he was a fellow law professor, also brought the memo to the meeting. Cheit has said that the memo was important in getting the

Regents to see that they could end the crisis without appearing to make new policy under pressure. In any event, the Regents did issue a statement declaring that their policies "do not contemplate that advocacy or the content of speech shall be restricted beyond the purview of the First and Fourteenth Amendments." That brought the events of the FSM to a more or less final close.

As some of the above recollections suggest, the events of the FSM semester show how intimately connected are the personal and the political when daily life comes under extreme political pressure. One might go further and suggest that political pressures may operate in a way that simulates some of the pressures of intimacy, loading one's daily actions and relationships with great emotional intensity. By ascribing the importance of grand events to daily actions, they create feelings of vulnerability or overinvestment in one's positions and increase the need for fellowship and approval. They tempt us to judge others' character on the basis only of their politics in the particular situation and to react with disproportionate affection or animosity to their political views. Yet one may well wonder whether it is not just these personal overreactions that provide the energy to power one's better efforts. Sometimes political behavior does reveal character, and this may have been true during the FSM, if less often than we thought. And occasionally, of course, it is precisely political pressure and the gravity of the consequences that reveal how good (or bad) a person's judgment can be.

A note about one other long-lived result of the FSM might be appropriate here. Budd Cheit, who became executive vice chancellor under the new chancellor, Roger Heyns, in the summer of 1965, asked me to draft the "time, place, and manner" rules for campus political activity that were called for by the December 8 resolution. I did, with consultation with key administrators, faculty, and students. In time issued by the chancellor, the rules were thoroughly shaped by the issues and experience of the FSM controversy. Although amended one way or another over the years, they are still in effect. Designed to promote speech while preventing "interference with the normal functions of the University," the FSM-informed "time, place, and manner" rules helped institutionalize free speech at Berkeley.

I stayed on as the chancellor's faculty consultant, joining Heyns, Cheit, and John Searle, who was now assistant to the chancellor. The post-FSM, Vietnam-era story could use a volume like this of its own. Suffice it to say that the experience added enormously to two lessons I had begun to learn in the FSM semester: that to serve with brilliant, thoughtful colleagues, acting and reflecting on events of great significance, is deeply formative and that the most heartfelt and enduring personal relationships are often forged in the trenches.

NOTES

1. Later printed in Seymour Martin Lipset and Sheldon S. Wolin, *The Berkeley Student Revolt: Facts and Interpretations* (Garden City, N.Y.: Doubleday), 201–4.

2. See CAF's report in "Notice of Meeting of the Berkeley Division of the Academic Senate," 5 Jan. 1965, University Archives, Bancroft Library, University of California at Berkeley; the text of our memorandum may also be found in Lipset and Wolin, 273–80.

The FSM

A Movement Lawyer's Perspective

Malcolm Burnstein

From the perspective of lawyers with a social conscience the decade of the 1960s was a dream come true. For me, nowhere was that sentiment more pertinent than in first counseling and later participating in the criminal defense of the participants in the Free Speech Movement. Movement lawyers were joined at the hip to the student protests from their early days, of course. Certainly that included, inter alia, the criminal defense of those arrested in the FSM.

Activities such as the FSM defense offered many opportunities for socially conscious lawyers to put our skills and our professional training to work for principles in which we believed. Our activist "clients" in the various civil rights and anti–Vietnam War sit-ins, picketing, and other demonstrations of that decade were almost uniformly grateful to the lawyers who volunteered their time. The truth was that most of us would have paid them for the chance to be involved.

In the context of the movements of the sixties, the FSM was vitally important. It won for the students of the University of California system the right to engage in political advocacy on campus. That victory was the result of months of struggle that included demonstrations, protests, negotiations, violations of regulations, suspensions from school, and ultimately, a mass arrest of almost eight hundred people, mostly students, that generated strong (though belated) faculty support. An overwhelming majority of the Academic Senate, the body representing the full membership of the Berkeley faculty, clearly moved by the courage of the students, finally acted to affirm the principles for which the FSM had been fighting. The University Regents did not have the will to continue to resist after the arrests and that faculty action. The FSM triumph brought about the adoption by the University of the constitutional principles for which the students endured arrest. In turn, the FSM victory sparked many other movement activities in the nation and around the world.

Paradoxically, however, and no matter how brave the intentions of the volunteer lawyers or how hard they toiled, the criminal defense of those arrested in the FSM sit-in resulted in an unvarnished legal defeat. The criminal trial resulted in conviction of 99 percent of those arrested and fines or jail sentences for the participants. Society is still paying the price of that legal defeat in the cynicism the convictions engendered in many of those arrested.

The principal reason for the convictions of the FSM defendants was the waiver of jury trials, a decision based on the felt need to expedite the proceedings and free the defendants for academic and other endeavors. That jury waiver and the resulting convictions taught a bitter lesson to both the lawyers and the activist defendants. The consequent message, never to waive jury in a political case no matter what personal hardship that decision entails, was put to good use in later demonstration arrest cases.

Despite the best efforts of both students and lawyers, the University and the court made arbitrary distinctions between those arrested. Once students were cited for manning tables on campus "illegally," hundreds of other students signed petitions asking for similar treatment for sharing the same motivation and the same goals. The University administration ignored them. The court, at the instance of the district attorney's office, separated the "leaders," who theoretically had brainwashed the other defendants into committing civil disobedience, and subjected them to heavier punishments. That condescending disregard for the conscious and individual choice of each of those involved was particularly galling to the students and their lawyers.

NEGOTIATIONS WITH THE UNIVERSITY

My initial involvement in the FSM was serendipitous. It started with the famous incident in which Jack Weinberg was arrested for violating the campus rules and placed inside a police car on the campus. The car was surrounded and prevented from moving for thirty-two hours by hundreds of students, at which point the campus administration agreed to a settlement with the demonstrators which included the creation of a twelve-person tripartite committee—the Study Committee on Campus Political Activity (Study Committee)—composed of an equal number of students, faculty and administration.*

---

*Editors' note: The committee was later renamed the Campus Committee on Political Activity (CCPA).

The Study Committee was created to "negotiate" the nature and scope of the exercise of political and civil rights on the campus. The campus administration, whose intransigence in banning political activity on campus had launched the dispute, initially appointed all members of the committee. Only protest by the students and the Academic Senate caused the administration to allow the students and the Senate to add two members each. At that point the students approached Robert Treuhaft to advise them on legal and constitutional issues. Bob was one of a handful of left-wing lawyers in the East Bay. He had been involved in many civil rights and civil liberties cases from the early 1950s. At that time there were few such lawyers around. Bob, Doris Walker (another radical lawyer), and I were in a small firm in Oakland at that time. Bob, who was then my boss, called me into the meeting with the delegation of students and asked me if I wanted the job. I gladly agreed.

It was clear by October 1964 that the University was grudgingly reconciled to allowing some forms of political speech on the campus. But it was equally apparent that the administration was determined to regulate the content of speech in order to prohibit the advocacy of what it determined to be "illegal" conduct (such as sit-ins and some picketing) and fund-raising for off-campus political activity. Indeed, I am fully convinced that the administration went into the meetings of the Study Committee with those limitations as its already established secret agenda, set by the office of the Regents' general counsel.

The FSM was composed of numerous varied political and issues-oriented student groups. They had many divergent substantive views. They were united, however, in opposing the silencing of all their views by the UC administration. A Steering Committee of representative members of the FSM was appointed to hash out most issues. Periodically FSM Steering Committee meetings were quite long and went very late. They were, however, extremely democratic. I enjoyed participating in these meetings to answer questions about legal issues and to absorb the dynamics of the movement. Contrary to the caricature of the FSM drawn by California conservatives hoping to ride to power by appealing to the public's fears of Berkeley student radicalism, revolution was far removed from the debates inside the FSM Steering Committee. Indeed, the overriding issue that created much of the fervor behind the FSM was commitment to the nonviolent civil rights struggles then being waged in the South, as well as, lest we forget, in Berkeley, Oakland, and San Francisco. The battle in 1964 between the pro- and anti-Goldwater forces for the soul of the Republican Party also played a role. Indeed, evidence suggests that a complaint from the late (conservative) Senator William Knowland (perhaps through one of the reporters of the Knowland-owned *Oakland Tribune*) to a UC dean caused the University to begin the confrontation in the first place.

In any event, my recollection of the issues most important in the meetings of the FSM Steering Committee was that democratic process in decision making was foremost, followed by substantive concerns with civil rights and First Amendment rights. Each Steering Committee meeting attempted to reach a consensus, since the disparate nature of the FSM would not permit any one interest group to force its will on the rest of the movement. Substantively, it was clear to me that the new University regulations were invalid. Consequently, I advised the students that, constitutionally, the only thing that could be regulated was the "time, place, and manner" of the exercise of political speech on campus. Any attempt to restrict the content of student speech was, by command of the First Amendment, entirely out of bounds.

The meetings of the Study Committee required agreement among all three groups represented to take any action. The students pushed to get the full measure of political rights allowed by the Constitution. The constitutional principle is a simple one: the University of California is a public institution, subject to the First and Fourteenth Amendment restriction on the right of government to regulate political freedom. Generally, government can reasonably regulate the time, place, and manner of political speech but not its content. Thus, the University can prevent interruptions of classes and obstruction of its streets, but it cannot do so on a selective basis based on the content of the speech. And a public university cannot prevent political speech entirely in its public areas any more than a city can prevent political speech on its city streets. To simply prevent tables on areas of campus that students frequent, where those tables did not obstruct the flow of pedestrian traffic, is as impermissible as barring some speech because of its content while allowing other speech deemed less offensive.

The administration revealed its plan in the course of the Study Committee meetings. It called for allowing the students to solicit for lawful off-campus activities but not unlawful ones, such as sit-ins. Had the FSM agreed to that position, it would of course have put the University in the unconstitutional position of judging the content of and thereby exercising prior restraint on the students' speech and of usurping the functions of a court in judging what is lawful and what is not.

The Study Committee meetings soon became pretty much of a formal minuet designed by the administration to reach a foregone conclusion: preserving to the administration as much autonomy over the exercise of political rights on campus as possible. After it became clear that the students would not accept a compromise of constitutional rights, the chancellor dissolved the committee.

Advising the student members of the Study Committee was definitely good training for a movement lawyer. Despite some popular misconceptions about lawyers, we were (and still are) socialized within the system to compromise, if necessary, to achieve a speedy and "decent" result for clients with as little strife as possible. The students, however, were interested in knowing what the Constitution required of the University and saw no legal or moral reason to settle for less. The administration representatives as well as the faculty members on the committee supported giving the students half a loaf, perhaps even three-quarters, by allowing them some political advocacy on the campus but prohibiting them from encouraging illegal actions such as sit-ins and similar acts of civil disobedience. Although in retrospect I now believe that the students' position was the right one, at the time, with a total victory by no means assured, I was inclined to argue for accepting the compromise offer. But once advised of the constitutional limitations on the University's authority in the area of free speech and advocacy, the students saw no reasonable grounds for allowing the University to provide less than what was constitutionally necessary, so they refused all offers to compromise their constitutional rights. It turned out that through their uncompromising strategy the students won a full measure of freedom rather than the fraction they would have received had they followed the advice of their sympathetic elders. It was a humbling and important lesson for a young lawyer.

THE SIT-IN AND VICTORY

Once the Study Committee was dissolved in November all negotiations ceased. Also, throughout November the FSM demonstrations slowly tailed off as outrage died down. The FSM Steering Committee sensed the waning of the student protest on campus as finals and other activities came to occupy students' time and thoughts. But the University snatched defeat out of the jaws of its prospective victory. As it had done in the past, when the interest of the campus community appeared to be flagging, it committed another highly visible and flagrant outrage, thereby reenergizing the protest's momentum. On November 25 the University charged four prominent FSMers with violations of the old University rules for acts committed in early October. That outraged and reinvigorated the student population and led directly to the December 2–3 sit-in at Sproul Hall.

It was, of course, that sit-in that culminated in the arrests of 773 people, commencing in the early hours of December 3, 1964. Those arrested were charged with trespass (failure to leave a public building after hours when ordered to do so by a regularly employed custodian) and failure to disperse from a place of unlawful assembly. Those who went limp instead of walking once they had been arrested were also charged with resisting arrest. Many of those arrested were treated extremely roughly by the sheriff's deputies who conducted the arrests (and who blocked off the windows to prevent the press from watching their conduct). After the arrest there was extreme confusion and some unpleasant behavior by the deputy sheriffs at the various jails and makeshift jails to which the students were taken: lack of food, failure to provide phone calls, and delays in processing so that some students were held in jail for more than a day before they were allowed bail.

THE TRIAL

The arrests galvanized the community around the FSM, particularly the academic and legal communities. Once those arrested had been bailed out, numerous lawyers volunteered to assist in the defense. Some of the defendants were provided with lawyers by their worried families. Initially, more than thirty-five lawyers attended an emergency meeting to discuss what aid they could provide to those arrested. Many more lawyers called to volunteer their services. Ultimately we had close to a hundred lawyers on our volunteer list, and we communicated with them all numerous times during the course of the defense. These lawyers were not only "movement" lawyers; many lawyers with no particular political bent were moved by the sacrifice made by the students and offered their help. As an example of the disparate nature of the volunteers, we had both Joseph Alioto, noted antitrust lawyer and future mayor of San Francisco, and J. Tony Serra, a movement lawyer specializing in drug possession and related cases, on the list of volunteer lawyers. Eight of the volunteer lawyers later became judges. Many of these lawyers met with the arrested students and provided initial counsel and answered questions from those who, forty-eight hours earlier, had never considered that they would ever need the services of a criminal defense lawyer. Because I had been advising the students before the arrest and because I knew and was known to a number of those arrested, it fell to me to coordinate the defense and the lawyers.

Rather quickly the vast majority of those arrested decided that a unified defense was the only way to honor the unified principles that had led to the sit-in. The logistics of accomplishing that were daunting. If this was not the largest mass arrest in U.S. history, it was certainly the largest mass arrest in memory in this area. We had some 780 clients to consult, to keep track of, to inform of facts, procedures, and problems. Those tasks appeared almost impossible. Fortunately, the defendants themselves provided the wherewithal to make a stab at it. Thanks particularly to Kathy Frank, one of the arrested students who devoted many hours to the mundane tasks at hand, we were able to more or less keep track of the defendants during the proceedings, to keep them informed of what was going on, and to obtain their decisions on the crucial questions. Simply learning who had been arrested and finding a way to facilitate communication were very difficult. This was, after all, decades before everyone was on e-mail.

The procedural situation in which the FSM defendants found themselves was designed by the prosecution to disadvantage the defendants. The Alameda County district attorney's office had charged those arrested in seventy-eight groups of ten defendants each. That meant that unless we did something about it, there would be seventy-eight separate trials. In those days Berkeley had only two judges and two courtrooms. Assuming each trial took only a week and the court devoted both judges and both courtrooms to these trials, eschewing all other business, the trials would have consumed thirty-nine weeks. But of course, given the complexity of the defenses, the trials would not take only one week each.[1] Nor could the court devote all its time to these cases, since there were other civil and criminal cases that needed to be heard. Indeed, we projected that trials in groups of ten could have taken several years. Most of those arrested were students; they had varying times left remaining at school, and most wanted to have the matter settled relatively quickly and then get on with their lives. Further, separate trials would have led inevitably to different results for people who had done similar things, depending on the variables of each jury. This possibility flew in the face of the principle that unified the FSM in the first place, a collective challenge to repressive rules. In short, we were looking at trial procedures that could have proven morally and logistically disastrous for the defendants.

The major issue for defense counsel was how to cope with the problem of getting a fair trial, that is to say, a trial in which serious defenses would have a reasonable chance to be heard on their merits, yet also a speedy trial, in which the defendants would not have to await trial for years and face potentially divergent results. The defense formally moved for a mass jury trial of all defendants on those issues common to everyone. Our motion was objected to by the prosecution and denied by the court. The defense then moved for a representative jury trial of a negotiated number of defendants, with the remaining defendants agreeing to be bound by the results of this trial. That would have allowed a jury from the community to judge the validity of the demonstrators' claims that, inter alia, they resorted to a sit-in only after exhausting all other avenues to redress their grievance for the denial of their constitutional rights. The prosecution objected; and again the trial judge, Rupert Crittenden, ruled that the prosecution controlled the format of the trial. He denied our motion and allowed the district attorney to continue the practice of separating those arrested into groups of ten and trying them in such groups, despite the obvious strain on the court. Whether the prosecution would have stuck to its opposition to a single jury trial if the defendants had insisted on jury trials or was just bluffing we will probably never know. Certainly the district attorney's office could not have been thrilled to commit that degree of resources to one case for so long. The District Attorney at that time, however, J. Francis

Coakley, was a far right-wing politician who had demonstrated great public antipathy toward both student and civil rights demonstrations and civil rights and civil liberties generally.[2]

Finally the prosecution proposed that all defendants waive jury and have a trial to the judge of a representative number of defendants, with the other defendants agreeing to submit their cases to the court on the evidence adduced at the trial. Thus, if those in the trial were acquitted, so would everyone else; conversely, if those on trial were convicted, everyone else would receive the same fate. There were minor variances in that those charged with resisting arrest could contest that charge if they did not go limp when arrested. The lawyers painstakingly met with every defendant to explain the options: to not waive jury and possibly be tried in groups of ten over several years, or waive jury and have just one trial to the judge. Some of those arrested saw no issue at all. They believed they had committed civil disobedience and simply wanted the punishment to be imposed; 101 defendants thus pleaded "no contest."

The lawyers discussed in great detail the chances of an acquittal from the judge. Stanley Golde, one of the FSM's trial lawyers, had been Judge Crittenden's law partner for many years, and others of the lawyers, myself included, had practiced before him. He was generally considered a fair judge. At that time many of the lawyers believed that we had a fighting chance with Crittenden.

A vocal minority of the defendants, including some of the more politically committed ones, argued against waiving jury. They contended, correctly as it turned out, that keeping juries, whatever the price in personal inconvenience, was the only way to prevent convictions. A mass trial, on the other hand, had the greater possibility of press coverage for the issues involved and thus could become a vehicle for community organizing. The debate between those favoring jury waiver and those favoring jury trials became somewhat sharp. Ultimately, the pragmatic interests of the students in avoiding a lengthy and uncertain proceeding, coupled with the mere possibility of a judicial victory, led to an overwhelming decision to waive jury and proceed to a mass trial. The decision was formally made under protest that the court had effectively denied the defendants their right to a jury trial as the only way it would accord them their right to a speedy trial. That argument did not impress Judge Crittenden.

Once the decision was made for a mass court trial, the lawyers and defendants decided on a trial team. Five lawyers were selected to conduct the proceedings for the defense. I was one of those lawyers because I had had the most contact with the FSM and had come to understand its goals pretty well. Unfortunately for the defendants, I was still relatively young and inexperienced. The others chosen were Stanley Golde, a leading East Bay criminal defense lawyer; Henry Elson, a prominent Berkeley lawyer;

Richard Buxbaum, a young law professor at Berkeley who was perhaps risking the most by becoming identified with the defense in this battle with the University; and Norman Leonard, an experienced progressive lawyer from San Francisco whose son was one of those arrested. There were also a number of juveniles arrested who were processed through the courts separately. They were represented by others of the volunteer lawyers. Of course, a number of other lawyers did much significant work, most particularly Sigfried Hesse, who did most of the legal research.

We had bargained for and received the right to select most of the trial defendants. The lawyers and the defendants then selected a representative group of 155 defendants to take part in the actual trial. Most of the spokespersons associated with the FSM, that is, the "leaders," mainly members of the FSM's Steering Committee, were part of the trial group.

After the defendants had committed to a jury waiver based in part on the perceived fairness of the judge, the evidence began to mount that Judge Crittenden was predisposed to convict the students either because of his own hostility to the student's disrespect for conventional avenues of redress of grievances or, conceivably, because of what certainly would have been a highly improper approach to the judge by the governor's office. The governor, Edmund G. "Pat" Brown, had, after all, ordered the arrests, and an acquittal would have shown the folly of his decision. Crittenden's predisposition was evidenced by a number of rulings unnecessarily hostile to the defense and contrary to law. For example, although California law allowed people charged with misdemeanors to appear for motions and other preliminary proceedings by counsel and not in person, Crittenden ordered the defendants to personally appear for all matters. He refused to explain why he had issued such an order. There were other examples of his proprosecution bias in this case. In the aftermath of the FSM trial, Crittenden was, not coincidentally, in my view, appointed to the Superior Court by the same governor who had ordered the arrests.

The prosecution team was headed by Assistant District Attorney D. Lowell Jensen. He was eagerly assisted by Edwin Meese, the deputy district attorney, who soon became Ronald Reagan's right-hand man in California and later, in my opinion, one of the least distinguished attorneys general of the United States in the history of the Republic. Although Jensen's instincts were not as politically to the right as those of his second in command, he was after all a prosecutor, and he was of course under directions from his boss, District Attorney Coakley, to obtain a conviction. Each day of trial, Meese insisted on taking roll of the defendants, and he asked for a bench warrant for the arrest of any defendant who was either not present or for whom an excuse had not been obtained. Judge Crittenden obliged. Nevertheless, however grim and stressful for the most part, the trial had its amusing moments. For example, defendant David Lance Goines, a talented and now very well known artist, used to drive the marshals who guarded the courtroom crazy by whistling classical music, on key, during recesses of the trial.

Given the size of the trial and the public interest in at least parts of it, the Berkeley courtrooms were far too small. Trial was therefore held in an auditorium of the Veteran's Building in downtown Berkeley. We presented evidence to show that the students had explored every avenue of redress open to them, that the substantive position of the students was constitutionally proper, that the administration had not taken any serious efforts to address the constitutional issues raised by the student protest, that the statutes under which the students were charged were either unconstitutional or were not designed to be applied to situations of political protest, and that the sit-in was peaceful and not destructive of property. All to no avail. Judge Crittenden acquitted the defendants of failing to disperse from an unlawful assembly but convicted them of trespass and, for those who went limp after arrest, of resisting arrest. Because sentencing could be the same whether the defendants were convicted of one, two, or three charges, we believe Crittenden, by acquitting the defendants of one charge, was trying to show that he was not entirely in the prosecution's pocket.

SENTENCING AND FURTHER PROCEEDINGS

What was left of the trial was sentencing. Judge Crittenden asked each defendant to write him a letter explaining why she or he had engaged in the mass protest of a sit-in. Because the judge completely ignored these letters in actual sentencing and instead gave generally similar sentences for all but the alleged "leaders," it became apparent that the judge expected apologies and expressions of regret. When he did not receive what he wanted, he disregarded a remarkable collection of documents, now at the Bancroft Library at the University of California. Those letters—an extremely moving portrait of a generation charged with idealism—reveal that the defendants, although convicted, were respectfully unrepentant for what they believed they had been forced to do to secure their constitutional rights.

What the court never learned, or simply ignored, and what the politicians and the district attorney (to be somewhat redundant) never could get straight or deliberately refused to recognize is that there were no leaders in the FSM who had the power or the desire to make a group of other people do things they would not otherwise do. Leadership, such as it was, fell to those who could better articulate the issues, those whose passion and compassion allowed them to articulate the thoughts of other students. The FSM was not the creature of a core of leaders who duped the multitude that blindly followed. The failure to make this distinction was most critical at sentencing, where those whom the district attorney's office considered leaders (sometimes with no basis in fact) were given harsher sentences than everyone else. Just as the FSM started with many students signing petitions admitting equal culpability with those cited by the deans, only to be ignored by the University administration, so too the court trivialized the conscious decision making of 770 people by refusing to recognize that the sit-in was not a preprogrammed response of mindless lemmings marching off the cliff to the tune of Mario Savio's oratory. Consequently, although the vast majority of students received only fines or "jail in the alternative," ten so-called leaders received between 30 and 120 days in jail plus fines and probation.

In sentencing, the judge again demonstrated a distaste for the militancy of the defendants. Those defendants who refused a sentence that included a period of probation, during which the defendants were expressly enjoined from committing civil disobedience, were given a greater fine (or jail in the alternative) than those who accepted that condition of probation. As further evidence of the judge's leanings, he generally sentenced those who refused to waive their right to appeal more harshly than those who agreed not to appeal.

Sentencing went on for weeks after the end of the trial. Much of it was handled by other volunteer lawyers. But the sentencing was far from the end of the FSM case from the standpoint of the lawyers' involvement. First came the appeal. After conviction of a misdemeanor in a municipal court there was the right to an appeal to the appellate division of the Superior Court. Approximately three-quarters of the 770 defendants exercised their right to appeal the conviction and a massive and comprehensive 400-plus-page brief was written on their behalf. Volunteer lawyer Sigfried Hesse was most responsible for this effort. Some of the basic grounds of the appeal were the following: (1) the defendants were effectively denied a right to trial by jury. (2) The statutes under which the defendants were convicted were unconstitutionally vague and unconstitutional as applied to the facts. (3) The court effectively denied the defendants their right to counsel. (4) The facts in the record did not support the convictions. There were many other issues raised in the appeal.

In a blatant departure from the usual practice of discussing the merits of the arguments presented in our brief, the Appellate Department of the Superior Court upheld the convictions in a one-page order, ignoring all the procedural and substantive issues raised by the case. We next sought review in the California Court of Appeals but were denied a hearing. Finally, we petitioned the U.S. Supreme Court for a hearing but were again denied. That ended our legal fight.

The trial and appeal were not, however, the end of the matter for either the lawyers or the defendants. The defendants were, after all, the cream of our young people of 1964. They were at the University to prepare them-selves for professions and jobs requiring, in some cases, state licenses and certifications. For years following the trial we received calls from numbers of defendants seeking assistance in obtaining state licenses where the FSM conviction was being used to deny the license by overzealous or timid state bureaucrats. Many of the volunteer lawyers took part in those unsung appearances in Sacramento before various state agencies, primarily the agency charged with credentialing teachers. Additionally, because Califor-nia law allows some misdemeanor convictions to be expunged after proba-tion has been successfully completed, we had to deal with numerous requests for that procedure. After thirty-five years we still receive inquiries from defendants asking us if their convictions have been expunged or if they can be.

Subsequent to the case, like any large cohort, numerous FSM defen-dants experienced their share of garden-variety legal problems such as a divorce or personal injury case. The lawyers who conducted the trial and appeal handled many of those problems, and the bond between us grew stronger. To this day, I still represent in various matters many of the people with whom I became so close so many years ago.

CONCLUSION

As I look back on the FSM, it demonstrates the adage that liberty must never be taken for granted and must be fought for from time to time. Fortunately, there were still many people with sufficient commitment to principle to take up the fight despite the risks to their futures. There is little doubt that the FSM was a major victory for civil liberties and constitu-tional rights. It was also of enormous collateral benefit to the Civil Rights Movements in Berkeley, northern California, and around the nation. It contributed to the continuing rise of student activism on other major issues of the decade. It spawned, among other things, the anti–Vietnam War teach-ins.

But that victory was the direct result of the willingness of almost eight hundred young people to endure arrest, gratuitous rough handling by the police, and an uncertain cloud over their future professional endeavors. It is not accidental that a great many of those politicized by the FSM remained politically aware and, in many cases, politically active. More than thirty-five years later, current events tell us that idealism is not yet extinct. One needs only look at the massive peaceful demonstrations against the WTO in Seattle in late 1999 (along with a great many other examples of altruism among young people) to know that the spirit of the FSM is not obsolete.

The FSM was also a shining example of the part that lawyers were allowed to play in the struggles of that decade. I know those opportunities again exist for socially conscious lawyers in arenas such as employment, women's rights, civil rights, civil liberties, ecology, and immigration, and that there are many lawyers taking up the banner.

NOTES

1. The actual trial took eleven weeks, of which a minimum of four would have been needed no matter how many or few were on trial.

2. Coakley was infamous for having successfully prosecuted a number of black sailors who refused to load munitions at Port Chicago, California, during World War II after an explosion killed hundreds of other black munitions loaders.

PART FOUR

Aftermath

Mario Savio and Berkeley's "Little Free Speech Movement" of 1966

Robert Cohen

It is one of the ironies of history that movements for social change often face some of their most severe tests, challenges, and opposition *after* they have passed their prime. This was the case, for example, with the Civil Rights Movement, which in the decades following the 1960s confronted a tidal wave of opposition seeking to roll back many of its earlier gains. Similarly, if on a much smaller scale, the Berkeley student movement confronted renewed opposition more than a year after the FSM disbanded. At stake was the free political forum the FSM had won in the Sproul Steps area, which in 1964 had become the site for mass amplified rallies. In 1966 Chancellor Roger Heyns tried to move the free speech area away from this central campus location and relegate it to a more secluded spot, down in what activist students called "the pit," a relatively isolated outdoor dining area on what was usually called "Lower Sproul" or "the Lower Plaza." Antiwar activists and FSM veterans, including Mario Savio, viewed the chancellor's initiative as an attempt to gag the campus left and roll back the free speech victory of 1964. The question activists faced in 1966 was whether the FSM's legacy was sufficiently strong and the political tradition it created sufficiently popular to facilitate the assembling of a new free speech movement that could rally the University community in defense of the gains made by the FSM. They answered this question affirmatively by mobilizing the campus in a new free speech struggle, one that Savio later referred to as "the little free speech movement." Examining this little known movement will enable us to explore the FSM's enduring impact on the Berkeley campus and on Savio himself.[1]

There seems little mystery as to why Mario Savio would fight as hard for student political rights in 1966 as he had in 1964. A semester of FSM struggle over student rights had transformed him into a civil liberties organizer on a mass scale. In 1964 he and his allies had had to demonstrate to the University community that the free speech issue really mattered and was not simply a technical dispute over obscure regulations. Once this was accomplished, they had to convince thousands of students (as well as the faculty) that the FSM had been correct in its rather complex and controversial arguments on behalf of student rights. The administration, in one of its early compromises, had agreed to remove the campus ban on political tables but only on the condition that activists confine themselves to disseminating information and avoid political advocacy. This left Savio and the FSM with the unenviable task of explaining why the administration's apparent concession was unacceptable and how it would still compromise student rights; they had to prove that the distinction between free speech and advocacy was spurious, that the two were indivisible. Representatives of the chancellor and the University president, as Savio put it,

> wanted to reserve to the administration the authority . . . to restrict speech on the basis of content. . . . That's just not acceptable. . . . There was no chance they were going to win on that! And if they lost on that they would lose on everything. . . . They wanted to stop the [civil rights] demonstrators and couldn't do it without stopping free speech. . . . We got into very . . . detailed civil liberties hang-ups with the administration and they wanted to find every possible way to . . . work things out so they could finally get what they wanted. And so they insisted on . . . the distinction between informing and advocating. [It] would really take a Solomon . . . to draw this line. . . . And we couldn't give them that. . . . I was really impressed by the sophistication of the university community about these very issues. [But] we had to persuade people, first of all to try to understand that [civil liberties] issue. . . . We really had to work very hard to raise a kind of level of sophistication of what was, after all, at the start a very sophisticated community, to the point where they could recognize that absolutely there could not be tolerated the slightest limitation by the university itself on the rights of free speech and advocacy![2]

More difficult still, when President Kerr and the Regents later (November 1964) conceded to students the right to advocacy on behalf of *legal* political actions, meaning that unlawful off-campus protests still could not be advocated or not in a proactive way (organizing, mounting, and the like), Savio and the FSM then had to persuade students and faculty that even this concession was insufficient, since it still entailed constraints that could stifle the organization of civil rights protests employing civil disobedience.[3] By December 8 they had succeeded.

In the course of this process of promoting dialogue, criticism, and activism on free speech issues, Savio and his FSM comrades had emerged as successful organizers of the largest campus free speech movement in American history. With the faculty's December 8 resolutions barring the regulation of the content of speech, the FSM had extended political liberty on campus far beyond where even First Amendment experts had thought it would ever go. They had won Sproul Plaza and the adjacent steps as a free political space and won it at a high personal cost in missed classes, suspensions, and arrests. This free speech victory mattered to Savio, who cherished the freedom that he had helped to win on the Plaza and on the steps that now bear his name. He wanted that freedom to endure, and in the little noted epilogue to the FSM that took place in 1966, he proved himself willing, as he had been in 1964, to jeopardize his academic career for its sake.[4]

Having recently returned from a year of study in England, Savio in 1966 was alarmed by what looked to him like a provocative offensive by the administration to drive amplified political rallies from Sproul Plaza. He could, of course, have left others to fight this battle. It would have been very much in his academic self-interest to sit out this round of conflict. Savio was in the process of applying for readmission to Berkeley at a time when conservatives—empowered by Ronald Reagan's gubernatorial campaign and anxious to strike a blow at campus radicalism—were publicly demanding that Savio be barred from rejoining the student body. In fact, at the very moment in October 1966 that this new struggle to "save the steps" was escalating, conservative Regent John Canaday was making headlines urging Kerr and the UC Regents to hold a hearing on Savio, evidently hoping to close the door to his readmission. In this political climate, Savio knew he would be placing his readmission at great risk if he played a conspicuous role in a new campus political struggle. Yet throw himself into that conflict he did.[5]

The new conflict arose in part because the FSM had failed to settle definitively certain tangential but ultimately significant questions, most notably that of "time, place, and manner" regulation. The December 8 resolutions had established the basic principle that the administration could not regulate the content of political expression, while reserving to the University the authority to regulate the time, place, and manner of such expression so as to ensure that it not interfere with the normal educational and intellectual functions of the campus community. Although in principle the FSM endorsed this restriction, when in the post-FSM semesters the campus administration began to put it into practice, new tensions were quick to arise. To achieve a consensus over precisely what constituted reasonable "time, place, and manner" regulations, at least a modicum of trust was needed. But such trust, already in short supply in the wake of the conflicts of 1964, would disappear entirely under the pressures of a campus left made ever more militant and alienated by the horrors of the Vietnam War and the actions of a campus administration warily facing an anti-Berkeley backlash in California's rightward-drifting political environment, which carried Ronald Reagan to the governorship. The angry tone of the post-FSM campus left offended the administration and its faculty allies, while the administration's rulings regarding "time, place, and manner" infuriated many student radicals, who saw them as a backdoor way of regulating the content of advocacy and hence a gross violation of the December 8 resolutions.[6]

By 1966 anger on the left was especially intense over the administration ruling that an individual student group could reserve the Sproul Steps and microphone for rallies only once a week. In a less tense political climate, such regulations—if administered judiciously—might have seemed reasonable. Since Berkeley was a large campus with many political groups, one could argue that this rule would promote a more open forum by keeping the Sproul Steps and its microphones accessible to all and prevent them from being monopolized by one particularly active group (one that might preempt others by reserving the steps day after day before others could do so). One could easily imagine political activists functioning effectively within this once-a-week system, leafleting and setting up recruitment and informational tables four days a week, and holding a big Sproul rally once a week. But the militant mood of the campus antiwar leadership combined with the injudicious manner in which the once-a-week policy was administered by campus officials to breed a cycle of bad feeling, defiance, and reprisals. For example, one week in February 1966 the Vietnam Day Committee (VDC), Berkeley's leading antiwar group, was denied permission to hold a second rally *even though no other group had requested the use of Sproul Steps that day*. Being barred in this manner from an idle plaza left VDC organizers convinced that the administration was interested not in regulating Sproul fairly but in curbing both campus radicalism and the antiwar movement. This sense of grievance helped provoke a defiant response. Had the VDC wanted to, it probably could have evaded this ruling by asking another group to sponsor the rally. But instead, the VDC, as a way of expressing its anger and resisting what it saw as political harassment, opted to break University rules, rallying without permission on Sproul Steps and using its own sound system. This, in turn, was viewed by the administration as rank insubordination, unjustifiable rule breaking, and an attempt to provoke a needless confrontation so as to generate free publicity and campus sympathy. The violation led to disciplinary action, generating further protest as the cycle of distrust and discord continued.[7]

Administrators were not the only ones drawn into free speech conflicts with the post-FSM student left. Even faculty who had supported the FSM and shared the VDC's opposition to the war were angered at times by the VDC's provocative tactics and insensitivity to the free speech rights of others. In March 1966, for example, Reginald Zelnik, then an active antiwar professor in the history department, publicly criticized VDC organizers for trying to "cut off" historian Charles Sellers, himself an antiwar activist and key faculty supporter of the FSM, from speaking at the microphone. Further, Zelnik complained that he had been treated little better than Sellers. When trying to speak at Sproul Steps in opposition to the VDC's "work transfer" campaign, Zelnik wrote to the *Daily Californian*, "with the VDC monopolizing the microphone for three straight days, I was refused ten minutes to speak against the plan, and when I finally got 30 seconds to clarify my position, was told by the chairman of the rally how he wanted me to word my clarification so as not to influence people against the work transfer." Zelnik also accused some VDC activists of engaging in "character assassination" against some members of the administration and was offended by leaflets that dubbed one campus official "Dean Fuzz"—seeing in all this a retrogression from the luminous days of the FSM: "The current behavior of what was once a meaningful student protest movement on this campus has nothing but the most superficial and insignificant connection with the high level of personal morality and serious dedication of the FSM," he wrote in sorrow.[8]

This perception that the post-FSM left was abusing the freedom that had been won by the FSM spread to a small but vocal segment of more traditional student groups. The shift in perspective was reflected in the senate of the Berkeley student government (ASUC), which by a 13–6 margin passed a resolution in March 1966 urging the removal of the free speech area from Sproul Steps. The senate majority, unhappy with conduct of the radical speakers and the crowds on Sproul Plaza, argued that "the use of the microphone to attract a crowd, and the mob scene caused by congestion of a thoroughfare seems [*sic*] . . . to be antithetic[al] to the concept of free speech and open debate." The ASUC senate wanted the student government to control the scheduling of speakers when the free speech area was moved down to Lower Sproul, which it thought would "encourage a wide[r] spectrum of speakers and topics."[9]

This vote was in part the outgrowth of a conflict between VDC activists and nonpolitical student representatives of the freshman class in February 1966. Apparently the freshmen had reserved Sproul Steps for a noon skit to publicize a Valentine's Day dance, and the success of the skit hinged upon their being able to surprise the crowd about their identity as representatives of the freshman class. But when they arrived in the area on the day of the skit, the freshmen found VDCers about to hold a noon rally on the very steps they had reserved. When the freshmen told rally organizers that they had reserved the steps, the VDCers informed them that the dean had erred in scheduling two events simultaneously. The freshman class and VDC organizers then agreed to a compromise in which the antiwar rally would be delayed for the five or ten minutes necessary to complete the skit. But in explaining this to the crowd, the VDC announced that the freshman class was putting on a skit, which took away the desired element of surprise, leading the freshmen to cancel the skit and simply make an announcement about their dance.[10]

This conflict with the freshman class representatives can be subject to a variety of interpretations. One can read it as an honest misunderstanding over who had reserved the steps. There is no clear evidence indicating that VDCers were lying when they said they thought they had permission to use the steps for a rally. And the antiwar group did negotiate with the freshman organizers once they argued that they had reserved the Plaza, culminating in the VDC's agreement to give up part of their rally time for the skit. The VDC's ruining of the element of surprise required for the skit seemed inadvertent, and it is hard to see in this clear evidence of intimidation or a free speech violation. Yet such was the climate of the polarized campus that—outside of radical circles, in any case—the incident was viewed as evidence of left intimidation and disdain for free speech—setting the stage for the student government's vote for moving the free speech area off Sproul Steps.[11]

Nor is there much doubt that the Heyns administration contributed to this polarization even in this particular conflict. As soon as the freshmen had finished their announcements and relinquished the microphone to the VDC, John Searle, then a special assistant to the chancellor, came running over to criticize them for having "let them [the VDC leaders] talk us out of the steps and take them away from us."[12] Once the strongest of faculty supporters of the FSM, soon after entering the administration Searle had undergone—as historian Carl Schorske put it—"a visible switch, from a radical stress on political rights to a radical stress on academic order," becoming in the eyes of many the nemesis of the campus left.[13] As an aggressive and tough administrator, Searle, now severely disappointed with the campus left, often exacerbated political tensions on campus, enforcing rules with what at times seemed excessive rigidity. He was denounced harshly by campus radicals, who viewed him as a "sellout." Such personal attacks only served to fuel Searle's anger, encouraging him to view radical behavior in the most negative light. One faculty critic colorfully likened Searle to a fighter pilot whose judgment had been clouded by battle fatigue: He "has flown his 100 operational missions; he should be relieved from duty."[14] Having been taken to task by Searle for not standing up to the radicals, the freshmen argued—with what degree of exaggeration it is hard to say—that they had been intimidated by the VDC, and this perception spread to the ASUC senate, helping to pave the way for the vote to ban microphoned rallies from Sproul Steps.

The idea of moving the free speech area off of Sproul was not new. Faculty members who were disturbed by the growth of student activism began advocating this move soon after the FSM had established the Sproul area as a site for political rallies. In May 1966, for example, renewing an effort he had begun in 1965, chemistry professor George P. Pimentel urged Heyns to remove voice amplification from Sproul Steps, contending that the rallies, with their powerful microphones, were too intrusive and "unfair to those who, by their use of this main thoroughfare entrance to the University become a captive audience." He argued that pedestrians who entered the campus were forced to walk into political rallies and hear their speakers whether or not they wanted to listen to them and so had been denied "freedom of choice." But it was not so much the decibel level as the tone of the radical discourse on Sproul that motivated Pimentel's complaints. That discourse was saturated with "slander and abuse," he declared. "This vituperation has been heaped upon the President of the United States, the Governor, President Kerr, many of our respectful [sic] colleagues, and, indeed, it seems upon anyone who disagrees with the speaker of the moment."[15]

Pimentel's allusion to "vituperation" was particularly explosive. It was, after all, an argument that hinged on the *content* of speech, the very issue that had been at the heart of the FSM. To student activists, the move to drive political rallies off the steps seemed a serious violation of the December 8 resolutions, since it was removing speech from a central campus location precisely because that speech was considered offensive.[16] Now the question was whether the faculty, administration, and student body were so disillusioned with the campus left (which had dominated political life on "liberated" Sproul Plaza) that they would stand for a move that seemed an affront to the FSM's legacy.

As the Heyns administration picked up on the student senate's initiative and tried to persuade the faculty to endorse a removal of the free speech area from Sproul Steps, it claimed that such a move would not violate free speech rights. Aware that it could be politically disastrous to appear to reverse the outcome of the FSM, Heyns argued that there was no conflict between the December 8 resolutions and his proposed move. After all, the students were not being asked to stop holding rallies or even to cease using microphones. They were free to hold such rallies and advocate whatever political ideas they chose. All they were being asked was to conduct these political activities in a place the administration found more convenient, an area 134 yards to the west known as Lower Sproul.[17] In short, changing the site for amplified rallies did not violate the letter of the December 8 resolutions; it fell within the authority those resolutions reserved to the University to regulate the time, place, and manner of campus political expression, and all that was being changed was the *place* where students mobilized politically.

Taken in isolation, this argument might have carried a great deal of weight. But Heyns was too angry at the campus left to make the drive to push amplified rallies off Sproul sound politically neutral. His remarks to the Academic Senate defending this drive indicated that he was motivated by disgust at the political and intellectual content of radical speech on Sproul and was searching for a way to make the campus left less conspicuous. Heyns told the Academic Senate that something had to be done to counter the radicals who had exploited the Sproul forum and

> whose mode of sensibility is destructive of academic values, with the worst manners [and] the most anti-intellectual posture.... Their presence and possessiveness [of the Sproul forum] has tended to drive out other student groups. We have ample evidence that people who are not heroes of these groups, are reluctant to use the steps or are badly treated when they do. I won't go into detail on the quality of the performances but I can assure you they are pretty wretched. This would not trouble me if the wretchedness did not have the effect of driving out something better. I am not impressed by the quality of our public forum and neither are most of our visitors![18]

Heyns thought the Sproul forum had become too "attractive as a weapon" for radicals because of its "crowd mobilizing function." Located so centrally at Sproul, armed with "the microphone [that] has the power... because of its commanding presence, its insistent compelling voice, [radicals could enlist] the daily crowd of the curious, the fascinated, the idle, the 'action seekers,' the TV cameras." All of this, in Heyns's view, made it too easy to mobilize an angry crowd. "Grievances, distortions, accusations, all of these assume enormous proportions and have a great potential for mischief." Worse still to Heyns was the fact that the target of such mobilizations was "the university and its administration."[19] Heyns argued that the Sproul forum was privileging politics over intellectual life in a way that was inappropriate for an institution of higher learning: "The central, highly visible Sproul Plaza gives political activity and organization a centrality that is out of proportion to its true importance in the University."[20]

Although he did not admit it publicly, Heyns seemed to be aware that he was violating the December 8 resolution against regulating the content of speech. In his Academic Senate speech he frankly acknowledged the "lurking suspicion that we have control of content in view" in the drive to remove amplification from the steps. To be sure, he denied any such intent, assuring the Senate that in proposing a change of venue he simply aimed to regulate the "manner, not content" of student speech. But in the draft of this speech were words Heyns edited out, in which he grudgingly acknowledged that "indeed our criticism of quality [of speech on Sproul] is, I guess, a criticism of content."[21]

The initial confrontation over the chancellor's initiative occurred at the meeting of the faculty-student Campus Rules Committee in May 1966. The most forceful statement against the continued use of Sproul Steps as a staging area for political rallies came from historian Martin Malia, a vocal faculty critic of the student left. Malia, reading a letter he had written to the *Daily Californian* (hereafter *Daily Cal*), told the committee that free speech would not be jeopardized in the least by banning microphoned political rallies from Sproul. In fact, he argued, the format of Sproul political gatherings, with their amplified speakers, had *not* been conducive to an open forum and the free exchange of ideas, since

> by its very nature a microphone is a commanding and rather imperialistic instrument.... An "open forum" is founded on the premise that truth and understanding ... emerge from dialogue, rebuttal, and mutual criticism—as in a parliament or, especially in a university. But the Sproul Steps forum, whatever it may represent in theory, in fact has developed as the exact antithesis of this. For the amplified voice of the microphone means a monopoly of one point of view, without the possibility of criticism (a counter-tirade the next day or week is no substitute for a living confrontation of ideas). It produces a harangue rather than a debate; it leads to exhortation rather than argument, to domination rather than dialogue. In short, it represents the exercise of power rather than of thought.[22]

In a variation on the "captive audience" argument, Malia contended that drawing a crowd from Sproul Steps was too easy: "[B]y providing an arena so central and commanding that speakers do not have to prove themselves or make their case in order to win attention [UC Berkeley was] encouraging the lowest level of ideological barking and political exhibitionism. It would be far better both for student politics and intellectual standards of the university if campus orators had to work a little harder to make people want to hear them on the Lower Plaza."[23]

Student dissent at the Rules Committee meeting was heated. Accusing the University of bowing to off-campus pressures, former FSM leader Bettina Aptheker charged that a ban on amplified rallies on Sproul Steps violated the December 8 resolutions and student free speech rights. FSM veteran Marvin Garson threw insults at the Rules Committee, terming it "stupid" and suggesting that "the chancellor was using it as a puppet to impose his own will." Other students were equally vitriolic; one threatened that, if the administration forced the steps issue, Heyns would lose his job just as Chancellor Strong had lost his during the FSM, and "expressed the opinion that Mr. [Earl] Cheit should resign as Vice Chancellor or be damned."[24] Such speeches were not persuasive intellectually to the committee's faculty majority, but they did suggest how explosive the steps issue was and thereby added weight to the arguments of those liberal faculty who urged a delay in the move at least until students and professors could be canvassed more thoroughly. In a close 6–4 vote (all of the negative votes came from the student representatives), the Rules Committee supported the move from the Sproul Steps to Lower Sproul; but the committee also voted to delay its implementation until the end of fall quarter 1966, and it recommended that before making a final decision the chancellor first consult with student groups and faculty.[25]

The dispute over the Sproul Steps was renewed in fall 1966, but this time it was linked to a broader set of conflicts. Most tellingly, new rules were announced in September restricting nonstudent participation in campus politics. These rules allowed nonstudents to belong to student organizations but only as "inactive" members, barred from holding office, soliciting funds, distributing leaflets, sitting alone at informational tables, or issuing statements in the name of the group. The administration saw the rules as a way of insuring that off-campus agitators not be able to form and dominate student front groups designed to exploit the campus forum. Student radicals saw the new rules as a politically motivated attempt to cut them off from the outside community and from former classmates who had recently postponed their studies in order to work full time as antiwar activists.[26] By October the administration would go even further, denying Students for a Democratic Society permission to use University facilities for a black power conference on the grounds that there was "convincing evidence of extensive non-student involvement in the conception and planning of the event."[27] Although, after considerable protest, the administration dropped its ban on the conference, the nonstudent rules remained. Adding to the contentiousness of the campus political scene was a gubernatorial election in which candidate Ronald Reagan was pledging that if elected governor he would enlist a former CIA director to oversee an investigation of Berkeley student radicals.[28]

Taken together with the attempt to drive amplified rallies off Sproul Steps, these initiatives left student radicals convinced that they were under siege from a hostile administration bowing to pressure from off-campus conservative interests. Nor was there much doubt that the Sproul Steps' status as a free political space was in serious jeopardy, since the Campus Rules Committee, the chancellor, and even the ASUC senate had gone on record as favoring the proposed move. Although the administration had agreed to delay the move pending more consultation with the University community, high-ranking campus officials were clearly eager to act. In an October 1966 internal memorandum, for example, Searle had likened the microphone used in Sproul rallies to "a permanent knife at the throat of all authority in the University, and particularly at the throat of the administration." He saw those rallies as breeding "simple naked hatred. All of the pus of the campus is drained onto the Sproul Hall steps."[29]

Clearly the move off Sproul Steps could be stopped only if student activists could mobilize the campus against the move. To their good fortune, the activists now had as an ally the most famous nonstudent in Berkeley, Mario Savio, just recently returned from England. Savio had sought readmission to the student body for the fall 1966 quarter but, having missed the deadline, applied for winter quarter instead.[30] Despite his nonstudent status, Savio, seeing the victory of 1964 at risk, sought to help build an FSM-style opposition to the move off Sproul. He later recalled that

> once we realized that they were serious about this [attempt] to move free speech out of the center of campus . . . we quickly reassembled . . . a thin facsimile of the old FSM coalition and issued a . . . rather long leaflet titled "Our Traditional Liberties." I remember Tina [Apteker] saying to me; "Once I saw that leaflet I knew Mario was involved in this again because it was very lengthy, philosophically argued in the style of what the old FSM leaflets had been. . . ." FSM leaflets were frequently lengthy and well argued and people were interested in reading them. There was something really to read and discuss in many of the leaflets that FSM issued. And this was a return to that . . . tradition . . . we had established.[31]

Savio made civil liberty and the FSM settlement the cornerstones of his broadly conceived defense of the steps. Even the title of the first leaflet he helped write in this campaign, "Our Traditional Liberties," indicated his intent to appeal to the University community as a whole rather than just to radicals. The leaflet called upon the campus to rally not on behalf of some radical leftist cause but rather in defense of the liberties the FSM had already won. Thanks to the FSM, the Sproul Steps had been established as an amplified free speech area, and they must remain so unless it could be shown that use of that location constituted "interference with the normal functions of the university," the language of the December 8 resolutions. In almost lawyerlike fashion, Savio took on the arguments of administration and hostile faculty, holding that although their criticisms of the quality of the Sproul rallies might be valid, they were ultimately irrelevant. Savio acknowledged that critiques of the low intellectual level of the rallies were "not without some appeal to the academic mind." He conceded the possibility that the smaller meetings that the administration hoped would result from moving off the steps might "be more likely to produce genuine dialogue" and thereby "further the primary 'normal' function of the University . . . the discovery and dissemination of truth . . . since dispassion and questioning contribute to and further this purpose." But, he concluded, "even if this were a *valid* argument," it remained "irrelevant" because the December 8 resolutions did not obligate organizers of campus rallies to *further* the normal function of the University—promoting a dispassionate search for truth—but only obligated them "not to *interfere* with the normal functions of the University." In other words, the administration was trying to take away an established right by changing the criteria, raising the standards of permissible amplified speech on Sproul, and such an extreme revision would violate the agreement that had ended the FSM crisis. Savio's leaflet pointed out: "The central intent of the December 8 Resolutions was to protect *advocacy*"; it was to serve a broad "civil libertarian purpose" rather than the narrower educational vision of some administrator. And, he continued, this civil libertarian purpose remained important because in 1966 with antiwar activists, as in 1964 with civil rights activists, the administration was using its power to "harass and isolate those whose opinions and activities are most in conflict with American society."[32]

This is not to say, however, that Savio agreed with those who held that the Sproul Steps free speech tradition lacked educational value. Actually, in his first leaflet on the steps controversy, Savio warned against underestimating "the purely educational value of unrestricted *persuasive* speech," or the idea that one could learn from "those whose primary purpose may be to persuade rather than to enlighten." America was a society that closed off its media and electoral process to those who advocated radical positions. A university could serve its educational mission well by giving a prominent forum to those dissidents who, having been so marginalized, could never get their views out to the rest of society. According to Savio's leaflet, in a nation

> which increasingly has become a captive audience for a dangerously narrow spectrum of political opinion, the interests and purposes of a free university are best served when the University community makes available to all dissenters the most effective access to an audience not particularly interested— initially—in what the dissenters have to say. We have shown above that the "educational" argument for moving the microphones is irrelevant; but now we see that it is also only partly valid. For who would suggest that the wide range of opinion presented from Sproul Steps is a normal part of instruction at the University? And who any longer expects genuine debate in the mass media? Clearly, then, it is the duty of the University in pursuit of its primary educational objectives to make the very center of campus life—the Upper Plaza—the site of unlimited debate and dissent.[33]

By the standards of Berkeley student politics in 1966, Savio's message was restrained. He had avoided revolutionary rhetoric, seeking instead to rally students around a faculty document, the December 8 resolutions. Although this approach was well designed to attract a wide spectrum of students and faculty, it was not sufficiently revolutionary for some prominent members of the campus left—most of whom were associated with the Free University, Berkeley's alternative college, committed to experimental education. In their leaflet "Fight!! For December 8??," the Free University radicals displayed little interest in Savio's civil liberties arguments and demonstrated none of his reverence for the December 8 resolutions. Instead, they offered a revolutionary message that stressed "Student Power" as opposed to faculty-student cooperation; they demanded a radical restructuring of the university:

"December 8"? Don't talk to us of December 8. Talk rather of Student Power.
. . . What was December 8? The day when the faculty expressed what they "had
always believed." The day when students were patted on the head and mis-
took legitimacy for success. It was a day, in short, far less significant than
October 2 or December 3 [the days of mass student sit-ins during the FSM]. If
the provisions of December 8 were upheld, would it be enough? Is it enough
to win a formal victory if the Administration's power to restrict and regiment
our education goes unchallenged? THEN WHY MAKE IT OUR SYMBOL?
. . . We are not interested in solving their problems, but in becoming and
remaining a problem for them. Rather than demanding more liberties, more
speech, more of what we have—we should begin to think of qualitative
changes in the goals and means of education. . . . Rights are abstract and
meaningless without the means of defending them. We must organize for
Student Power or see student freedom vanish. December 8 was only a shadow
of FSM. If we restrict ourselves to fighting for that shadow, our movement
becomes the shadow of a shadow.[34]

It quickly became evident, however, that Savio's approach rather than
the Free University's set the tone for the movement to save the steps. The
high point of this movement came on November 4, 1966, when a "Save the
Steps" rally was held on Sproul Plaza. The speakers included Dan Rosenthal, representing campus conservatives, Bettina Aptheker, then a leader
of Berkeley's antiwar movement, and graduate student Brian O'Brien, of
Berkeley's TA union, all of whom pledged to mobilize the campus to
defend the free speech area. But the main event at this gathering was
the appearance of Savio, whose first campus speech in more than a year
attracted a huge crowd—some five thousand—to the rally. Although this
speech (like the "little free speech movement" it helped to ignite) has
attracted no attention from historians, it was in its own way as daring and
memorable as any of Savio's famous FSM orations.[35]

Understanding the way that power actually worked on campus, Savio did
not utter a word about "student power" in the style of the 1966 student left.
Instead, he began his speech appealing to "the people with *preponderant*
power in this university, the faculty." Savio said that his talk was directed
"maybe even more than to those who are prepared to fight for the steps, to
a lot of faculty members who were our allies once who are unsure whether
they should be our allies *today.*" He quoted the message that Berkeley
physics professor Owen Chamberlain had sent out to faculty at other UC
campuses at the end of the FSM crisis, explaining why the Berkeley faculty
had voted for the December 8 resolutions: "some of our best students are
supporters, and ardent ones, of the FSM. I am trying to listen and I ask
you to listen. See if they are not saying: 'Respect our civil disobedience. It
is sometimes better than forgoing the rights you believe to be yours. Show
us that we have the full rights of all citizens whether we are this year on
the learning end or the teaching end of the University. Show us, *please,*

that whether or not you approve of our form of morality, at least you have heard it.'"[36]

Appealing for just such a hearing in 1966, Savio expressed the hope that "professor Chamberlain and other members of the faculty are listening today. We have something to say and I hope they hear it."[37]

Savio eloquently linked the steps controversy to the founding principles of the FSM. While using the December 8 resolutions to appeal to the faculty, he presented that document not as a "pat on the head" from the professoriate but as one whose ideas derived from the FSM itself. Since he had helped lead the revolt that inspired those resolutions, Savio was, in a sense, one of their prime authors and could speak with authority to their applicability to the current controversy. In those resolutions, Savio explained to the crowd, "the faculty adopted essentially the civil liberty demands of the Free Speech Movement." And the central FSM demand, which the December 8 resolutions "provide *explicitly,*" is "that speech and advocacy shall be regulated *only* to the extent that the normal function of the university will be reasonably protected." Since Sproul Steps rallies did not disrupt the University's normal functioning, there was no way that they could be forcibly removed without violating the resolutions. As in his leaflet, Savio acknowledged that smaller meetings on Lower Sproul might be more educational because the smaller crowds would allow for more dialogue and questions (and also, to much applause, noted that this same objection was raised by students who criticized the large lecture format upon which Berkeley's academic life was so dependent) but, he again concluded, this was "completely *irrelevant*. The question is civil liberties. The faculty resolutions of December 8 say nothing at all about speech" on the steps having to be sufficiently educational so that it "contributes to or *furthers* the normal functions of the University but rather speech which does not *interfere* with the normal functions. These two criteria are vastly different and one is much weaker than the other and we will stand only for the civil libertarian criterion in the faculty resolutions of December 8."

Savio argued that forcing students off the steps into a more isolated meeting place was a violation of their free speech rights. The Lower Plaza was a remote sanctuary whose very isolation would tend to make political discourse inaccessible when compared with speech at the central entryway to the campus. Savio reminded the crowd that during the FSM

> it became clear to all, students and faculty alike, that part of what was meant by protected speech content—by Free Speech—was speech which is effective, and that meant ... my speech is not free unless I have access to a large audience, potentially one that is interested in what I am saying, [though] initially not necessarily interested. During the early days of the Free Speech Movement, Clark Kerr tried to palm off on us the Lower Student Union plaza—it's not a new question. We said "we'll take it ... but not only." And the reason we

could not accept only the Lower Plaza was exactly why we will not accept it today; it isolated us from the many passers-by who might not . . . have (given) a damn what we had to say. . . . We felt then, if we were isolated in that way we would not have access to that potentially large audience not initially interested; so we insisted on not being restricted to the "Pit."

After this careful critique of the new policy's implications, Savio's logic gave way to emotion, as he expressed anger and "*amazement* that the Administration would consider such an *outrageous* action." Reminding everyone that political repression had backfired on Berkeley officials in the past, Savio told the crowd, "I think that the University greatly benefited by the *purging* which it received, self-inflicted, during the Free Speech Movement. I seriously doubt it would survive a second showing. However, they may force it on us."[38]

The speech's most dramatic point came when Savio turned from the dispute over Sproul Steps to the new restrictions on nonstudents. Savio denounced these regulations as "befitting more a *prison* than a university." Moving beyond rhetoric, Savio then took defiant action, asking the crowd to *watch*. "I am now going to *violate* a University regulation! I take full personal responsibility for the dire consequences. I'd like you to watch please." Savio, the nonstudent, then stepped away from the microphone to pass out copies of the leaflet he had written in defense of free speech on campus and in so doing broke the University's new rules barring nonstudents from leafleting. He told the crowd that he expected no justice should the administration seek to penalize him for this act of defiance: "there's no way to *violate* this regulation and then *test* it in a University *hearing* because we have no judicial review on the question of the December 8 resolutions." The administration would allow no internal review of the constitutionality of these restrictions on nonstudent speech or on their compatibility with the December 8 resolutions. In any campus hearing, Savio predicted (quite accurately), the only "question would be, 'Did you hand out the leaflet?' Well, of *course* I did; everybody *sees* I did. I have no reason to *deny* that I handed it out."

Savio predicted that if the administration ignored the protests against the removal of amplified rallies from Sproul Steps, a political storm would ensue. He expressed the hope that "we would not have to resort to the painful . . . tactics of sit-in" but implied that either such civil disobedience or a student strike would occur as students rallied to save their free speech forum. "I want to make that *clear* and I made it clear to Vice Chancellor Boyd, to Dean Arleigh Williams, everyone hears it now including Mr. O'Mara from the Berkeley 'Red Squad' (laughter). No question about it: we mean *business* and I hope they understand." Despite this threat, however, Savio wanted to avoid such a confrontation, and toward that end he closed his speech as he had started it, with "an appeal to sentiments expressed by Professor Owen Chamberlain when he defended the faculty's action....I want the faculty to stand up for what they once thought was worth defending. If they do that there will be no fight. They could have prevented the first fight had they acted sooner than they did. They have to be buttressed, if you will; that requires something amounting to a standing army. That's us, a non-violent army. I *hope* they're listening."[39]

The administration rather than the faculty was the first to demonstrate publicly that it was listening. Heyns was outraged that in front of this huge crowd Savio had denounced and defied campus regulations. His immediate response was punitive: henceforth, rallies on Sproul would be held on a "trial" basis only, with the allotted amount of time reduced from an hour to forty minutes. He threatened that any further defiance of University regulations, such as Savio's "public, deliberate, and provocative rule violation," would lead to an immediate end to the use of the steps as a site for amplified rallies. Again attacking the quality of discourse, Heyns pledged to monitor the rallies closely and punish those "who use our free forum for slander, intimidation, and deliberate misrepresentation." In an apparent reference to Savio's incendiary speech, Heyns warned that "the days of doing business in this campus by coercion or threat of coercion are over."[40] Student activists found the chancellor's choice of words ironic in light of the threats he was making against them and their free speech area. Thus in a leaflet they put out soon after Heyns's speech, they agreed that threats and coercion should stop, adding "STOP THREATENING US!"[41]

The chancellor's tough response to Savio elicited some faculty support. Four days after the "Save the Steps" rally, when Heyns, at an Academic Senate meeting, announced these restrictions on the use of Sproul Steps, he received a thirty-second standing ovation.[42] At this meeting Heyns claimed that most of the faculty he had spoken to favored the move off Sproul Steps, but he also acknowledged that even many who thought "the microphone should be moved...feared the possible effect of this action on the peace and decorum of the community." His words dripping with sarcasm, Heyns expressed frustration that what to him seemed a perfectly justifiable move—a mere 134 yards—was linked by so many members of the campus community to "issues of apparent cosmic significance," including "the true meaning of the FSM, the Free Forum, the First Amendment of the Constitution, the Declaration of the Rights of Man, the December 8 resolution, the political rights of students....There are so many romantic notions about the microphone in the present location. I am troubled by the fact that we are still not able to discuss the simple question of the proper location and style for a free forum without evoking all the rhetoric and emotion of bygone days."[43]

As this expression of frustration implies, Savio's appeal to the faculty had evoked "the rhetoric,...emotion," and civil liberties idealism of the FSM, an event clearly too fresh in the minds of liberal-minded professors to be dismissed as belonging to "bygone days." In the aftermath of Savio's speech and his own Academic Senate address on the Sproul forum, Heyns received mail from influential Berkeley faculty members indicating their opposition to his plan to move the rallies. In a particularly impressive letter, professors of geology, physics, German, zoology, English, and statistics, all of whom were associate deans, told him, "We are distressed by statements in your address to the senate which appear to imply that the content of speech may be used as one of the criteria for governing whether the microphone is to be moved. . . . We hope that in future statements and actions the Administration will make it clear that no attempt is being made to regulate the content of speech."[44] Seventeen members of the history department signed a petition urging that the free speech area not be moved, and two members of that department met with Heyns to ask him to delay any such move. A delay was also requested by the chairman of the Academic Senate's Student Affairs Committee.[45] Among the most prominent faculty members to write to Heyns in defense of the steps was Owen Chamberlain:

> I have found that the practice of having speakers at noon on Sproul Steps has been most pleasant and refreshing. I like the feature that as one walks through Sather Gate one hears a few sentences and can then decide whether to tarry or move on. I think it has added to our campus life a very positive tone. . . . I have heard that Sproul Steps has become a symbol of student defiance of the Administration. I am afraid I also feel that the Sproul Steps may have become a symbol in the Administration of its ability to show the students who is master in this house. I think I too am guilty a bit of symbolism. I feel that the use of voice amplification at noon on Sproul Steps stands as a symbol of freedom of speech on the Campus. No one will ever be able to support a charge that there is no freedom of speech on this campus as long as the noon talks on Sproul Steps continue.[46]

If such faculty dissent was bad news for Heyns, even worse was the flood of information he received on the state of student opinion. Most devastating was the survey that Dean of Students Arleigh Williams completed in early November.[47] Williams asked the presidents of all registered student organizations to express their views on moving the free speech area off Sproul. Dozens of student organizations, some political, others academic, responded, with the vast majority opposing the move. The dean and his staff were so taken aback by the breadth and depth of this student support for the old free speech area that they recommended "strongly" against any attempt to tamper with the current site. Williams was quite candid with his superiors regarding the administration's failure to win or even clearly articulate its case:

> Historically we had serious difficulty because of our failure to inform, prepare, or educate our community before critical administrative action was initiated. In this instance, we may have believed that we have handled the

problems of communications well, but it is obvious that we have not gotten the message to our students. Further, as much as I may not like to admit it, our anticipated move means the destruction of a symbol which is considered to be of value by most of our student body. If we change a popular "tradition" and if our actions are not understood or are considered to be accomplished by purposes which are not considered to be appropriate, we can expect nothing but serious conflict.[48]

It is highly unusual for an upper-echelon Berkeley administrator to write so pessimistically to a chancellor about a policy that the chief campus officer was so obviously anxious to implement. That Williams wrote such a memo is a testament not only to his political intelligence and candor but also to the magnitude of the consensus he had found when he canvassed the student body. The consensus was a measure of the lasting success of the FSM and the strength of its political legacy. Although the student senate had sought to challenge that legacy (at least with regard to Sproul Steps), it found precious few students willing to support its position, not even among the more moderate and less political. Even students who loathed some of the strident radical rhetoric emanating from Sproul Steps insisted on maintaining Berkeley's free speech tradition. This was evident, for example, in the report made by Bari Bradner, sorority representative to the ASUC senate. Having asked the presidents of twenty sororities to poll their members on the issue, she found that eighteen houses favored maintaining the current free speech area, most by heavy majorities. The total sorority vote was 553 members in support of the Sproul Steps, with only 174 favoring a move to Lower Sproul—a stunning vote when one considers that the Greek system was traditionally the most conservative segment of the student body.[49] If the administration could not even come close to winning sorority students to its side, it seemed certain to lose any contest with Savio for the allegiance of the larger and more liberal non-Greek majority of the student body.

What this suggests is that the chancellor, in addition to being at odds with the campus left, had momentarily lost touch with mainstream students. He had not understood their sensitivity, in the wake of the FSM, to even the appearance of a free speech violation. Nor had he been aware that so many students valued having a free speech forum at the center of campus, wishing to judge for themselves which speakers and causes were or were not attractive. The FSM had left even nonradicals wary of the administration and its perceived tendency to abuse its power. The influence that these values, sensitivities, and fears had over the minds of mainstream students is movingly expressed by Robert R. Cross, a student member of the Order of the Golden Bear—a forum for Berkeley's most traditional students, faculty, administrators, and alumni—in his mid-November letter to the chancellor. Cross had already spoken to Heyns (and written to Williams) against the move off the steps. In his letter he expressed the wish that the various groups . . . on the campus could discuss this, and every other subject which concerns us with honesty and respect. Unfortunately, that seldom happens when politically significant matters confront us. I certainly agree with you that demagoguery, falsehoods, maliciousness, and slander can often be found on the campus and reflect both a latent anti-intellectualism and a failure of the university to establish standards of respect and integrity. The question which interests me is how are we (students, faculty, and administration) going to pull our debate out of the bog in which it seems to be sinking? I contend we are not going to inculcate respect when these values and the rules which follow from them are established by fiat from above. It may be that talk of a "callous and impersonalized university machine" is trite and meaningless. Nevertheless a great many of us normally apathetic students were stirred and touched deeply by such charges made during the turmoil of the FSM. I need hardly remind you that the administration, through arbitrary acts and a stubborn harshness . . . drove probably a majority of students and faculty into sympathy with the aims of the FSM. It would be intemperate of me to use the experience of the FSM as a club to beat the administration into accepting whatever certain activists think is right. What the FSM does show is that unless we begin to act as a community, in deed as well as words, we are going to be involved in continual infighting and disunity. The chaos of the FSM . . . I hope will not ever be repeated; the basic distrust and division which gave birth to this movement is still with us. . . . The issue of the steps is an example of our difficulties. . . . Most of the students at Berkeley are fond of having rallies on the steps, although one might go to very few of those presented. We fully realize that these rallies are frequently of low intellectual quality—so we move on. We are also aware that a good many of the rallies are of high quality and of immediate significance to issues which concern us. We are willing to undergo a bit of inconvenience caused by bad rallies in order that we may not miss the outstanding rallies. . . . There is legitimate indignation when the small body of individuals known as the "administration" presumes to judge on a perfectly subjective basis what is good and what is bad on the rally scene. The fact is that no two of us agree on which are the good and which are the bad rallies. . . . The content and quality of rallytalk should be judged by . . . the "community" . . . the whole university body [not] the administration.[50]

To his credit, Chancellor Heyns, despite his anger at Savio and his ardent desire to move the rallies, responded positively to such criticism. He carefully canvassed student and faculty opinion and heeded the faculty who advised him to delay moving the amplified free speech area. At the end of the academic year, in June 1967, Heyns abandoned his campaign to move the rallies off the steps, declaring that he had been

gratified by an improvement in the use of the rallies over the past six months. With a few exceptions, there has been a restoration of civility. Moreover, a number of important national voices have been heard through the initiative of students. The cause of the free forum has certainly been advanced. . . .

Complete freedom to speak and to be heard must be our objective—and I believe that is the goal for most of this student body. In recognition of the progress which has been made, the Sproul Plaza will continue to be used for rallies next fall.[51]

If judged by this outcome, the little free speech movement had a happy ending. Students and some faculty rallied in support of free speech. The dean spoke truth to power. Sproul Steps was saved as a site for amplified political rallies. The chancellor backed away from pointless confrontation, suggesting that he had handled a serious free speech crisis better than his predecessor, Chancellor Strong. The conflict ended without the mass arrests and the bitterness of the FSM. Indeed, its very success in avoiding the headlines and pain of 1964 is undoubtedly a key reason why the story of this later free speech conflict has been largely forgotten by both the public and by historians.

·   ·   ·

There was another, more personal level, however, at which the little free speech movement's ending was far from happy. For Savio, as it turns out, the victory was by no means painless. In the little free speech movement, as in the FSM, protesters learned that there was a price to be paid for political success. This time, instead of hundreds of demonstrators paying fines and several leaders going to jail, the movement and the campus lost one of their most valued voices.[52] Savio's participation in the unrest of 1966 served as a pretext for a vindictive and effective administration effort to bar him from the student body.

The story of Savio's attempt to gain readmission to Berkeley began in December 1965, when, writing from England, he asked the UC registrar about his eligibility to return. (He had withdrawn from the University in mid-December 1964.) The registrar informed him that he was "academically eligible" but could be readmitted only with permission from the dean of letters and sciences.[53] Although Savio wasn't told this, the dean (and his superiors) had a great deal of discretion regarding admissions and could keep him out even if he was academically qualified. The very idea of Savio rejoining the student body aroused fear among high-ranking campus administrators. In late June 1966, as Savio was preparing to reapply, Vice Chancellor Earl Cheit and UC vice president and general counsel Thomas Cunningham quietly searched for legal means to avoid readmitting him. Apparently without actually questioning Savio's academic qualifications, Cheit had begun by asking Cunningham if the University could "lawfully refuse to readmit Mario Savio as a student."[54]

Cunningham responded that the University could keep Savio out even if his academic record was good, but only if it could find examples of

misconduct that affected his "suitability as a student." The problem, however, was that at the Greek Theater meeting of December 7, 1964, near the
end of the FSM, President Kerr had pledged not to discipline activists for
any actions they had taken prior to December 3. Thus, according to Cunningham, any misconduct (whether on campus or off) used to justify
denial of admission to Savio must have taken place after that date. Since
most of Savio's defiant actions in the FSM had preceded December 3,
they could not be used to bar his readmission.[55] In a second memorandum
to Cheit, however, Cunningham suggested that enough evidence of
post–December 3 misconduct existed to deny Savio readmission. This
alleged "misconduct" consisted of Savio's attempt "without permission" to
speak at the Greek Theatre meeting and his resistance to the campus
police who attempted to drag him off the stage as he tried to speak. Cunningham also wrote that Savio's criticism of the judge at the FSM trial constituted "a particularly intemperate contempt of court. . . . I think such off-
campus misconduct can be considered as affecting Savio's 'suitability as a
student.'"[56]

None of these internal machinations was known to the public at the
time. The public record, in fact, was misleading with regard to the fairness
of the University in handling Savio's application for readmission. President
Kerr's public rhetoric and actions in fall 1966 suggested that the University
would be judicious and nondiscriminatory in handling Savio's application.
In October 1966 Kerr fended off an attempt by Regent John Canaday to
initiate a special hearing on Savio designed to bar him from UC. Canaday
was actually the second conservative regent to go after Savio. In summer
1966 regent Max Rafferty, who was also the California superintendent of
public instruction, had written a public letter to the chair of the Board of
Regents saying that it would be "nuts" to readmit this troublemaker and
that if the Board allowed Savio back into the University, "I suggest we
regents submit ourselves forthwith to group therapy."[57] But Kerr properly
took the position that Regental interference in the admissions process
would violate the power of individual chancellors to decide on admissions,
and this position prevailed. So though it looked to the public as if the
autonomy and neutrality of the University had been protected, along with
due process, in fact, privately, Berkeley campus officials had been months
ahead of Canaday in searching for ways to bar Mario, a search they continued through the fall term.

When Mario violated campus regulations by leafleting at the November
4 "Save the Steps" rally, the Berkeley administration seized upon this as the
kind of "misconduct" Cunningham had said they needed to bar Savio's
readmission. The timing of the denial of Savio's admission and the manner
in which it was implemented both attest to its special nature, leaving no
doubt that the admissions process had been politicized. Savio had applied

for winter quarter readmission in August 1966. The University failed to reach a decision for over three months. Mario defied the leafleting ban on November 4, a Friday. On the very next business day, November 7, Boyd, vice chancellor for student affairs, sent out a letter informing Mario that his application was denied.[58] Indeed, so eager was the Berkeley administration to bar Savio that it ignored the University counsel's warning about the need for due process. Cunningham had advised the chancellor that "the safe and prudent legal course would be to provide Mr. Savio with a letter setting forth his alleged misconduct and extending to him the opportunity for a hearing as to those matters before a decision is made on his application."[59] Instead the chancellor opted to deny admission without first allowing such a hearing.

Had he wanted to, Savio would probably have been able to mobilize his many campus supporters to protest the administration's unfair conduct. And, in fact, some such protest did occur spontaneously. But Mario, affirming that he did not believe in movements centering on leaders, would not hear of Berkeley students mounting a reinstatement drive on his behalf.[60] Nonetheless, he and his lawyer did try to challenge the administration on free speech grounds, arguing in a meeting with campus officials that a hearing should be held to determine the validity and constitutionality of the nonstudent leafleting policy. But the campus administration, refusing to consider this constitutional issue, announced that the only hearing it would hold would be one to determine whether Savio had actually violated University regulations, thereby making him ineligible for readmission.[61] Since Mario had no interest in a hearing unless it would consider the relevant free speech issue, he did not pursue an appeal. As he explained to the press, "The only hearing I will attend is on their right to deny me, a nonstudent, the right of putting out a leaflet on campus. . . . If these hearings are not bound by the December 8 (1964) resolutions, then I consider the school unworthy of my attendance."[62]

Mario's readmission bid would have ended differently had the University's ostensibly neutral admissions process not been polluted politically. A document recently made public by the UC archives indicates that had the decision concerning Savio been left where admissions decisions normally are made—at the campus admissions office—the campus's most famous student radical would have enjoyed another opportunity to earn his Berkeley degree. In this "most confidential" June 1966 memo from UCB admissions officer F. T. Malm to Vice Chancellor Cheit, Malm concluded that Savio

> entered [UC] with an outstanding [academic] record. . . . Savio is . . . officially in good [academic] standing and entitled to readmission under existing University regulations . . . unless a block were imposed by the Dean of Students or the Chancellor. . . . I do not feel competent to judge whether such a block be

imposed, given the variety of circumstances and problems which must be considered by the Dean of Students and the Chancellor in such an unusual case. It is my feeling, however, that Savio's intellectual capacity is such that he certainly should be successful as a student upon his return; and moreover, that . . . his own circumstances (marriage and family obligations; change of major) have changed so that the situation is very difficult [i.e., different] from that of Fall 1964 when his leadership &/or catalytic effort had so immense an effect on the University and the whole educational scene. In short, my personal recommendation would be: READMIT.[63]

Politically it made perfect sense for the administration to ignore this admissions officer's recommendation. Even as a nonstudent, Mario in December 1966 would play a leading role in a controversial anti-ROTC sit-in at Berkeley's student union—which sparked a student strike. Had Mario remained a student, his great skills as an organizer and orator obviously would have been enlisted in furthering the antiwar movement and, perhaps even more disturbing to the administration, pressing it to honor more robustly the still rather fragile December 8 resolutions. The denial of his readmission was, moreover, not the only evidence of the administration's profound fear of Savio's presence. The week after Berkeley officials had vetoed his readmission, Savio was the subject of further high-level administration machinations. In executive session during the November 17, 1966, meeting of the Board of Regents, General Counsel Cunningham, "at the request of Chancellor Heyns," sought authorization from the Regents to obtain an injunction against Savio (along with VDC leaders Jerry Rubin and Stewart Albert) to prevent him from coming on to campus—believing that this would help the administration combat what they alleged was his "program of disruptive activities on the campus."[64]

Something was lost, however, when the University closed its doors to its most eloquent critic. And that something can best be sensed from the letter of protest that Reginald Zelnik, Robert Brentano, and three other Berkeley historians sent in Savio's defense to the Berkeley Academic Senate's Academic Freedom Committee after the University turned down his application:

Mr. Savio's readmission seems to us in a sense a touchstone of this University's character. No doubt he has been one of its most difficult and irritating members. Nevertheless . . . Mr. Savio is also symbolic of the positive achievement of the resolutions presented by the academic freedom committee and passed on December 8, 1964. One measure of our ability to deal with the full—and inevitably controversial—range of the world of ideas is our willingness and ability to make a place for Mr. Savio in this institution. To exclude him on the grounds now argued seems to us in a profound sense a violation of the University's academic freedom.[65]

But the Academic Freedom Committee did not share this sense of loss regarding Savio or see the denial of his readmission as a violation of academic freedom. Thus the only academic body with the power to challenge the administration's decision refused to do so.

It should come as no surprise that Savio suspected that the chancellor's move against him was politically motivated. Since the denial of his readmission came on the eve of the gubernatorial election, Savio saw it as linked to the resurgence of the Republican right in California and to Ronald Reagan's campaign promise to launch a political investigation of the Berkeley campus. "I'm only speculating," Savio told a San Francisco newspaper, "but maybe the chancellor . . . is fearful that Ronnie Reagan will win the election and wants to indicate that he doesn't need an investigation, that the university can provide internal protection."[66] These were logical deductions. What Savio could not have known, however, was that efforts by Berkeley administrators to exclude him from the student body had quietly begun almost a half-year before the gubernatorial election.

.   .   .

Historians have barely begun to explore the story of the New Left's actual relationship to free speech. As this subject comes under careful scrutiny, it seems almost certain to generate controversy, for there was controversy over the student movement's free speech record in the sixties almost as soon as there was a student movement. Foes of 1960s radicalism have always viewed the New Left as an intolerant movement that diminished rather than increased freedom of speech on campuses, and some even blame the FSM for starting this decline. In September 1966, for example, the *Atlantic Monthly* cover story by Lewis Feuer, a former Berkeley professor and caustic critic of the New Left, indicted Savio's generation of campus activists as "The New Tyrants of Berkeley." There is a whole antiradical frame of mind that holds that the New Left, as historian C. Vann Woodward once put it, "inflicted grievous injuries on the academy," trampling academic freedom and free speech via coercive strikes, demonstrations, building takeovers, library trashings, and harassment of nonradical speakers.[67] In other words, the FSM pioneered a new and ultimately destructive style of mass student action, one that politicized the university and ended the reign of civility within the college gates. The epilogue to this story would be the alleged takeover of the university in the closing years of the twentieth century by former sixties activists who became the "tenured radicals," those "politically correct" police who used their faculty power to stifle and gag nonradicals on campus.[68]

One serious problem with this scathing view of sixties radicalism is that it glosses over the diversity of the campus left. There has always been an illiberal segment within the American left, a radical contingent that cared little about free speech (except for itself), and this was as true in the New Left as it was in the Communist-dominated Old Left.[69] But the left has also had a strong tradition of championing free speech and criticizing the use of state power to suppress dissent, a tradition that dates back at least as far as the anarchists' and IWW's free speech struggles in early-twentieth-century America.[70] New Left activists so often had to contend with attempts by campus officials and police to suppress their protests that many developed a distaste for any form of political repression. This does not mean, however, that they were completely consistent in their application of First Amendment principles. Even thoughtful radicals at times agonized over how far their commitment to free speech should extend, especially with regard to foes who seemed to them fascistic (a category that seemed to grow broader with time), and over how in such cases they could reconcile their commitments to radical change with the First Amendment.[71]

The 1966 political wars at Berkeley do not lend themselves to a simple verdict regarding the movement's commitment to free speech. There were certainly moments when Berkeley radicals proved, at the very least, insensitive to the rights of those with whom they disagreed—as when the VDC sought to silence faculty who questioned their tactics. Such events suggest that some radical activists were not immune from the temptation to abuse their new-found campus political power. But any final evaluation of the movement's free speech record will not be convincing unless it is sufficiently balanced to explain not only such abuses but also the strong commitment to free speech that the FSM, the little free speech movement of 1966, and Mario Savio himself came to symbolize. The FSM may have left in its wake a small group of militants who felt empowered to act out their illiberal tendencies, behaving as if Sproul Plaza was their exclusive turf and a site where the expression of more moderate or conservative sentiment would not be tolerated. But the FSM also left many more students convinced that the victory of 1964 had established Sproul Plaza as a free political forum, one whose importance was such that when it seemed threatened in 1966, not merely radicals but many mainstream students, faculty, and even the fraternities and sororities rose to its defense.[72]

This profound commitment to the principle of free speech would endure long beyond the semester of the little free speech movement. It was visible, for example, in the way the *Daily Cal* covered the start of the prison sentence that Savio faced in 1967 for his role in leading the Sproul Hall sit-in of 1964. On his way to jail Mario encountered a *Daily Cal* reporter who asked whether four months in prison was too high a price to pay for his role in the FSM. Would serving this jail time "hurt his son's future?" Savio replied that "for my son's sake it was a good thing." The FSM's victory for free speech was, in Savio's words, one of the "most important events in the history of American higher education." The editors of the *Daily Cal* (which in 1964 had initially opposed the FSM!) echoed these sentiments, concluding that by now "the FSM is almost a legend here, and throughout the world." Wherever the struggle for student rights goes on," they continued, "college students remember the name of Berkeley and are encouraged by our successes. [The FSM was] a foothold in the door of campus liberty. Mario Savio will spend four months in jail for helping to get that foothold established."[73] Future generations of Berkeley students would agree with that sentiment, not out of nostalgia for a rebellion that most would have been too young to have witnessed but out of appreciation for what they saw and heard as they walked through Sproul Plaza; the bustling activity—speeches, debates, rallies, and tables staffed by activists championing diverse political causes—was and is powerful evidence that they were beneficiaries of the student rebellion that had won them the right to free speech and advocacy on campus. This view has recently been adopted by the Berkeley administration itself, which in the wake of Mario's death renamed the Sproul Steps in his honor and endorsed the creation of a Free Speech Movement café on campus.

There were so many campus revolts in America in the late 1960s and early 1970s that it would be absurd to argue that the story told in this essay can be taken as emblematic of the national student movement. Still, whatever the record on free speech might be in late-sixties rebellions at other campuses and at Berkeley itself, it should not obscure the history that Savio helped to make. That history included not only his well-known role in leading the largest campus free speech movement in American history but also his largely forgotten role in inspiring a second, if much smaller free speech movement in 1966. This post-FSM chapter of his career as a civil liberties champion at Berkeley reveals Savio at his most idealistic, daring, and selfless. Even as his academic future was jeopardized, Savio defended the steps, defied the ban on nonstudent leafleting, and demanded an appeals process that adhered to the First Amendment and the December 8 resolutions. It seems almost paradoxical, if not implausible, that a campus so renowned for its liberalism would be so illiberal as to draw Savio into this seemingly unending spiral of free speech conflicts and, ultimately, into a kind of political martyrdom. Yet that is what happened in 1966. From the dawn of the FSM through the days of the little free speech movement, Savio struggled to push the administration in a free speech direction, and this rendered him too radical even for Berkeley in the sixties.[74]

.   .   .

Mario's role in the little free speech movement was a courageous one, as he jeopardized his academic career in the service of free speech. To end the story here, however, would leave him as a kind of free speech icon, a martyr fit for a civil liberties hall of fame rather than a flesh and blood human being. We need to move for the moment from political history to biography to consider *why* Mario, at the height of the 1966 free speech fight, was so willing to put his readmission in jeopardy. The principled political reason for this is clear: an intense desire to preserve the gains won at such a high cost by him and his fellow students. The personal considerations involved in his willingness to sacrifice his academic future are harder to decipher because he never discussed them in public. But some of his private conversations in 1966, together with bits of other evidence, enable us to draw some tentative conclusions about the intersection between Mario the person and Mario the political martyr.

From a post–1960s perspective, in which we tend to view a college education as a step on the career ladder, Mario's political behavior in 1966 seems not only fearless but reckless. There he was, in public view, in front of thousands of people, defying campus regulations, essentially daring the campus administration to discipline him at a time when his readmission and the resumption of his academic career hung in the balance. From a professional or career perspective, such behavior made no sense. But then again, as Mario makes clear in the 1995 talk reprinted in this volume, he was not a careerist. He had approached his education in a highly idealized way, as the final stage of a spiritual quest to sort out—through intensive study of philosophy and science—his moral universe in the wake of his loss of faith in Catholicism. Engaged, as he put it, in an effort to "save my soul," Mario put ideas ahead of material or career considerations and came to feel that the willingness of others to do the same (though arguably for less spiritual reasons) was one of the key elements that gave rise to the student movement of the 1960s. And so in 1966 when Mario faced a choice between his ideals and his academic self-interest, this seemed hardly a choice at all.

Mario had also been troubled by all of the celebrity and attention that rained down on him as a result of the FSM. His coronation by the media as *the* leader and *the* spokesman of the FSM offended him and clashed with his belief that the FSM was a grassroots movement of thousands of students that was too egalitarian to need a maximum leader. Finding the media spotlight so distasteful, he also found it virtually impossible to focus on his studies when he was expected to be the perpetual leader and personification of Berkeley's insurgent students. This was one reason he had left Berkeley for England following the FSM.

In England too, however, Mario had had trouble focusing upon his studies. This inability to focus, as Suzanne Goldberg suggests, had a psychological dimension and may have been linked to inner conflicts Mario carried with him from his childhood. But there also seems to have been a connection between Mario's new academic problems and his tumultuous political life. Scholarly concentration requires a degree of peace and emotional tranquility that can be difficult to find after the excitement and turmoil that comes with leading a mass protest movement. It was thus difficult for Mario to settle down to a placid life of scholarship in the wake of the FSM.[75] He was not unique in experiencing such difficulties. Some of the leading figures in the black student movement that launched the southern civil rights sit-ins and SNCC, as David Halberstam has shown, had similar problems in returning to conventional academic work after their tumultuous years in civil rights agitation.[76]

Although, after returning from England, Mario had reapplied to Berkeley and planned to resume his studies, he remained ambivalent about both UC and the pursuit of an academic career. The new round of protests in 1966, to which he could not help but lend his name and energy, only added to his doubts about the possibility of studying in the political pressure cooker that Berkeley had become. In this context, Savio's defiance of campus regulations can be seen as a way of resolving his ambivalence about returning to his studies while engaging in a powerful gesture for his beloved free speech cause. That defiance was the act of *both* a courageous political leader and a troubled young man who, like many other college-age youths of his generation (and every college generation), was confused about his future.

Mario's confusion, and perhaps a lack of confidence about his ability to persevere in an academic career route, were also evidenced by his behavior after Berkeley closed its doors to him in 1966. Given his fine academic record and the respect he had won from some of Berkeley's most eminent faculty, who were prepared to support him in a variety of ways, Mario could easily have transferred to another university. But instead, in 1966 he seemed to have given up on academia and began working as a bartender. The former valedictorian, whose brilliance and interests seemed to naturally suit him to the academic world, would spend the rest of the decade outside of that world, drifting from one unskilled job to another. The full story of Savio's personal history awaits his future biographer, but to judge by what we know of it now, his story calls to mind historian David Farber's poignant words about the sixties as a time when "Americans dared to chance grand dreams and they paid for it."[77]

ADDENDUM

Mario Savio was a radical in the tradition of that part of the American left that was deeply committed to free speech. But his passion for radical social change was as strong as his love of free speech. On one of those very rare occasions when these two passions collided, Savio—driven by sympathy for the victims of oppression—allowed his egalitarianism to take precedence over his civil libertarianism, temporarily weakening his normally thoroughgoing commitment to free speech as a value in itself. The occasion was post-sixties Berkeley's most famous free speech controversy, which occurred at the height of the Reagan era. Here a free speech litmus test appeared in February 1983 in the form of Jean Kirkpatrick, U.S. ambassador to the UN, a widely loathed architect and advocate of the Reagan administration's Central America policy, which allied the United States with far-right regimes such as El Salvador's, with its notorious death squads. Kirkpatrick's speech disrupted by angry campus activists angry and, she consequently canceled a second previously scheduled talk. The disruption of her speech sparked heated debate over whether she should have been allowed the freedom to promote Reaganite propaganda on campus.

The Kirkpatrick incident put Savio's free speech ideals to a difficult test. Since he found the struggle for human rights and radical change in Central America deeply inspiring, Savio loathed the counterrevolutionary line Kirkpatrick was promoting. The question was whether Savio would conclude that someone whose politics he so detested should have her free speech rights protected and, indeed, enjoy the campus liberty that he had worked so hard to win. Initially, his free speech commitment faltered. In private conversations he revealed that he was drawn to the side of those who approved of the Kirkpatrick incident and echoed some of their arguments. Zelnik recalled an intense living-room discussion "where Mario defended the idea, not without qualms, that the First Amendment etc. was meant to restrict the actions of the state, not of private parties, so that whereas the University Administration had no right to restrict JK's speech, there was at least some argument to be made that the audience did. Some others on campus took a more 'revolutionary'—to hell with free speech—position, which Mario never took. He was ever trying to take the Constitution seriously."[78] Technically Savio and like-minded defenders of the Kirkpatrick incident were correct about the First Amendment being a bar to governmental rather than private restraint on speech. But this still did not erase the larger free speech and academic freedom problems arising from the serious disruption of a speech by hecklers and the question of how such behavior could be squared with the ideal of the university as the setting for the free exchange of ideas. In the Berkeley context, moreover, the legacy of the FSM, as codified in the Academic Senate's December 8 resolutions, included specific ground rules for political activism: "that the time, place, and manner of conducting political activity should be subject to reasonable regulation, to prevent interference with the normal functions of the university." If one included among those "normal functions" the presenting of a controversial political speaker to the campus community, then in the Kirkpatrick incident that function had been impaired by the disruptive hecklers, who violated the terms under which free speech had been guaranteed by the FSM and the December 8 resolutions.

Perhaps prodded by his recognition of the shallowness of a free speech position that exempted unpopular government officials, Savio changed his mind on the Kirkpatrick incident. At a 1985 Berkeley forum on the state of free speech at the University, he publicly acknowledged Kirkpatrick's right to speak on campus—while still, of course, passionately and publicly opposing her views. Here Savio was asked directly whether a right-wing government official such as Kirkpatrick should have the right to speak freely from a University podium at Berkeley. Savio answered "yes" and, shaking his head, acknowledged that although it was painful to have the University serve as a platform for someone advocating such vile policies, the principle of free speech had to be maintained, especially at Berkeley.[79]

NOTES

1. Mario Savio interview with Robert Cohen and David Pickell, Berkeley, 29 Sept. 1984, transcript in Free Speech Movement records, CU-309 (hereafter cited as FSM Records), University Archives, Bancroft Library, University of California at Berkeley. Neither the general studies of the New Left nor Verne A. Stadtman's 1970 centennial history, *The University of California 1868–1968* (New York: McGraw-Hill) mentions the 1966 free speech conflict; there is a paragraph on it in W. J. Rorabaugh, *Berkeley at War* (New York: Oxford University Press, 1989), 108–09. See also Sheldon S. Wolin and John Schaar, *The Berkeley Rebellion and Beyond* (New York: New York Review Press, 1970), 48, 50–51.

2. Savio interview with Cohen and Pickell.

3. Ibid.

4. Ibid. There was, of course, much continuity between Savio's civil rights work in Mississippi and in the Bay Area and his free speech organizing in Berkeley, an issue discussed in detail in the contributions of Martin, Freeman, and Weissman to this volume.

5. *Daily California* (hereafter *DC*), 21 and 24 Oct. 1966; *San Francisco Examiner*, 9 Sept. 1966. For brevity's sake I will generally use *Sproul Steps* to denote the amplified free speech area that extends from the steps of the administration building, Sproul Hall, to upper Sproul Plaza. Speakers used the steps as a podium from which to address the crowd.

6. *DC*, 2 Apr. 1965; 3, 11, and 23 Feb. 1966; 16 and 22 Mar. 1966; 6 May 1966.

7. *DC*, 3 and 11 Feb.1966; Jim Lemmon to Peter Camejo, 12 Aug. 1966, records of the office of the chancellor, University of California, 1952–1971, CU-149 (hereafter cited as Chancellor's Records) University Archives, Bancroft Library, University of California at Berkeley; John R. Searle to Nathan Glazer, 15 Mar. 1966; Heyns speech to Academic Senate, 22 Mar. 1966, 1–4, both in Chancellor's Records.

8. *DC*, 7 Mar. 1966.

9. Jerry Goldstein to Lloyd Ulman, 9 March 1966, Chancellor's Records.

10. Freshman class of '69 to Roger W. Heyns, 10 Feb. 1966, Chancellor's Records.

11. Ibid.; *DC*, 7 Mar. 1966.

12. Freshman class of '69 to Heyns, 10 Feb. 1966.

13. Carl E. Schorske, "Intellectual Life, Civil Libertarian Issues, and the Student Movement at the University of California, Berkeley, 1960–1969," oral history conducted in 1996 and 1997 by Ann Lage, Regional Oral History Office, Bancroft Library, University of California at Berkeley, 2000 (hereafter Schorske Oral History), 111.

14. C. Kittel to Heyns, 1 Dec. 1966, Chancellor's Records.

15. Pimentel to Heyns, 20 May 1966, Chancellor's Records. In this letter Pimentel also alluded to a letter he had sent to Heyns in September 1965 that urged barring amplified rallies from the Sproul area. On other faculty who in 1965–1966 had pushed for the removal of amplified rallies from this area, see John H. Lawrence to Martin Malia, 26 May 1966, ibid.

16. "December 8th or Fight," [Nov. 1966], Chancellor's Records.

17. Heyns, "Notes on Discussion: Re microphone," 27 Oct. 1966, Chancellor's Records.

18. Heyns, speech to Berkeley division of the Academic Senate, 8 Nov. 1966, Chancellor's Records; *DC*, 9 Nov. 1966.

19. Note, however, that in his speech to the Academic Senate Heyns deleted the words *and its administration*, apparently to demonstrate that his sole concern in banning the Sproul rallies was to protect the University—when in fact his initial draft more candidly acknowledged that he was giving at least equal weight in this decision to preserving the power of his administration. See Heyns's initial draft in "Notes on Discussion Re: microphone," 27 Oct. 1966.

20. Heyns, speech to Academic Senate, 8 Nov. 1966.

21. Heyns, "Re: microphone."

22. *DC*, 19 May 1966; Minutes of Campus Rules Committee, 20 May 1966, Chancellor's Records.

23. *DC*, 19 May 1966.

24. Minutes of Campus Rules Committee.

25. Ibid.; *San Francisco Examiner*, 30 Sept. 1966.

26. *San Francisco Examiner*, 30 Sept. 1966; *Oakland Tribune*, 5 Oct. 1966. Although the tough new rules inhibiting nonstudent activism came in September 1966, the first steps toward a crackdown on such activism came earlier. See Daniel E. Teodoru to Heyns, 10 Mar. 1966; Teodoru and Cal Conservatives for Political Action, "The 'Non-Student' and Freedom of Speech at Berkeley"; Glazer to Searle, 4 Feb. 1966; Searle to Glazer, 15 Mar. 1966; "Statement of Cited Students," 22 Mar. 1966, all in Chancellor's Records. Early outside pressure on the administration to act against nonstudents who used the campus as a base for antiwar organizing came from the Alameda County Grand Jury, which complained that tens of thousands of dollars in law enforcement expenses were incurred by local communities policing VDC-sponsored events. See Henry A. Bruno to Superior Court, 27 Jan. 1966; and Kerr to Heyns, 2 Feb. 1966, both in ibid.

27. Memo on SDS Black Power Conference [Oct. 1966]; Henry Mayer to Heyns, 5 Oct. 1966, both in Chancellor's Records. The administration had also justified its initial refusal to allow the black power conference on campus on the grounds that the event would serve no educational purpose. On faculty criticism of this position, see Charles Sellers to Heyns, 4 Oct. 1966, ibid.

28. On Reagan's pledge see *San Francisco Examiner,* 9 Sept. 1966, and *New York Times,* 27 Nov. 1966.

29. Searle, "Arguments in Favor of Moving the Mike to the Lower Plaza," 28 Oct.1966, Chancellor's Records.

30. "Chronology-mtg. w. Bernstein," 15 Nov. 1966, Chancellor's Records.

31. Savio interview with Cohen and Pickell, 29 Sept. 1984.

32. "Our Traditional Liberties," [fall 1966], FBI file SF100-54060 (FBI file of Savio), part 4.

33. Ibid.

34. "Fight!! For December 8??," [fall 1966], Chancellor's Records.

35. *The SAVE THE STEPS RALLY: Friday November 4, 1966: A Complete Transcription of the Speeches: Mario Savio, Bettina Aptheker, Dan Rosenthal, Brian O'Brian* (Berkeley: Academic Publishing, 1966); *Oakland Tribune,* 5 Nov. 1966.

36. *SAVE THE STEPS RALLY,* 7, 10. It was no accident that the faculty member Savio cited so approvingly was Chamberlain, a distinguished physicist and Nobel laureate. Savio loved physics, very much admired Chamberlain's scholarship, and hoped to work with him. This is just one out of many pieces of evidence of Savio's love of learning and reminds us that while disdaining insensitive administrators, he did not loath the University or its faculty as such.

37. This and following quotations from Savio's "Save the Steps" rally speech are, unless otherwise noted, from *SAVE THE STEPS RALLY,* 7–9.

38. In speaking of the University's self-inflicted purging, Savio seems to have had in mind the collapse of Chancellor Strong's administration in the wake of the FSM.

39. *SAVE THE STEPS RALLY,* 10. Savio's central role in the rally led to his election to the steering committee of the Council of Campus Organizations, the group that was coordinating the fight to preserve the old free speech area; see *San Francisco Chronicle,* 9 Nov. 1966. The week after the "Save the Steps" rally about eight hundred protesters marched on the chancellor's office to oppose the move off Sproul; they presented the administration with petitions signed by some three thousand students; see *DC,* 10 Nov. 1966.

40. *DC,* 9 Nov. 1966.

41. "December 8th or Fight."

42. *DC,* 9 Nov. 1966.

43. Heyns, speech to the Academic Senate, 8 Nov. 1966, Chancellor's Records; *DC,* 9 Nov. 1966.

44. Mark N. Christensen, Leroy T. Kerth, Joseph Mileck, Oscar H. Paris, Norman Rabkin, and Elizabeth Scott to Heyns, 16 Nov. 1966, Chancellor's Records.

45. Faculty Petition, Nov. 1966, asserting the "belief that the public forum on the Sproul Steps is in keeping with the general campus rules for speech and advocacy [and has] become the symbol of increasing communication among the various elements on this campus, and to restrict or abolish it would . . . symbolize a breakdown in the growing sense of community which has been established with such great effort over the past two years"; Robert Middlekauff and Irwin Scheiner to Heyns, 10 Nov. 1966; Frederich Tubach to Arthur Kip, 4 Nov. 1966, all in Chancellor's Records.

46. Owen Chamberlain to Heyns, 4 Nov. 1966, ibid.

47. Arleigh Williams to presidents of all registered student organizations, 26 Oct. 1966; Williams to William Boyd (cc to Heyns), 7 Nov. 1966, both in Chancellor's Records.

48. Williams to Boyd, 7 Nov. 1966. Williams was right in warning about the potential for serious conflict. There was both broad support for the Sproul location among mainstream students and a determination on the campus left to use militant tactics if that was what it took to prevent the change. The week after the "Save the Steps" rally, Savio was asking students to sign a "Declaration of Intent" pledging themselves to participate in illegal rallies on Sproul if the steps were forbidden to them and to refuse to participate in hearings that might be held to punish them. See *San Francisco Chronicle*, 19 Nov. 1966; *DC*, 17 Nov 1966.

49. Bari Bradner, report on sorority sentiment concerning the location of noon rallies, 7 Nov. 1966, Chancellor's Records.

50. Cross to Heyns, 15 Nov. 1966, ibid.

51. *DC*, 1 July 1967.

52. On the punishments that the court imposed on FSMers who sat in at Sproul Hall, see David Lance Goines, *The Free Speech Movement: Coming of Age in the 1960s* (Berkeley: Ten Speed Press, 1993), 526–74.

53. Savio to office of the registrar, 10 Dec. 1965; Clinton Gilliam to Savio, 20 Dec. 1965; Heyns to Kerr, 11 July 1966, all in Savio disciplinary file, Chancellor's Records.

54. Cunningham to Cheit, 29 June 1966, Savio disciplinary file, Chancellor's Records.

55. Ibid. Neither Savio nor his attorney, Mal Burnstein, had the slightest inkling that the administration had been secretly seeking ways to deny Savio readmission months before the November rally. These Cunningham memos came to light only after Savio's death, when the University archives released his disciplinary files to me. When I showed these documents to Burnstein, he reacted with consternation, insisting that if he had known of the Cunningham documents back in 1966, these would have been grounds for a lawsuit that could easily have won Savio's readmission. See Burnstein interview with the author, Berkeley, 13 July 1999 (audiotape in my possession).

56. Cunningham to Cheit, 19 Aug. 1966, Chancellor's Records. There is no direct evidence as to why the chancellor did not immediately follow Cunningham's advice to use Savio's Greek Theatre and courtroom behavior as grounds for denying his readmission. But a September 1966 memo from another University lawyer to Vice Chancellor Boyd suggests that this lack of immediate action may have been linked to the fact that the administration's legal team was not completely confident that those grounds would stand up in court. Here Boyd was told that Cunningham's memoranda indicate that "a denial of readmission to Mr. Savio would be justified, and not subject to reversal by the court if based on reasonable grounds (in view of University policy). While my uninformed hunch is that this is so, I would look much more closely at whether such 'reasonable grounds' do in fact exist here" (JDB to W[illiam] B. B[oyd], 13 Sept. 1966, Chancellor's Records).

57. *Berkeley Daily Gazette*, 2 July 1966; *DC*, 21 and 24 Oct. 1966. It is striking that Kerr stopped Canaday from using political criteria to bar Savio, whereas Heyns and his staff behaved in a Canaday-like manner by politicizing the admission process. In

a recent interview, Kerr did not recall having had any knowledge of the Heyns administration's covert search for ways to deny Savio readmission (interview with Cohen and Zelnik, Berkeley, 12 July 1999, audiotape in editors' possession). However, a July 1966 Heyns letter to Kerr indicates that the chancellor did keep him posted on Savio's readmission and had shared with him Cunningham's first (29 June 1966) memo on Savio's case (Heyns to Kerr, 11 July 1966, Chancellor's Records). At first glance it may be puzzling as to why Kerr would have prevented Canaday but not Heyns from politicizing the admissions process. Note, however, that Kerr opposed Canaday's move against Savio on the grounds that admissions decisions must be left to individual chancellors. He was defending not Savio's rights but the power of the chancellors and their independence from Regental interference.

58. Boyd to Savio, 7 Nov. 1966, Savio disciplinary file, Chancellor's Records. In this letter Boyd cited Savio's "deliberate violation . . . of the university rule prohibiting non-students from distributing literature on campus" as the primary reason for denying readmission. But in addition to this rule breaking, Boyd also cited Savio's defiant statements to the press and his "Save the Steps" speech as further grounds for denying him admission: "In admissions cases where conduct is an issue, the practice of this University has been to favor admission or readmission where the applicant shows reasonable promise that he will obey the rules and regulations. The evidence of recent days, far from suggesting such an assumption in your case, strongly supports the conclusion that if readmitted you will not comply with University regulations with which you did not agree. Your reported statements of October 31 advocating disobedience of duly constituted authority has been followed by similar public statements . . . on the plaza last Friday." To prepare for any possible appeal by Savio, UC attorneys compiled a list of defiant quotations that Savio made throughout the little free speech movement (JDB to W[illiam] B. B[oyd], 18 Nov. 1966, Chancellor's Records).

59. Cunningham to Heyns, 7 Nov. 1966, Chancellor's Records.

60. When Berkeley's leading activist coalition, the Council of Campus Organizations, raised the idea of mobilizing students to protest the decision to bar his readmission, Savio objected on the grounds that he was "philosophically opposed to student movements on behalf of individual persons"(*DC*, 9 Nov. 1966).

61. Transcript of meeting of Savio and Mal Burnstein with Cheit, Boyd, and Milton Gordon, 15 Nov. 1966; Boyd to Malcolm Burnstein, 20 Dec. 1966, both Savio disciplinary file.

62. *San Francisco Chronicle*, 9 Nov. 1966; *Berkeley Barb*, 11 Nov. 1966.

63. Malm to Cheit, 20 June 1966, Savio disciplinary file.

64. Thomas J. Cunningham, item for action to the Regents of UC, executive session, "Injunctions against Certain Non-Students," 17 Nov. 1966, Chancellor's Records.

65. Zelnik, Richard Tyler, Brentano, Edward L. Paynter, George W. Stocking, Jr., to the Academic Freedom Committee of the Academic Senate, 11 Nov. 1966, Chancellor's Records.

66. *San Francisco Chronicle*, 9 Nov. 1966.

67. Lewis Feuer, "The Decline of Freedom at Berkeley," *Atlantic Monthly* (Sept. 1996): 78–87; C. Vann Woodward, "The Siege," *New York Review of Books* (25 Sept. 1986): 10.

68. Roger Kimball, *Tenured Radicals: How Politics Has Corrupted Our Higher Education* (New York: Harper and Row, 1990).

69. On New Left abuses of free speech see Donald Alexander Downs, *Cornell '69: Liberalism and the Crisis of the American University* (Ithaca: Cornell University Press, 1999); on the Old Left's uneven free speech record on campus see James Wechsler, *The Age of Suspicion* (New York: Primus, 1981), 54; Robert Cohen, *When the Old Left Was Young: Student Radicals and America's First Mass Student Movement, 1929–1941* (New York: Oxford University Press, 1993), 29–30, 61–68, 98–133, 372; Eileen Eagan, *Class, Culture, and the Classroom: The Student Peace Movement of the 1930s* (Philadelphia: Temple University Press, 1981), 73–79; Ruth Rubin, "I Heckled Luther," *Student Review* 3, no. 2 (Jan. 1934), 7–8.

70. David M. Rabban, *Free Speech in Its Forgotten Years* (New York: Cambridge University Press, 1997).

71. For an example of how one such radical, Savio himself, agonized over the extension of free speech rights to those whose political views he loathed, see the addendum to this essay.

72. Still, almost four decades after the FSM, the Berkeley left's free speech record remains uneven. A recent example of this ambiguous legacy occurred when protesters blocked the entrance to the off-campus theater in Berkeley where former Israeli Prime Minister Benjamin Netanyahu was scheduled to speak—leading him to cancel his appearance. Some protesters and a few FSM veterans defended this disruption and even invoked the FSM in so doing, while others, including former FSM leaders (Savio's widow among them), condemned the disruption as contrary to the FSM's free speech principles (see *San Francisco Chronicle*, 10 Dec. 2000; *DC*, 29 and 30 Nov. 2000; Lynne Hollander Savio et al. to *San Francisco Chronicle*, 5 Dec. 2000).

73. *DC*, 30 June and 3 July 1967.

74. It would not be until fall 1970, the semester after Kent State, when student activism had fallen off, that Savio was finally readmitted to UC Berkeley, but he would never return to complete his degree work there. On his readmission, see *Oakland Tribune*, 19 Sept. 1970.

75. In her essay in this volume Suzanne Goldberg, Mario's wife at the time, suggests that the personal and academic problems Mario experienced during the mid- and late 1960s had primarily psychological roots and evolved from abuse he suffered in childhood. And in a telephone interview with the author (3 Feb. 2000), she interpreted Mario's educational and career problems during these years and beyond in exclusively psychological terms. While I have no basis for either questioning or confirming her account of Mario's inner "demons," I do not find in it a sufficient explanation of the ups and down of his academic career. Whatever his psychological difficulties (and Goldberg is not the only author in this volume to allude to them), they clearly did not affect his academic performance in high school, where he graduated with high honors as valedictorian. Mario's serious problems with academic work and career progress did not occur until after he emerged as a leader of the Berkeley student movement. It therefore makes sense to at least ask whether there was any connection between his new political role and the problems he then experienced pursuing his studies. Mario's personal discussion of these problems with Zelnik in 1966 suggested that the political leadership expectations

placed on him after the FSM did make it more difficult for him to return to his studies and left him ambivalent about matriculating as a Berkeley student (Zelnik to Cohen, 19 Dec. 1999, personal communication). Moreover, the similarity between Mario's problems and those of some other leading sixties activists leaves me skeptical of a monocausal interpretation based in childhood trauma. It is noteworthy, however, that whether his academic problems were more powerfully driven by the factors Goldberg stresses or by more politically derived stress factors, Mario ultimately managed to cope effectively with both, earning bachelor's and master's degrees in the 1980s and becoming—as Jonah Raskin's essay in this volume describes—an accomplished college teacher.

76. David Halberstam, *The Children* (New York: Fawcett Books, 1998), 357–58.

77. Wade Green, "Where Are the Savios of Yesteryear?" *New York Times Magazine,* 12 July 1970, 7; David Farber, *The Age of Great Dreams: America in the 1960s* (New York: Hill and Wang, 1994), 3.

78. Zelnik e-mails to the author, 9 Nov. 1999 and 27 Feb. 2002, copies in author's possession.

79. See *New York Times,* 13 Mar. 1983; Art Goldberg, "Right to Heckle," *Nation,* 2 Apr. 1983, 387; "The Mob vs. Kirkpatrick," *Newsweek,* 23 Mar. 1983, 77; *DC,* 16, 17, and 22 Feb. 1983); Savio speech, Sproul Plaza, 1 Oct. 1984, reprinted in Cohen, ed., "The FSM and Beyond," 55. See also Savio, "Beyond the Cold War," *DC,* 1 Oct. 1984. This panel, which occurred on the thirty-first anniversary of the FSM, focused on the administration's encroachments on the rights of protesters in Berkeley's anti-Apartheid divestment movement. The central issue was the use of videotaping by campus police to gather evidence against protesters who allegedly broke campus rules. Savio termed this taping "Orwellian" and denounced the "general nastiness" of campus police who had torn down protest signs. (I was in the audience at the time.) Perhaps because the forum was focused on these ongoing free speech disputes, the *Daily Cal* failed to mention Savio's important remarks on the Kirkpatrick incident (see *DC,* 2 Oct.1985). Further confirmation of Savio's change of mind on the Kirkpatrick incident can be found in Zelnik e-mail to author, 9 Nov. 1999.

The Limits of Freedom

Student Activists and Educational Reform at Berkeley in the 1960s

Julie A. Reuben

In 1968 a Berkeley student, Larry Magid, invited Eldridge Cleaver to teach a course at UC Berkeley. Magid, a member of a student organization called the Center for Participant Education (CPE), had attended a meeting at which a number of black students complained about the dearth of classes dealing with their experiences and political struggles. The CPE had been created to offer the kind of education many Berkeley students perceived they needed but were not getting, so Magid decided that the group should do something to address the students' complaints. Cleaver at the time was a notorious figure. Many activists viewed Cleaver, minister of public information for the Black Panther Party, presidential nominee for the California branch of the Peace and Freedom Party, and author of the best-selling book *Soul on Ice*, as an articulate new spokesperson for black liberation. But others saw Cleaver, a convicted rapist, then under indictment for assault with a deadly weapon, as a dangerous advocate of violence and racial hatred. To Magid, Cleaver offered a perspective not represented on the Berkeley faculty and therefore seemed the perfect choice for a course on race.[1]

After Cleaver accepted his invitation, Magid went to the Board of Educational Development (BED)—a faculty committee that the faculty's Academic Senate created in the wake of the FSM to encourage educational experimentation—for approval to offer the course for University credit. Soon after BED was created, students from CPE had begun bringing courses to the board for sponsorship. By the time Magid contacted Cleaver, students had successfully offered a number of courses through the board, and they naturally assumed that they could win approval for this one. Although BED required that the students make some changes in their initial plans, it approved the course for fall quarter 1968, designating it

"Social Analysis 139X: Dehumanization and Regeneration of the American Social Order."[2]

Everyone involved with the creation of 139X recognized that the course would be controversial, but no one had fully anticipated the storm it would produce. University officials, reasoning that they could contain public reaction better if they announced the course rather than letting it be "discovered" by the media, issued a timely press release. When the University was then inundated with angry phone calls, it issued a second press release meant to assuage hostile opinion: the course was only experimental, it would be offered only once, no University funds were to be used, Cleaver had not been appointed to the faculty, and four regular faculty members were responsible for overseeing the course.[3]

But the new announcement failed to stem the tide of outrage. Governor Ronald Reagan and other leading politicians soon demanded that Cleaver's appointment be dropped. Reagan described Cleaver as an "advocate of racism and violence" and called his appointment "an affront and an insult to the people of California." Legislators in Sacramento threatened to cut off the University's funding if the course went forward, but instead the state senate voted to censure University officials. Buoyed by thousands of letters and telegrams complaining about the course, Reagan asked the Regents to bar Cleaver from teaching at the University. The Regents, having enacted a rule that forbade people without appropriate instructional appointments to lecture in University courses more than once, now voted to apply the new rule retroactively to Cleaver. They refused to grant credit to 139X, and they censured University officials and the Berkeley faculty for approving the course.[4]

At Berkeley the Regents' actions produced more conflict. Student activists charged that the Regents' action was racist and violated their academic freedom. "We, not politicians and administrators, have the right to control our education," one leaflet declared. "Campus autonomy and academic freedom can only exist when students and faculty jointly initiate and determine the nature of the courses, the granting of credit, and the broader curriculum." The Regents canceled 139X, another leaflet asserted, "to prevent students from learning about the black liberation movement, to separate white from black—that is racism." To protest the denial of credit for the course, students sat in at Sproul Hall, and on the next day, students occupied and barricaded Moses Hall. The two days of protest yielded 174 arrests, which in turn sparked a hunger strike by the president of the student government and a call by the CPE and TA union for a boycott of classes.[5]

Although not united in support of the course, the faculty viewed the Regents' action as a violation of its academic freedom. The BED, after all, was a faculty body and had approved the course. Worse still, the Regents' rule regarding guests went beyond this specific course and restricted what faculty viewed as their right to control the content of classes. The Academic Senate condemned the Regents for violating academic freedom and also asserted that students' academic freedom had been violated because they were not allowed to take an approved course. Senate members urged their colleagues to offer the course as planned, and in later actions they voted defiantly to grant it credit (but were unable to enforce this decision). They also voted to grant degrees to students who were unable to graduate because of the denial of credit to 139X. Finally, they supported a suit brought by faculty and students against the Regents.[6]

On the face of it, this episode entailed a classic academic freedom case. The Board of Regents intervened in the internal affairs of the University because it found the ideas being taught there offensive. The administration tried to act as a buffer and soften the blow but ultimately could not stop the Board's intrusion. The faculty then united to defend the freedom of ideas on campus and to resist outside interference. Embedded within the Cleaver case, however, was another kind of struggle over academic freedom—an internal struggle among students, faculty, and administrators over the very nature of students' academic freedom.[7]

This second struggle had been developing since the late 1950s as student activists at Berkeley and at other campuses across the nation increasingly demanded changes in their education and in the structure of the university. The FSM was a key turning point in this struggle. Not only did that movement win greater political freedom for students, it also energized student activists who were critical of the University's educational policies and forced faculty and administrators to consider educational reform more seriously.

But the reform efforts of Berkeley faculty did not satisfy many student activists, some of whom were quick to challenge the faculty's claim to exclusive control over the curriculum. They rejected the notion that faculty, because of their expertise, had final authority in academic matters and claimed for students the right to design their own education. Some radical student activists wanted to share the kind of academic freedom that had previously been accorded to faculty only. But although a number of faculty supported them in this effort, most did not. To be sure, in the years following the FSM, students successfully renegotiated some of the boundaries defining the roles of students, faculty, and administration; but they never won the right to the kind of academic freedom faculty claimed for themselves. As it turned out, the Cleaver case was a key incident defining the limits of students' academic freedom.

Historically, the issue of students' academic freedom had not received as much attention as faculty's, and there was little agreement on what, if any, rights students had in this area. In the mid-1950s the National Student

Association (NSA) began a program on academic freedom. Much of it focused on educating students about McCarthyism and its threat to faculty's academic freedom. But the NSA also raised issues of students' academic freedom, encouraging students to challenge restrictions on their political activity, oppose institutional censorship of student-sponsored events, and lobby for greater student input into campus affairs. Although the NSA could not change institutional practices, it did open up discussion about the nature of students' academic freedom.[8]

In the early 1960s, the American Association of University Professors (AAUP) created a committee to draft an authoritative statement on students' academic freedom. Although the AAUP had a long history of defending academic freedom for faculty, its committee found it difficult to develop a statement on academic freedom for students. Whereas faculty's claim to academic freedom was based largely on their expertise, students, as committee member Phillip Monypenny explained, "are essentially in a position of dependence, subject to the authority of the institution from which they hope to receive their degrees, subject to the authority of their teachers." Therefore, the issues central to faculty's academic freedom—their control over "the content of instruction, the standard of instruction, the selection of staff, or the direction of institutional development"—were irrelevant to students. Students' academic freedom seemed to involve a separate set of issues, such as due process in disciplinary procedures, censorship over publications, and confidentiality of records.[9]

Given the difference of status between students and professors, many faculty thought it misleading to talk about student academic freedom. Sidney Hook, then a philosophy professor at New York University and a prominent authority on academic freedom, asserted that it was "nonsense to speak of 'academic freedom' for students. Students have a right to freedom to learn. The best guarantee of freedom to learn is the academic freedom of those who teach them." In the 1960s, however, student activists challenged this subordination of students' academic freedom to that of the faculty and tried to expand the meaning of the concept. At campuses across the country, students rejected the notion that faculty, based on their expertise, should have sole authority over academic matters. Asserting their "existential" authority, students countered that they knew, in a way that others could not, the kind of education they needed.[10]

EDUCATIONAL REFORM AND STUDENT ACTIVISM

By the early 1960s the rumblings of a reform movement in higher education could be detected. Nationally, faculty and administrators critical of the status quo, such as Harold Taylor, Nevitt Sanford, David Reisman, Robert Hutchins, and Paul Goodman, were gaining an audience among their colleagues. The federal government and some foundations responded by sponsoring programs to stimulate interest in educational experimentation. Planning for alternative colleges, such as Hampshire in western Massachusetts and UC Santa Cruz, and experimental colleges at Wayne State and the University of Michigan received considerable attention among educators. Some students took an interest in these issues, as well. Encouraged by the NSA, they began lobbying for changes in grading policy, student evaluation of courses, and other reforms. Faculty and students shared many concerns and advocated similar changes. However, students' views about the causes and solutions to the problems in higher education diverged in important ways from that of most faculty reformers. As student activism gained momentum, these differences would become more apparent and divisive.[11]

At Berkeley a small group of faculty joined the call for educational reform. Faculty such as Martin Trow and Nathan Glazer published essays criticizing in loco parentis and the structure of education relying on large lecture classes and rote examinations. The prominent faculty critic of contemporary undergraduate education, Philosophy professor Joseph Tussman, founded the "experimental program" at Berkeley in 1965. Tussman believed that undergraduate education lacked intellectual depth, with students having to endure a series of disjointed courses taught by faculty concerned more about their specialized disciplines than about the intellectual development of students. His small alternative program excluded courses as they are normally understood and engaged students and faculty in intensive reading and discussion of texts. The first year of its two-year lower-division program examined ancient Greece and seventeenth-century England; the second, America. Students focused on one book at a time so that, in contrast to the regular program, their attention would not be scattered. To insure that students were motivated by the intrinsic value of learning rather than external rewards, they received no grades. Tussman sought to create "education for the ruling function," with "the companion conviction that since everyone in a democracy is to share in the ruling function, everyone needed to share in the education reserved, in elitist societies, to the ruling class."[12]

A few Berkeley faculty shared Tussman's enthusiasm for alternative colleges. They hoped that Berkeley might adopt the model being planned for the new campus at Santa Cruz—multiple small undergraduate colleges within the structure of a large research university. They found this model appealing because they thought that the massive, impersonal College of Letters and Sciences made it impossible to overcome what they saw as the major educational problem of the University—the intellectual indifference of the average undergraduate. Small colleges were expected to facilitate personal relationships based on intellectual interests. In addition, the small-college structure would not force faculty to agree on an ideal curriculum or pedagogical approach. One college could use a St. Johns's "Great Books" curriculum, another could engage students in original research; one could abandon grades and rely on comprehensive examinations, another could use tutorials and independent study. Faculty could associate with the college that fit their own predispositions.[13]

Some students in SLATE, the activist political party, shared an interest in educational reform. Like reformist faculty, they criticized the existing structure of university education. SLATE member Brad Cleaveland, for example, described undergraduate education as "five courses, fifteen units, fifteen tests, a few superficially written papers, and overwhelming bibliographies. This is repeated incessantly . . . rammed down our throats by the coercion of grades." SLATE sought to attract support by giving voice to the common complaints of undergraduates: large classes taught by TAs or uninterested faculty, requirements that could be fulfilled only by taking courses of dubious value, inadequate advising, superficial assignments, arbitrary grading, long lines, and inefficient bureaucracy. SLATE members assumed that the most disaffected students were the serious ones, those who had come to Berkeley "to get an education." The more vocationally oriented students, wrote SLATE member Jo Freeman, just "want to hurry up and get their degree so they can go out and get a good job and live happily ever after in stagnation." Cleaveland agreed: "It is the highly intelligent and sensitive student who suffers the most. He is painfully aware that there is not time to think, few places to think, and fewer students interested in or capable of extended dialogue." The general picture that SLATE presented was similar to that of faculty critics—undergraduate education was not intellectually engaging.[14]

Students and faculty shared many of the same concerns—large classes, passive pedagogy, dominance of the curriculum by academic disciplines, superficiality, inappropriate standards of evaluation, and the burdens of in loco parentis. Because of this, reform-oriented faculty and students, at least initially, saw each other as allies. Nevertheless, student activists' analysis differed from that of most faculty in two important respects. First, students viewed the problems of the University as inextricably connected to the larger problems of the society. To students, educational reform was part of the broader movement for peace and social change that shook the American campus world of the 1960s. Second, they insisted that as part of educational reform, students must gain power within the institution. They rejected the idea that students were "intellectual" dependents and that faculty should have exclusive authority based on their expertise. Student activists asserted their own "existential" authority and envisioned a university in which students and faculty viewed each other more as colleagues than as teacher and pupil.[15]

In contrast to activist students, many faculty did not tie educational reform to other social and political agendas. Although Tussman did conceive of the purpose of the experimental program in broadly political terms, he viewed the causes of the undergraduates' problems not as political but as a consequence of the University's emphasis on research and graduate instruction. The harm was an unintended byproduct of the very different goals and needs of undergraduate and graduate education. Like other reform-minded faculty, Tussman accepted institutional political neutrality as an important ideal (if not a perfect description of reality) and thought that educational reforms should be justified primarily on intellectual grounds.[16]

Student activists, in contrast, saw the problem as largely political and saw the inadequacies of undergraduate education as having important political consequences. Cleaveland even went so far as to argue that students' education was designed to encourage political passivity. He warned undergraduates that they were being trained "in the capacity for unquestioning obedience to a complex flood of trivial bureaucratic rules. In the name of human learning you acquire the capacity to be docile in the face of rules." In contrast to faculty like Tussman, Cleaveland and other activists thought that the political lessons implicit in the structure of undergraduate education were intentional.[17]

Student activists related the problems of undergraduate education to the University's political role. SLATE's Committee on Educational Reform emphasized the University's ties to the military and industry, which, they argued, controlled the University directly through the Regents and indirectly through the influence of their money on the University's programs and general orientation. Corporations and the military wanted skilled technicians, not critical thinkers who might challenge the status quo. This line of analysis received an unexpected boost from the publication of Clark Kerr's *Uses of the University*, where he described the growth of federal research funding since World War II, characterized the University as a "knowledge industry," and coined the term *multiversity*. Activists constantly referred to the book as proof that the University provided the kind of education its powerful patrons wanted—not the kind that students needed. They argued that the idea of institutional neutrality was a sham, masking the University's real political role. Activists, however, did not want to divorce the University from society but to reorient it to serve social justice.[18]

Although student activists agreed with many of the specific reforms proposed by faculty, they did not want faculty to control the process. They insisted on "the establishment of a permanent student voice that is effective (that is, independent) in running university affairs," so that students and faculty share responsibility for the curriculum. FSM leader Michael Rossman explained that this would necessarily transform student-faculty relations: "Student attempts to gain control of curriculum, degree requirements, the hiring, firing and tenure of faculty, and all the other broad aspects of their academic lives, are natural and essential consequences of the drive toward autonomy.... The possession of such power will deeply change the nature of student relationships with faculty, other students, and their own work." Rossman and others envisioned a more equal relationship between professors and students. "The line between teacher and student will blur, despite its present sanctity," he predicted.[19]

In advocating student power, activists attacked the faculty's claim to authority based on expertise. In its place, they asserted authority based on their own experience—they knew the kind of education that would meet their needs. In this manner, they claimed for students a right that conflicted with faculty's understanding of their own academic freedom. Students' demand for a powerful role in academic affairs would drive a wedge between student activists and many faculty. Even reformers like Tussman thought that students had very little to contribute to curriculum building or other educational matters.[20]

Of course faculty reacted to students' position on institutional neutrality and student power in different ways. A few agreed and supported the activists' efforts. Others saw it as harmless youthful enthusiasm, best dealt with sympathetically and channeled in constructive ways. But many others saw it as evidence of a dangerous anti-intellectualism, proof that activists would, if not resisted, destroy the values of the University.[21]

THE FSM AND EDUCATIONAL REFORM

The FSM focused on students' political freedom rather than their academic freedom. Rejecting the idea that the University must limit students' political activity in order to protect its own neutrality, students argued that normal rules governing freedom of speech should apply on campus. "Civil liberties and political freedoms which are constitutionally protected off campus," the FSM asserted, "must be equally protected on campus for all persons."[22] After some three months of conflict between the students and the administration over rules governing political activity, the great majority of Berkeley faculty sided with the students. The faculty was simultaneously dealing with an academic freedom case involving a professor who had been a member of the Communist Party, and many members were therefore particularly sensitive to the dangers involved in protecting institutional neutrality at the cost of political freedom. They therefore agreed with the leaders of the FSM that students should not have to give up their rights as citizens while on University grounds.

Although the demands of the FSM focused on students' political rights, criticism of the University as an educational institution became one of the prominent motifs of the movement. As Jack Weinberg observed,

> Two of the most basic themes that began to emerge in the very first speeches of the protest and which have remained central throughout have been a

condemnation of the University in its role as a knowledge factory and a demand that the voices of the students must be heard. These themes have been so well received because of the general feeling among the students that the University has made them anonymous; that they have very little control over their environment, over their future; that the University society is almost completely unresponsive to their individual needs. The students decry the lack of human contact, the lack of communication, the lack of dialogue that exists at the University. Many believe that much of their course work is irrelevant, that many of their most difficult assignments are merely tedious busy work with little or no educational value.[23]

The leaders of the FSM, particularly Mario Savio, popularized the image of the University as a machine, run by bureaucrats, controlled by business and government, and indifferent to students. A survey of 439 students conducted shortly after the FSM found that most students were satisfied with their education yet revealed at the same time the appeal of Savio's critique. "A large majority of interviewees," reported the researcher, "considered the campus 'factory-like' and 'impersonal' and desired changes in the University's structure as well as an increase in student influence on its operations." No longer the province of a small group of disaffected students in SLATE, the demand for a student voice in education became part of the common parlance of Berkeley students.[24] Leaders of the FSM further emphasized the centrality of educational issues when in January 1965, having won their basic demands, they published a manifesto entitled "We Want a University." In it, they reiterated the critique of the University echoed throughout the fall: The University does not provide students with a real education. It forces them to jump through a series of hoops that keeps them busy and anxious but prevents them from thinking and learning. The University is there to serve the needs of government and industry, not the students. The content and form of education does not allow students to "know the realities of the present world-in-revolution, and have an opportunity to think clearly in an extended manner about the world." The manifesto ended with a call to create the "Free University of California," a new institution that would invite visiting intellectuals, offer seminars on issues not addressed in the official curriculum, and create a setting for genuine intellectual engagement. The ultimate purpose was to "bring humanity back to campus."[25]

The popularity of the FSM made it difficult for the administration and faculty to ignore calls for educational reform. Soon after his appointment as Berkeley's acting chancellor, Martin Meyerson addressed the Academic Senate on issues of educational reform, including general education requirements, the possibility of creating several distinct undergraduate colleges, increasing faculty involvement in undergraduate education, the proper use of TAs, and the role of students in formulating and implementing educational policy. He recommended that the Senate form a special commission to address "the state of education at Berkeley." This commission, "bringing together and clarifying the many ideas being suggested on the campus, could then develop for our consideration specific proposals for the revitalization of our educational aims and practice." Meyerson affirmed that the faculty was responsible for "the educational offerings of the university" but suggested that the commission consider "the best ways to access students' assistance" in order to understand their needs and interests. The Senate responded by creating the Special Select Committee on Education (SCOE), chaired by Professor Charles Muscatine of the English Department.[26]

For faculty who favored educational reform, the challenges from the FSM and the creation of SCOE provided a unique opportunity. Muscatine realized that the recent campus crisis had produced a rare opening for reform, and he was determined to take advantage of it. He therefore insisted that SCOE act quickly lest the campus return to normal and the moment be lost. To this end he decided that the committee would produce a preliminary report before the end of the semester, which would then serve as a basis for a campuswide discussion. The committee would then continue its investigations over the summer and submit its final recommendations during the next academic year.[27]

SCOE issued its preliminary report in May, disseminating it widely to faculty, students, and the press. Critical of education at Berkeley and generally sympathetic to student activists, the committee focused most of its attention on general education. The report maintained that departments geared their courses to future majors and ignored the needs of other students. It found the general education requirements both rigid and incoherent. The courses tended to be large and impersonal, and faculty were generally uninterested in teaching nonspecialist students. "Too often," the committee concluded, "the student's experience outside the major neither answers his personal desires nor has the compensating validity of being socially useful or intellectually coherent." To rectify this, the committee suggested that a General Studies Council be created to identify student needs and develop classes that met those needs, working with faculty to design interdisciplinary general education courses and integrated curricula as an alternative to fulfilling general education requirements. In a nod to student activists, the committee suggested that the council also could "receive and implement student proposals for ad hoc courses on subjects of current serious interest." The report also chastised the faculty, suggesting that professors had become overspecialized and recommending that the campus investigate ways to recruit senior scholars "of recognized intellectual breadth." It described the faculty as distracted by its outside contacts and contracts and suggested that the University consider developing guidelines regarding "the proper division of a professor's time and commitment among teaching, research, administration, public service, and private professional practice."

Among the committee's specific recommendations, the most controversial one involved exploring "the feasibility of a highly simplified system of grading.... Such a system should reduce the competition for grades, emphasize learning for its own sake, and encourage the student to experiment." Through such recommendations, including support of student course evaluations, the committee aligned itself, at least in part, with the activists' critique of the University's educational policies. The committee also seemed supportive of the activists when it asserted that "students will benefit from increased responsibility for their own education." However, the committee stopped short of recommending student control over educational policy; it discussed students' increased responsibility only in terms of allowing much greater freedom to choose among options, and it did not endorse an active student role in the development of the curriculum.[28]

The faculty's response to the preliminary report was mixed. Only a few supported the report as a whole or even sympathized with most of its recommendations. Others, though not entirely hostile, strongly disagreed with specific recommendations, particularly those regarding grading and course evaluations. Another group resented the report's critical tone, especially its implication that faculty neglected their duties and ignored their students. These critics maintained that Berkeley offered students an excellent education and that the committee offered no evidence to the contrary. Some criticized the committee for romanticizing the students and denounced granting students greater freedom as irresponsible. "It is essential," a small group of chemists argued, "for a University to set minimum standards, not only for entrance and performance, but as to breadth and depth of certain knowledge. If the faculty does not know just what it believes are the essentials of an education, how can the inexperienced student hope to make a worthwhile choice? It would be unfair to the student to permit him just to wander for four years." These faculty reminded the committee that it should not recommend educational reforms "simply to eliminate the unrest of a generation." The faculty, they argued, had to take responsibility for students' education, irrespective of the political consequences.[29]

By the time SCOE submitted its final report in early 1966, it had toned down its criticism and abandoned its more controversial recommendations. For example, instead of recommending large-scale changes in the grading system, the committee proposed that students in good standing be allowed to take one course each quarter "pass/fail" and that faculty, on an experimental basis, be allowed, with permission of their departments, to offer one of their courses pass/fail. In the final report, the committee also distanced itself from student activists' demands for a greater voice in formulating educational policy: "[students] do not have, nor can they be expected to have, professional responsibility for educational policy. We believe that campus-wide faculty committees should consult student opinion in the same way that they consult other sources of information before reaching decisions on educational policy. We do not believe that more direct student participation will necessarily lead to an atmosphere of greater intellectual and political trust."

In discussing the FSM the committee carefully explained that it viewed the level of student activism as an indication of problems but did not accept the activists' radical analysis of the University. Indeed, the committee called upon the faculty to "convince the students of the value of free and independent inquiry, of the need of the University for autonomy from all quarters." Committee members wanted to assure their colleagues that the reforms they were advancing served educational not political purposes.[30] Eschewing ideology, the final report did not suggest any single model for educational reform but instead proposed the creation of the Board of Educational Development (BED), another body that would generate and test proposals for educational change. BED would "stimulate and promote experimentation and innovation in all sectors of the Berkeley campus." It could also initiate and approve experimental courses, "for which neither departmental nor college support is appropriate or feasible." To expedite educational reform, the report recommend that the Academic Senate create a new vice chancellorship for educational development charged with administering BED programs and raising funds for educational experimentation. Finally, SCOE recommended the creation of the Council for Special Curricula, composed of members of BED and the Academic Senate Committee on Educational Policy. The council would have the authority to approve a limited number of degrees for students who pursued experimental courses of study rather than following the graduation requirements of one of the colleges.[31]

One SCOE member, George Pimentel, a popular chemistry professor, issued a dissenting report objecting to the powers granted to BED and warning that it could circumvent existing Academic Senate controls for course and degree approval. He noted that the board was not being placed under direct control of the Senate. "We have here a University within a University—its own Vice-Chancellor—its own . . . fund sources—its own courses subject to no prior review—its own faculty insofar as it chooses to establish curricula that are incompatible with existing colleges—even its own degrees, through the Council. We may well find it difficult to live with our own creation." If Pimentel cautioned the faculty not to create an agency that could implement programs of which the faculty might not approve, that was precisely the committee's intent: BED was designed to allow reformers to try new ideas without having to convince academically conservative colleagues of their merit. Experiments could be tried and tested before having to overcome the natural resistance of tradition.[32]

As an alternative to that approach, Pimentel recommended the status of the new administrative officer be changed to that of an assistant chancellor under the vice chancellor of academic affairs, thereby creating more formal ties to the Academic Senate's Committee on Educational Policy. He also proposed instituting a formal review of BED in five years. In a private review of these recommendations, one of the chancellor's advisors argued that, though Pimentel's suggestions were sound, they were not essential if the "right" people were appointed to BED. The Senate ultimately decided to follow Pimentel's recommendation regarding the status of the assistant chancellor and to require a review of BED in its sixth year. But it chose not to change the board's structure to make it more accountable to the Committee on Educational Policy. BED thus became the primary educational legacy of the FSM and the body responsible for educational reform at Berkeley.[33]

STUDENTS AND *BED*

Student activists who wanted a direct voice in educational policy were unhappy with the limited nature of the reforms that were instituted. FSM veterans, according to Muscatine, had ignored invitations to consult with the committee, possibly because, in Savio's words, they had "grave doubts that any commission which did not include students as voting members would take the evils of the existing educational system very seriously." Mario charged that the report ignored the larger political forces that shaped education at Berkeley and that it was a timid document, one that allowed for only small-scale experiments not of a kind that would affect larger institutional practices. "No one can speak for students but students," he asserted. "And we will secure the right to a decent education only when we have organized ourselves independently of both faculty and administration." Similar sentiments were voiced to the Academic Senate by other students, some of whom unsuccessfully petitioned the Senate to include student members on BED.[34]

As former leaders of the FSM increasingly turned their attention to the antiwar movement, a new group of students, who had not been at Berkeley during the FSM but still identified with it, took up the mantel of educational reform. These students found that they could use BED as an entrée into the curriculum. In winter quarter 1966–1967, soon after BED began to operate, Rick Brown, a new graduate student and former Berkeley undergraduate, approached the student government (ASUC) about funding a student group devoted to educational reform. Brown had been a graduate student in psychology at San Francisco State University, where he became involved in an evaluation of the Experimental College, an alternative institution sponsored by the student government. He was impressed with the college and became enamored with the possibilities of student-initiated educational reform. A few students at the ASUC were already interested in educational reform, and they, along with Brown, convinced the student government to found and fund a new reform organization, the Center for Participant Education (CPE). Brown prodded mathematics professor John Kelly, the first chair of BED, who was both sympathetic to student activists and involved in the antiwar movement, to commit the board to considering course proposals from students. Developing courses and helping other students do so soon became the CPE's primary activities.[35]

When BED first started receiving proposals from students, its members were uncertain how they should respond. Kelly proposed conferring initially with the relevant department chairs. Other members felt the Board should sponsor such courses but were concerned about standards. After students from CPE began to submit numerous proposals, this became a pressing problem. One member of BED, English professor Thomas Parkinson, though sympathetic to students, expressed reservations about approving their courses. "I am very troubled," he wrote to his colleagues on the board, "by the concept of the student-initiated course because it seems... in danger of becoming... a student-run and assessed course and... it seems likely that many of the courses will cover material that it is legitimate for students to study but not for the university to accredit." Parkinson recommended that the board adopt criteria and procedures that would insure that student-initiated courses met University standards. He wanted a Berkeley professor to be actively involved in each class, particularly in the process of evaluating student work. He therefore suggested that BED require more than simply a signature of a faculty sponsor. He wanted a letter "of some length" from the faculty member, explaining his or her role in the course. He also wanted the proposal to include enough detail about the topics covered, the readings, and other assignments to assure the board that the student-initiated courses would be intellectually demanding.[36]

BED members agreed with Parkinson's concerns and in June 1967 adopted a set of criteria for student-initiated courses. These included a letter from the faculty sponsor, a rationale for the course, and a detailed description of lecture and discussion topics, and readings and other assignments. BED also established procedures for reviewing student-initiated courses. One member was assigned to each proposal and was responsible for creating an ad hoc committee to review it. Thereafter, BED frequently requested more information or changes in plans for student-initiated courses, requests that were officially addressed to the faculty sponsor rather than the student representative from CPE. This reflected BED's reluctance to give students independent authority in academic matters.[37]

BED's preoccupation with standards conflicted with the aims and ideological perspectives of CPE students. Rick Brown recalled that CPE had a "liberation perspective"—its members wanted to free students from "the yoke of university standards" that they believed were used to suppress people. CPE was founded on the principle "that students should take responsibility for their own educations, that their perceptions of their needs and their views of what would best fulfill those needs are the best available determinants of the shape and content of their educations." Students associated with CPE assumed that this would produce "courses with relevance in a generally irrelevant curriculum." They also thought that the structure of these courses would be different; they would encourage "dialogue, independence and critical sensitivity." Finally, they believed that student-initiated courses would serve a political end—"the development of a new consciousness in students, a 'class consciousness,'" that included awareness of the way the University oppressed students and was involved in "the means of oppression of our society."[38]

Despite their conflicting philosophies students from CPE continued to work with the BED to get their courses certified for credit. This was important, they insisted, "not because we believe in credit, but because we think it will facilitate students' academic survival, and . . . it makes our challenge more direct." Credit symbolized CPE's claim in the name of students to the academic freedom faculty reserved for themselves—freedom to direct and control courses, not just select among them. CPE therefore accepted, however reluctantly, BED's criteria for course approval. CPE learned to work within those guidelines, while the board approved many of their courses. Students in CPE also served as intermediaries between other students and BED by helping them prepare proposals that fit the BED model.[39]

In the course of academic year 1967–1968 CPE students and BED faculty developed a reasonably good working relationship. In May 1968 CPE members tried to renegotiate their role to make it an even closer partnership. They began by requesting that BED appoint three student members. Board members would not agree to this, reiterating that students could not participate in course approval, but they did suggest that CPE students attend those meetings where their courses were discussed and that other means of regular communication, such as a student advisory committee, could be set up. Having failed to gain direct membership, CPE then made a number of additional proposals that were intended to strengthen the ties between the two groups. For example, CPE requested help with its secretarial needs. Here BED was more open, with one member suggesting that "in view of the service CPE provides indirectly to the Board," these funds could be provided by the chancellor's office via BED. If BED faculty were not willing to welcome students as equal partners, they were at least willing to acknowledge that they played a legitimate role in the process of educational reform.[40]

THE CLEAVER CONTROVERSY AND THE DEMISE OF THE *BED*

In the summer of 1968, when Larry Magid brought forward the proposal for the course involving Cleaver as primary lecturer, BED treated it as it did any other student-initiated course, granting approval contingent on a few changes. The most significant change was to limit the number of students taking the course for credit; this was meant to ensure that faculty, not volunteer student TAs (as Magid originally proposed), lead the discussion sections and grade all student work. This change was consistent with BED's concern that faculty sponsors have real responsibility for the courses they sponsored, particularly the evaluation of student work.[41]

But others on campus saw the course as an affront to academic standards. Four professors wrote BED to express their opposition: "we have come to the conclusion that this course, as presently planned, does not conform to minimal academic standards. . . . Cleaver does not have the qualifications of an academic teacher," they explained. "[His] record indicates that he cannot present the kind of balanced and critical assessment of problems appropriate in the classroom." The Berkeley administration debated canceling the course. One of the chancellor's advisors, Charles Wilke, recommended that they overrule BED because Cleaver was indeed the de facto instructor. "According to my concepts of appointment standards," Wilke explained, "he is disqualified for faculty status on at least two counts: (1) he is an established felon and currently under indictment for additional criminal acts, and (2) his extremist views on race relations make it questionable that he could present an objective view of the subject in class." Heyns, however, chose a milder course: he suggested that BED and the faculty sponsors change the structure of the course to minimize Cleaver's role and allow for other points of view.[42]

Although the faculty voted to condemn the Regents' actions against the course, some did so reluctantly. Professor Stuart Bowyer of astronomy, for example, wrote that it was "indeed unfortunate that the regents' recent resolution forces us to alienate a generally unsympathetic public in the necessary defense of academic freedom. It is more than unfortunate, it is tragic, that the issue arose over a course which was constituted in a form which was clearly not in the best traditions of academic scholarship." UC president Charles J. Hitch's compromise put the faculty in an awkward position. He cleverly steered the Regents away from targeting Cleaver as a spokesperson for certain views and instead framed the issue in terms of expertise and legitimacy. He maintained that only a person who had passed through the rigorous process of being appointed to the faculty should enjoy full freedom in the classroom. Faculty could bring in appropriate guest speakers, but they could not let someone who has not been appointed to the faculty teach their courses. According to Hitch, students' freedom to learn did not involve the right to design and control the curriculum. He also maintained that students' constitutional rights were not being violated: "Whatever is pertinent to the University concerning these First Amendment rights, they do not extend to the classroom. The classroom is, and properly so, a special place. . . . To have it otherwise would be, necessarily, to interfere with both the course-authorizing power and supervision of the Senate and the appointment powers of the administration and Regents in consultation with the Senate." From this perspective, the faculty's right to control the curriculum depended on a distinction between academic freedom and freedom of speech. If students enjoyed such constitutional freedoms on the campus, they did not enjoy academic freedom in a sense that was parallel to that of faculty. Academic freedom—the right to control the intellectual content of the classroom—was the exclusive preserve of certified scholars. Although the faculty could not ignore that the Regents had overruled a decision of an authorized faculty body, many on the faculty probably agreed with Hitch's reasoning in regard to limits on students' rights in the classroom.[43]

The controversy over the Cleaver course led to the demise of BED. After the Regents' intervention, Leonard Machlis, assistant chancellor for educational development, insisted that BED revise its procedures for the approval of courses. These revisions made it much more difficult for students to initiate courses and would prevent, without explicit approval from the administration, politically controversial courses from being offered. Students in CPE, not surprisingly, balked at such restrictions. When BED postponed action on the proposals, Machlis recommended that Heyns exert administrative control over BED by requiring that the assistant chancellor rather than the chair of the board sign the forms authorizing the instructional staff, and that his signature be required before the board could approve courses. "These two actions," Machlis explained, "would have the effect of giving me veto power." When BED approved courses for the winter term before these safeguards were implemented, Machlis suggested that Heyns take "the drastic action of . . . banning, by denying space and the issuance of class cards (i.e., the giving of credit), . . . all new BED courses." Machlis felt that the risk of alienating BED and many students was worth preventing the approval of another course like Social Analysis 139X.[44]

Machlis, the administrator charged with implementing BED's policies, had now turned against the board. He did so because he believed that Kelly, its chair, had become an irrational "supporter of maximum freedom for the students" and had politicized the board through its relationship with CPE, a relationship that inappropriately empowered the student group, giving it "a quasi-official status." Machlis feared that CPE was trying to embarrass the administration through new course proposals involving instruction by controversial activists; hence the authority of BED had to be circumscribed.[45]

The Regents had required that the campuses report back to them regarding their procedures for approving experimental courses. BED was asked to review its procedures and, if necessary, recommend changes to the Academic Senate. This led to a discussion about the structure of the board. In anticipation, members of BED exchanged ideas regarding its future. Kelly's recommendations dominated the initial discussions. His first recommendation was that BED be "guided, not by political considerations, but solely by academic objectives." Kelly intended this as a challenge to Machlis, who insisted "that the Board should use extreme caution in approving courses which might prove politically embarassing [*sic*] to the University." Other members agreed with this principle, but not all were convinced that BED needed to "nail it to the masthead." Kelly's next recommendations were designed to give BED more power and independence. He successfully argued to his BED colleagues that the board needed its own budget and faculty positions. The final issue he discussed involved course approvals. Most members of BED thought that the long time spent reviewing course proposals had precluded it from considering other important matters. Kelly suggested that they solve this problem by giving the students authority over their courses. He recommended that BED be allowed on an experimental basis to delegate authority to approve up to ten courses per quarter to a committee of the ASUC, but no other member of the Board agreed.[46]

Kelly then drastically changed his strategy. At the next board meeting he presented a draft report addressed to the Academic Senate. He suggested that members of BED submit their resignations to the Senate and cease all activity. He argued that the board was no longer operating as a legitimate committee of the Senate; it had been taken over by administration, and all efforts at experimentation and innovation had been blocked. After discussing Kelly's recommendation, however, the other members decided not to resign. They wanted to go to the Senate with a proposal for strengthening the board and in the meantime continue their activities. Kelly decided to submit his draft as a minority report and resign from BED.[47]

On February 21, 1969, the remaining members of the board (except Machlis) submitted a report to the Senate that closely followed Kelly's original recommendations. Arguing that "a policy which deliberately avoids potentially controversial issues is absolutely destructive of education," the report asserted that BED should dispose of a significant budget and faculty positions and have the authority to approach foundations directly for funding. The report reiterated the importance of student input but stopped short of recommending that students be given the authority to approve courses, suggesting instead that the ASUC appoint a seven-member committee to consult with the board. Finally it recommended that the assistant chancellor for educational development no longer be a member, proposing instead that the chancellor have the authority to select the BED chair from a list of seven members designated by the Academic Senate.[48]

Having received the BED's report, the Senate then had the opportunity to review BED and make recommendations concerning its future. It sought, however, not to further empower BED but to control it. Ignoring BED's recommendations, it proceeded to appoint a new committee, headed by music professor Joseph Kerman, to review the board. That committee, in turn, recommended that BED no longer be authorized to sponsor or approve courses. Instead, it recommended the creation of yet another body, the Division of Experimental Courses (DEC). DEC's procedures for reviewing courses would more closely resemble existing Senate rules. The Senate also instituted a number of other policies that restricted students' ability to design courses. It passed a resolution declaring that "only regularly appointed officers of instruction holding appropriate instructional titles may have substantial responsibility for the content and conduct of approved courses." The Senate's Committee on Educational Policy also supported restrictions on the number of independent study credits a faculty member could authorize in a given quarter. This was intended to prevent sympathetic faculty from giving groups of students credit for CPE courses.[49]

Without the authority to authorize courses, BED was supposedly free to investigate ways to promote educational innovation. In 1969–1970 the Senate appointed a new board headed by the structural engineering professor T. Y. Lin. Lin encouraged the board to take its new charge seriously but soon ran into problems working with Machlis. One of the projects the board decided to focus on was "student-designed education" (SDE). The board envisioned a program whereby a certain number of faculty were freed from regular teaching duties to help students design their own programs. These programs might include some regular course work and independent readings with faculty, as well as field studies, small student-run seminars, or other unconventional contexts for learning. Machlis, who was hostile to the idea from the beginning and kept returning proposals to BED for further elaboration, soon fell into the same pattern he had established in dealing with Kelly. Fearing that BED was planning to associate the administration with a controversial plan, he tried to block its actions by withholding funds and confidentially asking his superiors in the administration to reject its proposals. Lin resigned in frustration at the end of the academic year, complaining of the lack of independent funds and administrative cooperation. No one was appointed to replace him, and after 1970 BED largely ceased functioning.[50]

In contrast to BED, immediately after the Cleaver incident CPE thrived. It attracted a tremendous amount of attention, with various campus activists offering to teach courses. But the changes instituted by the faculty soon took their toll. Although DEC had been created in spring 1969, it did not operate during the following academic year, because the chancellor failed to appoint a chair. CPE students tried to pressure him to appoint a chair sympathetic to student-initiated courses, but he would not consider the names suggested by the students or, indeed, any faculty associated with leftist activism. With DEC not operating and with new restrictions on independent study credit, CPE could not offer credit for its courses. Students thus lost their ability to directly shape the curriculum.[51]

CONCLUSION

In their responses to the Regents' actions against Social Analysis 139X, it seemed that faculty and students might have finally joined together in common cause. Student activists clearly wanted to view the case as a violation of their and the faculty's right to determine the content of courses, and to extend their constitutional right to political advocacy beyond the physical space of the campus into the academic space of the classroom. Within certain limits, a small minority of faculty agreed. Through the process of educational reform, they had come to see students as junior partners in educational matters. However, this position was not broadly accepted on the campus. In the aftermath of the Cleaver episode, the administration moved, with the faculty's approval, to limit students' ability to sponsor classes.

Nevertheless, student activists continued to struggle to change the University and to gain more power, and they even won some important concessions. The Academic Senate eventually agreed to allow student members on some of its committees, including BED, and the faculty in the College of Letters and Science, where most undergraduates studied, approved a student-initiated proposal for changes in its graduation requirements, significantly expanding students' freedom in the realm of course selection. In the fight over ethnic studies, some students again pushed for direct power in academic affairs. But the administration and most faculty continued to resist this demand. They would not concede to students academic rights that were similar to those of faculty. Nor was this a cause that sparked the enthusiasm of most Berkeley students.[52]

Faculty at other institutions shared their Berkeley colleagues' reluctance to include students among those entitled to full academic freedom. The Center for Research and Development in Higher Education at Berkeley conducted a survey of professors at six institutions, soliciting their views on students' rights. It found that only 9 percent of professors thought students should have an equal voice with faculty on academic matters, while slightly more than a third approved of student membership on committees that dealt with academic affairs. The same faculty overwhelmingly approved, however, of ending in loco parentis rules. The majority agreed that students should have the freedom to advocate political ideals on campus grounds. They even should have a good deal of freedom to select their own courses. But determining the content of those courses was beyond the pale.[53]

Ultimately, the majority of faculty accepted President Hitch's views on academic freedom—students enjoyed First Amendment rights on campus grounds but not in the classroom. As a physical space, the University would tolerate students' freedom of speech, but not as an instructional space. Freedom within the classroom was limited to those people who had earned the right to speak with intellectual authority—those faculty who had been trained in the rigors of an academic discipline and acknowledged by their colleagues as experts in their field.

NOTES

I am grateful to the following people for assistance with this essay: the members of my writing group—Elizabeth Abrams, Catherine Corman, Hildegard Hoeller, Jill Lepore, and Laura Saltz—Bruce J. Schulman, and editors Robby Cohen and Reggie Zelnik. The students in my class on the 1960s at the Harvard Graduate School of Education talked about the challenges of researching this essay and read the first draft. Bill Roberts helped me identify archival collections at the University of California Archives, Bancroft Library. The Spencer Foundation provided funds to support the research for this essay. I would particularly like to thank the following people for agreeing to share their Berkeley experiences: Richard Brown, Lawrence Magid, Bradford Cleaveland, Charles Webel, Jack Schuster, Earl Cheit, Robert Connick, Charles Muscatine, and Peter Dale Scott.

1. Reuben interview with Lawrence Magid, 27 Feb. 2000, (notes in author's possession). On Cleaver, see John Kifner, "Eldridge Cleaver, Black Panther Who Became G.O.P. Conservative, Is Dead at 62," New York Times, 2 May 1998, B8.

2. Interview with Magid; Leonard Machlis, memo to Roger Heyns, 10 Sept. 1968, Records of the Office of the Chancellor, University of California, 1952–1971, CU-149 (hereafter cited as Chancellor's Records), box 56, University Archives, Bancroft Library, University of California at Berkeley.

3. Office of Public Relations, "Press Release re: Social Relations 139X," 9 Sept. 1968, box 56, Chancellor's Records; Daryle E. Lemke, "U.C. Clarifies Status of Cleaver in Program," Los Angeles Times (hereafter LAT), 13 Sept. 1968, 22.

4. Reagan and Unruh quoted in Jerry Gillam, "State Senate Votes Censure of UC Officials over Cleaver," LAT, 18 Sept. 1968, 1, 26. See also William J. Drummond, "Cleaver Dispute: Reform at UC Is on the Spot," LAT, 18 Sept. 1968, 1, 27; John Dreyfuss, "Regents Vote to Allow One Lecture by Cleaver at UC," LAT, 21

Sept. 1968. Committee on Educational Policies, executive session minutes—19 Sept. 1968, box 56, Chancellor's Records.

5. Striking students, "STUDENTS STRIKE!" 25 Oct. 1968; Campus Students for a Democratic Society, "Strike to Win," 29 Oct. 1968; Charles J. Hitch to Donald A. Ford, 15 Nov. 1968, all in box 56, Chancellor's Records.

6. "Summary of 1968–69 Actions of the Berkeley Division Re: Social Analysis 139X," ibid.

7. For an account of the case on these terms see Angus E. Taylor, *The Academic Senate of the University of California: Its Role in the Shared Governance and Operation of the University of California* (Berkeley: Institute of Governmental Studies Press, 1998), 82–99.

8. Robert Kernish, *The History of United States National Student Association* [USNSA] (Washington, D.C.: USNSA, 1965). Records of the NSA academic freedom program are in the Papers of the United States Student Association, box 108, State Historical Society of Wisconsin (hereafter cited as USSA).

9. Phillip Monypenny, "Toward a Standard for Student Academic Freedom," in Hans W. Baade, ed., *Academic Freedom: The Scholar's Place in Modern Society* (Dobbs Ferry, N.Y.: Oceana Publications, 1964), 196, 195. There is a rich literature on the development of notions of academic freedom in the United States. See, for example, Richard Hofstadter and Walter P. Metzger, *The Development of Academic Freedom in the United States* (New York: Columbia University Press, 1955); Neil Hamilton, *Zealotry and Academic Freedom: A Legal and Historical Perspective* (New Brunswick, N.J.: Rutgers University Press, 1995); William W. Van Alstyne, ed., *Freedom and Tenure in the Academy* (Durham, N.C.: Duke University Press, 1993); Ellen W. Schrecker, *No Ivory Tower: McCarthyism and the Universities* (New York: Oxford University Press, 1986); Mary O. Furner, *Advocacy and Objectivity: A Crisis in the Professionalization of American Social Science, 1865–1905* (Lexington: University of Kentucky Press, 1975); Walter Metzger, ed., *The American Concept of Academic Freedom in Formation: A Collection of Essays and Reports* (New York: Arno Press, 1977). For the important role played by the AAUP in these debates, see AAUP, *Policy Documents and Reports* (Washington, D.C.: AAUP, 1977); AAUP, "General Report on the Committee on Academic Freedom and Academic Tenure (1915)," reprinted in Van Alstyne, 404; AAUP, "1940 Statement of Principles on Academic Freedom and Tenure," reprinted in ibid., 407–8.

10. Sidney Hook, "Academic Freedom and the Rights of Students," in Seymour Martin Lipset and Sheldon S. Wolin, eds., *The Berkeley Student Revolt: Facts and Interpretations* (Garden City, N.Y.: Doubleday, 1965), 433.

11. Nevitt Sanford, ed., *The American College: A Psychological and Social Interpretation of the Higher Learning* (New York: John Wiley, 1962); Robert Maynard Hutchins, *The University of Utopia* (Chicago: University of Chicago Press, 1953, 1964); Paul Goodman, *Compulsory Mis-Education and the Community of Scholars* (New York, Horizon Press: 1964); Harold Taylor, *On Education and Freedom* (New York: Abelard-Schuman, 1954). The U.S. Department of Education helped publicize reforms. See, for example, Winslow R. Hatch and Ann Bennet, "Independent Study," *New Dimensions in Higher Education,* no. 1 (Washington, D.C.: Office of Education, 1960); Winslow Hatch, "The Experimental College," *New Dimensions in Higher Education,* no. 3 (Washington, D.C.: Office of Education, 1960); Charles C. Coll, Jr., and

Lanora G. Lewis, "Flexibility in the Undergraduate Curriculum," *New Dimensions in Higher Education*, no. 10 (Washington, D.C.: Office of Education, 1962).

12. Excerpts of Martin Trow, "The Campus Viewed as Culture," and Nathan Glazer, "The Wasted Classroom," are reprinted in the SLATE Summer Conference Papers, 27–28 July 1963, Free Speech Movement records, CU-309 (hereafter cited as FSM Records), University Archives, Bancroft Library, University of California at Berkeley (this SLATE document is available via the FSM Digital Archive at <http://lib.berkeley.edu/BANC/FSM/>); Joseph Tussman, *The Beleaguered College: Essays on Educational Reform* (Berkeley and Los Angeles: University of California Press, 1997), 5; idem, *Experiment at Berkeley* (New York: Oxford University Press, 1969).

13. See, for example, proposals from Alan Searcy, Carl Schorske, Martin Trow, box 57, Chancellor's Records.

14. Bradford Cleaveland, "Education Controversy Ignored by Faculty," and Jo Freeman, "Freshman's First Course: How to Beat the System," both in *California Reporter*, 13 May 1963 (both available on the FSM Digital Archive); Bradford Cleaveland, "Education, Revolution and Citadels" (Sept. 1964), in Lipset and Wolin, 91.

15. Activists now view their relationship with faculty in different ways. Cleaveland, for example, has come to see faculty as the primary barrier to reform, whereas Charles Webel views select faculty as student activists' most important allies. Interviews with Cleaveland, 3 May 2000, and Webel, 18 May 2000 (note in author's possession).

16. For a classic statement of this position, see Jacques Barzun, "The Danger of 'Public Service,'" in Immanuel Wallerstein and Paul Starr, eds., *The University Crisis Reader*, vol. 1, *The Liberal University under Attack* (New York: Random House, 1971), 123–30.

17. Cleaveland, "A Letter to Undergraduates," *SLATE Supplement Report 1*, no. 4 (Sept. 1964), reprinted in Lipset and Wolin, 69.

18. "SLATE Educational Reform Committee Meeting, 10 March," *SLATE Newsletter*, no. 3 (1963). For examples of activists' use of Kerr, see Hal Draper, "The Mind of Clark Kerr," Oct. 1964; and Gerald Gray and David Rynin, "Critique: The Uses of the University," in SLATE Summer Conference Papers, 27–28 July 1963. (Both SLATE items in this note are available via the FSM Digital Archive.)

19. Cleaveland, "A Letter to Undergraduates," 80; Michael Rossman, "The Movement and Educational Reform," 1967, reprinted in idem, *The Wedding Within the War* (Garden City, N.Y.: Doubleday, 1971), 158, 155.

20. On Tussman's position, see Robert Schmid, "Memo to File L68-3 re: Undergraduate Education at Berkeley," 29 May 1968, Grant 68-841, Reel 2380, Grant Files, Ford Foundation Archives, New York, N.Y.

21. A review of articles listed in the *Readers Guide to Periodical Literature* found that the published faculty commentary on student activism in the 1960s was overwhelmingly negative: Caroline Daniels, "The Persistence of Memory: The Use of History in Faculty Criticism of Radical Students in the 1960s" (unpublished essay, Harvard Graduate School of Education, 2000). A great deal of faculty hostility focused around the fear that student activists were destroying the University by disregarding the importance of institutional neutrality. For a telling example of this position see Nathan Glazer, "The Campus Crucible," *Atlantic* 224 (July 1969): 43–56. Faculty who defended and agreed with students on the issues of institutional

neutrality and student power would most likely identify themselves as radicals. For an example of this position see the New University Conference, "The Student Rebellion," 1969, New University Conference Papers, box 11, State Historical Society of Wisconsin. But even faculty who were active in leftist politics did not necessarily agree that the classroom should be a democracy (interview with Peter Dale Scott, 23 June 2000 [notes in author's possession]). The middle position could take various forms. One example was expressed in the report of the Study Commission on University Governance (UCB), *The Culture of the University: Governance and Education* (San Francisco: Jossey-Bass, 1968), which justified student involvement in curricular planning in terms of its educational benefits. This commission, which had both student and faculty members, was clearly more sympathetic to some form of student power than most Berkeley faculty.

22. "The Position of the Free Speech Movement on Speech and Political Activity," in Lipset and Wolin, 201.

23. Jack Weinberg, "Two Fronts in the Same War: The Free Speech Movement and Civil Rights," *Campus CORE-lator,* Jan. 1965 (available via the FSM Digital Archive).

24. Conclusions from Kathleen Gale's April 1965 survey of 439 students, Academic Senate, Berkeley division records, box 101, University Archives, Bancroft Library. Faculty at Berkeley debated whether this survey proved that student dissatisfaction with their education fueled the FSM. For an attempt to make sense of this issue, see [Charles Muscatine, et al.], *Education at Berkeley: Report of the Select Committee on Education* (Berkeley: University of California Press, 1968), 12.

25. FSM, "We Want a University," 4 Jan. 1965, in Lipset and Wolin, 215–16.

26. Martin Meyerson, "Speech on Educational Reform," 1 Mar. 1965, box 57, Chancellor's Records.

27. Muscatine does not recall the committee's preliminary report (interview with Muscatine, 13 June 2000 [notes in author's possession]). I am attributing this position to him based on a letter from George Pimentel, a member of the SCOE who eventually issued a dissenting report. He wrote, "I am brought back to the question of why we must proceed so rapidly on matters of such great import. . . . I would not like to believe that we are motivated by a 'strike-while-the-iron-is-hot' opportunism, nor that we are intimidated by student pressure. I do not sense that the Division is pressing for quick action. I am unmoved by the argument that a slower pace prolongs undesirably the life of the committee" (Pimentel, memo to members of SCOE, 1 Sept. 1965, Records of the Select Committee on Education, box 4 (hereafter SCOER), University Archives, Bancroft Library.

28. "Preliminary Report of the Special Select Committee on Education," 24 May 1965, Box 57, Chancellor's Records.

29. Chemists W. G. Dauben, D. S. Noyce, and A. Streitweiser to Muscatine, 1 Sept. 1965, box 4, SCOER. Copies of the faculty's responses to the preliminary report can be found in box 4, SCOER.

30. *Education at Berkeley,* 99, 35.

31. Ibid., 114–17.

32. Ibid., 218–19.

33. Ibid., 245–46; EWM, "Memo re: Muscatine Recommendations nos. 19, 20 and 21," 30 Mar. 1966, box 57, Chancellor's Records.

34. Interview with Muscatine, 13 June 2000; Mario Savio, "The Uncertain Future of the Multiuniversity: A Partisan's Scrutiny of Berkeley's Muscatine Report," *Harper's Magazine,* Oct. 1966, 88, 94; Report of Special Committee to Consider the Select Committee Report on Education 21 Mar. 1966, box 57, Chancellor's Records. On activists' response to the report, see also "FUB [Free University of Berkeley] Free-for-All on Muscatine Report," *Berkeley Barb,* 20 May 1966, 2.

35. Interview with Richard Brown, 7 Mar. 2000 (notes in author's possession).

36. Board of Educational Development, minutes of 11 Nov. 1966 meeting, Records of the Board of Educational Development, box 1 (hereafter BEDR), University Archives, Bancroft Library; T. Parkinson, letter to BED regarding student initiated courses, 18 Mar. 1967, box 1, BEDR.

37. BED, minutes of 4 April 1967 meeting, box 1, BEDR.

38. Interview with Brown; CPE and Individuals Representing the Campus Community, "The University and the Cleaver Course Controversy" [1968], box 110, USSA.

39. CPE, "One Year after the Revolution," 28 Sept. 1969, box 10, USSA. Students in CPE did complain about the restrictive criteria, but BED insisted on its obligation to maintain standards. BED, minutes of 10 May 1967 meeting, box 1, BEDR.

40. The three former CPE members I interviewed, Brown, Magid, and Webel, recall good relations with most of the BED faculty. See also BED, minutes of 23 May 1968 meeting, box 1, BEDR.

41. Leonard Machlis, "Memo to Heyns re: Cleaver Course," 10 Sept. 1968, box 56, Chancellor's Records. In this report Machlis mentioned that CPE dropped its request that Cleaver be appointed as a visiting lecturer. There is no other record indicating that the BED demanded that CPE make this change. CPE students may have done so on their own or under pressure from a member of the faculty or administration. Machlis also reported that he blocked a request for funding for the course, saying that he could not commit any funds for BED courses. During the controversy, the University repeatedly pointed out that Cleaver was not being paid with University funds and had not been appointed to the faculty, which suggests that, though the BED refused to consider the political nature of the course when it authorized it, the administration was very conscious of this issue.

42. Kenneth M. Stampp, Carl Landauer, Martin E. Malia, and Ernst B. Haas to BED, 18 Sept. 1968; Charles R. Wilke to Heyns, 18 Sept. 1967 [*sic*], both in box 56, Chancellor's Records. It is difficult to know how many faculty shared this point of view. Muscatine claims that, had he not been in Europe, he would have found a way to block approval of the course and that he believed that the majority of the faculty disapproved of it (interview with Muscatine). Peter Dale Scott supported the course but thought it unfortunate (interview with Scott).

43. Stuart Bowyer to A. C. Helmhoz [*sic*], 16 Oct. 1968, Academic Senate, Berkeley division records, box 95, University Archives; Charles J. Hitch, "Statement to the Academic Assembly Regarding Resolutions Proposed by University-Wide Academic Freedom Committee," 18 Nov. 1968, box 56, Chancellor's Records.

44. Machlis, memo to Heyns, 14 Nov. 1968, box 55, Chancellor's Records; Machlis, "B.E.D. Procedures—Preliminary Draft for Discussion," 17. Oct. 1968, ibid.; Machlis, memo to Heyns, 20 Nov. 1968, box 53, Chancellor's Records.

45. Machlis, memo to Heyns, 29 Dec. 1968, box 55, Chancellor's Records.

46. BED, "Notes on B.E.D. Policy Conference," 18 Jan. 1969, box 56, Chancellor's Records; "Position Paper by J. L. Kelley for BED Conference on Policy of 18 January 1969," box 55, Chancellor's Records.

47. BED, minutes of 23 Jan. 1969 meeting, box 56, Chancellor's Records; Kelley, "Minority Statement" [1969], box 55, Chancellor's Records.

48. James L. Jarrett et al., "Report of the Board of Educational Development," 21 Feb. 1969, box 56, Chancellor's Records.

49. "Summary of the 1968–69 Actions of the Berkeley Division re: Social Analysis 139X (Dehumanization and Regeneration in the American Social Order)," box 57, Chancellor's Records; Machlis, memo to Heyns, 12 May 1969, box 55, Chancellor's Records; Machlis, "Fall-Out from the Social Analysis 139X Controversy," 18 Oct. 1969, box 56, Chancellor's Records.

50. Jesse Reichek, "Draft Proposal for a Committee for Student Designed Education," 15 Aug. 1969; T. Y. Lin, "Memo to BED re: Committee for Student Designed Education—A BED Proposal," 20 Aug. 1969; BED Minutes 12 Sept. 1969; Machlis, Memo to Lin, 22 Sept. 1969, all three in box 56, Chancellor's Records; Machlis, Memo to Vice Chancellor Connick, 3 April 1970; Lin, "Final Report of the Board of Educational Development" June 1970; Minutes of the Special Meeting of the Representative Assembly of the Berkeley Division, 6 June 1972, all three in box 55, Chancellor's Records.

51. David S. Kemnitzer to Heyns, 14 March 1970, box 55, Chancellor's Records; Heyns to Kemnitzer, 23 March 1970; R. A. Cockrell, "IN CONFIDENCE," memo to Heyns, 27 Feb. 1970, all in box 55, Chancellor's Records. On CPE's difficulty see untitled call for a meeting of interested groups to address problems of education at Berkeley, Nov. [1969]; and CPE, "One Year after the Revolution," 28 Sept. 1969, both in box 10, USSA; interview with Webel.

52. John McKenzie, "Student Participation and the Academic Senate," Nov. 1969, Box 10, USSA; Robert Schmid, "Memo to File L68-3 re: Undergraduate Education at Berkeley," 29 May 1968, Grant 68-841, reel 2380, Grant Files; interview with Robert Connick, 3 May 2000 (notes in author's possession). On the struggle over black and ethnic studies at Berkeley, see Karen K. Miller, "Race, Power and the Emergence of Black Studies in Higher Education," *American Studies* 31, no. 2 (fall 1990): 83–99.

53. Fred M. Hechinger, "Student-Teacher Battle Next?" *New York Times*, 17 Aug. 1969, sec. 4, 9.

The FSM, Berkeley Politics, and Ronald Reagan

W. J. Rorabaugh

The Berkeley Free Speech Movement transformed politics in the city of Berkeley and throughout California. After the FSM's final victory in December 1964, student activists mobilized thousands of supporters, mostly Berkeley residents, as an important new force in local politics. In June 1966 Robert Scheer's anti–Vietnam War congressional campaign lost in the larger district but carried the city of Berkeley, and a year later a white-black coalition elected the first self-styled radical, the African American Ron Dellums, to the Berkeley city council. In 1970 Dellums was elected to Congress, and the following year the radical Berkeley coalition elected a mayor and three council members. Since the 1970s, self-styled progressives have often controlled the city government or at least commanded a large plurality. Meanwhile, Ronald Reagan in 1966 used the "mess" in Berkeley to propel himself into the governorship. Thus, quite ironically, the politics spawned by the FSM enabled both radicals and conservatives to thrive in different venues.[1]

The activists who created the FSM shared a unique worldview that had emerged in Berkeley by the beginning of the 1960s. Many of them were influenced by the eclectic radicalism of the nation's first listener-supported, noncommercial radio station, KPFA, and by the Beat subculture's sneering disapproval of tradition and middle-class propriety. To quote one FSM song, they were "questioning authority." They were also, somewhat paradoxically, influenced by the excitement of John Kennedy's New Frontier and especially by the new Peace Corps, even though they often felt that the president represented established Cold War interests. Frightened by nuclear war, they were anti-anti-Communists, increasingly disgusted by the Cold War. Some of them embraced the New Left, which proposed a bold transformation of society, including participatory democracy and either a greatly enhanced welfare state or socialism. The most important influence upon the idealistic young, however, was the Civil Rights Movement. Berkeley activists despised racism, admired southern black protest, usually adopted the doctrine of nonviolence, and demonstrated against racism locally.[2]

Participants in the FSM found their experience in the movement exhilarating and life transforming. For some, the FSM marked an epiphany. Nineteen-year-old freshman David Goines's consciousness changed when he was cited for violating the campus ban on political advocacy. Graduate student Michael Rossman's flash of transcendent truth came during the thirty-two hours when students spoke from atop a trapped police car. For many of the more than one thousand who sat in at Sproul Hall on December 2, the crucial moment was either the solemn, almost religious entry into the building or being arrested inside. For thousands outside the building, including twenty-four-year-old Loni Hancock, the mass arrests called into question basic values and assumptions. At one level, the FSM was about the way that intense personal experience overturned habit and challenged both participants and onlookers to explore new ideas, to change modes of living, and to remake politics. As with other movements in the 1960s, ranging from civil rights to the women's movement, the personal was political.[3]

These simultaneous individual explosions, akin to those in a religious revival, yielded a collective search for community. Shaken by events that mocked traditional values and conventional worldviews, participants sought out others who shared their experience. Establishing a "community of the beloved" became an important political goal. The era's radical politics, whether in the streets or at the ballot box, has to be understood in terms of this desire.[4] However, because the initial moment of change was personal, emotional, and psychological rather than rational or ideological, the basis for a common enterprise proved to be vague and often difficult to articulate.

Cultural values, personal experiences, and communitarian needs shaped Berkeley's emerging radical politics. In October 1965 veterans of the FSM and others active in the Vietnam Day Committee (VDC) helped lead one of America's first large anti–Vietnam War marches. The march went well in Berkeley, but it ran into trouble in neighboring Oakland, which stationed hundreds of police, under the direction of Assistant District Attorney Edwin Meese, to stop the demonstrators. Meese was already familiar to the protesters. On the night of the final FSM sit-in he had told Governor Pat Brown, erroneously, that protesters had broken into a University office. This report had convinced Brown to authorize the arrests, which Meese then directed. He also served as liaison with the FBI. Although the VDC march proved that radicals enjoyed power in Berkeley's streets, it also showed that conservatives controlled the county government, including police and security agencies. The VDC responded by mounting an electoral challenge.[5]

When Robert Scheer ran for Congress in 1966, he was already well-known as a leader of the VDC. This was the first time Berkeley radicals tried to elect one of their own number to high office. Scheer, age twenty-nine, who had once worked in Lawrence Ferlinghetti's City Lights bookstore and who had grown a beard in honor of Castro after visiting Cuba, tapped the large community of activists from the FSM and VDC. A democratic socialist, he ran in the Democratic Party primary hoping to defeat the incumbent congressman, Jeffery Cohelan, who generally defended the Johnson administration's Vietnam policies.[6]

Scheer's effort expressed his antiwar sentiments in a larger, radical context. Scheer and other leftists in his campaign rejected both conventional liberal anti-Communism and the policy of containment. Viewing the war primarily as an imperialist venture, Scheer presented an analysis that was consistent both with a Marxist notion of the right of the Vietnamese to make a communist revolution and with a more pacifist vision that called for American military self-restraint or even isolationism.

Scheer had participated in Bay Area civil rights demonstrations, and, like many of those in the FSM, had been profoundly affected by the experience. The pacifist doctrine of nonviolence questioned all war, while the black demand for rights both drew attention to the issue of human rights globally and caused a profound shift away from large-scale politics focused on the nation-state to matters involving individual suffering at the community level. In this new conception, politics was not to be imposed from the top down but was to rise from the bottom up. This change, along with the belief that politics had to be morally based, marked the core of the new radical sensibility.

Scheer's campaign slogan, "Peace and Freedom," suggested that only peace would enable the country to end poverty and the racism that accompanied it. Radicals like Scheer and his campaign associates advocated massive public expenditures far beyond Lyndon Johnson's Great Society, although they often disagreed on whether existing liberal structures should be reinforced or society should be reorganized on a socialist basis. They could not agree on a fundamental approach because the search for a spiritually driven community of the beloved was not a rigid political program. Rather, it was a work in progress, open to experimentation and subject to change. At the center was an open heart, compassion for the unfortunate, sensitivity to the other, and the desire to heal the wounds of racism.

The reconceptualization of politics as a locally constructed moral imperative led directly to new political methods consistent with that ideal. In a pattern copied by Eugene McCarthy and Robert Kennedy in 1968, Scheer used more than a thousand fervent supporters to organize voters precinct by precinct. In the long run, this careful attention to the grass roots was to pay handsomely for Berkeley's progressives. Numerous radical-sponsored community meetings, some broadcast on KPFA, encouraged mass political interest, which the New Left heralded as participatory democracy. The Civil Rights Movement and the FSM had also stressed mass involvement.

Scheer's campaign, unlike media-driven politics, cost little, depended heavily on volunteers, engaged residents in meaty dialogues with the candidate, and connected strongly with voters. Because Scheer and his white supporters had worked for civil rights, he was able to form a biracial coalition with African Americans in Berkeley (and to a lesser extent in Oakland). On primary election day, he carried Berkeley but lost the district because his campaign lacked enough volunteers to penetrate Oakland. White precincts there favored Cohelan, while turnout in that city's black precincts was low. The absence of an activist community in Oakland or, indeed, in most other noncollege settings signaled the limitations that radicals faced as they tried to extend their politics outside Berkeley, Madison, Wisconsin, and other college towns. More than most radicals admitted, success depended upon the ability to field large numbers of educated, articulate, and dedicated volunteers for direct, personal contact with voters.[7]

In 1967 many of the activists who had backed Scheer supported Ron Dellums's campaign for the Berkeley city council. In those days Berkeley held at-large elections for the council, and the combination of black votes and radical white votes, many drawn from precincts near campus where students and other young people lived, elected Dellums. African Americans were then about a quarter of the city's electorate (few ethnic Asians or Hispanics lived in Berkeley at the time). Then in 1970 the antiwar Dellums, who as an African American excited black voters in a way that Scheer had not, defeated Cohelan in the Democratic primary and then became the first black candidate elected to the House of Representatives by a mostly white district. By 1970 the war's growing unpopularity enabled radicals to bring more and more disaffected antiwar liberals into their biracial coalition. The bitter liberal split over the war was an important ingredient in creating a new left-liberal majority in Berkeley.[8]

In 1971 radicals in Berkeley elected a mayor and three council members. Their victory was largely due to superb organization and to the eighteen-year-old vote, established by the Twenty-Sixth Amendment. Twenty thousand young noncollege whites, many of them hippies, now lived in Berkeley. Also important were issues that Jerry Rubin had first raised to attract young voters in a losing campaign for mayor in 1967 when he had called for legal marijuana, rent control, and parks. The victors in 1971 included three African Americans, two of whom had civil rights backgrounds. The fourth was Loni Hancock, a former peace activist drawn into electoral politics after learning that the city planned to demolish her daughter's day care center.[9]

Radicals captured Berkeley, but conservatives won California. When Reagan ran for governor in 1966, he made the "mess" in Berkeley a central campaign theme. He got expert advice from Edwin Meese, who used his security ties to coach the candidate. At a press conference Reagan waved in his hand a "secret" security report. He claimed that it revealed that the University had condoned a VDC-sponsored dance on campus at which strobe lights projected pictures of nude bodies while students gyrated in shocking positions amid clouds of marijuana smoke. Declaring the material too obscene to be quoted, Reagan conflated radicalism and the counterculture, condemned both as immoral and abnormal, blamed the University, and thereby created an effective conservative moral issue.[10]

Reagan won in a landslide and, to prove that he was serious about changing Berkeley, encouraged the Regents to fire President Kerr. Meese became Reagan's chief of staff and helped the new governor confront Berkeley's radicals. In a method that recalled fifties anti-Communism, Reagan also obtained security information through Professor Hardin Jones, a staunch conservative and personal friend whose lab used federal science funds to monitor radicals. Jones investigated organizations on campus, attended meetings, took notes, sometimes used a tape recorder hidden under his coat, and frequently shot and developed photographs of radicals. He also maintained a massive newspaper clipping file and hired student and nonstudent informers.[11]

Reagan was not the only one concerned about Berkeley radicals. After the FSM started, the FBI stationed two full-time agents on campus. Both University officials and the city police "Red Squad" attended radical meetings, and the police often took photographs. Surveillance could easily turn into sabotage. A former CIA employee stationed in San Jose later confessed to more than forty antiradical burglaries in the Bay Area, including one at the *Ramparts* magazine office in San Francisco. Such break-ins increased fear and disoriented the victims. In 1966, after a dynamite bomb destroyed the VDC's Berkeley headquarters, embittered VDC leaders responded with a self-destructive campaign of street violence.[12]

Even after Meese joined the Reagan team in Sacramento, he continued to show unusual interest in Berkeley. In fall 1968 he led the raid on campus demonstrators who had barricaded themselves inside Moses Hall. Although no one was injured, considerable property was destroyed. Radicals charged that the police had damaged the building after removing the protesters. In May 1969 Meese took an active role in the battle over People's Park. On the day that James Rector was fatally shot in that conflict, Meese was spotted in Berkeley wearing a gas mask. The mask suggested that he expected trouble or, as some radicals believed, that he had planned it. Years later

Sheriff Frank Madigan said that the police shootings had not been his idea and that events that day had been directed from "higher up." He declined to elaborate, but on the fateful day in Berkeley no one outranked Reagan's chief of staff.[13]

Because young people felt committed to peace, life, the earth, and small-scale, self-directed communities, they favored People's Park against opposition from the University bureaucracy, state government, police, and the National Guard. At a deeper level, some radicals sought revolution, while conservatives were eager to crush Berkeley activists once and for all. Local elected officials, including the radical Ron Dellums, held a precarious position. University administrators were also caught in the middle. For years Hardin Jones, along with his friend and Reagan-appointed Regent John Lawrence, had waged a furtive campaign to have Berkeley chancellor Roger Heyns, who was too liberal to their liking, fired. The People's Park episode and Reagan's refusal to compromise over the park can be seen as a cynical attempt by Reagan, Meese, Lawrence, and Jones to destroy Heyns and gain conservative control over the University. Heyns and Dellums survived, but conservatives knew that People's Park gave them an enormous advantage statewide.[14]

It would be tempting to conclude that both radicals and conservatives gained from the FSM, from the VDC marches, and from People's Park. These various controversies, especially when they were mishandled by authorities, as they often were, fed radical growth in Berkeley. Progressive electoral activity began in the aftermath of the FSM, although triumph came after, not before, People's Park. The same events, however, viewed from *outside* Berkeley, moved California voters to the right. For the statewide majority, morally based politics meant traditional conservative values, not the beloved community. In a distinctly uneven outcome, electoral radicals won Berkeley, but conservatives took California and eventually, with Reagan's election to the presidency, the nation. Ed Meese became the U.S. attorney general, an office far more powerful than any held by a Berkeley radical. Progressive values and methods that worked in Berkeley generally failed elsewhere. Although radicals never succeeded in organizing much beyond their youthful, idealistic base, few noticed how conservatives and security agencies manipulated events, including protests, for their own benefit, and one wonders to what extent conservative power was created and maintained by surreptitious means.

NOTES

1. The politics may be followed in Harriet Nathan and Stanley Scott, eds., *Experiment and Change in Berkeley* (Berkeley: Institute of Government Studies, University of California, 1978); and W. J. Rorabaugh, *Berkeley at War* (New York: Oxford University Press, 1989).

2. On KPFA see Matthew Lasar, *Pacifica Radio* (Philadelphia: Temple University Press, 1999). The song is from [FSM], *Free Speech Songbook* (Berkeley: S.N., 1964), 17, copy in Free Speech Movement records, CU-309, University Archives, Bancroft Library, University of California at Berkeley. On the Peace Corps see Rorabaugh, 8; on Cold War weariness, ibid., 87–123; on civil rights, ibid., 71–74.

3. On the FSM as an epiphany see David Lance Goines, *The Free Speech Movement: Coming of Age in the 1960s* (Berkeley: Ten Speed Press, 1993), 137–40; Michael Rossman, "Twenty Years Later," *Express*, 28 Sept. 1984, 1ff; Loni Hancock quoted in Nathan and Scott, 366–67. Numerous testimonials are in Mark Kitchell's film, *Berkeley in the Sixties* (New York: First Run Features, 1990). See also Sara Evans, *Personal Politics: The Roots of Women's Liberation in the Civil Rights Movement and the New Left* (New York: Vintage Books, 1979); and James J. Farrell, *The Spirit of the Sixties: The Making of Postwar Radicalism* (New York: Routledge, 1997).

4. An insightful overview is Wini Breines, *Community and Organization in the New Left, 1962–1968: The Great Refusal* (New Brunswick, N.J.: Rutgers University Press, 1982). See also Robert S. Ellwood, *The Sixties Spiritual Awakening* (New Brunswick, N.J.: Rutgers University Press, 1994); and Douglas C. Rossinow, *The Politics of Authenticity: Liberals, Christians, and the New Left in America* (New York: Columbia University Press, 1998).

5. On Meese and the VDC see Rorabaugh, 96–97; on Meese and the sit-in, see *Berkeley Daily Gazette*, 3 May 1965; *Daily Californian* (hereafter *DC*), 4 May 1965; *San Francisco Examiner*, 4 May 1965; *The Defender: Free Speech Trial Newsletter*, 18 Apr. 1965, 3, 5, 6 (a copy is preserved in Free Speech Movement records, box 4). On Meese and Brown see Lou Cannon, *Ronnie and Jesse* (Garden City, N.Y.: Doubleday, 1969), 301; *San Francisco Bay Guardian*, 4 Apr. 1984, 9; *San Francisco Sunday Examiner-Chronicle*, 22 June 1986, "This World" section, 7. See also Gerard J. De Groot, "Ronald Reagan and Student Unrest in California, 1966–1970," *Pacific Historical Review* 65 (Feb. 1996): 107–29.

6. This paragraph and those that follow draw on Serge Lang, *The Scheer Campaign* (New York: W. A. Benjamin, 1967). In 1968 Scheer, Hancock, and other radicals founded the Peace and Freedom Party. On Peace and Freedom, see Rorabaugh, 83, 110–11.

7. On Madison see Paul Buhle, ed., *History and the New Left* (Philadelphia: Temple University Press, 1990). Other case studies are in Pierre Clavel, *The Progressive City: Planning and Participation, 1969–1984* (New Brunswick, N.J.: Rutgers University Press, 1986).

8. On the 1967 election see Rorabaugh, 110–13; on the liberal split, ibid., 111.

9. On the 1971 election see ibid., 166, 176; on Rubin, ibid., 112; on Hancock, ibid., 154–55, 166. The daughter of the New York activist Rev. Donald Harrington, Hancock was elected mayor in 1986. On the 1970s see Joseph P. Lyford, *The Berkeley Archipelago* (Chicago: Regnery Press, 1982).

10. An extract from the press conference is in the film *Berkeley in the Sixties*. On the dance see California Senate Fact-Finding Committee on Un-American Activities, *Thirteenth Report Supplement* (Sacramento, 1966), 133; *Berkeley Barb*, 25 Mar. 1966, 8; *Oakland Tribune*, 12 Apr. 1966; *Sunday Ramparts*, 6 Nov. 1966, 1.

11. On firing Kerr, see Alex C. Sherriffs, "The University of California and the Free Speech Movement: Perspectives from a Faculty Member and an Administrator," oral history conducted in 1978 by James H. Rowland, Regional Oral History

Office, Bancroft Library, University of California at Berkeley, 1980, 74; Hardin B. Jones to Edwin Pauley, Aug. 21, 1966, box 40, Jones Papers, Hoover Institution, Stanford, California. On Jones see Elinor Heller, "A Volunteer Career in Politics in Higher Education, and on Governing Boards," an oral history transcript, Berkeley, Calif., University of California, 1984 (available in Bancroft Library, 3:562a–562b). Jones's lab was funded with a rare direct grant, without peer review, from the Atomic Energy Commission. Jones's assistant, Alexander Grendon, was a retired U.S. Air Force intelligence officer who had no science background. Their activities monitoring radical meetings can be followed in notes and tape transcripts in the Jones Papers (e.g., Jones notes, 2 Dec. 1965, box 2; notes [ca. Feb. 1967], box 40; Jones memo, 20 Nov. 1967, box 45; Grendon notes, 7 July, 16 Sept., 4 Nov. 1965, box 60; Campus Draft Opposition transcripts, 1968, box 23; meeting transcript, 24 Apr. 1968, box 4). See also the paid informant Walter Hucul to Jones, 5 Feb., 30 May 1968, box 4. (Hucul was a former Berkeley graduate student who had received a Ph.D. there in Russian history. His targets included Reginald Zelnik.)

12. On the FBI agents see Frederick L. Terman memo of Sterling-Strong conversation, n.d. [before Jan. 1965], section III, box 57, folder 2, Terman Papers, Stanford University Archives. Police reports are in the chancellor's and president's files, both at Bancroft Library, University of California at Berkeley. Photographs in the Edmund G. Brown, Sr., Papers have since been transferred to the Bancroft's photographic collection. The CIA burglar is discussed in Frank J. Donner, *The Age of Surveillance* (New York: Vintage, 1980), 437; on the VDC bomb, see ibid., 145, 435–40.

13. On Moses Hall see Rorabaugh, 84, 219 n89; on People's Park see ibid., 162, 251 n87.

14. On John Lawrence see his papers, Hoover Institution.

Mario Savio's Second Act

The 1990s

Jonah Raskin

Sixties radicals have rarely been allowed second acts on the stage of American history and almost never on the obituary pages of the national press. Mario Savio was no exception. Predictably, Savio's obituaries—in the *New York Times, Los Angeles Times*, and *Washington Post*—emphasized his dramatic role during the Free Speech Movement of the sixties and ignored his complex and impassioned though less flamboyant life afterward. Savio himself, had he written his own obituary, might well have highlighted his career at Sonoma State University (SSU), where he taught as an untenured lecturer from 1990 to 1996 and where he was reborn an older and perhaps wiser campus radical. Certainly students and teachers at SSU felt that Savio's life there in the nineties deserved far more than a footnote in history.

Had his classmates at Berkeley in 1964 told Savio that he would be teaching at SSU in the nineties, he no doubt would have shaken his head in disbelief. Ever since it was founded in 1960, SSU has belonged to a strikingly different world than UC Berkeley, though only an hour separates them by car. Far smaller and far more insular than UC Berkeley, SSU has never been an academic powerhouse. The student body at SSU—unlike the diverse student body at Berkeley or at San Francisco State University—was and still is predominantly white (nearly 75 percent). During Savio's six years at SSU, the campus became increasingly homogenous—African American enrollment declined sharply—and the administration defined SSU as an elite campus—"the public ivy," in the words of Ruben Armiñana, president of the University. These developments were antithetical to Savio's vision of the California State University as a tuition-free institution accessible to all. In large part, the social transformation of the student body contributed to his decision, midway through his career at SSU, to become a major player again on the political stage.

In the early seventies, SSU boasted a vocal antiwar movement. Later in the decade, campus feminists rocked the academic boat. By 1990, however, students were on the whole apathetic if not cynical about causes and movements, and that mood too troubled Savio. Sadly, he noted that whole pages from the history of protest, especially the history of the Civil Rights Movement, had been lost to at least two generations of American college students.

Unlike the largely apolitical undergraduates, a hefty segment of the faculty had a history of radical activity that went back to the sixties. For decades before Savio's arrival in 1990, SSU had provided from time to time a sanctuary of sorts to blacklisted teachers, or teachers who had been on the barricades so often they were unable to find steady work on college campuses. Savio quickly found himself at home here, and especially in the ranks of the California Faculty Association, the faculty union, where he became an advocate for the rights of untenured lecturers.

Of course most faculty members knew Savio by name and reputation, if not by sight. Some professors couldn't quite believe that the lanky, white-haired instructor they saw striding across campus with books under his arms was the same person as the youthful protester they remembered from the sixties. "Are you *the* Mario Savio?" he was frequently asked. Bemusedly he would reply, "Well, someone has to be." What most of his colleagues didn't know and what Savio rarely if ever discussed was the life he had led after the FSM. Savio himself created the impression that he had been on the political sidelines for years. Accordingly, many colleagues and administrators, including President Armiñana, regarded him as a man of mystery who had returned as though from exile or the underground.

Initially Savio was hired to teach remedial mathematics (University 39) in the Intensive Learning Experience (ILE), a division of the University created to help students (largely from minority groups) who were inadequately prepared for basic college courses. Although he had taught mathematics at Urban High School in San Francisco in the mid-1980s and was a master of mathematical logic, he was not primarily a math teacher. After receiving a B.A. (1984) and then an M.S. in physics (1989)—both degrees from San Francisco State University—he had taught physics at SFSU and at Modesto Junior College.

Elaine Sundberg, the director of the ILE, hired Savio in part because he came highly recommended and in part because he had been the leader of the FSM. "As a high school student in 1964, I read about Mario, and I wanted to join the protests at Berkeley," she said. "Curiously, when I received his résumé there was nothing at all about the FSM. When I got to know him I learned that he didn't want to be known for his past activities. He kept a very low profile when he first got to SSU. Then, somehow or other word got out that he was here, and there was a continual barrage of calls from the media, including *Parade* magazine, asking for interviews, but he turned them all down."

Savio's desire to maintain a low profile was understandable. Granted, he had a great many friends who respected and even revered him. But there were also citizens who reviled him for his role during the FSM, and he was often reminded of the hostility he had once engendered. Soon after he began to teach at SSU, he encountered Gene Benedetti, a trustee of the University, who told him, "I hated you in the sixties," a comment that distressed him. Unwilling to become a target of derision or to provoke the trustees, he literally watched what he said.

Still, it proved impossible for him to remain silent for long. In the spring 1991 semester, he emerged, albeit tentatively, from his self-created cocoon. The catalyst for his return to action was one of his own math students, an indignant African American woman who showed him a two-page collage in the *Star*, the campus newspaper, that was composed of headlines from previous issues. One headline—"The Student as Nigger"—seemed to scream out. Originally published in 1967, it had been accompanied by an article that described the University as a plantation and undergraduates as slaves in the educational system. Savio was, of course, familiar with the provocative phrase "the student as nigger." He had read the Jerry Farber book that popularized it, and indeed as a sixties radical he had criticized the idea of the university as a factory for the mass production of docile workers for American corporations.

For Savio's students, the sixties were ancient history. Unfamiliar with Farber's book and unaware of the context in which the phrase "the student as nigger" had been used decades earlier, African American students were livid. The word *nigger* had been hurled at them on campus and in the surrounding community, they explained to Savio, and the publication of the epithet in the pages of the campus newspaper, as one student put it, felt "like the lash of a whip across our collective face."

In the midst of the racial controversy that developed, I met Savio face-to-face for the first time one afternoon in the cramped quarters of the *Star*. I remember feeling pleasantly surprised. As a sixties radical with a legacy of my own, I was delighted to have company from that era of protest, and over the next few years we would often compare notes about our experiences on picket lines and at meetings. In the spring of 1991, as chairman of the communication studies department, which provided an academic home for the newspaper, I found myself in the midst of a volatile situation. The African American students had poured into the newspaper office to express their anger and frustration, only to find the student reporters and editors and the faculty adviser, Andrea Granahan, unsympathetic and intransigent.

While the all-white staff of the newspaper invoked the First Amendment, the all-black contingent of protesters insisted that they had the right to work and study in an environment uncontaminated by racist remarks. As Savio and I knew, similar conflicts had taken place on campuses across the country in the eighties. Universities had created speech codes to regulate what could and could not be said, and the courts had consistently declared them unconstitutional. Neither Savio nor I was anxious to see the matter that was before us in court. What we wanted was learning about racial issues and the responsibility of the media, and though we tried to make our case, no one seemed to be listening.

As Savio explained in the office of the *Star,* "I don't see why reporters and students can't sit down together to discuss the issues. This isn't about censorship. It's about dialogue." Granahan, the faculty adviser—who was also the editor and publisher of a local weekly newspaper—expressed the fear that Savio meant to muzzle the *Star.* On her own initiative, she phoned the *Press Democrat,* the leading newspaper in Sonoma County, and explained that she had a hot news story: the former leader of the FSM, she said, was now against freedom of speech. Savio himself refused to be interviewed, and with only Granahan and the editor of the *Star* as sources, the reporter wrote a story that characterized Savio as an ideological turncoat who had made a radical passage "from free speech to censorship."[1]

Given his misgivings about the mass media and the blatant misreporting about him in the *Press Democrat,* it is not surprising that Savio rededicated himself to teaching remedial math. In the fall 1991 semester and for the entire 1992 academic year, he continued to work at the ILE and to remain quiet about campus issues. Then, in the spring of 1993, friends in the philosophy department persuaded him, after nearly a year of discussion, to give a public accounting of himself. On April 20, 1993, the Philosophy Department Club sponsored a talk entitled "The Philosophy of a Young Activist," in which Savio, for the first time on campus, talked openly about his past. His remarks were, in his own words, "shamelessly autobiographical," and indeed he seemed to feel a sense of embarrassment talking candidly about his own life in the sixties. The audience was made up of faculty members and undergraduates, some of them reentry students in their forties and fifties who were anxious to learn what had become of the Mario Savio they had known and admired.

Perhaps the highlight of Savio's talk was his admission that he was trying to create "distance on the historical figure Mario Savio." To symbolize the gap between who he had been and who he was striving to become, he explained, he had inserted the letter *E* (for Elliot) in his name. He was now Mario E. Savio, he said, and indeed, on his résumé and his course syllabi that is how he identified himself. Of course leaving his sixties legacy behind and creating a new identity at SSU proved to be a lot more difficult then simply inserting a letter between his first and last names, but he worked at it consistently.

What many of us found endearing about his talk to the Philosophy Department Club was his willingness to open up, to "confess" as more than one listener described it. In fact, there were hefty servings of candid self-criticism. As a student at Berkeley he had been "earnest but a snob," he said. As much as anything else—in the irreverent sixties—he had enjoyed the spectacle of watching administrators, like UC Berkeley president Clark Kerr, "hoisted by their own petards." Then, too, he admitted, he had experienced a "real problem moving from the FSM to antiwar action, in part because Vietnam seemed so far away." On the subject of philosophy and political action, he told the audience that early in life, he had adopted Immanuel Kant's categorical imperative as his moral yardstick. "You always treat humanity as an end and never as a means to an end," he explained. "And you act, not because you *want* to act, but because you *ought* to act."

The April 1993 talk proved to be a turning point for Savio. Beginning in August 1993, he moved out of the ILE's "academic ghetto," as African American students described it, and into the Hutchins School of Liberal Studies, an interdisciplinary college within the university that offered intellectually stimulating classes. In this creative atmosphere, Savio blossomed as an innovative teacher.

Professor Les Adler, a graduate of UC Berkeley and the provost of the Hutchins School, hired Savio and encouraged him to devise his own experimental courses. "Mario was fascinated by the two cultures," poetry and physics, said Adler. "He saw the possibility of building bridges between them and, of course, he knew both physics and poetry and he was ideally suited to teach courses that combined the two fields." Beginning in the fall 1993 semester, Savio threw himself passionately into teaching two classes he created specifically for the Hutchins School: "Discovery of Time" and "Science and Poetry," probably his favorite class because it allowed him "to synthesize the scientific and the poetical sides of himself." Science and Poetry also allowed him to teach his favorite authors, among them Galileo and T. S. Eliot, especially Eliot's passionate and philosophical poem "The Four Quartets." For the most part, students raved about Savio as a teacher, though there were grumblings here and there. "At times, it was difficult for students to restrain him and get a word in edgewise," Adler said. "But whenever he began to take over, students would remind him that it was a seminar not a lecture, and he would sit back and allow them to present their own ideas."

Catharyn Hatcher-England, a student in Science and Poetry, observed that "Mario's love of the subject and his ability to express himself both intellectually and emotionally was wonderful to experience as a student." And, she added, "I will never forget him reading in Italian the poetry we were discussing one day and his openly weeping at the beauty of the words." Mette Adams, another student in the class, noted, "Mario inspired me to learn. He enabled me to see the beauty and the accessibility of the language of science. Because of his class I came to realize that scientific writing doesn't have to be obscure or dull. It can be as inspiring as poetry."

In the spring of 1994, Savio continued to teach in the Hutchins School, and at the same time he began to teach two classes in the philosophy department, "Introduction to Logic" and "Critical Thinking," which was required for all undergraduates. Savio wasn't the only faculty member at SSU who moved from one academic department to another, but no one seemed to move from department to department as gracefully or as passionately as he did.

As one might have expected, he had his closest colleagues in the philosophy department: David Averbuck, Roger Bell (an undergraduate at Berkeley in 1964), Philip Clayton, Edward Mooney, Dianne Romain, and Joel Rudinow. Savio had been, after all, a philosophy major at Berkeley; moreover, it was metaphysics, not physics, that awakened his deepest intellectual passions. "We were on the same page," Professor Mooney explained. "We had read the same books and thought about the same philosophical questions, and we spoke the same philosophical language."

David Averbuck, a lecturer in the department, had met Savio for the first time at Melvin Belli's law office in San Francisco following the 1964 Sproul Hall arrests. Three decades later, they renewed their friendship and spent hours talking passionately about perennial philosophical topics: uncertainty, time, causality. "Mario was trying to construct a new approach to logic," Averbuck said. "He didn't like syllogisms that did not allow for ambiguity, and he was creating his own theory of the syllogism that allowed for the unknown."

Savio also developed an intense intellectual and personal relationship with Professor Philip Clayton, the chairman of the philosophy department. "Mario was preoccupied with metaphysical questions about the nature of good and evil," Clayton said. "He reminded us that philosophy was the pursuit of wisdom. I was in awe of him and also occasionally puzzled because in private he seemed insecure and even self-deprecating. Rehearsing for a lecture or a speech, he would struggle awkwardly not only to find the right words but to discover what he wanted to say. Then, when he performed before an audience, he was not only self-confident but eloquent."

At the same time that he was in the thick of intellectual activity, Savio became increasingly involved in political action. Indeed, he seemed to find his stride again at long last, and not simply or only in the public arena. He and his wife, Lynne Hollander, bought a house in Sebastopol—"Berkeley North," he called it—and ventured far beyond Sebastopol, too, traveling to Italy for an exhilarating vacation. Moreover, Savio was enjoying his relationships with his sons Daniel and Nadav, both of whom, he was proud to report, were radicals. "The fruit falls not far from the tree," he would say. "Thank God!"

Before he arrived at SSU, Savio had appeared at rallies and had spoken out about controversial issues. In the eighties, he had denounced President Reagan's foreign policy in Central America and the system of apartheid that existed in South Africa. Then, in the mid-nineties, he became more vocal in his condemnation of the rise of the religious right and the revival of conservatism. On the thirtieth anniversary of the FSM he blasted the election of the "barbarians"—as he called them—including Newt Gingrich.

To those who heard Savio, it was clear that the old fire was in his belly once more. Edward Mooney—who first heard him speak in 1964—described a vivid moment at SSU when he addressed his colleagues: "His delivery became intense and his arms began to move in that way of his familiar to Sproul spectators. He seemed to be in a spell—no longer the shy instructor but an orator fully in command of the multiple depths of his topic, and his passion fully alive to those transfixed before him."

In 1993 Savio was delighted when President Clinton nominated University of Pennsylvania law professor Lani Guinier to serve as assistant attorney general for civil rights, and he was then quickly disappointed when the president withdrew his nomination in the wake of conservative attacks on Guinier as "the quota queen." Even more disturbing to him were developments in his own political backyard. At the polls California voters approved Proposition 187, which denied education and health benefits to undocumented workers, and Proposition 209, which called for the end of affirmative action. "It looks like almost everything that the civil rights and the women's movements achieved over the past 35 years may be undermined," he said. Outraged by the "counterrevolution," he began to take part in a series of statewide campaigns with three important goals: to protect the civil rights of women and minority groups, to guarantee a free college education for all citizens, and to work toward a society based on social justice.

In 1995 he played a major part in building the Campus Coalitions for Human Rights and Social Justice, a northern California organization of women and men from diverse ethnic backgrounds that was committed to "an end to the disgrace of a massive 'underclass' in a land of such phenomenal wealth and promise."[2] With his son Nadav he wrote an impassioned political pamphlet, *In Defense of Affirmative Action,* that argued that California was at a "crossroads" and that citizens would have to choose between two clear paths: "One leads to a society whose people are healthy, well-educated and gainfully employed; the other to a society whose men and women, whose ethnic and racial groups are trapped in endless struggle."[3]

Savio intensified his political activity in Sonoma County. He walked picket lines with health workers at Santa Rosa's Kaiser Permanente Hospital who were protesting reductions in health care services, and he marched with members of the United Farm Workers seeking attention for the plight of agricultural laborers. At the annual American Civil Liberties

Union dinner, which was held in Sebastopol in 1995, he explained that he had not voted in the 1994 elections and that his son Daniel had challenged him to "do something" to stem the reactionary tide. To the *Press Democrat,* he said, "I have been pretty much quiet, but I feel that we are moving toward another moment in history in which people will have to take sides." And he added, "I don't want my children to ask me what the hell I was doing teaching logic courses when all this was going on."[4]

Perhaps Savio's most intense battle in the mid-nineties was waged on the campus of SSU, where President Armiñana urged students to approve a referendum that would have required them to pay an additional $300 a year in fees. If the fee increase was approved, Savio argued, SSU would become financially prohibitive for students from minority and working-class families, and the University would turn into an exclusive enclave for the sons and the daughters of the white middle classes. Clearly, he made a powerful personal identification with minorities. "I'm not white," he would say. "I'm Italian American." It was one of his most endearing one-liners.

In 1996, the last year of his life, Savio engaged in a series of seemingly unending battles at SSU that gave him a tremendous sense of joy. "I haven't had this much fun since the sixties," he told Mette Adams, a student in his Science and Poetry class and a campus activist who was inspired by his moral integrity. "Mario changed my life," Adams said. "He had an intense desire to create a just world in which all people could thrive, and that desire was contagious."

Savio's battles surely jeopardized his health. Though he had long been diagnosed with a congenital heart condition, he pushed himself to the limit, and it showed. When Adams told Savio that he appeared to be physically exhausted from the battle against the $300 fee increase, he explained, "I only have two speeds: zero and one hundred." When David Averbuck said, "You take things too much to heart; it's going to kill you," he replied tersely, "I know." In fact, he was working overtime and at twice his normal speed. Many of his colleagues urged him not to make the fee increase a do-or-die issue, but he insisted on going ahead full steam.

During the debate about the fee increase, Savio argued that SSU administrators had monopolized the channels of communication and were disseminating one-sided, if not misleading, information. "Mario thought that the administration was trying to control political debate in much the same way that the elites in Mississippi controlled debate before blacks won the right to vote," Elaine Sundberg said. Fueled by his outrage, he spoke against the fee everywhere on campus. "We need open, fair and objective discussion before this comes to a vote," he said. And he noted that while the administrators in favor of the fee increase were "good people," he added that "sometimes even good people do bad things," a remark that didn't win him new friends or allies.

On Friday, November 1, 1996, he took part in a bitter, drawn-out debate with President Armiñana that was witnessed by a handful of faculty members and a few dozen students. For years Armiñana had gone out of his way to be on good terms with Savio and to avoid following in Clark Kerr's footsteps. (Armiñana aptly described Savio as "Clark Kerr's nemesis.") Then, too, Savio had gone out of his way to be on good terms with Armiñana; there were meetings in Armiñana's office and genuine cordiality. Consistently, Savio avoided the confrontational relationship that had developed with Kerr. But now that pattern changed: Savio and Armiñana were locked in public, political combat that neither of them apparently wanted.

Listening to Savio speak against the fee increase, it seemed clear to me, though not to everyone, that he had pushed himself to the edge and that there was little if any chance of his coming back to a more balanced position. He himself was unhappy with his confrontational style and volatile temper, which he felt had gotten the best of him. "He recognized what he felt were some of the less attractive parts of his personality, and he didn't like them," Elaine Sundberg said. Accordingly, he wrote and delivered a letter of resignation to Professor Adler, provost of the Hutchins School, in which he explained that he planned to leave SSU. To Mette Adams he remarked, "When you spend more time fighting the administration than you do on teaching, it's time to go."

On Saturday, November 2, the day following his debate with Armiñana, he began to draft a document that indicted the University for failing to abide by legal procedures concerning the fee referendum. Before he could finish writing, he suffered a heart seizure, then went into a coma, and never regained consciousness. Four days later Lynne Hollander gave doctors at Palm Drive Hospital permission to disconnect her husband from his life support system, and Mario Savio died on November 6, 1996, one month short of his fifty-fourth birthday. That December, a memorial service on the SSU campus paid homage to Savio as "husband, father, son, teacher, friend, mentor, activist, colleague." The Free Speech Movement was barely mentioned, though it surely was on everyone's mind. "Mario was raised a Catholic," Lynne Hollander said. "He felt the one moral principle he took from his religious education was this: resist evil. He had no conviction that we would prevail, but he said that we have to be prepared to struggle even if we do not know we are going to win."

After his death Savio continued to be a moral presence on campus. In 1997 the $300 fee increase was defeated, in large part because of his individual effort. And in 1999, when the faculty engaged in a protracted battle with the administration for a new contract, Savio served as the guiding spirit. At rallies, meetings, and picket lines his name was often invoked. "Don't mourn for Mario, organize!" was a cry I often heard. Elaine Sundberg maintained the Mario Savio Memorial Bulletin Board and kept the campus informed of local issues and radical causes. Each year, the local branch of the ACLU offers the Mario Savio Student Activist Award, which has encouraged young people to work for social justice. Savio's supporters urged SSU to create a Mario Savio Free Speech Area on campus, but administrators balked at the idea; even in death he was controversial.

Obviously, Savio enjoyed a lively second act at SSU. Indeed, he fought tenaciously for a second act, and that act reverberated with a sense of integrity and dignity. Still, it seems fair though difficult to say that what Savio said and did at SSU did not match historically what he said and did at Berkeley. There was no gesture as dramatic as climbing on top of a police car or trying to speak from the podium at the Greek Theater. There was no arrest at SSU and no single speech as powerful as the speech in which he said, "There is a time when the operation of the machine becomes so odious, makes you so sick at heart, you can't take part"—though he felt much the same way in the mid-nineties. Moreover, by 1999 the Campus Coalitions for Human Rights and Social Justice, the organization he helped to build and for which he had such high hopes, ceased to exist on more than paper, though the issues of human rights and social justice obviously had not disappeared.

Many of Savio's SSU friends felt that he'd become a fuller, wiser person in the nineties. "He certainly aged well," Averbuck said. Others didn't see much point measuring Savio the young student against Savio the middle-aged teacher. "Who says Act II has to be bigger and better than Act I?" Elaine Sundberg wondered. For many of us Savio served as a living reminder that sixties activists had neither vanished into thin air nor blended cautiously into the corporate woodwork, as the mass media so often claimed.

At SSU we saw bits and pieces of Savio's many-sided personality. For Averbuck he was a "Jewish Catholic, a man with a rabbinical mind and a saintly heart." For Victor Garlin, the president of the SSU chapter of the California Faculty Association, he was a "dedicated, loyal union member." In an obituary I wrote for the *Press Democrat,* I described Savio as a moral crusader, a kind of Don Quixote.

Surprisingly, President Armiñana perceived as many sides of Savio as anyone else on campus. "Mario came out at SSU after being nearly invisible and in a state of self-imposed political exile," Armiñana observed of the man he had both battled and befriended. He continued:

> There was a big difference between the Mario I knew in private and the Mario who appeared in public. He was an outstanding teacher here, and he galvanized some students about civic responsibility. Anyone who thought that he was an anarchist didn't understand him. He was extremely disciplined in his thinking and highly responsible. He believed passionately in the law, and he was profoundly moral, perhaps even more moral than he himself recognized.

NOTES

A Note on Sources: In preparation for this essay I interviewed students in Savio's classes and students who took part in campus politics—Mette Adams, Catharyn Hatcher-England, Aaron Pava, and Dee Swanhuyser. I also interviewed Savio's colleagues—Les Adler, David Averbuck, Sterling Bennett, Philip Clayton, Victor Garlin, Benet Leigh, Edward Mooney, Dianne Romain, Elaine Sundberg, David Walls, and J.J. Wilson. SSU president Ruben Armiñana talked about his relationship with Savio. Judith Hunt, the associate vice president for university affairs, provided records of Savio's employment at SSU. The librarians at the *Press Democrat* in Santa Rosa provided the text of articles about Savio that appeared in the paper from 1991 to 1996. Lynne Hollander patiently answered questions. Mark Kitchell, the director of the documentary *Berkeley in the Sixties,* shared his recollections of Savio. Jaleah Winn served as a research assistant and fact checker. Notes from all of the interviews used in this essay are in the author's possession.

1. Bob Norberg, "SSU Instructor: From Free Speech to Censorship," *Press Democrat,* 2 May 1991, A1.

2. Campus Coalitions for Human Rights and Social Justice, "California at a Crossroads: Social Strife *or* Social Unity," Oakland, 1995, inside front cover.

3. Nadav Savio and Mario Savio, *In Defense of Affirmative Action: The Case Against Proposition 209* (Oakland: Campus Coalitions for Human Rights and Social Justice, 1996), 26.

4. Bleys W. Rose, "Free-Speech Figure Savio Breaks Silence: SSU Teacher Ready to Battle Conservative Wave," *Press Democrat,* 21 Feb. 1995, A1.

PART FIVE

Thoughts about Mario Savio

Mario Savio and the Politics of Authenticity

Doug Rossinow

I am not a political person. My involvement in the Free Speech Movement is religious and moral.
MARIO SAVIO, *1965*

UNUSUAL CHARISMA

Try though he did to prevent such an identification, the Free Speech Movement always comes back to Mario Savio. His effect on his contemporaries was powerful, and his face, voice, and words remain mesmerizing. He was a charismatic presence among the activists of 1964; his comrades testify movingly to his character. Michael Rossman attests to his "authenticity," a personal state or quality that young people in the 1960s esteemed highly.[1] Savio's is an elusive personality to the historian. It is not easy to integrate what we know of his public persona with what we read of his private self. His friends quickly draw contrasts between the two. Was his authenticity both a public and a private quality? What was the source and character of Savio's charisma, which seems largely to have been a public phenomenon? He undeniably had the capacity to move people, and authenticity and charisma are perhaps useful labels for the attributes that enabled him to do so. Before probing the meaning of these labels and the nature of these qualities, and considering what they tell us about the 1960s, we do well to clarify Savio's role in the FSM. We usually think, after all, of charismatic figures as undisputed leaders of movements that they gather around themselves. But the question of Savio's power and leadership was a vexing one for him. His was an unconventional charisma.

The FSM was impressive in its size and scale. Some fifty groups sent delegates to its Executive Committee, running the political gamut from Students for Goldwater to the Communist-led Du Bois Club. Perhaps over a thousand students occupied Sproul Hall on December 2–3, 1964, and almost eight hundred were arrested.[2] Such FSM mobilizations summoned hundreds of students for dramatic action, foreshadowing the mass movement of political youth whose force was felt across the country in the following years. The lingering image of this mass aspect of the FSM is the crowd of students who, for more than a night and a day surrounded a police car that held Jack Weinberg. However, in popular historical memory, documentary films, and history textbooks, that image of collective action competes for space with Savio's image and words just before the occupation of Sproul Hall, when he delivered his famous, brief speech. Savio's indelible statement about bodies, gears, and levers remains the quintessential expression of the FSM and of much that came in the years afterward. Mario became, as Bettina Aptheker says with some regret, "*the* icon of student activism."[3]

This apparently bothered Savio a good deal. According to Weinberg, "For Mario, media attention was troubling," and this was a matter of principle, not mere shyness. Barbara Garson recalls him "literally running (he had very long legs) away" from journalists who wanted interviews. Savio desperately wanted the general public to grasp that democracy and group leadership governed the FSM. What was Savio's true position within the FSM? In public he often looked like the movement's main spokesperson, and to some critics he appeared as a pied piper, leading more innocent students into hasty actions. If we look behind the scenes, the picture is murkier. Savio was a member of the Steering Committee, the real command center of the FSM. It usually had ten or twelve members, among whom no distinctions of office obtained.[4] According to comments from other members, Savio was not first among equals in this group's deliberations. Perhaps because all the committee's members understood this, Savio was at pains to make his humble status within the FSM elite clear to the press. In early 1965, amid the flush of analysis and debate that followed the final victory of the FSM, A. H. Raskin of the *New York Times* traveled to California to interview Savio and Clark Kerr, who were, Raskin thought, the two main antagonists in the drama just ended. Savio's "first words," Raskin recounted, were "a flat refusal to participate in any interview if I intended to focus on him as the communicator for the F.S.M. 'Anything like that will just perpetuate a misrepresentation that the press has already done too much to build up. . . . This is not a cult of one personality or of two personalities; it is a broadly based movement and I will not say anything unless it is made clear that the F.S.M. is not any single individual.'" The interview proceeded but with a group of seven "members of the collective leadership," including Savio. (Kerr, I assume, met alone with Raskin.)[5]

Savio wished to take the focus off himself. At least this was true outside the FSM's moments of public theater, as on the Sproul Hall steps or at Berkeley's Greek Theater on December 7, when his body was perhaps as effective as his voice could have been on its own. Campus policemen dragged him off stage as he tried to address the crowd, and reportedly this spectacle had a galvanizing effect on student and faculty opinion. Savio gravitated to the spotlight at such moments. His presence at scenes of confrontation had become important. What he really wished to do was to separate his leading role in these dramas from a perception that he was directing the FSM. He wrote little for public consumption. He rarely gave interviews, and as we have seen, he sometimes attached conditions when he did.

Still, Savio was in the spotlight, and so long as the FSM continued, he hardly could turn it off and on again at will. He scarcely could withdraw from the FSM before the basic questions of political freedom on campus were resolved, having done so much to push the movement forward, to inspire others to take militant, even illegal, action. But the FSM did not last through the spring 1965 semester, giving Savio the opportunity to withdraw gracefully from the public stage. And this, notwithstanding some brief return engagements in the following years, is exactly what he did. Some FSM activists went on to other fights: working for racial justice, organizing opposition to the Vietnam War, or building a student left. They and uncounted thousands like them roamed the country, living on nothing, sleeping in sympathetic homes, lending the activism of the 1960s its apostolic aspect. But Savio did not take this path. He went to prison for four months, with other FSM activists, when their negotiation of the criminal justice system turned out badly. For him, this time in jail was not a station on the way to further, deepening agitation, as it has been for so many radicals in the past. In later years he led a quiet, very private life. He occasionally resurfaced politically, speaking at the mammoth antiwar teach-in at Berkeley in May 1965 and running a half-hearted campaign for a seat in the California legislature (on the Peace and Freedom Party line).[6] But these were brief appearances, and Savio was never a major leader in protest activity beyond Berkeley's free speech fights.

Savio's comrades made this long retreat into privacy an integral part of his legend. In private, even during the FSM, Savio is said to have been astonishingly different from his public persona. His personal manner was not self-aggrandizing, as his melodramatic public style might suggest. Stew Albert calls him "extraordinarily modest." "He was not interested in personal power," says Aptheker. The difference most often noted between the public and private Savio pertains to his patterns of speech. In his youth Savio had a stammer. Friends still discerned this speech impediment in later years, but Savio stated in late 1964 that he had been able to overcome this handicap, surprisingly, through public speaking. He delivered the valedictory address at his high school graduation. "I stumbled on the first words and then the rest came out smooth; and then thereafter, over a period of a couple of years the stammer gradually disappeared. An unusual pattern." Fellow leaders of the FSM convey the impression of a person still not exactly fluent in private. Mark Shechner recalls, "People close to him in the movement would complain that Mario could be confused behind the scenes and spoke in sentences so intricate that nobody could unravel them." Barbara Garson goes far along these lines, recalling that during the FSM Savio's "mind was so childlike that we sometimes had to explain to him that when the march arrived at Point B it wouldn't still be at Point A."[7] Others disagree strongly with her characterization. Whatever was the case in private, in public his thought and speech became focused into a sharpness that was breathtaking to his friends and, one suspects, terrifying to his enemies.

The portrait that emerges from these remarks, of a person with a commanding public presence but who in private shrank naturally from authority, forms a second type of 1960s icon. It is the picture not of the students' hot-eyed spokesman but of the perfect democratic leader, beloved and respected but allergic to power, unafraid to show and perhaps unable to help showing his confusion and vulnerability to his comrades. He commands no one; he merely expresses the movement's will. The angry, eloquent Savio is the icon of public consumption, but the gentle, inarticulate Savio, in tandem with his public role, is an icon for 1960s activists imbued with the spirit of participatory democracy. Understood in this latter way, the discrepancy between persona and private self makes Savio an even more powerful figure, frustrating his and others' desire to downplay his celebrity. His flight from the public square is seen as the ultimate expression of his resistance against the lure of power and manipulation, and he thus becomes a moral exemplar. He becomes almost a white Bob Moses, a Moses for the white radicals of the 1960s.

OUTSIDERS AND INSIDERS

The Freedom Summer civil rights project that Moses helped to organize in the heart of violently racist Mississippi made a profound impression on young white participants like Savio. The Civil Rights Movement gave a strong boost to the notion that personal liberation and political emancipation were best pursued in tandem. Furthermore, many activists, including prominent FSMers, were radicalized by their time in the Deep South.[8] FSM leaders seemed to take back to Berkeley from the South a deeper sense of a malignant power at work in their society. Beneath the smiling surface of tolerant, permissive America, they appeared to think, even in a bastion of liberalism like Berkeley, there lurked a monstrous power, vicious when truly challenged. That the youthful rebellion on the campuses began with a battle against this University, headed by a liberal of national prominence, Clark Kerr, was an obvious irony of the FSM, noted continually by observers. But FSM leaders did not think they had much in common with liberals of Kerr's stripe. "We have a very bad society," Savio observed, whereas establishment liberals of the Kennedy-Johnson era thought American society was sound, full of unprecedented opportunity, despite its lingering imperfections, and governed by benign liberals.[9] Savio and the other young radicals thought there was a crusade to be fought; to Kerr this must have seemed absurd.

Raising the stakes to a cosmic level, Savio asserted, sounding a bit like Reinhold Niebuhr, "The reason why liberals don't understand us is because they don't realize there is evil in the world."[10] This statement may seem surprising in light of the conservative charge that the movements of the 1960s infected American society with the virus of moral relativism. Savio, like many 1960s leftists, directed a similar accusation, that of amorality and lack of scruple, against liberals. Radicals wished to restore a sense of moral urgency and stringency to American life. The hippie counterculture may have evinced a sort of moral relativism, but New Left activists could more plausibly be accused of moral dogmatism. Savio's sense of evil in the world might have originated in his Roman Catholic religious training. But if so, it comported as well with the lessons that many young activists took from the civil rights struggle.

The close personal connection between FSM leaders and the Civil Rights Movement provided many FSM participants and observers with the readiest explanation for the FSM itself. Weinberg was collecting money for the Congress of Racial Equality when he was arrested, precipitating the police car incident. Many FSM activists asserted that the UC administration cracked down on student civil rights agitation in response to the complaints of Bay Area businesses affected by student protest activities. Such FSM critics as Nathan Glazer insisted that the students' central goal was to use the University as a base for organizing civil disobedience off campus. Therefore, he said, the planning of illegal activities, which the administration at one point proposed making the only specifically prohibited form of student political activity, became the real sticking point in negotiations.[11]

To FSM partisans the broader social struggle between foes and friends of the Civil Rights Movement, and not a narrow legalistic question, was the real issue on campus. Savio put the matter plainly. During the fall he announced, "Last summer I went to Mississippi to join the struggle there for civil rights. This fall I am engaged in another phase of the same struggle, this time in Berkeley . . . a struggle against the same enemy." This was a harsh judgment on liberal UC administrators. Those who buckled to pressure from enemies of the Civil Rights Movement were considered allies of such reactionaries; if you faced a choice and did not act for the Civil Rights Movement, you were against it. Indeed, to some extent, those FSM activists who had participated in Freedom Summer were motivated by a desire to reaffirm, now that they were no longer in the South, their own commitment to the civil rights struggle. Savio reflected years later, "For us it was a question: whose side are you on? Are we on the side of the civil-rights movement? Or have we now gotten back to the comfort and security of Berkeley,

California, and can we forget the sharecroppers whom we worked with just a few weeks before?"[12] To the FSM leaders, this really was not just a fight about restrictions on student liberty at Berkeley.

But was it not exactly that? In fact, Savio strengthened the link between the FSM and the Civil Rights Movement by emphasizing the civil liberties aspect of both fights. Here was a way of arguing that the FSM really was a movement for free speech and simultaneously of connecting the Berkeley movement to the struggle in the Deep South. "The same rights are at stake in both places, the right to participate as citizens in democratic society and the right to due process of law," he said. By 1964 student radicals all over the United States were far along the path of political agitation, and attempts from any quarter to restrict their activities would naturally elicit their strong resistance. In this sense, free speech was the real issue in the FSM but not only because free speech was valued in the abstract; free speech was also fundamental to the purpose of building a radical youth movement that could, along with the Civil Rights Movement, change America. In this way the FSM is part of the American tradition of left-wing civil liberties advocacy that stretches back to the free speech fights of the IWW in the early twentieth century. Typically in the 1960s this issue was phrased in terms of democracy. African Americans were denied their citizenship rights, most obviously the right to vote, in the South. Students, said Savio, were denied a voice in the universities. This was poor training for democratic citizenship and an unacceptable anomaly within a supposedly democratic society. Writing in 1966 of students and universities, he noted, "Those of us whose lives are directly involved are denied any effective voice in [the] decisions which structure and pervert our immediate daily environment. What has become of the 'consent of the governed'?"[13] He might have been a black American issuing a radical criticism of American society.

Here surfaced the most basic link that Savio drew between the FSM and the Civil Rights Movement: students were victims, too. No doubt this notion was startling to moderate observers like Henry May, the Berkeley history department's chairman, who objected: "Surely it is not the same thing to stay in a restaurant for the purpose of insisting on one's moral and even legal rights and to occupy a university building for the stated purpose of obtaining a 'capitulation' on matters of university regulations. Defying a dean, or even risking academic units, does not call for the same kind of heroism or the same degree of danger as defying an Alabama sheriff and risking one's life." Yet Savio drew a parallel between the plight of African Americans and the situation of university students and did so too emphatically to be dismissed. Referring to the campus and its surrounding area as the "Berkeley ghetto," Mario explained that "you bear certain stigmas" there. "[N]ot the color of your skin . . . but the fact that you're an intellectual, and perhaps a moral Nonconformist. . . . Students are excited about political ideas. . . . But [that] means you have no use in American society . . . unless they are ideas which are useful to the military-industrial complex. . . . There's a lot of aimlessness in the ghetto. [There are people with] student mentalities who never grew up; they're people who were active in radical politics, let's say, in the Thirties, people who have never connected with the world. . . . You can see the similarity between this and the Harlem situation."[14]

Here he echoed the disquiet that animated liberal and social-democratic observers in the early 1960s, from Michael Harrington to Daniel Patrick Moynihan, over both "social disorganization" and political alienation among the American poor.[15] Savio, however, reflected the mix of outrage and hope that New Left radicals expressed when contemplating such phenomena among American society's "out-groups." The estrangement of the poor from the political system and perhaps from its dominant values made the poor a likely source of social disruption. Most 1960s radicals welcomed such disruption, especially if it were to take the form of a politically coherent challenge to "the system." Earlier leftists had looked to the industrial working class, but New Left activists viewed blue-collar workers as too comfortable, too enamored of society's dominant values, to play the revolutionary role. The New Left looked to African Americans, the poor, and students to step into the vacuum in radical politics created by the proletariat's embourgeoisement.

However, the hope that radicals attached to outcast status remained obscure to most observers, and even FSM leaders themselves seemed ambivalent. Most often, when they drew the parallel between students and blacks it was to decry their common victimization and demand redress. Again, Savio was explicit in this regard. Whereas the positive potential of students and blacks flowed from their alienation from the system, his expressions of moral outrage at students' situation emphasized their exploitation *within* that system. Savio cited the authority of Paul Goodman to assert that "students are the exploited class in America, subjected to all the techniques of factory methods: tight scheduling, speedups, rules of conduct they're expected to obey with little or no say-so. . . . For efficiency's sake, education is organized along quantifiable lines." Indeed, Goodman, who broadcast his sympathy with the FSM widely, argued that students were more exploited than African Americans: "At present in the United States," Goodman wrote in January 1965, "students—middle-class youth—are the major exploited class. (Negroes, small farmers, the aged are rather outcaste groups; their labor is not needed and they are not wanted.)"[16]

It is difficult to see how university students could have been both outcasts, as Savio said, and economically central in the way Goodman claimed, with Savio's approval. The first thesis drew a parallel between students and blacks, while the second quietly gave students pride of place in the radical analysis of American society. Despite these contradictions, the thought of people like Savio accommodated both theses.

As the 1960s progressed, the idea that students were central to the social system, fulfilling a role similar to that of industrial workers, gained ground among New Left radicals. It became known as the theory of the "new working class." This class was, the theory went, a social stratum of college-educated employees, whose central place in a new information-based economy would give them the former role of the industrial proletariat in future revolutionary scenarios. In *The Uses of the University*, which became something of a handbook of FSM social criticism, Kerr heralded the arrival of just such an economy, within which he saw the research university, if not its students, occupying a fundamental location. While New Left critics of American higher education sometimes termed students the products of a "knowledge factory," the theory of the new working class cast students as future workers whose education was there just to train them for productive labor. In order to create a society where they would be free of such glorified wage slavery, theorists of the new working class predicted that this new class would revolt against the system that gave birth to them. The university was the place where the new working class first espied its fate, and it was also a key element in the process of tying them to that fate. Therefore, a rebellion within and against the university system was likely and logical.

This somewhat bloodless theory, with its neo-Marxist tone of historical inevitability, required a moral ballast. Student militants all over the country had been moved more by the moral drama of the Civil Rights Movement than by any notion of the significance of that struggle to a broader process of social change. They needed a moral justification if they were to shift their emphasis to their own plight, and the idea of the student as victim provided this moral ballast. Savio made the case for this switch as strenuously as anyone, with an assertion that still makes us sit up and take notice decades later. He wrote, rather counterintuitively, "It is far easier to become angry when others are hurt. . . . Fighting for others' rights cannot engender nearly so great a guilt as striking rebelliously at one's own immediate environment. Also, it's simply easier to see the injustice done others—it's 'out there.'"[17] Was altruism truly easier than self-concern? Human history seems to teach a different lesson.

Nonetheless, this was Savio's explanation for the outpouring of concern for the less fortunate that sprang from America's college-educated youth in the 1960s. The FSM started as a movement in sympathy with the civil rights struggle; as he said in 1965, "It was easy to draw upon this reservoir of outrage at the wrongs done to other people; but such action usually masks the venting, by a more acceptable channel, of outrage at the wrongs done to oneself. I am far from propounding a psychoanalytic theory of politics, yet most people whom I have met who are committed to radical political innovation are people who have experienced a good deal of personal pain, who have felt strong frustration in their own lives."[18]

Some observers, like Berkeley Professor Lewis Feuer, sought to discredit New Left politics by interpreting it as the product of personal difficulties. Yet Savio clearly felt that political radicalism actually was justified by its personal roots. People were not unhappy without a reason. And pushing his rhetoric as far as he could, he asserted, "The Berkeley students now demand what hopefully the rest of an oppressed white middle class will some day demand: freedom for all Americans, not just for Negroes!"[19]

This move toward the idea of an oppressed white middle-class student population was exactly the direction taken by the New Left as a whole in the mid-sixties. SDS leaders Greg Calvert and Carl Davidson were making this case by 1966, promoting the theory of the new working class. But Savio did it earlier, drawing upon ideas the FSM had developed. In 1963 and 1964 SDS had concentrated on inner-city organizing, but by 1965 its leaders felt they had reached the limits of this approach to social change. One founder of SDS derided the "cult of the ghetto," urging a renewed emphasis on radicalizing university students.[20] Ironically, activists like Savio (who was not a member of SDS and who came to his radicalism through a different route) made this change in focus acceptable only by asserting that the campus *was* another ghetto.

EDUCATION AND ALIENATION

Once student radicals targeted the universities as both a locus of oppression and the seat of social change, they began devoting energy to "university reform." Some observers of the FSM were quick to identify the dissatisfaction of students with life and education in the "multiversity," and not political conflict over the Civil Rights Movement, as the FSM's cause. Raskin, the *Times* reporter, wrote, "The longer my conversation with the students went on, the clearer it became that the political battle was only a symptom of a larger revolt against the bigness and impersonality of the 'multiversity' itself." Hal Draper disagreed. "It is true," he acknowledged, "that... a wing of FSM activists emphasized... educational reform." But he insisted that, "while it is widely and warmly agreed that the result of this new interest in university betterment was valuable, it was a by-product of the movement, not its spur."[21] Students might complain about big classes, research-obsessed professors, or impersonal campus administrative routines, but these had not been the issues to spark the FSM. For a long time Savio's speech about gears and levers has evoked the critique of the University as a machine, complete with IBM computer cards that reduced students to mere numbers. However, at the time of the speech, the machine of which Savio spoke seemed to describe society overall. When he spoke during the

FSM of "bureaucracy" as the students' enemy, he referred not to student malaise but to an evil social system, evoking theories of totalitarianism then current. "In California, the privileged minority manipulates the University bureaucracy to suppress the student's political expression. That 'respectable' bureaucracy masks the financial plutocrats; that impersonal bureaucracy is the efficient enemy in a 'Brave New World.'"[22]

Although the matter is complicated, Draper got the chronology largely right. Educational reform was a concern of a few FSM activists from the start, but it emerged as a leading issue for student radicals only following the FSM. Indeed Draper and Glazer agreed, even though they squared off in debate over the FSM, that the alleged unhappiness among Berkeley students with their educational experience had been exaggerated.[23] When Robert H. Somers, a Berkeley sociologist, surveyed the students in November 1964, he concluded that support for the FSM was not closely linked to dissatisfaction with the educational program. "On the contrary, we found a remarkable amount of satisfaction with courses, professors, and so on, and appreciation of the efforts made by the administration to provide top-quality education for students here." Somers's data suggested "that a great deal of the steam for the protest came from the twin issues of paternalism" or, to put it differently, democracy on campus "and of civil rights."[24]

This is not to say that student militants were unconcerned about the state of American higher education. However, these concerns sometimes were conflated with the issue of student "alienation" so as to suggest that students were alienated primarily by and from the university. Student radicals developed a critique of American society, including the central charge that it alienated the young and the affluent as well as the poor, and then indicted the universities as it became clear how those institutions were entangled in the larger apparatus of injustice. Savio's most trenchant criticism of UC was expressed at this institutional level; Kerr was putting the University at the service of "the corporate establishment of California, plus a lot of national firms, the government, especially the Pentagon. It's no longer a question of a community of students and scholars, of independent, objective research but rather of contracted research, the results of which are to be used as those who contract for it see fit.... Why should the business community ... dominate the board of regents?" Such comments as these indicate the leftist cast of Savio's thought at least as early as February 1965. Research universities had become enmeshed in the military-industrial complex. Students like Savio wanted universities to return to an older concept of higher education, according to which "only people engaged in it—the students and teachers—are competent to decide how it should be done." Administrators, in this educational world, simply "should tend to keeping the sidewalks clean, to seeing that we have enough classrooms." Critics of student radicals claimed the militants wanted to politicize the university, by making it "relevant" to burning social issues. Savio said, on the contrary, that he wished universities would issue "a declaration of independence and 'autonomy from all quarters,'" to truly pursue "free and independent inquiry."[25] He wished to see students involved in social struggles; but where teaching and research were concerned, he was far more attracted to a vision of the university as an ivory tower than was Kerr.[26]

Draper wrote dismissively, after citing a standard account of "depersonalization" in the multiversity, "About all that is missing in this summary is a reference to Alienation." In 1965 the alienation of youth was already a cliché. Young persons' preoccupation with the issues of alienation and authenticity earned them the sobriquet "existentialist." One supporter of the FSM expressed a widely held view when he said, "Theirs is a sort of political existentialism."[27] Even if, as I noted earlier, the issues of alienation, educational reform, and plain political conflict were conflated in the aftermath of the FSM, each of them was real and important in the minds of FSM activists. Draper might have been uninterested in the psychological sources of student radicalism, but Savio was not. Like Savio, New Left radicals around the country did come to see universities as productive of alienation, even if these two concerns were not initially yoked together, and they committed themselves to developing alternative forms of education that were not only morally and politically sound but conducive to authenticity. Sometimes they used other terms to mean basically the same things: *real* or *natural* or *alive* or *organic* or *free,* all meant "authentic," whereas *plastic* or *dead* or *unfree* might, in the proper context, mean "alienating." These young militants sought social justice and authenticity simultaneously, their conviction growing over time that America was both radically unjust and a society full of alienation and that these conditions could only be overcome together.

But what did young radicals really mean by *alienation* and *authenticity?* Alienation had been a prominent topic of social scientific discussion since the 1950s (and an important concept in more speculative social thought for many decades). It had taken on many different meanings, lending discussion of the subject a sometimes maddening ambiguity. For social scientists in the early Cold War decades, the concept generally referred to the failure of individuals to internalize the norms and beliefs of their society. This was the alienation that Savio suggested in his discussion of the Berkeley "ghetto." However, in these same years, another meaning of *alienation* had gained ground. This referred to a subjective feeling of floating adrift, a sense of being unanchored to anything compelling or deeply felt. Those influenced by existentialists like Jean-Paul Sartre spoke of nausea, the absurd, or simply of meaninglessness. They felt, like Savio, that individuals had to create their own meaning in life through purely voluntary acts for which they took responsibility and that they could never ultimately justify through recourse to anything but their own decision. He said of his involvement in the FSM,

"I don't know what made me get up and give that first speech. I only know I had to. What was it Kierkegaard said about free acts? They're the ones that, looking back, you realize you couldn't help doing." Henry May, displaying considerable sensitivity, interpreted the FSM in this light as well: "What Savio was demanding, when he urged in a peak of passion that students throw their bodies on the administrative machine and bring it to a grinding halt, was something like an existentialist *acte gratuit,* a gesture of self-identification." May also heard in Savio "the voice of an exalted, quasi-religious romantic anarchism."[28] Existentialist philosophy traced its origin to Kierkegaard, a Christian thinker, and contemporary religious writers reemphasized the religious dimension of the idea of alienation. To them humans were alienated because they were cut off from God; this was the "ground of Being" of which Paul Tillich spoke, seeking to make theology acceptable to a seemingly postreligious generation.[29]

Leftist thinkers of the 1960s, eager to connect the student discussion of alienation to the socialist tradition, promoted Karl Marx's 1844 *Economic and Philosophical Manuscripts,* in which the concept of alienation, as it is experienced under capitalism, plays the central role. Indeed, Savio assimilated this concept too. Seymour Martin Lipset and Paul Seabury relate part of a talk that Savio gave to the Berkeley branch of the Young Socialist Alliance: "The most important concept for understanding the student movement is Marx's notion of alienation. Its basic meaning is that the worker is alienated from his product, but the concept is applicable to students too. . . . The students are frustrated; they can find no place in society where alienation doesn't exist, where they can do meaningful work." Perhaps Savio was tailoring his message to his audience. Perhaps he simply thought the Marxist concept of alienation and the contemporary existentialist doctrine of the free act stemmed from the same basic insights into the modern condition and that both were compatible with his interpretation of his participation in the FSM as "religious." Indeed, the Catholic monk Thomas Merton, in the midst of a Cold War diatribe against godless communism, paused to identify the concept of alienation as the element worth salvaging from Marxist thought.[30]

Savio's repertoire of alienations was impressive, and its eclecticism reflected the main line of thought within the New Left. There are differences among all these concepts of alienation. Yet they all share a belief that there is something essential in human existence from which one can become estranged and that such an estrangement is tragic. Contemporary theories of alienation held that this condition results in feelings of meaninglessness and anxiety. As Lionel Trilling put it in 1970, the feeling of alienation is "the sense of something intervening between man and his own organic endowment." Whether this essence, this "ground of Being" from which one was cut off was viewed as God, or as one's own labor power, or as humanity, or as the cosmos, or as one's ethnic identity, the goal was always an end to this state of estrangement. This reconnection, which would restore a sense of deep and vital existence, was what the existentialist radicals of the 1960s meant by the state of authenticity. The striving for authenticity became freighted with moral and, ultimately, political significance; "the natural processes of human existence have acquired a moral status in the degree that they are thwarted."[31]

AUTHENTICITY AND PROPHECY

Widespread reports of subjective alienation provided the most basic evidence supporting Savio's contention that university students had legitimate grievances to press against American society. His individual concern with achieving authenticity seems palpable, and characteristic of his generation. Mario, the son of a Sicilian immigrant, recalled that his father wanted the family to assimilate into American culture. Mario strove to do so but not without ambivalence. Only when he began school in Berkeley did he go by the name *Mario*, "instead of the more prosaic Bob of his childhood." This seems to anticipate the cultural preoccupation with a "symbolic ethnicity" that arose powerfully in the United States starting in the late 1960s. This way of asserting authenticity was virtually undiscussed in the 1950s and early 1960s, but it became perhaps the most popular one in later years. In W. J. Rorabaugh's words, Savio at Berkeley "appeared to be searching for new roots."[32]

The issue of authenticity had been brought forcefully into a political context by the Civil Rights Movement. In this struggle, activists seemed to achieve a personal authenticity as they worked for a just society. They explicitly stated that they wished to heal American society, to end its social alienation. Within the Civil Rights Movement itself, activists upheld an ideal of the "beloved community," a group bonded to one another in perfect equality, and this model of community became, for young American idealists of all races, the antithesis of the larger society. "There was a loving community in the Civil Rights Movement," Savio recalled. "One of the things that was absent in that America that I [knew] was any sense of a greater community."[33] Whites who participated in the Civil Rights Movement routinely spoke of it and of its cause of racial justice and reconciliation as authentic, as "real." It "was attractive, because it was real," Savio said. Unlike John Kennedy, whom Savio did not greatly admire, "it wasn't flash. It wasn't a fake. It wasn't a fantasy land." A genuine commitment to social justice, a deep engagement with the great social issues of the day, were hallmarks of the authentic person.[34]

This sense of being "real" was linked, for Savio, to his desire for excitement. This may seem strange as a moral and political concern, but for Savio it was meaningful. In his 1964 article "An End to History" he criticized liberals for thinking that American society had been essentially completed, that no great social accomplishments remained for the future. This was not true, Savio was convinced, and moreover, the prospect of a finished society left college students "looking toward a very bleak existence." He suggested that young people needed challenges in order to learn and grow, but, he said, "society provides no challenge. American society in the standard conception it has of itself is simply no longer exciting.... America is becoming ever-more the utopia of sterilized, automated contentment." But all hope was not lost: "The most exciting things going on in America today are movements to change America." Struggle was the key to authenticity, and excitement was an index to the presence of struggle. Savio sealed this connection when he reflected that his time in Mississippi did for him what, developmentally, the Great Depression had done for his parents. His father had served in the U.S. military in World War II but had not fought in battle. "He saw no combat. I didn't either. This [civil rights activism] was that kind of experience of initiation, the thing that was most real for me at that crucial time in my life." In dramatic fashion, Savio used a military metaphor to strengthen his warning to the older generation: "an important minority of men and women coming to the front today," he said, "have shown that they will die rather than be standardized, replaceable, and irrelevant."[35]

From the Civil Rights Movement the mental link between authenticity and struggle passed into the New Left, and the cause of free speech, joined in Berkeley, was a momentous stopping point on this journey. As noted earlier, the FSM cared about free speech because political organizing could not proceed in its absence. However, these young activists also embraced a more abstract belief in free speech as the indispensable means of expressing one's essence as a free political being, a free human being. The politics of authenticity commonly took the form of a radical humanism according to which alienation was a state in which one was less than fully human. Savio, citing the authority of Diogenes, one of the ancients he studied in his philosophy classes, said on one occasion, "To me, freedom of speech is something that represents the very dignity of what a human being is.... That's what marks us off from the stones and stars.... It is almost impossible for me to describe. It is the thing that marks us as just below the angels."[36] Such FSM detractors as Glazer never understood that student radicals had a deep commitment to free speech as an issue in its own right. The New Left's distinct version of civil libertarianism, although it was to be qualified or rejected in favor of revolutionary politics in some quarters, was sincere. It was not always easily recognized by liberals, since New Left radicals embraced the cause of free speech in the abstract less to maximize liberty than to open the floodgates of authentic being. This was libertarianism of a different color.

When Savio called his involvement in the FSM "religious," he offered a tantalizing hint of a link between 1960s student radicalism and the discussion of authenticity that had been circulating in American intellectual life since the 1940s. Did his Catholic upbringing plant the seeds of his radicalism? He averred that he had become estranged from the Catholic Church by the time he entered college, finding it "sectarian" and intellectually constricting. He gravitated toward Jewish friends (both his marriages were to Jewish women) as a kind of rebellion; he saw Jewish culture as one "in which there was much more respect for critical thinking than there was in the Catholic culture I was born into." Although this is something of a stereotype, it reveals that, even as Savio embraced an ethnic identity, at the same time he aspired to a cosmopolitanism that underlined his critical reflection upon his Catholic background.[37]

Despite this estrangement from Catholicism, Savio's early life was one of earnest devotion. He felt that his family had communicated to him during his boyhood the hope that he might become a priest. Before the Savios moved to California, "Bob" attended Manhattan College, run by the Christian Brothers order of priests. Most striking is his work in rural Mexico on a Church-run relief project one summer before he went to Mississippi; for him, Freedom Summer was not without precedent. Savio may have learned the value of social justice from his Catholic boyhood, his falling away from the Church notwithstanding. He noted casually, "I think that there was a religious basis, very clearly, to my political involvement." There is little mystery here.[38]

There is no reason to think Savio was deeply engaged with the truly historic changes that emerged from the Second Vatican Council between 1962 and 1965 or with contemporary Catholic theology. He was familiar with the work of Gabriel Marcel, the best-known Catholic existentialist, but apparently was no more influenced by Marcel than by Kierkegaard. More relevant than Savio's earlier education, perhaps, was the Berkeley course in the "philosophy of existence" that he took during the semester before he left for Mississippi. Albert Camus was another specific influence. "I had read *The Stranger*. Everybody was reading *The Stranger*."[39] Camus, like Sartre, was an atheist; yet Camus's brand of existentialism bore the imprint of his early Catholicism, just as did Savio's activism. Camus demanded heroic acts of defiance from those who wished to be truly human, a call to which young people in the 1960s responded with gusto, contributing to the dramaturgy that marked their politics.

Savio had been shaped by an ensemble of intellectual influences—Catholicism, existentialist moralism, humanist Marxism—that he blended and interpreted as a kind of cosmopolitan religious existentialism. We can place him among those who felt that the essential being to which the pursuit of authenticity would return us was located in the realm of the spirit. Bettina Aptheker says that his life was "a practicum in search of meaning, in search of wholeness." This "was a deeply personal quest, and a deeply spiritual one. This was a freedom beyond the conventional understanding of the [word], a freedom that included the political but went beyond it." To her and other friends, Savio is a model of spiritual-moral authenticity. Although she goes on to evoke a kind of contemplative authenticity, it was the fiery Savio of denunciation and demand that etched itself in American historical memory in 1964.[40]

This returns us to the question with which this essay began: What was the nature of Savio's leadership? Why did students respond to his public call? His charisma did not derive from any philosophic ingenuity. His apparent authenticity, in 1964, was not a token of some perfect integration of his public and private selves. "Integrity" is a quality that Savio's comrades ascribe to him.[41] In his case the term conveys not only the usual meaning that here was a sincere man who honored his word but also the existentialist ideal of a person whose various parts form a whole; it is akin to the romantic imperative "that the person be an integer."[42] But the reconstruction of Savio's life to fit this concept is just that, a retrospective attempt to make him fit an ideal of personal authenticity, blending public and private, that has reemerged powerfully in our culture in the decades since the FSM. Savio did indeed project a sense of authenticity to his fellow students in 1964, but it was a different kind of authenticity whose character is not easy to recapture today.

Savio thundered against iniquity with the voice of a prophet. This may be a useful way of thinking about his persona and its effects upon his contemporaries. His sense of injustice was stronger than his concept of justice, he said. He felt this was the gift of his Italian American childhood. It also is typical of the prophet, according to the influential Jewish theologian Abraham Heschel.[43] A prophet establishes a connection with a transcendent realm that has been lost by the people; he rains God's word down upon the wayward flock. In terms of existentialist politics the prophet's voice is the most authentic of all; he is a kind of portal to the "ground of Being" but without recourse to such gentle euphemisms. We need not hold any religious belief whatever to see that when Savio the stammerer stepped onto the public stage and erupted with a torrent of outrage and denunciation, he was in a religious state. He trembled and his eyes burned.

Whence his sudden fluidity, we do not know. But to the children of Berkeley he was a man possessed of some deep power, and they responded to it. Savio's arresting public performances and his lack of egotism conform well to the following characterization of prophetic or shamanistic figures: "The behavior of these divine spokesmen is often thought to have been ecstatic, frenzied, or abnormal in some way, which reflected their possession by the deity *(and the absence of personal ego)* at the time of transmission."[44] Should we really wonder that he seemed different in private? When in communion with otherworldly power the prophet "becomes radically transformed; he is 'turned into another man' (I Sam. 10:6)." Reflecting upon his youthful religious training, Savio told an interviewer that individuals can have extraordinary moments: "It's possible for people to be holy, for some period of time, anyway. Right actions done with great power." He felt that the Civil Rights Movement had been holy.[45] Perhaps he was, too, for a brief time. Neither history making nor prophecy is necessarily a lifetime occupation.

The prophet knows that righteous works are to be done in history. "Others have considered history from the point of view of power; . . . the prophets look at history from the point of view of justice, judging its course in terms of righteousness and corruption." "To the prophets, man's home is in history. [H]istory is the vessel for [divine] action and the material for man's achievement."[46] Savio, whatever the phenomenological reality of his experiences and whatever his own religious beliefs, knew that the demand of righteousness implies unmistakably that there is more history to be made.

NOTES

1. Michael Rossman, "Mario's Last Day/Perspectives on Mario," Nov. 1996, available at <http://www.fsm-a.org/stacks/rossman_mario.html>.

2. According to the editors of *California Monthly*, approximately one thousand sat in at Sproul Hall (Andrew L. Pierovich [managing editor], "Chronology of Events: Three Months of Crisis," *California Monthly* 75 [Feb. 1965], reprinted in Seymour Martin Lipset and Sheldon S. Wolin, *The Berkeley Student Revolt: Facts and Interpretations* [Garden City, N.Y.: Doubleday, 1965], 163). The Berkeley sociologist Robert H. Somers put this number at "over 1,000"; and Hal Draper, more of a partisan of the FSM, wrote, rather elastically, that "about 1,000 to 1,500" were in the building (Somers, "The Mainsprings of the Rebellion: A Survey of Berkeley Students in November, 1964," in Lipset and Wolin, 533; Draper, *Berkeley: The New Student Revolt* [New York: Grove Press, 1965], 98–99). A total of 773 were arrested (W. J. Rorabaugh, *Berkeley at War* [New York: Oxford University Press, 1989], 33).

3. Bettina Aptheker, "In Memory of Mario Savio," December 1996, available at <http://www.fsm-a.org/stacks/rossman_mario.html>.

4. Jack Weinberg, in Mark Shechner et al., "Remembering Mario Savio," *Tikkun* 21 (Jan.–Feb. 1997): 29; Barbara Garson, "Me and Mario Down by the Schoolyard: Recollections of the Free-Speech Movement," *The Progressive* 61 (Jan. 1997): 24; Draper, 62. Doug McAdam makes the case for Savio as the real leader of the FSM on the basis of his public role (McAdam, *Freedom Summer* [New York: Oxford University Press, 1988], 163–64).

5. A. H. Raskin, "The Berkeley Affair: Mr. Kerr vs. Mr. Savio & Co.," in Lipset and Wolin, 420–21.

6. Robert Randolph, "12,000 at UC Teach-In on Vietnam," in Louis Menashe and Ronald Radosh, eds., *Teach-ins, U.S.A.: Reports, Opinions, Documents* (New York: Frederick A. Praeger, 1967), 33.

7. Stew Albert, in Shechner et al., "Remembering Mario Savio," 29; Aptheker, "In Memory of Mario Savio"; "Mario Savio on Free Speech," available at <http://www.fsm.-a.org/stacks/covers/savio_gilles.html>; Shechner in Shechner et al.; Garson, "Me and Mario."

8. Aptheker's and Starobin's family-based involvements in the American Communist movement are well known. Other FSM activists, such as Barbara Garson,

Sydney Stapleton, and Jackie Goldberg, were involved in various left-wing activities before the FSM began (Rorabaugh, 24; Rorabaugh does not say that these last three came from leftist families. The important point is that they, like the "red-diaper babies" at Berkeley, were not radicalized by the events of 1964; they were already radicals.)

9. Savio [interview with Jack Fincher], "The University Has Become a Factory," *Life,* 26 Feb. 1965, 101.

10. Quote in Rorabaugh, 46.

11. Nathan Glazer, "What Happened at Berkeley," *Commentary,* Feb. 1965, reprinted in Lipset and Wolin, 297–300. Glazer expressed the view that "free speech" was not the real concern of the FSM but a clever turn of phrase designed to gain the students the moral high ground and divert attention from their actual agenda.

12. Quoted in McAdam, 168–69.

13. Quoted in ibid., 169; Mario Savio, "The Uncertain Future of the Multiversity: A Partisan Scrutiny of Berkeley's Muscatine Report," *Harper's,* Oct. 1966, 94.

14. Henry May, "The Student Movement at Berkeley: Some Impressions," in Lipset and Wolin, 460; Savio, "The University Has Become a Factory," 100.

15. See Michael B. Katz, *The Undeserving Poor: From the War on Poverty to the War on Welfare* (New York: Pantheon Books, 1989), 16–43. Conservative scholars such as Edward Banfield concurred in this analysis even at this time, but during the Kennedy years this "culture of poverty" thesis was most identified with liberals.

16. Savio, "The University Has Become a Factory," 100; Paul Goodman, "Thoughts on Berkeley," *New York Review of Books,* 14 Jan. 1965, reprinted in Lipset and Wolin, 316.

17. Mario Savio, "Introduction," in Draper, 5

18. Ibid., 6.

19. Ibid. Years later Savio referred specifically to Feuer's work (Lewis S. Feuer, *The Conflict of Generations: The Character and Significance of Student Movements* [New York: Basic Books, 1969]): "It seemed to me a shame to have some really significant issues raised in so lurid a way." Savio interview with Bret Eynon, 5 Mar. 1985, Columbia University Oral History Project, Columbia Oral History Project, 73, available at <http://www.lib.berkeley.edu/BANC/FSM>.

20. This was Alan Haber, quoted in James Miller, *"Democracy Is in the Streets": From Port Huron to the Siege of Chicago* (New York: Simon and Schuster, 1987), 190.

21. Raskin, "Berkeley Affair," 460; Draper, 154. Raskin's view doubtless was influenced by the presence among the FSM leaders he interviewed of Myra Jehlen and Robert Starobin. Both expressed concern over educational issues and both went on to distinguished academic careers (Starobin's ending tragically.)

22. Savio quoted in McAdam, 169.

23. Glazer reported that in his experience undergraduates seemed pleased with their Berkeley education but that dissatisfaction might run far higher among graduate students. Glazer, "What Happened at Berkeley," 294. He also bemoaned "the indifference to educational reform of both faculty and students," surely an overstatement; but by how much, one is not sure. Glazer, "Reply to Goodman," in Lipset and Wolin, 320.

24. Somers, "Mainsprings," 534, 548.

25. Savio, "The University Has Become a Factory," 100; Savio, "The Uncertain Future of the Multiversity," 94.

26. Savio's respect for a traditional approach to university education became clear in his support for the embattled Tussman plan during the 1964–1965 school year. This plan proposed an alternative course of study oriented toward the "Great Books." This episode is discussed by David Hollinger in this volume.

27. Draper, 153; Paul Jacobs, quoted in Raskin, "Berkeley Affair," 421.

28. Savio, "The University Has Become a Factory," 100; May, "Student Movement," 460, 459.

29. Tillich's most widely read works were: *The Shaking of the Foundations* (New York: Scribner, 1948); *The Courage to Be* (New Haven: Yale University Press, 1952); *The New Being* (New York: Scribner, 1955).

30. Seymour Martin Lipset and Paul Seabury, "The Lesson of Berkeley," in Lipset and Wolin, 344; Thomas Merton, "Christianity and Totalitarianism," in *Disputed Questions* (New York: Farrar, Straus and Cudahy, 1960), 146.

31. Lionel Trilling, *Sincerity and Authenticity* (Cambridge, Mass.: Harvard University Press, 1972), 127, 128. This book was based on lectures delivered in spring 1970. I think May may have had this subjective experience of alienation in mind when he wrote, "The alienation of our students is social rather than political, and it is to this alienation that Mario Savio is best able to speak" ("Student Movement," 459).

32. Rorabaugh, 22; Herbert J. Gans, "Symbolic Ethnicity and Symbolic Religiosity: Towards a Comparison of Ethnic and Religious Acculturation," *Ethnic and Racial Studies* 17 (Oct. 1994): 577–92.

33. Rorabaugh, 23, 22.

34. Savio interview with Eynon, 5 Mar. 1985, 23, 13, 18.

35. Mario Savio, "An End to History," *Humanity*, Dec. 1964, reprinted in Draper, 182; Savio interview with Eynon, 41.

36. "Mario Savio on Free Speech."

37. Savio interview with Eynon, 3, 5, 6.

38. Ibid., 3, 5; Rorabaugh, 21; Draper, *Berkeley*, 38.

39. Savio interview with Eynon, 34.

40. Aptheker, "In Memory of Mario Savio."

41. Aptheker speaks of his "absolute and transparent integrity"; Aptheker ("In Memory"). Rossman honors "the simple authenticity of his example, his metabolic integrity" ("Mario's Last Day").

42. Trilling, 99.

43. Savio interview with Eynon, 4; Heschel, *The Prophets: An Introduction* (New York: Harper Colophon, 1962), 204.

44. Gerald T. Sheppard and William E. Herbrechtsmeier, "Prophecy: An Overview," in Mircea Eliade, ed., *The Encyclopedia of Religion* (New York: Macmillan, 1987), 12:8 (emphasis added). Savio's friends indicate that he was modest at all times, publicly and privately.

45. Heschel, 22; Savio interview with Eynon, 74.

46. Heschel, 171, 169.

Remembering Mario

Lynne Hollander Savio

The Mario Savio I knew for thirty-two years and lived with for eighteen was a person of great intellectual and emotional complexity, engaged by many ideas and ideals. Yet there is little doubt in my mind that the single greatest influence upon his politics and upon his life, apart from that of family dynamics, was his early exposure to Catholicism. Although by high school he was beginning to reject Catholic doctrine (I think he found most of it—virgin birth, resurrection, and so forth—impossible to swallow as a description of reality, while its sexual strictures were too guilt provoking), the search for a God he could believe in was a driving force in his life. In his early teens, he had wanted to be a priest, and, in a sense, that ambition never quite left him. His interest in physics, although in part motivated by an aesthetic love for astronomy, was also driven by a compulsion to understand the grand scheme of the universe—that is, to see God. What is the nature of reality? What is the nature of time? How can one explain the emergence of consciousness? Where is the boundary between that which has consciousness and that which does not? The poets he loved most were the religious poets—Emily Dickinson, Wordsworth, and the great Anglo-Catholic poets John Donne, Gerard Manley Hopkins, and T. S. Eliot. One would think he had little in common with the archconservative Eliot, and yet the spiritual quest of Eliot's *Four Quartets* spoke to a deep, and never fulfilled, longing within him.

The basic principle of Catholic morality was what drove his politics, as he made explicit on a number of occasions: do good; resist evil. Interestingly, although choices presented themselves to him in those terms (to act is to do good/to act is to resist evil), he was not prone to oversimplifying issues. Aware of the complexities, aware that *all* the good was never on one side, *all* the bad on the other, he was reluctant to demonize others. But in the end,

Mario felt one could, and should, make judgments and then act upon them. In his talk "Reflections on the FSM," reprinted in this volume, he makes clear his readiness to engage in such activism. During the sixties, that meant choosing to fight for civil rights against the forces of racism and repression; he saw the Civil Rights Movement as "an example of God working in the world." (It was rather ironic that the FBI tailed this particular young radical in the hopes of linking the movement to "Godless Communism.")

To the end, Mario was unable to totally relinquish even the negative aspects of his Catholic heritage—he could reject it intellectually, but to free himself emotionally was far more difficult. Nor was he able to fully embrace an alternative faith. He toyed sometimes with the idea of converting to Judaism, loved the Jewish holidays we participated in together, and would have gladly attended services if I had been interested in doing so. He valued what he saw as Jewish respect for critical thinking and intellectual inquiry. Yet he made no attempt to seriously involve himself in a study of the religion; I'm not sure why. He became more involved with Buddhism, reading and meditating on a regular basis with a little statue of the Buddha. He was particularly drawn to the figure of Green Tara—the principle of compassionate action in the world—with whom he liked to identify. The idea of oneness in the universe was consonant with both his understanding of physics and with his morality and ethics (a favorite joke: "What did the Buddhist say to the hot dog vendor?" "Make me one with everything."). But he could not accept the Buddhist principles—at least as depicted in the West—of resignation and all-inclusiveness; "resist evil" was too ingrained in Mario, philosophically, psychologically, temperamentally.

Mario was in love with language—its meanings, its sounds, its rhythms. He thought that his sensitivity to the rhythms of speech, so apparent in his public addresses, was due to the years of attempting to overcome his severe stutter by "fanatic listening" to the structure of speech rhythms. Beyond this, he was rigorous about using language precisely; in our house he was known as the "dictionarian" because of his love of the family dictionary and his frequent use of it to check meanings. He was, of course, extremely sensitive to the connotative meanings of words in addition to the denotative, and with his strong access to unconscious processes (both his own and others) he was a gifted interpreter of poetry, as well as a lover of it. In addition to English, he spoke Italian fluently, Spanish well, and French grammatically, though hampered by a lack of vocabulary.

For someone so in love with words, Mario was surprisingly visually oriented, and he thought that if the times had been different, if his life had been different, he would have most loved being an art history major. He could—and did—pore over each (it seemed like each at the time) stained glass panel in Chartres Cathedral, resulting in one of our (fairly infrequent) squabbles. The mosaics in the churches of Ravenna and St.

Mark's delighted him; he loved the cloisters and cathedrals—the enclosing, intimate Romanesque more than the soaring Gothic—and Japanese brush painting. The fee increase fight at Sonoma State University, which preceded (and may even have hastened) his death, kept him from following through on plans to study painting.

One of Mario's great pleasures in life was good dining. Blessed with the capacity to eat heartily without putting weight on his six-foot-two-inch frame, he found food a delight, a conflict-free arena in which he could indulge at no great cost. His tastes were wide and varied, but, with the exception of his somewhat quaint predilection for "afternoon tea and scones," it was the simple, honest foods of the Mediterranean peasant kitchen he loved most—pasta, basil, garlic, garden tomatoes (particularly in a Greek salad loaded with feta), chunks of chewy bread with olives and Romano cheese, Parmesan and grapes for dessert, plenty of red wine to drink. One of our treasured memories was an evening meal on the waterfront in Naxos, where the two of us gorged on three full portions of fried calamari, along with the ubiquitous Greek salad. Mario loved the feeling of having had as much calamari as one could possibly eat—and the luxury and recklessness (albeit on a small scale) of the self-indulgence.

He was so funny—in a myriad of ways, witty, teasing, ironic, sarcastic, silly. He was totally without personal malice or barbs, even when he was sarcastic; I don't think anyone ever experienced him as hurtful in his humor. He liked to tell a story about an occurrence when he was in Santa Rita jail, locked up with some very tough characters. One day—and I can't remember what might have provoked this—he proposed to one of his fellow inmates, a man substantially larger and stronger than Mario, with a considerable reputation for toughness, that he, Mario, could pour a cup of water on this man's head and not be retaliated against. The other prisoner was astonished at the chutzpah of this greenhorn—he probably figured this was going to be the easiest bet he'd ever won. He readily agreed to the peculiar wager. At which point, Mario filled two cups of water and simultaneously poured one over the other man's head and one over his own. Of course, Mario won the bet.

What were the characteristics that made Mario have such an impact on people? Certainly one factor was a moral purity—the sense that he gave people of not only knowing, seeing clearly, the right and wrong of a situation but, perhaps as important, that he appeared so ego free that one never felt he had an interest in power, position, status, or publicity for himself. This was deeply true, not merely an "appearance," although I am hard put to pin down what it was in his behavior that so quickly convinced people of this; maybe it was the *absence* of something. But he had frequently—in fact almost always when he was not righteously indignant about some injustice or deceit—a diffidence, even an apologetic quality if he disagreed with or found flaws in your position. This obviously was both a strength and a weakness; he was, as we sometimes joked but meant quite literally, "modest to a fault." At times, after an argument in which he had strongly asserted a position, he would worry about whether he had hurt or antagonized the other person by being too vehement, or too rejecting, or too scornful—or even too intelligent. He was, of all people I have known, the most courteous.

He was also a man of immense charm, which he knew and about which he felt ambivalent. Our son, Daniel, describes it as the capacity to devote himself wholly to the other person, to participate without reservation in whatever his companion was saying or doing, even if he had no particular interest in the activity. Certainly this was true of his relations with his children. With adults, I think people experienced him as being fully responsive and fully engaged. Just as it was maddening trying to get his attention if it were fixed elsewhere (on a math problem, for instance), so it was gratifying to feel, when you were talking with him, that to him you were, at that moment, the most fascinating person in the room. Although at bad moments he would denigrate these personal qualities and refer to himself as "the chatty wind-up Mario doll," he in fact had a genuine interest in other people and an enjoyment in communicating with nearly everyone. This quality, which one could perhaps see as that of a smooth politician, was actually totally lacking in artifice, which was what made it so incredibly effective. Mario would talk to anyone, in any place, and at length, about anything. Daniel and I would often writhe in embarrassment while he struck up conversations with the checker or the person next in line at the supermarket—though that person was obviously delighted to be engaged in dialogue.

Mario's genius was an acute sensitivity—a *hyper*sensitivity—to everything, really: to the feelings of others, to issues of politeness, to hints, to the nuances of language and logic, to relationships, to words and silences, to moral issues. Can all these sensitivities be considered a single quality? Surely it was both his genius and, at least in part, what made life a torment for him much of the time. Although his sensitivity may well have been honed within his extended family, with all the intense stated and unstated conflicts between its various members, it's hard not to believe that fundamentally this was an innate quality. This sensitivity included an unusual closeness/alertness to the unconscious, both his own and that of others. It made him brilliant at dream analysis and, as I mentioned, at the analysis of poetry. But it's not so good for the boundary between conscious and unconscious to be an overly permeable membrane.

Mario was a contemplative soul—the Italian motto *dolce far niente,* "how sweet it is to do nothing," spoke to him. He loved to look at the stars and had his favorites—the Pleiades and the Andromeda galaxy. He would often wake up late at night or early in the morning and, from our bedroom window on Petaluma Hill Road, watch "a giant cosmic merry-go-round" as the

Dipper rotated through the night. He liked to listen to water—to rain, fountains, rivers, oceans—to watch the snow, to smell the sweet fragrance of jasmine and Victorian box. He enjoyed taking walks and bike riding, but that was about as active as he wanted to get. He loved flowers, gardening, picnics, and sunrises. Although he indulged my taste for sunsets, he found them a source of melancholy; sunsets, he said, spoke to him of death.

Mario, Personal and Political

Suzanne Goldberg

It is often said that the personal is political: the women's movement of the seventies and eighties raised our consciousness of the impact that social and political institutions have on how we think about ourselves and define our abilities. And in turn, how we define ourselves determines much of our perspective on social and political institutions and issues.

I would like in this essay to describe some personal aspects of Mario Savio that had a direct impact on his role in the FSM. There is not the space here to explicate these connections but only, roughly, to sketch some of them and hope that my suggestions shed some light on one aspect of a remarkable person in a remarkable time.

For Mario and the FSM, 1964 was one of those historical moments in which the personal and public came together to address a profound personal and social-political problem: the abuse of power and the consequent disappointment and loss of faith in leaders.

It has been over thirty-six years since the events of 1964 and my own transformation from a graduate student in philosophy to an activist critic of our socializing institutions. Mario Savio caught my attention as I walked through the University of California, Berkeley, campus on my way to and from classes. As a teaching assistant I took my work seriously. But the eloquence and honesty of Mario's words struck me for their lack of the usual manipulative rhetoric of political speeches, for his sensitivity and intelligence. It was impossible for me just to walk by and dismiss his struggle as someone else's. He was asking the University community to be involved in an important moral struggle and it felt immoral to walk away. I often stopped and listened to his speeches.

I was in my second year as a teaching assistant in the philosophy department, having received my master's degree in philosophy from the City

557

University of New York. I had begun my political awakening at Cornell University aware of the Freedom Rides and lunch counter sit-ins but still fairly naive and removed from politics. In New York City, while a student at CCNY/CUNY I participated in antiwar demonstrations (1962–1963) and occasionally attended a political discussion group.

I enjoyed my students; loved the role of teacher—loved to try to explain complicated ideas simply so as to make them accessible to my students. (The love of making complicated ideas accessible is something Mario and I shared.) Yet I found the moral imperative so passionately and compellingly enunciated by Mario that I would have felt I was betraying my own moral integrity to go on about my business just because I didn't want to risk hurting my career.

This sort of personal experience was repeated all over the country at that time and was one of the forces that drove the Civil Rights Movement that preceded the FSM. I recently heard Bernice Johnson Reagon speaking about music and the Civil Rights Movement, describing how people "woke up with [their] mind on freedom"; and how once that happened— the waking up—you couldn't do anything else but step off the path you were on and attend to this profound moral issue that screamed for your participation.

I had experienced hypocrisy and lack of consistent moral stance in my family. I often heard my parents proclaim high ideals and values, only to watch them behave in a manner inconsistent with those values. I had thus become skeptically critical—even hypersensitive—of anyone exhorting people to act on the basis of stated principles without demonstrating that their own deeds did not belie what they spoke. With this skepticism I watched Mario to see what positions he would take in the hours and hours of talk and debate in FSM meetings. He always took the moral stance, adhering to principle in making decisions concerning tactics or strategy. He was never an opportunist. I fell in love.

My own anger and passion against injustice were aroused and found a political outlet. I soon became a graduate student representative to the FSM. As a member of the FSM Steering Committee, I gave speeches at rallies and became immersed in discussion and debate analyzing daily tactics and, generally, the political situation within the University and the University's situation vis-à-vis the state of California. Frequently I would state a position in meetings that would be ignored, only to be restated later by either Jack Weinberg or Mario. Then they would be taken seriously. I would feel that I had not stated my position forcefully enough or effectively. Twenty-five years later I learned from Jackie Goldberg, who was often present at meetings, that for years she used my predicament as an example of sexist behavior for street theatre she produced. For this was, after all, before the women's movement, and yes, sexism existed in the FSM.

Often Mario and I worked together, staying awake all night to write the next day's leaflet to be distributed on campus. It would announce that day's rally and any action planned, providing a rationale for that action and an interpretation of current developments on the campus.

Mario never wished to destroy the University. He was never violent. He wished to reform the University's leaders (perhaps assuming here a religious model of redemption). He wished to persuade them of the right way so that faith in them might be restored and the University could get on to its proper role—as a true educator and moral leader in the community. I say this aware that there was a certain ironic ambivalence in Mario's manner. He held up the ideals leaders professed for them and for us to see, calling upon them to adhere to the ideals they professed, at the same time knowing their motivations were elsewhere. Yet a part of him wanted to believe that in their hearts they were good.

Mario did not hesitate to use the power of mass resistance to help persuade but he was polite and respectful and always willing to engage in dialogue even when others of us were more cynical and less willing to believe that anything but power would convince the University administration to change its course.

Mario and I had worked very closely in an intense situation with mutual respect. We fell in love and were married the year after the FSM, during the trials. (We had been arrested for trespassing and resisting arrest during a major demonstration on the Berkeley campus, the Sproul Hall sit-in.) There were signs from the beginning of our relationship that something disturbing lurked deep inside Mario. He even warned me that something was wrong. In the winter following the FSM Mario had had very intense and, as he described them, frightening and repulsive hallucinations under the influence of marijuana in a social situation where his friends were quietly enjoying themselves. I was twenty-five (Mario was twenty-two) and naive and thought that as long as we loved each other all would be well—having been brought up on the "and they lived happily ever after" myth of Hollywood fiction.

We believed the world to be wide open to us. And so I asked Mario what he most wanted to do. He replied, "To study physics." Where is the best place to do that? "Oxford, England." (UC Berkeley's physics department was excellent then, too, but we both felt that Mario needed to be away from Berkeley, where everyone seemed to need something from him and constantly pressured him to be something for them.) And so, with the assistance of liberal-minded people here and in England, we arranged for Mario to begin studies at St. Catherine's College, Oxford.

It was at this time that Mario's compulsive thinking became more apparent. I remember after a bus ride with Mario his incredible intelligence focused on a problem he described having to do with passing telephone poles on the road. He spent hours analyzing such problems instead of working on problems assigned at St. Catherine's. When he worked on the latter he would get lost in one small part of a problem and never get to the others—so much so that even he was disturbed.

I am suggesting that this compulsive focus might be seen as Mario's desperate need to get at the truth of something he perceived to be unexplained. This was harmless in some contexts and at times even led to brilliant insights. (Years later, for example, when Mario attended and received a master's degree from San Francisco State, he came up with deeply perceptive insights and later published a paper describing one of them.) In other situations, however, this compulsiveness became crippling to him and kept him from being productive. I believe the origins of his compulsiveness to lie in Mario's early childhood experiences, which were deeply disturbing and unresolved.

We had to leave Oxford and St. Catherine's after a few months because Mario's internal pressures became too great for him.

Mario's focus on truth also took the form of debating people who would approach him with views conflicting with his own. He believed that anyone who saw all of the facts would have to agree on the truth. And so he would explain his view to his opponent with infinite patience or obsessive determination—depending on one's view. I found him both admirable and foolish in this, for he spent his time without discriminating among the people he spoke with. Perhaps his religious training (Jesuit College) along with his mother's wish for him to be a second Christ created the burden of an impossible standard to live up to but also the motivation and drive to be a moral leader. It created what was both impressive in him—for someone to treat each human being fully equally—and, as I said, foolish—because, though in some way his view made sense, it failed to account for wide disparities in intellectual capacity and the ability of entrenched ideology and prejudice to prevent change.

It was with the same intensity and without discrimination that Mario focused on "small" events in daily life. I recall an incident years later, after my divorce and remarriage, when Mario visited our younger son. There had been some unpleasant interchange, in our son's presence, with an obstructionist clerk in a store. The incident was so trivial that I have forgotten the details. But I vividly recall how Mario analyzed and described astutely what had gone on as though it were *so* important and of such consequence that it might have had a damaging effect on our son. He focused obsessively, unable to put the incident in a context as either disturbing but trivial or as representing some greater truths about human behavior.

We had two sons together: Stefan was born in 1965. He was a very difficult child from the start. He would cry inconsolably with what we thought was colic but turned out never to go away, later taking the form of frequent tantrums.

Mario was always kind with Stefan. He understood a child's point of view and would play with children on their level. He also respected them. Perhaps too much. Stefan, who is mentally retarded, would be consulted by Mario as to his wishes with the same care and attention I described earlier when Mario would patiently explain his truth to someone who disagreed, no matter who they were or what their mental capabilities. This would end with Stefan being anxious and confused.

I relate this because it illustrates two of Mario's qualities: (1) his respect for and attention to others—without sufficient perspective—based on philosophical and religious principles and his own inner drives; and (2) his concern for and projection of disappointment as a major issue in his life and one to be carefully guarded against. Mario was deeply disappointed in himself. It is my conjecture that, along with an incident of abuse he experienced in childhood, he must have suffered betrayal at the hands of someone he loved and on whom he depended, and that his (unconscious) disappointment in that person or persons was never distinguished from disappointment in himself.

I believe that is why in interpersonal reactions he so focused on disappointment as an issue. For example, on another visit with our younger son, Nadav, who was ten or eleven, a small child damaged a book Nadav had with him. Instead of simply recognizing Nadav's feelings, Mario belabored with Nadav how disappointed Nadav must be that his book was damaged. In projecting his own disappointment and its intensity, he was unable to help his son go beyond his experience, label it, and put it in context.

These are examples of Mario's preoccupation with issues of power (the clerk versus the customer) and disappointment (something not found in a store, or a book damaged), a preoccupation that interfered on a personal level with his effective functioning. Yet on a political level these were themes that organized Mario's perspective and informed his passion, making him a powerful and charismatic leader.

The FSM was an exceptional time for all of us. For Mario it enabled him to soar—to function way beyond his personal conflicts and focus in the social-political sphere on issues that plagued him in the personal sphere: the arbitrary and abusive use of power and the dishonesty of an authority (UCB) that presented itself as a moral leader and educator while succumbing to political or practical pressures and thereby subverting its own integrity. It was, as I have said, one of those historical moments in which the personal and public came together to address a profound set of problems, both personal and social-political.

With compelling, passionate exhortations, Mario appealed to the University community not to accede to the political demands of the Republican

Party and political leaders of the state of California; he urged the University administration not to betray the trust of the students, and he urged the students to uphold the morality they had been taught, not to become cynical nor to "sell out."

Perhaps because the events were outside himself and happening to others as well as himself, Mario was able to focus his genius on analyzing and placing them in a historical context. He had an extraordinary ability to pick out details of behavior and astutely describe and explain them. In more personal situations this process could become oppressive, but during the FSM he brilliantly demonstrated truths at the core of the University's functioning. He used simple parables along with accurate retelling of events to make evident existing biases and propose corrective action.

I look back with great fondness on those times and the way the FSM experience revolutionized the University community. For the University did become a community. It became energized by the urgency of a real situation and emerged from its "ivory tower." Faculty, graduate students, and undergraduates spoke with each other across department and generational lines. We became engaged with one another and developed lifelong friendships.

After the FSM experience, the University would never be the same. An educational reform movement developed that examined the University's role in society. The University emerged as a more diverse place offering courses more relevant to students' varied concerns, interests, and backgrounds. Its legacy was a more questioning, less complacent student body and faculty that saw themselves in a continuing activist role.

Elegy for Mario Savio

Wendy Lesser

He wasn't, in the strictest sense of the word, an author. He never published a book. He was even a bit wary of publishing, as I learned when I set out to print one of his commemorative speeches in a 1995 issue of *The Threepenny Review*. He confessed to me, with an almost painful nervousness, that he hesitated to engage in any sort of publication for fear of losing the copyright; and when I assured him that I was acquiring one-time rights only, and that he would retain all further copyright, he explained to me the source of his anxiety. Early in his career he had allowed some of his speeches to be published, only to discover that in doing so he had unwittingly given away the rights to them. That such a thing was possible—that he could be deprived of the possession of his own sentences—surprised and wounded him. He had thought of speech as something free; it shocked him to see it treated as a salable commodity, a product divorced from its maker.

But if he was not an author in the book sense of the word, Mario Savio was nonetheless a poet. He was the only political figure of my era for whom language truly mattered. He was the last American, perhaps, who believed that civil, expressive, precisely worded, emotionally truthful exhortation could bring about significant change. He was the only person I have ever seen or met who gave political speech the weight and subtlety of literature. The irony is that his power lay entirely in the spoken word, so that what he said on any given occasion could never quite be captured in print. His voice—the very sound of it, its accent and emphasis and pitch—was physically a part of the meaning of his words. And with his death on November 6, 1996, that voice was silenced.

·   ·   ·

I hardly knew Mario Savio (and in this respect I was unusual in Berkeley, where half the population seemed to consider him an old friend). I met him only once, talked to him on the phone about printing his speech, saw him occasionally at a rally or a memorial service. I wasn't even around to hear his fiery early speeches, because in 1964, when he was making history as part of Berkeley's Free Speech Movement, I was still a junior high school student in Palo Alto, down on the quiet peninsula, away from all the action. But I heard about him then, and when, twenty or thirty years later, I saw videotapes of his speeches, I instantly understood what I had missed. I lived through the late sixties on college campuses and heard an endless number of protest speeches, but I had never heard political speech like Mario Savio's. He spoke without notes of any kind, and he spoke at length, directly addressing his audience with passion and imagination. But that, in a way, was the least of it. The sentences he spoke were complicated and detailed, with clauses and metaphors and little byways of digression that together added up to a coherent grammatical whole. When he spoke, he seemed inspired—literally so, as if he were breathing thought through language. That's how natural it seemed.

Apparently he had stammered in his youth, so much so that he was nearly unable to deliver his own valedictorian speech in high school. It was not until he came to Berkeley that he found his gift, and he was to lose and find it more than once after that, for the times weren't always right for someone of his strengths and vulnerabilities. He brought an innocence to the world—a pure, ingenuous, trusting sense of righteousness and compassion—that the world was ill equipped to handle. Sometimes, even before he died, I would think of him as a sainted Dostoyevskian fool, like Prince Myshkin in *The Idiot*. Since I have always been a confirmed atheist, such thoughts do not come easily to me, but when I think of Mario Savio, I find it difficult to conceive of him in any other way. It goes against my grain to think in terms of martyrdom, but something of the martyr's unusual power is there in his story. He did not set out to be a martyr, certainly, but he was willing to lose in the name of justice; there were more important things to him than winning. "We are moving right now in a direction which one could call creeping barbarism," he said in 1994. "But if we do not have the benefit of the belief that in the end we will win, then we have to be prepared on the basis of our moral insight to struggle even if we do *not* know that we are going to win."

He was gentle, even to those who behaved brutally, and he was decent, even when he was angry. In 1964, when he clambered up on a police car to protest the arrest of a fellow student, he took off his shoes first so he wouldn't damage the car. Such gentleness did not prevail in American politics. In that sense, Mario Savio had no direct inheritors. His was a political pathway that led nowhere, a dead end in our evolutionary development.

This is our loss. We were unable to learn what he had to teach us, because we were unable to conceive of political language that could be truthful rather than just persuasive. Mario Savio's literary gifts were intimately tied to his political perceptions: he could not have cared about fairness or equality or humanity in exactly the way he did without caring about language in exactly the way he did. Yet such precision came, in the practical world of politics, to seem irrelevant, inconvenient, worse than useless. A complexity of language meant a complexity of thought, and a complexity of thought meant that you couldn't win an election. But Mario Savio's politics weren't just about winning elections; they were about changing the way people thought about each other and the world.

He died of a heart attack, shortly after a debate with the president of his university over the issue of raising student fees. (Ironically, and typically, it was the *president's* heart he was worried about when they finished the stressful debate.) Raising student fees at the state university would, he argued, make it increasingly difficult for poor kids to go to college. He knew exactly what he was talking about: Mario Savio, the son of a machinist, had earned all his degrees at state universities. The student-fee problem was something that everyone else at the university probably would have swept under the carpet if Mario Savio hadn't single-handedly turned it into a cause. He was always making extra trouble for himself, finding causes where other people found only problems to ignore. He couldn't help himself.

"At least he died fighting," said my husband, who works at the same university where Mario Savio taught remedial math, formal logic, and physics. "There are worse ways to go."

"I think it's more that there was no other way for him to live," I said.

His death has moved and upset me more than I could have predicted, considering how little I knew him. I feel as if something very old and valuable, something irreplaceable, has been taken away from me and destroyed. I feel as if the last surviving member of a rare and beautiful species has disappeared from the earth. I take the loss personally, and I long to hear the kinds of comforting words that Mario Savio himself could have provided, in his secular-humanist, quasi-religious, saintly-priestly way. But the only voice that could have offered such comfort is one that we won't, any of us, hear again.

On Mario Savio

Greil Marcus

In the fall of 1964 at the University of California at Berkeley the United States entered a new stage in its history: in places of privilege, ordinary people once again began to make history. The previous spring, students had helped organize highly effective protests against racist hiring practices in the San Francisco Bay Area. Regional business interests demanded an end to what they considered harassment, and the University—defined by its then-president, Clark Kerr, as a "knowledge factory" meant to serve American productivity—responded by banning all political activity on campus: distributing literature, collecting donations, circulating petitions, publicizing meetings. But some students on campus had just returned from Mississippi, where they had spent the summer in an effort to open a new public space where black Mississippians could exercise their rights as citizens; three of their coworkers had been murdered. Now they found their own rights in question.

Among those students was Mario Savio, who died November 6, [1996], at the age of fifty-three, in Sebastopol, California. In 1964, he was a twenty-one-year-old majoring in philosophy. Savio helped found the Free Speech Move-ment, whose members ranged from Students for Goldwater to the communist W. E. B. Du Bois Club. As Savio put it in 1965, looking back, "The Berkeley students now demand what hopefully the rest of an oppressed white middle class will some day demand: freedom for all Americans, not just for Negroes!"

That idea was a paradox in those days, when the campuses of great universities were almost all white, and throughout the fall of 1964 the entire university community was convulsed by it. There were fruitless negotiations, sit-ins, daily rallies, and at the end, with the arrest of nearly eight hundred demonstrators and police violence in the midst of a grand convocation, historic events. Finally, nobody talked about anything else—but everybody talked, many as never before.

From the first, Mario Savio emerged as the principal spokesperson of the FSM. There was often a scary rush in his speeches, sometimes a tense, brittle calm, but always vehemence—an insistence that choices were being made as you listened, which meant that you too had to choose. "He took the mantle," Rolling Stone editor Jann Wenner said when we talked over Savio's death; we were both undergraduates at Berkeley in the fall of 1964. "He rose to it. That probably took five years off his life." Savio seemed to embody not just will but also doubt, and the need to speak and act in the face of doubt.

"We have an *autocracy* which runs this university," Savio said on December 2, 1964, speaking to a huge crowd moments before beginning the climactic demonstration of the Free Speech Movement. "It's *managed*. I ask you to consider"—those last five words by now, thanks to Savio, the common watchword of the FSM, "I ask you to consider" forming an invitation to judgment, turning a crowd into an assembly of thinking individuals who might decide to act in concert, and might not—"I ask you to consider, if this is a firm, and if the Board of Regents are the board of directors, and if President Kerr is in fact the manager, then I tell you something: the faculty are a bunch of employees, and we're the raw material! But we're a bunch of raw material that don't mean to be, to have any process put upon us—don't mean to be made into any product—don't mean, don't mean to end up being bought by some clients of the university, be they government, be they industry, be they organized labor, be they anyone. We're human beings!"

Then came the words with which Savio's name will always be linked. "There's a time," he said—with the word *time* extended as Van Morrison might have extended it, rolled out, then pulled back in—"when the operation of the machine becomes so odious, makes you so sick at heart, that you can't take part; you can't even tacitly take part, and you've got to put your bodies upon the gears and upon the wheels, upon the levers, upon all the apparatus and you've got to make it stop. And you've got to indicate to the people who run it, to the people who own it, that unless you're free, the machine will be prevented from working at all."

And that, over the next days, is just what happened. Over the next several years, all across the country, it happened again and again.

.   .   .

At the thirtieth anniversary FSM reunion, in 1994, only a certain bitter burr was missing from Savio's voice. He had long since absented himself from public life; perhaps following the example of civil rights leader Bob Moses, he had understood from the beginning that, in public affairs, one's own celebrity only absolves others from having to make their own choices. This day, three decades later, he had been asked, he said with a laugh, to talk about "spiritual values." "This isn't my job," he said. "I know what my job has been, all these years. This isn't my job. But I'm going to try to do it anyway."

Savio didn't explain that day what his job had been; in a way, his death explained for him. His job was never to betray the history he and others had once made. That was the best way to ensure that it was a story that would hold its shape and continue to be told. Savio's job was never to trade away whatever moral authority had attached itself to him—not for power, respectability, comfort, or peace of mind.

In his last months, Savio was again speaking out—in his own community, at the state university in Sonoma, California, where he was teaching—against Proposition 209, the state ballot initiative that promised to end all affirmative action against discrimination based in race or gender in California. It passed just four days after Savio suffered the heart attack that would kill him; it passed the day before he died.

Had history come full circle? The purpose of Proposition 209 was to inaugurate a movement to roll the country back to the days when, as in 1964 in the San Francisco Bay Area, there was only one form of affirmative action, for white men. To protest the initiative, the day after Savio's death five Berkeley students chained themselves to the Campanile, the campus tower, and were arrested; hundreds more marched through the campus. "We are able to do what we're doing because of Mario Savio," one student, Anthony Weathington, told a reporter. "When he died, he passed the torch on to us."

Rolling Stone, December 26, 1996

Mario Savio

Avatar of Free Speech

Reginald E. Zelnik

He was tall and somewhat gangly, and when he hovered above the mike on the steps overlooking Sproul Plaza, he cut an extraordinary figure. That was where I first heard him speak. His face was exceptionally mobile, at times telegraphing the thought that was still being formulated or whose utterance was delayed by an occasional stutter. When he spoke, Mario made full use of his arms and hands, perhaps revealing his Italian origins. ("Sicilian!" his father, a retired machine-punch operator, once corrected me.) He sounded like the New Yorker he was, raised mainly in Queens. Unappreciative at first, I had no idea that I was listening to the most original public speaker I would ever hear, nor that we would become lifelong friends.

Writing a century ago, a Russian Marxist (Georgii Plekhanov) maintained that circumstance created Napoleon: had Napoleon not existed, someone else would have filled his shoes. Well, I came to know everyone who might have been Mario if Mario hadn't existed, and I know that only Mario could have done what he did. In three months he turned thousands of students into a united voice for free speech, persuading a complacent faculty to accede to the Free Speech Movement's demands.

Though known for his leadership skills, he was a complex mix of activist, philosopher, and lover of the smaller beauties of life. Nor have I met anyone as politically engaged who was so ready to admit doubt, give ground to others, raise a point that weakened his own case.

The piercing words of Mario's speech that preceded the sit-in of December 2 are often quoted: "There is a time when the operation of the machine becomes so odious...you've got to put your bodies upon the gears...you've got to make it stop." But there were many other Savio speeches before that one, and without them one cannot imagine why so many students followed him to the sit-in, risking expulsion and jail. The dialogical quality of his speeches engaged students at the level of their own apprehensions; they were not being fed dogma but were invited to a forum. Mario was able to personalize and even feminize the idiom of the movement. He was not afraid of words like *love.*

The FSM helped ignite the anti–Vietnam War protests. Given the horror of that war, the quality of movement rhetoric changed. Denunciation became more common, cynicism infected all camps. With time, all this may have contributed to Mario's depression. There were lulls in his activism, as he struggled to support his family and slowly put himself through school (a master's degree in physics) while battling ill health. Yet none of this stopped him from continuing to defend affirmative action and, of course, students' rights, which he vigorously supported at Sonoma State University, where he taught before his death. In the end Mario was doing the things he loved to do alongside the people with whom he wanted to be.

New York Times Magazine, December 29, 1996 (slightly modified)

SELECTED BIBLIOGRAPHY

BANCROFT COLLECTION ORAL HISTORIES

All the Bancroft Collection oral histories listed below are cited in the notes with the interviewee's last name followed by the words *Oral History;* e.g., "Constance Oral History."

Lincoln Constance. "Versatile Berkeley Botanist: Plant Taxonomy and University Governance." Oral history conducted in 1986 by Ann Lage, Regional Oral History Office, Bancroft Library, University of California at Berkeley, 1987.

Henry F. May. "Professor of American Intellectual History, University of California, Berkeley, 1952–1980." Oral history conducted in 1998 by Ann Lage, Regional Oral History Office, Bancroft Library, University of California at Berkeley, 1999.

Carl E. Schorske. "Intellectual Life, Civil Libertarian Issues, and the Student Movement at the University of California, Berkeley, 1960–1969." Oral history conducted in 1996 and 1997 by Ann Lage, Regional Oral History Office, Bancroft Library, University of California at Berkeley, 2000.

Alex C. Sherriffs. "The University of California and the Free Speech Movement: Perspectives from a Faculty Member and an Administrator." Oral history conducted in 1978 by James H. Rowland, Regional Oral History Office, Bancroft Library, University of California at Berkeley, 1980.

Kenneth M. Stampp. "Historian of Slavery, the Civil War, and Reconstruction, University of California, Berkeley, 1946–1983." Oral history conducted in 1996 by Ann Lage, Regional Oral History Office, Bancroft Library, University of California at Berkeley, 1998.

Chancellor Edward W. Strong. "Philosopher, Professor and Berkeley Chancellor, 1961–1965." Oral history conducted in 1988 by Harriet Nathan, Regional Oral History Office, Bancroft Library, University of California at Berkeley.

Katherine Towle. "Dean of Students, Administration and Leadership." Interview in 1967 by Harriet Nathan, Series Director, University History Series, Bancroft Collection, University of California at Berkeley, 1970.

Arleigh Williams. "Dean of Students Arleigh Williams: The Free Speech Movement and the Six Years' War, 1964–1970." Oral history conducted in 1988 and 1989 by Germaine LaBerge, Regional Oral History Office, Bancroft Library, University of California at Berkeley, 1990.

FREQUENTLY CITED AND ESSENTIAL PUBLISHED WORKS

Academic Senate Minutes (meetings of October–December 1964, University of California, Berkeley Division).

Breines, Wini. *Community and Organization in the New Left, 1962–1968: The Great Refusal.* New Brunswick: Rutgers University Press, 1989.

"Chronology of Events: Three Months of Crisis." *California Monthly* 75 (Feb. 1965): 35–74.

Cohen, Robert, ed. "The FSM and Beyond: Berkeley Student Protest and Social Change in the 1960s." Unpublished manuscript, 1994. Photocopy in editors' possession.

Draper, Hal. *Berkeley: The New Student Revolt.* New York: Grove Press, 1965.

Eynon, Bret. "Community in Motion: The Free Speech Movement, Civil Rights, and the Roots of the New Left." *Oral History Review* 17 (spring 1989): 39–69.

Foote, Caleb, Henry Mayer, and Associates. *The Culture of the University: Governance and Education* [report of the Study Committee on University Governance, University of California, Berkeley]. San Francisco: Jossey-Bass, 1968.

Gitlin, Todd. *The Sixties: Years of Hope, Days of Rage.* New York: Bantam Books, 1987.

Goines, David Lance. *The Free Speech Movement: Coming of Age in the 1960s.* Berkeley: Ten Speed Press, 1993.

Heirich, Max. *The Spiral of Conflict: Berkeley 1964.* New York: Columbia University Press, 1971.

Heirich, Max, and Sam Kaplan, "Yesterday's Discord." *California Monthly* 75 (Feb. 1965): 20–32.

Horowitz, David. *Student.* New York: Ballantine Books, 1962.

Kaplan, Samuel. "Revolt of an Elite: Sources of the FSM Victory," *Graduate Student Journal,* no. 4 (spring 1965): 77.

Kerr, Clark. *The Gold and the Blue: A Personal Memoir of the University of California 1949–1967,* vol. 1: Academic Triumphs; vol. 2: *Political Turmoil* (Berkeley and Los Angeles: University of California Press, 2003).

———. *The Uses of the University.* Cambridge, Mass.: Harvard University Press, 1963. Reprint, 1995.

Lipset, Seymour Martin, and Sheldon S. Wolin, eds. *The Berkeley Student Revolt: Facts and Interpretations.* Garden City, N.Y.: Doubleday, 1965.

Marwick, Arthur. *The Sixties: Cultural Revolution in Britain, France, Italy, and the United States, c. 1958–1974.* New York: Oxford University Press, 1998.

Miller, Michael V., and Susan Gilmore, eds. *Revolution at Berkeley: The Crisis in American Education.* New York: Dell, 1965.

[Muscatine, Charles, et al.]. *Education at Berkeley: Report of the Select Committee on Education.* Berkeley: University of California Press, 1968.

Pierovich, Andrew L. "A Season of Discontent." *California Monthly* 75 (Feb. 1965): 13–15.

Rorabaugh, W. J. *Berkeley at War*. New York: Oxford University Press, 1989.

Rossman, Michael. *The Wedding Within the War*. Garden City, N.Y.: Doubleday, 1971.

Seaborg, Glenn T., with Ray Colvig. *Chancellor at Berkeley*. Berkeley: Institute of Governmental Studies Press, 1994.

Searle, John. *The Campus War: A Sympathetic Look at the University in Agony*. New York: World Publishing Company, 1971.

Stadtman, Verne A. *The University of California, 1868–1968*. New York: McGraw-Hill, 1970.

Starobin, Robert. "Graduate Students in the FSM." *Graduate Student Journal*, no. 4 (spring 1965): 17–26.

Taylor, Angus E. *The Academic Senate of the University of California: Its Role in the Shared Governance and Operation of the University of California*. Berkeley: Institute of Governmental Studies Press, 1998.

Margot Adler is a correspondent for National Public Radio and has been reporting for NPR since 1978. Before then she reported news and public affairs for Pacifica and hosted free-form radio shows on WBAI-FM. She is the author of *Drawing Down the Moon* and *Heretic's Heart: A Journey through Spirit and Revolution.* She graduated from UC Berkeley in 1968, after which she received her M.A. from the Columbia School of Journalism. In 1982 she was a Nieman Fellow at Harvard.

Bettina Aptheker is professor and chair of women's studies at UC Santa Cruz. She was on the FSM Steering Committee and was later active in the movement against the Vietnam War and the movement to free Angela Davis. Her books include *The Morning Breaks: The Trial of Angela Davis; Woman's Legacy: Essays on Race, Sex, and Class in American History;* and *Tapestries of Life: Women's Work, Women's Consciousness and the Meaning of Daily Experience.* She is at work on a memoir, "Brooklyn Tracks."

Malcolm Burnstein is a prominent Bay Area movement lawyer. He has been active in that capacity since the late 1950s. In the 1960s he used his legal training in behalf of such causes as the Free Speech Movement, including the legal defense of the students arrested in Sproul Hall on December 3, 1964. He retired from his practice in 2001.

Keith Chamberlain, a retired Presbyterian minister, has lived and worked in Germany since 1971. In addition to campus ministry positions in Berkeley, Berlin, and Frankfurt, he has been a parish minister and chaplain at the Frankfurt airport, where he was involved with the problems of refugees. He was acting University pastor at Westminster House, the Presbyterian campus center, at the time of the FSM.

Robert Cohen is director of New York University's Social Studies Program and associate professor in NYU's Department of Teaching and Learning, with an affiliated appointment in the history department. He received his Ph.D. at Berkeley in 1987. He is author of *When the Old Left Was Young: Student Radicals and America's First Mass Student Movement, 1929–1941,* and editor of *Dear Mrs. Roosevelt: Letters from Children of the Great Depression.* He is preparing an edited volume of Mario Savio's speeches and writings.

Robert H. Cole is professor of law emeritus at Boalt Hall, the law school of UC Berkeley. His main fields are constitutional law, torts, and professional ethics. He received his LL.B. from Harvard, where he was book review editor of the *Harvard Law Review,* and later served as a law clerk at the U.S. Supreme Court. Shortly after the FSM, he served a term as faculty consultant to the new Berkeley chancellor, Roger Heyns.

Kate Coleman, a veteran Bay Area journalist, has written for numerous publications, including *Ramparts, New West, Ms., Women Sports,* the *Los Angeles Times Magazine, LA Weekly, San Francisco,* and *Salon.* She has written extensively on the Black Panther Party as well as on such cultural figures as Miss America, Jane Fonda, Michael Douglas, and Zsa Zsa Gabor. She is currently writing a biography of Earth First activist Judi Bari.

Jo Freeman received her B.A. from UC Berkeley in 1965, her Ph.D. in Political Science from the University of Chicago in 1973, and her J.D. from New York University School of Law in 1982. She is the author of three books, including *A Room at a Time: How Women Entered Party Politics,* and numerous articles and is editor or coeditor of seven volumes, most recently the coedited *Waves of Protest: Social Movements since the Sixties.*

Jackie Goldberg is currently a California State Assembly member. She previously served as a member and president of the Los Angeles Board of Education and as a member of the Los Angeles City Council. She was a member of the FSM Steering Committee in the fall of 1964.

Suzanne Goldberg is a practicing psychotherapist and an artist. During the Free Speech Movement she was a delegate of the Graduate Coordinating Committee to the FSM Steering Committee and was a frequent public speaker in behalf of the FSM.

David A. Hollinger, who received his Ph.D. from the UC Berkeley history department in 1970, is now the Preston Hotchkis Professor of American History in that department. His most recent books are *Postethnic America: Beyond Multiculturalism* and *Science, Jews, and Secular Culture.*

Clark Kerr is professor emeritus of economics and business administration at UC Berkeley and president emeritus of the University of California. He served as the Berkeley chancellor in 1952–1958 and as president of the University in 1958–1967. His publications include *The Uses of the University* and *The Gold and the Blue: A Personal Memoir of the University of California, 1949–1967*, vol. 1: *Academic Triumphs;* vol. 2: *Political Turmoil.*

Wendy Lesser is the editor of *The Threepenny Review*. She was educated at Harvard, Cambridge, and UC Berkeley. The author of six books and editor of one, she has received fellowships from the Guggenheim Foundation, the NEH, the ACLS, the Columbia Journalism School, and other institutions. She lives in Berkeley with her husband and their son.

Lawrence W. Levine taught for thirty-two years in the UC Berkeley history department; since 1994 he has been on the faculty at George Mason University. His books include *Black Culture and Black Consciousness, Highbrow/ Lowbrow: The Emergence of Cultural Hierarchy in America, The Opening of the American Mind,* and (with Cornelia Levine) *The People and the President: America's Conversation with FDR.*

Leon F. Litwack is Alexander F. and May T. Morrison Professor of American History at UC Berkeley, where he received both his B.A. and Ph.D. degrees. His 1980 book, *Been in the Storm So Long: The Aftermath of Slavery*, received the Pulitzer Prize in History. His most recent books are *Trouble in Mind: Black Southerners in the Age of Jim Crow* and (as coauthor) *Without Sanctuary: Lynching Photography in America*. He is coeditor of *The Harvard Guide to African American History.*

Jeff Lustig, who received his Ph.D. at UC Berkeley, is professor of government at the State University of California at Sacramento and is currently an officer of the California Faculty Association. He is the author of *Corporate Liberalism: The Origins of Modern American Political Theory* as well as numerous articles on American politics and political thought.

Greil Marcus attended UC Berkeley as an undergraduate in 1963–1967 and as a graduate student in political science in 1967–1972. He taught the American studies seminar "Prophecy and the American Voice" at both Berkeley and Princeton in 2000. He is the author of *Lipstick Traces; The Old, Weird America;* and *The Dustbin of History*, among other books. He lives in Berkeley.

Waldo Martin is professor of history at UC Berkeley, where he received his Ph.D. in 1980. He specializes in African American political, social, and cultural history. He is the author of *The Mind of Frederick Douglass* and *Brown v. Board of Education: A Brief History with Documents* and coeditor of *Civil Rights in the United States: An Encyclopedia.*

Henry Mayer is the author of *All On Fire: William Lloyd Garrison and the Abolition of Slavery*, which won the J. Anthony Lukas Book Prize and was nominated for the National Book Award, and *A Son of Thunder: Patrick Henry and the American Republic.* During the FSM he was a history delegate to the Graduate Coordinating Committee. In 1967 he was cochair (with Caleb Foote) of Berkeley's Study Commission on University Governance, and he was co-author of its published report, *The Culture of the University: Governance and Education.* His death in July 2000 was a terrible loss to his friends, his loved ones, and American letters.

Robert Post is the Alexander F. and May T. Morrison Professor of Law at Boalt Hall, the law school of UC Berkeley. He is the author of *Constitutional Domains: Democracy, Community, Management* and the editor of *Censorship and Silencing: Practices of Cultural Regulation.*

Jonah Raskin is the chair of the communication studies department at Sonoma State University. He is the author of *For the Hell of It: The Life and Times of Abbie Hoffman* and *Out of the Whale: Growing up in the American Left.*

Julie A. Reuben is professor of education at the Harvard Graduate School of Education. She is the author of *Making of the Modern University: Intellectual Transformation and the Marginalization of Morality.* She is currently completing a book tentatively titled "Campus Revolts: Politics and American Higher Education in the 1960s."

W. J. Rorabaugh received his Ph.D. from UC Berkeley in 1976. His publications include *Berkeley at War: The 1960s* and *Kennedy and the Promise of the Sixties.* He is professor of history at the University of Washington in Seattle.

Doug Rossinow is associate professor of history and chair of the Department of History, Religious and Women's Studies at Metropolitan State University in Minneapolis. He is the author of *The Politics of Authenticity: Liberals, Christians, and the New Left in America.* His current book project is called "The Vital Margin: Interpreting 'Progressive' Politics in Modern America."

Michael Rossman is a writer and mathematics teacher. He is currently the president of FSM-A, an organization dedicated to the gathering, preservation, and dissemination of materials related to the FSM, and editor of the *FSM-A Newsletter.* He is the author of *The Wedding Within the War* and *New Age Blues* and coauthor of the Rossman Report (the subject of his essay in the present volume).

Martin Roysher was a member of the FSM Steering Committee. He received both his B.A. degree (history) and his Ph.D. degree (sociology) at UC Berkeley. In 1967 he was a member of the Study Commission on University Governance. A specialist in the fields of urban politics and society and public health, he has held a variety of positions in both the public and the private sectors.

Lynne Hollander Savio, who studied at Bryn Mawr College and graduated from UC Berkeley, was an active participant in the FSM and one of the coauthors of the Rossman Report. She now lives in Sonoma County, where she works as a public school librarian. She is the widow of Mario Savio and heads the board of directors of the Mario Savio Memorial Lecture and Young Activist Award.

Mario Savio, a veteran of the Bay Area and southern civil rights movements, was the FSM'S most influential orator and its most famous organizer. Educated at Manhattan College, Queens College, UC Berkeley, and San Francisco State University, he received his B.S. (summa cum laude, with designation as "outstanding science student") and M.S. degrees in physics from the last-named school. He taught mathematics, logic, and interdisciplinary courses in science and literature at Sonoma State University. In addition to his political and social writings, he published "AE (Aristotle-Euler) Diagrams: An Alternative Complete Method for the Categorical Syllogism," *Notre Dame Journal of Formal Logic* (fall 1998). Many aspects of his rich and often complicated life are treated in the present volume. Mario died in 1996 at the age of fifty-three. This book is dedicated to his memory.

Steve Weissman has been an editor of *Ramparts* and a television producer for the BBC. His films appeared on PBS. He has written for newspapers and magazines throughout the world and coauthored *The Islamic Bomb.* Now living in France, he is working on a book called "Phantoms of Lost Liberty: Free Speech and the Terrorists." In 1964 he was a member of the FSM Steering Committee and a leader of the Graduate Coordinating Committee.

Leon Wofsy is professor emeritus of molecular and cell biology/immunology at UC Berkeley. He joined the Berkeley faculty in 1964, just before the birth of the FSM. From 1949 to 1955 he was national chairman of the Labor Youth League, a Marxist youth organization. He is the author of many scientific papers and articles on social issues and of a memoir, *Looking for the Future.* He is editor of a book on the Cold War, *Before the Point of No Return.*

Reginald E. Zelnik, who received his Ph.D. from Stanford, is professor of history at UC Berkeley and former chair of that department. He was a new acting assistant professor at Berkeley at the time of the FSM. In 1967 he was a member of the Study Commission on University Governance. His most recent books are *Law and Disorder on the Narova River: The Kreenholm Strike of 1872* and the edited volume *Workers and Intelligentsia in Late Imperial Russia: Realities, Representations, Reflections.*

INDEX